THE NEW CAMBRIDGE SHAKESPEARE

GENERAL EDITOR
Brian Gibbons, *University of Münster*

ASSOCIATE GENERAL EDITOR
A. R. Braunmuller, *University of California, Los Angeles*

THE TRAGEDY OF KING LEAR

For this updated critical edition of *King Lear*, Lois Potter has written a completely new introduction, taking account of recent productions and reinterpretations of the play, with particular emphasis on its afterlife in global performance and adaptation.

The edition retains the Textual Analysis of the previous editor, Jay L. Halio, shortened and with a new preface by Brian Gibbons. Professor Halio, accepting that we have two versions of equal authority, the one derived from Shakespeare's rough drafts, the other from a manuscript used in the playhouses during the seventeenth century, chooses the Folio as the text for this edition. He explains the differences between the two versions and alerts the reader to the rival claims of the quarto by means of a sampling of parallel passages in the Textual Analysis and by an appendix which contains annotated passages unique to the quarto.

THE NEW CAMBRIDGE SHAKESPEARE

All's Well That Ends Well, edited by Russell Fraser
Antony and Cleopatra, edited by David Bevington
As You Like It, edited by Michael Hattaway
The Comedy of Errors, edited by T. S. Dorsch
Coriolanus, edited by Lee Bliss
Cymbeline, edited by Martin Butler
Hamlet, edited by Philip Edwards
Julius Caesar, edited by Marvin Spevack
King Edward III, edited by Giorgio Melchiori
The First Part of King Henry IV, edited by Herbert Weil and Judith Weil
The Second Part of King Henry IV, edited by Giorgio Melchiori
King Henry V, edited by Andrew Gurr
The First Part of King Henry VI, edited by Michael Hattaway
The Second Part of King Henry VI, edited by Michael Hattaway
The Third Part of King Henry VI, edited by Michael Hattaway
King Henry VIII, edited by John Margeson
King John, edited by L. A. Beaurline
The Tragedy of King Lear, edited by Jay L. Halio
King Richard II, edited by Andrew Gurr
King Richard III, edited by Janis Lull
Love's Labour's Lost, edited by William C. Carroll
Macbeth, edited by A. R. Braunmuller
Measure for Measure, edited by Brian Gibbons
The Merchant of Venice, edited by M. M. Mahood
The Merry Wives of Windsor, edited by David Crane
A Midsummer Night's Dream, edited by R. A. Foakes
Much Ado About Nothing, edited by F. H. Mares
Othello, edited by Norman Sanders
Pericles, edited by Doreen DelVecchio and Antony Hammond
The Poems, edited by John Roe
Romeo and Juliet, edited by G. Blakemore Evans
The Sonnets, edited by G. Blakemore Evans
The Taming of the Shrew, edited by Ann Thompson
The Tempest, edited by David Lindley
Timon of Athens, edited by Karl Klein
Titus Andronicus, edited by Alan Hughes
Troilus and Cressida, edited by Anthony B. Dawson
Twelfth Night, edited by Elizabeth Story Donno
The Two Gentlemen of Verona, edited by Kurt Schlueter
The Two Noble Kinsmen, edited by Robert Kean Turner and Patricia Tatspaugh
The Winter's Tale, edited by Susan Snyder and Deborah T. Curren-Aquino

THE EARLY QUARTOS
The First Quarto of the Merry Wives of Windsor, edited by David Lindley
The First Quarto of Hamlet, edited by Kathleen O. Irace
The First Quarto of King Henry V, edited by Andrew Gurr
The First Quarto of King Lear, edited by Jay L. Halio
The First Quarto of King Richard III, edited by Peter Davison
The First Quarto of Othello, edited by Scott McMillin
The First Quarto of Romeo and Juliet, edited by Lukas Erne
The Taming of a Shrew: The 1594 Quarto, edited by Stephen Roy Miller

THE TRAGEDY OF KING LEAR

Third Edition

Edited by

JAY L. HALIO

Emeritus Professor of English, University of Delaware

With a new introduction by

LOIS POTTER

Emeritus Professor of English, University of Delaware

Textual Introduction edited, with a new preface, by

BRIAN GIBBONS

CAMBRIDGE
UNIVERSITY PRESS

CAMBRIDGE
UNIVERSITY PRESS

University Printing House, Cambridge CB2 8BS, United Kingdom

One Liberty Plaza, 20th Floor, New York, NY 10006, USA

477 Williamstown Road, Port Melbourne, VIC 3207, Australia

314–321, 3rd Floor, Plot 3, Splendor Forum, Jasola District Centre,
New Delhi – 110025, India

79 Anson Road, #06–04/06, Singapore 079906

Cambridge University Press is part of the University of Cambridge.

It furthers the University's mission by disseminating knowledge in the pursuit of
education, learning, and research at the highest international levels of excellence.

www.cambridge.org
Information on this title: www.cambridge.org/9781107195868
DOI: 10.1017/9781108164412

First published 2020

Printed in the United Kingdom by TJ International Ltd, Padstow Cornwall

A catalogue record for this publication is available from the British Library.

ISBN 978-1-107-19586-8 Hardback
ISBN 978-1-316-64697-7 Paperback

IN MEMORIAM
PHILIP BROCKBANK, 1922–1989

CONTENTS

Contents

ILLUSTRATIONS

PREFACE TO THE THIRD EDITION

This edition of *King Lear* retains the text established by Jay L. Halio, which is based on the version published in 1623 in the collection of Shakespeare's plays known as the First Folio. It also retains the magisterial textual introduction, slightly shortened by General Editor Brian Gibbons, in which Professor Halio shows the complexity of the arguments about the relationship of the Folio text to the one published in 1608. I have also retained Professor Halio's notes.

My contribution has been the writing of a new critical introduction. In doing this, I have been conscious of two enormous differences between my situation and that of my predecessor. First, my readers will have access, on the internet, to far more information than a single introduction can summarize. Second, much current academic study is 'presentist' – that is, more concerned with the reception of a work in the present than with how it might have looked to its original public.

I have tried to indicate how *King Lear* has been transformed over the centuries in accordance with changing expectations and desires. This has meant paying more attention than usual to adaptations of the play and to modern productions that have challenged what they took to be its attitude to family, gender, authority, and religion. This is not a definitive account of *King Lear*; it simply indicates the richness of creative and critical responses that it has inspired. Professor Halio's notes to the play offer a more consistent interpretation and thus provide an alternative to my approach. I hope that readers will arrive at their own interpretations of the play by choosing among the various alternatives presented here. There are as many *Lear*s as there are productions and critical interpretations of the play. Some of these are 'wrong' in the sense that they approach the play from perspectives that can be shown not to have existed when it was first performed, and yet 'right' in that they speak to the needs of a modern reader or spectator. It is important to bear this distinction in mind.

Professor Halio, a former colleague at the University of Delaware, has been consistently generous in his response to my work. Brian Gibbons, the General Editor of this series, has been very helpful, as has Emily Hockley of Cambridge University Press. I have benefitted greatly from their suggestions. Thanks also to Leigh Mueller, my copy-editor, and to Margaret Berrill, for reading the proofs. For permission to use their photographs, I thank the British Library, the Folger Shakespeare Library, the Schomburg Center for Research in Black Culture at The New York Public Library, the Stratford Festival of Canada, Mark Douet, Jonathan Keenan, and Sara Krulwich. I am particularly grateful to Nancy Meckler for helping me get a photograph of her 2017 production for Shakespeare's Globe.

PREFACE TO THE FIRST EDITION

In the quarto and the Folio, *King Lear* presents two significantly different versions of Shakespeare's play, one closer to the composition as he originally conceived it (Q), the other closer to an actual staged production after revision (F). The two versions involve a host of variant readings in addition to unique passages, alternative speech assignments, missing stage directions, and other divergences, besides numerous printer's errors. Editors have hitherto thought that by conflating, or splicing, the two versions they could approach what they assumed to be the 'ideal' form of the play, apparently lost; but this belief violates theatrical tradition and otherwise has little to support it.

Establishing the definitive text of such a fluid enterprise as a play is in its evolution from conception through performance under a variety of exigencies becomes impossible, unless one arbitrarily decides (as past scholars usually have done) that the last published version in the author's lifetime in which the author had a hand is 'definitive'. Questions about the soundness of this procedure aside, what if the author had no hand in the publication of the work? Shakespeare was dead before half of his plays were published, and it is uncertain what role, if any, he played in the publication of any of the others, including *King Lear* in 1608. Although he oversaw the printing of his long poems, *Venus and Adonis* and *The Rape of Lucrece*, dedicated to his patron Southampton, he apparently cared much less about the publication of his dramatic works, leaving to generations of scholars the fascinating problems of establishing an authentic, if not definitive, edition of his plays. An authentic, not definitive, edition of *King Lear* is the goal of this one. Founded on a fresh examination of the texts as well as on the best available scholarship and criticism regarding the text, the total historical context (including theatrical data), and the study of extant sources, this edition tries to provide a clear, up-to-date, readable, and reliable version based on the Folio text of Shakespeare's *King Lear*. Throughout, the emphasis is upon the play *as a play*, not just a literary document, though it is that too, of course, and the Commentary accordingly ignores neither aspect of the work.

Modern editors of Shakespeare owe enormous debts to the countless scholars, editors, critics, and theatre professionals who have preceded them. Wherever possible, I have tried to record specific debts in footnotes or Commentary, but more generalized and personal debts must be acknowledged here. Many friends and scholars have lent assistance by reviewing various parts of the typescript in preparation and making invaluable suggestions and often corrections of error or misunderstanding. Donald Foster, Trevor Howard-Hill, and Gary Taylor all read the Textual Analysis in its original form; it appears here much changed as a result of their suggestions and those of Philip Brockbank who, until his death, served as General Editor of the New Cambridge Shakespeare. Thomas Clayton, Richard Knowles, and George Walton Williams read the original *and* the revised versions of that analysis – a service well beyond the call of collegiality and friendship. Indeed, Thomas Clayton read all of the Introduction, except the stage history, which Marvin Rosenberg read in an earlier form. Philip Brockbank also vetted the original version of the section on dates and sources, which (like the Textual Analysis) has been entirely reorganized and revised according to his recommendations. I am sure, had he lived, he would have made further recommendations concerning other sections of the Introduction, which then would have profited from his advice and counsel. Since his death, Brian Gibbons, who has succeeded him as General Editor, has been of great assistance, offering many suggestions and not a few corrections of detail. It was, in fact, his suggestion to follow the example of John Hazel Smith's edition of *Bussy D'Ambois*, and include a sampling of parallel passages from quarto and Folio to highlight the kinds of changes that occur between them. The Associate General Editors, Robin Hood and A. R. Braunmuller, have also been most helpful in making suggestions and corrections. Sarah Stanton has advised me on various aspects of format and procedure, and Paul Chipchase's copy-editing has been both thorough and acutely perceptive. To all of these dedicated professionals, I express my gratitude and exempt them from any errors or infelicities that remain. They are of my own making and my own responsibility.

Several scholars have generously permitted me to see their work in typescript or in proof. Among them are J. Leeds Barroll, Peter Blayney, Frank Brownlow, G. Blakemore Evans, F. D. Hoeniger, Arthur King, Alexander Leggatt, and Stanley Wells. Others have kindly sent me offprints or pre-prints of articles or have answered queries concerning some aspect of *King Lear*. These scholars have demonstrated once again that Shakespearean – indeed, all – scholarship at its best is always a collaborative venture.

I must also express gratitude to the following libraries and their staffs, who have been unfailingly co-operative and helpful: the University of Delaware Library, the Folger Shakespeare Library, the British Library, the Shakespeare Centre Library, and the Library of Congress. Several graduate students and secretarial staff have assisted in various aspects of research or preparation: Kate Rodowsky, Patience Philips, Susan Savini, Suzanne Potts, and Victoria Gray cheerfully carried out duties that must often have seemed at least tedious. To the Trustees of the University of Delaware, I owe thanks for awarding me a sabbatical leave in the autumn term of 1987 and for a research grant in the summer of 1988. Such assistance has greatly facilitated work on this edition.

J. L. H.

ABBREVIATIONS AND CONVENTIONS

Shakespeare's plays, when cited in this edition, are abbreviated in a style modified slightly from that used in the *Harvard Concordance to Shakespeare*. Other editions of Shakespeare are abbreviated under the editor's surname (Theobald, Duthie) unless they are the work of more than one editor. In such cases, an abbreviated series title is used (Cam.). When more than one edition by the same editor is cited, later editions are discriminated with a raised figure (Rowe[2]). All quotations from Shakespeare, except those from *King Lear*, use the text and lineation of *The Riverside Shakespeare*, under the general editorship of G. Blakemore Evans.

1. Shakespeare's Plays

Ado	*Much Ado About Nothing*
Ant.	*Antony and Cleopatra*
AWW	*All's Well That Ends Well*
AYLI	*As You Like It*
Cor.	*Coriolanus*
Cym.	*Cymbeline*
Err.	*The Comedy of Errors*
Ham.	*Hamlet*
1H4	*The First Part of King Henry the Fourth*
2H4	*The Second Part of King Henry the Fourth*
H5	*King Henry the Fifth*
1H6	*The First Part of King Henry the Sixth*
2H6	*The Second Part of King Henry the Sixth*
3H6	*The Third Part of King Henry the Sixth*
H8	*King Henry the Eighth*
JC	*Julius Caesar*
John	*King John*
Lear	*King Lear*
LLL	*Love's Labour's Lost*
Mac.	*Macbeth*
MM	*Measure for Measure*
MND	*A Midsummer Night's Dream*
MV	*The Merchant of Venice*
Oth.	*Othello*
Per.	*Pericles*
R2	*King Richard the Second*
R3	*King Richard the Third*
Rom.	*Romeo and Juliet*
Shr.	*The Taming of the Shrew*
STM	*Sir Thomas More*

Temp.	*The Tempest*
TGV	*The Two Gentlemen of Verona*
Tim.	*Timon of Athens*
Tit.	*Titus Andronicus*
TN	*Twelfth Night*
TNK	*The Two Noble Kinsmen*
Tro.	*Troilus and Cressida*
Wiv.	*The Merry Wives of Windsor*
WT	*The Winter's Tale*

2. Other Works Cited and General References

Abbott	E. A. Abbott, *A Shakespearian Grammar*, 1894
Bell's Shakespeare	[Francis Gentleman], note to *King Lear* in *Bell's Edition of Shakespeare's Plays, as they are now performed at the Theatres Royal in London*, 9 vols., 1774, II
Berlin	Normand Berlin, *The Secret Cause: A Discussion of Tragedy*, 1981
Bevington	*King Lear*, ed. David Bevington, 1988 (Bantam)
Blayney	Peter W. M. Blayney, *The Texts of 'King Lear' and Their Origins*, 2 vols., I (1982)
Booth	Stephen Booth, *'King Lear', 'Macbeth', Indefinition, and Tragedy*, 1983
Boswell	*Third Variorum Edition of Works of William Shakespeare*, ed. Edmond Malone, 21 vols., 1821
Bradley	A. C. Bradley, *Shakespearean Tragedy*, 2nd edn, 1905
Bratton	*King Lear*, ed. J. S. Bratton, 1987 (Plays in Performance)
Brockbank	Philip Brockbank, *'Upon Such Sacrifices'*, The British Academy Shakespeare Lecture, 1976
Bullough	*Narrative and Dramatic Sources of Shakespeare*, ed. Geoffrey Bullough, 8 vols., 1957–75, VII (1973)
Cam.	*The Works of William Shakespeare*, ed. W. G. Clark, J. Glover, and W. A. Wright, 1863–6 (Cambridge Shakespeare)
Capell	*Mr William Shakespeare his Comedies, Histories, and Tragedies*, ed. Edward Capell, 10 vols., 1767–8, IX
Cavell	Stanley Cavell, *Must We Mean What We Say?*, 1969
Cercignani	Fausto Cercignani, *Shakespeare's Works and Elizabethan Pronunciation*, 1981
Chambers	E. K. Chambers, *William Shakespeare: A Study of Facts and Problems*, 2 vols., 1930
Clayton	Thomas Clayton, ' Is this the promis'd end?': revision in the role of the king', in *Division*, pp. 121–41
Colie	Rosalie Colie, 'The energies of endurance: biblical echo in *King Lear*', in *Some Facets*, pp. 117–44
Collier	*The Complete Works of William Shakespeare*, ed. J. P. Collier, 6 vols., 1858
Colman	E. A. M. Colman, *The Dramatic Use of Bawdy in Shakespeare*, 1974
conj.	conjecture
corr.	corrected
Cotgrave	Randall Cotgrave, *A Dictionarie of the French and English Tongues*, 1611

Danby	John F. Danby, *Shakespeare's Doctrine of Nature*, 1948, reprinted 1961
Davenport	A. Davenport, 'Notes on *King Lear*', *N&Q*, n.s., 98 (1953), 20–2
Dent	R. W. Dent, *Shakespeare's Proverbial Language: An Index*, 1981
Division	Gary Taylor and Michael Warren (eds.), *The Division of the Kingdoms: Shakespeare's Two Versions of 'King Lear'*, 1983
Doran	Madeleine Doran, *The Text of 'King Lear'*, 1931, reprinted 1967
Duthie	*King Lear: A Critical Edition*, ed. George Ian Duthie, 1949
Dyce	*The Works of William Shakespeare*, ed. Alexander Dyce, 6 vols., 1857
ELR	*English Literary Renaissance*
Elton	William Elton, *'King Lear' and the Gods*, 1966
F	*Mr William Shakespeares Comedies, Histories, and Tragedies*, 1623 (First Folio)
F2	*Mr William Shakespeares Comedies, Histories, and Tragedies*, 1632 (Second Folio)
F3	*Mr William Shakespeares Comedies, Histories, and Tragedies*, 1663–4 (Third Folio)
F4	*Mr William Shakespeares Comedies, Histories, and Tragedies*, 1685 (Fourth Folio)
FQ	Edmond Spenser, *The Faerie Queene*, 1596
Furness	*King Lear*, ed. Horace Howard Furness, 1880 (New Variorum)
Globe	*The Globe Shakespeare*, ed. W. G. Clark and W. A. Wright, 1864
Goldring	Beth Goldring, '*Cor.*'s rescue of Kent', in *Division*, pp. 143–51
Granville-Barker	Harley Granville-Barker, *Prefaces to Shakespeare*, 2 vols., 1946, I
Greg, *Editorial Problem*	W. W. Greg, *The Editorial Problem in Shakespeare*, 1942, 2nd edn, 1951
Greg, *SFF*	W. W. Greg, *The Shakespeare First Folio*, 1955
Greg, *Variants*	W. W. Greg, *The Variants in the First Quarto of 'King Lear'*, 1940
Halio	*King Lear*, ed. Jay L. Halio, 1973 (Fountainwell)
Hanmer	*The Works of Shakespear*, ed. Thomas Hanmer, 1743–4
Harbage	*King Lear*, ed. Alfred Harbage, 1958 (Penguin)
Harsnett	Samuel Harsnett, *A Declaration of Egregious Popish Impostures*, 1603
Heilman	Robert Heilman, *This Great Stage: Image and Structure in 'King Lear'*, 1948, reprinted 1963
Hinman	Charlton K. Hinman, *The Printing and Proofreading of the First Folio of Shakespeare*, 2 vols., 1963
Hoeniger	F. D. Hoeniger, *Medicine and Shakespeare in the English Renaissance*, 1992
Holland	Norman N. Holland, *The Shakespearean Imagination*, 1964
Hunter	*King Lear*, ed. G. K. Hunter, 1972 (New Penguin)
Jackson	MacDonald P. Jackson, 'Fluctuating variation: author, annotator, or actor', in *Division*, pp. 313–49
Jennens	*King Lear*, ed. Charles Jennens, 1770
Johnson	*The Plays of William Shakespeare*, ed. Samuel Johnson, 8 vols., 1765, VI
Joseph	Sister Miriam Joseph, *Shakespeare's Use of the Arts of Language*, 1947
Kerrigan	John Kerrigan, 'Revision, adaptation, and the Fool in *King Lear*', in *Division*, pp. 195–245

King	Arthur King, *Materials for the Study of 'King Lear'* (in preparation)
King Leir	*The History of King Leir* (1605) (Malone Society Reprints), 1907
Kittredge	*King Lear*, ed. George Lyman Kittredge, 1940
Knight	*The Pictorial Shakespeare*, ed. Charles Knight, 6 vols., 1839
Kökeritz	Helge Kökeritz, *Shakespeare's Pronunciation*, 1953
Mack	Maynard Mack, *'King Lear' in Our Time*, 1965
McLeod	Randall McLeod, '*Gon.* No more, the text is foolish', in *Division*, pp. 153–93
Malone	*The Plays and Poems of William Shakespeare*, ed. Edmond Malone, 10 vols., 1790, VIII
Massai	Sonia Massai, 'Nahum Tate's revision of Shakespeare's *King Lears*', *SEL* 40 (2000), 435–50.
Meagher	John C. Meagher, 'Vanity, Lear's feather, and the pathology of editorial annotation', in Clifford Leech and J. M. R. Margeson (eds.), *Shakespeare 1971*, Toronto, 1972, pp. 244–59
MLR	*Modern Language Review*
Montaigne	*The Essayes of Michael Lord of Montaigne*, trans. John Florio, 6 vols., 1897 (Temple Classics)
MP	*Modern Philology*
Muir	*King Lear*, ed. Kenneth Muir, 1963 (Arden)
N&Q	*Notes and Queries*
Noble	Richmond Noble, *Shakespeare's Biblical Knowledge*, 1935
NS	*King Lear*, ed. George Ian Duthie and John Dover Wilson, 1960, 1968 (New Shakespeare)
OED	*Oxford English Dictionary*
Onions	C. T. Onions, *A Shakespeare Glossary*, enlarged and revised, Robert D. Eagleson, 1986
Oxford	*William Shakespeare: The Complete Works*, gen. eds. Stanley Wells and Gary Taylor, 1986
Partridge	Eric Partridge, *Shakespeare's Bawdy*, 3rd edn, 1969
PBSA	*Papers of the Bibliographical Society of America*
Peat	Derek Peat, 'And that's true too: *King Lear* and the tension of uncertainty', *S.Sur.*, 33 (1980), 43–53
Perrett	Wilfrid Perrett, *The King Lear Story from Geoffrey of Monmouth to Shakespeare*, Berlin, 1904
Pope	*The Works of Shakespear*, ed. Alexander Pope, 1723–5
Q	*M. William Shake-speare: HIS True Chronicle Historie of the life and death of King Lear and his three Daughters*, 1608 (first quarto)
Q2	*M. William Shake-speare, HIS True Chronicle Historie of the life and death of King Lear, and his three Daughters* [1619] (second quarto)
Qq	quartos
Reibetanz	John Reibetanz, *The Lear World*, Toronto, 1977
RES	*Review of English Studies*
Riverside	*The Riverside Shakespeare*, gen. ed. G. Blakemore Evans, 1974
Rosenberg	Marvin Rosenberg, *The Masks of 'King Lear'*, 1972
Rowe	*The Works of Mr William Shakespeare*, ed. Nicholas Rowe, 6 vols., 1709, V

Rowe²	*The Works of Mr William Shakespeare*, ed. Nicholas Rowe, 2nd edn, 8 vols., 1714
Rubenstein	Frankie Rubenstein, *A Dictionary of Shakespeare's Sexual Puns and Their Significance*, 1984
Salingar	Leo Salingar, *Dramatic Form in Shakespeare and the Jacobeans*, 1986
SB	*Studies in Bibliography*
Schmidt	Alexander Schmidt, *A Shakespeare-Lexicon*, 3rd edn, Breslau, 1901
Schmidt 1879	*King Lear*, ed. Alexander Schmidt, Berlin, 1879
SD	stage direction
SFNL	*Shakespeare on Film Newsletter*
SH	speech heading
Shaheen	Naseeb Shaheen, *Biblical References in Shakespeare's Tragedies*, 1987
Sisson	C. J. Sisson, *New Readings in Shakespeare*, 2 vols., 1956, II
Some Facets	Rosalie L. Colie and F. T. Flahiff (eds.), *Some Facets of 'King Lear': Essays in Prismatic Criticism*, 1974
SP	*Studies in Philology*
Spurgeon	Caroline Spurgeon, *Shakespeare's Imagery and What It Tells Us*, 1935
SQ	*Shakespeare Quarterly*
S.St.	*Shakespeare Studies*
S.Sur.	*Shakespeare Survey*
Stampfer	Judah Stampfer, 'The catharsis of *King Lear*', *S.Sur.* 13 (1960), 1–10
Staunton	*The Plays of Shakespeare*, ed. H. Staunton, 1858–60
Steevens	*The Plays of William Shakespeare*, ed. Samuel Johnson and George Steevens, 15 vols., 1793, XIV
Stone	P. W. K. Stone, *The Textual History of 'King Lear'*, 1980
subst.	substantively
Taylor, 'Censorship'	Gary Taylor, 'Monopolies, show trials, disaster, and invasion: *King Lear* and censorship', in *Division*, pp. 75–119
Taylor, 'Date and authorship'	Gary Taylor, '*King Lear*: the date and authorship of the Folio version', in *Division*, pp. 351–468
Taylor, 'New source'	Gary Taylor, 'A new source and an old date for *King Lear*', *RES* 132 (1982), 396–413
Taylor, 'War'	Gary Taylor, 'The war in *King Lear*', *S.Sur.* 33 (1980), 27–34
Textual Companion	Stanley Wells and Gary Taylor, with John Jowett and William Montgomery, *William Shakespeare: A Textual Companion*, 1987
Theobald	*The Works of Shakespeare*, ed. Lewis Theobald, 7 vols., 1733, V
uncorr.	uncorrected
Urkowitz	Steven Urkowitz, *Shakespeare's Revision of 'King Lear'*, 1980
Urkowitz, 'Editorial tradition'	Steven Urkowitz, 'The base shall to th'legitimate: the growth of an editorial tradition', in *Division*, pp. 23–43
Warburton	*The Works of Shakespeare*, ed. William Warburton, 8 vols., 1747, VI
Warren, 'Albany and Edgar'	Michael Warren, 'Quarto and Folio *King Lear* and the interpretation of Albany and Edgar', in David Bevington and Jay L. Halio (eds.), *Shakespeare: Pattern of Excelling Nature*, 1978, pp. 95–107
Warren, 'Diminution'	Michael Warren, 'The diminution of Kent', in *Division*, pp. 59–73

Warren, R.	Roger Warren, 'The Folio omission of the mock trial: motives and consequences', in *Division*, pp. 45–57
Werstine	Paul Werstine, 'Folio editors, Folio compositors, and the Folio text of *King Lear*', in *Division*, pp. 247–312
Wiles	David Wiles, *Shakespeare's Clown*, 1987
Wittreich	Joseph Wittreich, *'Image of that Horror': History, Prophecy, and Apocalypse in 'King Lear'*, 1984

Biblical quotations are taken from the Geneva Bible, 1560

INTRODUCTION

King Lear, a play about an unstable society, is itself an unstable text. For much of its theatrical history it has been adapted and altered, either because it was considered too difficult to perform as written or because it was felt to be artistically defective. It exists in two published versions (called a 'History' in 1608, a 'Tragedy' in 1623). The *Lear* published in 1623 differs from the earlier one in large ways – two scenes are omitted – and in a great many small ones, such as the spelling of characters' names.[1] The reasons for these differences are still the subject of scholarly debate. The traditional view is that both derive from a common original and that the differences can be explained, on the one hand, by the incompetence of the printer in 1608 (he had never printed a play before) and, on the other, by alterations made by someone in the acting company and/or, later, by the editor employed to work on the massive 1623 Folio of Shakespeare's collected plays.[2] Editors and directors who work on this assumption base their edition on both texts, making choices between them where they differ and thus producing what is really a third version.

The other view is that the Folio represents Shakespeare's revision of the quarto and that the two texts should be treated separately.[3] However, the word 'revision' may be misleading, if it means the author's later, perhaps final, view of the play. As Leah Marcus writes, 'These are two "local" versions of *King Lear* among other possible versions which may have existed in manuscript, promptbook, or performance without achieving the fixity of print.'[4] It is now recognized that plays were adapted for different occasions: they might be shortened for some performances and, for others, lengthened with songs and dances. For plays at court, actors were expected to be well dressed and spectacle was important, especially since some spectators, such as foreign ambassadors, would not know much English. Touring productions may have had fewer actors at their disposal; plays in private houses or at the Inns of Court (law schools) may have had their own requirements – for instance, long plays might have had a refreshment break in the middle. The early published versions of many of Shakespeare's most popular plays – *A Midsummer Night's Dream*, *Romeo and Juliet*, *The Merry Wives of Windsor*, *Hamlet*, and *Othello* – differ from the ones published in 1623. We do not know whether the *King Lear* seen at court late in 1606 resembled the one published in 1608, or in the Folio of 1623, or neither. Tests of vocabulary and diction in the new material have suggested that it

---

[1] The spelling of Edmond and Gonerill in this Introduction is that of the Folio, but quotations from other writers will often give the more conventional quarto spellings, Edmund and Goneril.

[2] Brian Vickers, *The One King Lear*, 2016. His argument is summarized on p. 328.

[3] See the essays in *Division*, and many of those in James Ogden and Arthur H. Scouten (eds.), *'Lear' from Study to Stage*, 1997. R. A. Foakes, 'A shaping for *King Lear*', the final chapter of his *Hamlet versus Lear: Cultural Politics and Shakespeare's Art*, 1993, is a close study of how, in his opinion, the alterations work.

[4] Leah Marcus, *Puzzling Shakespeare*, 1988, p. 151.

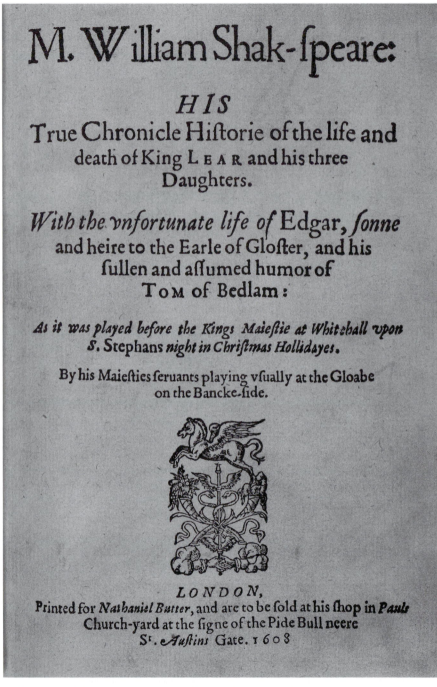

M. William Shak-speare:

HIS

True Chronicle Historie of the life and death of King LEAR and his three Daughters.

With the vnfortunate life of Edgar, *sonne* and heire to the Earle of Gloster, and his sullen and assumed humor of TOM of Bedlam:

As it was played before the Kings Maiestie at Whitehall vpon S. Stephans *night in Christmas Hollidayes.*

By his Maiesties seruants playing vsually at the Gloabe on the Bancke-side.

LONDON,
Printed for *Nathaniel Butter*, and are to be sold at his shop in *Pauls* Church-yard at the signe of the Pide Bull neere St. *Austins* Gate. 1608

1   Title page of the 1608 quarto of *King Lear*. Leaf A4 recto: title page

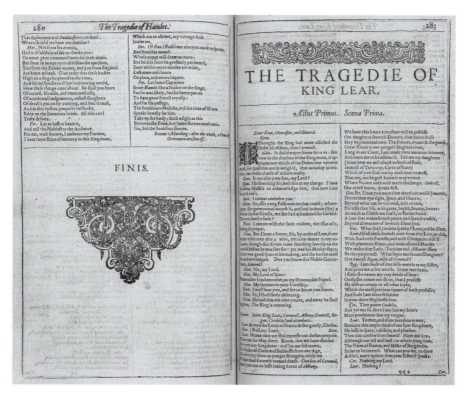

2   First page of *King Lear* in the 1623 Folio. Leaf qq1 verso (page 280), leaf qq2 recto (page 283)

dates from around 1610, but the amount of text on which this conclusion is based is very small. Even if the changes were made around the time Shakespeare was writing *Cymbeline* (also based on early British history), the play remains an early Jacobean work rather than an example of 'late Shakespeare'.[1]

Whatever one thinks about the origins of the two texts, the argument for editing the quarto and Folio plays separately is that it enables readers to make their own decisions about the differences between them. This edition prints the text of the play as it appeared in the 1623 volume of *Mr William Shakespeares Comedies, Histories, and Tragedies*. The first New Cambridge Shakespeare edition of this play, by Jay L. Halio, included a full discussion of these two texts. A slightly shortened version is reprinted here, introduced by Brian Gibbons, and the reader who wants to know more about this complex subject should look to pp. 50–79, 249–72. Passages that exist only in the quarto are printed in an Appendix.

The play's date is less controversial. It must be later than 1603, which is the publication date of one of its sources, Samuel Harsnett's *Declaration of Egregious Popish Impostures* (see p. 8, below). The title page of the play's first edition says that

[1] See Gordon McMullan, *Shakespeare and the Idea of Late Writing: Authorship in the Proximity of Death*, 2007, pp. 294–313, for the idea that the two-text theory attracts those who want a play about old age to be a late play.

it was performed at the court of James I at Whitehall on 26 December 1606. It is possible that this was its first performance, though it is more likely that the actors had already played it in public or private locations. Gloucester seems to assume that his onstage and offstage listeners will know what he means by 'These late [recent] eclipses in the sun and moon' (1.2.91); he may or may not be referring to the eclipses that had taken place in September and October 1605.

The play's most important theatrical source is an earlier play called *The True Chronicle History of King Leir and His Three Daughters*. This play (anonymous to us, but probably not to Shakespeare) could have been acted as early as 1589, and there are records of its performance at the Rose Theatre in April 1594 by a company that combined the personnel of two acting companies, the Queen's Men and the Earl of Sussex's Men. It was first entered into the Stationers' Register in May 1594 (to establish ownership) but apparently not published; it was entered again in May 1605 and published later that year. Richard Knowles, who finds that *Lear* recalls *Leir* in 'nearly a hundred significant details', thinks that Shakespeare could have acquired such familiarity only from reading the published text and thus that his play must have been written mainly in 1606.[1] To many scholars, however, the echoes of *Leir*'s plot and language – which have been found in other Shakespeare plays as well – seem like the result of long acquaintance rather than recent skimming. Although there is no evidence that Shakespeare ever belonged to the Queen's Men, several of their most popular plays became the basis for his own, and it remains possible that he saw or even acted in *Leir* when it was new.[2] The general view at present is that Shakespeare was probably writing *King Lear* in 1604–5 and planning *Macbeth* at about the same time.

EXPERIENCING THE PLAY

While *King Lear* is usually a gripping play in performance, it gets off to a difficult start. Its first scene, overloaded with characters and information, is difficult for an audience to take in. Actors notoriously find it difficult as well; Ian McKellen, who has played Lear several times, writes that he kept 'saying to myself: Once upon a time there was a King with Three Daughters' in order to believe in the improbable things he had to do.[3] The initial dialogue between Kent and Gloucester emphasizes Gloucester's two sons, legitimate and illegitimate, who are then forgotten for some 270 lines. Lear's plan to divide his kingdom among his daughters and their husbands is apparently known at least to these two courtiers, but his idea of basing his division on a 'love-test' may be either a secret plan or a sudden inspiration on his part. It is difficult for the five prospective heirs to the kingdom (and Cordelia's two suitors, who enter later) to

---

[1] Richard Knowles, 'How Shakespeare knew *King Leir*', *S.Sur.* 55 (2002), 12–35: 35. Knowles argues that Shakespeare is not known to have been part of the Queen's Men, who owned the play, and must have known it only from reading the published text.

[2] For example, Jacqueline Pearson, '*Much Ado* and *King Leir*', *N&Q* (April 1981), 128–9, and Alan Stewart, *Shakespeare's Letters*, 2008, p. 215. For other parallels, see Meredith Skura, 'What Shakespeare did with the Queen's Men's *King Leir* and when', *S.Sur.* 36 (2010), 316–25, and Janet Clare on the *Leir* play in *Shakespeare's Stage Traffic: Imitation, Borrowing, and Competition in Renaissance Theatre*, 2014, pp. 210–29.

[3] Ian McKellen, 'King Lear', in Julian Curry, *Shakespeare on Stage*, II, London, 2017, p. 157.

establish their characters and relationships in the few lines they are given. The love-test itself is an interpretive puzzle. The mood can be that of a lighthearted game, suddenly turning nasty when Cordelia refuses to play, or a deadly serious trial. Kent's interruption gives the audience something like an outside perspective on the action. Since France and Burgundy are said to have been courting Cordelia for a 'long' time (1.1.42), productions sometimes indicate, as the text does not, whether she (or Lear) has a preference for either of them. Her departure as the future Queen of France can feel like a fairytale ending, but her farewell warning and the brief, hasty exchange between Gonerill and Regan suggest that there is more to come.

When the action shifts to Gloucester's family and Edmond's plot, Gloucester's lament over the events at court keeps the Lear story in view. It also helps Edmond's deception, since the old man thinks he sees a parallel between Lear's unnatural treatment of his daughter and Edgar's supposed plot against his father. The audience's first look at Edgar is too brief to establish him as a counterweight to the attractive Edmond, whose plot takes effect with amazing speed. The action moves, like Lear, to the house of Gonerill and Albany, where Lear's stipulation that he should always be attended by a hundred knights is infuriating Gonerill. Kent, disguised as a servant, is taken on by Lear and at once has a confrontation with Gonerill's confidential servant Oswald. The Fool – the only major character not already seen – makes a surprise entrance and immediately dominates the stage. His increasingly bitter songs and jokes emphasize the breakdown of Lear's relation with Gonerill, which reaches a climax when Lear calls down a curse on his daughter and storms out of her house. Act 1 (the Folio *Lear*, unlike the quarto, is divided into acts and scenes) ends with a short conversation between Gonerill and her bewildered husband Albany, whose allegiance is still unclear; Oswald and Kent are sent, separately, with letters to Regan; and the Fool tries to amuse the unhappy Lear and the audience before setting off with him to visit the second daughter. It is not clear whether Lear's palace and the houses of Gonerill, Regan, and Gloucester are imagined as near each other.

From Act 2 onwards, everyone seems constantly on the move. Edgar is tricked by Edmond into fleeing from Gloucester's house and is at once replaced by Regan and Cornwall, who have abandoned their own residence for reasons which at this point are obscure. They proceed to make themselves at home in Gloucester's, even adopting Edmond in the process. Another confrontation between Kent and Oswald, which at first seems unmotivated, leads to Kent's humiliating punishment in the stocks. Significantly (see note to 2.2.156), he probably remains visible, supposedly at Gloucester's house, during the soliloquy in which Edgar, who has just fled from there, explains his intended disguise as an insane beggar. When Lear arrives, it finally becomes clear that Oswald's arrival with a letter from Gonerill not only interrupted Kent's delivery of Lear's letter but also made Regan and Cornwall leave home at once. Lear has somehow learned of Regan's whereabouts and come to Gloucester's house, where, furious at the treatment of his messenger, he confronts Regan and Cornwall. When Gonerill arrives, and all three join forces against him, he is overwhelmed by the collapse of the world he thought he knew. Again, he rushes out of a house, this time saying, 'I abjure all roofs' (2.4.201).

Act 3, an extraordinary piece of writing, divides the characters into those outside in the storm and those who remain indoors. On the Elizabethan stage, all this movement would be indicated by long entrances and exits through the doors at the back of the stage. Thunder and lightning provide a background against which human voices can be hard to hear. Kent and the Fool have managed to find Lear; when they try to enter a shelter, they are confronted by the disguised Edgar as Poor Tom, mankind reduced to its lowest possible level, and the sight precipitates Lear's descent into madness. Gloucester finds somewhere for them to go *in*, but almost at once returns to warn them to go *out* again, carrying the sleeping Lear. The Fool is never seen again. Running parallel to the scenes of Lear's madness are the quieter ones in Gloucester's house, where Edmond betrays his father. The blinding of Gloucester (3.7) is the most shocking event of the play, but also a turning point. Cornwall's servant, revolted by the act, kills his master; Gloucester finally learns the truth about his two sons. But the servant himself is killed and Gloucester's knowledge only adds to his wretchedness. Most productions put the interval either just before or just after this scene, as Gloucester is thrown out of his own house.

In Act 4, everyone seems to be converging on Dover, but characters frequently meet each other on the way in unspecified locations. When Edgar leads his blinded father onto the stage, the audience, like Gloucester, has to take his word that they are approaching Dover Cliff. Gloucester attempts suicide by jumping from it but Edgar has deceived him (and perhaps some of the audience) in the hope of curing his despair. Lear rejoins them, but the dialogue between mad king and blind man, another high point of the play, ends abruptly when Lear runs away from the soldiers sent by Cordelia to rescue him. Meanwhile, short scenes have indicated the crumbling of the alliance among Lear's enemies: Albany is estranged from Gonerill; Cornwall's death has made Regan a danger-ous rival for Edmond's love. Gloucester has a price on his head, so Oswald, now travelling with a letter from Gonerill to Edmond, tries to kill the old man. He is killed by Edgar, who discovers the incriminating documents that he was carrying. The act ends with the great scene in which Lear awakes in Cordelia's presence, gradually recognizes her, and asks her forgiveness. Like her departure for France in 1.1, her insistence that she has nothing to forgive seems about to bring the story to a happy ending.

Throughout the first four acts, there has been talk of war, first between Albany and Cornwall, then between France and England – or, rather, between supporters of Lear, helped by a French army, and the armies of Albany and Edmond, who has replaced Cornwall as general. Act 5 finally brings the battle that everyone has been expecting, and, as often noted, it is an anticlimax. Possibly Shakespeare was avoiding the dramatization of a French invasion of England; possibly this part of the play depended on spectacle that would have been worked out in rehearsal rather than recorded in the text. Modern productions often depict the battle only through sound effects, heard by the blind Gloucester. He is finally led away by Edgar, who has seen the defeat of Lear's forces.

Unlike the battle, the trial by combat between Edgar and Edmond ends with victory for the 'right' side and with the one genuinely effective revelation in the play – 'My name is Edgar, and thy father's son' (5.3.159). But Edmond's defeat, which leads to the exposure and death of Gonerill, shows evil destroying itself (Gonerill has already poisoned Regan). Albany has the women's bodies brought on stage to make this visible for the audience and the other characters. Edmond belatedly tries to undo his worst action, ordering the deaths of Lear and Cordelia, and is taken to die, like his father, offstage. The subplot is finished, and Edgar remains as an appalled spectator when Lear's entrance with the dead Cordelia shows that there will be no victory for good. As in the opening scene, the king is with his daughters, urging Cordelia to speak. Perhaps, as he dies, he thinks she is about to answer him, but the meaning of his last words is mysterious. A sense of exhaustion hangs over the survivors. Albany, technically the heir to the throne, apparently attempts to divide his kingdom between Kent and Edgar (but does 'rule in this realm' mean the whole of Britain, or only part of it?). Neither explicitly consents (unless the 'we' in Edgar's final speech is a royal we). Kent exits, saying that he will follow Lear in death, and the concluding couplets may be deliberately flat. What do we feel? What ought we to say?

Contexts

PUBLIC EVENTS

James I had arrived from Scotland in the summer of 1603. *King Lear*, like *Macbeth*, belongs to the period when Shakespeare and his colleagues were looking for the right kind of play for a new king and a new court. This meant, among other things, a movement away from English history, in which the Scots often figured as villains, and towards 'British' or classical history, likely to be more familiar not only to the Scots but also to visiting foreign dignitaries. The play's apparently casual opening line – 'I thought the king had more affected the Duke of Albany than Cornwall' – must have attracted attention at the court performance in 1606, since the king's sons, Henry and Charles, had recently been given these titles. In the play, they apparently refer to Scotland and Wales (with England presumably intended as Cordelia's portion), though the exact boundaries are left deliberately vague. But Gloucester's reply, with its reference to 'the division of the kingdom' (1.1.3–4), would have been still more significant. James's reuniting of the crowns of England and Scotland had already been celebrated officially; the play will show its audience the fatal moment at which Britain was divided. The word 'British', as used in *Lear*, not only refers to the period in which the play is set but also has topical significance. James wanted to unite his kingdom under the name of 'Great Britain' – something that would not officially happen for another 100 years.[1] Albany was Prince Charles's Scottish title, and the Duke of Albany is given the play's last lines in the quarto, perhaps foreshadowing Scotland's later importance; the lines were given to Edgar in the Folio, perhaps because this point no longer needed to be made.

---

[1] See James Shapiro, *1606: William Shakespeare and the Year of Lear*, 2015, pp. 48–9. Though it has been suggested that the opening line refers to James's preference of one son over the other, the boys were only 12 and 6 at the time of the court performance. In *Shakespeare and the Popular Voice*, 1989, pp. 106–7, Annabel Patterson argues that Lear offered a thinly veiled critique of James I's love of hunting and his fondness for his court fool, as well as his self-justifying rhetoric.

Leah Marcus has pointed out that St Stephen's Night, when the play was given at court, was associated with hospitality and charity (it was the day when poor boxes in churches were broken open and the money distributed to the poor). The fact that the 1608 title page makes a point of the performance date might, she thinks, alert readers to a way of reading the play, with its references to beggars and the homeless.[1] The version printed in 1623 does not make this connection, since the Folio, though it emphasizes Shakespeare's close relationship with the King's Men, omits references to performance conditions. Published twenty years after James's accession (and only two years before his death), the Folio *Lear* was already becoming a less topical work.

The public theatres were closed because of plague between 5 October and 15 December 1605, and November saw the discovery of the Gunpowder Plot to blow up the Houses of Parliament – the result of the disappointment and anger of some Roman Catholics who had hoped that the change of reigns might lead to greater toleration for their religion. In the circumstances, it is unlikely that Shakespeare could have finished the play, or that his company could have rehearsed it, in time for the Christmas season of court performances in 1605–6. Even without this traumatic event, religion was a major topic of discussion at the time of *Lear*'s first performance. The king's reign had begun with a conference about religion at Hampton Court (January 1604), and the commissioning of a new translation of the Bible. The measures that Gloucester takes to keep Edgar from leaving the country ('All ports I'll bar': 2.1.79) are like those taken against the plotters and their supporters.

One of the play's odder sources, Samuel Harsnett's *Declaration of Egregious Popish Impostures*, is an anti-Catholic polemic. The author revisits an episode of 1585–6, recently investigated again, in which Roman Catholic priests had claimed to exorcise servants suffering from demonic possession. He argues that the susceptible servants, mainly women, had been led to give spectacular accounts of their sufferings by the suggestions of their interrogators. It was from this book that Shakespeare took the names of the devils by whom 'Poor Tom' claims to have been possessed, and the situation of the servants in their chair (something Harsnett insists on several times) may have helped to create the awful image of Gloucester bound to a chair and tortured. The name Edmund (or Edmunds) occurs frequently in Harsnett's account; however, both Edmund and Edgar were also the names of kings before the Norman Conquest.

In 1603–4, there had been a curious parallel to the story of Lear. The elderly Sir Brian Annesley had three daughters, though only two were involved in the legal battle over whether he was too senile to be allowed to act for himself; the one who argued that his wishes deserved respect was, significantly, named Cordell. When Sir Brian died in 1604, one of the executors of his will was a man probably known to Shakespeare, Sir William Harvey, husband of the Countess of Southampton, who later married Cordell himself (her father had left her everything). It is not likely that this episode inspired Shakespeare's play, or even the name of the heroine, since there are other sources for both, but Shakespeare may have been struck by the way in which life sometimes imitated art.

---

[1] Marcus, *Puzzling*, pp. 153–4.

LITERARY AND THEATRICAL INFLUENCES

Knowing the sources of *Lear* is perhaps as close as one can ever come to observing the creative process by which Shakespeare made his play. It can also help to avoid unnecessary questions, such as, 'Why doesn't Cordelia just tell her father what he wants to hear?' The basic starting point – the king who asks his three daughters to say how much they love him – was not Shakespeare's invention. Many cultures have a story about someone who asks his three children how much they love him, fails to appreciate the honest answer of (always) the youngest one, and eventually realizes that she or he was right.

The 'chronicle histories' that served as sources for many plays in the 1590s tended to make up for the absence of hard facts with traditional anecdotes, especially for the poorly documented earlier periods. Geoffrey of Monmouth, in *Historica Anglicana* (*c.* 1135), was the first to connect the love-test with the division of the kingdom, and to ascribe it to a King Lear. There was no historical Leir or Lear: his name may have been invented to explain the name of the town of Leicester, interpreted as the Roman fort (*caster*) of Leir (compare Old King Cole, supposedly resident at Colchester). According to Geoffrey, Cordelia led an army that restored Lear to his throne, and became queen after his death. Later, her sisters' children rebelled and threw her into prison, where she hanged herself. This story is retold in *The Chronicles of England, Scotland, and Ireland* (1587), published under the name of Raphael Holinshed. This was probably Shakespeare's main source but he could also have read a condensed account in Edmund Spenser's *Faerie Queene* (1590). Another popular work was *The Mirror for Magistrates* (1574), a series of verse monologues by various writers in which the ghosts of famous people describe their miserable fates. It includes Cordelia's account of her imprisonment and suicide.

By calling itself *The True Chronicle History*, the anonymous *Leir* play acknowledges its indebtedness to sources like these, but gives events a romantic and folkloric turn, ending with Leir's restoration to his throne. Tolstoy, in a famous essay, said that it was superior to Shakespeare's version.[1] Certainly, it tells its story more clearly than Shakespeare does, partly because it has no subplot. Although there is no Fool, there are a number of comic characters and scenes; despite some harrowing and pathetic moments, there is rarely much doubt that the story will end happily and that virtue will be rewarded.

In the *Leir* play, as in Holinshed, all three daughters are unmarried at the beginning, but the love-test is designed to trap Cordella, who has said that she wants to marry for love: once she professes her love, Leir plans to make her prove it by marrying the man of his choice. Since the two older sisters have already been tipped off that their father plans to marry them to the men they prefer, they have no hesitation in expressing unconditional love and obedience; Cordella, however, defeats his plan by refusing to flatter him. The king of 'Gallia' (France – but the name perhaps emphasizes how long ago all this is happening) visits England in disguise in order to find out whether

---

[1] 'Tolstoy on Shakespeare: A critical essay on Shakespeare' (translated from the Russian by V. Tchertkoff and I. F. M.), published as a preface to Ernest Crosby's *Shakespeare's Attitude to the Working Classes* (1907). This essay is easiest to find on the internet, in the online transcription by Project Gutenberg.

i i

leire builded cayre laire
now caled leicester he had
three daughters, govorell,
ragan, and cordell, which
cordell succeded him in
the kyngdom, when hee
had raigned 40 years

Cordila was sore vexed
by her two nephus, Mor-
gan of Albanye, and cone-
dagus of Camber, who caste
her in prison, where she
slewe selfe when she had
raigned 5 yeares: sssss

3   Thomas Trevelyon, Leire and Cordila [*Trevelyon Miscellany*], 1608. Folio 73 verso

English women are as pretty as he has heard; he meets the banished Cordella and falls in love at once. Meanwhile, Leir's other daughters show their evil natures: Ragan pays someone to kill her father and his loyal friend Perillus, but the murderer is frightened off by heaven's thunder. In desperation, the two old men travel to France, where they meet Cordella and her husband, again in disguise, and have a touching reunion. The author handles the tricky problem of dramatizing a successful French invasion by making it comic. All the characters trade pre-battle insults; there is plenty of onstage fighting; the sisters' husbands run away; and Leir, a wiser man, is restored to his throne. It is made clear that the Gallian king is there only on Leir's behalf and that he and Cordella will return to France at once.

As Janet Clare has pointed out, the title page of the 1608 edition of *Lear* 'advertised its relationship and continuity with the recently published *Leir* play'.[1] It also emphasized its difference: *this* version of *The Chronicle History of King Lear* is by William Shakespeare, depicts not only the life but also the death of the king, and includes new material. This statement was necessary, because the Stationers' Company (the equivalent of a publishers' and printers' union) protected its members by making it difficult for anyone to publish a work that was likely to duplicate and thus damage the sales of one already in existence. The emphasis on the role of Edgar also ensured that prospective readers and spectators would not be expecting just another retelling of a story they already knew.

The subplot involving Gloucester and his two sons reinforced the theme of parent–child relations and provided more good roles for the company's actors. Shakespeare based it on an episode in one of the most prestigious and popular works of the Renaissance, Sir Philip Sidney's *Arcadia* (first published in 1590). Two young princes are sheltering from a storm when they overhear a young man arguing with an old, blind man. The old man turns out to be the king of Paphlagonia, whose son has refused to lead him to the top of a rock, realizing that his father wants to throw himself off. As in *Lear*, the king has previously been deceived by his bastard son, though Sidney's characters do not explain (as Shakespeare's play does) how the deception was carried out. The two princes intervene, restore the old man to his throne, and reward his virtuous son, though this happy ending is as temporary as the happy ending of Cordelia's story in the chronicles. As Geoffrey Bullough has shown in his massive source study, Shakespeare drew on more than one part of the novel, as well as on its fatalism and its serious debates about the meaning of life. Perhaps, too, the spectacular storm that opens this episode suggested the one in *Lear*.[2]

Among Shakespeare's own works, the plays most often compared with *Lear* are *Titus Andronicus*, an early work, and *Timon of Athens*, probably begun around the same time as *Lear* but left unfinished. Both plays have a Fool or Clown among the characters, and a hero who sometimes sounds like Lear in his rage.[3] But *Lear* also resembles the comedy

---

[1] Clare, *Traffic*, p. 224.
[2] Bullough, pp. 284–6.
[3] Both plays also appear to have been collaborations, with George Peele and Thomas Middleton, respectively.

As You Like It, acted around 1600 but not printed until 1623. The song that a courtier sings in the Forest of Arden –

> Blow, blow, thou winter wind,
> Thou art not so unkind
> As man's ingratitude   (*AYLI* 2.7.174–6)

– sounds as if it belongs in *King Lear* rather than in a comedy where ingratitude is not a prominent theme. When Kent tells Lear that 'Freedom lives hence, and banishment is here' (1.1.175), he echoes Celia's claim that she and Rosalind, in leaving the court, will go 'To liberty and not to banishment' (*AYLI* 1.3.138).[1] Structurally, too, both plays have several 'false endings'. In *As You Like It*, these take the form of rhyming couplets and a cue for dance, twice interrupted; in *Lear*, Albany makes similar unsuccessful attempts to draw the play to an end. The brief snatch of song from Lear's Fool, 'He that has and a little tiny wit' (3.2.72), echoes the Fool's final song in *Twelfth Night* (1601).

King *Lear* is the only one of Shakespeare's major tragedies to make use of disguise, which, as Peter Hyland has noted, is used primarily in comedy and tragicomedy (including the comic scenes in the chronicle histories).[2] The old *King Leir* included several disguised characters, though not the same ones as in *Lear*. A character in disguise usually gains power by knowing something that others don't, and the disguises of Kent and Edgar create the expectation that they will bring about a happy ending – as in Shakespeare's *Measure for Measure* and John Marston's *The Malcontent*, both of which are usually dated 1603–4. Yet the disguises in *Lear* result mainly in humiliation and Edgar's final triumph rings hollow.

Another comedy – *Eastward Ho!* (1605) – has also been suggested as a source.[3] This collaboration by George Chapman, Ben Jonson, and John Marston contains several joking references to *Hamlet*, as well as an obvious parody of a line from *Richard III*, so it is likely that Shakespeare would have wanted to see or at least read it. The resemblances that Gary Taylor finds in *Lear* (an ironically inverted father–daughter relationship; the wildness of the apprentice Quicksilver, which resembles Edgar's narrative of his past as Poor Tom; the importance of a storm at the centre of the play; and an improvised trial scene) may be – like the echoes of the old *Leir* play – Shakespeare's transformation of theatrically striking moments in a new context. But the dates of the two plays are uncertain; the influence may have worked either way.

If the literary sources of the play, apart from the *Arcadia*, are essentially comic, the 'historical' accounts contain tragic events. Lear apparently dies of old age, but Cordelia's suicide in a state of despair would, to a Christian reader, have condemned her to hell, which is why Alexander Leggatt argues that murder is a 'more merciful'

---

[1] Frank McCombie calls it 'another version of *As You Like It*'. See 'Medium and message in *As You Like It* and *King Lear*', *S.Sur.* 33 (1980), 67–80, and Jane Kingsley-Smith's chapter, '"Hereafter, in a better world than this": the end of exile in *As You Like It* and *King Lear*', in Kingsley-Smith, *Shakespeare's Drama of Exile*, 2003, pp. 106–36.

[2] Peter Hyland, *Disguise on the Early Modern English Stage*, 2011, p. 72. Disguise in tragedy, Hyland notes, is usually used by a revenger.

[3] Gary Taylor, 'A new source and an old date for King Lear', *RES* 33 (1982), 396–413.

end for her than suicide.[1] The old *Leir* play ended happily because it ended before that point. Shakespeare did not really turn a comedy into a tragedy, as is often said; he compressed the events of many years into a play. Moreover, the design of this early Jacobean play requires the division of the kingdom to have disastrous consequences. The implication (though most people are unlikely to have believed it, even in 1606) is that the happy ending, a thousand years in the future, will be James I.

Afterlife: In the Theatre

EARLY RESPONSES

The lack of surviving contemporary reaction to *King Lear* makes it difficult to know whether its first audiences took it as a political work or simply as a powerful theatrical experience. Richard Burbage was the leading actor of the King's Men, and Lear is mentioned as one of his roles in an elegy on his death.[2] The line 'And my poor fool is hanged' (see the note on 5.3.279) has led some scholars to think that the parts of Cordelia and the Fool were doubled by a boy actor, while others believe that Robert Armin, who had recently joined the company, played the Fool. Armin, short and ugly, was a clever actor who also wrote plays and, in 1608, perhaps to accompany *Lear*'s appearance in print, published a book on fools called *A Nest of Ninnies*. William A. Ringler, however, has argued for the Fool–Cordelia doubling, on the grounds that Armin's versatility made him better suited to Edgar.[3] The fact that many female roles in the major tragedies are those of mature women suggests that the company now had older boy actors who were convincing in these roles. The smallness of Cordelia's part may be due to its being written for a new, less experienced boy. There is one other casting possibility. In English drama, *Lear*'s most obvious influence was on John Webster's *The Duchess of Malfi* (1613). Bosola, a villain with a conscience, echoes both *Lear* and the *Arcadia* in describing life as 'a shadow or deep pit of darkness' and claiming that 'we are merely the stars' tennis balls'. To a dying man, he murmurs, 'Break, heart!' in an obvious echo of Kent's words over the dying Lear: 'Break, heart, I prithee break' (5.3.286). This line is given to Lear in the quarto, but Webster must have heard it spoken by Kent in the theatre (as it is in the Folio). John Lowin, a leading actor in the King's Men, played Bosola; he may have played Kent as well.

In 1609–10, a King Lear play was performed at a private house in Yorkshire. It might have been the old *Leir*, but it is more likely that the company chose the one published in 1608, which would have been new to a provincial audience. The actors got into trouble for putting on a play about Saint Christopher, and their patron was suspected of Catholicism. Stephen Greenblatt suggests that they must have felt that *Lear*, despite its use of the anti-Catholic Harsnett, 'was not hostile, was strangely

---

[1] Alexander Leggatt, *King Lear*, 1988, p. 7.

[2] He is called 'kind Lear'; unless this is a printer's error for 'king', it may indicate how the character was perceived.

[3] 'Shakespeare and his actors: some remarks on *King Lear*', in Ogden and Scouten (eds.), *'Lear' from Study to Stage*, pp. 127–32.

sympathetic even, to the situation of persecuted Catholics'.[1] A play called *Lear König in Englelandt*, presumably based on Shakespeare's, was performed by an English company in Dresden (a Protestant city) on 26 September 1626. It was never printed, but, if it was like other surviving German versions of English plays, it would have been heavily cut, with emphasis on the mad scenes and clowning.

The public theatres were closed at the start of the English Civil War in 1642 and remained closed until the restoration of the Stuart monarchy in 1660. Sir William Davenant, one of the two theatre managers appointed at that time, had his company perform the play in 1664 and 1675. Unfortunately, Samuel Pepys did not see it, and there are no records of its reception – which suggests that it was unsuccessful. In 1681, however, the same company performed an adaptation by the poet and dramatist Nahum Tate, with the finest actor of the age, Thomas Betterton, as Lear. This version, which is also the first conflation of quarto and Folio,[2] became the acting text for the next 150 years.

NAHUM TATE'S ADAPTATION, 1681–1838, AND AFTER

Although Tate used to be mentioned only as an object of ridicule, many of his changes not only reflect the taste of the late seventeenth century but also represent good playwriting practice. Theatres after 1660 were using representational scenery (painted on flats) and hence found it difficult to stage a series of short scenes like those in Acts 3 and 4. Women had replaced boys in female roles, and needed to be given more to do. Like many modern directors, Tate cut and conflated minor characters. He also removed one major one, the Fool – and not only because the character had become old-fashioned. As Sonia Massai points out (p. 436), his disappearance removed 'the main source of the vexing criticism the king is exposed to in the Shakespeare originals'. The newly restored monarchy had every reason to be nervous about such criticism.

Tate's main innovation was to create a romantic relationship between Edgar and Cordelia, a decision that turned Cordelia's small part into an important one. She now has a motive for defying her father in the first scene, in order to avoid marrying Burgundy (the King of France, obviously, is not part of this play, so Cordelia never leaves the country). Lear also has a better motive for his anger against her, since he believes the negative view of Edgar that Edmond has disseminated (Massai, pp. 437–8). Edgar himself is so distracted by his concern for Cordelia that he is easily duped by Edmond, and he remains in the country to watch over her. Because he has a recognizable personality before he goes into disguise, the audience is not confused by his Poor Tom impersonation.

In this context, there was no doubt as to the evil of Gonerill and Regan. Although for the first two acts they maintain that their quarrel is with Lear's entourage, not with him, a common practice among rebels in the English history plays (and Parliament in the 1630s) was to claim that they wanted only to remove the corrupt

---

[1] Stephen Greenblatt, 'Shakespeare and the exorcists', in *Shakespearean Negotiations: The Circulation of Social Energy in Renaissance England*, 1988, p. 122.

[2] Massai, pp. 438–9.

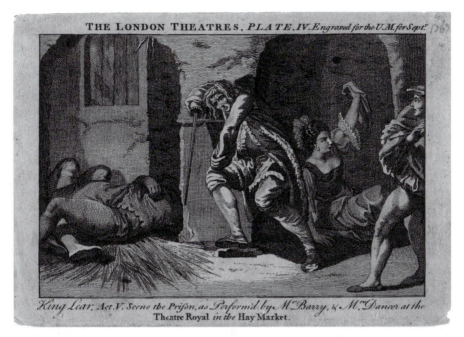

4   Anonymous artist, 'King Lear, act V, scene the Prison [III], as perform'd by Mr. Barry & Mrs. Dancer at the Theatre Royal in the Haymarket'

favourites around the ruler. Edmond's relations with the sisters are those of a Restoration rake, but he also lusts after Cordelia and sends ruffians to carry her off, so that Edgar is able to rescue her and prove his worth. Tate set the final scene in prison where Lear, asleep with his head in Cordelia's lap, is finally able to enjoy, as he had hoped in 1.1, 'her kind nursery'. The audience sees the old man heroically fighting off the murderers sent by Edmond, and his exhausted collapse afterwards was one of the highpoints of eighteenth-century performances. Albany and Edgar arrive with rescue just in time, and Lear abdicates in favour of Edgar and Cordelia. Tate retained two of the play's most shocking scenes, the blinding of Gloucester and his attempt to throw himself off a non-existent cliff. By the eighteenth century, however, the blinding was happening off stage, where it seems to have remained until well into the twentieth century. Developing a hint in Shakespeare (4.4.12–13), Tate made Gloucester decide to use the spectacle of his blindness to raise a popular rebellion against the sisters. Kent, whose role in the second half of Shakespeare's play is disappointingly subdued, becomes the leader of Cordelia's army. These changes create their own difficulties: Gloucester's energy seems inconsistent with his desire for death, and, the more emphasis there is on the rallying of Lear's forces, the harder it is to understand why the wrong side wins. Royalists in Restoration England may, however, have seen the defeat of Lear's cause as a parallel to their own in the recent Civil War. The ending, with its emphasis on restoration, was equally significant. 'By making Lear both the "Martyr-King" and the restored king, Tate reverses the act of regicide.'[1] In 1681, when the childless Charles II was being urged to divert the succession from his Roman Catholic brother James to his illegitimate son, the Protestant Duke of Monmouth, no one could miss the relevance of a play in which a villainous bastard plots to disinherit his brother. In 1688, other political events made the conclusion too awkwardly topical. Facing rebellion, James II fled to France and was replaced by his daughter Mary and her husband, William of Orange. He was declared to have abdicated (like Lear, in favour of a daughter and son-in-law), though in fact he and his successors made several attempts to regain the throne. One of his supporters accused Mary of being 'worse than cruel, lustful Goneril'.[2] Tate's *Lear* was not performed again until five years after Mary's death in 1694.

It was largely David Garrick's playing of the role, from 1742 to his retirement in 1776, that made it a popular success. By the end of that period, however, the editing of Shakespeare's text was becoming a high-profile activity and there were calls for the original play to be performed. Garrick's marked-up acting copy, now in the British Library, shows that in the course of his career he removed some of the Restoration language and restored 255 lines of the original. Nevertheless, the play still ended with Lear's heroic fight, the last-minute rescue, and the happy ending of the love story. Francis Gentleman's notes to *Bell's Shakespeare* (1774), the acting edition used in the London theatres, were obviously written with Garrick's performance in mind; they emphasize the pathos in the role and the opportunities for a versatile actor in the king's rapid transitions of mood.[3]

The play again became uncomfortably topical when, in 1788, George III began showing signs of insanity. In a letter of 18 December 1788, recently published online, a doctor informed the Prince of Wales that his father had been 'agitated and confused, perhaps from having been permitted to read King Lear'.[4] The king may even have tricked his doctors into giving him the play.[5] Though he recovered from this attack, in 1811 his condition became permanent, and *Lear* was not performed again until after his death in 1820, when both London theatres rushed to revive it. The great actor of the Romantic period, Edmund Kean, played Lear successfully in that year, and his literary friends persuaded him to try the tragic ending in 1823, but it was a failure.

[1] Nancy Klein Maguire, 'Nahum Tate's *King Lear*: the king's blest restoration', in Jean I. Marsden (ed.), *The Appropriation of Shakespeare*, 1991, p. 38.

[2] Anon., 'The female parricide', in *Poems on Affairs of State: Augustan Satirical Verse, 1660–1714*, Vol. V, *1688–1697*, ed. William J. Cameron, 1971, p. 157.

[3] *Bell's Shakespeare*, p. 32n.

[4] Camilla Tominey, 'George III's medical records put online', *The Telegraph*, 16 Nov. 2018, www .telegraph.co.uk/news/2018/11/16/george-iiis-medical-records-put-online-royal-first-revealing.

[5] From Dr John Willis's testimony on 13 Jan. 1789, in Richard Warren, Lucas Pepys, Francis Willis, George Baker, Henry Revell Reynolds, and Thomas Gisborne, *Report from the Committee appointed to examine the physicians who have attended His Majesty during his illness*, 1789, p. 223. (I should like to thank Marguerite Happé for directing me to this publication.) After Willis had refused to let him have the Shakespeare play, the king asked for and received a set of George Colman's plays which contained his adaptation of *Lear*. The two leading physicians contradicted each other about its effect, Dr Richard Warren saying that 'His Majesty's Observation on the Book affected me strangely' (p. 186) while Willis (obviously afraid of being blamed for providing it) insisted that the king was incapable of any sustained reading (p. 223).

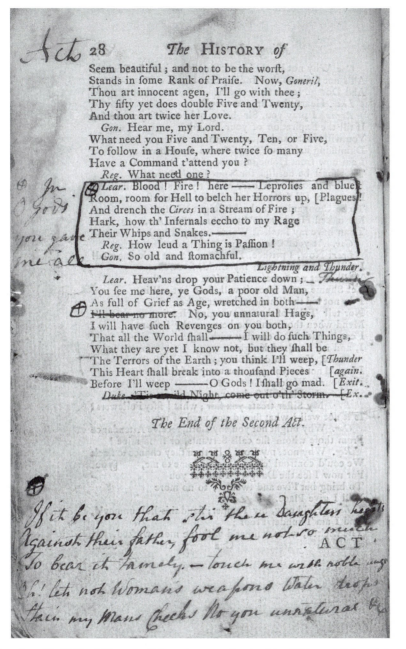

Seem beautiful ; and not to be the worſt,
Stands in ſome Rank of Praiſe. Now, *Goneril*,
Thou art innocent agen, I'll go with thee ;
Thy fifty yet does double Five and Twenty,
And thou art twice her Love.
　　Gon. Hear me, my Lord.
What need you Five and Twenty, Ten, or Five,
To follow in a Houſe, where twice ſo many
Have a Command t'attend you ?
　　Reg. What need one ?
　　Lear. Blood ! Fire ! here —— Leproſies and blue
Room, room for Hell to belch her Horrors up, [Plagues]!
And drench the *Circes* in a Stream of Fire ;
Hark, how th' Infernals eccho to my Rage
Their Whips and Snakes.——
　　Reg. How leud a Thing is Paſſion !
　　Gon. So old and ſtomachful.
　　　　　　　　　　　　Lightning and Thunder.
　　Lear. Heav'ns drop your Patience down ;
You ſee me here, ye Gods, a poor old Man,
As full of Grief as Age, wretched in both——
I'll bear no more. No, you unnatural Hags,
I will have ſuch Revenges on you both,
That all the World ſhall—— I will do ſuch Things,
What they are yet I know not, but they ſhall be
The Terrors of the Earth ; you think I'll weep, [*Thunder*
This Heart ſhall break into a thouſand Pieces [*again.*
Before I'll weep —— O Gods ! I ſhall go mad. [*Exit.*
　　Duke. 'Tis a wild Night, come out o' th' Storm. [*Ex.*

　　　　　The End of the Second Act.

5　Page from David Garrick's copy of the acting text, showing his additions and alterations to the Tate version

Kean's most important successor, William Charles Macready, played a tragic version (though still without the Fool) in 1834, but in 1838 he revived the play, heavily cut and rearranged, omitting all of Tate's lines and restoring the Fool. There were difficulties: actors found it hard to learn a new text, and his new leading lady, Helena Faucit, was reluctant to take the much reduced role of Cordelia. When Macready worried that the Fool 'will either weary and annoy or distract the spectator' someone suggested that the part should be played by a woman.[1] Though later revivals did not necessarily follow this example, they generally depicted the Fool as frail and wistful, cutting his bawdier lines. The restoration of the original text went along with historical sets and costumes that placed the play's events in a more 'primitive' age. Though Lear was still treated as a pathetic figure, Macready also found 'a heartiness, and even jollity in his blither moments, in no way akin to the helplessness of senility'.[2] The comedy, of course, was in the service of a sympathetic characterization. The Tate version continued to have a life in America until Edwin Booth played a condensed but totally Shakespearean version in 1875.

LEAR IN EUROPE BEFORE 1900

In the eighteenth century, as Shakespeare began to be known outside the Anglophone world, the early French and German translators felt free to adapt a play which had already been adapted. The German version published in 1778 was by the actor Friedrich Schröder, who based it on an accurate prose translation by C. M. Wieland (1762). Unlike Tate, he retained the Fool, a character type that had remained popular in central Europe, and he omitted the Edgar–Cordelia love affair. Some of his changes were minor improvements. Lear asks the disguised Kent's name when they first meet, so that the audience isn't confused by hearing him called Caius at the very end of the play.[3] Edgar is not quite so easily manipulated as in Shakespeare. Other changes reduce the number of characters and scene changes. 1.1 is cut: Kent simply tells Gloucester about the love-test and his banishment. Thus, Kordelia does not appear until Act 4 and her role is greatly reduced.

Schröder, who had great success in the role of Lear, departs most from the original in his treatment of the ending. As in Tate's version, the final scene takes place in prison, where Lear, who has never recovered his sanity, fantasizes about singing 'like birds in the cage', and puts an imaginary Gonerill and Regan on trial. Though he kills the soldier who is trying to hang Kordelia, she faints; thinking that she is dead, he dies of grief, while she apparently survives to become Queen of England. Even Goethe, who produced the play at Weimar in 1796 and 1800, believed that Schröder had the right idea about staging Shakespeare, whose numerous scene changes he considered impossible.

---

[1] William Charles Macready, *Reminiscences*, ed. F. Pollock, 1875, p. 438.
[2] *Ibid.*, p. 156.
[3] *König Lear, Ein Trauerspiel nach Shakespear*, 1778, 1.3., p. 17. In Jonathan Munby's Chichester and London production (2017–18), the disguised Kent, rather improbably, started to say 'Kent' and corrected it to Caius at the last minute.

Because of the international dominance of French in the eighteenth and nineteenth centuries, the very different *Lear* (or *Léar*) of Jean-François Ducis was still more influential. Ducis, though he knew no English, had access to a better Shakespeare translation than for his earlier *Hamlet* and *Othello*. His version was performed in 1783 before Louis XVI at Versailles and was the first Shakespeare play acted at the Comédie Française. Following his usual practice, Ducis reduced the size of the cast, changed the names of some characters, and, like Schröder, opened the play after its most improbable episode, the love-test, had already taken place. He omitted the subplot but gave Kent two sons, both virtuous, who fight to restore Léar. What this version retained above all were the spectacular effect of characters speaking against the background of a storm and the touching reunion of the feeble and confused Léar with his daughter. Still more than in Tate, the emphasis is on family relationships: when Helmonde (Cordelia), prompting Léar's memory, asks him whether he was a king, he replies, 'No, but I was a father.'[1] The omission of the subplot gives room for an even more prolonged display of madness than in Schröder, continuing into the inevitable prison scene; Léar finally recovers when he hears that Helmonde has been saved from death.

At a time when English was still not widely known, translators in other countries often followed the French or German adaptation. Although a fuller translation of the play by Josef Schreyvogel was performed in Vienna's Burgtheater in 1822, the censor insisted that Lear and Cordelia must be allowed to live. Rather than rewrite the final scene, the translator followed the Shakespeare text until Lear said 'Look there!' – 'only to have Cordelia revive and the curtain descend on the rapturous reunion of father and daughter'.[2] Even when, late in the century, the play finally included Cordelia's death, 'it seemed merely a natural step towards their final reunification' (Williams, *German Stage*, p. 126). Ira Aldridge, the great African-American actor, played Lear in whiteface on the European continent and in provincial English theatres between 1858 and his death in 1867. Reviewers saw him as 'a just and kind king who . . . is blinded and confused by his good nature'.[3] When he played in non-anglophone countries, he used a heavily cut text; it apparently included the love between Edgar and Cordelia, though in some performances at least he also played Lear's death scene.[4]

Both translation and scholarship on Shakespeare developed rapidly during the nineteenth century, particularly in Germany. Important evidence about the Elizabethan theatre came from the discovery in Utrecht in 1880 of what is usually called the 'Swan drawing', a rare surviving view of an Elizabethan playhouse interior. In 1889, a newly designed auditorium in Munich's Residenztheater, later known as the Shakespeare Stage, gave *Lear* as its first production, showing how a permanent set could enable rapid movement from scene to scene.[5] It was not an

---

[1] Jean-François Ducis, *Le Roi Léar* [1783], 4.5, p. 58.
[2] Simon Williams, *Shakespeare on the German Stage*, Vol. i, *1586–1914*, 1990, p. 116.
[3] N. J. Nazarov, 'Aldridge in *King Lear*', *Ruskii Vestnik* 42 (1862), 24–7, quoted, in translation, Bernth Lindfors, *Ira Aldridge: The Last Years, 1855–1867*, 2015, p. 184.
[4] *Ibid.*, pp. 89, 140–50, 159. Some reviewers complained about the Edgar–Cordelia love story, which by then they knew to be non-Shakespearean. Aldridge may have used the original text in later years.
[5] Dennis Kennedy, *Looking at Shakespeare: A Visual History of Twentieth-Century Performance*, 2nd edn, 2001, pp. 3–8.

Айра Олдридж в роли короля Лира

Из собраний Гос. Центрального театрального музея
им. А. Бахрушина

6   Ira Aldridge as Lear, *c.* 1860, in white make-up

accurate reconstruction, but it inspired many other attempts at 'Elizabethan' methods. The twentieth century would find other ways – technical advances in scenery and lighting, an unlocalized stage – to speed up performances and thus enable the playing of a fuller text.

7   Lear's denunciation of Cordelia, as played at Munich's 'Elizabethan' theatre, *c.* 1890, on a semi-permanent set, with the 'early English' costumes typical of nineteenth-century productions

THE ROLES: CHANGING PERSPECTIVES SINCE 1900

Lear

Audiences once expected 'cosmic grandeur' from the actor of Lear, particularly in the curse on Gonerill and the storm scene. This phrase, though it might have applied to many Lears, was in fact used by Edith Sitwell about Donald Wolfit in 1940. However, it seemed 'an outdated idea' to Michael Pennington when he wrote in 2016 about the experience of playing Lear himself.[1] For one thing, political – and especially feminist – criticism tends to be hostile to Lear, at least in the early part of the play. Moreover, very few productions are now, like Wolfit's, dominated by an actor who is also the director. In Anglophone productions at least, directors are now likely to care more about the family story than the 'cosmic' one, and to attempt to do justice to all the characters. Nevertheless, Lear continues to dominate discussions of the play, and reviews still focus largely on the actor who plays the part.

Richard Burbage was probably about 40 when he first played Lear; Garrick was 25, Gielgud 27. For them, the part of the 80-year-old king was simply one more feat of impersonation (an actor playing someone totally unlike himself). Now, Lear is often played by actors at the peak of their careers, implying a kind of identity between actor and role. Laurence Olivier (who first played Lear in 1946) appeared in a television

[1] Michael Pennington, *King Lear in Brooklyn*, 2016, p. 43.

8   'Howl, howl, howl, howl': Colm Feore as King Lear and Sara Farb as Cordelia (background: Victor Ertmanis)

version in 1983, when he was 75 and terminally ill. Some of the effect of Robert Stephens's Lear in 1993 was due to his obvious frailty (he died two years later).[1] William Hutt, who played a famous King Lear at Canada's Stratford in 1988, appeared in the television series *Slings and Arrows* in 2006 at the age of 86, as an ageing actor who wants to play the part yet again.[2] Audiences who know the age of the

[1] See McMullan, *Late Writing*, pp. 314–15.
[2] https://en.wikipedia.org/wiki/William_Hutt_(actor).

actor playing Lear will watch with awe if he carries the dead Cordelia onto the stage. Ronald Harwood's *The Dresser* (1980) depicts the worry this causes for an old actor ('Sir') playing Lear. Gregory Doran at the first rehearsal of the *Lear* he directed in 2016 quoted the advice 'Get a Cordelia you can carry', attributing it to Donald Wolfit, the prototype for 'Sir'.[1] Many of Shakespeare's tragedies give the leading actor some opportunity at the end to impress the audience by fighting, as with Romeo, Richard III, Hamlet, and Macbeth. With the disappearance of Tate's version, Lear's heroic fight also disappeared, and, while rehearsing the role, Oliver Ford Davies wondered, 'Has the carrying on of Cordelia become the most famous piece of stage business in Shakespeare, the ultimate test of an ageing actor's virility?'[2] For an audience more involved in the story, however, Lear's entrance is both a shock and a moment of almost unbearable pain.

Garrick's Lear was, he said, based on his observation of an old man who had gone mad after accidentally killing a beloved child. Many actors since his time have also felt the need to study real examples of mental illness. Macready, knowing the frequency of mad scenes in the major theatrical roles, forced himself at the beginning of his career to visit an asylum and drew on his vivid memories when he played Lear.[3] Productions in the twenty-first century reflect increasing awareness of an ageing population's vulnerability to dementia. In Australia, according to Philippa Kelly, medical professionals speak of 'The *King Lear* syndrome' and society 'increasingly understands what it might feel like to be Goneril, Regan and Edmund, and to fear what it is like to be Lear or Gloucester'.[4]

In some productions, Lear shows symptoms of insanity from the beginning. Christopher Plummer's Lear (Stratford, Ontario, 2002) had trouble remembering the word 'Burgundy' in the opening scene, and in 4.6 his slurred speech suggested that he had had a stroke.[5] However, Alzheimer's is an irreversible condition, whereas the scene (4.6) in which Lear finally recognizes Cordelia is usually seen as the beginning of a return to sanity, though in a state of diminished energy (the doctor says that the 'great rage' has been 'killed' in him: 4.6.77–8). Simon Russell Beale researched mental illnesses before his performance at the National Theatre in 2014 and concluded that the king was suffering from the condition known as 'dementia with Lewys Bodies', characterized by restlessness and hallucinations like Lear's vision of 'the little dogs and all' barking at him. A doctor who reviewed the production, however, thought that Lear seemed less mad in the final scene than in Act 1.[6] Ian Stuart-Hamilton, the psychologist who talked to Antony Sher during rehearsals of Gregory Doran's *King Lear* (2016), argued that Lear at the beginning was capable of making plans and in good health, and his later behaviour could be explained as delirium resulting from fever and exposure to

[1]   Antony Sher, *The Year of the Mad King*, 2018, p. 173.
[2]   Oliver Ford Davies, *Playing Lear: An Insider's Guide from Text to Performance*, 2003, p. 123.
[3]   Macready, *Reminiscences*, pp. 141–2.
[4]   Philippa Kelly, *The King and I*, 2011, pp. 73–4.
[5]   Christopher Plummer, *In Spite of Myself*, 2008, pp. 641–2.
[6]   Roger Jones, 'The madness of the king', review of *King Lear*, National Theatre, *British Journal of General Practice* 64 (2014), 148. Peter Ustinov, who played Lear at Canada's Stratford in 1981, contended that Lear was mad at the beginning and regained his judgement in the course of the play (Maurice Good, '*Every Inch a Lear*', 1982, p. 9).

the elements.[1] Thus, his earlier fears of madness might be either emotional blackmail ('I prithee, daughter, do not make me mad': 2.4.211) or genuine fear of Alzheimer's. Lear himself recognizes the symptoms of *hysterica passio* (see notes to 2.4.52–3 and 2.4.114). The Lear of David Warner (Chichester, 2005) died, literally, of a broken heart,[2] as did Kevin McNally at the Globe in 2016.

The Fool

The relation of the Fool and Lear is almost symbiotic: Antony Sher, one of a number of actors who have played both characters in the course of their careers, writes that 'the two performances have to grow together in rehearsals'.[3] Perhaps for this reason, most Lear actors, though they call the Fool 'boy', do not want him to be boyish, and many Fools have been nearly as old as Lear.[4] But women are also cast in the role – for example, Linda Kerr Scott (RSC) and Emma Thompson (Renaissance Theatre Company), both in 1990 – and some performers, such as Ruth Wilson (New York, 2019), have doubled the role with Cordelia, as some think was the original practice. The early modern Fool was instantly recognizable by his costume, which, as David Wiles explains, consisted of motley clothing, a cockscomb (substitute crown), and a bauble (substitute sceptre).[5] In a

9 'Poor fool and knave': Kent (Louis Hillyer), Lear (Corin Redgrave), and Fool (John Normington). Royal Shakespeare Company 2004, directed by Bill Alexander

---

[1] Sher, *Year*, pp. 182–3.
[2] Michael Dobson, 'Shakespeare performances in England', *S.Sur.* 59 (2006), 335–6.
[3] Antony Sher, 'The Fool', in *Playing Shakespeare 2*, 1988, p. 154.
[4] See, e.g., Ford Davies, *Playing Lear*, p. 48; Sher, *Year*, p. 132.
[5] Wiles, p. 190.

modern-dress production, he may look like a music hall performer or red-nosed circus clown. Much of his humour depends on puns that are too ingenious for a modern audience – see this edition's notes on 'Take the fool with thee' (1.4.270) and 'cruel garters' (2.4.7) – so he usually needs to have other performance skills.

Directors are often tempted to bring him on in the opening scene, playing games with the king or watching, appalled, as Lear destroys his kingdom. The Fool in Irving's 1892 production reverently kissed the hem of Cordelia's robe as she departed.[1] But, as Oliver Ford Davies points out, 'the three mentions Lear makes of the Fool early in 1.4 are a deliberate build up to his first grand entrance. The Jacobean audience would have anticipated a turn, and the Fool obliges by dominating the scene for nearly a hundred lines.'[2]

Since the Fool was both a character and a recognized part of the acting company, his disappearance halfway through the play may not have needed an explanation. Critics point out that both Edgar and Lear take over his role, and this idea can be conveyed in performance: John Normington (RSC, 2004) handed Poor Tom his distinctive cap and bauble, walking not only off the set but out of the play. At a time when it was assumed that Lear's 'my poor fool is hanged' (5.3.279) referred to him rather than Cordelia, he was sometimes seen twisting a rope into a noose; suicide is still given as an explanation for his disappearance. In Adrian Noble's RSC production of 1982/3, Lear killed the Fool in his madness, an idea that has been taken up by other directors. In a Georgian production, a tyrannical Lear deliberately killed the Fool 'for mocking him'.[3] In Max Stafford-Clark's Royal Court production (1993), the Fool re-appeared in Act 5 and was hanged by soldiers for spraying subversive graffiti.[4] Munby's 2018 Lear brought the lights up for the interval just as the Fool was apparently about to be killed by Edmond. Some directors, such as Grigory Kozintsev in his film version, cannot bear to let the Fool disappear. Sher, as Lear, wanted to retain an echo of the character, so he illustrated his line about 'this great stage of fools' with a bit of the Fool's characteristic dance.[5]

Gonerill, Regan, and Cordelia

In the old Leir play, all three daughters are unmarried at the start. In Lear, the two older ones seem to have been married for some time, though they have not yet received their dowries, and both appear to be childless. They are often depicted as considerably older than Cordelia, though when Lear curses Gonerill with sterility he must assume that she is still capable of childbearing.[6] When they were assumed to be unproblematically evil from the beginning, they, and the women who played them, received very little critical attention. The theatre historian A. C. Sprague noted that

[1] Alan Hughes, Henry Irving, Shakespearean, Cambridge, 1981, p. 123.
[2] Ford Davies, Playing Lear, p. 113.
[3] Zdeněk Stříbrný, Shakespeare and Eastern Europe, 2000, p. 143.
[4] Jonathan Croall, Performing King Lear: Gielgud to Russell Beale, 2015, p. 180.
[5] Sher, Year, p. 214.
[6] It is only in the quarto that Kent says that the daughters are the offspring of 'one self mate and make' (see Appendix, xx, line 32). Ian McKellen thought that Cordelia was the daughter of a second, exceptionally happy marriage and indicated this by wearing two wedding rings, though he did not expect the audience to understand the implication: McKellen, 'King Lear', p. 135.

there is a great deal of information about how famous actors before 1900 delivered the curse on Gonerill, but virtually nothing about how she reacted to it.[1] A review by Francis Gentleman in 1770 says only, of the two sisters, that it would be 'a coarse compliment to say any ladies looked or played them thoroughly in character'.[2] Reluctance to be identified with vicious characters may have resulted in rather subdued performances.

Gonerill and Regan often used to look evil from the start. On the page, they can seem almost alike when they take part in their competition for Lear's love, but in performance they can be differentiated quite sharply.[3] Psychological readings often begin with birth order: Gonerill, the oldest, usually takes the initiative, while Regan builds on what others have said: 'she names my very deed of love. / Only she comes too short ... ' (1.1.66–7). Directors usually have more sympathy for Gonerill, at least in Act 1. Gonerill and Albany often seem to have a virtually sexless marriage, but in Rupert Goold's production (Liverpool and Young Vic, 2008–9) Gonerill was pregnant: 'Cursed by its grandfather while still in the womb, the baby was born in parallel motion to the storm scene.'[4] Regan may be weaker; Judi Dench gave her a stammer in 1976 (RSC), supposedly the result of a childhood of intimidation by her father. A statue of Lear towered over the daughters in the 2014 National Theatre production, perhaps to explain the extraordinary viciousness of Anna Maxwell Martin's Regan, who appeared sexually excited by the torturing of Gloucester. Jonathan Pryce's Lear (Almeida, 2012) suggested incestuous feelings towards his two older daughters.[5]

Cordelia leaves the play after the first scene and re-appears only in Act 4. When a production cuts all her asides, as is sometimes done in the interest of realism, her small role becomes even smaller and her behaviour even more abrupt. In Gregory Doran's production of 2016, she was something of a spoiled child: her speech ridiculing the idea of loving her father at the expense of her husband was made with the confidence of a woman used to finding approval, and it drew sympathetic laughter from the other characters, making Lear's violent response all the more shocking. Depending on how the King of France is played – Lear's later description of him as 'hot-blooded' (2.4.205) is rarely borne out in performance – it can seem strange that her only later mention of him is as 'great France' who has allowed her to bring an army to fight for her father. A few productions have tried to show how their marriage turned out, by bringing him back with her to England (giving him the lines of the Doctor) or by depicting her as pregnant (as at Glasgow Citizens', 2012).

---

[1] A. C. Sprague, *Shakespeare and the Actors: The Stage Business in His Plays (1660–1905)*, 1944, p. 187.

[2] *The Dramatic Censor*, 1770, I: 373, quoted in Kalman A. Burnim, *David Garrick Director*, 1961, p. 145.

[3] In 'Eel pie and ugly sisters in *King Lear*', in Ogden and Scouten (eds.), *'Lear' from Study to Stage*, Carol Rutter describes in detail a number of ways in which actresses have depicted the characters in the opening scene.

[4] Boika Sokolova, 'New recruits to the "maverick" squad: *Othello*, *King Lear*, and *The Merchant of Venice* in London, 2008/09', *Shakespeare Bulletin* 30.2 (2012), 87–97: 93.

[5] Croall, *Performing King Lear*, p. 195.

10   'But goes thy heart with this?' Lear (John Gielgud) in a 'Renaissance' setting, with Gonerill (Cathleen Nesbit), Regan (Fay Compton), and Cordelia (Jessica Tandy). Old Vic, 1940, directed by Lewis Casson and Harley Granville-Barker

Gloucester, Edgar, and Edmond

When Gloucester's blinding took place off stage, as happened before the twentieth century, it was possible for critics to claim that he suffers less than Lear because his suffering is 'only' physical rather than mental. No one is likely to say this after seeing most modern productions, where the blinding is depicted with horrible realism. Sometimes, it even encourages audience laughter. In Gale Edwards's production in

11 Lear (Simon Russell Beale) under his statue with Gonerill (Kate Fleetwood), Regan (Anna Maxwell Martin), and Cordelia (Olivia Vinall). National Theatre, 2014, directed by Sam Mendes

Adelaide, Australia, in 1988, 'the sensationally gory balls representing Gloucester's eyes were flung into the wings after his blinding'. Like Peter Brook, Edwards took the interval at this point, 'leaving the audience to dwell on what they had just laughed at'.[1]

Because of Gloucester's offensively flippant references in 1.1. to his adultery and his son, he is often played as a tyrannical father or as a fool. Surprisingly few productions play up his heroism ('If I die for it – as no less is threatened me – the king my old master must be relieved': 3.3.14–16), and even fewer make anything of the rapidity with which, when he learns of Edmond's treachery, he repents his own 'folly' towards Edgar and prays the 'Kind gods' to 'forgive me that, and prosper him' (3.7.91). Nahum Tate gave him a moving speech on his blindness, inspired by the opening of Book III of Milton's *Paradise Lost*, and allowed him to join Lear in retirement instead of dying.

Scholarly opinion is divided as to whether the scene of Gloucester's attempted suicide is meant to fool the audience as well as Gloucester, though Edgar is given lines that should make the deception clear ('I do trifle thus with his despair', 4.5.33, and 'Had he been where he thought', 4.5.44). The uncertainty is, of course, possible only on a stage without representational scenery, or in a film that controls what the audience can see. Brook's film version used 'only close shots . . . so the naïve spectator would have no way of knowing Edgar's plan until a long shot after Gloster's fall'.[2] In the 1998

[1] Elizabeth Schafer, *Ms-Directing Shakespeare: Women Direct Shakespeare*, 1998, p. 130.
[2] Rosenberg, p. 265n.

12   'Alive or dead?': the 'Dover cliff' scene, with Gloucester (Karl Johnson) and Edgar (Harry Melling). Old Vic, 2016, directed by Deborah Warner

film of Richard Eyre's National Theatre production (1997), the two actors moved in a fog that made it impossible to know where they were. The stylized background of Deborah Warner's 2016 production was equally ambiguous. Though early modern cures for madness sometimes suggest playing along with the delusions of the sufferer, many critics see nothing but cruelty in Edgar's behaviour. It has been suggested that he is indulging in a fantasy of both killing and saving the father who has rejected him.[1]

As Ian McKellen has written, Edgar is a very difficult role and Edmond an easy one,[2] but the latter usually gets better reviews, because of his humour and the fact that he confides in the audience. He becomes most complex in his last minutes, with the ambiguous 'Yet Edmond was beloved', but his last-minute repentance is often cut in order to speed up the ending. Although Edgar's poetic linking of Gloucester's blind-ness with 'the dark and vicious place' where Edmond was conceived has been condemned as self-righteous moralizing, Edmond himself accepts it, adding another traditional image, Fortune's wheel, to symbolize his situation.

An eighteenth-century audience would have been aware of Edgar the romantic lover behind Poor Tom, and may even have found the impersonation comic, since, as Francis Gentleman writes, 'feigned madness always caricatures real'.[3] In the Shakespeare text, the audience hardly knows Edgar before he takes on the role,

[1]   See, e.g., Simon Palfrey, *Poor Tom: Living* King Lear, 2014, pp. 160–1, 170–1.
[2]   McKellen, 'King Lear', p. 158.
[3]   *Bell's Shakespeare*, p. 5n.

and does not always appreciate the virtuoso performance of his various identities. His absence from the opening scene may mean that the actor had to double as France or Burgundy. Modern productions sometimes include him; Simon Russell Beale's Edgar (RSC, 1993) was seen reading a book while awaiting Lear's arrival. Otherwise, his first appearance in 1.2 may show him, at one extreme, in serious study or, at the other, reeling in from a night on the town. Either way, the lunatic is so much more vivid than the young aristocrat who impersonates him that Simon Palfrey, who has devoted a whole book to *Poor Tom*, suggests that the fictitious character is eerily interwoven with the 'real' one throughout the play; Edgar is 'not so much a character as a nest of possibilities'.[1]

The Knights, Kent, and Oswald

Lear's initial stipulation of a hundred knights would not have seemed odd at a time when aristocratic households contained a vast hierarchy of retainers. Given the importance of 'attendants' for establishing a character's status, it is likely that the Jacobean stage always had more people on it than one expects to see now. Theatres well into the twentieth century could press extras into service, including some who were recruited on the afternoon of the performance: Henry Irving, in 1892, had sixty on stage in the opening scene. In 2016, Gregory Doran had twenty-four 'supernumeraries' for his RSC *Lear*. Gonerill's complaints seem more justified when the stage is full of knights than when this entourage is represented only by the single knight with a speaking part. Peter Brook made these characters rowdy and violent in 1962 and they have been getting steadily worse: Trevor Nunn in 2007 and Jonathan Munby in 2018 had them carry off one of Gonerill's female servants to be raped.

Kent and Oswald, both loyal servants, used to be regarded as moral opposites. Coleridge described Kent as 'the nearest to perfect goodness of all Shakespeare's characters', and Oswald as 'the only character of utter unredeemable *baseness* in Shakespeare'.[2] When Macready wrote that the actor playing Kent 'requires powers for comedy and tragedy',[3] he was thinking mainly of the character's interactions with Oswald in 1.3 and 2.4, which, in some eighteenth- and nineteenth-century productions, went on for much longer than one would guess from the text. Oswald had further opportunities for clowning when Kent was safely in the stocks – apparently a 'farcical' punishment rather than a painful one.[4] If Francis Gentleman is representative of attitudes in 1774, they were extremely class-based: he objected to Kent's defiant behaviour in 2.4 ('Such conduct in presence of a sovereign prince is intolerable') but reported that Edgar's killing of Oswald 'never fails to create laughter' (*Bell's Shakespeare*, 65n.) Directors now are more likely to agree with an influential comment by Bertolt Brecht in the 1950s: 'What you cannot have is the audience, including those who happen to

---

[1] Palfrey, *Poor Tom*, p. 5.
[2] Terence Hawkes (ed.), *Coleridge on Shakespeare*, 1969, pp. 203, 204.
[3] William Charles Macready, *Diaries*, ed. William Toynbee, 2 vols., 1912, I: 147.
[4] See Sprague, *Shakespeare and the Actors*, pp. 285–8, for nineteenth-century comic business.

be servants themselves, taking Lear's side to such an extent that they applaud when a servant gets beaten for carrying out his mistress's orders.'[1] Modern productions rarely discard the comedy altogether, but they often stress the resemblance as much as the difference between the two characters.

Afterlife: Critical and Creative Responses

THE TRAGIC EXPERIENCE: PHILOSOPHY AND RELIGION

In his introduction to the 1972 Arden edition of *King Lear*, Kenneth Muir wrote that the Romantic poets and critics had arrived at 'a conception of the play not essentially different from that generally held today'.[2] Keats's sonnet 'On sitting down to read *King Lear* once again' (1818) brilliantly embodies this conception as, in his opening lines, he turns away from romance to something completely different:

> O golden-tongued Romance with serene lute!
> Fair plumed Syren! Queen of far away!
> Leave melodizing on this wintry day,
> Shut up thine olden pages, and be mute:
> Adieu! for once again the fierce dispute,
> Betwixt damnation and impassion'd clay
> Must I burn through; once more humbly assay
> The bitter-sweet of this Shakespearian fruit.
> Chief Poet! and ye clouds of Albion,
> Begetters of our deep eternal theme,
> When through the old oak forest I am gone,
> Let me not wander in a barren dream,
> But when I am consumed in the fire,
> Give me new Phoenix wings to fly at my desire.

This expectation that reading *King Lear* will be a consuming, painful, and life-changing experience is characteristic of a writer for whom Shakespeare was Scripture. It is also, as Muir says, characteristic of many readers and spectators of the play up to the time when he was writing, and probably still represents what most people want to find in it. To be burned by a literary work is to undergo *catharsis*, the famous and much discussed word that Aristotle used to explain the almost visceral reaction that great tragedy can evoke. The word evokes both purification and purging, and Aristotle seems to have thought that it should result in the acceptance of a supernatural order. This assumption has been questioned for much of the last century.

Keats's description of the play as a 'fierce dispute, / Betwixt damnation and impassion'd clay' implies a serious questioning of the situation of mortal humanity faced with a very real sense of evil. The word 'evil' seems somewhat excessive, when it is first used by Kent to Lear:

---

[1] *The Messingkauf Dialogues*, trans. John Willett, 1965, p. 62.
[2] Kenneth Muir, introduction to *King Lear*, 1972, p. xli.

Revoke thy gift
Or whilst I can vent clamour from my throat,
I'll tell thee thou dost evil.   (1.1.158–60)

What he means by 'evil' might be Lear's decision to give up his rule to Gonerill and Regan, or his treatment of Cordelia, or even the violence he has just shown (in some productions, the reference to 'my throat' follows Lear's attempt to throttle him). Cordelia does not use the word, and her reference to her sisters' 'faults', which she is reluctant to call by their right names (1.1.265), may apply simply to their flattery of their father. The play contains examples of what might be called *normal* moral dishonesty: after she has heard from Gonerill, Regan travels hastily to Gloucester's home so that she doesn't have to deal with Lear at her own residence; Edmond also leaves home at a crucial point, apparently ignoring the appalling implications of Cornwall's suggestion that 'The revenges we are bound to take upon your traitorous father are not fit for your beholding' (3.7.7–8). But nothing can explain the speed with which Gonerill and Regan go from irritation, to anger, to the chilling line (however it is spoken) 'O sir, you are old' (2.4.138, then to the smug claim that being out in the storm will teach him a lesson (2.4.295–7), and finally to Gloucester's report that they 'seek his death' (3.4.147). Perhaps the turning point comes when Cornwall calls to have Kent put in the stocks, saying, 'there shall he sit till noon', and Regan, building as usual on what others have said, corrects him: 'Till noon? Till night, my lord, and all night too' (2.2.122–3). By this time, the word 'evil' seems totally appropriate: 'What begins as common sense opens out into a terrifying blankness of moral idiocy.'[1]

It is possible to quote lines from *King Lear* to support almost any religious or philosophical outlook. Since it is supposedly set in pre-Christian times, Shakespeare can make Kent retort to Lear's 'by Apollo' with 'Now by Apollo, king, / Thou swear'st thy gods in vain' (1.1.154–5) without being accused of blasphemy. It can be argued that Shakespeare is deliberately depicting the horror of a world without Christianity, or, on the other hand, that 'the gods' who inflict so much cruelty are really 'God'. Cordelia's self-sacrificing love has led some to call her a Christ-figure and some of her words have biblical overtones (see the note to 4.3.23–4). Gloucester's astrological fatalism is ridiculed by Edmond but echoed by Kent, though only in the quarto, as a way of explaining the different moral characters of three children with the same parents.[2] Gloucester, when he prays to the gods, calls them 'kind' (3.7.91) and 'ever gentle' (4.5.208), perhaps in the folk belief that one must flatter them in order to get an answer to one's prayers. In the most famous lines of the play, he says that they treat human beings as inhumanely as boys treat flies (4.1.36–7).

Many religions are based on the idea that the events of this world seem unjust only when one is unable to perceive them in a spiritual context. A. C. Bradley's summary of what he takes to be the play's message could apply to many religions: 'Let us renounce the world, hate it, and lose it gladly. The only real thing is the soul, with its courage, patience, devotion.' He adds, however, that this is not 'the whole spirit of the tragedy' and, indeed,

---

[1] Leggatt, *King Lear*, p. 44.
[2] See Appendix, p. 285, xx, lines 30–3.

if pushed further, would 'destroy the tragedy' – as do the religious interpretations that imagine Lear and Cordelia reunited in heaven.[1] Tate's *Lear* ends with Cordelia exclaiming 'Then there are gods, and virtue is their care!' and Edgar, addressing her, states the moral:

> Thy bright Example shall convince the World,
> (Whatever Storms of Fortune are decreed)
> That Truth and Vertue shall at last succeed.   (V.vi.159–61)

Shakespeare's ending could hardly be more different. Most notoriously, Kent says, 'the gods reward your kindness' (3.6.5) to Gloucester who, some 100 lines later, is tortured and blinded for his actions; Albany's 'The gods defend her' (5.3.230), when he hears that Edmond has ordered the deaths of Lear and Cordelia, is immediately followed by Lear's entrance with her dead body.[2] In his RSC production in 2007, Trevor Nunn underlined the irony by giving the play a Christian setting. Everyone on stage knelt in prayer after Albany's line, and Lear's entry demonstrated 'the impotent misguidedness of religious faith'.[3]

THE ABSURD

In a famous essay published in 1930, G. Wilson Knight described examples in *Lear* of what he called the 'Comedy of the Grotesque', calling Cordelia's death 'the final grotesque horror in the play'.[4] His interpretation was a precursor to the Theatre of the Absurd, of which Samuel Beckett's plays are the most famous examples. It assumes that the absence of a divine creator means the absence of any meaning in life, and thus in the play itself. In 1962, Jan Kott's *Shakespeare Our Contemporary* was published, with a chapter on '*King Lear* and *Endgame*'. There is some doubt as to whether, as is often said, Kott's book influenced Peter Brook's 1962 production of *King Lear*, but Beckett was a constant influence. In 4.5, Lear and Gloucester looked like the tramps in *Waiting for Godot*. Brook saw Shakespeare, like Beckett, as depicting an 'absurd' universe, frustrating the desire of its characters – especially Edgar and Albany – to impose a moral explanation on events. Brook's production, seen on tour as well as in Stratford and London, was enormously influential. Charles Marowitz, who kept and published a diary of the rehearsal period, shows a constant desire to make the audience as uncomfortable as possible. It was his idea that the play should end with a faint rumble of thunder, threatening another storm, to counter what he called 'the threat of a reassuring catharsis'.[5] A generation later, some critics reacted against the production's bleakness (the film was bleaker still) and pointed out that this was the result of cuts to any mitigating elements, such as Edmond's attempt to save Lear and Cordelia. Others argued that a totally pessimistic interpretation has the same effect as the religious one that it rejects, since it makes positive action seem meaningless; the

---

[1] A. C. Bradley, *Shakespearean Tragedy*, 2nd edn [1905], 1992, p. 286.
[2] Both lines look to modern eyes like statements, but they are really prayers ('*May* the gods').
[3] Dobson, 'Shakespeare performances', p. 338.
[4] G. Wilson Knight, *The Wheel of Fire: Interpretations of Shakespearian Tragedy*, [1930] 1954, pp. 173–4.
[5] Charles Marowitz, 'Lear log', *Tulane Drama Review* 8.2 (1963), 103–21: 114.

13   'Hark in thine ear': Lear (Paul Scofield) with Gloucester (Alan Webb) and Edgar (Brian Murray). Royal Shakespeare Company 1962, directed by Peter Brook. Folger Shakespeare Library 267931.

'barren dream' that Keats feared is perhaps what Kiernan Ryan calls 'the complacent conclusion that this is how things were meant to be'.[1]

POLITICAL/HISTORICAL READINGS

Francis Gentleman's comment, in 1774, on the 'Poor naked wretches' speech – 'We could wish this speech read to certain great folks, every day!' (*Bell's Shakespeare*, p. 43n.) – shows that Lear's sudden awareness of social injustice was already, at the beginning of an era of revolutions, achieving something of its present importance. When Macready played Lear, it was noticed that he always emphasized 'those noble passages in which the poet contrasts the lots of rich and poor, of oppressor and thrall'.[2] This claim is borne out in the actor's diary entry for 18 Feb. 1839: 'Acted King Lear well. The Queen was present, and I pointed at her the beautiful lines: "Poor naked wretches!"'[3] The speech, A. C. Bradley wrote in 1904, is 'one of those passages which make one worship Shakespeare'.[4] Bill Clinton, then a Rhodes Scholar at Oxford, saw

[1]   Kiernan Ryan, *Shakespeare*, 2002, p. 71.
[2]   Westland Marston, *Our Recent Actors*, 1888, I: 69.
[3]   Macready, *Diaries*, I: 496.
[4]   Bradley, *Shakespearean Tragedy*, p. 249.

14   Is man no more than this?' Lear (Kevin McNally), and 'Poor Tom' (Joshua James). Shakespeare's
Globe, 2017, directed by Nancy Meckler

the play at Stratford-upon-Avon in 1968. According to a fellow-student, he was
'struck that Lear had been on the throne for decades before he learned the first
thing about how his subjects lived' and talked about the play all the way back on the
bus, 'relating it to his life' and his career plans.[1]

Unlike Lear's knights, the poor and homeless are not included in the cast of *Lear*,
but vast numbers of them appear in the films of *Lear* by Brook and Grigori Kozintsev
and they have been brought on stage in recent productions: at the Glasgow Citizens'

[1]   David Maraniss, *First in His Class: A Biography of Bill Clinton*, 1995, p. 144.

Theatre in 2012, they occupied more and more of the space as the play went on, and at Canada's Stratford in 1981 and the RSC in 2016 beggars hovered outside Albany's castle, a reminder of the suffering outside the subjective world of Lear. Nancy Meckler's Globe production in 2017 opened with a group of homeless people breaking into a theatre apparently under wraps and off limits to them. In the course of the performance, the theatre space gradually lost its ugly wrappings and became itself again, while the actors confronted 'the thing itself'.

Jonathan Dollimore insists, in an often-quoted comment, that empathy is not enough: 'where a king has to share the sufferings of his subjects in order to "care", the majority will remain poor, naked, and wretched'.[1] The political readings of *King Lear* exemplified by Annabel Patterson, Alan Sinfield, Jonathan Dollimore, and Kiernan Ryan, among others, reject any notion that suffering makes the sufferer a better person and insist that the injustices the play depicts can be changed only by a change in society.

FEMINISM

Feminist criticism of *Lear* initially focused mainly on the play's treatment of Gonerill and Regan, and on Lear's misogynistic rages, sometimes taking in the implications of Albany's 'Proper deformity shows not in the fiend / So horrid as in woman' (4.2.37–8), which is echoed in A. C. Bradley's statement that Edmond is the 'least detestable' of the play's three villains because he 'is at any rate not a woman'.[2] The contrast between the male and female villains is telling: Edmond addresses the audience eloquently and even wittily; he is chivalric in his fight with Edgar, recognizes the (perhaps dubious) justice of his fate, and tries to undo his most evil action. The two women die off stage – 'desperately', as Kent says – without any final moment of insight. Attempts to justify them sometimes emphasize the pain that might lie behind Gonerill's 'He always loved our sister most' (1.1.281–2), and sometimes even demonize Cordelia.[3] As noted above, most productions now treat them as complex characters and find sympathy for Gonerill, if not for Regan.

Some feminist critics also agree with Janet Adelman's psychoanalytic reading of the scene where Lear is reunited with Cordelia. Lear seems unable to think of his daughter as the wife of the King of France, but, Adelman argues, it is not only Lear but also Shakespeare who fails to respect her identity as a grown woman, turning her instead into 'the Cordelia of Lear's fantasy'.[4] Few productions, however, have taken an ironic look at a relationship which is responsible for the emotional highpoints of the play, and Kathleen McLuskie and Ann

[1] Jonathan Dollimore, *Radical Tragedy: Religion, Ideology and Power in the Drama of Shakespeare and his Contemporaries*, 1984, p. 191.

[2] Bradley, *Shakespearean Tragedy*, p. 260.

[3] See, e.g., Lesley Kordeci and Karla Koskinen, *Re-Visioning Lear's Daughters: Testing Feminist Criticism and Theory*, 2010.

[4] Janet Adelman, *Suffocating Mothers: Fantasies of Maternal Origin in Shakespeare's Plays, Hamlet to The Tempest*, 1992, p. 124.

Thompson have questioned whether a feminist response to *Lear* requires a sacrifice of the theatrical pleasure of empathy.[1]

ECOCRITICISM

In many ways, *Lear* seems an ideal play for the critical approaches that try to undo centuries of anthropocentric views by giving a primary role to the non-human elements, living or inanimate, in a literary work. In his 1982 production, Adrian Noble insisted 'that the storm should be considered as another character' rather than a sound effect.[2] Since theatre and film are extravagant users of all forms of energy, it is not easy for them to be environmentally conscious, though some small-scale productions have attempted it.[3] Most of the time, however, nature is used anthropomorphically: that is, 'The storm is not really poetry unless it is serving to signify something else.'[4] The relation between human beings and Nature is taken for granted in phrases like Lear's 'This tempest in my mind' (3.4.12), and becomes a political metaphor when Kent speaks of 'The tyranny of the open night' (3.4.2).

Rowe's 1709 edition of Shakespeare's works, the first to include editorial indications of location, specified that the storm took place on a heath. Many editors have followed him, but the only suggestion of the imagined landscape is Gloucester's statement that 'for many miles about / There's scarce a bush' (2.4.294–5).[5] The characters' wanderings may bring them into the more fertile world implied by some of Cordelia's language (Nicholas Hytner's 1990 RSC production located 4.1 in a cornfield). Grigori Kozintsev's book about the making of his Lear film, significantly called *King Lear and the Space of Tragedy*, shows an environmentalist's feeling for the natural world. He visualizes Edgar's 'Welcome, then, / Thou unsubstantial air that I embrace' (4.1.6–7) as 'the hunted, naked Edgar in the endless expanse of the earth – the free conversation of a free man with the wind'. Edgar, in a curiously pastoral line, tells his father to 'take the shadow of this tree / For your good host' (5.2.1–2). Kozintsev, who saw Peter Brook's production, recalled the striking image of the old man sitting alone on a bare stage, but regretted the absence of the 'poetry' of the shade of the tree, 'the reflection of love and compassion'.[6]

THE POLITICS OF CASTING

Whether or not the theatre can change society, it can change its own practices, and has done so in various ways – making theatre more affordable, taking it to people who

---

[1] Kathleen McLuskie, 'The patriarchal Bard: feminist criticism and Shakespeare: *King Lear* and *Measure for Measure*', in Jonathan Dollimore and Alan Sinfield (eds.), *Political Shakespeare: Essays in Cultural Materialism*, 1985; Ann Thompson, 'Are there any women in *King Lear*?', in Valerie Wayne (ed.), *The Matter of Difference*, 1991.

[2] Sher, 'The Fool', in Russell Jackson and Robert Smallwood (eds.), *Players of Shakespeare* 2, 1988, p. 160.

[3] For a production that attempted to focus audience attention on the environment, see Rob Conkie, 'Nature's above art: an illustrated guide', *Shakespeare Bulletin* 36 (2018), 391–408.

[4] Jennifer Mae Hamilton, *This Contentious Storm: An Ecocritical and Performance History of King Lear*, 2017, p. 12.

[5] Gwilym Jones, *Shakespeare's Storms*, 2015, p. 62.

[6] Grigori Kozintsev, *King Lear: The Space of Tragedy: The Diary of a Film Director*, trans. Mary Mackintosh, 1977, pp. 221–3.

15 'I will not swear these are my hands': Lear (Don Warrington) with Cordelia (Pepter Lunkuse). Talawa Theatre Company at Manchester Royal Exchange, 2016, directed by Michael Buffong

normally have no chance to see a play, encouraging acting in prisons, and, in 1991, taking *King Lear* to Broadmoor, a high-security psychiatric hospital.[1] A recent development, in major theatre companies in Britain and North America, has been the policy of 'gender and race balance' – that is, casting plays so that the proportion of women and other under-represented groups is roughly comparable to that in the population as a whole. The existence of many first-rate actors of colour has resulted in productions set in other cultures, like the highly praised Talawa Theatre Company *Lear* with Don Warrington at the Manchester Royal Exchange in 2016. This was the first production in a major British theatre to star a black actor, but James Earl Jones had played the role in 1973 in Joseph Papp's New York Shakespeare Festival production, later repeated on television.

In practice, casting can rarely be completely blind, since a production may want to use it for a purpose, as when (in Hamburg, 2018) Gonerill and Regan were played by men and Edmond by a woman – 'to make the point', a reviewer suggested, 'that evil is not binary'.[2] The desire to broaden the range of opportunities for women in a drama whose protagonists are mainly male has resulted in a number of female Lears.

[1] See Brian Cox, *The Lear Diaries: The Story of the Royal National Theatre's Productions of Shakespeare's* Richard III *and* King Lear, 1992. He notes (p. 4) that the Broadmoor audience particularly liked the relationship between Lear and the Fool and the Fool's disrespectful language.

[2] A. J. Goldman, 'Theatre review: in Germany Shakespeare gets revered, rewritten … and eaten', *New York Times*, 2 Nov. 2018.

16 'If thou wilt weep my fortunes, take my eyes': Lear (Glenda Jackson) with Gloucester (Jayne Houdyshell). Cort Theatre, New York, 2019, directed by Sam Gold

Marianne Hoppe played the part at the age of 77 in a production directed by Robert Wilson (Frankfurt, 1990). Her performance was described as 'age-worn sexlessness, all passion spent, that of the indomitable self in ultimate disgust of the world'.[1] Kathryn Hunter (Leicester Haymarket and Young Vic, 1997) played an old woman in a mental hospital who becomes King Lear. Two later Lears, Nuria Espert (Barcelona, 2015) and Glenda Jackson (Old Vic, 2016), apparently played the part as men, though in modern-dress productions gender distinctions are often unclear. Jackson observed in interview that 'as we get older, [...] those barriers, or rather boundaries, which define our gender begin to get foggy'.[2] When she played the part in New York (2019), not only did a woman double Cordelia and the Fool, but Gloucester was also played by a woman.

Kent was played not only by, but *as*, a woman in two 2017 productions: Nancy Meckler's Globe *King Lear* and Jonathan Munby's at the Chichester Festival, later transferred to London. Both productions redistributed lines to give the character a more obviously active role in organizing the English participation in Cordelia's invasion. Whereas most modern productions make very little of the discrepancy between Kent's status as Earl and the way he is treated in disguise, the awareness

---

[1] William Hortmann, *Shakespeare on the German Stage*, vol. II: *The Twentieth Century*, 1998, p. 450.
[2] Glenda Jackson, interview with Michael Witmore on *Shakespeare Unlimited* podcast. Published 14 May 2019. © Folger Shakespeare Library.

that Lear's servant was really a woman made the situation dramatically exciting. The Globe Kent, Saskia Reeves, began as a self-effacing civil servant and her confrontations with Oswald were a clumsy exaggeration of what she took to be masculine behaviour.

A pioneering and radical example of 'inclusive casting' was the *Lear* directed by Michael Kahn at the Shakespeare Theatre in Washington, DC (2000). Cordelia was played by a deaf actress, Monique Holt, whose signs in 1.1 were interpreted by the Fool. The King of France, who reappeared in Act 4, turned out to have learned sign language. Bradley D. Ryner describes the pathetic and moving attempts at communication in the reunion between father and daughter: Lear tried to 'invent signs' to show that he recognized her and she tried to speak her reply, 'And so I am, I am.'[1] As if to avoid implying that disability must always create sympathy, Sam Gold's New York *Lear* of 2019 gave the role of Cornwall to a deaf-mute actor.

TRANSFORMATIONS OF *LEAR*

Keats's subjection to a masterpiece is not a passive one. He may 'burn through' the play and be 'consumed' by it, but then, reborn from his own ashes, like the mythical phoenix, he will 'fly at my desire' – that is, transform the experience into his own creation. In fact, the sonnet itself represents the fulfilment of his wish.

Other creative responses have included plays offering a prequel or alternative vision: *King Lear's Wife* by Gordon Bottomley (1920), *Lear* by Edward Bond (1971), *Seven Lears* by Howard Barker (1989). It is hardly surprising that (as an internet search will quickly show) there are many plays called *Queen Lear*. Most of them take the point of view of the female characters, either the 'absent' wife or the daughters. Bond's *Lear*, the most famous theatrical response, conflates Lear with Gloucester (Lear is blinded) and makes Cordelia a revolutionary who eventually becomes a dictator. Despite the violence, the play ends with a faint possibility of hope. Lear, finally enlightened, tries to get rid of the wall that he had once begun. Government soldiers shoot him, but, as they go off, the stage direction says, 'One looks back', suggesting the (very small) extent to which political action may effect change.

Given the importance of parent–child relationships to novelists, it is not surprising that there have been many analogues to *King Lear*. The two most famous nineteenth-century examples, Honoré de Balzac's *Père Goriot* (1835) and Ivan Turgenev's *A King Lear of the Steppes* (1870) focus on the father–daughter story, transposing it to, respectively, fashionable Paris and the Russian countryside. Neither novel has a Cordelia; there are only two daughters and both are ungrateful. The fathers themselves, however, are far less sympathetic than the pathetic and wronged Lear of the contemporary theatre.[2] Both are stupid men, though physically powerful (Turgenev's hero dies like Samson, pulling down his house to avenge himself). In his deathbed

---

[1] Bradley D. Ryner, 'As performed: by the Shakespeare Theatre Company in Washington DC in 2000', in *King Lear: The Sourcebooks Shakespeare*, 2007, pp. 19–26. See also, in the same volume, Douglas Lanier, '"Unaccommodated man": *King Lear* in Popular Culture', pp. 27–38.

[2] Richard Proudfoot points out that the death of Lear had not yet been staged in England: 'Some Lears', *S.Sur.* 55 ('*King Lear* and its Afterlife'), 2002, 139–52: 145.

monologue, Goriot expresses what seem to be Balzac's views about the importance of patriarchy as the foundation for all stable government, but his maudlin obsession with his daughters is virtually incestuous. He dies happy (in a parody of the reunion of Lear and Cordelia) because he imagines that he can feel the tears his daughters are weeping for his death. The daughters have not arrived, and the tears are those of the two young men who have been looking after him in his last hours.

The most successful recent retellings of *Lear* can be read without previous knowledge of the play. Nearly all are hostile to Lear himself. In Jane Smiley's *A Thousand Acres* (1991), the narrator is Ginny/Gonerill, who gives a horrific account of her 'Daddy', a brutal giant of an Iowa farmer: 'He says, "You look me in the eye, girlie." He says, "I'm not going to stand for it." His voice rises. He says, "I've heard enough of this." His fists clench. He says, "I'm not going to be your fool."'[1] His death finally rates only a brief aside, with no cosmic implications. Ginny has already said, in another context, that 'There is not any wisdom to be gained from the death of a parent.'[2] This dry and disillusioned tone – and especially the depiction of Lear as an abusive father – has influenced some productions.

Christopher Moore's *Fool* (2009) uses Shakespeare's plot and characters, including the Gloucester family, and an early medieval setting, but his narrator is the Fool, who comes to loathe Lear's abuse of power, particularly in a sexual context. His intelligent, bawdy, and anarchic views colour the story, which has a suitably anarchic conclusion: neither the Fool nor Cordelia dies; instead, they go off together to France, where the king, who is gay, is quite willing to let them rule the country.

In Edward St Aubyn's *Dunbar* (2017), written for the Hogarth Press series of modern Shakespeare retellings, the Lear character is the head of a media empire, because St Aubyn felt that such figures are more powerful than political leaders.[3] In a brutal takeover scheme, Dunbar is drugged to make him seem insane, then committed to a mental institution from which he escapes with an alcoholic ex-comedian (the equivalent of the Fool). Though told from multiple viewpoints, this is the only novel sympathetic towards Lear, and the only one to suggest a spiritual journey. Because he genuinely loves his youngest daughter, the ending is harrowing, though it is clear that the evil characters will, as in the play, destroy each other.

The most ambitious recent novelistic treatment is *We That Are Young* (2017) by Preti Taneja, which, despite its setting in modern India, is surprisingly close to the play in ideas, and even, at times, in language. Taneja sees parallels between *Lear* and Indian society: 'the Partition of a country, huge turmoil; a civil war . . ., daughters being made to perform a kind of perfection for family honour'.[4] The story is seen successively through the eyes of the characters corresponding to Edmond, Gonerill, Regan, Edgar, and Cordelia, interspersed with brief monologues by the Lear character, revered like a god by the poor whom he exploits, but sadistic and probably

---

[1] Jane Smiley, *A Thousand Acres*, 1991, p. 306.
[2] *Ibid.*, p. 292.
[3] www.nytimes.com/2017/09/28/books/edward-st-aubyn-king-lear.htm.
[4] Interview with Preti Taneja by Martha Greengrass, posted 21 June 2018: www.waterstones.com/blog/the-interview-preti-taneja-on-desmond-elliott-prize-winning-novel-we-that-are-young.

insane. Sita (Cordelia), a committed environmentalist, has attended Cambridge. Jivan (Edmond), a graduate of Harvard Business School, is grieving for his mother, the 'absent' character ignored by most writers, and is partly motivated by anger at her treatment by the others.

Transformations and analogues of *Lear* in media that are primarily visual or aural are not only too numerous to mention, they can be found and appreciated much better on the internet; the rest of this section will simply make a few suggestions about what to look for. Like most of Shakespeare's best-known plays, *Lear* has its iconic images, reproduced on book jackets, theatre posters, and programmes: the king with a crown of weeds, the king carrying the dead Cordelia, the king with blind Gloucester, and the king and fool in the storm. Lear on the heath was 'the most frequently depicted Shakespearean scene in the middle years of the [eighteenth] century', the era of Garrick's theatrical dominance.[1] Artists suggest that the storm is as much within him as without; in one example, 'Lear's hair is blown by a wind that does not affect anyone else in the painting.'[2]

Nineteenth-century productions turned from modern dress to historical costumes and sets specially designed for the play, aiming not only for accuracy but for symbolic effect. The setting of Macready's *Lear* was described by a sympathetic critic as conveying 'the outward and visible sign, not only of Lear's strong and absolute will, but of the primitive, half-savage royalty that we associate with remote and legendary periods'.[3] Henry Irving's elaborate production (1892) depicted 'a time shortly after the departure of the Romans, when the Britons would naturally inhabit the houses left vacant'.[4] Alan Hughes saw the 'crumbling Roman palace' as 'a powerful metaphor for his mental state' and noted that 'scene by scene, Lear moved from protected enclosure to naked exposure'.[5] The actor's 'Make-up, expression and posture' were modelled on a painting, *Cordelia's Portion* (1875), by the pre-Raphaelite artist Ford Madox Ford.[6] As the theatre critic Benedict Nightingale has pointed out, modern productions frequently imply 'cosmic issues' less in the actors than through visual effects, particularly in the storm scenes.[7]

In film, as Yvonne Griggs has shown, the story of Lear is almost infinitely malleable – it 'translates with particular ease to a western or a gangster genre' but can become 'female-centred melodrama' (as in the adaptation of *A Thousand Acres* in 1997).[8] A 'road' movie can also become a version of King Lear's journey. The most famous films that take Shakespeare's *Lear* and its language as their starting point are those of Peter Brook (1971, considerably shortened and altered from his 1962 stage version) and Grigory Kozintsev (also 1971); Akira Kurosawa's *Ran* (1986) set the play in a beautiful and bloody version of

[1] Stuart Sillars, *Painting Shakespeare: The Artist as Critic, 1720–1820*, 2006, p. 83.
[2] Hamilton, *Contentious Storm*, p. 153.
[3] Westland Marston, *Our Recent Actors*, I: 67.
[4] Alan Hughes, *Henry Irving, Shakespearean*, 1981, p. 123.
[5] *Ibid.*, p. 139.
[6] *Ibid.*, p. 123; see illustrations on pp. 124–5.
[7] 'Some recent productions', in Ogden and Scouten (eds.), *'Lear' from Study to Stage*, p. 230.
[8] Yvonne Griggs, *Screen Adaptations: Shakespeare's King Lear: The Relationship between Text and Film*, 2009.

sixteenth-century Japan.[1] Jean-Luc Godard in 1987 made a notoriously free version, set in a post-Chernobyl world and resembling the play mainly in its anarchy. Macdonald P. Jackson's 'Screening the tragedies: *King Lear*' is a recent analysis of the best-known film and made-for-television versions of the play,[2] but the internet is constantly acquiring more material.

Lear's musical quality has often been noted; director Terry Hands has described it as 'an orchestral piece, in which all the instruments are given their full value'.[3] At times – as when Lear, the Fool, and Poor Tom are expressing their separate thoughts and emotions – it seems as if music, with its ability to represent multiple themes at once, would be a better medium than the spoken word. Giuseppe Verdi, who wrote three operas based on Shakespeare plays, dreamed of composing a *Lear*, but finally confessed himself 'frightened' by the scene of Lear on the heath. The great German baritone Dietrich Fischer-Dieskau was so convinced that the play could be fully expressed only in music that he urged several composers to take on the subject; in 1978, he starred in a work composed for him by Aribert Reimann, which has remained in the operatic repertory.[4] A Finnish *King Lear (Kuningas Lear)*, composed by Aulis Salinen to his own libretto, was premiered in 2000 and filmed in 2002. Both are available on CD and DVD; reviews and clips of both can be found on the internet.[5] The Suzuki *Tale of Lear* (see below) was made into an opera (by Toshio Hosokawa, 1998) with an English text.[6]

GLOBAL *LEARS*

By the end of the twentieth century, Shakespeare study and performance had become a global project. International theatre festivals brought diverse theatre groups together, culminating in the anniversaries of Shakespeare's birth and death (2014 and 2016, respectively). The fusion of Shakespeare's plots with ethnic traditions was sometimes exciting, sometimes disturbing. Though some European countries are justifiably proud of the quality of their translations, the title of Dennis Kennedy's Introduction to *Foreign Shakespeare* is 'Shakespeare without his language'.[7] Directors of non-English-language *Lear*s often work closely with a translator to fit the play to their interpretation.

Lear was one of Shakespeare's most popular works in Russia from the 1920s to the 1940s, even though Soviet Realism, which prescribed optimistic endings, clashed with the 'traditional Russian belief that suffering is the only true path

---

[1] For a discussion of this film, with a fuller translation than appears in the subtitles, see Jessica Chiba, 'Lost and found in translation: hybridity in Kurosawa's *Ran*', *Shakespeare Bulletin* 36.4 (2018), 599–633.

[2] In Michael Neill and David Schalkwyk (eds.), *The Oxford Handbook of Shakespearean Tragedy*, 2016, pp. 607–23.

[3] In Croall, *Performing King Lear*, p. 145.

[4] See Dieter Mehl's appreciative account, '*King Lear* in the opera house', in Tetsuo Kishi, Roger Pringle, and Stanley Wells (eds.), *Shakespeare and Cultural Traditions*, 1994, pp. 295–303.

[5] Mark Mazullo, 'Listening for Nothing in the operatic *Lear*: adaptations by Reimann and Sallinen', *Music and Literature*, 2015.

[6] Yasunari Takahashi, 'Tragedy with laughter: Suzuki Tadashi's *The Tale of Lear*', in Minami Ryuta, Ian Carruthers, and John Gillies (eds.), *Performing Shakespeare in Japan*, 2001, p. 118.

[7] Dennis Kennedy (ed.), *Foreign Shakespeare: Contemporary Performance*, Cambridge, 1993, p. 1.

to regeneration'.[1] Much as in western productions, interpretations of the play in the Soviet world moved through a phase of qualified optimism (Lear and Edgar, at least, learn something from their experiences; society as a whole will be better in the future), then, through the influence of Kott and Brook, to a more absurdist one. In oblique attempts at subversion, Lear in dictatorships was often depicted simply as a tyrant. In the post-communist era, however, 'The King can be a despotic patriarch, as in Lev Dodin's 2004 production in St. Petersburg, or a bank manager, as in various Hungarian and Polish productions, but he is invariably an easily recognizable, modern fixer-entrepreneur whose downfall is grotesque rather than tragic.'[2]

On the other hand, the play's focus on old age gives it considerable appeal outside the western theatrical tradition. Yvonne Brewster, the Jamaican-born artistic director of Talawa Theatre Company, explained that, 'from an African or a Caribbean perspective, old people are the people you revere'.[3] Lear's question 'Who is it that can tell me who I am?' is relevant to the postcolonial, multilingual world that many performers live and work in. *The Shadow King*, a free adaptation performed by a company of black Australians in a mixture of English and Kriol, emphasized the struggle for possession of a land cursed by generations of greed and misuse.

Asian actors once felt that in order to act Shakespeare they had to make themselves up with red wigs, and act in a 'western' style. Now they are more likely to transpose *Lear* to an Asian setting. 'As a play about dispossession, ownership, dis/embodiment of the subject, and the search for identity', Alexander Huang writes, '*King Lear* has become a central text for theatre artists in the Chinese and Asian diaspora'.[4] A *Lear* directed by David Tse (Shanghai and London, 2006) showed a Cordelia who had to say 'Nothing' because, western-educated, she could no longer communicate in her father's language.[5] *Lear and the Thirty-fold Practice of a Bodhisattva* juxtaposes Chinese translations of passages from the play with passages from a fourteenth-century Tibetan Buddhist text.[6] The Japanese *Lear* of the director Tadashi Suzuki (1984) is set in a nursing home: an 'old man' fantasizes that he is Lear while his Nurse reads the story to herself, cackling loudly. As Yasunari Takahashi writes, the effect of the ending, where the old man dies and the Nurse cackles, is 'absurdly comic without ceasing to be frighteningly tragic'.[7]

---

[1] Alexander Shurbanov and Boika Sokolova, '*King Lear* east of Berlin: tragedy under Socialist Realism and afterwards', in Anthony R. Guneratne (ed.), *Shakespeare and Genre: From Early Modern Inheritances to Postmodern Legacies*, 2011, p. 178. What follows is largely indebted to this excellent survey.

[2] *Ibid.*, p. 186.

[3] Schafer, *Ms-Directing Shakespeare*, pp. 135–6.

[4] Alexander C. Y. Huang, *Chinese Shakespeares: Two Centuries of Cultural Exchange*, 2009, pp. 216, 197.

[5] The full video of this stage production is available at https://globalshakespeares.mit.edu/king-lear-tse-david-2006.

[6] Huang, *Chinese Shakespeares*, pp. 206–16.

[7] Takahashi, 'Tragedy with laughter', p. 116.

The 1997 *Lear* by the Singaporean director Ong Ken Sen (revived in 2012 as a Noh drama called *Lear Dreaming*) was designed, according to the programme, to bring out the complexity of the new millennium: not only were the actors from five different countries, but each spoke in his own language 'and the Noh and Beijing Opera actors in the cast retained their own acting styles throughout performance, thus intentionally creating "discords" on various levels'.[1] The effect was to emphasize the universality of the story, liberating it from the domination of the written word and its original language.

The Genre of *Lear*: Contested Territory

Scholars and actors have traditionally wanted to understand Shakespeare better, through better editions or translations, and to find the 'right' way to perform him. Now, there is less faith in the existence of a 'right' way. *Lear* is performed frequently in major theatres and its long history of being considered unactable as written encourages directors to take liberties with both text and performance. The 'right' period for the play was once pre-historic or post-Roman Britain; Gielgud played a Renaissance ruler; many productions now choose the late Victorian age, as the last period in which patriarchal rulers and sword fights seem believable. But many productions are eclectic: in the opening scene of the 2016 RSC *King Lear*, the king (Antony Sher) was carried in state like a barbaric despot, while his daughters, who bore no resemblance to their father or to each other, wore modern evening dress.

In particular, the play has become a touchstone for attitudes to political and patriarchal authority. A nineteenth-century critic, seeing later portrayals of Lear and his daughters, might feel that, as Oswald says of Albany, the director

> had turned the wrong side out.
> What most he should dislike seems pleasant to him;
> What like, offensive.   (4.2.9–11)

For example, Nicholas Hytner, who directed the play in 1990, said, of Gonerill and Regan, that he was 'absolutely on their side', whereas he disliked Cordelia.[2] A Bulgarian production in 1985 made Edgar 'a ridiculous fop' and Edmond totally sympathetic.[3] Many actors, male as well as female, have said how much they dislike Lear at the beginning of the play (and sometimes throughout).[4]

Awareness of the textual problems in *King Lear* sometimes affects the rehearsal process. Oliver Ford Davies records that Jonathan Kent, directing *Lear* in 2002, had the actors consider whether, for instance, Cordelia should say that her love for her father was 'more richer' or 'more ponderous' than her tongue.[5] When David Warner

---

[1] Minami Ryuta, Ian Carruthers, and John Gillies, 'Introduction', in Ryuta, Carruthers, and Gillies (eds.), *Performing Shakespeare in Japan*, p. 8.

[2] Abigail Rokison-Woodall, *Shakespeare in the Theatre: Nicholas Hytner*, 2017, pp. 76, 79.

[3] Shurbanov and Sokolova, '*King Lear* east of Berlin', pp. 184–5.

[4] Bridget Escolme, 'Review of the Actors' Shakespeare Project's *King Lear*', *Shakespeare* 2.1–2 (2006), 77–81, argues that intellectual and emotional responses are not incompatible.

[5] Ford Davies, *Playing Lear*, p. 107.

17   Lear (Antony Sher) with Regan (Kelly Williams), Cordelia (Nathalie Simpson), and Gonerill (Nia Gwynne). Royal Shakespeare Company 2016, directed by Gregory Doran

was playing Lear in 2005, director Stephen Pimlott had the actors 'produce our own acting text … In the early rehearsals we actually had a lot of different editions around and made choices between them, sometimes making small emendations of our own.'[1] Most directors choose the Folio as their basic text, but even Hytner's 1990 production, meant to be entirely Folio-based, included the 'Mad Trial', found only in the quarto, and Tim Piggott-Smith, who played Lear in 2011, wrote, 'I cannot imagine any actor wanting to take on Lear without playing that scene.'[2]

For most readers from the eighteenth century to the mid twentieth, *King Lear* was a powerful emotional experience. It may seem strange that this was also true in the theatre, where, for 150 years, audiences were seeing a version in which Lear and Cordelia did not die. Matthew Steggle, who has studied evidence of laughing and weeping in Renaissance drama, finds that the moments for which we have evidence of a tearful response do not usually come at the end of the play; rather, 'onstage weeping induces audience weeping'.[3] Audiences wept in the great scene between Lear and Gloucester, where Gloucester himself wept for Lear; they responded above all to Lear's reconciliation with Cordelia and his 'Be your tears wet? Yes, faith' (4.6.69). The happy ending brought more tears of joy – because these audiences were not stupid; they knew that life was not like that. The word 'tragedy' is used much less than it used to be in discussions of *King Lear*, and its precise definition is uncertain, but most people who see a successful production of the play are likely to think that it is the right word for their experience.

Aristotle admitted in his *Poetics* that audiences preferred tragedies with a happy ending. Samuel Johnson defended Tate's alteration on the grounds that 'All reasonable beings naturally love justice', and Tolstoy preferred the old *Leir* play to *Lear* because its ending was 'more in accordance with the moral demands of the spectator'.[4] The term 'poetic justice' implies that art ought to be fairer than life, since, unlike life, it is in the artist's power. Aristotle, and the Renaissance and Enlightenment critics who followed him, wanted tragedy to depict suffering that was in some way deserved, so that the gods would not seem unjust, but not so thoroughly deserved that the audience lost sympathy with the sufferer. The problem for many *King Lear* productions is to get the balance right – not to make Lear and Gloucester totally pathetic or, at the other extreme, to destroy all sympathy for them.

Oddly enough, although few people now would argue in favour of a happy ending on the grounds that the characters deserve it, some have complained instead of the play's cruelty towards themselves – that is, the audience. Janet Adelman sees the dramaturgy as itself a form of torture: 'The oscillation of scenes throughout Act III – indoors and outdoors equally brutal – serves to intensify the audience's pain, as each promises momentary relief from the other and then drives in a different mode toward the same dark place.'[5] Ian McKellen points out that no one character knows as much

[1] David Warner, 'King Lear', in Michael Dobson (ed.), *Performing Shakespeare's Tragedies Today: The Actor's Perspective*, 2006, pp. 132–3.

[2] Piggott-Smith, *Do You Know Who I Am? A Memoir*, 2017, p. 281. The 'trial' follows 3.6.14 of the Folio text. It is, however, sometimes cut, as at the Globe in 2017, not only to shorten the play but also to reserve the full display of Lear's madness for his later scene with Gloucester.

[3] Matthew Steggle, *Laughing and Weeping in Early Modern Theatres*, 2007, p. 98.

[4] 'Tolstoy on Shakespeare', ch. 4, para. 64.

[5] Adelman, *Suffocating Mothers*, p. 111.

about the suffering in the play as the audience does: 'They go through all of it, they have to suffer the blinding and the poisonings, and Edgar's anguish. Lear only experiences his part of it.'[1]

At the same time, the 'grotesque' quality of the play means that audiences sometimes react even to the suffering with laughter. Jonathan Miller, knowing that Christopher Plummer wanted to act in a comedy, urged him to play Lear in Stratford, Ontario, on the grounds that *Lear* was 'one of the funniest plays ever written'.[2] Not many would agree with him; but, from the actor's point of view, giving a character a sense of humour humanizes him. Stage madness was popular in early modern drama and one reason is that it could be funny, as Lear's madness sometimes is ('Ha! Gonerill with a white beard?' – 4.5.94). A writer who makes a Fool an important character in his tragedy can hardly wish to eliminate laughter, but it is often hard to judge the tone of unfamiliar language and conventions. Oliver Ford Davies noticed the 'uncertain smiles' evoked when Lear, after railing at Regan, says, 'I'll not chide thee', or, with 'casual cruelty', tells Gloucester, 'I remember thine eyes well enough': 'Time and again the absurdity, the grotesqueness of the moment, leaves the audience floundering.'[3] At the press night of the RSC *Lear* in 2018, Antony Sher was upset to hear 'a big laugh' at his climactic 'reason not the need' speech (2.4.257–79), where Lear incoherently expresses his rage and grief, then rushes out into the storm. The playwright David Edgar assured him afterwards that this reaction was good: the audience had 'laughed, and then we caught ourselves, thinking, "That could be my dad."'[4] A speech that has traditionally been one of the high points of a performance of 'cosmic grandeur' had reminded everyone of the behaviour of ordinary human beings.

The power of *King Lear* is due to the fact that it touches both on common social issues (family relationships, old age, poverty, mental illness) and on larger questions (why evil and suffering exist, and, indeed, why goodness exists), which may have both political and cosmic answers. Many Renaissance plays make generalized, sometimes proverbial, comments on life. But in *Lear*, more than in most plays, these statements arise out of the extreme situations in which the characters find themselves. It seems only right for Gloucester, after what has happened to him, to say, 'As flies to wanton boys are we to th'gods' (4.1.36). Lear's words 'When we are born, we cry that we are come / To this great stage of fools' (4.5.174–5) do not come out of nowhere; they are a response to Gloucester's weeping. As Marjorie Garber writes, after quoting one of Edgar's moments of illumination, 'It is for perceptions like these, and not for its commentary on seventeenth-century monarchy or the plight of early modern mendicants, that the play is regarded as one of Shakespeare's most magnificent achievements.'[5]

These are sometimes called 'timeless' truths, but they are not necessarily true, except to the character who is speaking them, and they become more or less topical,

---

[1] McKellen, 'King Lear', p. 150.
[2] Plummer, *In Spite of Myself*, p. 639.
[3] Ford Davies, *Playing Lear*, p. 170.
[4] Sher, *Year*, p. 235.
[5] Marjorie Garber, *Shakespeare After All*, 2005, p. 677.

more or less admired, as circumstances change. Francis Gentleman in 1774 wrote enthusiastically of a speech which Michael Pennington in 2016 described as 'a picture of Cordelia so mawkish that it almost makes the part unplayable'.[1] In 2016–18, when there were a number of productions of *Lear* in England, the lines that most often provoked audible responses from the audience were Lear's sarcastic 'Dear daughter, I confess that I am old; / Age is unnecessary . . . ' (2.4.146–7) and Gloucester's ''Tis the time's plague, when madmen lead the blind' (4.1.47). The first spoke directly to a modern audience who were, or had, aged parents; the second struck many as a meaningful generalization. The play is both personal and cosmic; the challenge, for critics and performers, is to do justice to both aspects.

[1] Pennington, *Lear in Braoklyn*, 176.

TEXTUAL ANALYSIS, PART 1

Preface by Brian Gibbons

King Lear exists in two early quarto editions, 1608 and 1619, and in the Folio of 1623. To make a modern-spelling critical edition of the play is a complex and difficult task. A short preface is therefore offered to those for whom this subject is new; then follows the full 'Textual Analysis' by the play's editor, Jay Halio, giving a detailed account of the early *King Lear* texts, of the modern hypotheses about their origins, and (p. 79) of the editor's principles and practice in creating the present edition.

In Shakespeare's time, a play belonged, legally speaking, to the dramatic company that produced it on the stage – in the case of Shakespeare's *King Lear*, this was the King's Men (of which Shakespeare was a shareholder). Later, it would belong to the publisher who purchased it from the dramatic company. Some of Shakespeare's plays were published in his lifetime but no manuscripts of Shakespeare's plays have survived, there are only books printed from lost manuscripts, whether authorial drafts or copies of them. Nor does there seem to be evidence that Shakespeare (unlike Ben Jonson) saw any of his plays through the press or checked proofs.

To create the original text of a play, Shakespeare wrote in longhand with a quill on separate sheets of paper. The resulting manuscript, when complete and tied in a bundle, might contain occasional false starts, second thoughts or deletions, corrections, or additions, making it untidy and difficult to read in places. This first manuscript was termed 'foul papers'.

The next stage was for a transcript suitable for theatrical use to be made by either the author or a professional scribe. This second manuscript is known as a 'fair copy'.

Then, a member of the acting company would mark it up, specifying theatrical business wherever the author might have left it unclear. Now, so far as the acting company was concerned, this was the most valuable version. Once it had been officially licensed by the Master of the Revels, it was known as the 'book' and used by the 'bookkeeper' (prompter) during performances. The individual 'parts' to be acted (lines and cues) were separately copied from 'the book' and distributed to the appropriate players.

Early printed versions of Shakespeare's plays are in two forms, 'quarto' and 'Folio'. The printer used a large piece of paper, the 'sheet': for a 'quarto', a sheet was folded twice to make four leaves (eight pages front and back), measuring 7 by 9 inches. For a 'Folio' (a large book), it was folded once to make two leaves (four pages front and back) measuring 9 inches by 14. Pages were not printed in numerical order when a sheet was laid flat on a printing press, first on one side, then, after the ink dried, on the other. For a 'Folio', pages 1 and 12 were printed on one side, and then pages 2 and 11 on the reverse side. The amount of handwritten (manuscript) text that would fill twelve pages had to be estimated or 'cast off', a job that required an experienced workman. If too much or too little space was estimated, this would only become clear during type-setting, and then compositors might awkwardly crowd or stretch their text.

The printing process in the print-shop began with compositors reading the part of the manuscript assigned to them, then selecting pieces of metal type from a large case divided into boxes containing the various letters and punctuation marks. These selected pieces of type were placed into the frame to form words, then were locked into the bed of the press. A blank sheet was pressed onto the bed and imprinted; it was then removed and proofread.

Two compositors usually set the type simultaneously, one beginning at page 6 and working backwards to page 1, the other beginning on page 7 and working forwards to page 12. The side of the sheet containing pages 6 and 7 was set and printed first, then the other side, pages 5 and 8, was set and printed. When this was complete, the pieces of type were unlocked, extracted, sorted, and replaced in their respective boxes to be ready for further use. (The compositors who set Folio *King Lear* are discussed under the heading 'The Copy for F' on pp. 55–7.)

There was scope for textual error at each stage: an author's or scribe's hand-writing might be careless or partly indecipherable, or marred by spelling errors. Compositors might misread their copy, or have differing habits of spelling and punctuation, or make mistakes in choosing type. Sometimes type became damaged in printing. To sift the evidence of these kinds of error is an important part of the editor's work.

There are also issues of more general scope. Although the reader may in solitude encounter it as a work of literature, a play is destined for live perfor-mance, in which success depends on collaboration. Shakespeare was not only a writer but also an actor in the leading theatrical company, the King's Men. As a 'Sharer' in it, he also shared managerial responsibility. Although the first public performances of *King Lear* took place at the Globe, the company's open amphitheatre playhouse, there was also a select indoor performance for the court at Whitehall. After 1610, the King's Men regularly performed in winter at Blackfriars, their recently acquired, additional, indoor playhouse, and when touring in the provinces they performed at a variety of playing spaces. Evidently, therefore, the Company had to be adaptable.

Rehearsals and perhaps first performances of *King Lear* (and also its subse-quent revivals over a number of years) involved both amplifications and cuts to the text. The section of the 'Textual Analysis' headed 'Playhouse Adaptations' (pp. 66–9), and the 'Appendix' (pp. 273–89), provide full discussion of this matter. It is remarkable that, in addition to many minor differences between quarto and Folio throughout, an entire scene, 4.3. in the quarto text, was cut – it is missing in the Folio – and so was the mock trial episode after 3.6.14 (which is discussed in the 'Textual Analysis part 2' on pp. 253–4 below), while the characterization in the quarto of Gonerill, Kent, Edgar, and Albany is signifi-cantly changed in the Folio: indeed, the last speech in the play, which is spoken by Albany in the quarto, is transferred to Edgar in the Folio (see p. 248).

Textual Analysis, Part 1

In Register C, folio 161b, of the Company of Stationers of London, under the date 26 November 1607, the following entry appears:

Na. Butter   Entred for their copie vnder thandes of Sr Geo.
Io. Busby   Buck knight & Thwardens A booke called. M^r
           William Shakespeare his historye of Kinge Lear
           as yt was played before the kinges maiestie at
           Whitehall vppon S' Stephans night at Christmas
           Last by his mai^{ties} servantes playinge vsually
           at the globe on Banksyde   vj^d

The play was subsequently printed in quarto by Nicholas Okes for Nathaniel Butter during the period from mid-December 1607 to early January 1608.[1] The title page of this first quarto (Q) reads:

M. William Shak-speare: / *HIS* / True Chronicle Historie of the life and / death of King LEAR and his three / Daughters. / *With the unfortunate life of* Edgar, *sonne* / and heire to the Earle of Gloster, and his / sullen and assumed humor of / TOM of Bedlam: / *As it was played before the Kings Maiestie at Whitehall upon* / S. Stephans *night in Christmas Hollidayes.* / By his Maiesties servants playing usually at the Gloabe / on the Bancke-side. / [Printer's device, McKerrow 316] / *LONDON*, / Printed for *Nathaniel Butter*, and are to be sold at his shop in *Pauls* / Church-yard at the signe of the Pide Bull neere / S^t. *Austins* Gate. 1608.

This quarto, also known as the 'Pied Bull' quarto, contains forty-two unnumbered leaves (signatures A2 B–L4). It has occasioned controversy about its authority, the nature of the copy from which it derives, and its relation to the version in the Folio (F).

A second quarto (Q2), printed in 1619 by William Jaggard, bears the false date and imprint, 'Printed for *Nathaniel Butter*. / 1608.' It was one of a group of ten plays intended originally as a collection of works by Shakespeare (or attributed to him) to be published by Jaggard's friend, Thomas Pavier. Essentially a reprint of Q, the Pavier quarto is nevertheless important because of its possible influence on the printing of the Folio text and for a unique reading of a part-line inserted before 4.5.189. The third quarto, a poor reprint of Q2, was published in 1655 by Jane Bell and has no textual authority whatsoever.

The third edition of the play (F) appeared in 1623. It occupies pages 283–309 (signatures qq2^r–ss3^r) of the tragedies, situated between *Hamlet* and *Othello*. The text differs significantly from Q, lacking some 285 lines and containing about another 115 not found in Q. Moreover, many different readings of individual words and phrases appear, punctuation and lineation vary decidedly, and speech designations are sometimes altered. F was long regarded as the authoritative text and Q a pirated one, but many scholars now believe that the quarto and Folio represent different versions of the play, F being a revision of the text found in Q and a form the play took on the boards after its initial performances. This version was reprinted in 1632 (F2), 1663 (F3), and 1685 (F4). Although these reprints correct some errors, they introduce

---

[1] Blayney, pp. 148–9.

others, and none has any textual authority. Not until 1709, when Nicholas Rowe edited a new collection of Shakespeare's works, was the text scrutinized again. Rowe used F4 as his copy-text, adding stage directions, scene locations, and other details, while also frequently correcting lineation and punctuation. It is with his edition that the history of modern printed editions of the play may be said to begin.[1]

THE Q TEXT

King Lear was the first play that Nicholas Okes, who had only recently become a master printer, attempted to print. Inexperience may explain, in part, the poor quality of Q, but difficult copy must also share the responsibility. Early theories held that this copy was a reported text of some kind, a version of the play taken down from memory ('memorial reconstruction') or in shorthand by someone in the theatre. W. W. Greg (1933) maintained that the text derived from a shorthand report.[2] While agreeing that Q represents a pirated text, Leo Kirschbaum argued instead that the copy derived from a memorial reconstruction, not shorthand[3] – a position also taken in 1949 by G. I. Duthie.[4] Madeleine Doran had taken the opposite view in *The Text of 'King Lear'* (1931). She held that the quarto text derived directly from Shakespeare's rough draft, or foul papers,[5] which contained many revised and rewritten passages. This theory partly explained the poor printing in Okes's shop, while at the same time it afforded Q more textual authority than it could possibly have as a reported text.

In what amounts to a kind of compromise among these competing theories, Alice Walker (*Textual Problems of The First Folio*, 1953) proposed that Q *Lear* derived from a transcript of Shakespeare's foul papers stolen by the boy actors who played Gonerill and Regan. In dictating the play to each other, they occasionally depended more upon their memory than on the manuscript before them and thus memorially 'contaminated' some of the scenes, such as 1.1 and 5.3, where their roles were prominent. Michael Warren, in 1978, argued not only that Q and F represent alternative versions of the play, but that Q, for all its problems, is an authoritative text.[6] P. W. K. Stone, while advancing the alternative versions hypothesis in *The Textual History of King Lear* (1980), argued (pp. 13–40) that Q nonetheless represented a reported text, though not a memorial reconstruction. He attributed the multitude of aural errors,

[1] Steven Urkowitz notes that some handwritten collations of Q and F exist on a copy of F3 that may have been prepared as a prompt-book for Dublin's Smock Alley Theatre in the 1670s, and Nahum Tate collated Q and F for his adaptation of the play. But Alexander Pope was the first *editor* to begin conflating the two texts, a tradition that has remained almost unbroken up to the present time. See Urkowitz, 'Editorial tradition', pp. 24–5.

[2] See Greg, *Variants*, pp. 138, 187.

[3] *The True Text of 'King Lear'*, 1945, esp. pp. 6–7.

[4] *Elizabethan Shorthand and the First quarto of 'King Lear'*, 1949. The case for memorial reconstruction is argued at length in Duthie's critical edition of the play, pp. 6, 21–116.

[5] In 'Narratives about printed Shakespeare texts: "foul papers" and "bad" quartos', *SQ* 41 (Spring 1990), 65–86, Paul Werstine questions the use of this term, especially as W. W. Greg 'idealised' it, referring to it as the author's final draft before a fair copy was made. 'Foul papers' could exist in a variety of states.

[6] Warren, 'Albany and Edgar', pp. 95–107.

mislineation, and faulty punctuation to a longhand, not stenographic, report by someone in the theatre who attended the play more than once. This report was then used as copy by Okes's compositors, who committed further errors, especially where the manuscript was difficult to follow.

Steven Urkowitz (1980) in *Shakespeare's Revision of 'King Lear'* revived the 'foul papers' theory and brought further arguments in support of it, analysing misassigned speeches, 'anomalous' spellings, punctuation, and mislined verse. Rejecting Alice Walker's theory of 'memorial contamination' of foul papers, he concluded that Q was printed directly from Shakespeare's drafts and not from a transcript of them.[1] His study also strongly supported Warren's argument against the single 'ideal' text theory and in favour of the two-text hypothesis.

Peter W. M. Blayney's exhaustive study of Nicholas Okes and Q *Lear* (1982) examined the quarto text both in itself and in the context of other work produced by Okes and his immediate predecessors, particularly during the years 1605–9.[2] Though without specifying the exact nature of the manuscript copy used for printing Q, he remarks that it was evidently very difficult copy.[3] He confirmed E. A. J. Honigmann's contention[4] that more than one compositor worked on Q *Lear*, although the second compositor did not become involved until late. Blayney referred to them as 'B' and 'C' and thought that 'C', who worked more slowly and less competently than 'B', may have been an apprentice.[5] Difficult copy and inexperience in setting a play-text from manuscript doubtless led to numerous errors, some of which were discovered after press-work began.[6] Since the proofreader was free to work with or without reference to copy, which may have been indecipherable or just not handy, he could make a calculated guess, as in the correction of Q uncorr. 'crulentious' to Q corr. 'tempestious'.[7] Moreover, his corrections were not always accurately made by the compositors – or indeed made at all.[8] Although Q *Lear* shows evidence of an unusual amount of proof-correction, it was after all just a play, of by no means the same importance as, say, a sermon, such as John Pelling's 'Of the Providence of God' (1607), which took precedence over *Lear* in the schedule of printing and publication.[9] In any case, the play was already a year old, although the title page advertisement and dating tend to obscure that fact. *Lear* was not immediately reprinted; the second edition did not appear until the abortive collection projected by Thomas Pavier eleven years later. If it was not a highly profitable commodity, then, the case for 'stolne, and surreptitious' copy (the phrase used by Heminge and Condell in their preface to the Folio to stigmatize previously published editions of Shakespeare's plays) accordingly weakens.

[1] Urkowitz pp. 7–11, 191–2.
[2] Blayney, p. 8.
[3] *Ibid.*, p. 184.
[4] 'Spelling tests and the first quarto of *King Lear*', *The Library*, 5th ser., 20 (1965), 310–15.
[5] Blayney, p. 186.
[6] Greg, *Variants*, pp. 43–57, 191–2.
[7] *Ibid.*, p. 164. Compare F 'contentious', 3.4.6.
[8] Blayney, pp. 245–7.
[9] *Ibid.*, pp. 81ff.

THE F TEXT

The other authoritative text for *King Lear*, one which is generally recognized as at least better printed than Q, is the one that Heminge and Condell included in the Folio of 1623. Using cast-off copy, Compositors B and E in Jaggard's printing shop set by formes, as Charlton Hinman showed. Subsequent scholarship has confirmed his analysis, modifying only slightly the identification of specific formes or part-formes set by either one.[1]

That Compositor E's pages were more carefully proofread than B's is hardly surprising, since E was only an apprentice. Hinman has recorded the corrections – which tend to show the kinds of mistakes an apprentice might make.[2] Jaggard was also more interested in the appearance of the pages than the accuracy of the text.[3] For example, at 1.1.164 uncorrected Folio (F uncorr.) reads 'To come betwixt our sentence, and our power', where corrected Folio (F corr.) has '. . . sentences, and . . .' As Hinman explains, F corr. is clearly wrong.[4] What probably happened is that Compositor E mistook the 'dele' sign in the margin (ꝯ) for an (ſ) – that is, 's' in secretary hand – and, instead of removing the extraneous comma intended for deletion, added an 's' to 'sentence', thereby corrupting sense and metre.

THE COPY FOR F

P. A. Daniel first advanced in 1885 the theory that F was set from an annotated copy of Q, one that had been collated against a theatrical manuscript, probably the prompt-book.[5] Greg, using the evidence of errors reproduced in F from Q, maintained that the annotated quarto contained at least one sheet (D) in the corrected state and two sheets (H and K) uncorrected (possibly also E and G). The state of sheets C and F he could not determine, and sheets B, I, and L are invariant in all extant copies.[6]

Stone concluded that compositor E used an annotated copy of Q2 for his share in the pages of F *Lear* whereas compositor B used manuscript copy.[7] Hinman had argued that compositor E was too inexperienced to set from manuscript; this was left for his

---

[1] Textual scholars now believe that Compositor B, more experienced but more prone to take liberties in setting from copy, set pages qq2, 3ᵛ 5, rrIᵛ (column b), 2ᵛ, 3ᵛ–6ᵛ, or (in the Folio numbered pagination) pages 283, 286, 289, 294b, 296, 298–304 (Hinman, II: 277, 293). These pages correspond to 1.1.1–83, 1.2.19–135, 1.4.183–293, 2.4.138–93, 3.1.3–2.89, 3.4.74–4.5.271. Compositor E, whom Hinman (I: 200–26) identified as an apprentice, set the rest of the play, or almost twice as much as B.

[2] Hinman, I: 304–12. Hinman's summary on p. 325 shows that, of twenty-three pages in *Lear*, thirteen were proof-corrected; of fifty-one variants, forty-five were in material set by Compositor E. Recalculated according to Trevor Howard-Hill's reattributions ('New light on compositor E of the Shakespeare First Folio', *The Library*, 6th series, 2 (1980), 159, 273–8), all but one of the variants occur in material set by E.

[3] Hinman, I: 235–9. Hinman identifies the proof-corrector as none other than Isaac Jaggard himself (who took over the running of the printing-house from his father at about this time) and notes that correction was usually not made against copy.

[4] Hinman, I: 304–6.

[5] Introductory notice to a facsimile of the 1608 quarto, ed. Charles Praetorius.

[6] Greg, *Variants*, pp. 138–49. The summary of findings appears on p. 148.

[7] Stone, pp. 129–40. In Appendix DI, pp. 257–67, as elsewhere, Stone assigns pages ss1 and ss3 to Compositor B instead of E, apparently unaware of Howard-Hill's reattributions, with which Stone's tallies fit more closely, obviating the need for any special pleading. Stone's conclusions are supported by MacD. P. Jackson, 'Printer's copy for Folio *Lear*', in *Division*, pp. 346–9.

partner, compositor B.[1] Gary Taylor, having first agreed with Stone's conclusions,[2] later argued that both compositors B and E used annotated Q2 copy while setting the Folio text.[3] However, as Taylor acknowledges in a footnote, E might have been deliberately stretching his copy to fill up space, the result of inaccurate casting-off of copy.[4]

Similarly, much of the other evidence Taylor uses to demonstrate the dependence of F upon annotated Q2 for both compositors is subject to alternative interpretation. It derives from shared Q2/F spellings of fairly common words[5] and from similar kinds of evidence, such as altered speech ascriptions[6] and punctuation.[7] Of course, neither the resemblances between Q2 and the presumed copy for F, nor any other extant bibliographical evidence can *prove* that Q2 was Compositor B's copy as well as E's; other alternatives are possible, as Taylor says.[8] The main point is that Q2 was a major influence on the printing of F, however it was used.

From the evidence of spelling, punctuation, and speech ascriptions, Howard-Hill claimed that F used manuscript copy primarily but with some reference to Q2. The theory he finally proposes is that the manuscript underlying F derives from a copy of Q2 used to interpret the playhouse prompt-book that was transcribed for use in Jaggard's printing-house – now many years old, and probably damaged – which could explain anomalous readings and errors. Thus, for orthography and accidentals, the transcriber would be most influenced by Q2; for substantives and the unusual spellings, the prompt-book would have greater influence. The process of scanning first the quarto, then the manuscript (to locate additions and corrections), best accounts (in Howard-Hill's view) for the mixture of forms that characterizes the Folio text.[9]

A fresh transcript would seem to be decidedly more desirable for printer's copy than a heavily annotated exemplar of a quarto, given the myriad changes that distinguish F from Q and Q2. Howard-Hill rejects the alternative theory supported by Taylor, that the manuscript copy for F was prepared by first collating Q2 against the prompt-book and then copying the annotated exemplar to provide a clean transcript for the printer. Howard-Hill's objection to this alternative is not only that it assumes the collator failed to see early on that what he was producing was unacceptable as printer's copy, but also, more importantly,

---

[1] Hinman, I: 220–6; Charlton K. Hinman, 'The prentice hand in the tragedies of the Shakespeare First Folio: Compositor E', *SB* 9 (1957), 3–20.

[2] 'The Folio copy for *Hamlet*, *King Lear*, and *Othello*', *SQ* 34 (Spring 1983), 44–61.

[3] 'Folio compositors and Folio copy: *King Lear* and its context', *PBSA* 79 (1985), 17–74.

[4] *Ibid.*, p. 26, n. 9. Compare Hinman, II: 507–8.

[5] *Ibid.*, pp. 30–41, 57–65.

[6] *Ibid.*, pp. 41–5, 52–5.

[7] *Ibid.*, pp. 65–9.

[8] *Ibid.*, p. 56. Compare *Textual Companion*, p. 531.

[9] Trevor Howard-Hill, 'The problem of manuscript copy for Folio *King Lear*', *The Library*, 6th ser., 4 (1982), 1–24: 23.

that the collator failed to correct the numerous errors that persist in F when he had the playhouse copy in front of him. Moreover, the failure of many distinctive Q spellings to survive in F, as well as the similarity of the non-distinctive orthography of Q2 and F, suggested to him that his proposed theory (actually, the procedure long ago suggested by Madeleine Doran) was closer to the mark. Peter Blayney weighed the evidence for and against annotated Q2 as copy for F and came to the same conclusion as had Howard-Hill: that manuscript, not printed copy, was what both Folio compositors used, although Blayney believed that the manuscript was neither the original prompt-book nor a transcript of it, but rather a transcript of an annotated exemplar of Q either annotated by the reviser or altered by the reviser as he copied it out. This transcription then became the new prompt-book.[1]

THE PRESENT EDITION

That manuscript copy was used together with an exemplar of Q2 in some fashion now seems, on the evidence, the most plausible theory upon which to proceed in editing. Manuscript copy best explains a number of misreadings and errors in F, although the exact relation of the manuscript to the prompt-book is still unclear. Whether the manuscript was the prompt-book itself or a transcription of it made by consulting Q2 or possibly even an autograph or scribal fair copy (made for presentation or some other purpose),[2] we shall probably never know for certain, but both a manuscript and an exemplar of Q2 did influence the setting of the Folio.[3] The numerous deletions from Q in the manuscript, including a whole scene, strongly suggest theatrical adaptation; hence, the manuscript copy for F very likely was, or derived from, a prompt-book, despite the fact that several prompt-book indicators are missing, such as the names of actors, duplicated stage directions, and warnings for the use of some stage

---

[1] I am greatly indebted to Dr Blayney for generously providing me with the relevant chapter of his typescript for *The Texts of 'King Lear' and Their Origins*, Vol. II.

[2] Taylor, *'King Lear* and its context', p. 74. Compare the chapter on 'The manuscript "copy" for F' in Stone, esp. pp. 104–12.

[3] Compare *Textual Companion*, pp. 530–1. Greg disregarded Q2 as a mere reprint of Q and argued that F had to be set from an exemplar of Q with K4^V in the uncorrected state. His evidence focused on the omission of 'and appointed guard' inserted and partially turned over in Q corr. but lacking in both Q uncorr. and F (Greg, *Variants*, pp. 140–1). In 'Q1 and the copy for Folio *Lear*', *PBSA* 80 (1986), 427–35, Howard-Hill argues that Greg's case does not hold up, since the F collator might have missed the insertion in the margin of his manuscript, just as Okes's compositor did. But if the manuscript was the theatre prompt-book, a fair copy of the corrected foul papers, why would the words again be inserted in the margin? In that case, the person who prepared the fair copy also missed the insertion and then, like the proof-corrector of Q, went back and added it in the margin in such a way that it could be overlooked once more by the F compositor. This is perhaps too coincidental to be plausible, especially since Q2, the exemplar which was collated, has the words which are missing in Q uncorr. and F. Howard-Hill therefore argues that the words were inserted in the prompt-book in such a manner as to be ambiguous. Since underlining was used to indicate deletion as well as interlineal insertion, Compositor E understandably became confused by the apparent conflict in authority and opted to follow the prompt-book, which apparently marked 'and appointed guard' for deletion.

properties.[1] In general, then, substantive readings and alterations derive from the manuscript; accidentals and orthography from Q2.

The implications of this distinction for an editor are important. As Howard-Hill has said, 'Depending upon whether the copy was manuscript or print, the editor may more exactly determine the sources of textual corruption and resolve cruxes.'[2] If the copy for F was (or derived from) an authoritative playhouse manuscript, then the editor can with some confidence correct mistakes that originate in certain misreadings (such as minim errors) and try to determine non-authorial interventions (such as theatrical cuts or actors' interpolations). Although accidentals and orthography will have little or no bearing on the preparation of a modern-spelling text, the editor must be on the lookout for mislined verse, ambiguous or erroneous speech headings, and the like. Especially if the copy was the playhouse prompt-book (or a transcription of it) modified by the book-keeper and then collated against an exemplar of Q2, the tendency will be to retain F readings against Q variants, except where the collator or compositor has bungled his job. The editor must then determine between the original Q reading and the intended reading that F has garbled in so far as it can be 'decoded'. In the example of Q 'strange newes' versus F 'strangenesse', the editor will adopt Q's reading, since not altered copy but a misreading of the manuscript underlies the F variant. On the other hand, where both Q and F have acceptable readings, F will be preferred as the presumably authoritative alteration or revision of the original text: 'presumably', because we cannot always know certainly that it was the author who effected the change, as in F 'sterne' for Q 'dearne' (3.7.62). Finally, in a few instances where both Q and F are doubtful, Q may provide a guide to the intended alteration or correction. For example, at 1.1.104, Q 'mistresse' has been clumsily altered to F 'miseries', whereas 'misteries' (F2 'mysteries') was probably the intended reading.

F AND Q TRANSMISSION

Strong support for a revision-hypothesis has grown among scholars and has led to the discrete editing of Q and F *Lear* as differing versions of the play, as in the complete Oxford Shakespeare of 1986. It is possible, however, that differences between Q and F are mixed and cumulative, and that autonomy can be claimed for neither in isolation. If Q derives from Shakespeare's own rough draft – his foul papers in some state or other – it can be argued that this version, as reflected in Q, was not a finished product but just a stage in the development of the play. Changes doubtless occurred when a fair copy of the manuscript was made either by Shakespeare or by a scribe, and when the fair copy became the prompt-book

---

[1] Taylor, '*King Lear* and its context', p. 74; *Textual Companion*, p. 530. But compare Stone, 'The manuscript "copy" for F', pp. 107–11, who comments on several of these omissions but finds that, on the whole, F reflects prompt-book deviation.
[2] Howard-Hill, 'The problem of manuscript copy', p. 3.

further alterations were introduced, a practice no doubt typical of theatrical production then as now.[1] These alterations included deletions of varying lengths, additions and amplifications, rewriting and recasting as well as substitutions. Moreover, changes need not have occurred all at once.[2] Theatrical practice demonstrates that playscripts tend to evolve over time, especially after initial performances, and now and then when a play is revived.[3] The author may have been a willing participant in any or all of the alterations, or he may not have been: the text as found in the Folio version may reflect one or more compromises between him and his fellow shareholders in the King's Men.

Finally, other stages in the transmission of the text, for which we have no record, may have intervened between the initial performances (not fully represented by Q) and the text as it exists in F. It is possible, for example, that after Butter issued the Pied Bull quarto, Shakespeare got hold of a copy and began tinkering with it, revising many individual words and phrases and altering some passages and scenes on a larger scale as well.[4] Stylistic evidence, particularly a study of the vocabulary used in substitutions and additions, indicates that revision was by Shakespeare and that it was quite late.[5] Adding these new revisions to the prompt-book, already marked up with alterations, must have seemed impractical, and a new prompt-book was prepared by collating the annotated quarto and the old prompt-book. This new prompt-book (or a transcript of it) became the copy for F, which was printed in consultation with Q2, copies of which were available in Jaggard's printing-house.

Demonstrating with certainty each step in the transmission of the text is difficult, and evidence is admittedly sensitive to editorial predisposition. The presentation of materials in this section of textual analysis is meant to provide a perspective for their interpretation. The proposed stemma somewhat simplifies transmission from foul papers to Folio. Some intervening stages have been postulated, but to include every possibility would unduly complicate matters without shedding sufficient light on the problems involved. Briefly, then, the following stemma is a graphic representation of the transmission of the *King Lear* text:

---

[1] In a review otherwise severely critical of many of the essays in *Division*, Richard Knowles supports the claims of Jackson (pp. 333–5) that revisions could have occurred during the rehearsal process. See Knowles, 'The case for two *Lears*', *SQ* 36 (Spring 1985), 117.

[2] Compare Taylor, 'Date and authorship', p. 351: 'Indeed, even to speak of "*the* date" and "*the* authorship" of the redaction presumes something we have no right to presume: that all the changes between the Quarto and Folio versions were made at the same time and by the same man.'

[3] For a modern instance, see Thomas Clayton, 'The texts and publishing vicissitudes of Peter Nichols's *Passion Play*', *The Library*, 6th ser., 9 (1987), 365–83, which includes references to Tom Stoppard's *Jumpers* as well.

[4] See Kerrigan, pp. 195–245, and Taylor, 'Date and authorship', pp. 351–468.

[5] Compare Taylor, 'Date and authorship', pp. 376–95, 462–4.

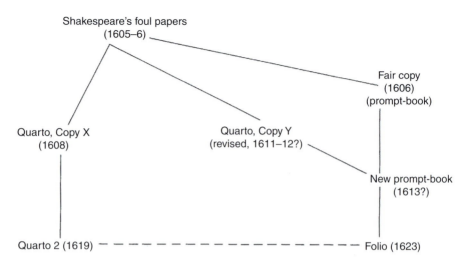

The solid lines on the stemma indicate direct transmission; the broken line indicates collateral influence. Dates for revision are estimates, therefore queried. The stemma shows essentially three separate but related lines of transmission. The first, from foul papers to Q2, is firmly established. The second, from foul papers through revised Q to F, is admittedly speculative. The third, from foul papers to fair copy and prompt-books 1 and 2 culminating in F, is also a speculative but, like the second line, seems the best way to take account of available evidence. Collation of the old prompt-book with revised Q is necessary to explain all the revisions, including changes in vocabulary, speech ascriptions, deletions, and other alterations involving both authorial 'tinkerings' and production decisions.

THE NATURE OF INTERVENTIONS
The kinds of intervention by the author or others in the text of *King Lear* (and any other Shakespearean or Elizabethan play-text) are simple in outline but become intricate and extensive when set down in detail. Conclusive evidence is often impossible to marshal; one must proceed by using knowledge of printing practices and theatrical experience; stylistic analysis; and finally supposition, logic, and inference. Since available evidence is frequently ambiguous, alternative explanations are possible. The purpose here is to explain specifically the types of difference between Q and F and the nature of the Folio text as a revised acting version of the play.

OMISSIONS AND CUTS
Omission of one or more lines usually, but not necessarily, indicates a cut. Cuts may originate with a revising author, scribe, or book-keeper; or they may originate in the printing-house, where a compositor may have skipped a line accidentally or, finding copy badly cast-off, may have deliberately dropped a line. The omission after 1.1.98,

for example, could be the result of eye-skip by the Folio compositor,[1] or it may be the result of revision, eliminating a redundancy from lines 94–5 (and an irregular half-line):[2]

> Why have my sisters husbands, if they say   94
> They love you all?. . .
> Sure, I shall never marry like my sisters   98
> [To love my father all].

Omission of several lines often signals a theatrical cut, marked in the prompt-book with a stroke through the text and a vertical line in the margin. The marks could have been misunderstood, and either too much or too little deleted (see below, p. 68). Adjoining lines sometimes invited or required rewriting, as at 1.4.185–91, erroneously printed as prose in the quarto and otherwise in need of correction (see below, p. 64). More often, blocks of lines (in one instance, the entire scene following 4.2) were cut. Where there is no disruption in the adjoining lines, we may suspect a theatrical cut, but *King Lear* is seldom abridged simply to shorten the play. Although the Folio text is some 200 lines shorter than Q, reducing performance time cannot have been the only or even the principal reason for many of the deletions, which demonstrably alter the ethos of several characters and are sometimes offset by additions or amplifications. True, most of the cuts occur in the latter half of the play, from 3.6 onwards, where anxiety about wearying the audience might have been a factor.[3] These include the omissions at the end of 3.6, the concluding lines of Acts 3 and 4, and at 5.3.195. But elsewhere, as in the cuts in Gonerill's speeches or Kent's, many of the alterations directly if subtly change characterizations and suggest authorial rather than theatrical intervention.[4]

AMPLIFICATIONS AND ADDITIONS

Amplifications that elaborate the style or content of an existing speech or passage may sometimes be distinguished from additions of entirely new material, which modify character or dramatic structure. As Thomas Clayton has shown, Lear's first long speech, amplified in F (1.1.31–49), contains additions closely correlated with substantive variants.[5]

---

[1] As Duthie, p. 166, and Stone, p. 233, believe.
[2] Compare Taylor, 'Censorship', p. 87.
[3] Taylor, 'War', p. 29, notes that although F contains significant additions to the Q text in 1.1, 1.4, 2.4, and 3.2, between the beginning of 3.6 and the end of 4.3 the Folio omits 157 lines while adding only 7; i.e. approximately half of the F omissions occur in these scenes. Compare Jackson, p. 331, and David Richman, 'The *King Lear* quarto in rehearsal and performance', *SQ* 37 (1986), 381–2.
[4] See, for example, Warren, 'Albany and Edgar', pp. 95–105, and McLeod, pp. 164–88. Taylor, 'War', pp. 28–30, shows how the cuts in Acts 3–4 'streamline the plot', strengthen the 'narrative momentum', and otherwise tighten the dramatic structure of the play.
[5] Clayton, pp. 121–41. See also the edited parallel passages, pp. 71–2 below.

Q: *Lear.* Meane time we will expreſſe our darker purpoſes,
The map there, know we haue diuided
In three, our kingdome, and tis our firſt intent,
To ſhake all cares and buſines of our ſtate,   35
Confirming them on yonger yeares,
The two great Princes *France* and *Burgundy,*
Great ryuals in our youngeſt daughters loue,
Long in our Court haue made their amorous ſoiourne,
And here are to be anſwerd, tell me my daughters,

  Which of you ſhall we ſay doth loue vs moſt,
  That we our largeſt bountie may extend,
  Where merit doth moſt challenge it,
  Gonorill our eldeſt borne, ſpeake firſt?

F: *Lear.* Meane time we ſhal expreſſe our darker purpoſe.
Giue me the Map there. Know, that we haue diuided
In three our Kingdome: and 'tis our faſt intent,
To ſhake all Cares and Buſineſſe from our Age,
Conferring them on yonger ſtrengths, while we   35
Vnburthen'd crawle toward death. Our ſon of *Cornwal,*
And you our no leſſe louing Sonne of *Albany,*

  We haue this houre a conſtant will to publiſh
  Our daughters ſeuerall Dowers, that future ſtriſe
  May be preuented now. The Princes, *France & Burgundy,*   40
  Great Riuals in our yongeſt daughters loue,
  Long in our Court, haue made their amorous ſoiourne,
  And heere are to be anſwer'd. Tell me my daughters
  (Since now we will diueſt vs both of Rule,
  Intereſt of Territory, Cares of State)   45
  Which of you ſhall we ſay doth loue vs moſt,
  That we, our largeſt bountie may extend
  Where Nature doth with merit challenge. *Generill,*
  Our eldeſt borne, ſpeake firſt.

The complex effects of this amplification are essentially threefold: (1) anticipation of Lear's firmness, as in the alteration of Q 'our first intent' to F 'our fast intent' (line 33),[1] and the added 'We haue this houre a constant will' (line 38); (2) provision of more detailed and rational-sounding motives for abdication, as in the desire to confer responsibility of the realm on 'yonger strengths' (line 35) and the wish to prevent 'future strife' by immediately publishing the daughters' dowries (lines 38–40); (3) contributions to the patterns of imagery involving clothing and nakedness, as in the announcement that Lear will 'divest' himself of rule, territory, and responsibility for the state (lines 44–5). Careful comparison of the entire speech in F with its shorter – and different – form in Q, combined with other changes later in the Folio version of the play that Clayton notes, strongly suggest, though they cannot prove, authorial second thoughts and subsequent revision.[2]

---

[1] Of course, 'first' could be a misreading of 'fast', which F corrects; but compare 'I am firm' (240), which F adds.

[2] Compare Jackson, pp. 332–9, for another analysis, which comes to similar conclusions. He cites E. A. J. Honigmann, *The Stability of Shakespeare's Text*, 1965, who notes how Shakespeare's 'after thoughts' sometimes made his revised verses irregular.

Similarly, alterations in Gonerill's character involve not only cuts but additions and amplifications as well. While basically she remains an ungrateful daughter, headed (as in Q) for collision with her equally strong-willed father, her nature in F is softer. If she seems in Q 1.3–4 almost out of control raging against her father, in F she is cooler, a woman much more capable of responding to provocation 'slowly and in proportion', as Randall McLeod says.[1] The omissions after 1.3.15 are complemented by revision of 1.4.267 (F 'Pray you content' for Q 'Come sir no more') and the addition of 1.4.276–87, which shows her mastering emotion and countering Albany's demurrer with rational argument. Again, in 2.4, F alters Gonerill's entrance from her aggressive behaviour in Q, still harping on mistreatment of her servant, to a more restrained initial silence, broken only by coming to her sister's defence (2.4.188).[2] Gonerill's speech on entering is given to Lear in F, with an appropriate change in wording (2.4.181):

Q: *Duke.* What meanes your Grace ?   *Enter Gon.*
     Gon. Who ftruck my feruant, *Regan* I haue good hope
     Thou didft not know ant.
     Lear. Who comes here ? O heauens !
     If you doe loue old men, if you fweet fway allow
     Obedience, if your felues are old, make it your caufe,
     Send downe and take my part,
     Art not afham'd to looke vpon this beard?
     O *Regan* wilt thou take her by the hand ?
     Gon. Why not by the hand fir, how haue I offended?

F: *Enter Goneril.*
     Lear. Who ftockt my feruant? *Regan*, I haue good hope
     Thou did'ft not know on't.
     Who comes here ? O Heauens !
     If you do loue old men ; if your fweet fway
     Allow Obedience ; if you your felues are old,
     Make it your caufe : Send downe, and take my part.
     Art not afham'd to looke vpon this Beard ?
     O *Regan*, will you take her by the hand ?
     Gon. Why not by'th'hand Sir? How haue I offended?

Michael Warren has shown how Albany's character is also affected by both deletions and additions in F.[3] In Act 1, Albany seems not quite so weak in F as he does in Q, mainly because in 1.4 F adds a few judiciously spoken lines in his dialogue with Gonerill and Lear. For example, Albany cautions Gonerill, 'Well, you may fear too far' (1.4.282), and he urges patience to the furious Lear (217). These additions, which somewhat strengthen his moral character, contrast with the later weakening that occurs in Acts 4 and 5. The outrage against his wife's treatment of Lear in 4.2 is substantially reduced; and in 5.3 Albany seems less sure of himself in his role as

---

[1] McLeod, pp. 175–81.
[2] *Ibid.*, p. 181.
[3] Warren, 'Albany and Edgar', pp. 99–101.

commander. Together with corresponding alterations in Edgar's role, they make ceding the kingdom to the younger man appropriate.[1]

REWRITING, SUBSTITUTION, AND RECASTING

Passages might be changed significantly either by local emendations or the substitution of new text, and recasting could involve moving speeches, changing the order of dialogue, and altering speech headings. Local emendations, sometimes of little or no significance, occur throughout the Folio text of *King Lear*, as in the alteration of the number of days Lear gives Kent in which to depart (1.1.167). Such minor (and minute) changes, or tinkerings, are typical of an author, as Kerrigan has shown,[2] not of a theatrical abridger, who would scarcely care how many days Lear gave Kent to leave the kingdom (four days in Q, five in F).

At 2.4.17, two brief speeches in Q are omitted in F; in their place F adds a new line (see below, p. 252). At 3.1.14–21, eight lines in F replace twelve and a half lines in Q. Although some editors believe both sets of lines in these examples were intended for inclusion in F[3] (and appear thus in modern conflated texts), they are badly spliced and otherwise point to substitution, not amplification (see below, p. 253).

Recasting is clearly evident in a number of places in the Folio *King Lear*. At 1.4.183–92, F recasts Lear's speech (printed as prose in Q), making several corrections, cutting some lines at the end, and assigning to the Fool an important response (see below, p. 251):

Q: whoop *Iug* I loue thee.
 Lea. Doth any here know mee? why this is not *Lear*, doth *Lear* walke thus? speake thus? where are his eyes, either his no-tion, weaknes, or his discernings are lethergie, sleeping, or wake-ing; ha! sure tis not so, who is it that can tell me who I am? *Lears* shadow? I would learne that, for by the markes of soueraintie, knowledge, and reason, I should bee false perswaded I had daughters.
 Foole. Which they, will make an obedient father.
 Lear. Your name faire gentlewoman?
 Gon. Come sir, this admiration is much of the fauour of other

F: Whoop Iugge I loue thee.
 Lear. Do's any heere know me?
This is not *Lear*:
Do's *Lear* walke thus? Speake thus? Where are his eies?
Either his Notion weakens, his Discernings
Are Lethargied. Ha! Waking? 'Tis not so?
Who is it that can tell me who I am?
 Foole. *Lears* shadow.
 Lear. Your name, faire Gentlewoman?
 Gon. This admiration Sir, is much o'tn' fauour

---

[1] Compare Urkowitz, pp. 80–128. His fuller analysis of the differences between Q and F Albany comes to conclusions similar to Warren's, but he tends to see every change in F as a deliberate alteration of character, whereas some changes, such as the cut following 5.3.195, may have been dictated as much – or more – by considerations of theatrical shortening. Of course, all such alterations modify character; it is a question of assessing the motives – and the source – that underlie the changes, and these are often impossible to determine with certainty.

[2] Kerrigan, pp. 205–17.

[3] For example, Duthie, pp. 394–5; compare Stone, pp. 70–5.

The reassignment of Gonerill's speech on entering at 2.4.181 has already been noted, but not the revision that goes with it (see above, p. 63). In 5.3 a good deal of rewriting and recasting has occurred, most notably at the very end. Lear's last words are new, one of his speeches is reassigned to Kent, a stage direction is added, and several other alterations of the text appear:[1]

Q: *Lear*. And my poore foole is hangd, no, no life, why fhould a
dog, a horfe, a rat of life and thou no breath at all, O thou wilt
come no more, neuer, neuer, neuer, pray you vndo this button,
thanke you fir, O, o, o, o.   *Edg*. He faints my Lord, my Lord.
     Lear. Breake hart, I prethe breake. *Edgar*. Look vp my Lord.

F: *Lear*. And my poore Foole is hang'd: no, no, no life?
Why fhould a Dog, a Horfe, a Rat haue life,
And thou no breath at all? Thou'lt come no more,
Neuer, neuer, neuer, neuer, neuer.
Pray you vndo this Button. Thanke you Sir,
Do you fee this? Looke on her? Looke her lips,
Looke there, looke there.   *He dies.*
     Edg. He faints, my Lord, my Lord.
     Kent. Breake heart, I prythee breake.

Finally, F assigns the last speech in the play to Edgar rather than Albany, their difference in rank notwithstanding. This is one of the alterations that concern the modified characters of both men (see pp. 259–60 below).

THE TIMING OF INTERVENTIONS

Previous discussions of the evolution of the F text have tended to freeze the revisions at a single point in time, although (as noted) theatrical practice demonstrates that changes could be introduced at intervals over an extended period.[2] There seems little necessity, therefore, to fix precisely upon a single moment for all the differences between Q and F. Hypothetically, several stages in the evolution of the text may be posited, from pre-performance alterations to playhouse adaptations and finally to preparation for publication.

Pre-performance Alterations

The process of alteration or revision could have begun with the transcription of foul papers to produce a fair copy. If Shakespeare himself transcribed his autograph draft, he might have begun tinkering with it then. Probably, however, a playhouse scribe was commissioned to prepare a fair copy for use as the prompt-book. In that event, alterations would have occurred from the scribe's failure to interpret the manuscript or from his deliberate intervention for the sake of lucidity or tidiness.[3]

---

[1] See Clayton, pp. 128–38.

[2] See above, p. 59, and compare Knowles, 'The case for two *Lears*', pp. 119–20, who believes changed playing conditions could account for variations, for example, in 4.6.

[3] Stone, pp. 105–6, attributes to a playhouse scribe precisely such indifferent variants as later appear in F, but he believes they were introduced at a later stage, i.e. in the preparation of the new prompt-book *c.* 1613.

As Stone remarks,[1] the nature of Q misreadings suggests that the manuscript copy was sometimes illegible, not because of sloppiness or crowding or wilful distortion but because of hasty composition. A number of the corrections or alterations in F may be the result, then, of scribal intervention in the preparation of fair copy rather than authorial revision. Impossible though it may be to determine when and by whom these changes were introduced, Q 'straied', F 'strain'd' (1.1.163) and Q 'bitt', F 'kill' (4.1.37) – to cite just two examples from Stone's list of Q misreadings – may represent scribal corrections or 'tidyings' of Shakespeare's autograph.[2]

Playhouse Adaptations

It is likely that during the rehearsal process the author, the book-keeper, or some other member of the company introduced other alterations. To the book-keeper fell the responsibility for recording routine clarifications of performance, such as the insertion of entrances and exits, speech assignments, sound effects, and the use of properties. The Q text notoriously lacks many such designations, especially entrances and exits, most of which F supplies, also adding or altering a number of other stage directions, as at 1.1.28 and 2.1.36.[3] In addition, the book-keeper would have the responsibility for indicating deletions from the prompt-book, although others in the company might have suggested the cuts. Elimination of the scene following 4.2, for example, could have been proposed during the first rehearsals. For all its lovely poetry, as in the Gentleman's lines on Cordelia (Appendix, pp. 284–5 below, xx, 12–24), the scene adds little to the forward progress of the action; it is essentially a lyric interlude. Whether or not it was ever performed, or whether Shakespeare or another member of his company suggested the cut, we may never know. Likewise, the deletions in the last scene, such as the Captain's two-line speech after 5.3.35 or Edgar's longer passage after 195, might have been proposed by Shakespeare or someone else as inessential material that could be omitted.

It is also possible – indeed likely, on the basis of stylistic analysis – that major revisions including many additions and 'tinkerings' occurred sometime after the King's Men occupied the Blackfriars private theatre in 1609. If Shakespeare was asked to introduce act intervals for performance there, he might have taken that occasion to revise and correct the text, especially if he used a copy of Q.[4] At that or some other time, it might have been decided to eliminate many of the references to

---

[1] Stone, p. 177.

[2] Of course, Stone attributes the manuscript not to Shakespeare, but to a reporter.

[3] F simplifies or omits a number of Q's descriptive stage directions, as at 2.2.37, 3.3.0, 3.7.80. Many of the omissions may have occurred through compositor error, or the book-keeper or collator may have considered them redundant, as at 4.5.194, 233, 239. Altered stage directions may also indicate a change in staging or playing conditions, as at 4.3.0, 4.6.21. See below, p. 67, and compare Taylor, 'War', p. 30, and Knowles, 'The case for two *Lear*s', p. 119.

[4] George Walton Williams, review of *Division of the Kingdoms* in *Medieval and Renaissance Drama in English* 2 (1985), 347. Compare Taylor, 'Date and authorship', p. 428, and Stone, p. 107.

France as the invading power. Was censorship involved? Gary Taylor has argued that
if a censor intervened, he would have been more likely to cast a critical and disapprov-
ing eye upon other matters in the play, specifically those alluding to domestic
problems that date from the accession of James I.[1] Since France under Henri IV
and Britain under James I were now at peace and had been for years, an invasion set
long ago in virtual pre-history would hardly be stepping on sensitive political corns.
Or would it? Of course, as Taylor reminds us, at a time when England had much to
fear from foreign invasion, the old play *King Leir* (*c.* 1590) was more explicit concerning the French landings in Britain than Shakespeare's *King Lear* is, even in the quarto.
Moreover, England under James I was at peace not only with France, but with all the
great powers of Europe. Nevertheless, diplomatic relations between Henri and James
were never easy or relaxed. James was concerned about the war between Spain and the
Dutch and the role France played in it, as well as about payment of the French debt to
Britain. Since an incident involving protocol at one of Queen Anne's masques had
strained or at least chilled diplomatic relations between the two countries,[2] discretion
might advise the muting of hostilities in a play performed by the king's own company,
especially if, like the masque, the performance would be at court. In the light of
James's known pursuit of policies favouring peace, this deliberate muting becomes still
more credible. Although we do not know and perhaps cannot know how it happened
or when it happened, the fact is that almost all references to France and the French
king as the invader in *King Lear* disappear in the Folio text; the omissions are
undoubtedly made with a purpose.[3]

   Changed playhouse conditions, such as a change of cast, an actor's indisposition,
special performances for particular audiences, tours, and so forth may also have led to
alterations in the text. The changes in both the cast and the sound effects in 4.6 may
owe something to such changed conditions. The quarto's 'Doctor' becomes the
'Gentleman' of 3.1, and the call for music to awaken Lear is omitted. If the play was
taken on tour, perhaps the musicians (except those for trumpet and drums) were left

[1] 'Censorship', p. 80. Taylor later acknowledges (pp. 102–5) that censorship occasioned the cut after
   1.4.119, since the lines contain pointed allusions to King James's mismanagement of the realm. But see
   Philip J. Finkelpearl, '"The comedians' liberty": the censorship of the Jacobean stage reconsidered', *ELR*
   16 (1986), 123–38.
[2] Maurice Lee, *James I and Henri IV: An Essay in English Foreign Policy, 1603–1610*, 1970, p. 103. Lee's
   essay details the perennial difficulties in James's foreign policy regarding France under Henri IV.
[3] Doran, p. 73, notes that 'references to invasion by a foreign power remain untouched when the power is
   unnamed and when the circumstances of the invasion are shrouded in vagueness', but 'they are generally
   missing from the folio when France is directly named'. She believes that this is evidence of censorship,
   since the Master of the Revels was 'on guard to catch any matter in plays which might be offensive to the
   court or to foreign ambassadors'. But knowing this, the King's Men could themselves have made the
   alterations without having been told to do so. In 'War', p. 31, Taylor analyses these differences between
   quarto and Folio and makes several astute observations, but he does not speculate upon political or other
   motivations for the changes that are essentially extrinsic to the drama. Finkelpearl, ' "The comedians'
   liberty" ', does not treat *King Lear* but discusses the many loopholes in the system and quotes abundant
   testimony to show that scandalous and libellous plays were, in fact, performed; objectionable material
   apparently could be added *after* licensing. Furthermore, while the deletion of verbal allusions to France
   suggests self-censorship by the King's Men, on the other hand F introduces visual indications of
   nationality in altered stage directions, e.g. at 4.3.0, 5.1.0, 5.2.0, as Honigmann notes in 'Do-it-yourself-
   Lear', *New York Review of Books*, 25 October 1990, p. 59.

behind and the cast reduced.[1] Again, this is entirely speculative: unfortunately, we have sparse records of performance for *King Lear* in the early seventeenth century (see above, p. 13). It bears repeating that just as no single motive or person need have been responsible for all the alterations in the Folio, no single occasion is necessary to mark them. On the contrary, some evidence points to several stages of alteration. At 1.4.119, Q has fifteen lines of dialogue between Lear and his Fool. F lacks the passage, except for the first three lines, which were probably marked for omission as well, since an obvious hiatus is left; but Compositor E missed the notation or it was not indicated clearly enough on his manuscript.[2] The three lines in F, however, vary not only in accidentals but in two substantive readings:

Q: *Lear*. A bitter foole.
   Foole. Doo'ſt know the difference my boy, betweene a bitter foole, and a ſweete foole.
   Lear. No lad, teach mee.
   Foole. That Lord that counſail'd thee to giue away thy land, Come place him heere by mee, doe thou for him ſtand,

   The ſweet and bitter foole will preſently appeare,
   The one in motley here, the other found out there.
   Lear. Do'ſt thou call mee foole boy ?

   Foole. All thy other Titles thou haſt giuen away, tha . thou waſt borne with.
   Kent. This is not altogether foole my Lord.
   Foole. No faith, Lords and great men will not let me, if I had a monopolie out, they would haue part an't, and Ladies too, they wc:ll not let me haue all the foole to my ſelfe, they'l be ſnatching; giue me an egge Nuncle, and ile giue thee two crownes.

F: *Lear*. A bitter Foole.
      Foole. Do'ſt thou know the difference my Boy, be-
   tweene a bitter Foole, and a ſweet one.

      Lear. No Lad, teach me.
      Foole. Nunckle, giue me an egge, and Ile giue thee two Crownes.

What apparently happened was that a reviser originally altered the passage, which at a later time was marked for deletion in the playhouse manuscript (by a vertical line in the left-hand margin and a diagonal line through the passage).[3] Possibly the marks did not extend fully enough or clearly enough from the beginning of the passage; hence, Compositor E mistakenly set the first three lines that were intended for omission along

---

[1] Compare Greg, *SFF*, pp. 386–7. Taylor argues, however, that musicians regularly toured and in any case no evidence exists of *Lear* going on tour (*Textual Companion*, p. 538).

[2] Compare Stone, p. 234. Taylor, 'Censorship', pp. 106–7, seconded by Kerrigan, pp. 218–19, rejects Stone's conjecture and believes Shakespeare intended the lines to stand in F as they are.

[3] Alternatively, as Professor Howard-Hill advises me, a revising author might have begun adjusting the passage, then decided it was better to omit it altogether.

with the rest of the passage. In the process, besides changing the spelling of 'Doo'st' and capitalising 'boy' and 'foole', he kept the variant readings introduced earlier: the added 'thou' and the substitution 'one' for 'foole'.

Preparation for Publication

Since Shakespeare had died several years before publication of the Folio collection was planned by his fellows, and since he apparently showed no interest in the publication of his plays during his lifetime, preparation of copy for the printing of either Q or F by the author may be ruled out. The book-keeper, the Folio compilers, or a printing-house editor, however, might have taken some care to see that the manuscript was properly prepared before printing began. Q gives little evidence that Okes or anyone else in his printing-house edited the manuscript before printing began. Q2, on the other hand, shows some attempts to correct lineation and other Q errors, and F (also printed by Jaggard) shows further attempts to correct, regularize, and otherwise update spelling and punctuation, not always accurately, as we have seen. The heavier Folio punctuation and capitalization are doubtless the work of Compositors B and E and reflect Jaggard's house style, although the heavier use of parentheses might be a scribe's. Italics for stage directions are common for Q and F, but F uses italics for the letters in 1.2 and 4.5 as well. Either the author, an editor, or the book-keeper had introduced act and scene divisions in the copy for F, but whoever it was forgot to renumber the last scene in Act 4 correctly (see Commentary 4.6.0). Compositors might attempt local emendation – certainly B might, though not E – but neither was above stretching or compressing his copy to fit his measure, or breaking or combining verse lines as the available space required (see above, p. 55). Most likely we owe the better state of the Folio text more to the relative tidiness of the prompt-book manuscript, collated and corrected in the theatre, than to the attentions of a printing-house editor or the compositors.

THE TEXTUAL DATA AND EDITORIAL PROCEDURE

Variants are of two kinds, substantive and accidental. For the editor of a modern-spelling text, orthography and punctuation usually have little significance, although some ambiguous spellings in the copy-text may require decisions or emendations, as in the spelling of F 'mettle' (1.1.64), which could be 'mettle' or 'metal' (Q has 'mettall'), and the use of question marks, which were often used for exclamation marks. Where accidentals of this kind may have substantive implications, they are recorded in the collation.

More important than accidentals are the nearly 1,500 substantive variants between Q and F that require choices for a modernized text. Where both readings are acceptable, F is usually preferred, in accordance with the revision-hypothesis generally accepted for this edition, but both readings are recorded in the collation. Q readings usually preferred by editors are discussed in the Commentary, as in the case of Q 'rash'/F 'sticke' (3.7.57) and Q 'dearne'/F 'sterne' (3.7.62). Where F is clearly wrong and Q right, the Q reading is adopted, as at 3.6.27, Q 'Bobtaile tike'/F 'Bobtaile tight', though the spelling is modernized. Again, these variants are all recorded in the collation.

Quarto and Folio Compared: Some Parallel Passages

The many detailed changes that occur between Q and F are graphically illustrated in the series of parallel passages below, which are edited with collation (but no other annotation) and modernized, like the rest of this edition. Words, phrases, lines unique to one text or the other appear in bold type, with spaces left to indicate where cut or added passages appear. The reader may thereby get a general idea of the revision process, whereas the Textual Analysis (Part 2, pp. 249–72 below) and the Commentary provide more detailed information.

In the first pair of passages, the revision of stage directions as well as Lear's opening speeches are prominent. Not only are additions and deletions noticeable, but words and phrases are altered, for various reasons (see Textual Analysis, pp. 61–2 above). In the next pairs of passages, similar changes occur that, again, may be variously explained. As the collation reveals, the Folio sometimes corrects the quarto, and vice versa. Other emendations of both Q and F may also be required for clarity or sense, as in the emendations of Tom o'Bedlam's mad rant. In the final example, Shakespeare apparently took some pains to alter Lear's last speech, substituting for the long sigh in Q ('O, o, o, o') lines that emphasize the changes in his character by the end of the play. Two important speech ascriptions are also altered. The first makes ambiguous in F what was straightforward in Q (does Kent wish his heart, or Lear's, to break?); the second gives the concluding lines in F to Edgar rather than Albany and thus makes an important thematic and political statement. An appropriate final stage direction is added or restored.

The reader who wishes to study all the differences between Q and F in detail should seek out *The Complete 'King Lear'*, ed. Michael Warren, 1990, or *'King Lear': A Parallel Text Edition*, ed. René Weis, 2nd edn, 2010 – or, better still, both. Warren, arguing that F is a revision of Q, produces the two texts in parallel form in facsimile reproduction, including the corrected and uncorrected states of each passage in which they occur. Weis, whose edition was first published in 1993, gives the edited and annotated texts in modern spelling; the second edition includes a preface arguing against the revision theory. Brian Vickers also argues against it, in still more detail, in *The One 'King Lear'*, 2016. So the debate goes on.

[Quarto: Act 1, Scene 1]

Sound a Sennet. Enter one bearing a Coronet, then Lear, then the Dukes of Albany and Cornwall, next Gonerill, Regan, Cordelia, with Followers

LEAR Attend **my** lords of France and Burgundy, Gloucester.
GLOUCESTER I shall, my **liege**.   [*Exit*]   30
LEAR Meantime we shall express our darker **purposes**.
        The map there. Know, we have divided
        In three our kingdom, and 'tis our **first** intent
        To shake all cares and business **of** our **state**,
        Confirming them on younger **years**.   35

        The **two great** princes, France and Burgundy,   40
        Great rivals in our youngest daughter's love
        Long in our court have made their amorous sojourn,
        And here are to be answered. Tell me, my daughters,

        Which of you shall we say doth love us most,
        That we our largest bounty may extend   45
        Where **merit** doth **most** challenge **it**? Gonerill,
        Our eldest born, speak first.

30 SD *Exit*] F; *not in* Q; *Exeunt Gloucester with Edmond. / Capell*   **48–9** Gonerill, / Our ... first] F; Gonerill, our ... first Q (*one line*)

[Quarto: Act 1, Scene 2]

GLOUCESTER He cannot be such a monster.   85
EDMOND **Nor is not, sure.**
GLOUCESTER **To his father, that so tenderly and entirely loves him.**
        Heaven and earth! Edmond, seek him out: wind me into him, I pray
        you. Frame **your** business after your own wisdom. I would unstate
        myself to be in a due resolution.
EDMOND **I shall** seek him, sir, presently, convey the business as I shall **see**
        means, and acquaint you withal.   90
GLOUCESTER These late eclipses in the sun and moon portend no good to
        us. Though the wisdom of nature can reason thus and thus, yet nature
        finds itself scourged by the sequent effects. Love cools, friendship falls
        off, brothers divide. In cities, mutinies; in countries, **discords**; palaces,
        treason; the bond cracked **between** son and father.   95

[Folio: Act 1, Scene 1]

Sennet. Enter KING LEAR, CORNWALL, ALBANY, GONERILL, REGAN, CORDELIA, *and Attendants*

LEAR Attend **the** lords of France and Burgundy, Gloucester.
GLOUCESTER I shall, my **lord**.   *Exit*   30
LEAR Meantime we shall express our darker **purpose**.
    Give me the map there. Know, **that** we have divided
    In three our kingdom, and 'tis our **fast** intent
    To shake all cares and business **from** our **age**,
    Conferring them on younger **strengths while we**   35
    Unburdened crawl toward death. Our son of Cornwall,
    And you our no less loving son of Albany,
    We have this hour a constant will to publish
    Our daughters' several dowers, that future strife
    May be prevented now. The princes, France and Burgundy,   40
    Great rivals in our youngest daughter's love,
    Long in our court have made their amorous sojourn,
    And here are to be answered. Tell me, my daughters
    (Since now we will divest us both of rule,
    Interest of territory, cares of state),   45
    Which of you shall we say doth love us most,
    That we our largest bounty may extend
    Where **nature** doth with **merit** challenge? Gonerill,
    Our eldest born, speak first.

[Folio: Act 1, Scene 2]

GLOUCESTER He cannot be such a monster.   85

    Edmond, seek him out: wind me into him, I pray you. Frame **the**
    business after your own wisdom. I would unstate myself to be in a due
    resolution.
EDMOND I **will** seek him, sir, presently, convey the business as I shall **find**
    means, and acquaint you withal.   90
GLOUCESTER These late eclipses in the sun and moon portend no good to
    us. Though the wisdom of nature can reason **it** thus and thus,
    yet nature finds itself scourged by the sequent effects. Love cools,
    friendship falls off, brothers divide. In cities, mutinies; in countries,
    discord; in palaces, treason; **and** the bond cracked 'twixt son and   95
    father. **This villain of mine comes under the prediction: there's**
    son against father. The king falls from bias of nature, there's
    father against child. We have seen the best of our time. Machina-
    tions, hollowness, treachery, and all ruinous disorders follow us
    disquietly to our graves. Find out this villain, Edmond, it shall lose   100
    thee nothing. Do it carefully. And the noble and true-hearted Kent
    banished; his offence, honesty. 'Tis strange.   *Exit*

[Quarto: Act 2, Scene 2]

CORNWALL   Fetch forth the stocks!
      As I have life and honour, there shall he sit till noon.
REGAN Till noon? Till night, my lord, and all night too.
KENT Why, madam, if I were your father's dog,
          You **could** not use me so.
REGAN   Sir, being his knave, I will.   125
                  [*Stocks brought out*]
CORNWALL This is a fellow of the selfsame **nature**
          Our sister speaks of. Come, bring away the stocks.
GLOUCESTER Let me beseech your grace not to do so.   128
          His fault is much, and the good king, his master,
          Will check him for't. Your purposed low correction
          Is such as basest and contemned'st wretches
          For pilferings and most common trespasses   128d
          Are punished with. The king must take it ill
          That **he's** so slightly valued in his messenger
          Should have him thus restrained.
CORNWALL   I'll answer that.
REGAN My sister may receive it much more worse
          To have her gentleman abused, assaulted.
          For following her affairs. – Put in his legs.   133a
                  [*Kent is put in the stocks*]
          Come, my **good** lord, away.
                          [*Exeunt all but Gloucester and Kent*]
      Find out this villain, Edmond, it shall lose thee nothing. Do it carefully.   100
      And the noble and true-hearted Kent banished; his offence, honesty.
      Strange, strange!   [*Exit*]

121–2 Fetch... noon] F *lineation; divided* honour, / There Q **122** sit] F, Q *corr.;* set Q *uncorr.* **124–5** Why ... so] F *lineation; as prose* Q **125** SD] F; *after 125* Dyce; *not in* Q **127** speaks] F; speake Q **128c–d** Is ... trespasses] *Pope's lineation; two lines divided* valued / In Q **128c** basest] Q *corr.;* belest Q *uncorr.* **128c** contemned'st] *Capell;* contaned Q *uncorr.;* temnest Q *corr.,* Q2 **128e–131** Are ... that] *Oxford lineation; lines end...* with, /... valued /... restrained. /... that. Q **133a** SD] *After 127, Rowe; not in* Q, F **134** Come ... away] F *assigns this line to Cornwall* **134** SD] Dyce; *Exit* Q2, F; *not in* Q **101** offence, honesty.] F; *not in* Q **102** SD] F; *not in* Q

[Folio: Act 2, Scene 2]

CORNWALL   Fetch forth the stocks!
        As I have life and honour, there shall he sit till noon.
REGAN Till noon? Till night, my lord, and all night too.
KENT Why, madam, if I were your father's dog,
        You **should** not use me so.
REGAN   Sir, being his knave, I will.   125
                        Stocks brought out
CORNWALL This is a fellow of the selfsame **colour**
        Our sister speaks of. Come, bring away the stocks.
GLOUCESTER Let me beseech your grace not to do so.

        The king his master **needs** must take it ill
        That **he**, so slightly valued in his messenger,
        Should have him thus restrained.
CORNWALL   I'll answer that.
REGAN My sister may receive it much more worse
        To have her gentleman abused, assaulted.   133

                [Kent is put in the stocks]
CORNWALL Come, my lord, away.
                        [Exeunt all but Gloucester and Kent]

133 sd] *After 127 Rowe; not in* Q, F   134 sd] *Dyce; Exit.* F, Q2; *not in* Q

[Quarto: Act 4, Scene 1]

GLOUCESTER   Sirrah, naked fellow.
EDGAR Poor Tom's a-cold. [*Aside*] I cannot **dance** it **farther**.
GLOUCESTER Come hither, fellow.
EDGAR Bless thy sweet eyes, they bleed.
GLOUCESTER Know'st thou the way to Dover?   55
EDGAR Both stile and gate, horseway and footpath. Poor Tom hath been
    scared out of his good wits. Bless **the good man** from the foul fiend.
    Five fiends have been in poor Tom at once: of lust, as Obidicut;
    Hobbididence, prince of dumbness; Mahu, of stealing; Modo, of
    murder; Flibbertigibbet, of mopping and mowing, who since   58c
    possesses chambermaids and waiting-women. So, bless thee,
    master!
GLOUCESTER Here, take this purse, thou whom the heavens' plagues
    Have humbled to all strokes. That I am wretched   60
    Makes thee the happier. Heavens deal so still.
    Let the superfluous and lust-dieted man
    That **stands** your ordinance, that will not see
    Because he does not feel, feel your power quickly.
    So distribution should **under** excess,   65
    And each man have enough. Dost thou know Dover?
EDGAR Ay, master.
GLOUCESTER There is a cliff whose high and bending head
    Looks **firmly** in the confinéd deep.
    Bring me but to the very brim of it,   70
    And I'll repair the misery thou dost bear
    With something rich about me. From that place
    I shall no leading need.

52 a-cold] *Rowe;* a cold Q, F   **56–58e** Both ... master] *as prose* F; *entire passage as verse, lines ending...* foot-path, /... wits, /... fiend, /... once, /... dumbnes, /... of /... chambermaids /... maister. Q   **58c** Flibbertigibbet] *Pope;* Stiberdigebit Q   **58c** mopping and mowing] *Theobald;* Mobing, & *Mohing* Q   **72–3** With ... need] F *lineation; lines end* ... me, /... need Q

[Folio: Act 4, Scene 1]

GLOUCESTER   Sirrah, naked fellow.

EDGAR Poor Tom's a-cold. [*Aside*] I cannot **daub** it **further**.

GLOUCESTER Come hither, fellow.

EDGAR [*Aside*] **And yet I must.** – Bless thy sweet eyes, they bleed.

GLOUCESTER Know'st thou the way to Dover?   55

EDGAR Both stile and gate, horseway and footpath. Poor Tom hath been
    scared out of his good wits. Bless thee, **goodman's son**, from the foul
    fiend.

GLOUCESTER Here, take this purse, thou whom the heavens' plagues
    Have humbled to all strokes. That I am wretched   60
    Makes thee the happier. Heavens deal so still.
    Let the superfluous and lust-dieted man
    That **slaves** your ordinance, that will not see
    Because he does not feel, feel your power quickly.
    So distribution should **undo** excess,   65
    And each man have enough. Dost thou know Dover?

EDGAR Ay, master.

GLOUCESTER There is a cliff whose high and bending head
    Looks **fearfully** in the confinèd deep.
    Bring me but to the very brim of it,   70
    And I'll repair the misery thou dost bear
    With something rich about me. From that place
    I shall no leading need.

54 And . . . bleed] *Capell's lineation and punctuation; two lines divided* must: / Blesse F   **57** scared] Q; scarr'd F   **57** thee,
goodman's son,] thee good mans sonne, F; the good man Q

[Quarto: Act 5, Scene 3]

LEAR And my poor fool is hanged. No, no, life?
Why should a dog, a horse, a rat have life,   280
And thou no breath at all? **O thou wilt** come no more,
Never, never, never. Pray you, undo
This button. Thank you, sir. **O, o, o, o.**

EDGAR   He faints. My lord, my lord!   285a
LEAR Break, heart, I prithee break.
EDGAR   Look up, my lord.
KENT Vex not his ghost. O, let him pass. He hates him
That would upon the rack of this tough world
Stretch him out longer.   [*Lear dies*]
EDGAR   O, he is gone indeed.
KENT The wonder is he hath endured so long.   290
He but usurped his life.
ALBANY Bear them from hence. Our present business
Is **to** general woe. Friends of my soul, you twain
Rule in this kingdom and the gored state sustain.
KENT I have a journey, sir, shortly to go: 295
My master calls, and I must not say no.
ALBANY The weight of this sad time we must obey,
Speak what we feel, not what we ought to say.
The oldest have borne most; we that are young
Shall never see so much, nor live so long.   300
                              [*Exeunt with a dead march*]

279–81 And... more] F *lineation; as prose* Q   280 have] F; of Q   282–3 Never... O] *Oxford lineation; as prose* Q   287–
9 Vex... longer] F *lineation; lines end... passe, /... wracke, /... longer.* Q   289 SD] *Oxford; not in* Q (*compare* F)   300
SD] F; *not in* Q

[Folio: Act 5, Scene 3]

LEAR And my poor fool is hanged. No, no, **no** life?
       Why should a dog, a horse, a rat have life,   280
       And thou no breath at all? **Thou'lt** come no more,
       Never, never, never, **never, never.**
       Pray you, undo this button. Thank you, sir.
       Do you see this? Look on her! Look, her lips.
       Look there, look there.   *He dies*
EDGAR   He faints. My lord, my lord!   285
KENT Break, heart, I prithee break.
EDGAR   Look up, my lord.
KENT Vex not his ghost. O, let him pass. He hates him
       That would upon the rack of this tough world
       Stretch him out longer.
EDGAR   He is gone indeed.
KENT The wonder is he hath endured so long.   290
       He but usurped his life.
ALBANY Bear them from hence. Our present business
       Is general woe. Friends of my soul, you twain
       Rule in this **realm** and the gored state sustain.
KENT I have a journey, sir, shortly to go: 295
       My master calls **me**; I must not say no.
EDGAR The weight of this sad time we must obey,
       Speak what we feel, not what we ought to say.
       The oldest **hath** borne most; we that are young
       Shall never see so much, nor live so long.   300
               Exeunt with a dead march

NOTE ON THE TEXT

The text for this edition is based on the First Folio (1623), not on the first quarto (1608). The quarto and Folio texts, while in the main running parallel to each other, are also significantly different in places: some words, phrases, and passages are unique in each, and some show minor alterations of various kinds. Some modern scholars argue that the differences – in which the Folio omits some of the quarto and adds new material – constitute evidence that the Folio is a revised version of the play, largely carried out by Shakespeare himself. In the present edition, spelling has been modernized, and abbreviations and punctuation regularized. The spelling of characters' names in speech headings and stage directions is made uniform and consistent with spellings used in F; hence, Edmond, Gonerill. Punctuation has been kept as light as possible, except where syntax requires clarification; significant departures from punctuation in the copy-text are recorded in the collation.

In the format for the collation, the authority for this edition follows immediately after the lemma (the quotation from the text, enclosed by a square bracket). Other readings follow in chronological order. Significant departures from F are noted in the collation by an asterisk, and all Q-only passages (not found in F) are presented in an Appendix, pp. 273–89 below. Discussions of substantial passages unique to either Q or F appear in the Textual Analysis, pp. 249–72 below.

Elisions in F are generally retained, when consistent with the metre. All *-ed* endings are assumed to be elided, where they would be today, except when the metre requires otherwise and *-èd* is used. Other elisions are often signalled in the Commentary. Although Shakespeare was at the height of his powers when writing *King Lear*, and irregular lines (short or long) may be found throughout the text, the iambic pentameter line has been taken as the normal verse structure, and relineation is made accordingly. This means that sometimes two half-lines, found to equal a single pentameter or (occasionally) hexameter line, will be so arranged in the text.[1]

The present edition generally omits locations for each scene or a detailed time scheme for the play. In keeping with its emphasis on the play as a performance script, especially for a modern audience, every effort is made to stress the fluid and rapid movement from scene to scene as well as within scenes. Although act and scene designations (which the Folio introduces) may appear as impediments to that end, they can be regarded as useful aids for tracking events in the play, nothing more.

The 'Through Line Numbers', as established by Charlton Hinman in *The Norton Facsimile: The First Folio of Shakespeare*, copyright © by W. W. Norton & Company, Inc., are used in this volume with the kind permission of Norton & Co. They appear at the top of each page of the play text and include the first and last lines on those pages according to Hinman's Folio numbering.

---

[1] On joining half-lines, see George T. Wright, *Shakespeare's Metrical Art*, 1988, pp. 103–5, 143–5, and compare David Bevington (ed.), *Ant.*, 1990, pp. 266–70.

The Tragedy of King Lear

LIST OF CHARACTERS

LEAR, *King of Britain*
GONERILL ⎫
REGAN ⎬ *Lear's daughters*
CORDELIA ⎭
The King of FRANCE
The Duke of BURGUNDY
The Duke of ALBANY, *husband to Gonerill*
The Duke of CORNWALL, *husband to Regan*
The Earl of GLOUCESTER
EDGAR, *his elder son*
EDMOND, *his bastard son*
The Earl of KENT
CURAN, *a courtier*
A GENTLEMAN
OSWALD, *Gonerill's steward*
An OLD MAN, *Gloucester's tenant*
A CAPTAIN
A HERALD
FOOL, *in Lear's service*
Knights, Gentlemen, Soldiers, Attendants, Messengers, Servants

THE TRAGEDY OF KING LEAR

1.1 *Enter* KENT, GLOUCESTER, *and* EDMOND

KENT I thought the king had more affected the Duke of Albany than
Cornwall.

GLOUCESTER It did always seem so to us: but now in the division of
the kingdom, it appears not which of the dukes he values most,
for qualities are so weighed that curiosity in neither can make   5
choice of either's moiety.

KENT Is not this your son, my lord?

GLOUCESTER His breeding, sir, hath been at my charge. I have so
often blushed to acknowledge him, that now I am brazed to't.

KENT I cannot conceive you.   10

GLOUCESTER Sir, this young fellow's mother could; whereupon
she grew round wombed, and had indeed, sir, a son for her
cradle ere she had a husband for her bed. Do you smell a fault?

Title] F; M. William Shak-speare / HIS / Historie, of King Lear. Q   **Act 1, Scene 1**   1.1] *Actus Primus. Scoena Prima.*
F; *not in* Q   0 SD] F; *Enter Kent, Gloster, and Bastard.* Q   **4** kingdom] F; kingdomes Q   **5** qualities] F; equalities
Q   **9** to't] too't F; to it Q

Act 1, Scene 1

0 SD GLOUCESTER F spells the name this way in
some SDs and *Gloster* in others. In SHS, *Glouc.* is
most frequently used, though Compositor E tends
to prefer *Glo.* or *Glost.* In dialogue, 'Glouster' is
Compositor B's preferred spelling, 'Glouster'
Compositor E's. Q consistently uses 'Gloster',
which reflects the proper pronunciation.

0 SD EDMOND This is the F spelling here and at
21; in 1.2 and afterwards F usually uses *Bastard* in
SDs and *Bast.* in SHS, like Q, but either 'Edmond'
or (especially in Acts 3–5) 'Edmund' in the dialogue, where Q uses 'Edmund' consistently. The
name was probably suggested by Father Edmonds,
the exorcist in Harsnett's *Declaration*, and by
Edmond Peckham, in whose home the exorcisms
took place.

1 affected inclined to, loved.

1 Albany When Brute, the first King of Britain,
divided his realm, he gave his youngest son
Albanact the territory north of the Humber as far
as Caithness. Thus it was called Albania and later
Albany.

3–4 but . . . kingdom Lear has not revealed all of

the plan to his closest advisers. Compare 'darker
purpose' (31). As these lines and 32–3 indicate,
Lear has already divided up the realm; hence, the
love contest that follows is a sham and not really
meant to determine who gets what share. It appears
from 81 that he intends to favour Cordelia, and the
incentive in 47–8 is false.

4 values rates.

5 qualities i.e. their qualities. F changes Q's
'equalities'.

5 weighed balanced.

5–6 that . . . moiety that the most careful examination of either one's portion cannot determine any
preference.

5 curiosity careful examination, scrutiny.

6 moiety share, portion.

8 breeding (1) upbringing, (2) parentage.

9 brazed brazened, hardened.

10 conceive understand. Gloucester plays on the
biological sense.

11–13 Sir . . . bed Gloucester's coarse humour
must be offensive to Edmond, if he overhears
his father speaking thus, as Rosenberg assumes
(p. 12).

KENT   I cannot wish the fault undone, the issue of it being so proper.

GLOUCESTER   But I have a son, sir, by order of law, some year elder   15
than this, who yet is no dearer in my account; though this knave
came something saucily to the world before he was sent for, yet
was his mother fair, there was good sport at his making, and the
whoreson must be acknowledged. Do you know this noble
gentleman, Edmond?   20

EDMOND   No, my lord.

GLOUCESTER   My lord of Kent; remember him hereafter as my
honourable friend.

EDMOND   My services to your lordship.

KENT   I must love you and sue to know you better.   25

EDMOND   Sir, I shall study deserving.

GLOUCESTER   He hath been out nine years, and away he shall
again. The king is coming.

Sennet. Enter KING LEAR, CORNWALL, ALBANY, GONERILL,
REGAN, CORDELIA, *and Attendants*

LEAR   Attend the lords of France and Burgundy, Gloucester.

GLOUCESTER   I shall, my lord.   *Exit*   30

---

16 account;] *Theobald;* account, Q, F   17 to] F; into Q   22 Kent; remember] Kent: / Remember F; Kent, remember
Q   28 SD] F; *Sound a Sennet, Enter one bearing a Coronet, then Lear, then the Dukes of Albany, and Cornwell, next Gonorill,
Regan, Cordelia, with followers.* Q   30 lord] F; Leige Q   30 SD] F; *not in* Q; *Exeunt Gloucester and Edmond. / Capell*

14 fault (1) transgression, (2) lost scent, as in
hunting, (3) female genitals (Rubenstein, King).
Compare *Venus and Adonis* 691–6, where 'fault' is
used in sense (2), and *AYLI* 4.1.174, where 'fault' is
used in senses (1) and (3).

14 issue (1) result, (2) offspring.

14 proper (1) good-looking, (2) right.

15 order of law i.e. legitimate.

15 some year about a year; compare 1.2.5.

16 account estimation.

16 knave fellow; often applied to servant or
menial. Hence, with an implication of low condition
(see *OED* sv *sb* 2).

17 something somewhat.

19 whoreson bastard son (like 'knave' above,
said jocularly).

26 study deserving 'I shall make every effort to
be worthy of your favour' (Kittredge). But the
words carry an ominous implication.

27 out abroad. Renaissance nobles often sent
their children to be brought up in other noble-
men's homes, sometimes in their own country,
sometimes abroad.

27–8 away … again 'Perhaps these words seal
Gloucester's doom' (Muir).

28 SD Sennet A set of notes played on a trumpet
or cornet to signal a ceremonial entrance or exit.

28 SD GONERILL F spelling of this name is consistent. Compare the older form 'Gonorill' preferred by Q.

28 SD Q indicates that a 'coronet' is carried in
as part of the procession – the one intended for
Cordelia, Perrett and Muir believe. It is not
clear why F omits this part of the SD. See 133
n. below.

29 Attend Wait upon, escort. Lear's entrance
will be conditioned as much by the size and stature
of the actor playing the role as by his interpretation
of it. See Rosenberg, pp. 22–32.

30 SD Most modern editions include Edmond in
this exit, but neither Q nor F gives any indication
when he leaves. In the light of subsequent events
and the development of his character, there may be
justification in keeping him on stage throughout
these momentous proceedings until the general
exodus at 261. Compare Granville-Barker, p. 229.

LEAR Meantime we shall express our darker purpose.
        Give me the map there. Know, that we have divided
        In three our kingdom, and 'tis our fast intent
        To shake all cares and business from our age,
        Conferring them on younger strengths while we   35
        Unburdened crawl toward death. Our son of Cornwall,
        And you, our no less loving son of Albany,
        We have this hour a constant will to publish
        Our daughters' several dowers, that future strife
        May be prevented now. The princes, France and
                Burgundy,   40
        Great rivals in our youngest daughter's love,
        Long in our court have made their amorous sojourn,
        And here are to be answered. Tell me, my daughters
        (Since now we will divest us both of rule,
        Interest of territory, cares of state),   45

---

31 shall] F; will Q   31 purpose] F; purposes Q   32 Give me] F; *not in* Q   32 that] F; *not in* Q   33 fast] F; first Q   34 from our age] F; of our state Q   35 Conferring] F; confirming Q   35 strengths] F; yeares Q   35–40 while we . . . now.] F; *not in* Q   40 The princes] F; The two great princes Q   44–5 (Since . . . state)] F; *not in* Q

31–49 Meantime . . . first See Textual Analysis, pp. 71–2 above, for Folio revisions in this passage.

31 we The royal plural.

31 darker purpose secret intention. The sinister sense of 'darker' is submerged.

32 Give me the map Perrett (p. 144), following Koppel, says that Gloucester or Kent carries the map in when they enter, discussing the division. Mack (pp. 89–90) argues that despite its many interrogatives, the play's dominant rhetorical mood is imperative. Berlin (p. 92) disagrees: Lear's progress is *from* imperative *to* interrogative, 'from a sure sense of self to a confrontation with mystery'.

33 In three i.e. into three parts, but not equal thirds. See 3–4 n.

33 fast (1) firmly fixed, (2) swift.

34–5 To shake . . . strengths This is Lear's motivation for dividing the kingdom in Q. F expands it and adds a further motive at 44–5. 'Q's "state" compresses several relevant meanings, including the political and the personal . . . F unfolds the implications in "state", partly by developing the hint in Q's "Confirming"' (Jackson, p. 333).

36 crawl Lear speaks figuratively. Although some actors have made him appear weak and senile from the outset, Lear's old age appears vigorous throughout this scene and later, certainly in F. Gary Taylor, 'Censorship', p. 96, discusses F's 'deliberate retrenchment of anything which might too directly suggest

senility, the comic *senex iratus*, or the doddering old man . . .'

36 son i.e. son-in-law. In the sources, none of the daughters has a husband until after the love contest.

38 constant will unswerving intention. Characteristically, as at 33, Lear speaks in absolute terms.

38 publish publicly proclaim.

39 several separate (*OED* sv *adj* 1).

39–40 that . . . now The wisdom of Lear's motive here is arguable. Shakespeare's audience would have recognized the dangers, and James I would have been particularly concerned (see p. 7 above). NS cites Matt. 12.25: 'Every kingdom divided against itself is brought to desolation.' In any event, Lear's good intention does not succeed. At 2.1.6–11, Curan speaks of impending wars between the dukes, and at 3.1.11 Kent mentions 'division' between them.

40 prevented forestalled.

40 France and Burgundy Shakespeare assumes that in the time of which he writes France was not a unified kingdom and that the Duke of Burgundy shared equal status with the King of France. Their rivalry for Cordelia's hand is Shakespeare's invention.

44 both Used elsewhere by Shakespeare before more than two nouns, as in *WT* 4.4.56.

45 Interest Possession; compare *John* 4.3.147, where 'interest' = ownership.

Which of you shall we say doth love us most,
That we our largest bounty may extend
Where nature doth with merit challenge? Gonerill,
Our eldest born, speak first.

GONERILL   Sir, I love you more than word can wield the matter,   50
Dearer than eyesight, space, and liberty;
Beyond what can be valued, rich or rare,
No less than life, with grace, health, beauty, honour;
As much as child e'er loved, or father found;
A love that makes breath poor, and speech unable;   55
Beyond all manner of so much I love you.

CORDELIA   [*Aside*] What shall Cordelia speak? Love, and be silent.

LEAR   Of all these bounds even from this line, to this,
With shadowy forests and with champains riched
With plenteous rivers and wide-skirted meads,   60
We make thee lady. To thine and Albany's issues
Be this perpetual. What says our second daughter,
Our dearest Regan, wife of Cornwall?

REGAN   I am made of that self-mettle as my sister
And prize me at her worth. In my true heart   65

---

48 nature doth with merit challenge? Gonerill,] F; merit doth most challenge it, / *Gonorill* Q   50 Sir, I love] F; Sir I do love Q   50 word] F; words Q   51 and] F; or Q   54 as] F; a Q   54 found] F; friend Q   57 SD] *Pope;* not in Q, F   57 speak?] F; doe, Q   59 shadowy] F; shady Q   59–60 and with ... rivers] F; *not in* Q   61 issues] F; issue Q   63 of] F; to Q   64 I] F; Sir I Q   64 that self-mettle as my sister] F; the selfe same mettall that my sister is Q

48–50 Where ... matter Metrically irregular lines. F's revision of Q is incomplete or incompletely transcribed. In 48 'Gonerill' is elided (= 'Gon'rill'); in 50 'Sir' may be an actor's interpolation (Schmidt, *Zur Textkritik*, cited by Furness).

48 Where ... challenge Where natural affection along with desert may claim it as due.

50 more ... matter more than language can convey.

51 eyesight, space, and liberty King notes the dramatic irony behind Gonerill's first comparison, to 'eyesight', and her demand at 3.7.5 that Gloucester should be blinded, which perhaps explains the curious inclusion of this abstraction with the others.

51 space, and liberty 'freedom from confinement, and the enjoyment of that freedom' (Hunter).

53 grace favour, happiness.

55 breath poor (1) speech inadequate, (2) language impoverished, i.e. by love (King).

55 unable incapable, weak.

56 Beyond ... much i.e. 'I love you beyond limits, and cannot say it is *so much*, for how much soever I should name, it would yet be more' (Johnson).

58 Of ... to this Lear points to the map (32).

59–60 and ... rivers Q's omission is probably the result of the compositor's eye-skip. See Textual Analysis, p. 260 below.

59 champains level, open country; compare Italian *campagna*.

59 riched enriched.

60 wide-skirted meads broad meadows.

64 self-mettle (1) self-same spirit (mettle), (2) self-same substance (metal). Shakespeare uses 'mettle' and 'metal' interchangeably, often playing on both senses regardless of spelling. Compare *2H4* 1.1.116: 'For from his metal was his party steeled'. The pun conveys dramatic irony: Regan's mettle/metal, like her sister's, is hard (King).

65 prize ... worth estimate my value to be the same as hers. Kittredge believes the form is imperative: 'value me'.

I find she names my very deed of love.
Only she comes too short, that I profess
Myself an enemy to all other joys
Which the most precious square of sense possesses,
And find I am alone felicitate   70
In your dear highness' love.

CORDELIA [*Aside*]   Then poor Cordelia,
And yet not so, since I am sure my love's
More ponderous than my tongue.

LEAR   To thee and thine hereditary ever
Remain this ample third of our fair kingdom,   75
No less in space, validity, and pleasure
Than that conferred on Gonerill. Now our joy,
Although our last and least, to whose young love
The vines of France and milk of Burgundy
Strive to be interested. What can you say to draw   80

66–7 I . . . profess] F; *two lines divided* short, / That Q   67 comes too] F; came Q   *69 possesses] Q; professes F   71 SD] *Pope; not in* Q, F   73 ponderous] F; richer Q   77 conferred] F; confirm'd Q   77 Now] F; but now Q   78 our last and least, to whose young] F; the last, not least in our deere Q   78 least,] *Hanmer;* least; F   79–80 The vines . . . interested] F; *not in* Q   *80 interested] *Jennens;* interest F   80 draw] F; win Q

66 **very deed** actual document (from which she can read her love).

67 **that** in that.

69 **the most precious square of sense** Of uncertain meaning, the phrase has been variously interpreted. Riverside glosses 'square of sense' as figurative for 'the human body' or 'human life' and cites *FQ* II, ix, 22. In Pythagorean terms, the square is an emblem of the material world, or the world of sense, the physical universe; the circle, an emblem of the conceptual world, even God Himself. (See S. K. Heninger, *Touches of Sweet Harmony*, 1974, p. III, and compare Leonardo's famous drawing of the human figure inscribed within a square superimposed upon the same figure with outstretched limbs inscribed within a circle – a design that derives from Vitruvius. See G. L. Hersey, *Pythagorean Palaces*, 1976, pp. 88 ff.)

69 **possesses** Most modern editors follow Q since the F compositor may have erred through the proximity of 'professe' in 67.

70 **felicitate** made happy.

73 **More ponderous** Weightier. A short, hypermetrical line at the end of a speech is not unusual in Shakespeare's mature drama. On short and shared lines (like 71, also), see George T. Wright,

Shakespeare's Metrical Art, 1988, pp. 116–42. Wright notes the variety of Shakespeare's metrics in *King Lear* and analyses a passage (138–48 below) on pp. 104–5.

76 **validity** value. Compare 5–6.

78 **our last and least** In revising (or correcting) Q, F makes a more clear-cut distinction in Lear's attitude to Cordelia and reintroduces the France–Burgundy rivalry for her love. Cordelia was not only the youngest daughter but smallest in stature, hence 'least' in both senses.

79 **milk of Burgundy** Furness and others cite Eccles: 'The pastures of Burgundy, the effect for the cause'. But Burgundy was a great wine-producing country, then as now, and 'milk' contrasting with 'vines' may signify a rich wine; compare 'Bristol milk'. Compare 253, however, where the King of France refers to 'waterish Burgundy', and n.

80 **interested** Most modern editors emend F's 'interest', a variant spelling of the past participle form of 'interess' = 'to admit to a privilege' (*OED* Interess *v* 1: '*to be interested*, to have a right or share', quoting this passage).

80 **draw** win. 'The gambling metaphor is significant' (NS).

A third more opulent than your sisters? Speak.

CORDELIA   Nothing, my lord.

LEAR   Nothing?

CORDELIA   Nothing.

LEAR   Nothing will come of nothing, speak again.   85

CORDELIA   Unhappy that I am, I cannot heave
My heart into my mouth: I love your majesty
According to my bond, no more nor less.

LEAR   How, how, Cordelia? Mend your speech a little,
Lest you may mar your fortunes.

CORDELIA   Good my lord,   90
You have begot me, bred me, loved me. I
Return those duties back as are right fit,
Obey you, love you, and most honour you.

---

81 opulent] Q; opilent F   81 Speak.] F; *not in* Q   83–4 LEAR Nothing? / CORDELIA Nothing.] F; *not in* Q   85 Nothing]
F; How, nothing Q   86–8 Unhappy … less] F; *as prose,* Q   88 no more] F; nor more Q   89 How, how, Cordelia?
Mend] F; Goe to, goe to, mend Q   90 you] F; it Q   91–2 You … fit] *Pope's lineation; lines divided* me. / I Q, F

81 **A third more opulent** This exposes the pretence of the contest, since only a third remains. Contrary to modern usage of the word 'third', these thirds are three very unequal parts of the whole. If it is more opulent, the division of the realm and the awards must have been decided beforehand. The ways Lear may address, or 'tempt', Cordelia these lines are numerous and various (see Rosenberg, pp. 55–6). Nevertheless, Cordelia refuses to humour her father and adheres rigidly to her 'bond' of filial duty.

81 **Speak** Cordelia's first response may be silence (compare 57). F's addition, besides completing the line metrically, increases the dramatic tension occasioned by Cordelia's hesitation. Jill Levenson contrasts Cordelia's response to that of most of her precursors in the Lear story and relates it to folktale and scriptural sources ('What the silence said: still points in *King Lear*', in Clifford Leech and J. M. R. Margeson (eds.), *Shakespeare 1971*, 1972, pp. 215–29).

82 **Nothing** J. S. Gill, *N&Q* 31 (1984), 210, suggests Matt. 27.12–14 as a possible analogue or source for Cordelia's response, and Matt. 27.11–26 as a whole for the love test.

83 **Nothing?** Lear's question may reflect incredulity or unsure hearing or both. The F additions (83–4) not only make Cordelia's response emphatic, but provide the actor playing Lear with space for further reaction.

85 **Nothing … nothing** Proverbial: *Ex nihilo*

nihil fit (Tilley N285).

86–7 **I cannot heave … mouth** Noble and Shaheen both cite Ecclus. 21.26: 'The heart of fooles is in their mouth: but the mouth of the wise is in his heart'; but compare Sidney's *Arcadia* (1590), Bk II, ch. 2, where Zelmane begins speaking 'with such vehemencie of passion, as though her harte would clime into her mouth, to take her tongues office'. On Cordelia's linguistic behaviour and later Kent's, Colie (p. 126) cites 1 John 3.18: 'let vs not loue in worde, nether in tongue onely, but in dede and trueth'.

87–8 **I love … less** Compare *King Leir*, 279–80: 'But looke what love the child doth owe the father, / The same to you I beare, my gracious Lord' (Bullough, p. 344). On Cordelia's reply as it evolved from Geoffrey to Shakespeare, see Perrett, pp. 228–40.

88 **bond** i.e. the bond between child and parent, filial obligation. Salingar (pp. 96–7) discusses the ambiguity in 'bond' = (1) fetter, (2) covenant, legal agreement.

91–3 **You … honour you** Cordelia explains what she means by her 'bond'. Shaheen compares the Catechism: 'To love, honour, and succour my father and mother', and Eph. 6.1–2, Exod. 20.12, and Deut. 5.16. Seeing Cordelia as a 'dramatized emblem', Reibetanz notes Cordelia's reply as a close paraphrase of the wedding response (pp. 30–1) – a fact noticed also by some psychoanalytically oriented critics.

Why have my sisters husbands, if they say
They love you all? Happily, when I shall wed,   95
That lord whose hand must take my plight shall carry
Half my love with him, half my care and duty.
Sure, I shall never marry like my sisters.

LEAR   But goes thy heart with this?

CORDELIA   Ay, my good lord.

LEAR   So young, and so untender?   100

CORDELIA   So young, my lord, and true.

LEAR   Let it be so, thy truth then be thy dower.
For by the sacred radiance of the sun,
The mysteries of Hecate and the night,
By all the operation of the orbs   105
From whom we do exist and cease to be,
Here I disclaim all my paternal care,
Propinquity and property of blood,
And as a stranger to my heart and me
Hold thee from this forever. The barbarous Scythian,   110
Or he that makes his generation messes
To gorge his appetite, shall to my bosom

94–8 Why . . . sisters.] F; *lines end* . . . you all, / . . . hand / . . . him, / . . . neuer / . . . father all. Q   98 sisters.] F; sisters, to loue my father all. Q   100 untender?] F; vntender, Q   104 mysteries] F2; mistresse Q; miseries F   104 night,] F; might, Q   111–13 Or . . . relieued] F; *lines end* . . . generation / . . . appetite / . . . relieued Q   112 to my bosom] F; *not in* Q

94–8 Why . . . sisters Cordelia's logic here is irrefutable, but Lear is in no mood for logic. He only registers what seems to him his daughter's cold response to a repeated invitation to tell the world how much she really loves him, as her sisters have just done. As 99 and 100 show, he cannot believe what he hears or understand what is happening.

95 Happily i.e. haply, perchance. F's spelling (a variant form) suggests a possible pun, though the pronunciation is disyllabic.

96 plight troth-plight, promise to wed.

98 Sure The sarcastic effect of 'Sure' is better appreciated in America, where the idiom has survived, than in Britain (King). Q's additional half-line makes Cordelia's point more emphatic but repeats the sense of 95.

99 thy heart King notes a possible pun on Cordelia's name (Latin *cor, cordis* = 'heart'). In the next twenty lines Lear twice refers to his heart as severed from her (109, 120).

101 true In the preceding line, Hunter detects a play on 'untender' = (1) hard, (2) inflexible, stiff in

opinion; 'true' would then = (1) unerring, (2) growing straight.

104 mysteries secret rites.

104 Hecate Pagan goddess of the lower world, patroness of witchcraft (usually performed at night) and of the moon, she appears in *Mac* 3.5 and 4.1.

105 operation of the orbs The movement, and therefore astrological influence, of the heavenly bodies.

108 Propinquity and property of blood i.e. close relationship, kinship, consanguinity.

110 from this from this time (Steevens). But Lear may be gesturing from his breast. In *Ham.* 2.2.156, Polonius similarly gestures, using demonstrative pronouns.

110 Scythian Inhabitant of Asia known from classical times for barbaric practices. Tamburlaine, in Marlowe's play, was a fierce Scythian shepherd whose cruelty was dramatized but did not include cannibalism.

111–12 Or he . . . appetite A reference to the barbaric custom among some cannibalistic peoples of feeding upon their infant children or their

        Be as well neighboured, pitied, and relieved,
        As thou my sometime daughter.

KENT   Good my liege –

LEAR   Peace, Kent,   115
        Come not between the dragon and his wrath.
        I loved her most, and thought to set my rest
        On her kind nursery. Hence and avoid my sight!
        So be my grave my peace, as here I give
        Her father's heart from her. Call France. Who stirs?   120
        Call Burgundy. – Cornwall and Albany,
        With my two daughters' dowers digest the third.
        Let pride, which she calls plainness, marry her.
        I do invest you jointly with my power,
        Pre-eminence, and all the large effects   125
        That troop with majesty. Ourself by monthly course,
        With reservation of an hundred knights
        By you to be sustained, shall our abode
        Make with you by due turn; only we shall retain
        The name and all th'addition to a king: the sway,   130

---

114 liege –] *Rowe;* Liege. Q, F   115–16 Peace … wrath.] F; *one line* Q (*turned over*)   121 Burgundy. –] *Theobald;* *Burgundy,* Q, F   122 dowers … the] F; *dower … this* Q   124 with] F; *in* Q   129 turn … shall] F; *turnes … still* Q   130 th'addition] F; *the additions* Q   130 king: the sway,] F; King, / The sway, Q

parents ('generation' = either 'offspring' or 'progenitors'; 'messes' = 'dishes of food'). According to Harrison's *Description of Britain*, ch. 4, the ancient Scots were of mixed Scythian and Spanish blood, and practised cannibalism (Perrett, p. 292).

114 sometime former.

114 liege sovereign.

116 dragon … wrath Although the dragon was on the crest of ancient British kings (Kittredge; NS), Shakespeare may refer simply to a type of fierceness (as in *Cor.* 4.7.23), and to wrath as a property of that fierceness, not its object.

117 set my rest Another metaphor from gambling (compare 80). In the card game primero, to set up one's rest meant 'to stand upon the cards in one's hand', thus to stake one's all. But as Kittredge and others note, 'rest' also carried the suggestion of repose, to which Lear looked forward in retirement. These ambiguities are present in *Rom.* 4.5.6–7, 5.3.110.

118 nursery i.e. care. The inversion of roles involving Lear's second childhood is the subject of much psychoanalytical commentary.

118 Hence Get away, leave; addressed to

Cordelia, who disobeys.

120 Who stirs? i.e. jump to it! 'The courtiers are shocked into immobility' (Muir).

122 digest consume, assimilate.

123 Let pride … marry her i.e. let her pride, which she terms candour, be her dowry and get her a husband.

125 all … effects all the outward shows, accompaniments. Compare *Ado* 2.3.107. But note the qualifiers below.

126–9 Ourself … turn Although Shakespeare borrowed the idea of a retinue from an earlier source than *King Leir* (probably the *Mirour for Magistrates*), he increased the number to a hundred knights and added the stipulation of alternating monthly visits (Perrett, pp. 187–90). How Gonerill and Regan react here to Lear's unexpected stipulation of monthly visits is open to interpretation.

127 reservation '*Law.* The action or fact of reserving or retaining for oneself some right or interest in property which is being conveyed to another' (*OED* sv 2); Compare 2.4.245.

130 addition titles, honours.

Revenue, execution of the rest,
Beloved sons, be yours; which to confirm,
This coronet part between you.

KENT   Royal Lear,
Whom I have ever honoured as my king,
Loved as my father, as my master followed,   135
As my great patron thought on in my prayers –

LEAR   The bow is bent and drawn, make from the shaft.

KENT   Let it fall rather, though the fork invade
The region of my heart. Be Kent unmannerly
When Lear is mad. What wouldst thou do, old man?   140
Think'st thou that duty shall have dread to speak
When power to flattery bows? To plainness honour's
        bound,
When majesty falls to folly. Reserve thy state,
And in thy best consideration check
This hideous rashness. Answer my life, my judgement: 145
Thy youngest daughter does not love thee least,

---

133 between] F; betwixt Q   136 prayers –] *Rowe;* prayers. Q; praiers. F   138–46 Let ... least] F (*except 142, divided*
bowes? / To); *nine lines ending* ... rather, / ... heart, / ... man, / ... dutie / ... bowes, / ... folly, / ... consideration / ...
life / ... least, Q   140 mad] Q2, F; man Q   140 wouldst] F4; wouldest F, F2–3; wilt Q   142 When ... bound] *Johnson's*
lineation; two lines divided bowes / To F   143 Reserve thy state] F; Reuerse thy doome Q

131 Revenue Accented on second syllable.

133 This coronet Shakespeare uses 'coronet' for
the diadem of a nobleman in *1H6* 5.4.134, *JC*
1.2.238, and elsewhere. In *H5* 2 Chorus 10 and in
Temp. 1.2.111–16 he explicitly contrasts 'crowns
and coronets'. In view of 131, moreover, it is unlikely that Lear gives his sons-in-law his own crown
to divide between them (compare Greg, *SFF*, p.
384 n.), although in stage performances he sometimes does, ironically emphasizing the folly of
dividing his kingdom by so doing. Probably Lear
refers to the coronet he meant for Cordelia, which
an attendant carries during the entry procession, as
Q directs (28 SD n.) See Perrett, pp. 151–4, and
Rosenberg, p. 67, for stage business here, and compare G. W. Williams, 'Lear's coronet', *American
Notes & Queries* 9 (1971), 99–100, who argues that
'coronet' means Lear's crown.

137 make from i.e. let go. Lear's metaphor
refers to Kent's elaborate preamble; impatient, he
wants Kent to get to the point. But some commentators (e.g. Muir, Kittredge) interpret the passage
differently and gloss 'make from' as 'avoid', i.e. get
out of the way of (the arrow of) my anger.

138 fork An arrowhead with two forward points,
or 'forkhead'.

140 When ... old man? Abandoning the figure
of parrhesia, or respectful protest (Joseph, p. 276),
Kent changes his idiom to direct, blunt address,
using the familiar second-person pronoun, appropriate only to subordinates and children, and an
appellation ('old man') that is stunning in its
impudence.

142 plainness blunt, frank speaking; as at 123
and 2.2.91.

143 Reserve thy state i.e. do not relinquish
your kingdom. Furness cites Johnson: 'I am
inclined to think that *Reverse thy doom* was
Shakespeare's first reading, as more conducive
to the present occasion, and that he changed it
afterwards to "Reserve thy state," which con-
duces more to the progress of the action.' Other
commentators (e.g. Duthie, p. 125; Granville-
Barker, p. 303) suggest that in F Kent is thinking more of Lear's safety than of Cordelia, who
in the Q reading is uppermost. Jackson (p. 338)
says the F readings stress Lear's political folly in
surrendering his kingdom; Q, more closely following the source play, emphasizes his error in
condemning Cordelia.

145 Answer ... judgement Let my life be
answerable for my opinion.

> Nor are those empty-hearted whose low sounds
> Reverb no hollowness.

LEAR   Kent, on thy life no more.

KENT   My life I never held but as a pawn
> To wage against thine enemies, ne'er feared to lose it,   150
> Thy safety being motive.

LEAR   Out of my sight!

KENT   See better, Lear, and let me still remain
> The true blank of thine eye.

LEAR   Now by Apollo –

KENT   Now by Apollo, king,
> Thou swear'st thy gods in vain.

LEAR   O vassal! Miscreant!   155

ALBANY, CORNWALL   Dear sir, forbear.

KENT   Kill thy physician, and thy fee bestow
> Upon the foul disease. Revoke thy gift,
> Or whilst I can vent clamour from my throat,
> I'll tell thee thou dost evil.

LEAR   Hear me, recreant,   160
> On thine allegiance hear me.

147–8 low sounds / Reverb] F; low, sound / Reuerbs Q   150 thine] F; thy Q   *150 ne'er feared] *Oxford (Furness conj.);* nere feare F; nor feare Q   151 motive] F; the motiue Q   154 Apollo –] Q2; Appollo, Q; Apollo, F   154–5 Now … vain.] F; *one line* Q   155 O vassal! Miscreant] F; Vassall, recreant Q   156 ALBANY … forbear] F; *not in* Q   156 SH CORNWALL] *Cor.* F; CORDELIA *Halio, Oxford*   157–60 Kill … evil.] F; *lines end* … Physicion, / … disease, / … clamour / … euill. Q   157 Kill] F; Doe, kill Q   157 thy fee] F; the fee Q   158 gift] F; doome Q   160–1 Hear … me.] *Capell's lineation; one line* Q, F   160 recreant] F; *not in* Q   161 thine] F; thy Q

148 Reverb no hollowness Do not reverberate hollowly; with a quibble on 'hollowness' = 'emptiness' and 'insincerity' (Riverside). Compare *H5* 4.4.67–9: 'I did never know so full a voice issue from so empty a heart; but the saying is true, "The empty vessel makes the greatest sound."'

149 pawn stake; as in a wager.

150 wage wager, risk. The preposition 'against' may suggest some form of waging war (Muir), and 'pawn' (149) may involve a metaphor from chess (Capell).

152–3 See … eye Kent, as the wise counsellor, asks Lear to continue using him as his instrument for seeing better. 'Blank' refers to the white centre of a target, the concentric rings of which resemble the pupil of an eye. Like Cordelia, Kent disobeys Lear's command to get out.

154 Apollo An appropriate pagan god, Apollo was the archer god and the sun god, or the god of clear seeing (Hunter). He was also the god of diseases and their cure; compare 157–8.

155 vassal base wretch.

155 Miscreant Villain (literally, infidel); as in *R2* 1.1.39. Some editions (e.g. NS) follow Rowe and add SD, *Laying his hand on his sword*, as occasioning Albany and Cornwall's interjection (156). But other stage business suggesting violence is possible (Rosenberg, p. 72; compare Urkowitz, pp. 32–3).

156 SH CORNWALL F's *Cor.* can indicate either Cordelia or Cornwall. Following Goldring's suggestion (pp. 143–51), Oxford makes Cordelia the speaker here and later (see 182 SH n. below).

157–8 Kill … disease Compare *Ham.* 3.4.145–9, where Shakespeare uses the disease metaphor for moral corruption, and 4.3.65–7, where he uses it for mental disorder.

158 Revoke thy gift Seeing what has happened, Kent opposes the plan of dividing the kingdom, regardless of what he may have thought earlier (see 3–4 n. above).

160 recreant traitor.

That thou hast sought to make us break our vows,
Which we durst never yet; and with strained pride,
To come betwixt our sentence and our power,
Which nor our nature nor our place can bear,   165
Our potency made good, take thy reward.
Five days we do allot thee for provision
To shield thee from disasters of the world,
And on the sixth to turn thy hated back
Upon our kingdom; if on the tenth day following   170
Thy banished trunk be found in our dominions,
The moment is thy death. Away! By Jupiter,
This shall not be revoked.

KENT   Fare thee well, king, since thus thou wilt appear,
    Freedom lives hence, and banishment is here.   175
    [*To Cordelia*] The gods to their dear shelter take thee,
        maid,
    That justly think'st and hast most rightly said.
    [*To Gonerill and Regan*] And your large speeches may your
        deeds approve,
    That good effects may spring from words of love.
    Thus Kent, O princes, bids you all adieu,   180
    He'll shape his old course in a country new.   *Exit*

Flourish. Enter GLOUCESTER *with* FRANCE *and* BURGUNDY
[and] Attendants

CORDELIA   Here's France and Burgundy, my noble lord.

---

162 That] F; Since Q   162 vows] F; vow Q   163 strained] F; straied Q   164 betwixt] F; betweene Q   *164 sentence] Q, F *uncorr.*, F2; sentences F *corr.*   167 Five] F; Foure Q   168 disasters] F; diseases Q   169 sixth] F4; fift Q; sixt F   170 tenth] F; seventh *Collier*   174 Fare] F; Why fare Q   *174 since] Q; sith F   175 Freedom] F; Friendship Q   176 SD] *Hanmer; not in* Q, F   176 dear shelter] F; protection Q   177 justly think'st] F; rightly thinks Q   177 rightly said] F; justly said Q   178 SD] *Hanmer; not in* Q, F   181 SD.1 *Exit*] F; *not in* Q   181 SD.2] F; *Enter France and Burgundie with Gloster.* Q   182 SH CORDELIA] *Halio, Oxford; Cor.* F; *Glost.* Q

162 **That** Seeing that.
163 **strained** excessive.
166 **Our ... good** i.e. our royal power being effected. Lear has not yet relinquished his kingship (note 'our dominions', 171), as the subsequent dialogue with Burgundy and France also shows.
171 **trunk** torso, body.
174–81 **Fare ... new** 'After the storm comes the equanimity of Kent's rhymed couplets' (Craig, cited by NS).
174 **since thus** Crowding may have prompted Compositor E to substitute awkward 'sith' for Qq 'since' (*Textual Companion*, p. 532), thus avoiding a turned-over line.
175 **Freedom ... here** An early indication of

topsy-turviness, or inverted order, in the play. (See NS, p. xxviii.)
178 **approve** make good, confirm.
179 **effects** deeds, actions.
181 **old course** customary conduct.
181 SD.2 *Flourish* A fanfare; compare '*Sennet*', 28 SD.
182 SH CORDELIA F alters Q's *Glost.* to *Cor.*, which most editors take to indicate Cornwall. Cordelia seems a more appropriate speaker, since Burgundy and France are her suitors. See 156 n., and compare Duthie, p. 168, who adopts Q's SH, and Urkowitz, pp. 39–40.
182 **Here's** A singular verb preceding a plural subject appears often in Shakespeare; compare 3.3.16.

LEAR   My lord of Burgundy,
      We first address toward you, who with this king
      Hath rivalled for our daughter. What in the least   185
      Will you require in present dower with her,
      Or cease your quest of love?
BURGUNDY   Most royal majesty,
      I crave no more than hath your highness offered,
      Nor will you tender less?
LEAR   Right noble Burgundy,
      When she was dear to us, we did hold her so,   190
      But now her price is fallen. Sir, there she stands.
      If aught within that little seeming substance,
      Or all of it, with our displeasure pieced
      And nothing more, may fitly like your grace,
      She's there, and she is yours.
BURGUNDY   I know no answer.   195
LEAR   Will you with those infirmities she owes,
      Unfriended, new adopted to our hate,
      Dowered with our curse, and strangered with our oath,
      Take her, or leave her?
BURGUNDY   Pardon me, royal sir,
      Election makes not up in such conditions.   200
LEAR   Then leave her, sir, for by the power that made me,
      I tell you all her wealth. [*To France*] For you, great king,
      I would not from your love make such a stray

183–93 My ... pieced,] F; *ten lines ending* ... towards you, / ... daughter, / ... present / ... loue? / ... what / ... lesse? /
... to vs [*turned over*] / ... fallen, / ... little / ... peec'st, Q   184 toward ... this] F; towards ... a Q   187 Most] F; *not in*
Q   188 hath] F; what Q   194 more] F; else Q   196 Will] F; Sir will Q   198 Dowered] F; Couered Q   199 her?]
Rowe; her. Q, F   199–200 Pardon ... conditions.] F; *divided* vp / On such Q   200 in] F; on Q   202 SD] *Pope; not in* Q,
F

184 **address toward** direct our speech toward
(Schmidt).

185 **rivalled** competed.

189 **less?** Modern editors change the question
mark, found in both Q and F, to a full stop, which
makes Burgundy's reply sound too peremptory.
Caught off guard by Lear's question, the duke
does not know what to make of it and responds
with a query of his own.

190 **so** i.e. dear, worth much (with a pun on 'dear'
= 'beloved').

192 **that little seeming substance** The ambiguity of 'seeming' (it can go with either 'little' or
'substance') suggests two interpretations: either (1)

that person who rejects the slightest hint of insincerity, or (2) that small piece of unreality (that looks
like a person).

193 **pieced** added, eked out.

194 **like** please.

196 **infirmities** i.e. disabilities (enumerated in
197–8).

196 **owes** owns, has.

198 **strangered** made a stranger, disowned.

200 **Election ... conditions** No choice (election) is possible under the terms thus set out.

202 **tell** (1) report to, (2) count (Hunter).

202 **For** As for.

203 **make such a stray** be so aberrant.

To match you where I hate; therefore beseech you
T'avert your liking a more worthier way   205
Than on a wretch whom nature is ashamed
Almost t'acknowledge hers.

FRANCE   This is most strange,
That she whom even but now was your best object,
The argument of your praise, balm of your age,
The best, the dearest, should in this trice of time   210
Commit a thing so monstrous to dismantle
So many folds of favour. Sure, her offence
Must be of such unnatural degree
That monsters it, or your fore-vouched affection
Fall into taint; which to believe of her   215
Must be a faith that reason without miracle
Should never plant in me.

CORDELIA   I yet beseech your majesty –
If for I want that glib and oily art,
To speak and purpose not, since what I well intend,   220
I'll do't before I speak – that you make known
It is no vicious blot, murder, or foulness,
No unchaste action or dishonoured step
That hath deprived me of your grace and favour,

---

205 T'avert] F; To auert Q   207 t'acknowledge] F; to acknowledge Q   207–13 This ... degree] F; *six lines ending* ...
now / ... praise, / ... deerest, / ... thing, / ... fauour, / ... degree, Q   208 she whom] F; she, that Q   *208 best] Q; *not
in* F   210 The best, the] F; most best, most Q   214 your fore-vouched affection] F; you for voucht affections
Q   215 Fall] F; Falne Q   217 Should] F; Could Q   218–21 majesty – / If ... speak – that] Maiestie, / If ... speake,
that Q; Maiesty. / If ... speake, that F; majesty, / (If ... speak) that *Theobald*   *220 well] Q; will F   221 make known]
F; may know Q   223 unchaste] F; vncleane Q

204 **To** As to.
204 **beseech** I beseech.
205 **T'avert** To redirect.
205 **more worthier** Double comparatives and
superlatives are common in Shakespeare. Compare
e.g. 2.2.92, 3.2.62.
208 **whom** i.e. who. Compare *Temp.* 5.1.76–8.
208 **best object** most favoured object (to gaze
upon). Compare *MND* 4.1.170, *Cym.* 5.4.55–6.
209 **argument** theme, subject.
211–12 **dismantle ... favour** The image is of
removing many layers of clothing that drape, or
enfold, Cordelia in her father's favour. On the imagery of clothing and divestment, see Heilman,
pp. 67–87.
214 **monsters it** i.e. makes it (the offence)
monstrous.
214 **fore-vouched affection** previously proclaimed love.

215 **Fall into taint** i.e. must (from 213) now
appear to be insincere, hence discredited.
215 **her** 'Emphatic. Of the two alternatives
France chooses the second, for the first is to him
incredible' (Kittredge).
215–17 **to believe ... me** i.e. to believe
Cordelia guilty of so monstrous an offence
requires a faith that reason alone cannot instil
in me; it would require a miracle to get me to
believe it.
219 **If for** If (it is) because. Cordelia's broken
or ungrammatical syntax (as well as her somewhat repetitious speech) may be the result of
her emotional state, as some commentators
believe.
219 **want** lack (also at 225).
220 **purpose** intend (to fulfil).
222 **vicious blot** moral stain.
223 **dishonoured** dishonourable.

But even for want of that for which I am richer –   225
A still-soliciting eye, and such a tongue
That I am glad I have not, though not to have it,
Hath lost me in your liking.

LEAR   Better thou
Hadst not been born than not t'have pleased me better.

FRANCE   Is it but this? A tardiness in nature,   230
Which often leaves the history unspoke
That it intends to do? My lord of Burgundy,
What say you to the lady? Love's not love
When it is mingled with regards that stands
Aloof from th'entire point. Will you have her?   235
She is herself a dowry.

BURGUNDY   Royal king,
Give but that portion which yourself proposed,
And here I take Cordelia by the hand,
Duchess of Burgundy.

LEAR   Nothing, I have sworn; I am firm.   240

BURGUNDY   I am sorry then, you have so lost a father
That you must lose a husband.

CORDELIA   Peace be with Burgundy;
Since that respect and fortunes are his love,
I shall not be his wife.

FRANCE   Fairest Cordelia, that art most rich being poor,   245
Most choice forsaken, and most loved despised,
Thee and thy virtues here I seize upon.

---

225 for want] Q, F; the want *Hanmer*   225 richer] F; rich Q   227 That] F; As Q   228–9 Better thou / Hadst . . . better.]
Pope's lineation; Better thou hadst, / Not . . . better. F; Goe to, goe to, better thou hadst not bin borne, / Then . . . better.
Q   229 t'have] F; to haue Q   230 but this?] F; no more but this, Q   231–6 Which . . . dowry.] F; *five lines ending* . . . to
do [*turned under*] / . . . Lady? / . . . sta[n]ds [*turned under*] / . . . haue her? / . . . dowre. Q   231 Which] F; That
Q   *232 do?] *Pope;* do, Q; do: F   233 Love's] F; Loue is Q   234 regards] F; respects Q   235 th'entire point. Will]
Steevens; the intire point wil Q; th'intire point, will F   236 a dowry] F; and dowre Q   236–9 Royal . . . Burgundy.] F;
three lines ending . . . portion / . . . Cordelia / . . . Burgundie, Q   236 king] F; Leir Q; Lear Q2   240 I am firm.] F; *not in*
Q   242–4 Peace . . . wife.] F; *two lines divided* respects / Of Q   243 respect and fortunes] F; respects / Of fortune Q

---

225 for which i.e. for lack of which.
226   still-soliciting   always   importuning,
begging.
228 liking 'Cordelia deliberately uses a colder
word than love' (Muir, following Kittredge).
230 tardiness in nature i.e. slowness in
disposition.
231 history 'Frequently used for what passes in the
inner life of man' (Schmidt 1879, cited by Furness).
Used in this sense in *MM* 1.1.28, *R3* 3.5.28.
233–5 Love . . . point Compare Sonnet 116,
where Shakespeare develops the idea more fully.
234–5 mingled . . . point adulterated with

considerations (such as a dowry) completely irrelevant to the main issue (love).
243 Since that Since.
243 respect and fortunes consideration of
wealth (hendiadys). Compare 1.2.45, etc., and Q
'respects / Of fortune'.
245–6 most rich . . . despised Noble and
Shaheen compare the paradoxes in 2 Cor.
6.10: 'As poore, and yet making many rich: as
hauing nothing, and yet possessing all things'.
Shaheen adds 2 Cor. 8.9: 'Our Lord Iesus
Christ, that he being riche, for your sakes became
poore'.

Be it lawful I take up what's cast away.
Gods, gods! 'Tis strange, that from their cold'st neglect
My love should kindle to inflamed respect.   250
Thy dowerless daughter, king, thrown to my chance,
Is queen of us, of ours, and our fair France.
Not all the dukes of waterish Burgundy
Can buy this unprized precious maid of me.
Bid them farewell, Cordelia, though unkind;   255
Thou losest here a better where to find.

LEAR   Thou hast her, France, let her be thine; for we
Have no such daughter, nor shall ever see
That face of hers again. Therefore be gone,
Without our grace, our love, our benison.   260
Come, noble Burgundy.

Flourish. Exeunt [Lear, Burgundy, Cornwall, Albany, Gloucester,
Edmond, and Attendants]

FRANCE   Bid farewell to your sisters.
CORDELIA   The jewels of our father, with washed eyes
Cordelia leaves you. I know you what you are,
And like a sister am most loath to call
Your faults as they are named. Love well our father: 265
To your professèd bosoms I commit him.
But yet, alas, stood I within his grace,
I would prefer him to a better place.

---

251 my] F; thy Q   253 of] F; in Q   254 Can] F; Shall Q   257–8 Thou ... see] F; *divided* thine, / For we Q   260
benison.] F; benizon? Q   *261 SD] *This edn; Exit Lear and Burgundie.* Q; *Flourish. Exeunt.* F; *Exeunt Lear, Burgundy,*
Cornwal, Albany, Gloster, and Attendants. / Capell   262–5 The ... father:] F; *lines end* ... father, / ... you are, [*turned*
over] / ... faults / ... Father, Q   265 Love] F; vse Q

249–60 Gods ... benison The couplets not only
conclude the major action of this scene, they also
formalize the attitudes involved, as Hunter notes.
Reibetanz, p. 32, regards this speech of 'rhymed
paradoxy' as evidence that France is 'from another
world' than Lear's dark one.

250 inflamed respect passionate regard.

251 thrown ... chance cast to my luck (another
gambling metaphor).

253 waterish (1) well-watered (with streams and
rivers), (2) weak, insipid. Compare 79 n.: the king
may be casting a slur on the wine of Burgundy as
well!

254 unprized precious unvalued, unappre-
ciated (by others) but dear (to me).

255 though unkind i.e. though they have been
unkind or unnatural.

256 here ... where Used as nouns. Kittredge
compares *Oth.* 1.1.137.

260 benison blessing.

261 SD *Exeunt* 'Lear seems to take his leave,
but in fact he flees ... Flight – and pursuit –
will weave throughout the whole play now, its
effect will be ... pervasive' (Rosenberg, p. 79).
Drawing parallels with classical Greek tragedy,
Fredson Bowers considers the climactic aspects
of this scene in 'The structure of *King Lear*',
SQ 31 (1980), 7–20.

262 jewels A term of endearment (NS), spoken
sarcastically.

262 washed eyes (1) tear-filled eyes, (2) eyes
cleared of illusion, cleansed, as in *R3* 4.4.389–90,
Ado 4.1.153–4.

265 as ... named by their actual names.

266 your professèd bosoms i.e. the nurture
and love you have declared (as opposed to what
you may really feel and intend).

268 prefer recommend.

So farewell to you both.

REGAN   Prescribe not us our duty.

GONERILL   Let your study   270
Be to content your lord, who hath received you
At fortune's alms. You have obedience scanted,
And well are worth the want that you have wanted.

CORDELIA   Time shall unfold what plighted cunning hides;
Who covers faults, at last with shame derides.   275
Well may you prosper.

FRANCE   Come, my fair Cordelia.

Exeunt France and Cordelia

GONERILL   Sister, it is not little I have to say of what most nearly
appertains to us both. I think our father will hence tonight.

REGAN   That's most certain, and with you; next month with us.

GONERILL   You see how full of changes his age is; the observation   280
we have made of it hath not been little. He always loved our
sister most, and with what poor judgement he hath now cast
her off appears too grossly.

REGAN   'Tis the infirmity of his age; yet he hath ever but slenderly
known himself.   285

---

269 both.] F; both? Q   **270** SH REGAN] F; *Gonerill.* Q   **270** duty.] F; duties? Q   **270** SH GONERILL] F; *Regan* Q   **270–3** Let … wanted.] F; *lines end* … Lord, / … almes, / … scanted, / … wanted. Q   **273** want] F; worth Q   **274** plighted] F; pleated Q   **275** covers] Q, F; cover *Jennens;* cover'd *Hanmer, Capell*   **275** with shame] F; shame them Q   **276** my] F; *not in* Q   **276** SD *Exeunt*] F3; *Exit* Q, F, F2   *277–8 Sister, … tonight.] *As prose, Capell; three verse lines ending* … say, / … both, / … night. Q, F   **277** little] F; a little Q   *281 not] Q; *not in* F   **283** grossly] F; grosse Q

---

270 study aim, endeavour.

272 At fortune's alms As a charity, a poor gift of fortune.

272 scanted stinted, slighted.

273 the want … wanted the absence of that which you have lacked (i.e. love). Bevington says 'want' may also refer to her dowry. The alliteration and word-play (anadiplosis) emphasize Gonerill's sarcasm.

274 Time … hides Martha Andresen notes Cordelia's version of the Renaissance commonplace *sententia Veritas filia temporis* ('Truth the daughter of Time') and its relation to divestiture imagery ('"Ripeness is all": sententiae and commonplaces in *King Lear*', in *Some Facets*, pp. 155–6).

274 plighted pleated, folded, hence concealed (Onions). Compare 211–12.

275 Who … derides The F reading is acceptable. As Duthie says, 'The F version of the speech sounds more awkward and stilted than that of Q: but the speech is a sentatious one, and it may well have left Shakespeare's pen more rather than less stilted.' 'Who' takes 'Time' as its antecedent, not 'cunning',

and 'faults' is the object of both 'covers' and 'derides' (Schmidt, cited by Duthie). NS and Oxford emend 'covers' to 'covert', following Mason (cited by Furness), so that 'cunning' is still responsible for covering faults. But Sisson, p. 231, defends the F reading: 'Time at first covers faults, but at last (unfolds them and) derides them with shame.'

276 Well … prosper Again, spoken sarcastically. Noble and Shaheen cite Prov. 28.13: 'He that hideth his sinnes, shall not prosper.' Shaheen notes that the Authorized Version (1611) uses 'covereth' instead of 'hideth'.

278 will hence will go hence (a common ellipsis).

279 with you Lear has not actually stipulated with whom he will first reside (126–9), but Regan rightly assumes that Gonerill, as the eldest daughter, will be first.

281 not Compositor E has apparently dropped the negative in this crowded line (and column), but Schmidt 1879 and Oxford follow F.

283 grossly obviously.

GONERILL   The best and soundest of his time hath been but rash;
then must we look from his age to receive not alone the
imperfections of long-engraffed condition, but therewithal the
unruly waywardness that infirm and choleric years bring with
them.   290

REGAN   Such unconstant starts are we like to have from him as this
of Kent's banishment.

GONERILL   There is further compliment of leave-taking between
France and him. Pray you, let us sit together. If our father carry
authority with such disposition as he bears, this last surrender   295
of his will but offend us.

REGAN   We shall further think of it.

GONERILL   We must do something, and i'th'heat.

Exeunt

1.2 *Enter* EDMOND

EDMOND   Thou, Nature, art my goddess; to thy law
My services are bound. Wherefore should I

---

287 from his age to receive] F; to receiue from his age Q   288 imperfections] F; imperfection Q   288 long-engraffed]
Pope; long ingraffed F; long ingrafted Q   289 the unruly] F; vnruly Q   294 Pray you, let us sit] F; pray lets hit Q; pray
you let vs sit F   295 disposition] F; dispositions Q   297 of it] F; on't Q   **Act 1, Scene 2**   1.2] *Scena Secunda.* F; *not in*
Q   0 SD] *Enter Bastard.* F; *Enter Bastard Solus.* Q   1–26 Thou ... news?] F; *as prose* Q   1 SH EDMOND] *Bast.* Q, F
(*generally throughout*)

---

286 The best ... rash Even when in his prime
and in good health, i.e. not infirm of age (284), Lear
has been impetuous.

287 look expect.

287 alone only.

288 imperfections ... condition faults
implanted for a long time in his disposition. Q's
'ingrafted' is closer to modern spelling; 'engraffed'
is an older variant form.

291 unconstant starts sudden fits (of passion).

293 compliment ceremony.

294 sit together take counsel with one another
(Schmidt). See *R3* 3.1.173, *Per.* 2.3.92. Q's 'hit' =
'agree' or 'strike' is more generally adopted by editors, but F makes sense and does not require emendation. McLeod (pp. 157–65) questions Duthie's
preference for 'hit' on several important grounds.

294 carry bear, manage.

295–6 last surrender ... us i.e. his recent yield-
ing of authority will become a problem for us.
Gonerill is concerned that despite his abdication
Lear will still try to wield power.

298 do As opposed to Regan's 'think' (Muir).

298 i'th'heat at once. Apparently, Gonerill and
Regan fail to decide on a plan for immediate action.
Scenes 3 and 4 show Gonerill taking the offensive
against Lear and his hundred knights only after a

period of time has elapsed and she has endured
disruptions to her household.

Act 1, Scene 2

0 SD Gloucester's castle is the only location defi-
nitely named, besides Dover, though Perrett (p.
258) questions the description of Gloucester's
house as a 'castle' by Rowe and subsequent editors.

1–22 Thou ... bastards Edmond's soliloquy is
in the manner of the Vice of the old Morality plays
or Richard's opening soliloquy in *R3*, except that he
does not address the audience quite as directly as
they do while he reveals his vicious intentions. Like
Richard III, Edmond shares the Elizabethan
Machiavel's rationalism and ability to manipulate
others. See Danby, p. 63.

1 Nature The natural son of Gloucester,
Edmond naturally takes Nature as his deity. See
Danby, pp. 15–53, who discusses the conflicting
concepts of Nature in Shakespeare's time.
Heilman says nature for Edmond is 'a vital force,
the individual will, sexual vigor'. Compare Elton:
'In his libertine naturalism, Edmund witnesses [to]
the Jacobean disintegration of natural law and ethical absolutes' (p. 126).

1 law i.e. as opposed to religion's laws and those
of society.

Stand in the plague of custom and permit
The curiosity of nations to deprive me?
For that I am some twelve or fourteen moonshines   5
Lag of a brother? Why 'bastard'? Wherefore 'base'?
When my dimensions are as well compact,
My mind as generous, and my shape as true
As honest madam's issue? Why brand they us
With 'base'? with 'baseness'? 'bastardy'? 'base, base'?   10
Who in the lusty stealth of nature take
More composition and fierce quality
Than doth within a dull, stale, tired bed
Go to th'creating a whole tribe of fops
Got 'tween a sleep and wake? Well then,   15
Legitimate Edgar, I must have your land.
Our father's love is to the bastard, Edmond,
As to th'legitimate. Fine word, 'legitimate'.

---

4 me?] F; me, Q   6 brother?] F; brother, Q   6 'base'?] F; base, Q   9 issue?] F; issue, Q   10 With 'base'? with 'base-ness'? 'bastardy'? 'base, base'?] With Base? With basenes Barstardie? Base, Base? F; base, base bastardie? Q   13 dull, stale, tired] F; stale dull lyed Q   14 th'creating] F; the creating of Q   15 a sleep] Q, F; asleep *Capell*   15 then,] F; the Q   16 land.] land, Q, F   17 love] Q; loue, F   18 th'legitimate] F; the legitimate Q   18 Fine word, 'legitimate'] F; *not in* Q

3 custom convention, usage with the force of law.
4 curiosity of nations 'Edmund probably owes his word, *curiosity* – which he appears to use here in the sense of capricious refinement, with an overtone of officious meddling – to Florio, and the attitude behind it to Montaigne, who insistently contrasts Nature and Custom' (Salingar, p. 122). Salingar cites relevant passages from the *Essais*, and Muir from the *Apology for Raymond Sebonde*.
4 me? Most editors continue the query to 6, but F appears right in making the break here. Edmond is vexed at being 'deprived', or denied an inheritance; he then considers the two counts against him: he is a younger brother, and he is illegitimate.
5 For that Because.
5 moonshines months.
6 Lag of Behind, later than.
6 Why ... 'base' His bastardy concerns Edmond more than Edgar's seniority. Hence, in the following lines he wrings from the terms 'bastard' and 'base' and their derivatives (the two terms are not, however, etymologically related) as much of their meaning as he can, both through the figure of repetition and through what seems to him logical questioning. (Compare Falstaff on 'honour', *1H4* 5.1.127–41.) Edmond challenges the assumption

that being base-born implies being base in other respects. Salingar, pp. 123–4, believes this passage is indebted in part to Montaigne's essay, 'Upon Some Verses of Virgil'.
7 dimensions bodily proportions; as in *MV* 3.1.60.
7 compact composed, formed.
8 generous i.e. lofty, magnanimous, as befits a gentleman; as in *Ham.* 4.7.135.
8 true proper, correct, 'truly stamped' (Muir).
9 honest chaste.
11 lusty ... nature 'stealthy enjoyment of natural sexual appetite' (Riverside).
11–12 take ... quality Either (1) receive more physical and mental ingredients and energetic traits, or (2) require a greater and more vigorous physical and mental constitution. Both senses of 'take' may be active here.
13 a dull ... bed i.e. the result of a long marriage.
14 fops fools.
15 Got Begot.
15 a sleep Capell's emendation, making one word, is unnecessary.
17–18 Our father's ... legitimate The warrant for this statement is Gloucester's speech, 1.1.17–18 (Hunter).

Well, my legitimate, [*Takes out a letter*] if this letter speed
And my invention thrive, Edmond the base   20
Shall to th'legitimate. I grow; I prosper;
Now gods, stand up for bastards!

Enter GLOUCESTER

GLOUCESTER   Kent banished thus? and France in choler parted?
        And the king gone tonight? Prescribed his power,
        Confined to exhibition? All this done   25
        Upon the gad? Edmond, how now? What news?

EDMOND   So please your lordship, none. [*Putting up the letter*]

GLOUCESTER   Why so earnestly seek you to put up that letter?

EDMOND   I know no news, my lord.

GLOUCESTER   What paper were you reading?   30

EDMOND   Nothing, my lord.

GLOUCESTER   No? What needed then that terrible dispatch of it
        into your pocket? The quality of nothing hath not such need to
        hide itself. Let's see. Come, if it be nothing, I shall not need
        spectacles.   35

---

19 SD] *This edn; not in* Q, F   21 to th'] F; tooth' Q; top th' *Capell (conj. Edwards)*   23 thus? ... parted?] F; thus, ... parted, Q   24 tonight?] F; to night Q   24 Prescribed] F; subscribd Q   25 exhibition?] F; exhibition, Q   26 gad?] F; gadde; Q   27 SD] *Rowe; not in* Q, F   32 needed] F; needes Q   32 terrible] Q2, F; terribe Q

19 speed succeed.

20 invention device.

21 Shall to th'legitimate i.e. shall advance to, or take the place of, usurp, the legitimate. Nichols (cited by Furness) first proposed this interpretation of the Q, F reading in 1861–2 as against Edwards's emendation, 'top th' legitimate', which editors since Capell have generally adopted. Sisson, without citing Nichols, also defends the original reading, and articles by Thomas Clayton and Malcolm Pittock, both in *N&Q* 31 (June 1984), 207–10, present cogent arguments for 'disemending' the text. As Clayton says, 'Though differently arrived at, the forceful complementarity claimed for "top" ... is there still' (p. 208). Moreover, other F alterations in this passage make it unlikely that the Q reading was overlooked (pp. 207–8); and as Pittock shows, *OED* gives numerous examples of an ellipsis after 'to' (p. 209).

22 Now ... bastards Heilman (pp. 102 and 314 n. 16) notes the ambiguities here: since 'stand up' may refer to male sexual tumescence (as in *Rom.* 2.1.25, 3.3.88), Edmond's prayer becomes a phallic ritual; and he proceeds immediately to behave in the pejorative sense of 'bastard'.

23 thus? F's question marks throughout this speech, except for the last one, may be intended as exclamation points, as Muir interprets them, but a querying or wondering tone seems more appropriate for Gloucester here.

23 in choler Apparently something went wrong during the 'compliment of leave-taking' referred to at 1.1.293.

23 parted departed.

24 tonight last night; as in *Rom.* 1.4.50, *MV* 2.5.18.

24 Prescribed Limited, restricted.

25 Confined to exhibition Limited to an allowance. Compare *TGV* 1.3.68–9.

26 Upon the gad i.e. suddenly, as if pricked or goaded (a gad is a sharp spike or spear).

28 put up stow, conceal.

31 Nothing The word reverberates throughout the first half of the play. Compare 1.1.82–5, 1.4.113–15, 2.2.148, 2.3.21.

32 terrible dispatch extremely hasty disposition.

35 spectacles Spectacles are a symbol of what Gloucester does need. He does not see through Edmond's plot and shows himself entirely 'credulous' (Heilman, pp. 45, 154).

EDMOND   I beseech you, sir, pardon me; it is a letter from my
brother that I have not all o'erread; and for so much as I have
perused, I find it not fit for your o'erlooking.

GLOUCESTER   Give me the letter, sir.

EDMOND   I shall offend either to detain or give it. The contents, as   40
in part I understand them, are too blame.

GLOUCESTER   Let's see, let's see.

EDMOND   I hope for my brother's justification he wrote this but as
an essay or taste of my virtue.

                    [*Gives him the letter*]

GLOUCESTER   *Reads* 'This policy and reverence of age makes the   45
world bitter to the best of our times, keeps our fortunes from us
till our oldness cannot relish them. I begin to find an idle and
fond bondage in the oppression of aged tyranny, who sways not
as it hath power but as it is suffered. Come to me, that of this I
may speak more. If our father would sleep till I waked him, you   50
should enjoy half his revenue forever and live the beloved of
your brother. Edgar.' Hum! Conspiracy! 'Sleep till I waked
him, you should enjoy half his revenue.' My son Edgar, had he
a hand to write this? a heart and brain to breed it in? When
came you to this? Who brought it?   55

EDMOND   It was not brought me, my lord; there's the cunning of it.
I found it thrown in at the casement of my closet.

GLOUCESTER   You know the character to be your brother's?

EDMOND   If the matter were good, my lord, I durst swear it were
his: but in respect of that, I would fain think it were not.   60

---

36 SH EDMOND] *Bast.* F; *not in* Q *uncorr.*; *Ba.* Q *corr.*   37 and] F; *not in* Q   38 o'erlooking] ore-looking F; liking
Q   40–1 I . . . blame.] *As prose* Q; *three verse lines ending* . . . giue it: / . . . them, / . . . blame. F   44 SD] *This edn; not in* Q,
F   45 SD] F; *not in* Q, *which inserts* /A Letter / *after* 44   45–52 This . . . brother.] F *prints in italics,* Q *in roman*   45 and
reverence] F; *not in* Q   52 Sleep] F; slept Q   *52 waked] wakt Q; wake F   55 you to this] F; this to you Q

38 **o'erlooking** inspection, perusal.

41 **too blame** too blameworthy. As recorded in
OED Blame *v* 5, the dative infinitive, *to blame*, was
much used as the predicate after *be*. In the sixteenth
and seventeenth centuries, the *to* was misunderstood as *too*, and *blame* was taken as an adjective
meaning 'blameworthy, culpable'. Compare *1H4*
3.1.175: 'In faith, my lord, you are too willful
blame', cited *OED*, Schmidt. Bevington emends
'to blame', but says the Q/F reading, followed
here, may be correct.

44 **essay or taste** trial or sample, i.e. test. 'Essay'
is etymologically the same as 'assay'.

45 **policy ... age** policy of revering the old:

hendiadys (Schmidt). 'Policy' suggests 'a clever
trick on the part of the aged' (Kittredge).

46 **best ... times** best years of our lives.

47–8 **idle and fond** useless and foolish.

48–9 **who ... suffered** which rules not as though
it had real power, but because it is permitted
to do so.

57 **casement** A window opening on hinges.

57 **closet** private room; as in *Ham.* 2.1.74,
3.2.331.

58 **character** handwriting.

59 **matter** substance (of the letter's contents).

60 **that** i.e. the 'matter'.

60 **fain** gladly, willingly.

GLOUCESTER   It is his.

EDMOND   It is his hand, my lord, but I hope his heart is not in the
    contents.

GLOUCESTER   Has he never before sounded you in this business?

EDMOND   Never, my lord. But I have heard him oft maintain it to   65
    be fit that, sons at perfect age, and fathers declined, the father
    should be as ward to the son, and the son manage his revenue.

GLOUCESTER   O villain, villain – his very opinion in the letter!
    Abhorred villain, unnatural, detested, brutish villain – worse
    than brutish! Go, sirrah, seek him: I'll apprehend him.   70
    Abominable villain, where is he?

EDMOND   I do not well know, my lord. If it shall please you to
    suspend your indignation against my brother till you can derive
    from him better testimony of his intent, you should run a
    certain course; where if you violently proceed against him,   75
    mistaking his purpose, it would make a great gap in your own
    honour and shake in pieces the heart of his obedience. I dare
    pawn down my life for him that he hath writ this to feel my
    affection to your honour and to no other pretence of danger.

GLOUCESTER   Think you so?   80

EDMOND   If your honour judge it meet, I will place you where
    you shall hear us confer of this and by an auricular assurance have
    your satisfaction, and that without any further delay than this
    very evening.

---

61 his.] F; his? Q   64 Has] F; Hath Q   64 before] F; heretofore Q   65 heard him oft] F; often heard him Q   66
declined] F; declining Q   66 the father] F; his father Q   67 his] F; the Q   70 sirrah] F; sir Q   70 I'll] F; I Q; I, Q2;
Ay, *Cam.*   72 lord. If] F; Lord, if Q   74 his] F; this Q   78 that he hath writ] F; he hath wrote Q   79 other] F;
further Q

62 hand handwriting.

64 sounded searched, examined: a nautical
metaphor (Kittredge).

66 perfect fully mature.

66–7 father … revenue Citing references to
Pettie, Florio, and Montaigne, Muir suggests that
this notion (that aged parents should be under the
guardianship of their children) was not unfamiliar
in Shakespeare's time; indeed, it is now Lear's
position, as Verity (cited by NS) remarks.
Compare Lady Wildgoose's action against her
father, Sir Brian Annesley (p. 8 above).

69 Abhorred Abhorrent. 'Participles in *-ed* are
common in this use' (Kittredge).

69 detested detestable.

70 sirrah Familiar term of address to children or
subordinates.

71 Abominable The Q/F spelling,
'Abhominable', reflects the Elizabethan belief that
the term derived from Latin *ab* + *homine*, 'away
from man', hence 'unnatural', 'execrable'.

74–5 you … course your course of action would
be sure.

75 where whereas.

76 gap breach.

77 shake … obedience i.e. utterly destroy the
essence of his devotion.

78 pawn stake.

78 feel test.

79 pretence of danger dangerous purpose.
Compare *Mac.* 2.3.131.

81 meet fitting, proper.

82 auricular assurance i.e. certainty derived
from hearing directly.

GLOUCESTER He cannot be such a monster. Edmond, seek him   85
out: wind me into him, I pray you. Frame the business after
your own wisdom. I would unstate myself to be in a due
resolution.

EDMOND I will seek him, sir, presently, convey the business as I
shall find means, and acquaint you withal.   90

GLOUCESTER These late eclipses in the sun and moon portend no
good to us. Though the wisdom of nature can reason it thus
and thus, yet nature finds itself scourged by the sequent effects.
Love cools, friendship falls off, brothers divide. In cities,
mutinies; in countries, discord; in palaces, treason; and the   95
bond cracked 'twixt son and father. This villain of mine comes
under the prediction: there's son against father. The king falls
from bias of nature, there's father against child. We have seen
the best of our time. Machinations, hollowness, treachery, and
all ruinous disorders follow us disquietly to our graves. Find   100
out this villain, Edmond, it shall lose thee nothing. Do it
carefully. And the noble and true-hearted Kent banished; his
offence, honesty. 'Tis strange.   *Exit*

---

85 monster.] F *omits three lines here*   86 the] F; your Q   89 will] F; shall Q   90 find] F; see Q   92 it] F; *not in* Q   95 discord; in palaces] F; discords, Pallaces Q   95 and the] F; the Q   96 'twixt] F; betweene Q   96–100 This . . . graves.] F; *not in* Q   97 prediction:] prediction F   97 father.] Father, F   103 honesty. 'Tis strange.] F; honest, strange, strange! Q   103 SD] F; *not in* Q

85 monster F omits two lines here found in Q. See Textual Analysis, p. 249 below.

86 wind me insinuate yourself (ethical dative construction; compare *Oth.* 1.1.49).

86 Frame Fashion.

87–8 I . . . resolution I would divest myself of estate and rank to be resolved sufficiently of doubt. Gloucester's anxiety resembles Othello's in *Oth.* 2.3 and 3.3, and like Othello he jumps too quickly to conclusions. Like Iago, Edmond preys upon this weakness and even proposes eavesdropping (81–3; compare *Oth.* 4.1.81 ff.), although he apparently changes his plan (2.1.20 ff.). Edmond makes his fortune by two letters and is undone by a third (Mack, p. 95; see 3.5.8, 5.1.39).

89 presently immediately.

89 convey carry out.

90 withal therewith.

91 late eclipses A possible allusion to the eclipse of the moon on 27 September and of the sun on 2 October 1605 (see p. 4 above). Eclipses were regarded by superstitious men like Gloucester as auguries of evil, giving warning of such things as the machinations of the Catholic conspirators who intended to blow up king and parliament. The Gunpowder Plot, however, was uncovered in November 1605 – before it could be carried out.

92–3 Though . . . effects Nature is used in two senses here: (1) human nature, specifically human reason as embodied in natural philosophy, or science; (2) the world of nature, including but not limited to the world of humankind. Thus: human reason can explain these events scientifically, but all nature is afflicted nevertheless by what subsequently happens ('Love cools', etc.).

95 mutinies riots, insurrections.

96–100 This . . . graves On the absence of these lines in Q, see Textual Analysis, p. 261 below.

97–8 son . . . child This recalls Matt. 10.21: 'The brother shall betray the brother to death, and the father the sonne, and the children shal rise against their parents, and shal cause them to die.' See also Mark 13.8, 12; Luke 12.52–3, 21.16; Micah 7.6, and compare part 3 of the homily 'Against Disobedience and Wilfull Rebellion' (Shaheen).

98 bias of nature 'natural course or tendency. A figure from bowling. The *bias* is the curve that the bowl makes in its course' (Kittredge).

99 best . . . time our best years; as at 46.

99 hollowness emptiness, insincerity; as in Kent's reference to Gonerill's and Regan's speeches, 1.1.148.

100 disquietly unquietly.

103 honesty 'love of truth, upright conduct' (Schmidt).

EDMOND This is the excellent foppery of the world, that when we
          are sick in fortune, often the surfeits of our own behaviour, we   105
          make guilty of our disasters the sun, the moon, and stars; as if
          we were villains on necessity, fools by heavenly compulsion,
          knaves, thieves, and treachers by spherical predominance,
          drunkards, liars, and adulterers by an enforced obedience of
          planetary influence; and all that we are evil in, by a divine   110
          thrusting on. An admirable evasion of whoremaster man, to lay
          his goatish disposition on the charge of a star! My father
          compounded with my mother under the Dragon's tail, and my
          nativity was under *Ursa major*, so that it follows, I am rough and
          lecherous. I should have been that I am had the maidenliest   115
          star in the firmament twinkled on my bastardising.

                              Enter EDGAR

          Pat: he comes, like the catastrophe of the old comedy. My cue

---

105 surfeits] F; surfeit Q   106 stars] F; the Starres Q   107 on] F; by Q   108 treachers] F; Trecherers Q   108 sphe-
rical] F; spirituall Q   108 predominance,] Q; predominance. F   111 whoremaster man] Q; Whore-master-man
F   112 on] F; to Q   112 a star!] a Starre, F; Starres: Q   115 I should] F; Fut, I should Q   115 maidenliest] F3;
maidenlest Q, F, F2   116 in] F; of Q   116 bastardising.] F; bastardy Q   116 SD] Q2, F; *in margin* Q   117 Pat: he] F;
Edgar; and out hee Q   117 My cue] F; mine Q

104 **excellent** (1) supreme, (2) splendid (from
Edmond's point of view: Hunter).
  104 **foppery** foolishness.
  105 **sick in fortune** i.e. down on our luck.
  105 **surfeits** excesses.
  107 **on** by; as in *LLL* 1.1.148.
  107 **heavenly compulsion** i.e. astrological
influence.
  108 **treachers** traitors.
  108 **spherical predominance** Under the astrological concept of 'planetary influence' (110), if at
the time of one's birth a heavenly body was especially powerful because of its ascendant position,
one's disposition and destiny were accordingly controlled, or 'enforced'.
  109 **of** to.
  110–11 **divine thrusting on** supernatural
imposition.
  111 **whoremaster** lecherous.
  111–12 **lay ... charge of** impute his lustful
tendencies to (Schmidt). To Elizabethans, goats
were emblematic of lechery.
  113 **compounded** copulated.
  113 **Dragon's tail** The constellation Draco, an
especially malevolent astrological sign.
  114 **nativity** birth.
  114 *Ursa major* The constellation Great Bear, or
Big Dipper, in which (astrologically) Mars is

predominant but shares influence with Venus, making
it a malign constellation producing temperaments that
are not only daring and impetuous ('rough'), but also
lascivious ('lecherous'), as Hunter notes.
  115 See collation. The omission of 'Fut' (a variant
of the expletive 'foot' = 'Christ's foot') is probably the
result of purging away profanity in accordance with
the 'Acte to Restraine Abuses of Players' in 1606
(Duthie, p. 170). Taylor concurs and argues for
restoration ('Censorship', pp. 78, 109–10).
  117 **Pat** See collation. Because Q crowds *Enter
Edgar* into the margin immediately beside 'Edgar'
in Edmond's speech, some editors believe the F
collator may have become confused and dropped
Edmond's summons which, Duthie argues, p. 171,
makes 'Pat' pointless. The effect of Edmond's
speech, however, does not depend on such a direct
summons, and the F reading may stand.
  117 **catastrophe ... comedy** Early Tudor plays
often lacked dramatic motivation; the catastrophe,
or concluding episode, often arrived quite arbitrarily to suit the playwright's need to end a play.
Armado uses 'catastrophe' in *LLL* 4.1.77 to refer
to the concluding episode of an action.
  117 **cue** Edmond deliberately adopts theatrical
language in keeping with the role he is about to play.
On stage-managing in *King Lear*, see Reibetanz,
pp. 57–67.

is villainous melancholy, with a sigh like Tom o'Bedlam. – O
these eclipses do portend these divisions. Fa, sol, la, me.

EDGAR   How now, brother Edmond, what serious contemplation   120
are you in?

EDMOND   I am thinking, brother, of a prediction I read this other
day, what should follow these eclipses.

EDGAR   Do you busy yourself with that?

EDMOND   I promise you, the effects he writes of succeed un-   125
happily. When saw you my father last?

EDGAR   The night gone by.

EDMOND   Spake you with him?

EDGAR   Ay, two hours together.

EDMOND   Parted you in good terms? Found you no displeasure in   130
him by word nor countenance?

EDGAR   None at all.

EDMOND   Bethink yourself wherein you may have offended him,
and at my entreaty forbear his presence until some little time
hath qualified the heat of his displeasure, which at this instant   135
so rageth in him that with the mischief of your person it would
scarcely allay.

EDGAR   Some villain hath done me wrong.

EDMOND   That's my fear. I pray you have a continent forbearance
till the speed of his rage goes slower; and as I say, retire with   140
me to my lodging, from whence I will fitly bring you to hear my
lord speak. Pray ye, go; there's my key. If you do stir abroad, go
armed.

---

118 sigh] Q2, F; sith Q   118 Tom o'] F; them of Q   119 Fa . . . me.] F; *not in* Q   124 with] F; about Q   125 writes] F;
writ Q   125–6 unhappily.] F (*which omits seven lines here*); vnhappily, Q   126 When] F; when Q   127 The] F; Why,
the Q   129 Ay,] I, F; *not in* Q   131 nor] F; or Q   134 until] F; till Q   136 person] F; parson Q   137 scarcely] F;
scarce Q   139–44 I . . . brother?] F; *not in* Q

118 **villainous** wretched.
118 **Tom o'Bedlam** A common name for a real
or pretended madman (Bedlam, or Bethlehem, was
a London lunatic asylum). See 2.3.14.
119 **divisions** (1) conflicts (as in 94–6), (2) a
musical run.
119 **Fa . . . me** Edmond vocalizes to himself,
pretending to be unaware of Edgar's approach
while he is busy about something else, possibly a
book on astrology he is reading, as the subsequent
dialogue suggests (Taylor, 'Censorship', p. 86).
Some commentators, e.g. Hunter, think Edmond
is deliberately singing across the interval of an aug-
mented fourth, or 'the devil in music', a most
unpleasant sound suggesting the disharmony of
'divisions' (or the sound of a bedlamite?).
125 **effects** results (of the eclipses).

125 **succeed** follow.
125–6 **unhappily** Taylor suggests that
Edmond snaps his book shut and (in F)
abruptly changes the subject. F omits seven
lines here found in Q; see Textual Analysis,
p. 250 below.
131 **countenance** bearing, demeanour.
134 **forbear** avoid.
135 **qualified** mitigated, reduced.
136–7 **with . . . allay** i.e. even with bodily harm
to you his rage would not subside much.
139 **I pray . . . Brother** See Textual Analysis,
p. 262 below, on the lines missing from Q.
139 **have . . . forbearance** 'restrain yourself and
keep out of his presence' (Kittredge).
141 **fitly** at a suitable time.
142 **abroad** outside, out-of-doors.

EDGAR   Armed, brother?

EDMOND   Brother, I advise you to the best. I am no honest man, if   145
there be any good meaning toward you. I have told you what I
have seen and heard – but faintly, nothing like the image and
horror of it. Pray you, away.

EDGAR   Shall I hear from you anon?

EDMOND   I do serve you in this business.   150

Exit [Edgar]

A credulous father and a brother noble,
Whose nature is so far from doing harms
That he suspects none; on whose foolish honesty
My practices ride easy. I see the business.
Let me, if not by birth, have lands by wit.   155
All with me's meet that I can fashion fit.   *Exit*

1.3   *Enter* GONERILL *and [her] Steward* [OSWALD]

GONERILL   Did my father strike my gentleman for chiding of his
fool?

OSWALD   Ay, madam.

GONERILL   By day and night, he wrongs me; every hour
He flashes into one gross crime or other   5
That sets us all at odds. I'll not endure it.
His knights grow riotous, and himself upbraids us

---

145 best.] F; best, goe arm'd Q   **146** toward] F; towards Q   **150** SD] *As* Q; *after 149* Q2; *Exit* F (*after 149*)   **Act 1,
Scene 3** 1.3] *Scena Tertia.* F; *not in* Q   **0** SD] *Collier (subst.);* Enter Gonerill, and Steward F; Enter Gonorill and Gentleman
Q   ***3** SH] *Ste.* F; *Gent.* Q (*throughout*)   **3** Ay,] *Rowe;* I F; Yes Q   **4–5** By ... other] F; *divided* me, / Euery Q   **7**
upbraids] F; obrayds Q

147–8 image and horror true picture of the
actual horror (hendiadys).

154 practices plots, machinations. Edmond
then uses an equestrian metaphor.

154 I see the business Edmond's plot now
becomes clear.

156 All ... fit Everything is all right with me that
I can frame to my own purposes.

Act 1, Scene 3

0 SD In the fictional narrative, enough time is
supposed to have passed for Gonerill to experience
the disruptions in her household she says Lear and
his knights have caused.

0 SD OSWALD F consistently uses *Steward* in SDs
and SHs; Q uses *Gentleman* and *Gent.* in this scene
but *Steward* and *Stew.* in the next. At 1.4.268 and
281 Gonerill calls for Oswald, whose name was the
Anglo-Saxon word for a steward. He is foppishly
dressed, probably in Albany's cast-off garments (NS).

1–2 Did ... fool This is not only the first mention of the Fool, but the first mention of disorderliness caused by Lear and his entourage, giving
Gonerill the excuse to act as she does.

4 By ... night Either (1) an oath (compare
1.1.103–4), or (2) constantly (compare 'every hour').
F punctuation favours (1); Q, omitting the comma,
favours (2).

5 flashes breaks out.

5 crime offence.

7 His ... riotous The absence of actual evidence
for this behaviour in the play has led some commentators, e.g. Kittredge, to discredit Gonerill's asser-
tion, but some stage and film versions, such as Peter
Brook's, have graphically presented Lear's train as
unruly. In any event, a hundred knights and squires
given to hunting and other sports would doubtless
cause some problems, which Gonerill decides to
exacerbate, forcing a confrontation with her father.

On every trifle. When he returns from hunting,
I will not speak with him. Say I am sick.
If you come slack of former services,   10
You shall do well; the fault of it I'll answer.

[Horns within]

OSWALD   He's coming, madam, I hear him.

GONERILL   Put on what weary negligence you please,.
You and your fellows: I'd have it come to question.
If he distaste it, let him to my sister,   15
Whose mind and mine I know in that are one.
Remember what I have said.

OSWALD   Well, madam.

GONERILL   And let his knights have colder looks among you:
What grows of it no matter. Advise your fellows so.   20
I'll write straight to my sister to hold my course.
Prepare for dinner.

Exeunt

1.4 *Enter* KENT [*disguised*]

KENT   If but as well I other accents borrow
That can my speech defuse, my good intent

---

8 trifle. When] F; trifell when Q   11 SD] Capell (*after 12*); *not in* Q, F   13–16 Put . . . one.] F; *as prose* Q   14 fellows:]
F; fellow seruants, Q   14 to] F; in Q   15 distaste] F; dislike Q   15 my] F; our Q   16 one.] one, Q, F; F *omits four lines
here*   17 Remember . . . said] F; *as prose* Q   17 have said.] F; tell you. Q   18 Well] F; Very well Q   19–20 And . . . so.]
Hanmer's lineation; as prose Q, F   20 so.] so, Q, F; F *omits one and a half lines here*   21–2 I'll . . . dinner.] *This edn; as prose*
Q, F   21 course.] F; very course, Q   22 Prepare] F; goe prepare Q   22 SD] F; *Exit.* Q   Act 1, Scene 4 1.4] *Scena
Quarta.* F; *not in* Q   0 SD *disguised*] Rowe; *not in* Q, F   1–7 If . . . labours.] F; *as prose* Q   1 well] Q; will F

---

8 hunting The provision for Lear's hunting
appears in Layamon's *Brut*, which also includes a
hunting episode (Muir).

9 Say I am sick A transparent 'social' lie.

10 come slack of slacken, fall short of.

11 answer be answerable for.

12 I hear him Capell introduces SD, *Horns
within*, which many editors follow. (Compare 1.4.7
SD.)

13 weary negligence tiresome or irksome
neglect (of service).

14 come to question i.e. come to a head, made
an issue of.

15 distaste dislike.

15–16 let . . . one Apparently, though they may
not have decided upon any immediate course of
action, Gonerill and Regan have agreed not to put
up with much from Lear for very long. (Compare
1.1.298 n.)

16 one F omits four lines here found in Q and

two more after 19; see Textual Analysis, p. 250
below.

21 straight at once, straightaway.

Act 1, Scene 4

0 SD KENT [*disguised*] Kent reappears, his countenance altered (4) and wearing clothing more suitable for the servant, 'Caius', than for an earl. He
also tries to disguise his voice by adopting a different accent (usually the actor adopts a rustic brogue,
according to Rosenberg, p. 96) and a blunt, plainspoken manner. The Elizabethan convention of
'impenetrable disguise' operates here and throughout the rest of the play, until Kent drops the disguise in 5.3. Lear never identifies Caius with Kent,
even at the end, when Kent wishes it (5.3.257–63).

1 as well i.e. as well as I have disguised myself
otherwise.

2 defuse confuse, disorder; a variant of 'diffuse'.

2 my good intent i.e. to serve his master, Lear.

May carry through itself to that full issue
For which I razed my likeness. Now, banished Kent,
If thou canst serve where thou dost stand condemned, 5
So may it come thy master, whom thou lov'st,
Shall find thee full of labours.

Horns within. Enter LEAR, [*Knights,*] *and Attendants*

LEAR Let me not stay a jot for dinner. Go, get it ready.

[*Exit an Attendant*]

How now, what art thou?

KENT A man, sir. 10

LEAR What dost thou profess? What wouldst thou with us?

KENT I do profess to be no less than I seem, to serve him truly that
will put me in trust, to love him that is honest, to converse with
him that is wise and says little, to fear judgement, to fight when
I cannot choose, and to eat no fish. 15

LEAR What art thou?

KENT A very honest-hearted fellow, and as poor as the king.

LEAR If thou be'st as poor for a subject as he's for a king, thou art
poor enough. What wouldst thou?

KENT Service. 20

LEAR Who wouldst thou serve?

KENT You.

---

*4 razed] raz'd Q; raiz'd F 6 So … come] F; *not in* Q 6 lov'st] F; louest Q 7 labours] F; labour Q 7 SD] Rowe;
Hornes within. Enter Lear and Attendants. F; Enter Lear Q 8 SD] Malone; *not in* Q, F 18 be'st] F; be Q 18 he's] F; he is
Q 18 thou art] F; thar't Q

3 **full issue** complete or satisfactory outcome.

4 **razed** erased, obliterated. Muir suggests a
quibble on 'razor'.

4 **likeness** appearance.

4 **banished Kent** 'In case the audience have not
recognized his voice, he announces his identity'
(Hunter).

6 **So … come** Either (1) let it then happen that,
or (2) it may happen thus.

7 SD **Horns within** Lear has been hunting (compare 1.3.8).

7 SD **Knights** That knights as well as attendants
accompany Lear is clear from SHs at 44 ff. (Duthie).

8 **stay** wait.

10 **man** (1) a fully human being, (2) a servant.
Compare *Ham.* 1.2.187: "'A was a man, take him for
all in all.'

11 **profess** set up for, claim as a calling or trade.
Kent plays on the sense 'proclaim, declare' in his
reply.

13 **converse** associate, consort. Shaheen compares

Ecclus. 9.17: 'Let thy talke be with the wise', and Prov.
13.20, 17.27–8.

14 **fear judgement** Many commentators
assume a reference to the Last Judgement. (Noble
and Shaheen cite Psalms 1.5; Noble adds Jer. 8.7.)
Kittredge says such an allusion may accord with the
pagan religion of Lear's time, though not the following reference to abstaining from fish, which is
anachronistic (Catholics ate fish but not meat on
Fridays, the day of the Crucifixion). Kent may,
however, simply be declaring his desire to serve
well, fearing his master's censure.

15 **cannot choose** i.e. cannot help it.

15 **eat no fish** Three not incompatible glosses
are possible. Kent means: (1) he is no papist
(Warburton); (2) he is 'a jolly fellow, and no lover
of such meagre diet as fish' (Capell; compare *2H4*
4.3.90–5); (3) he is no womanizer.

17 **as … king** Kent risks the joke, but Lear takes
it good-humouredly.

LEAR Dost thou know me, fellow?

KENT No, sir; but you have that in your countenance, which I
would fain call master. 25

LEAR What's that?

KENT Authority.

LEAR What services canst thou do?

KENT I can keep honest counsel, ride, run, mar a curious tale
in telling it, and deliver a plain message bluntly. That which 30
ordinary men are fit for, I am qualified in, and the best of me is
diligence.

LEAR How old art thou?

KENT Not so young, sir, to love a woman for singing, nor so old to
dote on her for anything. I have years on my back forty-eight. 35

LEAR Follow me; thou shalt serve me, if I like thee no worse
after dinner. I will not part from thee yet. Dinner, ho, dinner!
Where's my knave? my fool? Go you and call my fool hither.

[*Exit an Attendant*]

Enter OSWALD

You, you sirrah, where's my daughter?

OSWALD So please you – *Exit* 40

LEAR What says the fellow there? Call the clotpoll back.

[*Exit a Knight*]

Where's my fool? Ho, I think the world's asleep.

[*Enter* KNIGHT]

How now? Where's that mongrel?

KNIGHT He says, my lord, your daughter is not well.

---

28 thou] F; *not in* Q 31 me] me, Q, F 34 sir] F; *not in* Q *37 dinner. I] *Jennens;* dinner, I Q, F 38 SD.1] *Dyce*
(following Capell); not in Q, F 38 SD.2 *Enter* OSWALD] *Capell (subst.);* Enter Steward. Q, F *(after 39)* 39 You, you] You
you F; you, Q 40 SD] F; *not in* Q 41 clotpoll] Clot- / pole F; clat-pole Q 41, 42 SD] *Dyce; not in* Q, F 44 SH] F;
Kent. Q; 44 daughter] Q; Daughters F

24 countenance demeanour, bearing.

25 fain gladly, willingly.

29 keep honest counsel keep honourable
confidences.

29–30 mar … telling it Proverbial: 'A good
tale ill told is marred in the telling' (NS, citing
Tilley T28). Kent underscores his plainspokenness
here.

29 curious elaborate, intricate.

34 to as to.

36–7 thou … dinner. Q/F punctuation is
ambiguous, but Lear's capricious attitude is clearer
with a full stop after 'dinner'.

37 Dinner, ho Lear repeatedly calls for dinner,
and modern editors insert directions for attendants

to exit, but no dinner is served (Rosenberg, p. 100).
Gonerill's instructions in 1.3 to slack off service are
taking effect.

38 knave boy. The word, often used familiarly,
could imply affection (Kittredge) and does not
necessarily refer to the Fool's age. Compare 1.1.16
and below, 80. At 3.4.26 Lear addresses the Fool as
'boy' but may be using the word similarly.

40 So please you A deliberate snub.

41 clotpoll blockhead. A 'clot' or (in dialect)
'clat' = 'a clod of earth'; 'poll' = head.

44 SH KNIGHT Here and later F assigns speeches
to a Knight, where Q assigns 44 to Kent and 46,
49–53, 55–6, 62–3 to a servant. Duthie notes the
Lear/Kent alternation of speeches (9–36) and

LEAR   Why came not the slave back to me when I called him?   45

KNIGHT   Sir, he answered me in the roundest manner, he would not.

LEAR   He would not?

KNIGHT   My lord, I know not what the matter is, but to my judgement your highness is not entertained with that cer-   50
emonious affection as you were wont. There's a great abatement of kindness appears as well in the general dependants as in the duke himself also, and your daughter.

LEAR   Ha? Sayest thou so?

KNIGHT   I beseech you pardon me, my lord, if I be mistaken, for   55
my duty cannot be silent when I think your highness wronged.

LEAR   Thou but rememberest me of mine own conception. I have perceived a most faint neglect of late, which I have rather blamed as mine own jealous curiosity than as a very pretence and purpose of unkindness. I will look further into't. But   60
where's my fool? I have not seen him this two days.

KNIGHT   Since my young lady's going into France, sir, the fool hath much pined away.

LEAR   No more of that, I have noted it well. Go you and tell my daughter I would speak with her.   65

[*Exit an Attendant*]

Go you, call hither my fool.

[*Exit an Attendant*]

46, 49, 55, 62 SH] F; *seruant.* Q   48 He] F; A Q   52 of kindness] F; *not in* Q   54 Sayest] F; say'st Q   57 rememberest] remember'st Q; remembrest F   60 purpose] F; purport Q   61 my] F; this Q   *62 lady's] *Rowe;* Ladies Q, F   64 well] F; *not in* Q   65 SD, 66 SD.1] *Dyce; not in* Q, F

says Q's SH for Kent here is a misassignment, but the others are the result of F's abridgement of the number of speaking characters. On altered SHs, see Textual Analysis, pp. 64–5 above.

46 roundest bluntest, most plainspoken. Compare 'round' in Polonius's admonition to Gertrude, *Ham.* 3.4.5, and in King Henry's to Williams, *H5* 4.1.203.

50 entertained treated. Although Gonerill has just given instructions to slight Lear (1.3.13–14) and the action between Scenes 3 and 4 is continuous, Shakespeare conveys the illusion of a greater passage of time.

50–1 ceremonious affection 'combination of the affection due to a father and the ceremony appropriate to a king' (Hunter).

52 general dependants i.e. household staff as a whole.

52–3 as in the duke This charge is inconsistent

with Albany's claim to be 'guiltless' (228) and with his general behaviour. Either the Knight is deliberately exacerbating the situation, or Shakespeare emphasizes Lear's isolation (Hunter).

57 rememberest remindest.

57 conception thought.

58 faint neglect Either Lear minimizes what the Knight has seen as 'a great abatement' (51–2) because he dreads the consequences of a confrontation, or the Knight, again, has exaggerated the situation.

59 jealous curiosity suspicious fastidiousness, i.e. paranoid concern over trifles.

59–60 pretence and purpose deliberate intention (synonyms).

62–3 Since ... away The Knight calls attention to the affection between the Fool and Cordelia, whose roles may have been doubled. (See p. 13 above.)

Enter OSWALD

Oh, you, sir, you, come you hither, sir, who am I, sir?

OSWALD   My lady's father.

LEAR   'My lady's father'? My lord's knave, you whoreson dog, you
    slave, you cur!   70

OSWALD   I am none of these, my lord, I beseech your pardon.

LEAR   Do you bandy looks with me, you rascal?

[Strikes him]

OSWALD   I'll not be strucken, my lord.

KENT *[Tripping him]*   Nor tripped neither, you base football player.

LEAR   I thank thee, fellow. Thou serv'st me, and I'll love thee.   75

KENT   Come, sir, arise, away, I'll teach you differences. Away,
    away. If you will measure your lubber's length again, tarry; but
    away, go to! Have you wisdom?

[Pushes Oswald out]

    So.

LEAR   Now, my friendly knave, I thank thee; there's earnest of thy   80
    service.

[Gives Kent money]

Enter FOOL

FOOL   Let me hire him, too; here's my coxcomb.

[Offers Kent his cap]

---

66 SD.2 *Enter* OSWALD] *Johnson (subst.); not in* Q; *Enter Steward.* F *(after 67)*   71 I ... pardon.] *As one line* Q; *divided*
Lord, / I F   71 these] F; this Q   71 your pardon.] F; you pardon me. Q   72 SD] *Rowe (subst.); not in* Q, F   73
strucken] F; struck Q   74 SD] *Rowe (subst.); not in* Q, F   75 I thank ... love thee.] *As one line* Q; *divided* fellow. / Thou
F   76 arise, away] F; *not in* Q   *78–9 go to! Have you wisdom? So.] *Theobald (subst.);* goe too, haue you wisdome, so
F; you haue wisdome. Q   *78 SD] *Theobald (subst.); not in* Q, F   80 my] F; *not in* Q   81 SD.1] *Capell (subst.); not in* Q,
F   82 SD] *Rowe (subst.); not in* Q, F

72 bandy bat back and forth (as in tennis),
exchange. NS adds SDs, *glares* and *glares back*, at 68
and 70. Oswald's insolence moves Lear to strike him.

74 base football player Tennis was played by
aristocrats, football by the lower classes. Thomas
Elyot, *The Boke of the Governour* (1531), warns 'al
noble men' against football, 'wherein is nothinge
but beastly furie and extreme violence' (NS).

76–9 Come ... So Kent roughly picks Oswald
up and shoves him out.

76 differences distinctions (of rank, position).

77 measure ... length Kent sent Oswald
sprawling to the ground (74), where he lay at full

length. Shakespeare uses the term in *MND* 3.2.429
and similarly in *Rom.* 3.3.69–70.

77 lubber clumsy lout.

80 earnest earnest-money, i.e. part payment to
bind a bargain.

82 coxcomb professional jester's cap. The cap
evidently varied somewhat, though its salient feature was a crest made of red flannel in the shape of a
cock's comb. It may also have had a bell, ass's ears,
and/or feathers attached. (See pp. 24–5 above.)
The Fool offers the symbol of his office to Kent as
someone who deserves it for following Lear, but
Kent demurs (84).

LEAR   How now, my pretty knave, how dost thou?

FOOL   [*To Kent*] Sirrah, you were best take my coxcomb.

LEAR   Why, my boy?   85

FOOL   Why? For taking one's part that's out of favour. [*To Kent*]
Nay, and thou canst not smile as the wind sits, thou'lt catch
cold shortly. There, take my coxcomb; why, this fellow has
banished two on's daughters and did the third a blessing
against his will; if thou follow him, thou must needs wear my   90
coxcomb. How now, nuncle? Would I had two coxcombs and
two daughters.

LEAR   Why, my boy?

FOOL   If I gave them all my living, I'd keep my coxcombs myself.
There's mine; beg another of thy daughters.   95

LEAR   Take heed, sirrah, the whip.

FOOL   Truth's a dog must to kennel. He must be whipped out,
when the Lady Brach may stand by th'fire and stink.

LEAR   A pestilent gall to me.

FOOL   Sirrah, I'll teach thee a speech.   100

LEAR   Do.

FOOL   Mark it, nuncle:

84 SD] *Oxford; not in* Q, F   85 LEAR Why, my boy?] F; *Kent.* Why Foole? Q   86 Why?] F; Why Q   86 one's] F, Q2; on's
Q   86 SD] *Oxford; not in* Q, F   88–9 has banished] F; hath banisht Q   89 did] F; done Q   94 all my] F; any
Q   97 Truth's] F; Truth is Q   97 dog must] F; dog that must Q   98 the Lady Brach] F; Ladie oth'e brach
Q   98 by th'] F; by the Q   99 gall] F; gull Q   102–12 Mark . . . score.] F *lineation; as prose* Q   102 nuncle] F; vncle
Q

85 LEAR **Why, my boy?** Duthie, p. 171, attributes
the changed SH in F to compositor eyeskip from 85
to 93 (and then back to 86). This seems unlikely in
view of F's other alterations in the passages that
follow.

87 **and** if; a common variant of 'an'.

87–8 **thou . . . shortly** i.e. if you cannot ingrati-
ate yourself with the powers that prevail, you will
soon be out in the cold and suffering.

89 **banished** Compare 1.1.175.

89 **on's** of his.

89–90 **blessing . . . will** Cordelia is now out of
Britain and Queen of France – hardly the cursed
existence Lear intended for her.

90 **must needs** A redundancy used for emphasis
(as often).

91 **nuncle** A contraction of 'mine uncle' (the
usual address of a jester to his master).

94 **If . . . myself** NS cites Tilley A187: 'He that
gives all before he dies is a fool.' Two coxcombs is
the equivalent of a double fool.

95 **There's mine** The Fool now offers his coxcomb to Lear.

96 **the whip** Fools, like children, were whipped
when they went too far out of line. Compare *AYLI*
1.2.84–5.

97–8 **Truth . . . stink** The Fool identifies himself with truth, imagined as an unwelcome, lowly
dog chased out of the house into a rude shelter;
whereas the bitch, flattery ('brach' = bitch),
enjoys a privileged place. The Fool hints at
Gonerill or Regan, 'braches of noble rank, and
sycophantic' (Sisson, p. 231), and implies an
identification between Truth and Cordelia
(Muir).

99 **pestilent gall** plaguey irritant. Lear probably
refers to the Fool's gibes, though he may be thinking of Oswald and his fellows or his own foolish
behaviour. In any event, the Fool tactfully changes
strategy here.

100 **Sirrah** Some editions follow Rowe and add a
SD, *To Kent*. But the Fool seems to address Lear,
who responds, not Kent. The Fool's licence permits
him to address Lear as 'Sirrah'.

> Have more than thou showest,
> Speak less than thou knowest,
> Lend less than thou owest,   105
> Ride more than thou goest,
> Learn more than thou trowest,
> Set less than thou throwest,
> Leave thy drink and thy whore,
> And keep in-a-door,   110
> And thou shalt have more,
> Than two tens to a score.

KENT This is nothing, fool.

FOOL Then 'tis like the breath of an unfeed lawyer; you gave me
nothing for't. Can you make no use of nothing, nuncle?   115

LEAR Why, no, boy; nothing can be made out of nothing.

FOOL [*To Kent*] Prithee, tell him so much the rent of his land
comes to; he will not believe a fool.

LEAR A bitter fool.

FOOL Nuncle, give me an egg, and I'll give thee two crowns.   120

LEAR What two crowns shall they be?

FOOL Why, after I have cut the egg i'th'middle and eat up the
meat, the two crowns of the egg. When thou clovest thy crown
i'th'middle and gav'st away both parts, thou bor'st thine ass on

---

113 SH] F; *Lear.* Q   114 'tis] F; *not in* Q   115 nuncle?] F; vncle? Q   116 Why ... nothing.] Q; *two lines divided* Boy, / Nothing F   117 SD] *Rowe; not in* Q, F   119 fool.] *This edn;* F *erroneously includes three lines here meant for exclusion* (*see p. 64 above*), *then omits fifteen lines*   120 Nuncle, ... egg,] F; giue ... Nuncle, Q   122 i'th'] F; in the Q   123 crown] Q; Crownes F   124 i'th'] F; it'h Q   124 gav'st] F; gauest Q   124 bor'st] F; borest Q   124 thine] F; thy Q   124–5 on thy] F; at'h Q

103–12 Have ... score This counsel of prudence is set in sing-song rhyme to emphasize its conventional wisdom, and accordingly earns Kent's response.

105 thou owest you own.

106 thou goest you walk; as at 3.2.92, where 'going' means walking.

107 Learn ... trowest i.e. don't believe everything you hear.

108 Set ... throwest i.e. don't gamble away your last penny.

110 in-a-door indoors. NS compares *MV* 2.5.53–5 on staying home and saving money.

111–12 thou ... score i.e. you will grow richer (Riverside).

113 nothing i.e. no big news. As at 85, F changes Q's SH. Kent's interruption is dramatically apt.

114 unfeed lawyer Alludes to the proverb 'A

lawyer will not plead but for a fee' (Tilley L125); 'breath' = speech, hence pleading.

115 use usury, interest. Compare *Ado* 1.1.278–9.

116 nothing ... nothing Compare 1.1.84–5.

117 his land Ironic: Lear is landless. He feels the Fool's gibe (119).

119 fool F includes three lines here that should probably have been cut along with the passage of twelve lines found only in Q that immediately follows: see Textual Analysis, pp. 68–9 above.

121 two crowns Compare 'two coxcombs', 91. The two crowns are obviously the two halves of the eggshell, but Lear is deliberately acting as a stooge (Muir).

123–4 When ... parts Compare 1.1.133 and n. The Fool alludes not to Lear's parting of the coronet but to the division of the kingdom.

thy back o'er the dirt. Thou hadst little wit in thy bald crown   125
when thou gav'st thy golden one away. If I speak like myself in
this, let him be whipped that first finds it so.

[*Sings*] Fools had ne'er less grace in a year,
    For wise men are grown foppish,
    And know not how their wits to wear,   130
    Their manners are so apish.

LEAR When were you wont to be so full of songs, sirrah?

FOOL I have used it, nuncle, e'er since thou mad'st thy daughters
thy mothers; for when thou gav'st them the rod and put'st down
thine own breeches,   135

[*Sings*] Then they for sudden joy did weep,
    And I for sorrow sung,
    That such a king should play bo-peep,
    And go the fools among.

Prithee, nuncle, keep a schoolmaster that can teach thy fool to   140
lie. I would fain learn to lie.

LEAR And you lie, sirrah, we'll have you whipped.

---

126 gav'st] F; gauest Q   128 SD] *Rowe; not in* Q, F   128 grace] F; wit Q   130 And] F; They Q   130 to] F; doe Q   133 e'er] ere F; euer Q   134 mothers] F; mother Q   134 gav'st] F; gauest Q   136 SD] *Rowe; not in* Q, F   136 Then they] *Theobald;* then they Q, F (*as part of preceding prose*)   136–9 for ... among.] F *lineation; as prose* Q   139 fools] Q; Foole F   141 learn to] F; learne Q *uncorr.;* learneto Q *corr.*   142 And] F, Q; If Q2   142 sirrah] F; *not in* Q

124–5 thou ... dirt An allusion to the fable of the old man who foolishly, out of a mistaken sense of kindness, carried his ass on his back instead of letting it carry him. The Fool's comments insistently point up inversions or perversions of the natural order.

126–7 If ... so i.e. let him who calls this foolish be whipped, not me. Compare 96–7. The Fool's baldness (to prevent lice) gives extra point to the passage if he removes his coxcomb to 'speak like myself in this' (Wiles, p. 190).

126 like myself i.e. like a fool.

128–31 Fools ... apish i.e. fools have never been more out of favour since wise men have become foolish and do not behave properly, their style becoming ridiculously imitative (of fools). Compare Lyly, *Mother Bombie* 2.3: 'I thinke Gentlemen had neuer lesse wit in a yeere' (Capell, cited by Furness). NS, citing Tilley F535, 'Fools had never less wit in a year', says the Fool is parodying either Lyly or the original proverb; hence the F reading is correct.

128 grace favour.

129 foppish foolish.

131 apish foolishly imitative. The off-rhyme with 'foppish' seems deliberate: see Kökeritz, p. 225.

133 used it i.e. made it a practice. Muir cites *Ham.* 3.2.45.

133–4 thou ... mothers i.e. you made your children your parents (another inversion, or perversion, of the natural order).

134–5 thou ... breeches i.e. the right to chastise has been transferred from parent to child.

136–9 Then ... among The Fool adapts the first stanza of the familiar old *Ballad of John Carelesse*: 'Some men for sodayne ioye do wepe, / And some in sorow syng: / When that they lie in daunger depe, / To put away mournyng' (Hyder E. Rollins, '"King Lear" and the ballad of "John Careless"', *MLR* 15 (1920), 87–90).

138 bo-peep 'A nursery play with a young child, who is kept in excitement by the nurse or playmate alternately concealing herself (or her face), and peeping out for a moment at an unexpected place, to withdraw again with equal suddenness' (*OED*). Apparently, the game was also played with naturals, or fools. Compare Skelton, *Image Hypocrisy*: 'Thus youe make vs sottes / And play with vs boopeepe' (cited Tilley B540).

142 And If.

FOOL I marvel what kin thou and thy daughters are: they'll have
me whipped for speaking true, thou'lt have me whipped for
lying, and sometimes I am whipped for holding my peace. I had   145
rather be any kind o'thing than a fool, and yet I would not be
thee, nuncle; thou hast pared thy wit o'both sides and left
nothing i'th'middle. Here comes one o'the parings.

Enter GONERILL

LEAR How now, daughter! What makes that frontlet on? You are
too much of late i'th'frown.   150

FOOL Thou wast a pretty fellow when thou hadst no need to care
for her frowning; now thou art an O without a figure. I am
better than thou art now; I am a fool, thou art nothing. [*To
Gonerill*] Yes, forsooth, I will hold my tongue, so your face bids
me, though you say nothing.   155

[*Sings*] Mum, mum:
    He that keeps nor crust, nor crumb,
    Weary of all, shall want some.
That's a shelled peascod.

GONERILL   Not only, sir, this, your all-licensed fool,   160
    But other of your insolent retinue
    Do hourly carp and quarrel, breaking forth
    In rank and not-to-be-endurèd riots. Sir,

---

144 thou'lt] F; thou wilt Q   145 sometimes] F; sometime Q   146 o'] F; of Q   147 o'] F; a Q   148 i'th'] F; in the
Q   148 o'] F; of Q   149–50 How ... frown.] F; *as verse, two lines divided* on, / Me Q   149 on? You] F; on, / Me thinks
you Q   150 of late] F; alate Q   150 i'th'] F; it'h Q   152 frowning] F; frowne Q   152 now thou] F, Q *corr.*; thou, thou
Q *uncorr.*, Q2   153–4 SD] *Pope; not in* Q, F   156 SD] *Rowe; not in* Q, F   156–7 Mum ... crumb,] *Capell's lineation; one
line* Q, F   157 nor crust] F; neither crust Q   *157 nor crumb] nor crum Q; not crum F   158–9 Weary ... peascod.]
Rowe's lineation; one verse line Q, F   160–73 Not ... proceeding.] F *lineation; as prose* Q   *163 In ... Sir,] *Capel* (*without
hyphens*); in ranke & (not to be indured riots,) Sir Q; In ranke, and (not to be endur'd) riots Sir. F

143–5 I marvel ... peace An example of the
'crocodile's argument', one that harms the opponent whichever way he chooses (Joseph, p. 202).
    146–8 yet ... middle i.e. if a fool is only a half-
wit, Lear is less: he has given his wits away along
with everything else.
    149 What ... on Gonerill enters wearing a front-
let = 'a cloth or bandage containing some medica-
ment' (*OED sv sb* ic; compare 44 above and 1.3.9,
where Gonerill instructed Oswald to tell Lear she is
sick). A frontlet also = a 'frowning cloth', i.e. a
forehead band worn by ladies at night to prevent
or smooth out wrinkles (*OED sb* Ia). Lear quibbles
on the two senses of 'frontlet', asking Gonerill why

she is wearing the cloth and commenting on her
demeanour.
    152 O without a figure i.e. a cipher; a zero with
no number before it to give it value (NS).
    154 forsooth An expletive: in truth, truly.
    156 Mum, mum Hush, hush; softly.
    157–8 He ... some i.e. he who foolishly gives
everything away, because he is tired of it all, shall at
the end of the day want some of it back.
    159 shelled peascod empty pea-pod, i.e.
nothing.
    160 all-licensed free to say or do anything.
    162 carp find fault, cavil.
    163 rank gross, excessive.

I had thought by making this well known unto you
To have found a safe redress, but now grow fearful,   165
By what yourself too late have spoke and done,
That you protect this course, and put it on
By your allowance; which if you should, the fault
Would not 'scape censure, nor the redresses sleep;
Which in the tender of a wholesome weal   170
Might in their working do you that offence
Which else were shame, that then necessity
Will call discreet proceeding.

FOOL   For you know, nuncle,
    The hedge-sparrow fed the cuckoo so long,   175
    That it's had it head bit off by it young.
  So out went the candle, and we were left darkling.

LEAR   Are you our daughter?

GONERILL   I would you would make use of your good wisdom,
    Whereof I know you are fraught, and put away   180
    These dispositions, which of late transport you
    From what you rightly are.

---

167 it] F; *not in* Q   169 redresses] F; redresse Q   170 Which] F; that Q   173 Will] F; must Q   173 proceeding] F; proceedings Q   174 know] F; trow Q   175–6 The . . . young.] *Pope's lineation; as prose* Q, F   176 it's] F; it Q   176 by it] F; beit Q   179–82 I . . . are.] F *lineation; as prose* Q   179 I] F; Come sir, I Q   180 Whereof . . . fraught,] Q; (Whereof . . . fraught), F   181 which] F; that Q   181 transport] F; transforme Q

164 I . . . you The line is hypermetrical unless the first two words are elided (= I'd) as well as 'known unto' (= known to). Similarly, in the next line, 'To have' = T'have. In correcting Q's prose, the F editor or reviser failed to make all the necessary adjustments to verse.
165 safe sure.
166 too late very recently.
167 put it on encourage it.
168 allowance i.e. failure to censure.
168–73 which . . . proceeding i.e. if you do approve of all this, then you are to blame and redress will be forthcoming, although the steps I take, designed to maintain a healthy state ('wholesome weal'), may offend you as they are carried out. In other circumstances these steps might indeed be shameful, but in this instance they will be considered an act of necessary discretion. Gonerill's rhetoric conveys 'an impression of cold venom' (Hunter). Her speech is formal, convoluted, and abstract; but Lear gets the point, which leaves him – and Kent – speechless; hence, the Fool fills the silence (Rosenberg, p. 117).
170 Which i.e. the redresses.

170 tender care.
175–6 The hedge-sparrow . . . young The cuckoo proverbially laid its eggs in other birds' nests, and its chicks were notorious for their murderous gluttony. (See *1H4* 5.1.59–64.) The Fool alludes figuratively to Gonerill's illegitimacy (compare 209) or usurpation and certainly to her ingratitude in taking over half the realm. The baby-talk ('it . . . it') heightens the grotesqueness.
177 So . . . darkling Possibly this is a nonsense tag to take off the edge of the Fool's bitter couplet, but even so it conveys a sense of disaster. 'Lear's folly has produced a figurative darkness in the kingdom, and darkness can be very frightening' (NS, p. xxx). The image of the snuffed candle may come from the Lear story in *FQ* II, x, 30 (Knight, cited by Furness).
177 darkling in the dark.
180 fraught furnished (literally, freighted).
181 dispositions moods, humours; as in *AYLI* 4.1.114.
181 transport passionately carry away; as in *WT* 3.2.158.

FOOL   May not an ass know when the cart draws the horse? Whoop,
    Jug, I love thee!

LEAR   Does any here know me? This is not Lear: 185
             Does Lear walk thus? speak thus? Where are his eyes?
             Either his notion weakens, his discernings
             Are lethargied – Ha! Waking? 'Tis not so!
             Who is it that can tell me who I am?

FOOL   Lear's shadow.   190

LEAR   Your name, fair gentlewoman?

GONERILL   This admiration, sir, is much o'th'savour
             Of other your new pranks. I do beseech you
             To understand my purposes aright:
             As you are old and reverend, should be wise.   195
             Here do you keep a hundred knights and squires,
             Men so disordered, so deboshed and bold,
             That this our court, infected with their manners,
             Shows like a riotous inn; epicurism and lust
             Makes it more like a tavern or a brothel   200
             Than a graced palace. The shame itself doth speak
             For instant remedy. Be then desired
             By her, that else will take the thing she begs,
             A little to disquantity your train,

---

*183–4 Whoop . . . thee!] Q (subst.); as separate verse line F (see Commentary)   185 Does . . . Lear:] Rowe's lineation; as prose Q; two lines divided me? / This F   185 Does] F; Doth Q   185 This] F; why this Q   186–9 Does . . . am?] F lineation; as prose Q   186 Does] F; doth Q   187 notion weakens,] F; notion, weaknes, or Q   188 lethargied –] Rowe; Lethargied. F; lethergie, Q   188 Ha! Waking?] F; sleeping or wakeing; ha! sure Q   *188 so!] so? F; so, Q   190 FOOL Lear's shadow.] F; no SH in Q; which continues as Lear's prose speech with four lines not in F   190 shadow] F; shadow? Q   192–210 This . . . daughter.] F lineation; as prose Q   192 This admiration, sir,] F; Come sir, this admiration Q   192 o'th'] F; of the Q   194 To] F; not in Q   195 old] Q; Old, F   197 deboshed] F; deboyst Q   200 Makes it] F; make Q   200 or a] F; or Q   201 graced] F; great Q   202 then] F; thou Q*

183 May . . . horse As Lear remains stunned by what he is hearing, the Fool again interposes, referring sarcastically to the proverbial inversion of the cart and the horse.

183–4 Whoop . . . thee Gonerill makes a threatening gesture that elicits this mock protestation of love, possibly the tag from an old song.

184 Jug Nickname for Joan, often = whore, as in *Cambyses* 251–2: 'Rufe. I wil give thee sixpence to lye one night with thee. *Meretrix*. Gogs hart, slave, doost thinke I am a sixpenny jug?' (NS).

187 notion understanding.

187–8 discernings . . . lethargied intellectual faculties or ability to discriminate is dulled, paralysed. Moved almost to incoherence, Lear does not complete the either/or construction. Compare 2.4.263.

188–90 Ha . . . shadow On F's revisions, see Textual Analysis, p. 251 below.

188 Ha! Waking? Lear pinches or shakes himself to be sure he is not asleep and dreaming.

192 admiration (pretended) astonishment, wonderment. Compare *Ham.* 1.2.192.

192 savour characteristic (literally, taste).

193 Of other your Of your other (anastrophe).

193 pranks childish misbehaviour. Gonerill's terminology reflects her attitude to her father.

195 should you should.

196–200 Here . . . brothel Compare 1.3.7 n.

197 disordered disorderly.

197 deboshed Variant of 'debauched'.

197 bold impudent.

199 epicurism gluttony.

201 graced endowed with graces, favoured, adorned with honour (Onions).

202 desired requested.

204 disquantity reduce the size or number of.

And the remainders that shall still depend   205
To be such men as may besort your age,
Which know themselves and you.
LEAR   Darkness and devils!
Saddle my horses; call my train together. –
Degenerate bastard, I'll not trouble thee;
Yet have I left a daughter.   210
GONERILL   You strike my people, and your disordered rabble
Make servants of their betters.

Enter ALBANY

LEAR   Woe that too late repents!
Is it your will? Speak, sir. Prepare my horses.
Ingratitude! Thou marble-hearted fiend,
More hideous when thou show'st thee in a child   215
Than the sea-monster.
ALBANY   Pray, sir, be patient.

---

205 remainders] F; remainder Q   207 Which] F; That Q   207 devils!] Q; Diuels. F   211–12 You ... betters] *Rowe's lineation; as prose* Q, F   212–16 Woe ... sea-monster.] F *lineation; as prose* Q   212 Woe] F; We Q   212 repents!] F; repent's, O sir, are you come? Q   *213 will? Speak, sir.] *Johnson;* will, speake Sir? F; will that wee Q   213 my] F; any Q   215 show'st] shew'st F; shewest Q   217 ALBANY Pray ... patient.] F; *not in* Q, *which continues Lear's speech without* SH

---

205 remainders ... depend i.e. the rest of your followers.

206 besort suit, befit.

207 Which ... you Who know their places and yours.

207 Darkness and devils Lear explodes with anger at this point. Peter Brook staged the scene thus: 'Incensed by [Gonerill's] words, Lear overturns the dinner-table and storms out. This is the cue for general pandemonium as the knights, following their master's example, tip chairs, throw plates and generally demolish the chamber' (C. Marowitz, 'Lear Log', *Tulane Drama Review* 8 (1963), 113). This representation is extreme (Rosenberg, p. 121). Lear's knights may appear disorderly in varying degrees; compare 218–21 below and Booth, p. 50.

208 Saddle ... together Lear's servants seem frozen here; thus, he must order them again at 227 (see n.) and 244. Nevertheless, Oxford adds SD *Exit one or more.*

212 Woe i.e. woe to him who.

213 Speak, sir Albany is astonished at what is happening.

213 Prepare my horses Again, no SD appears, though Oxford repeats *Exit one or more.* Either the servants ignore Lear's commands, or his attendants

and knights are paralysed by events. At 227 Lear urges his people out, but their departure seems further delayed until 244.

216 sea-monster No monster of the deep has been satisfactorily identified, but the ocean, traditionally a home of horrors, was also cold and pitiless. The sea-monster that destroyed Hippolytus probably best fits the context (Hunter). In the 1581 translation of Seneca's *Phaedra*, it has a 'marble neck' and is sent as a punishment for filial ingratitude.

217 ALBANY ... patient See Textual Analysis, p. 262 below.

217 be patient Coverdale's definition of patience is 'the precious pearl', the Christian virtue that guards against forsaking charity and falling into wrath (Danby, p. 29). 'Lear's passion rises. Albany – always the "moral fool" – calls out the advice from the devotionalists appropriate for the occasion ... Patience is the only remedy in cases such as Lear's. Lear, however, flings into the angry venom of his outburst against Goneril. Patience is something he has yet to learn' (Danby, p. 177). Compare Hoeniger, who notes that patience is the only virtue that can cure intemperate passion (p. 325). At 2.4.264 Lear prays for patience, and by 4.5.170 he preaches it to Gloucester.

LEAR [*To Gonerill*] Detested kite, thou liest!
My train are men of choice and rarest parts,
That all particulars of duty know,
And in the most exact regard support 220
The worships of their name. O most small fault,
How ugly didst thou in Cordelia show!
Which, like an engine, wrenched my frame of nature
From the fixed place, drew from my heart all love,
And added to the gall. O Lear, Lear, Lear! 225
Beat at this gate that let thy folly in
And thy dear judgement out. Go, go, my people.

ALBANY My lord, I am guiltless as I am ignorant
Of what hath moved you.

LEAR It may be so, my lord.
Hear, Nature, hear, dear goddess, hear: 230
Suspend thy purpose, if thou didst intend
To make this creature fruitful.
Into her womb convey sterility,
Dry up in her the organs of increase,
And from her derogate body never spring 235
A babe to honour her. If she must teem,
Create her child of spleen, that it may live

---

217 SD] *Rowe; not in* Q, F   217 liest!] F; list Q; lessen Q2   218 train are] F; traine, and Q   222 show!] shew? F; shewe,
Q   223 Which] F; that Q   225 Lear, Lear, Lear!] F; *Lear, Lear!* Q   228 SH] F; *Duke.* Q (*throughout scene*)   229 Of . . .
you.] F; *not in* Q   229–44 It . . . away!] F *lineation; as prose* Q   230 Hear] F; harke Q   230 goddess, hear] F;
Goddesse, Q

217 kite A carrion bird particularly despised by
Shakespeare. Muir cites Armstrong, *Shakespeare's
Imagination*, 1946, pp. 12, 17.
218 choice and rarest parts select and special
qualities.
220–1 in . . . name i.e. on every single point
justify and uphold their honourable reputation.
221 worships dignity, honour. 'Abstract nouns
are often pluralized when they refer to more than
one person' (Kittredge).
223 engine mechanical contrivance; here, one
used for levering, not the rack.
223–4 wrenched . . . place i.e. pried loose the
structure of my being from its foundations. The
metaphor is of an overturned edifice or building.
Lear implies that Cordelia was the centre of his
being.
225 gall bitterness; literally, bile, secreted by the
liver.
226 Beat . . . gate Pope and others add SD
Striking his head.
227 Go . . . people Some editors add SD *Exeunt

Kent and Knights, but their departure appears
further delayed until 244.
230 Nature The goddess Lear appeals to is very
different from Edmond's (1.2.1). It is closer to a
personification of the orthodox Elizabethan conception of nature as described, for example, by Richard
Hooker in *Of the Laws of Ecclesiastical Polity*, I.iii: ' . . .
God being the author of Nature, her voice is but his
instrument' (cited by Danby, p. 26). Lear's curse is
very much like those of the Old Testament. Hunter
cites Deut. 28.15, 18. In the eighteenth century (in
Tate's adaptation), this was regarded as a high point of
the drama.
230 dear precious.
235 derogate debased (Onions); but compare
Cotgrave: *derogé* 'disabled; also . . . abolished in
part'. If Gonerill's 'organs' were dried up, her
body would be 'derogate' in the latter sense.
236 teem be fruitful, have offspring.
237 of spleen i.e. entirely of malice, as in *Cor.*
4.5.91.

And be a thwart disnatured torment to her.
Let it stamp wrinkles in her brow of youth,
With cadent tears fret channels in her cheeks,   240
Turn all her mother's pains and benefits
To laughter and contempt, that she may feel
How sharper than a serpent's tooth it is
To have a thankless child. Away, away!

Exeunt [Lear, Kent, Knights, and Attendants]

ALBANY   Now, gods that we adore, whereof comes this?   245
GONERILL   Never afflict yourself to know more of it,
But let his disposition have that scope
As dotage gives it.

Enter LEAR

LEAR   What, fifty of my followers at a clap?
Within a fortnight?
ALBANY   What's the matter, sir?   250
LEAR   I'll tell thee. [*To Gonerill*] Life and death! I am ashamed
That thou hast power to shake my manhood thus,
That these hot tears, which break from me perforce,
Should make thee worth them. Blasts and fogs upon thee!
Th'untented woundings of a father's curse   255

---

238 thwart disnatured] F; thourt disuetur'd Q   240 cadent] F; accent Q   242 feel] F; feele, that she may feele Q   244 Away, away!] F; goe, goe, my people? Q   244 SD] *This edn; not in* Q; *Exit* F; *Exit Lear and Attendants* Rowe (*after 265*)   245 Now . . . this?] Q; *two lines divided* Q   246 more of it,] F; the cause, Q   248 As] F; that Q   248 SD] F; *not in* Q   249–50 What . . . fortnight?] F *lineation; as prose* Q   250 What's] F; What is Q   251 I'll . . . ashamed] *Rowe's lineation; two lines divided* thee: / Life F   251 SD] *Theobald; not in* Q, F   252–65 That . . . forever.] F *lineation (except 254); as prose* Q   253 which] F; that Q   254 Should . . . thee!] *Rowe's lineation; two lines divided* them. / Blasts F   254 thee worth them. Blasts] F; the worst blasts Q   254–5 thee! / Th'untented] F; the vntender Q *uncorr.;* the vntented Q *corr.*

---

238 **thwart** perverse, cross-grained.
238 **disnatured** unnatural, lacking natural feelings.
240 **cadent** falling.
240 **fret** make or form by wearing away.
241 **pains** care.
243 **How . . . is** The wording recalls Ps. 140.3: 'Thei haue sharpened their tongues like a serpent' (Malone).
247 **disposition** mood, humour.
248 **As** That.
249–50 **What . . . fortnight** Gonerill has said nothing to Lear about halving his train; presumably someone informs him of her order in the brief time he is off stage, and the news drives him back for further confrontation. But Hunter

rightly discounts explanations that depend upon realism and praises instead 'the bold foreshortening that makes the loss of fifty followers seem the consequence of an absence during which only four lines are spoken'.
249 **at a clap** at one stroke.
250 **Within a fortnight?** Either this is part of the ultimatum, or it suggests the length of time Lear has been with Gonerill so far.
253–4 **That these . . . them** That you appear to be worth the tears that uncontrollably fall from me.
254 **Blasts** Gusts of pestilential foul air.
255 **untented** untentable, i.e. too deep for probing with a tent (probe or absorbent wedge used for cleaning wounds: *OED sb*[3] 1 and 2).

Pierce every sense about thee. Old fond eyes,
Beweep this cause again, I'll pluck ye out
And cast you with the waters that you loose
To temper clay. Ha! Let it be so.
I have another daughter,   260
Who I am sure is kind and comfortable.
When she shall hear this of thee, with her nails
She'll flay thy wolvish visage. Thou shalt find
That I'll resume the shape which thou dost think
I have cast off forever.   *Exit*

GONERILL   Do you mark that?   265
ALBANY   I cannot be so partial, Gonerill,
To the great love I bear you –
GONERILL   Pray you, content.
What, Oswald, ho!
You, sir, more knave than fool, after your master.
FOOL   Nuncle Lear, nuncle Lear, tarry, take the fool with thee.   270
A fox, when one has caught her,
And such a daughter,
Should sure to the slaughter,

---

256 Pierce] F; peruse Q *uncorr.*; pierce Q *corr.*   256 thee. Old] F; the old Q   257 ye] F; you Q   258 cast you] F; you cast Q   258 loose] F; make Q   259 clay.] F; clay, yea, i'st come to this? Q   259 Ha! . . . so.] F; *not in* Q   260 I have another] F; yet haue I left a Q   261 Who] F; whom Q   265 forever.] F; for euer, thou shalt I warrant thee. Q   265 SD] F; *not in* Q   265 that?] F; that my Lord? Q   266–7 I . . . you –] F *lineation; as prose* Q   267 you –] Theobald (*subst.*); you, Q; you. F   267 Pray you, content.] F; Come sir no more, Q   268 What, Oswald, ho!] F; *not in* Q   269 You, sir,] F; you, Q   270 Nuncle . . . thee] *As prose* Q; *two verse lines divided:* Lear, / Tarry, F, Oxford   270 tarry,] F; tary and Q   270 with thee] F; with Q   271–5 A fox . . . after.] F *lineation; as prose* Q

---

256 **fond** foolish (as often).

257 **Beweep this cause again** If you cry over this once more.

258 **loose** let loose, release. But 'lose' is also possible, as the spellings were interchangeable. Muir suggests a quibble.

259 **temper** soften by moistening. Compare *2H6* 3.1.311: 'And temper clay with blood of Englishmen'.

259–60 **Ha! . . . daughter** An example of F substitution for Q. Compare Duthie, pp. 36, 172, and Stone, p. 234, who believe the Q half-line was accidentally omitted and should be restored. Some metrical disruption is manifest, but short lines are not uncommon in F, similar substitutions occur elsewhere (see Textual Analysis, p. 71–2 above), and other evidence of revision appears; hence, conflation (which does not perfect the metre) is unwarranted.

261 **comfortable** able to comfort, comforting.

267 **Pray you, content** Gonerill cuts Albany off in mid sentence in both Q and F, but the manner in F is somewhat gentler, as Duthie, p. 35, and McLeod, pp. 176–7, agree. On F's alterations of Gonerill's role, see Textual Analysis, p. 63 above.

270 **take . . . thee** 'An absolutely perfect pun. The literal sense is obvious; but the phrase was a regular farewell gibe: "Take the epithet 'fool' with you as you go!" ' (Kittredge).

271–5 **A fox . . . after** The rhymes here may have been phonetically exact, possibly involving a patchwork of colloquial pronunciations. Neither the *l* in 'halter' nor the *f* in 'after' was pronounced. Compare Ben Jonson's rhymes, *water: daughter: slaughter: after* in 'On the Birth of the Lady Mary', which Elizabethans would not have regarded as vulgar or rustic, but 'undoubtedly a source of amusement and appreciative comment' (Kökeritz, p. 183; compare Cercignani, p. 211).

273 **sure to** certainly go to.

If my cap would buy a halter;
So the fool follows after.   *Exit*   275

GONERILL   This man hath had good counsel. A hundred knights?
'Tis politic and safe to let him keep
At point a hundred knights? Yes, that on every dream,
Each buzz, each fancy, each complaint, dislike,
He may enguard his dotage with their powers   280
And hold our lives in mercy. Oswald, I say!

ALBANY   Well, you may fear too far.

GONERILL   Safer than trust too far.
Let me still take away the harms I fear,
Not fear still to be taken. I know his heart.
What he hath uttered I have writ my sister: 285
If she sustain him and his hundred knights
When I have showed th'unfitness –

Enter OSWALD

                          How now, Oswald?
What, have you writ that letter to my sister?

OSWALD   Ay, madam.

GONERILL   Take you some company and away to horse.   290
Inform her full of my particular fear,
And thereto add such reasons of your own
As may compact it more. Get you gone,
And hasten your return.

                                   [*Exit Oswald*]

---

275 SD] F; *not in* Q   276–87 This . . . th'unfitness –] F; *not in* Q   276 This . . . knights?] *Rowe's lineation; two lines divided* Counsell, / A F   *278 knights?] *Hanmer;* Knights: F   287 th'unfitness –] *Rowe;* th'vnfitnesse. F   287 SD] F; *not in* Q   287 How now, Oswald?] F; What *Oswald*, ho. *Oswald.* Here Madam. Q   288 that] F; this Q   289 Ay,] I F; Yes Q   290–300 Take . . . well.] F *lineation; as prose* Q   291 fear] F; feares Q   294 And hasten] F; *and after* Q *uncorr.,* Q2; & hasten Q *corr.*   294 SD] *Rowe; not in* Q, F

274 halter hangman's noose.
276–87 This . . . unfitness On F's addition, see Textual Analysis, p. 263 below.
276 This man i.e. Lear. Gonerill speaks sarcastically.
278 At point In (armed) readiness.
279 buzz whisper, rumour.
280 enguard put a guard around, protect.
281 in mercy in fee, at (his) mercy.
282 fear . . . trust too far Compare 'Fear is one part of prudence' (Tilley F135, cited by NS).
283 still always (as often).
284 Not . . . taken Rather than constantly live in fear of being overtaken by those dangers. Gonerill

uses the rhetorical device of antimetabole (Joseph, p. 81). Compare *Tro.* 3.3.178–9.
288 What . . . writ At 1.3.21, Gonerill says she will write to her sister at once, but the letter cannot contain what Lear has just said, and presumably she means she has commissioned Oswald to write for her.
291 full fully.
291 particular own.
293 compact strengthen, confirm.
294 return Although Gonerill orders Oswald to return, she meets him instead at Gloucester's castle (2.4).

No, no, my lord,
This milky gentleness and course of yours,   295
Though I condemn not, yet under pardon
You are much more ataxed for want of wisdom,
Than praised for harmful mildness.
ALBANY   How far your eyes may pierce I cannot tell;
Striving to better, oft we mar what's well.   300
GONERILL   Nay then –
ALBANY   Well, well, th'event.

                                                        Exeunt

1.5 *Enter* LEAR, KENT, *and* FOOL

LEAR   Go you before to Gloucester with these letters. Acquaint my
daughter no further with anything you know than comes from

---

294 No, no] F; Now Q   **295** milky] F; mildie Q *uncorr.*; milkie Q *corr.*   **296** condemn] F; dislike Q   ***297** You are] F2; y'are Q; Your are F   ***297** ataxed for] ataxt for *Duthie, conj. Greg*; alapt Q *uncorr.*, Q2; attaskt for Q *corr.*; at task for F   **298** praised] F; praise Q   **300** better, oft] F; better ought, Q   **302** th'event] the'uent F; the euent Q   Act 1, Scene 5 **1.5**] *Scena Quinta.* F; *not in* Q   ***0 SD*] Q2; *Enter Lear.* Q; *Enter Lear, Kent, Gentleman, and Foole.* F

295 milky ... course mild and gentle course of action (hendiadys). Compare *Tim.* 3.1.54.
296 Though ... not 'But she does' (NS).
296 under pardon pardon me.
297 ataxed taxed, censured: a famous crux. Greg, *Variants*, pp. 153–5, has convinced most recent editors that Q uncorr. 'alapt' is probably a misprint for 'ataxt' (*t* and *x* were often confused with *l* and *p*). The press readers wrongly corrected the word in Q corr. and F, although Q corr. 'attaskt' can be construed as a variant of 'ataxt', and F 'at task' may be a sophistication or regularization of Q corr. (Hunter). Noting the common origin of 'task' and 'tax' and their interchangeable spellings, T. Howard-Hill conjectures that F 'at task' derived from 'ataxt' through an intermediate manuscript 'in which the spelling may have already been varied' ('The problem of manuscript copy', 21–2). Compare 3.2.15, where F reads 'taxe' for Q 'taske'.
298 harmful mildness i.e. leniency, which results in further harm being done.
299 How ... tell i.e. I cannot tell how perceptive you are or how well you can predict future events.
300 Striving ... well Compare 'Let well enough alone' (Tilley w260), Bodenham, *Belvedere* (1600): 'Some men so strive in cunning to excell, / That oft they marre the worke before was well' (Dent, p. 246) and Sonnet 103.9–10.
302 Well ... event i.e. let's await the outcome. Albany has no stomach here for continuing the quarrel.

Act 1, Scene 5
0 SD Although F includes *Gentleman* in the SD, most editors delete it, as Lear directs Kent, not his Gentleman or Knight, to carry his letters. The Gentleman has no speaking role and is not needed until 38, where Theobald inserts his entrance. Oxford, following Jennens, retains the Gentleman here and has Lear give him letters for Gloucester and Kent a letter for Regan, after which each exits. While this arrangement attempts to resolve the problem of Regan and Cornwall's residence (see below), Gloucester in the next scene gives no indication of receiving word from Lear, as Regan does (2.1.122).
1 before i.e. before me, ahead.
1 Gloucester Perhaps Lear refers not to the Earl of Gloucester but to the town of that name, near where Cornwall and Regan may have a residence (Perrett, pp. 167–72). Bradley, p. 449, notes that Cornwall is Gloucester's 'arch and patron', 2.1.58. But NS sees a slip here for 'Cornwall' and emends accordingly. Shakespeare may simply have anticipated the later action.
1 these letters this letter; compare Latin *litterae*, a similar plural form with a singular meaning; see also 3 and 5 below, and 4.5.237, 244.
1–3 Acquaint ... letter Compare 1.4.288–93. Lear does not distrust Kent; unlike Gonerill, he is trying to keep a lid on the situation. Hunter implausibly says Lear distrusts Regan and does not want to give her any ammunition against him.

her demand out of the letter. If your diligence be not speedy, I
shall be there afore you.

KENT   I will not sleep, my lord, till I have delivered your letter.   5

Exit

FOOL   If a man's brains were in's heels, were't not in danger of
kibes?

LEAR   Ay, boy.

FOOL   Then, I prithee, be merry; thy wit shall not go slipshod.

LEAR   Ha, ha, ha.   10

FOOL   Shalt see thy other daughter will use thee kindly, for though
she's as like this as a crab's like an apple, yet I can tell what I
can tell.

LEAR   What canst tell, boy?

FOOL   She will taste as like this as a crab does to a crab. Thou   15
canst tell why one's nose stands i'th'middle on's face?

LEAR   No.

FOOL   Why, to keep one's eyes of either side's nose, that what a
man cannot smell out, he may spy into.

LEAR   I did her wrong.   20

FOOL   Canst tell how an oyster makes his shell?

LEAR   No.

FOOL   Nor I neither; but I can tell why a snail has a house.

LEAR   Why?

FOOL   Why, to put 's head in, not to give it away to his daughters,   25
and leave his horns without a case.

---

4 afore] F; before Q   6 were in's] F; where in his Q   6 were't] *Rowe*; wert Q, F   9 not] F; nere Q   12 crab's] F; crab is Q   12 can tell what] F; con, what Q   14 What canst] F; Why what canst thou Q   14 boy?] F; my boy? Q   15 She will] F; Sheel Q   15 does] F; doth Q   16 canst] F; canst not Q   16 stands] F; stande Q   16 i'th'] F; in the Q   16 on's] F; of his Q   18 one's] F; his Q   18 of] F; on Q   19 he] F; a Q   25 put 's] F; put his Q   25 daughters] F; daughter Q

3 **demand** question.
3 **out of** from, suggested by.
6 **were't** i.e. his brains, taken as singular.
7 **kibes** chilblains. The Fool refers first to Kent's promise of speedy service, then (11–13) to Lear's foolish journey that shows he has no wit, even in his heels.
9 **thy ... slipshod** your brains will not have to wear slippers (because of chilblains); you are witless to begin with (in going to Regan and thinking to find succour there). The joke has sometimes been used as a cue for actors playing the Fool to do handstands or somersaults (Rosenberg, p. 137).
11 **Shalt** Thou shalt.
11 **kindly** (1) affectionately, (2) according to her kind (the same as Gonerill's).
11–15 **though ... to a crab** The Fool makes an ironic joke, continuing the play on 'kindly': only a fool could think there is any real difference between Regan and Gonerill. Though Regan and Gonerill

look slightly different, they are essentially the same.
12 **like this** i.e. like this daughter.
12 **crab** crab-apple; a small, sour wild apple. Wright (cited by Furness) quotes Lyly, *Euphues*: 'The sower Crabbe hath the shew of an Apple as well as the sweet Pippin.'
15–19 **Thou ... into** An example of the Fool's rapidly shifting focus though the answer to his question adheres to the main issue of perception.
16 **on's** of his.
20 **I ... wrong** Lear broods on his treatment of Cordelia. Compare 'O most small fault' (1.4.221). D. G. James, *The Dream of Learning*, 1951, pp. 94–6, believes Lear refers to Gonerill.
23–5 **why a snail ... in** Compare Tilley, s580: 'Like a snail he keeps his house on his head' (NS).
25 **put 's** put his.
26 **horns** An allusion to the cuckold's horns; being cuckolded was the inevitable fate of married men, according to the standard (and much

LEAR   I will forget my nature. So kind a father! Be my horses ready?

FOOL   Thy asses are gone about 'em. The reason why the seven
stars are no mo than seven is a pretty reason.

LEAR   Because they are not eight.   30

FOOL   Yes, indeed, thou wouldst make a good fool.

LEAR   To take't again perforce. Monster ingratitude!

FOOL   If thou wert my fool, nuncle, I'd have thee beaten for being
old before thy time.

LEAR   How's that?   35

FOOL   Thou shouldst not have been old till thou hadst been wise.

LEAR   O let me not be mad, not mad, sweet heaven!
Keep me in temper, I would not be mad.

[*Enter* GENTLEMAN]

How now, are the horses ready?

GENTLEMAN   Ready, my lord.   40

LEAR   Come, boy.

FOOL   She that's a maid now, and laughs at my departure,
Shall not be a maid long, unless things be cut shorter.

Exeunt

28 'em] F; them Q   29 mo] F; more Q   31 indeed] F; *not in* Q   36 till] F; before Q   37–9 O ... ready?] *Pope's lineation; as prose* Q, F   37 not mad] F; *not in* Q   38 Keep] F; I would not be mad, keepe Q   38 SD] *Theobald; not in* Q, F   39 How now,] F; *not in* Q   40 SH] F; *Seruant.* Q   41 boy.] F; boy. *Exit.* Q   42 that's] F; that is Q   43 unless] F; except Q   43 SD] F; *Exit.* Q

repeated) Elizabethan joke. The legitimacy of
Lear's elder daughters is again brought into question, and Lear's destitution predicted.

27 forget lose.

27 nature Either (1) generally: character, disposition; or (2) specifically: paternal instincts; or (3)
both.

28 asses An obvious quibble.

28–9 The reason ... reason An example of the
fallacy of begging the question, i.e. when the conclusion, or question to be proved, stands as one of
the premises (Joseph, p. 198).

29 mo more.

31 thou ... fool 'There is bite in Fool's answer
... Fool's jokes are not working, line by line Lear
slips further away from communication ... as Fool
incites Lear to sanity, he baits him, too, and the
pitch rises' (Rosenberg, p. 139).

32 To take't again i.e. to resume his sovereignty. Lear's mutterings, when he does not
directly respond to the Fool, are not fully coherent.

As at 20 'her' could refer to either Cordelia or
Gonerill, here Lear may be thinking of Gonerill's
rescinding the privileges she agreed to grant him
(Steevens).

32 perforce by force.

37–8 O ... mad The fear is occasioned by
'wise' = in one's right mind, in the Fool's preceding
gibe (NS). Lear's passion is rising, and the 'unnatural' events are approaching a climax. Hoeniger
describes Lear's madness in Renaissance terms as
'acute hypochondriac melancholy developing into
mania' (p. 330) and traces it from here through 4.5.

42–3 She ... shorter The Fool addresses the
audience and warns *naïfs* against a simplistic (i.e.
merely humorous) interpretation of his role and (by
extension) of all experience. He puns on 'departure'
(pronounced like 'departer' and rhyming with
'shorter': Kökeritz, pp. 169, 226; Cercignani, pp.
114, 263), and on the bawdy sense of 'things',
perhaps putting his bauble (= a phallus) between
his legs as he mimes the lines (Wiles, pp. 190–1).

2.1 *Enter* EDMOND *and* CURAN, *severally*

EDMOND   Save thee, Curan.

CURAN   And you, sir. I have been with your father and given him
notice that the Duke of Cornwall and Regan his duchess will
be here with him this night.

EDMOND   How comes that?   5

CURAN   Nay, I know not. You have heard of the news abroad? I
mean the whispered ones, for they are yet but ear-kissing
arguments.

EDMOND   Not I; pray you, what are they?

CURAN   Have you heard of no likely wars toward 'twixt the Dukes   10
of Cornwall and Albany?

EDMOND   Not a word.

CURAN   You may do then in time. Fare you well, sir.   *Exit*

EDMOND   The duke be here tonight! The better, best.
This weaves itself perforce into my business.   15
My father hath set guard to take my brother,
And I have one thing of a queasy question
Which I must act. Briefness and Fortune, work!
Brother, a word, descend; brother, I say!

Act 2, Scene 1   2.1] *Actus Secundus. Scena Prima.* F; *not in* Q   0 SD] F; *Enter Bast. and Curan meeting.* Q   2–4 And . . .
night.] *As prose* Q; *four verse lines ending* . . . bin / . . . notice / . . . Duchesse / . . . night. F   *2 you] Q; your F   3 Regan]
F; *not in* Q   4 this] F; to Q   *6 abroad?] *Duthie;* abroad, Q, F   7 they] F; there Q   7 ear-kissing] F; eare-bussing
Q   9 Not I;] F; Not, I Q   10–11 Have . . . Albany?] Q; *not in* Q2, *which also omits 12; two verse lines divided* toward, /
'Twixt F   10 toward] F; towards Q   10 Dukes] Q; two Dukes Q   13 You . . . sir.] Q; *two lines divided* time. /
Fare F   13 do] F; *not in* Q   13 SD] F; *not in* Q   14–27 The . . . yourself.] F *lineation; as prose* Q   *14 better,] *Rowe;*
better Q, F   18 I must act. Briefness and Fortune, work] F; must aske breefnes and fortune helpe Q

Act 2, Scene 1

0 SD *severally* Edmond and Curan enter separately from different entrances.

1 Save thee i.e. God save thee (a common
greeting).

1 Curan Though unusual, as Hunter says, for so
minor a character to have a proper name, it is not
unprecedented (compare Conrad in *Much Ado*).
Curan is apparently one of Gloucester's men and
thus known by name to Edmond.

6 news abroad talk going around.

7 ear-kissing Q's 'bussing' may be a misreading
for 'kissing' since *k* could be misread as *b* – as e.g. at
4.1.37: Q'bitt', F 'kill'. Minim misreadings, *i* for *u*,
and vice versa, are common. On the other hand,
'kissing' may be a Folio sophistication (Duthie, p.
192, adopting Q). The two words mean the same,
but 'bussing' has the advantage of a possible pun on
'buzzing' (Collier, cited by Furness). Nevertheless,
the F reading is perfectly acceptable.

8 arguments subjects, topics.

10–11 wars . . . Albany A leitmotiv from here
on, showing disorder in domestic politics and con-
futing one of Lear's reasons for giving up the throne
(1.1.39–40).

10 toward impending.

14 The better, best i.e. this is better, in fact the
best news yet.

17 queasy question i.e. delicate nature.

18 Briefness and Fortune Whereas Fortune
was a standard allegorical figure, Edmond here personifies another 'natural' force, speed. During this
speech following Curan's exit, Edmond moves
towards his imagined lodging, where he has hidden
Edgar (1.2.140–2).

19 descend This is the only occasion in the play
where some kind of 'above' seems to be used.
Possibly Edgar drops down from the Lord's Room
above the rear centre stage, where he is hidden by
spectators seated there. Edmond is again stage-
managing the action, manipulating people and
events.

Enter EDGAR

My father watches: O sir, fly this place.   20
Intelligence is given where you are hid;
You have now the good advantage of the night.
Have you not spoken 'gainst the Duke of Cornwall?
He's coming hither, now i'th'night, i'th'haste,
And Regan with him. Have you nothing said   25
Upon his party 'gainst the Duke of Albany?
Advise yourself.

EDGAR   I am sure on't, not a word.

EDMOND   I hear my father coming. Pardon me,
In cunning, I must draw my sword upon you.
Draw, seem to defend yourself. Now, quit you well.   30
[*Shouting*] Yield! Come before my father! – Light ho,
        here! –
Fly, brother! – Torches, torches! – so, farewell.

                                        Exit Edgar

Some blood drawn on me would beget opinion
Of my more fierce endeavour.
                [*Wounds his arm*]
                      I have seen drunkards
Do more than this in sport. Father, father!   35
Stop, stop! No help?

---

*19 SD] *Theobald; in margin before 15* Q; after 18* F   **20** sir,] F; *not in* Q   **23** Cornwall?] F; *Cornwall ought,* Q   **24**
i'th'night] F; *in the night* Q   **24** i'th'haste] F; *i'th hast* Q   **26** 'gainst] F; *against* Q   **27** on't] F; *your –* Q   **28–36** I
... help?] F *lineation (except 30); as prose* Q   **29** cunning] F; *crauing* Q   **30** Draw ... well.] *Capell's lineation; two lines
divided* your selfe, / Now F   **30** Draw] F; *not in* Q   **31** SD] *This edn; not in* Q, F   **31** ho] F; *here* Q   **32** brother! –
Torches,] Brother, Torches, F; *brother flie, torches,* Q   **32** SD] F; *not in* Q   **34** SD] *Rowe; not in* Q, F   **36** No] Q, F; Ho
Oxford

21 Intelligence Information.
23 spoken 'gainst Edmond is not wildly spec-
ulating, but planting seeds of doubt in Edgar's mind
concerning his safety, as he does at 25–6.
24 i'th'haste i.e. in haste.
27 on't of it.
29–30 In cunning ... yourself Playing on his
brother's naïvety, as in 1.2, Edmond implies that
his 'cunning', or craft, is used on Edgar's behalf,
though in fact the opposite is true. Rosenberg, pp.
142–3, questions whether Edmond here intends to
kill Edgar (the 'queasy question', 17) and claim self-
defence. But citing the duel in 5.3, Rosenberg notes
that Edgar, a better swordsman, frustrates
Edmond's design, unless Edmond himself has a
change of heart at the last moment. 33–4 suggest,

however, that the duel is a sham from first to last,
even though Edmond might be better off with
Edgar dead.
30 quit you acquit yourself; with a possible play
on the sense 'leave'.
33–4 beget ... endeavour i.e. cause people to
think that my efforts were fiercer than they actually
were in the struggle.
34–5 drunkards ... sport Young gallants sometimes stabbed their own arms so that they could
drink the healths of their mistresses in blood
(Collier, cited by Furness). Several references to
the practice appear in dramatic literature; e.g.
Steevens cites a relevant passage from Marston's
The Dutch Courtesan 4.1, and Kittredge cites
Middleton's *A Trick to Catch the Old One* 5.2.198.

Enter GLOUCESTER *and Servants with torches*

GLOUCESTER   Now, Edmond, where's the villain?
EDMOND   Here stood he in the dark, his sharp sword out,
    Mumbling of wicked charms, conjuring the moon
    To stand auspicious mistress.
GLOUCESTER   But where is he?
EDMOND   Look, sir, I bleed.
GLOUCESTER   Where is the villain, Edmond?   40
EDMOND   Fled this way, sir, when by no means he could –
GLOUCESTER   Pursue him, ho! Go after.

                                    [*Exeunt Servants*]
                        'By no means' what?
EDMOND   Persuade me to the murder of your lordship,
    But that I told him the revenging gods
    'Gainst parricides did all the thunder bend,   45
    Spoke with how manifold and strong a bond
    The child was bound to'th'father; sir, in fine,
    Seeing how loathly opposite I stood
    To his unnatural purpose, in fell motion
    With his preparèd sword he charges home   50
    My unprovided body, latched mine arm;

---

36 SD] F; *Enter Glost.* Q   36 where's] F; where is Q   37–9 Here ... mistress.] F *lineation; as prose* Q   38 Mumbling] F; warbling Q   39 stand] F; stand's Q, *Oxford;* stand his Q2   *41 could –] Q; could. F   42 ho] F; *not in* Q   42 SD] Dyce (*subst.*); *not in* Q, F   43–84 Persuade ... capable.] F *lineation; as prose* Q   44 revenging] F; reuengiue Q   45 the thunder] F; their thunders Q   46 manifold] F; many fould Q   47 to'th'] F; to the Q   47 fine] F; a fine Q   49 in] F; with Q   51 latched] F; lancht Q

---

36 SD with torches Note the ironies of (a) Edmond's call for torches (32), when he does not really want to reveal what is happening, and (b) Gloucester's entrance with them, and their failure to illuminate what he most needs to see (Heilman, p. 46).

38–9 Mumbling ... mistress Edmond is playing upon Gloucester's superstitious nature, but the lines also show Shakespeare beginning to imagine Edgar as Tom o'Bedlam. Compare 1.2.118.

38–9 moon ... mistress Edmond alludes to Hecate. See 1.1.104 n.

39 stand be; 'his' is understood, though Q prints 'stand's' and Q2 'stand his'.

41 this way Edmond points in the wrong direction, of course, giving Edgar time to flee, just as in the preceding lines he has been deliberately stalling despite his father's repeated demands to know where Edgar is.

44 revenging avenging.

45 bend aim. The metaphor is from archery; compare 1.1.137.

47 in fine finally.

48 loathly opposite loathingly opposed.

49 fell motion fierce, deadly thrust.

50 preparèd unsheathed.

50 charges home makes a home thrust at (Muir).

51 unprovided i.e. unprotected, unarmed.

51 latched caught. In defending the F reading against Q's 'lancht' (= lanced), Duthie, p. 137, regrets that his best evidence is a 1535 quotation from a Scottish author cited by *OED* Latch *sb* 2. But compare *OED sb* 4, 'to receive ... a blow'; Bishop Hall in 1649: 'A man that latches the weapon in his own body to save his Prince'; and *Mac.* 4.3.195, also cited by *OED* under *sb* 4.

And when he saw my best alarumed spirits
Bold in the quarrel's right, roused to th'encounter,
Or whether ghasted by the noise I made,
Full suddenly he fled.

GLOUCESTER   Let him fly far,   55
Not in this land shall he remain uncaught;
And found, dispatch. The noble duke my master,
My worthy arch and patron, comes tonight.
By his authority I will proclaim it,
That he which finds him shall deserve our thanks,   60
Bringing the murderous coward to the stake;
He that conceals him, death.

EDMOND   When I dissuaded him from his intent
And found him pight to do it, with cursed speech
I threatened to discover him. He replied,   65
'Thou unpossessing bastard, dost thou think,
If I would stand against thee, would the reposal
Of any trust, virtue, or worth in thee
Make thy words faithed? No; what I should deny
(As this I would, ay, though thou didst produce   70
My very character) I'd turn it all
To thy suggestion, plot, and damnèd practice;
And thou must make a dullard of the world,

---

52 And] F; but Q   53 quarrel's right,] F; quarrels, rights Q   53 th'] F; the Q   54 ghasted] *Knight;* gasted Q, F   55 Full] F; but Q   *56–7 uncaught; / And found, dispatch. The] *Steevens (subst.);* vncaught / And found; dispatch, the F; vncaught and found, dispatch, the Q   61 coward] F; caytife Q   67 would the reposal] F; could the reposure Q   *69 I should] Q; should I F   70 *ay,] I, Q; *not in* F   72 practice] F; pretence Q

52 **best alarumed spirits** i.e. best energies called to arms (Kittredge).

54 **ghasted** frightened, scared. Compare *Oth.* 5.1.106. Muir suggests a possible pun on 'ghosted', since Edgar 'vanished like a ghost at cock-crow'. The two words are nevertheless etymologically distinct.

55 **Full** An intensive (= 'very', 'extremely').

55–7 **Let … dispatch** Either (1) however far he flies, we'll catch him and kill him, or (2) let him fly far from this land, for if he dares to remain I'll see that he is caught and exiled (Davenport, p. 20).

57 **And found, dispatch** i.e. and once he is found, he will be summarily executed.

58 **arch and patron** chief patron (hendiadys).

61 **to the stake** i.e. to the place of execution.

64 **pight** firmly set, determined; an archaic form of the past participle of 'pitch', as in 'to pitch a tent'. Compare *Tro.* 5.10.24 for its literal use.

64 **cursed** angry.

65 **discover him** i.e. reveal his purpose.

66 **unpossessing** Illegitimate children could not inherit property.

67 **I would** I should.

67 **reposal** placing.

68 **virtue, or worth** 'These words are not the objects of *of*; they are in the same construction as *reposal*: "Would our father's putting any confidence in you, or would any virtue or worthiness on your part", etc.' (Kittredge).

69 **faithed** believed.

71 **character** handwriting.

72 **practice** evil machination. Compare 106 below.

73–6 **thou … seek it** i.e. you must think the world is pretty stupid for people not to think that what you stood to gain from my death was a powerful incentive for you to seek it (by this stratagem).

> If they not thought the profits of my death
> Were very pregnant and potential spirits   75
> To make thee seek it.'
>   *Tucket within*
> GLOUCESTER   O strange and fastened villain!
> Would he deny his letter, said he?
> Hark, the duke's trumpets. I know not why he comes.
> All ports I'll bar, the villain shall not 'scape;
> The duke must grant me that. Besides, his picture   80
> I will send far and near, that all the kingdom
> May have due note of him; and of my land,
> Loyal and natural boy, I'll work the means
> To make thee capable.
>
>   *Enter* CORNWALL, REGAN, *and Attendants*
>
> CORNWALL   How now, my noble friend, since I came hither,   85
> Which I can call but now, I have heard strange news.
> REGAN   If it be true, all vengeance comes too short

---

75 spirits] F; spurres Q   76 SD] F; *after 77, Malone; not in* Q   76 O strange] F; Strong Q   77 said he?] F; I neuer got him, Q   *78 why] Q; wher F   82 due] F; *not in* Q   84 SD] F; *Enter the Duke of Cornwall.* Q   85–94 How ... father?] F *lineation; as prose* Q   *86 strange news.] Q; strangenesse F

75 pregnant and potential spirits i.e. spirits fertile and powerful in incitement. Many editors, ignoring a possibly mixed metaphor ('pregnant spurs'), adopt Q's reading as better suiting the sense. Duthie, p. 173, thinks the F collator or compositor may have misread 'spurres' and thus miscorrected Q. But Sisson, p. 232, argues that the sense and language of the whole speech points to 'spirits', with 'pregnant and potential' fitting evil spirits and referring back to 'damnèd practice' (72). Shakespeare often juxtaposes 'potent' and 'spirits' (Muir, adopting F, as does Riverside).

76 SD *Tucket within* Most editors place SD after 77, but space considerations did not force Compositor B to insert it earlier, and Gloucester's preoccupation with Edmond's news naturally suggests a delayed response. A tucket (from Italian *toccata*) is a succession of notes on a trumpet distinguished from a flourish. Gloucester recognizes the particular melody or sequence as Cornwall's (78).

76 strange (1) monstrous (of human species), (2) unnatural, alienated (of human kinship).

76 fastened confirmed, hardened.

77 said he? F's substitution for Q's 'I neuer got

him' leaves an irregular line, but conflation, as Duthie recommends (p. 173) and many editors read, does not help metrically. Duthie believes 'said he?' was meant as an addition, not a substitution, and was misinterpreted by the scribe or collator preparing copy for F. Gloucester's agitation lends itself to hypermetrical speech, interrupted by the trumpet announcing Cornwall and Regan's arrival.

79 ports seaports; but possibly gates of walled towns, too.

80–1 his picture ... near Before xerography or even photography, this method of apprehending malefactors was used. Furness cites *Nobody and Somebody* (1606): 'Let him be straight imprinted to the life: / His picture shall be set on euery stall, / And proclamation made, that he that takes him, / Shall haue a hundred pounds of *Somebody*.'

83 natural The ambiguity – (1) naturally loyal and loving, (2)illegitimate – is further compounded since 'natural' could also refer to a legitimate child. Thus Gloucester may already indicate that Edmond is his heir (Muir).

84 capable i.e. legally able to inherit patrimony.

Which can pursue th'offender. How dost, my lord?

GLOUCESTER   O madam, my old heart is cracked, it's cracked.

REGAN   What, did my father's godson seek your life? 90
He whom my father named, your Edgar?

GLOUCESTER   O lady, lady, shame would have it hid.

REGAN   Was he not companion with the riotous knights
That tended upon my father?

GLOUCESTER   I know not, madam; 'tis too bad, too bad. 95

EDMOND   Yes, madam, he was of that consort.

REGAN   No marvel, then, though he were ill affected.
'Tis they have put him on the old man's death,
To have th'expense and waste of his revenues.
I have this present evening from my sister 100
Been well informed of them, and with such cautions,
That if they come to sojourn at my house,
I'll not be there.

CORNWALL   Nor I, assure thee, Regan.
Edmond, I hear that you have shown your father
A child-like office.

EDMOND   It was my duty, sir. 105

GLOUCESTER   He did bewray his practice, and received
This hurt you see, striving to apprehend him.

CORNWALL   Is he pursued?

GLOUCESTER   Ay, my good lord.

CORNWALL   If he be taken, he shall never more 110
Be feared of doing harm. Make your own purpose

---

88 th'] F; the Q   89 O] F; *not in* Q   89 it's] F; is Q   92 O] F; I Q   94 tended] F; tends Q   96 of that consort] F; *not in* Q   99 th'expense and waste] F; these – and wast Q *uncorr.*; the wast and spoyle Q *corr.*   99 his] F, Q *corr.*; this his Q *uncorr.*   102–3 That . . . there.] F *lineation; one line* Q   103–5 Nor . . . office.] F *lineation; as prose* Q   104 hear] F; heard Q   104 shown] shewne F; shewen Q   105 It was] F; Twas Q   106 bewray] F; betray Q   110–16 If . . . on.] F *lineation; as prose* Q

88 **dost** i.e. dost thou. Since Regan never again addresses Gloucester in the second-person familiar, Furness believes the F2 emendation, 'does', should be adopted, though his text follows Q/F.

90 **my father's godson** Regan begins to make a series of associations connecting Edgar and Lear with mischief and disorder. Compare 93–4.

94 **tended upon** Although many editors follow Theobald and emend 'tended' to 'tend', thus preserving the metre, Abbott 472 (cited by Furness, Duthie) indicates that *-ed* was often not pronounced after a *d* or *t*; hence, the emendation, which also changes the tense, is unnecessary.

96 **consort** band, company; accented on second syllable.

97 **though** if.

97 **ill affected** badly disposed, disloyal.

98 **put him on** put him on or up to.

99 **th'expense** the spending.

99 **revenues** Accented on second syllable.

101 **them** i.e. Lear's knights.

103 **assure thee** be assured.

105 **child-like office** filial service.

106 **bewray** expose, reveal.

111–12 **Make . . . please** i.e. carry out your plan to capture Edgar, using whatever means in my name you please.

How in my strength you please. For you, Edmond,
Whose virtue and obedience doth this instant
So much commend itself, you shall be ours;
Natures of such deep trust we shall much need;   115
You we first seize on.

EDMOND   I shall serve you, sir,
Truly, however else.

GLOUCESTER   For him I thank your grace.

CORNWALL   You know not why we came to visit you?

REGAN   Thus out of season, threading dark-eyed night?
Occasions, noble Gloucester, of some prize,   120
Wherein we must have use of your advice.
Our father he hath writ, so hath our sister,
Of differences, which I best thought it fit
To answer from our home. The several messengers
From hence attend dispatch. Our good old friend,   125
Lay comforts to your bosom and bestow
Your needful counsel to our businesses,
Which craves the instant use.

GLOUCESTER   I serve you, madam;
Your graces are right welcome.

                                        Exeunt. Flourish

116–17 I . . . else.] *Pope's lineation; one line* Q, F   116 sir] F; *not in* Q   119 threading] F; threatning Q   120 prize]
F; prise Q *uncorr.;* poyse Q *corr.*   123 differences] F, Q *corr.;* defences Q *uncorr.*   123 best] F, Q *uncorr.;* lest Q *corr.*
*123 thought] Q; though F   124 home] F, Q *corr.;* hand Q *uncorr.*   126–8 Lay . . . use.] F *lineation; two lines divided*
councell / To Q   127 businesses] F; busines Q   128–9 I . . . welcome] F; *one line* Q   129 SD] F; (*Exeunt* Q (*after* vse,
127)

114 **ours** The royal plural.
115 **we . . . need** Cornwall alludes to impending broils with either Lear or Albany (Hunter).
116 **seize on** 'take legal possession of (a vassal)' (NS); but Cornwall may not be using the term technically.
118 **you?** Many editions (e.g. Muir, Oxford) follow Rowe and change the question mark to a dash, making Regan cut Cornwall off in mid speech. But by interposing herself and relegating Cornwall to second fiddle, Regan does not necessarily interrupt her husband (NS).
119 **out of season** i.e. untimely travel by night.
119 **threading dark-eyed night** A precise metaphor conveying the difficulties of travel along unlit roads and byways, with a quibble on the eye of a needle (NS).
120 **prize** importance. See collation. Oxford reads 'poise': Taylor argues, against Greg, that

here and again at 123 Q's press-corrections are authoritative and were simply overlooked by the F collator ('Date and authorship', pp. 362–3). Duthie, pp. 139–40, rejects Q corr. 'poyse', since he believes F's 'prize' came from a playhouse manuscript.
123 **which** Not the differences, or quarrels, but the letters (Delius, cited by Muir).
124 **To . . . home** Regan leaves her home so that she will have an easier way to put Lear off and to consult with Gonerill. But, dramaturgically, her arrival and Cornwall's at Gloucester's castle bring all the principal characters of the main plot together (except Cordelia and Albany) for the climactic episodes that end this act and the next (Bradley, p. 449).
124 **from** i.e. away from.
125 **attend dispatch** are waiting to be sent back (with replies).
128 **craves . . . use** demands immediate action.

2.2 *Enter* KENT *[disguised] and* OSWALD, *severally*

OSWALD   Good dawning to thee, friend. Art of this house?
KENT   Ay.
OSWALD   Where may we set our horses?
KENT   I'th'mire.
OSWALD   Prithee, if thou lov'st me, tell me.   5
KENT   I love thee not.
OSWALD   Why, then I care not for thee.
KENT   If I had thee in Lipsbury pinfold, I would make thee care
   for me.
OSWALD   Why dost thou use me thus? I know thee not.   10
KENT   Fellow, I know thee.
OSWALD   What dost thou know me for?
KENT   A knave, a rascal, an eater of broken meats, a base, proud,
   shallow, beggarly, three-suited, hundred-pound, filthy worsted-
   stocking knave; a lily-livered, action-taking, whoreson glass-   15
   gazing, superserviceable, finical rogue; one-trunk-inheriting

---

Act 2, Scene 2   2.2] *Scena Secunda.* F; *not in* Q   0 SD *severally*] F; *not in* Q   1 dawning] F; deuen Q *uncorr.*; euen Q *corr.*   1 this] F; the Q   5 lov'st] F; loue Q   *14 three-suited, hundred-pound,] three snyted hundred pound Q *uncorr.*; three shewted hundred pound Q *corr.*; three-suited-hundred pound F; three-suited, hundred pound F2   14–15 worsted-stocking] woosted-stocking F; wosted stocken Q *uncorr.*; worsted-stocken Q *corr.*   15 action-taking] F; action taking knaue, a Q   16 superserviceable, finical] F; superfinicall Q   *16 one-trunk-inheriting] F3; one truncke inheriting Q; one Trunke-inheriting F, F2

Act 2, Scene 2

1 **dawning** Q uncorr. 'deuen' (colloquial) was unnecessarily changed to Q corr. 'euen' (NS). F's neologism, 'Good dawning', is 'possibly an invention … to suit Oswald's euphuistic style' (Stone, p. 194). In any event, as 26–7 indicate, it is night-time before dawn.

1 **of this house** i.e. a servant here. Why Kent answers affirmatively is not clear, unless it is to give occasion for further attacks on Oswald (Hunter).

5 **if … me** A conventional, if affected, way of saying please (Hunter).

7–8 **care … care** A quibble: (1) like, (2) heed (NS).

8 **Lipsbury pinfold** Probably a pun on 'between my teeth' (Nares, cited by Furness). No town of Lipsbury is known; 'pinfold' = pound, or pen, for confining stray cattle or sheep.

10 **use** treat.

13 **broken meats** Leftover food or scraps, such as a menial would eat.

14 **three-suited** Servingmen were allotted three suits of clothes. Compare 3.4.120–2 and Jonson, *Epicoene, or The Silent Woman* 3.1.38–42 (Mrs Otter scolds her husband, whom she treats as a dependant): 'Who giues you your maintenance, I

pray you? Who allowes you your horsemeat, and man's-meat? your three sutes of apparell a yeere? your foure paire of stockings, one silke, three worsted?' (Wright, following Steevens; cited by Furness).

14 **hundred-pound** A large amount for a servingman, but probably a hit at James I's profuse creation of knights (Muir). Compare Middleton's *The Phoenix* 4.3.55: 'How's this? am I used like a hundred-pound gentleman?' (Steevens, cited by Furness).

14–15 **worsted-stocking** Silk stockings were very dear; servingmen wore woollen ones.

15 **lily-livered** cowardly.

15 **action-taking** i.e. preferring litigation to fighting.

15–16 **glass-gazing** given to self-admiration, vain.

16 **superserviceable** ready and willing to serve beyond one's duties, even dishonourably (Kent soon calls him a bawd and a pander). Compare 4.5.240–2.

16 **finical** fussily fastidious.

16 **one-trunk-inheriting** possessing only enough things to fill a single trunk.

slave; one that wouldst be a bawd in way of good service, and
art nothing but the composition of a knave, beggar, coward,
pander, and the son and heir of a mongrel bitch, one whom
I will beat into clamorous whining if thou deniest the least   20
syllable of thy addition.

OSWALD Why, what a monstrous fellow art thou, thus to rail on
  one that is neither known of thee nor knows thee!

KENT What a brazen-faced varlet art thou to deny thou knowest
  me! Is it two days since I tripped up thy heels and beat thee   25
  before the king? Draw, you rogue! For though it be night, yet
  the moon shines. I'll make a sop o'th'moonshine of you,
  [*Drawing his sword*] you whoreson cullionly barber-monger,
  draw!

OSWALD Away, I have nothing to do with thee.   30

KENT Draw, you rascal. You come with letters against the king,
  and take Vanity the puppet's part against the royalty of her
  father. Draw, you rogue, or I'll so carbonado your shanks –
  draw, you rascal, come your ways!

OSWALD Help, ho, murder, help!   35

KENT Strike, you slave! Stand, rogue! Stand, you neat slave, strike!

OSWALD Help, ho, murder, murder!

---

19 one] F; *not in* Q   *20 clamorous] Q *corr.*; clamarous Q *uncorr.*; clamours F   20 deniest] F; denie Q   21 thy] F; the
Q   22 Why] F; *not in* Q   23 that is] F; that's Q   23 thee!] thee. Q; thee? F   24 brazen-faced] F; brazen fac't
Q   25 me!] mee, Q; me? F   25 days . . . thee] F; dayes agoe since I beat thee, and tript vp thy heeles Q   26 yet] F; *not
in* Q   27 o'th'] F; of the Q   27 of you] F; a'you, draw Q   28 SD] *After 29,* Rowe; *not in* Q, F   31 come with] F; bring
Q   *33 shanks –] *Rowe*; shankes, Q; shanks, F   36 strike!] strike? Q *corr.*; strike. Q *uncorr.*, F   37 murder, murder!] murther,
murther. F; murther, helpe. Q

---

17 be a bawd . . . service i.e. do anything, no
matter how dishonourable, and consider it good
service.

18 composition compound.

19 heir 'A fine touch! – not merely the *son*, but
the *heir*, inheriting all the mongrel's qualities'
(Kittredge).

21 addition A mark of distinction, something
added to a man's name or coat-of-arms to denote his
rank, title (Onions); here used ironically.

24 varlet rogue, rascal.

27 sop o'th'moonshine Kent threatens to beat
Oswald so badly that he will be worthless except to
soak up moonlight. He may also allude to sopping
up 'eggs in moonshine', a dish of fried eggs and
onions (Nares, cited by Furness).

28 cullionly despicable.

28 barber-monger frequenter of barbershops;
hence, a vain fop.

32 Vanity the puppet's part Vanity as a
proud, self-admiring woman was emblematic,

virtually interchangeable with the figure of
Pride (one of the Seven Deadly Sins). The figure appears often in Renaissance iconography,
though not in any extant Morality plays, as
commentators (following Johnson) have been
misled into believing (Meagher, pp. 252–3).
Kent refers to Gonerill thus because as part of
her costume she wears a hand-mirror (compare
3.2.33–4); but Meagher fails to connect
Gonerill's vanity with her servant Oswald's,
which Kent detests. 'Puppet' is also a 'contemptuous term for a person (usually a woman)'
(*OED* sv *sb* 1, cited by NS). Compare 'poppet'
= darling, pet, or dolled-up woman.

33 carbonado cut crosswise for broiling.

34 come your ways come on, come along; as in
Tro. 3.2.44. Kent tries to get Oswald to fight, but he
comically keeps backing away, refusing the encounter. (Some editors follow Rowe and insert a SD after
36: *Beats him.*)

36 neat elegant, foppish.

Enter EDMOND, CORNWALL, REGAN, GLOUCESTER, *Servants*

EDMOND   How now, what's the matter? Part!

KENT   With you, goodman boy, if you please; come, I'll flesh ye; come on, young master.   40

GLOUCESTER   Weapons? Arms? What's the matter here?

CORNWALL   Keep peace, upon your lives; he dies that strikes again. What is the matter?

REGAN   The messengers from our sister and the king?

CORNWALL   What is your difference – speak!   45

OSWALD   I am scarce in breath, my lord.

KENT   No marvel, you have so bestirred your valour, you cowardly rascal. Nature disclaims in thee: a tailor made thee.

CORNWALL   Thou art a strange fellow – a tailor make a man?

KENT   A tailor, sir, a stone-cutter, or a painter could not have made   50
him so ill, though they had been but two years o'th'trade.

CORNWALL   Speak yet, how grew your quarrel?

OSWALD   This ancient ruffian, sir, whose life I have spared at suit of his grey beard –

KENT   Thou whoreson zed, thou unnecessary letter! My lord, if you   55
will give me leave, I will tread this unbolted villain into mortar
and daub the wall of a jakes with him. Spare my grey beard,
you wagtail?

---

37 SD] F; *Enter Edmond with his rapier drawne, Gloster the Duke and Dutchesse.* Q   38 Part!] Part. F; *not in* Q   39 if] F; and Q   39 ye] F; you Q   43 What is] F; what's Q   44 king?] F; King. Q   45 What is] F; Whats Q   50 A] F; I, a Q   51 they] F; hee Q   51 years] F; houres Q   51 o'th'] o'th F3; oth' F, F2; at the Q   52 SH] F; *Glost.* Q   53 ruffian] F; ruffen Q   *54 grey beard –] *Rowe* (subst.); gray-beard. Q, F   55–6 you will] F; you'l Q   57 wall] F; walles Q

37 SD Since Edmond's name precedes those of the others, who outrank him, he may actually enter first and try to separate Kent and Oswald (who may have drawn his sword by now). Oxford alters the SD accordingly. See collation: in Q, Edmond enters *with his rapier drawne*.

39 **With you** Kent here turns to Edmond, challenging him.

39 **goodman boy** A contemptuous term of address for a presumptuous young man.

39 **flesh** initiate (i.e. into tasting blood, fighting); as in *1H4* 5.4.130.

45 **difference** quarrel.

48 **disclaims in thee** disavows, renounces having any part in you.

48 **a tailor made thee** Referring to Oswald's fancy clothes but hollow character, Kent alludes to the proverb, 'The tailor makes the man' (Tilley T17), as Guiderius does in *Cym.* 4.2.81–3, describing Cloten.

51 **years** Q's 'houres' is a vulgarization;

'Shakespeare knows that art is long' (Greg, *Editorial Problem*, p. 91).

55 **unnecessary letter** The letter *z* is 'unnecessary' because its function is largely taken over by *s*; dictionaries of the time ignored the letter, which is not used in Latin (Muir). As a parasite, Oswald is 'unnecessary'.

56 **unbolted** (1) unsifted (of flour or cement), hence (2) unmitigated, or (3) undiscovered, unexamined; (4) released of fetters or bolts (as a villain should not be); (5) effeminate, impotent (i.e. lacking a 'bolt').

57 **jakes** privy.

58 **wagtail** '(used as a term of contempt) obsequious person' (Onions); compare *OED* sv *sb* 3b, 'contemptuous term for a profligate or inconstant woman'. Oswald is too scared to stand still and, hopping about, resembles the actions of a bird, the wagtail (Kittredge). Kent may also strike out against him again, prompting Cornwall's response.

CORNWALL   Peace, sirrah.
        You beastly knave, know you no reverence?   60
KENT   Yes, sir, but anger hath a privilege.
CORNWALL   Why art thou angry?
KENT   That such a slave as this should wear a sword,
        Who wears no honesty. Such smiling rogues as these,
        Like rats, oft bite the holy cords a-twain,   65
        Which are too intrince t'unloose; smooth every passion
        That in the natures of their lords rebel,
        Being oil to fire, snow to the colder moods,
        Renege, affirm, and turn their halcyon beaks
        With every gall and vary of their masters,   70
        Knowing naught, like dogs, but following.
        A plague upon your epileptic visage!
        Smile you my speeches, as I were a fool?

59–60 Peace … reverence?] F *lineation; one line* Q   **60** know you] F; you haue Q   **61** hath] F; has Q   **64** Who] F; That Q   **65** the holy] F; those Q   **65** a-twain] F; in twaine Q   **66** too intrince] *Capell;* to intrench, Q; t'intrince, F   **66** t'unloose] F; to inloose Q   **68** Being] F; Bring Q   **68** fire] F; stir Q   **68** the] F; their Q   **69** Renege] Reneag Q; Reuenge F   **70** gall] F; gale Q   **71–3** Knowing … fool?] F *lineation; two lines divided* epileptick [*turned over*] / Visage Q   **71** dogs] F; dayes Q   **73** Smile] smoyle Q; Smoile F

61 anger … privilege Tilley L458, citing *John* 4.3.32: 'Impatience hath his privilege' (NS).

63 sword A symbol of manhood.

64 smiling rogues Compare *Ham.* 1.5.105–7, where Hamlet refers to Claudius as 'a smiling damned villain'.

65 rats, oft bite Compare Tilley M135: 'A mouse in time may bite in two a cable' (NS).

65 holy cords i.e. sanctified bonds (of matrimony). 'Kent hints that Oswald is "duteous to the vices" of his mistress' (NS).

65 a-twain in two.

66 too intrince too intertwined, tightly bound (compare 'intrinsicate', *Ant.* 5.2.304, and Stone, pp. 52–3). F's contraction may have been influenced, wrongly, by the contraction later of the preposition; *t'* for the adverb is not normal (*Textual Companion*, p. 534), though it is common for the preposition. Both words could be spelled the same, as they are in Q. (Compare Doran, p. 93, and Duthie, pp. 385–7.) Moreover, 'are' should be elided so that 'too' receives the accent.

66 smooth flatter, humour (Onions).

67 rebel i.e. against reason, which should control the passions.

68 Being Although in NS Duthie withdrew his earlier defence of F, his argument still makes excellent sense. Citing *2H6* 5.2.51–5, he says that 'flatterers *are* oil to the flame of their masters' wrath …

just as when their masters are in, say, a melancholy mood, which is a cold mood, the flatterers are snow to that mood, keep it cold' (pp. 142–3).

69 Renege Deny. Compare 4.5.94–7. Q is clearly right here; F results from Compositor E's misreading copy (Doran, p. 91; compare Duthie, pp. 13–14).

69 halcyon beaks The bird is the kingfisher, which when hung up by the neck or tail could serve as a weathervane. Compare Marlowe's *The Jew of Malta* 1.1.38–9: 'But now how stands the wind? / Into what corner peeres my Halcion's bill?' (Steevens, cited by Furness). Flatterers thus shift with their masters' passions.

70 gall and vary Most editors accept Q's 'gale' and treat the words as hendiadys. Duthie cites *OED*'s reference to 'gall-wind' and retains 'gall', since his is an old-spelling edition (NS adopts 'gale'). Oxford reads 'gall' (= 'a state of mental soreness or irritation', *OED sb*² 2), despite F2's emendation supporting Q (*Textual Companion*, p. 534). The hendiadys may then signify 'varying irritation', a less easy metaphor but not less Shakespearean.

72 epileptic visage 'Oswald pale, and trembling with fright, was yet smiling and trying to put on a look of lofty unconcern' (Muir).

73 Smile you i.e. smile you at.

73 as as if.

Goose, if I had you upon Sarum Plain,
I'd drive ye cackling home to Camelot.   75
CORNWALL   What, art thou mad, old fellow?
GLOUCESTER   How fell you out? Say that.
KENT   No contraries hold more antipathy
    Than I and such a knave.
CORNWALL   Why dost thou call him knave?
    What is his fault?
KENT   His countenance likes me not.   80
CORNWALL   No more perchance does mine, nor his, nor hers.
KENT   Sir, 'tis my occupation to be plain.
    I have seen better faces in my time
    Than stands on any shoulder that I see
    Before me at this instant.
CORNWALL   This is some fellow   85
    Who, having been praised for bluntness, doth affect
    A saucy roughness, and constrains the garb
    Quite from his nature. He cannot flatter, he;
    An honest mind and plain, he must speak truth.
    And they will take it, so; if not, he's plain.   90
    These kind of knaves I know, which in this plainness
    Harbour more craft and more corrupter ends
    Than twenty silly-ducking observants
    That stretch their duties nicely.

---

74 if] F; and Q   **75** drive ye] F; send you Q   **79–80** Why … fault?] F *lineation; one line* Q   **80** What is] F; what's Q   **80** fault?] F; offence. Q   **81** nor … nor] F; or … or Q   **84** Than] Then F; That Q   **85–94** This … nicely.] F *lineation; nine verse lines ending* … praysd / … ruffines, / … nature, / … plaine, / … so, / … know / … craft, / … ducking / … nisely. Q   **85** some] F; a Q   **87** roughness] F; ruffiness Q   **89** An … plain,] F; he must be plaine, Q   ***90** take it,] *Rowe*; take it F; tak't Q   **93** silly-ducking] F; silly ducking Q

74–5 Goose … Camelot Though the passage is variously interpreted, the main sense is clear. Oswald's laughter suggests the cackling of a goose and hence associations with Sarum (= Salisbury) Plain, not far from Winchester, where Camelot may have been located. But it is not certain that geese were, in fact, found on Sarum Plain, or why Shakespeare should make that association. Capell suspected an allusion to 'Winchester goose', i.e. a syphilitic person, but Muir thinks the association must have been largely unconscious and doubts that it would have been picked up by an audience. Compare E. A. Armstrong, *Shakespeare's Imagination*, 1963, pp. 57–8.

80 likes pleases.

86 affect put on, assume.

87–8 constrains … nature i.e. he distorts the style of plain speech from its inherent function, sincerity, and makes it a cloak for craftiness and corrupt ends (92) (Clarke, cited by Furness). In Shakespeare 'garb' = 'style, fashion (of speech or behaviour); never = "fashion in dress"' (NS).

88 his its.

90 And … plain i.e. if people will take it, fine; if not, his excuse is that he's plainspoken.

92 craft craftiness.

92 more corrupter Double comparatives, like double superlatives, are common in Shakespearean and Elizabethan usage.

93 silly-ducking observants obsequious servants who foolishly keep bowing.

94 stretch … nicely strain the exercise of their duties to a fine point.

KENT   Sir, in good faith, in sincere verity,   95
       Under th'allowance of your great aspect,
       Whose influence like the wreath of radiant fire
       On flick'ring Phoebus' front –
CORNWALL   What mean'st by this?
KENT   To go out of my dialect, which you discommend so much. I
       know, sir, I am no flatterer. He that beguiled you in a plain   100
       accent was a plain knave, which for my part I will not be,
       though I should win your displeasure to entreat me to't.
CORNWALL   What was th'offence you gave him?
OSWALD   I never gave him any.
       It pleased the king his master very late   105
       To strike at me upon his misconstruction,
       When he, compact, and flattering his displeasure,
       Tripped me behind; being down, insulted, railed,
       And put upon him such a deal of man
       That worthied him, got praises of the king   110
       For him attempting who was self-subdued,
       And in the fleshment of this dread exploit
       Drew on me here again.

---

95 faith] F; sooth Q   95 in] F; or in Q   96 great] F; graund Q   *98 flick'ring] *Duthie (subst.)*; flitkering Q; flicking F; flickering *Pope*   *98 front –] *Rowe*; front. Q, F   98 mean'st] F; mean'st thou Q   99 dialect] F; dialogue Q   103 What was th'] F; What's the Q   104–6 I . . . misconstruction,] F *lineation; two verse lines divided* maister / Very Q   107 compact,] F; coniunct Q   109 man] F; man, that, Q

95–8 Sir . . . front Kent parodies the style and manner of one of the 'silly-ducking observants', adopting the idiom of an Oswald (or an Osric).
95 sincere verity A deliberate redundancy for 'good faith'.
96 aspect (1) countenance, (2) astral position and influence (in astrology); accent is on the second syllable. Kent's inflated speech compares Cornwall to a powerful planet or star.
97 influence Another astrological term (compare 1.2.110).
98 Phoebus' front The sun's forehead. Phoebus was the sun god.
99 dialect idiom, manner of speaking.
100–1 He . . . knave Kent alludes to the person Cornwall described above, 85–94, and disassociates himself accordingly.
102 though . . . to't Unsatisfactorily explained. Kent probably means that nothing, not even the incentive of Cornwall's further displeasure, could induce him to be the kind of 'plain knave' Cornwall has described.

105 very late most recently.
106   misconstruction   misunderstanding, misconstruing.
107 compact in league with, in cahoots with (the king).
108 being . . . railed i.e. I being down, he insulted and railed at me.
109 put . . . man i.e. struck such an attitude of manliness.
110 That worthied him Either (1) that it made him appear very worthy, (2) that it raised him to honour or distinction (Onions), or (3) that it made a hero of him (NS). It is not clear, as Muir notes, whether the verb derives from the adjective (Abbott), or from the noun 'worthy' = hero (Schmidt), or from Middle English *wurthien* = dignify (Perrett).
111 For . . . subdued 'For attacking a man who offered no resistance' (NS).
112 fleshment 'Excitement resulting from a first success' (Onions). Compare 39 above.
112 dread exploit Oswald speaks ironically.

KENT   None of these rogues and cowards
            But Ajax is their fool.
CORNWALL   Fetch forth the stocks!
            You stubborn, ancient knave, you reverend braggart,   115
            We'll teach you.
KENT   Sir, I am too old to learn:
            Call not your stocks for me. I serve the king,
            On whose employment I was sent to you.
            You shall do small respects, show too bold malice
            Against the grace and person of my master,   120
            Stocking his messenger.
CORNWALL   Fetch forth the stocks!
            As I have life and honour, there shall he sit till noon.
REGAN   Till noon? Till night, my lord, and all night too.
KENT   Why, madam, if I were your father's dog,
            You should not use me so.
REGAN   Sir, being his knave, I will.   125
                    Stocks brought out
CORNWALL   This is a fellow of the selfsame colour
            Our sister speaks of. Come, bring away the stocks.
GLOUCESTER   Let me beseech your grace not to do so.
            The king his master needs must take it ill

113–14 None ... fool.] F *lineation; one line* Q   114 Ajax] F; A'Iax Q   114 Fetch] F; Bring Q   114 stocks!] F; stockes ho? Q   115 ancient] F; ausrent Q *uncorr.;* miscreant Q *corr.*   116–18 Sir ... you.] F *lineation; two lines divided* me, / I Q   116 Sir,] F; *not in* Q   118 employment] F; imployments Q   119 shall] F; should Q   119 respects] F; respect Q   121 Stocking] F; Stobing Q *uncorr.;* Stopping Q *corr.*   121–2 Fetch ... noon.] F *lineation; divided* honour, / There Q   122 sit] F, Q *corr.;* set Q *uncorr.*   124–5 Why ... so.] F *lineation; as prose* Q   125 should] F; could Q   125 SD] F; *after 127, Dyce and most later editors (except Oxford); not in* Q   126 colour] F; nature Q   127 speaks] F; speake Q   128 so.] so, Q, F (F *omits four lines here*)   129–31 The ... restrained.] F *lineation; two lines divided* valued / In Q   129 his master needs] F; *not in* Q

114 Ajax Kent's muttered response arouses Cornwall's fierce outburst because he believes Kent identifies him with the foolish Greek warrior who is easily duped by others (as in *Tro.*) (NS). Kent's pun, intentional or otherwise ('Ajax' – 'a jakes'), does not help matters.

114 stocks An ancient form of punishment for servants. In the fifth Earl of Huntingdon's household, disorderliness or unseemly behaviour towards one's betters was punished first by a spell in the stocks, as recorded in Rawdon Hastings MSS. iv (G. M. Young, *Times Literary Supplement*, 30 Sept. 1949, p. 633; cited by Muir).

115 reverend old. Cornwall is being sarcastic.

117 I ... king Kent reminds Cornwall that he is not his servant, but the king's (and thus should be treated with more consideration).

120 grace and person The position he holds as king and himself personally.

125 should would.

125 being i.e. since you are.

126 colour stripe, complexion.

127 sister i.e. Gonerill. Elizabethans took the marriage ceremony literally, husband and wife becoming 'one flesh'; hence, a sister-in-law was a sister.

127 Come ... stocks Some editors take this as the cue to bring out the stocks and move the previous SD (125) here. But the change is unnecessary; Cornwall sees the stocks at this point and directs them to be brought up.

129–31 The king ... restrained For F's revision and cuts here and at 133, see Textual Analysis, p. 251 below.

That he, so slightly valued in his messenger,   130
Should have him thus restrained.
CORNWALL   I'll answer that.
REGAN   My sister may receive it much more worse
To have her gentleman abused, assaulted.
                    [*Kent is put in the stocks*]
CORNWALL   Come, my lord, away.
                    [*Exeunt all but Gloucester and Kent*]
GLOUCESTER   I am sorry for thee, friend; 'tis the duke's pleasure,   135
Whose disposition all the world well knows
Will not be rubbed nor stopped. I'll entreat for thee.
KENT   Pray do not, sir. I have watched and travelled hard.
Some time I shall sleep out, the rest I'll whistle.
A good man's fortune may grow out at heels.   140
Give you good morrow.
GLOUCESTER   The duke's to blame in this; 'twill be ill taken.   *Exit*
KENT   Good king, that must approve the common saw,
Thou out of heaven's benediction com'st
To the warm sun.   145
Approach, thou beacon to this under globe,
That by thy comfortable beams I may

---

130 he] F; hee's Q   133 gentleman] F; Gentlemen Q   133 assaulted.] F; assalted Q; F *omits one line here*   133 SD] *After
134, Rowe; not in* Q, F   134 SH] F; *not in* Q, *where line is part of Regan's speech*   134 my] F; my good Q   134 SD] *Dyce;
Exit.* F; *not in* Q   *135 duke's] Dukes Q; Duke F   138 Pray] F; Pray you Q   139 out] F; ont Q   142 The ... taken.] Q
lineation; two lines divided this, / 'Twill F   *142 to] Q; too F   142 taken] F; tooke Q   142 SD] F; *not in* Q   143 saw] F,
Q *corr.;* say Q *uncorr.*   144 com'st] F; comest Q

133 SD **Kent ... stocks** '[T]he Morality-play
icon of virtue martyred in the stocks becomes
an icon of social transposition, of the confusion
of moral values' (Salingar, p. 99; compare Mack,
pp. 55–6).
134 **Come ... away** Cornwall addresses
Gloucester who, unhappy about the situation,
remains behind for a few moments.
137 **rubbed** A term from bowls, meaning
impeded or deflected. Kittredge compares *R2*
3.4.3–5.
138 **watched** stayed awake, been up.
140 **A good ... heels** With mordant humour
Kent reflects that the usual metaphor, or saying,
has become reality, for him, being in the stocks
(Furness). Colie compares Tilley H389. Colie compares
Job 13–27.
141 **Give** i.e. may God give.
142 **to blame** to be blamed; but see collation and

compare 1.2.41, where 'too blame' = too
blameworthy.
143 **approve** confirm, prove the truth of.
143 **saw** saying, proverb.
144–5 **Thou ... sun** Proverbial for going from
good to bad (compare Tilley G272, who quotes
Florio: '"Da baiante a ferrante": From bad to
worse, out of gods blessing into the warme sun,
out of the parlor into the kitchin'). Perhaps used
ironically: bad as Gonerill is, Lear is heading for
worse. Muir cites *King Leir* 1154: 'he came from
bad to worse'. Daybreak reminds Kent of the
proverb.
146 **thou beacon** The sun. Its beams may be
'comfortable' (147), i.e. comforting, in so far as
they will provide light for Kent to read
Cordelia's letter, whereas 'the warm sun' (145)
in context suggests less beneficent exposure to
the elements.

Peruse this letter. Nothing almost sees miracles
But misery. I know 'tis from Cordelia,
Who hath most fortunately been informed   150
Of my obscurèd course, and shall find time
For this enormous state, seeking to give
Losses their remedies. All weary and o'er-watched,
Take vantage, heavy eyes, not to behold
This shameful lodging. Fortune, goodnight,   155
Smile once more, turn thy wheel. [*He sleeps*]

2.3 *Enter* EDGAR

EDGAR   I heard myself proclaimed,
              And by the happy hollow of a tree
              Escaped the hunt. No port is free, no place
              That guard and most unusual vigilance
              Does not attend my taking. Whiles I may 'scape   5
              I will preserve myself, and am bethought

---

148 miracles] F; my rackles Q *uncorr.*; my wracke Q *corr.*   **150** most] F, Q *corr.*; not Q *uncorr.*   *151 course, and] Q; course. And F   *152 For] *Rowe*; From Q, F   **152** enormous] F; enormious Q   **153** their] F, Q *corr.*; and Q *uncorr.*   **153** o'er-watched] F; ouerwatch Q   **154** Take] F, Q *corr.*; Late Q *uncorr.*   **156** Smile once more,] F; smile, once more Q   *156 SD] *sleepes* Q; *not in* F   **Act 2, Scene 3   2.3**] *Steevens; not in* Q, F *(see Commentary)*   **1** heard] F; heare Q   **4** unusual] Q; vnusall Q2, F   **5** Does] F; Dost Q   **5** Whiles] F; while Q

148–9 Nothing … misery The most miserable are almost the only ones to witness miracles ('for, when we are in despair, any relief seems miraculous' (Kittredge)).

151–3 and … remedies A famous crux. Many editors follow Jennens and assume that Kent is reading excerpts from Cordelia's letter, or that the passage is corrupt and some words are missing. Perhaps Kent cannot fully make out the contents of the letter since it is not yet light enough (Muir). But such considerations may be irrelevant: 'Who' (150) can be understood as the subject of this clause, too. Rowe's emendation, 'For' for 'From', is simple and easy and makes sense of the lines (*Textual Companion*, p. 515).

152 enormous state monstrous situation, one full of enormities.

153 o'er-watched exhausted, used too much for 'watching'; compare 138 above.

154 Take vantage Take advantage (of your fatigue and fall asleep).

155 shameful lodging i.e. the stocks.

156 turn thy wheel Compare 5.3.164, where

Edmond also refers to Fortune's wheel.

156 SD *He sleeps* The SD, from Q, indicates that Kent remains asleep in the stocks as Edgar enters and gives his soliloquy. Modern editors follow Q, keeping Kent on stage (as he would have been at the Globe) during Edgar's speech. 'The juxtaposition is symbolic, not illusionistic, making a point about two banished men who must disguise themselves and endure humiliation while villains prosper' (D. Bevington, *Action Is Eloquence*, 1984, p. 121).

Act 2, Scene 3

0 SD Although the action is continuous, and probably the Globe stage would not be cleared, Edgar's soliloquy warrants a scene to itself; therefore, I preserve the traditional scene numbering.

1 proclaimed publicly declared (an outlaw).

2 happy opportune.

3 port Compare 2.1.79, where Gloucester orders all ports closed to Edgar.

5 attend my taking stand ready to capture me.

6 am bethought have an idea.

To take the basest and most poorest shape
That ever penury in contempt of man
Brought near to beast. My face I'll grime with filth,
Blanket my loins, elf all my hairs in knots,   10
And with presented nakedness outface
The winds and persecutions of the sky.
The country gives me proof and precedent
Of Bedlam beggars, who with roaring voices
Strike in their numbed and mortifièd arms,   15
Pins, wooden pricks, nails, sprigs of rosemary;
And with this horrible object, from low farms,
Poor pelting villages, sheep-cotes, and mills,
Sometimes with lunatic bans, sometime with prayers,
Enforce their charity. 'Poor Turlygod! Poor Tom!'   20
That's something yet: Edgar I nothing am.   *Exit*

---

10 elf] F; else Q   10 hairs in] F; haire with Q   12 winds] F; wind Q   12 persecutions] F; persecution Q   15 numbed
... arms] F; numb'd and mortified bare armes Q *corr.*; numb'd mortified bare armes Q *uncorr.*   16 Pins] F, Q *corr.*; Pies Q
uncorr.   16 wooden pricks] wodden prickes Q; Wodden-prickes F   17 from] F, Q *corr.*, Q2; frame Q *uncorr.*   17 farms]
F; seruice Q   *18 sheep-cotes] sheep-coates Q; Sheeps-Coates F   19 Sometimes] F; Sometime Q   20 Turlygod] F, Q
corr., Q2; *Tuelygod* Q *uncorr.*

8 in contempt of man holding humanity in
contempt.
  10 elf twist, tangle into 'elflocks' (*Rom.* 1.4.90).
  11 presented exposed, exhibited.
  11 outface brave, confront. As Edgar utters
these lines, he strips off his clothes and decorates
himself accordingly. The action is moreover significant if Edgar throws off conspicuously rich attire
(as a nobleman's son) to become 'nothing'. 'On this
pivot, Edgar's inward journey turns: he gives up,
not only clothes and person, but also a way of life,
from best to worst, and the peripety is evidently
steep' (Rosenberg, p. 151).
  13 proof example.
  14 Bedlam beggars 'Abram men', or vagabonds, who feigned madness or who actually
were discharged from Bedlam (i.e. Bethlehem
Hospital, the lunatic asylum in London) and
licensed to beg. Furness cites Awdeley's
Fraternitye of Vacabondes (1565): 'An Abraham
man is he that walketh bare armed, and bare
legged, and fayneth hym selfe mad, and caryeth a
packe of wool, or a stycke with baken on it, or such
lyke toy, and nameth himself poore Tom.' Furness
also quotes a longer passage adapted from
Harman's *Caueat or Warening for Commen*

Cvrsetors (1567) in Dekker's *Belman of London*
(1608), which gives a more detailed description
corroborating Shakespeare's.
  15 numbed i.e. with cold.
  15 mortifièd deadened to pain. See collation.
Duthie accepts the Q reading, which 'adds an effective touch to the picture' (it also helps the metre),
and explains F's omission as compositor oversight
(p. 175). But accenting *-ed* in 'mortified' makes the
metre regular.
  16 pricks skewers.
  17 object spectacle.
  17 low lowly, humble.
  18 pelting paltry, mean.
  19 bans curses.
  20 Turlygod Unexplained. Oxford prefers Q
uncorr. 'Tuelygod' and suggests some possible
derivations for the word (*Textual Companion*,
pp. 515–16). See collation.
  21 That's ... am i.e. Poor Tom is at least something, however base and despicable; I renounce my
identity as Edgar, who is doomed in any case. The
rhyme, 'Tom' – 'am', is probably dialectal
(Kökeritz, p. 224; compare Cercignani, pp. 113–
14); Edgar doubtless means to disguise his voice
as well as his person.

2.4 *Enter* LEAR, FOOL, *and* GENTLEMAN

LEAR   'Tis strange that they should so depart from home
         And not send back my messenger.
GENTLEMAN   As I learned,
         The night before there was no purpose in them
         Of this remove.
KENT   [*Waking*]   Hail to thee, noble master.
LEAR   Ha!   5
         Mak'st thou this shame thy pastime?
KENT   No, my lord.
FOOL   Ha, ha, he wears cruel garters. Horses are tied by the heads,
         dogs and bears by th'neck, monkeys by th'loins, and men by
         th'legs: when a man's overlusty at legs, then he wears wooden
         nether-stocks.   10
LEAR   What's he that hath so much thy place mistook
         To set thee here?
KENT   It is both he and she,
         Your son and daughter.
LEAR   No.
KENT   Yes.   15
LEAR   No, I say.
KENT   I say, yea.

Act 2, Scene 4   2.4] *Steevens; not in* Q, F   0 SD] F; *Enter King.* Q   1 home] F; *hence* Q   *2 messenger*] Q; Messengers
F   2 SH] F; *Knight.* Q   2–4 As . . . remove.] F; *two lines divided* was / No Q   3 in them] F; *not in* Q   4 this] F; his Q   4
SD] *Staunton; not in* Q, F   5–6 Ha! . . . pastime] *Steevens's lineation; one line* Q, F   5 Ha!] F; How, Q   6 thy] Q; ahy
F   6 KENT No, my lord.] F; *not in* Q   7–10 Ha, ha . . . nether-stocks.] *As prose* F; *five verse lines ending* . . . garters, /
. . . beares / . . . men / . . . at legs, / . . . neatherstockes Q   7 he] F; looke he Q   7 heads] F; heeles Q   8 by th'neck] F;
Byt'h necke Q   8 by th'loins] Q; bit'h loynes Q   8–9 by th'legs:] F; Byt'h legges, Q   *9 man's] mans Q; man F   9
wooden] Q; wodden F   11–12 What's . . . here?] *Rowe's lineation; three lines ending* . . . he, / . . . mistooke / . . . heere? F; *as
prose* Q   12–13 It . . . daughter.] F; *one line* Q   17 yea.] F *omits two half-lines here*

Act 2, Scene 4

0 SD The action may be regarded as continuous
from 2.2 (see at 2.2.156 SD n.). Lear and the others at
first do not see Kent in the stocks; he awakens at 4.

0 SD GENTLEMAN Q designates this speaker as
Knight, a member of Lear's reduced entourage (see
56 below). The speech headings are simply alternative appellations for the same small-part actors
(Duthie, p. 83).

1 they i.e. Regan and Cornwall.

2 messenger i.e. Kent.

4 remove change of residence.

6 pastime amusement; i.e. is this your idea of a
joke?

7 cruel garters The Fool refers of course to the

stocks, with a pun on 'crewel', thin worsted material. Compare *Two Angry Women of Abington* (1599):
'heele haue / His Cruel garters crosse about the
knee' (Muir).

9 overlusty at legs too eager to use his legs (for
running away from service or indenture); with a
quibble on the deadly sin of lust.

10 nether-stocks stockings. Upper-stocks were
breeches (Kittredge).

11 place (1) rank (as king's messenger), (2)
proper place for you to be (Hunter).

12 To As to.

13 son son-in-law; compare 2.2.127 n.

14–19 LEAR . . . swear ay See Textual Analysis,
p. 252 below.

LEAR   By Jupiter, I swear no.

KENT   By Juno, I swear ay.

LEAR   They durst not do't:
They could not, would not do't. 'Tis worse than murder,   20
To do upon respect such violent outrage.
Resolve me with all modest haste which way
Thou mightst deserve or they impose this usage,
Coming from us.

KENT   My lord, when at their home
I did commend your highness' letters to them,   25
Ere I was risen from the place that showed
My duty kneeling, came there a reeking post,
Stewed in his haste, half breathless, panting forth
From Gonerill, his mistress, salutations;
Delivered letters spite of intermission,   30
Which presently they read. On those contents
They summoned up their meiny, straight took horse,
Commanded me to follow and attend
The leisure of their answer, gave me cold looks;
And meeting here the other messenger,   35
Whose welcome I perceived had poisoned mine –
Being the very fellow which of late
Displayed so saucily against your highness –
Having more man than wit about me, drew.
He raised the house with loud and coward cries.   40
Your son and daughter found this trespass worth
The shame which here it suffers.

---

19 KENT By . . . ay.] F; *not in* Q   20 could not, would] F; would not, could Q   23 mightst] F; may'st Q   23 impose] F; purpose Q   26 showed] shewed Q, F   *28 panting] Q; painting F   31 those] F; whose Q   32 meiny] F; men Q   33–4 Commanded . . . looks;] F; *divided* leasure / Of Q   37 which] F; that Q

21 **upon respect** Either (1) against proper regard and deference (due to a king's messenger), or (2) deliberately, upon consideration (compare *MV* 1.1.74; *John* 3.4.90).
22 **Resolve me** i.e. free me from uncertainty or ignorance, satisfy, inform (Schmidt).
22 **modest** moderate.
24 **us** The royal plural.
25 **commend** deliver.
27 **reeking** steaming, sweating.
28 **panting** Duthie, p. 176, rightly suspects a minim misreading of manuscript copy. Oxford retains

F 'painting', defended in *Textual Companion*, p. 534.
30 **spite of intermission** in spite of interrupting me. Note that Cornwall and Regan not only permit the interruption, they extend it by reading the letters Oswald delivers.
31 **presently** immediately.
32 **meiny** body of retainers (Onions).
38 **Displayed** Acted, exhibited himself.
39 **more man than wit** more manliness or courage than sense.
39 **drew** i.e. his sword.
40 **raised** woke up.

FOOL   Winter's not gone yet, if the wild geese fly that way.
        Fathers that wear rags
           Do make their children blind,   45
        But fathers that bear bags
           Shall see their children kind.
        Fortune, that arrant whore,
        Ne'er turns the key to th'poor.
But for all this, thou shalt have as many dolours for thy   50
daughters as thou canst tell in a year.

LEAR   O how this mother swells up toward my heart!
    Hysterica passio! Down, thou climbing sorrow,
    Thy element's below. Where is this daughter?

KENT   With the earl, sir, here within.

LEAR   Follow me not, stay here.   55

                              Exit

GENTLEMAN   Made you no more offence but what you speak of?

KENT   None.
    How chance the king comes with so small a number?

FOOL   And thou hadst been set i'th'stocks for that question,
    thou'dst well deserved it.   60

KENT   Why, fool?

43–51 FOOL Winter's ... year.] F; *not in* Q   43 wild] F2; wil'd F   44–9 Fathers ... poor.] *Pope's lineation; three lines ending ... blind, / ... kind. / ... poore.* F   *53 Hysterica] F4; *Historica* Q, F, F2; *Hystorica* F3   55 here] F; *not in* Q   55 stay here.] F; stay there? Q   55 SD] F; *not in* Q   56 SH] F; *Knight.* Q   56 Made ... of?] *One line* Q; *two lines divided* offence, / But F   56 but] F; then Q   57 None] F; No Q (*as part of 53*)   58 the] Q; the the F   58 number]F; traine Q   59 And] F, Q; If Q2   59 i'th'] F; in the Q   60 thou'dst] F; thou ha'dst Q

43–51 FOOL ... year See Textual Analysis, p. 263 below, for F addition.

43 Winter's ... way i.e. we're in for more trouble (bad weather), judging from these portents.

43 wild geese A possible allusion to Sir John and Lady Grace Wildgoose? See p. 8 above.

44–9 Fathers ... poor Oxford inserts SD *Sings* before these lines (as later at 71). Possibly the verses were sung, but neither Q nor F indicates this, they do not sound like traditional ballad material (Hunter, p. 340), and actors often speak the lines, though in sing-song fashion.

45 blind i.e. to their father's needs.

46 bags money bags.

49 turns the key opens the door (as a prostitute would, admitting someone to her favours).

50 dolours (1) griefs, (2) dollars (from German *thaler*, a silver coin first struck in 1515 and worth about three marks, or about 15 pence).

50 for on account of, owing to (Muir).

51 tell (1) count, (2) relate.

52 mother hysteria. Compare 114 below. Richard Mainy, mentioned by Harsnett, suffered from the mother, also known as *Passio Hysterica*, which Harsnett describes as a disease that 'riseth ... of a wind in the bottome of the belly, and proceeding with a great swelling, causeth a very painfull colicke in the stomack, and an extraordinary giddiness in the head' (NS, citing Muir, 'Samuel Harsnett and *King Lear*', *RES* 2 (1951), 14).

53 Hysterica passio Hysteria, or the 'mother' (see 52 n.). In his chapter on 'The development of Lear's madness', Hoeniger traces the medical history of the illness, its symptoms, and Shakespeare's borrowing from Harsnett.

54 element sphere, place; 'a visceral symbol of the breakdown in hierarchy, when the lower elements climb up to threaten or destroy the superior ones' (Hunter).

58 How chance How comes it.

FOOL   We'll set thee to school to an ant, to teach thee there's no
labouring i'th'winter. All that follow their noses are led by their
eyes but blind men, and there's not a nose among twenty but
can smell him that's stinking. Let go thy hold when a great   65
wheel runs down a hill, lest it break thy neck with following.
But the great one that goes upward, let him draw thee after.
When a wise man gives thee better counsel, give me mine
again; I would have none but knaves follow it, since a fool gives
it.   70

That sir which serves and seeks for gain
    And follows but for form,
Will pack when it begins to rain
    And leave thee in the storm.
But I will tarry, the fool will stay,   75
    And let the wise man fly;
The knave turns fool that runs away,
    The fool no knave, perdy.

KENT   Where learned you this, fool?

FOOL   Not i'th'stocks, fool.   80

Enter LEAR *and* GLOUCESTER

LEAR   Deny to speak with me? They are sick, they are weary,

63 i'th'] F; in the Q   64 twenty] F; a 100. Q   *65 hold] Q; hold, F   66 following.] F; following it, Q   67 upward] F;
vp the hill Q   68 wise man] Q; wiseman F   68 gives] F *corr.*, Q; giue F *uncorr.*   68 counsel,] Q, F *uncorr.*; counsell F
corr.   *69 have] Q; hause F   71 which] F; *that* Q   71 and seeks] F; *not in* Q   73 begins] F; begin Q   76 wise man]
Q; wiseman F   80 i'th'] F; in the Q   80 fool] F; *not in* Q   *80 SD] As in* Q; *after 78* F   81 Deny ... weary,] *One line*
Q; *two lines divided* me? / They F   81 They are ... they are] F; th'are ... th'are Q

62–3 **We'll ... winter** The Fool alludes to the
proverbial ant, mentioned by Aesop, gathering its
food in harvest time (i.e. during times of plenty),
not in winter. Compare Prov. 6.6, 30.25 (cited by
Noble, NS, Shaheen). As he falls from prosperity,
Lear offers less attraction to hangers-on, as Kent
ought to realize. Even a blind man, the Fool continues, can detect someone's decaying fortunes
('him that's stinking' (65)).

64 **twenty** i.e. twenty blind men.

65–6 **great wheel** Compare *Ham.* 3.3.17–22,
where Rosencrantz uses the image similarly.

71–2 **That ... form** Compare *Oth.* 1.1.49–55:
Iago describes himself to Roderigo as one of those
self-serving individuals, 'throwing but shows of
service on their lords'.

71 **sir** man.

73 **pack** pack up and leave.

75–8 **But ... perdy** The Fool plays on different
senses of 'fool', 'wise man', and 'knave', using them

both ironically and straightforwardly. In one sense
it is mere foolishness for anyone to hang on to the
'great wheel' while it rolls down-hill; 'The better
part of valour is discretion', as Falstaff says (*1H4*
5.4.120). This is one kind of wisdom. Against it the
Fool posits absolute fidelity – adversity and self-
interest notwithstanding. The paradox that concludes the lines resolves itself thus: the knave is
foolish, finally, for running away and exposing his
true colours, and he is foolish in any higher moral
sense; the loyal fool – whatever else he may be – is at
least no knave, i.e. guilty of disloyalty and gross self-
interest.

78 **perdy** by God (from French *par Dieu*).

81 **Deny** Refuse.

81–2 **They ... they ... They** The pronouns
perhaps are stressed, as Lear may be sardonic;
he, after all, has 'travelled twice as far, wearily,
unfed, sickening in mind and body' (Rosenberg,
p. 157).

> They have travelled all the night? Mere fetches,
> The images of revolt and flying off.
> Fetch me a better answer.

GLOUCESTER   My dear lord,
> You know the fiery quality of the duke,   85
> How unremovable and fixed he is
> In his own course.

LEAR   Vengeance, plague, death, confusion!
> 'Fiery'? What 'quality'? Why Gloucester, Gloucester,
> I'd speak with the Duke of Cornwall and his wife.   90

GLOUCESTER   Well, my good lord, I have informed them so.

LEAR   'Informed them'? Dost thou understand me, man?

GLOUCESTER   Ay, my good lord.

LEAR   The king would speak with Cornwall, the dear father
> Would with his daughter speak! Commands – tends –
>   service!   95
> Are they 'informed' of this? My breath and blood!
> 'Fiery'? The 'fiery duke'? Tell the hot duke that –
> No, but not yet; maybe he is not well:
> Infirmity doth still neglect all office

---

82 have travelled all the] F; *traueled hard to* Q   **82** fetches,] F *corr.;* fetches F *uncorr.;* Iustice, Q   **83** The] F; I the Q   **84–90** My ... wife.] F; *as prose* Q   **88** plague, death] F; death, plague Q   **89** 'Fiery'? What 'quality'?] F; What fierie quality, Q   **91–2** Well ... man?] F; *not in* Q   **94** The ... father] *As in* Q; *two lines divided:* Cornwall, / The F   **94** father] F, Q *corr.;* fate Q *uncorr.*   **95** his] F, Q *corr.;* the Q *uncorr.*   **95** Commands – tends – service!] *This edn;* commands, tends, service. F; come and tends seruise, Q *uncorr.;* commands her seruice, Q *corr.*   **96** Are ... blood!] F; *not in* Q   **97** 'Fiery'? The 'fiery duke'?] F; The fierie Duke, Q *uncorr.;* Fierie duke Q *corr.*   **97** that –] F; that *Lear*, Q   **98** No] F, Q *corr.;* Mo Q *uncorr.*   **99–102** Infirmity ... forbear,] F; *three lines ending* ... health / ... oprest / ... forbeare, Q

---

82 fetches (1) contrivances, dodges, tricks, (2) (an allusion to) the nautical manoeuvre of 'tacking', by which a vessel sails indirectly to windward by alternating between two oblique courses, or 'tacks'. Milton uses a similar image to describe Satan's approach to Eve in the Garden of Eden (*Paradise Lost*, IX.510 ff.).

83 images ... off Lear sees in their refusal to see him the sign or symbol of serious disobedience, tantamount to 'revolt' and desertion, the breakdown of order.

85 quality character, disposition.

91–2 GLOUCESTER ... man See Textual Analysis, pp. 263–4 below, for F's addition here and at 96.

95 Commands – tends – service See collation. Q corr. is generally regarded as a proof-corrector's guess carried over into Q2, since 'tends' could not be a misreading of 'her'. Q uncorr., 'come and tends seruise', is possibly a misreading of what was in the original manuscript, which F may recover: 'tends',

an aphetic form of 'attends' = waits for. (See Greg, *Variants*, pp. 161–2; Duthie, pp. 143–4; but Duthie in NS adopts the Q corr. reading, withdrawing his earlier note.) Hunter suggests that 'commands true seruise', or something like it, may have been in the copy for Q, but he follows F.

97 'Fiery'? The 'fiery duke'? See collation. Again, the Q corrector erred and F (which restores or adds 96) may reflect the original wording (Greg, *Variants*, p. 162). Blayney, however, conjectures that in Q corr. the line, with punctuation emended, should have read: 'Fierie? the Duke? Tell the hot Duke that *Lear* – '; he then explains how the compositor might have failed to make corrections the proofreader had marked. He conjectures, further, that the second 'fiery?' was retained in F through faulty proof-correction or compositor error (pp. 245–6).

97 hot i.e. hot-tempered. Lear plays on 'fiery'.

99–100 Infirmity ... bound i.e. illness invariably makes us neglect duties which, when well, we

Whereto our health is bound. We are not ourselves   100
When nature, being oppressed, commands the mind
To suffer with the body. I'll forbear,
And am fallen out with my more headier will,
To take the indisposed and sickly fit
For the sound man. – Death on my state! Wherefore   105
Should he sit here? This act persuades me
That this remotion of the duke and her
Is practice only. Give me my servant forth.
Go tell the duke and's wife I'd speak with them,
Now, presently: bid them come forth and hear me,   110
Or at their chamber door I'll beat the drum
Till it cry sleep to death.

GLOUCESTER   I would have all well betwixt you.   *Exit*

LEAR   Oh me, my heart! My rising heart! But down.

FOOL   Cry to it, nuncle, as the cockney did to the eels when she put   115
’em i'th'paste alive; she knapped ’em o'th'coxcombs with a stick
and cried, 'Down, wantons, down!' 'Twas her brother that in
pure kindness to his horse buttered his hay.

Enter CORNWALL, REGAN, GLOUCESTER, [*and*] *Servants*

LEAR   Good morrow to you both.

---

101 commands] F; Cõmand Q   104–7 To … her] F; *three lines ending* … man, / … here? / … & her [*turned under*] Q   109 Go] F; *not in* Q   109 I'd] Il'd F; Ile Q   113 SD] F; *not in* Q   114 Oh … down.] F; O my heart, my heart. Q   115 cockney] F; Coknay Q *uncorr.*; Cokney Q *corr.*   116 ’em i'th'] F; vm it'h Q   116 paste] F; past Q *uncorr.*; pâst Q *corr.*   116 knapped ’em o'th'] F; rapt vm ath Q   118 SD] F; *Enter Duke and Regan.* Q

are obliged to perform.

100–2 We … body Compare 3.4.11–14, where Lear also notes psychosomatic effects.

102–5 I'll … man i.e. I'll desist, for I am upset that my violent impulse ('will') mistook the unhealthy condition for the well man. But this rationalization and the calm it induces are short-lived, as Lear catches sight again of Kent in the stocks and is reminded of the insult it represents.

105 state royal power.

107 remotion keeping aloof or remote; as in *Tim.* 4.3.342. But Lear may refer to Cornwall and Regan's removal from their home to Gloucester's (Malone, cited by Furness).

108 practice craft, trickery; as at 2.1.72.

109 and's and his.

110 presently immediately, at once.

112 Till … death i.e. till sleep is destroyed by the noise. Muir compares *Mac.* 2.2.39.

114 Oh … down A further symptom, or

aggravation, of the 'mother', *hysterica passio*; compare 52–3 above and n.

115–18 Cry … hay NS identifies two examples here of foolish tender-heartedness relevant to Lear's earlier dealings with his daughters: (1) the cockney cook who could not bear to kill eels before baking them in a pie, and when they tried to wriggle out, she could only rap them on the head and cry, 'Down'; (2) her brother, who thought he was favouring his horse by buttering its hay but actually was doing the opposite (horses dislike grease). Now that Lear's heart distresses him by 'rising', he is as ludicrous as the cockney crying 'Down!' For possible borrowing from or allusion to Lyly's *Euphues*, see Muir.

116 coxcombs heads.

117 wantons playful, frisky creatures.

118 SD Cornwall and Regan may be in night gowns, or they may be fully clothed, giving the lie to their 'social excuse' (Rosenberg pp. 161–2). But

CORNWALL   Hail to your grace.

                    Kent here set at liberty

REGAN I am glad to see your highness.   120

LEAR   Regan, I think you are. I know what reason
                 I have to think so. If thou shouldst not be glad,
                 I would divorce me from thy mother's tomb,
                 Sepulch'ring an adultress. [*To Kent*] O are you free?
                 Some other time for that. Belovèd Regan,   125
                 Thy sister's naught. Oh Regan, she hath tied
                 Sharp-toothed unkindness, like a vulture here –
                 I can scarce speak to thee – thou'lt not believe
                 With how depraved a quality – oh Regan!

REGAN I pray you, sir, take patience. I have hope   130
                 You less know how to value her desert
                 Than she to scant her duty.

LEAR   Say? How is that?

REGAN I cannot think my sister in the least
                 Would fail her obligation. If, sir, perchance
                 She have restrained the riots of your followers,   135
                 'Tis on such ground and to such wholesome end
                 As clears her from all blame.

LEAR   My curses on her.

REGAN O sir, you are old,
                 Nature in you stands on the very verge
                 Of his confine. You should be ruled and led   140

---

119 SD] F; *not in* Q   *121 you] Q; your F   123 divorce] F, Q *corr.;* deuose Q *uncorr.*   *123 mother's] mothers Q;
Mother F   123 tomb,] F; fruit, Q *uncorr.;* tombe Q *corr.*   124 SD] *Rowe; not in* Q, F   124 O] F; yea Q   126 sister's] F;
sister is Q   127 here] F; heare Q   128 thou'lt] F; thout Q   129 With] F; Of Q   129 depraved] F; deptoued Q *uncorr.;*
depriued Q *corr.*   130 you] F; *not in* Q   132 scant] F; slacke Q   132–7 Say? ... blame.] F; *not in* Q   139–43 Nature
... return;] F *lineation; four lines ending* ... confine, ['fine' *turned over*] / ... discretion, / ... your selfe, / ... returne,
Q   139 in] F; on Q   140 his] F, *Oxford;* her Q, *Duthie*

whatever Regan wears, she is 'gorgeous' (261).
    124 Sepulch'ring Entombing.
    126 naught wicked.
    126–9 Oh ... Regan The dashes (where F uses
commas or, at 129, a period) emphasize the gasping
cadences that Lear's overwrought condition
produces.
    126–7 tied ... here The image of a vulture
gnawing at Lear's innards derives from the torture
of Prometheus, familiar to Shakespeare's contemporaries. Harsnett mentions it, as Muir notes, along
with Ixion's wheel (compare 4.6.44).

129 quality nature, disposition.
    130 take patience Standard Renaissance coun-
sel. Compare 1.4.217 and n.
    130–2 I ... duty i.e. I hope you are less able to
estimate her merit than she is capable of slighting her
duty. The double negative, 'less know' and 'scant',
makes the syntax difficult, but the sense is clear.
    132–7 LEAR ... blame On F's addition, see
Textual Analysis, p. 264 below.
    135 She have i.e. she may have.
    135 riots carousals.
    140 his confine its limit, boundary area.

By some discretion that discerns your state
Better than you yourself. Therefore I pray you
That to our sister you do make return;
Say you have wronged her.

LEAR   Ask her forgiveness?
Do you but mark how this becomes the house?   145
[*Kneels*] 'Dear daughter, I confess that I am old;
Age is unnecessary: on my knees I beg
That you'll vouchsafe me raiment, bed, and food.'

REGAN   Good sir, no more: these are unsightly tricks.
Return you to my sister.

LEAR [*Rising*]   Never, Regan.   150
She hath abated me of half my train,
Looked black upon me, struck me with her tongue
Most serpent-like upon the very heart.
All the stored vengeances of heaven fall
On her ingrateful top! Strike her young bones,   155
You taking airs, with lameness.

CORNWALL   Fie, sir, fie.

LEAR You nimble lightnings, dart your blinding flames
Into her scornful eyes! Infect her beauty,
You fen-sucked fogs, drawn by the powerful sun

---

142 pray you] F; pray Q   144 her.] F; her Sir? Q   145 but] F; *not in* Q   146 SD] *Hanmer (subst.); after 147, Johnson; not in* Q, F   150 SD] *Collier; not in* Q, F   150 Never] F; No Q   154–6 All . . . lameness.] F; *two lines divided* top, [*turned over*] / Strike Q   156 Fie, sir, fie.] F; Fie fie sir. Q   157 SH] F; *not in* Q, *but line indented*   159 fen-sucked] F; Fen suckt Q

141 discretion i.e. a discreet person, the abstract for the concrete (Furness, who compares 3.4.26, 'houseless poverty').

141 state mental and physical condition; with a possible ironic play upon 'power, royalty' (Hunter).

144 Ask her forgiveness? Lear is stunned by Regan's response.

145 house Either (1) family, or (2) royal line.

146–8 Dear . . . food Deliberate bathos. Lear is hurt and angry but still has enough wit left for sarcasm.

147 Age is unnecessary Lear aptly summarizes Gonerill's and Regan's Darwinian outlook, in which survival of the fittest rules and the elderly are superfluous (compare Heilman, p. 143).

148 vouchsafe grant in condescension (Schmidt).

149 tricks i.e. rhetorical devices.

151 abated deprived.

155 top head.

155 young bones unborn child. Compare *King Leir* 844–7: Leir tries to excuse Gonorill's 'tutchy' behaviour by saying 'she breeds young bones'. Cursing Gonerill's unborn child is appropriate in the context of 'ingrateful top': Lear is obsessed with filial ingratitude. Compare 1.4.230–44, where Lear similarly curses Gonerill and a child she might bear, which he hopes will be deformed and torment her as she torments him. In both contexts, the serpent image occurs. But 'young bones' may refer to Gonerill herself; compare Gascoigne's *Supposes* 4.2.4: 'A rope stretche your yong bones', referring to a young man (Perrett, pp. 275–6).

156 taking airs blasting, pernicious vapours.

158–9 Infect . . . sun Noxious vapours produced by the sun's rays upon swampy fens were, like 'taking airs' (156), thought to be infectious.

	To fall and blister.	160
REGAN	O the blessed gods! So will you wish on me	
	When the rash mood is on.	
LEAR	No, Regan, thou shalt never have my curse.	
	Thy tender-hefted nature shall not give	
	Thee o'er to harshness. Her eyes are fierce, but thine	165
	Do comfort and not burn. 'Tis not in thee	
	To grudge my pleasures, to cut off my train,	
	To bandy hasty words, to scant my sizes,	
	And in conclusion, to oppose the bolt	
	Against my coming in. Thou better know'st	170
	The offices of nature, bond of childhood,	
	Effects of courtesy, dues of gratitude.	
	Thy half o'th'kingdom hast thou not forgot	
	Wherein I thee endowed.	
REGAN	Good sir, to th'purpose.	
LEAR	Who put my man i'th'stocks?	

Tucket within

CORNWALL	What trumpet's that?	175
REGAN	I know't, my sister's. This approves her letter	
	That she would soon be here.	

---

160 blister] F; blast her pride Q; blister her *Muir*   161–2 O … on.] Q *lineation; divided* Gods! / So F   162 mood is on.] F; mood – Q   164–7 Thy … train,] F *lineation; three lines ending* … or'e / … burne [*turned over*] / … traine, [*turned under*] Q   164 Thy tender-hefted] F; The tĕder hested Q   170 know'st] F; knowest Q   173 o'th'] F; of the Q   *175 SD *Tucket within*] Collier; *after 174* F; *not in* Q   176 letter] F; letters Q

160 fall and blister i.e. the action of the fogs and their effect. Furness compares *Temp.* 1.2.323–4: 'A south-west blow on ye, / And blister you all o'er!' The intransitive verbs have led editors to various emendations, unnecessarily, since F makes sense as it stands.

164 tender–hefted 'A heft or haft is a handle, and a nature tender-hefted is one which is set in a tender handle or delicate bodily frame' (Wright, cited by Furness); hence 'womanly, gentle' (Muir). Note Regan's differences from Gonerill: ' … her particular style of dress, her more feminine mode of offering tenderness to Lear, her kind manner toward Gloster, and, probably, Edmund, have so far in the text masked her capacity for hurt and hate … In the theatre she has been most effective – partly because it contrasts her with Goneril – when she has seemed sweet; in fact bittersweet, emasculating Lear with an insistent, tender concern' (Rosenberg, pp. 162–3).

168 bandy Compare 1.4.72 and n.

168 scant my sizes reduce my allowances. Compare 'sizar' = 'a poor scholar who used to obtain allowances from the college butteryhatch' (Muir).

169 oppose set over against, i.e. to lock. Compare *Tim.* 3.4.79: 'What, are my doors oppos'd against my passage?' Of course, this is exaggerated; Gonerill did not lock Lear out, although later Regan (297), seconded by Cornwall (301), will order Gloucester's doors shut up against Lear and his followers.

171 offices of nature duties that nature expects us to fulfil; specifically those relating to filial 'bonds'.

172 Effects Manifestations.

174 to th'purpose i.e. get to the point.

175 Who … stocks Lear repeats the question (181) and does not receive an answer until his third demand (191).

175 SD *Tucket within* See 2.1.76 SD n.

176 approves confirms.

Enter OSWALD

Is your lady come?

LEAR This is a slave whose easy-borrowed pride
　　　Dwells in the sickly grace of her he follows.
　　　Out, varlet, from my sight!

CORNWALL　　　　　　　What means your grace?　　　　180

Enter GONERILL

LEAR Who stocked my servant? Regan, I have good hope
　　　Thou didst not know on't. Who comes here? O heavens!
　　　If you do love old men, if your sweet sway
　　　Allow obedience, if you yourselves are old,
　　　Make it your cause; send down and take my part.　　185
　　　[*To Gonerill*] Art not ashamed to look upon this beard?
　　　O Regan, will you take her by the hand?

GONERILL　Why not by th'hand, sir? How have I offended?
　　　All's not offence that indiscretion finds,
　　　And dotage terms so.

LEAR　　　　　　　O sides, you are too tough!　　　　190

---

177 SD] *Dyce; after* that? (*175*) Q; *after* Stockes? (*175*) F 179 sickly] F3; fickly F, F2; fickle Q 179 her he] F; her a Q *uncorr.;* her, a Q *corr.* 180 varlet] F, Q *corr.;* varlot Q *uncorr.* 180 SD] F, Q; *after* on't (*182*) *Johnson, Duthie, and most later editors* 181 SH] F; *Gon.* Q 181 stocked] F; struck Q 182 Thou . . . heavens!] *Pope's lineation; two lines divided* ant. / *Lear.* Who Q; *two lines divided* on't. / Who F 182 on't] F; ant Q 183–5 If . . . part.]. F *lineation; lines end* . . . allow / . . . cause, / . . . part, Q 183 your] F; you Q 184 you] F; *not in* Q 186 SD] *Johnson; not in* Q, F 187 will you] F; wilt thou Q 188 by th'] F; by the Q

178 easy-borrowed Either (1) cool, derived; (2) easily assumed. Most editors follow Theobald and insert a hyphen, as Muir does, though he questions it and thinks 'easy' may mean 'coolly-impudent'.

179 sickly See collation. The copy for F corrected Q, most likely, but the compositor got the wrong ligature, probably through foul-case error. NS and Oxford reject 'fickle' on semantic grounds as well: the dig at Gonerill could result in sympathy for Oswald, which is certainly not desirable in this or any other context. By contrast, 'sickly grace' = diseased grace, a possible oxymoron, which could also mean 'causing sickness or ill health' (*Textual Companion*, p. 534).

180 varlet rogue, rascal.

180 SD *Enter* GONERILL. Many editors follow Johnson and move Gonerill's entrance to 182 after 'here', but in the growing tumult, Lear may not at first see her. On the differences between Q and F, see Textual Analysis, p. 63 above.

182 on't of it.

184 Allow Sanction, approve of.

185 it i.e. what is due to parents and the elderly.

186 Art Art thou.

186 beard Symbol of aged reverence.

187 O . . . hand ' . . . with four quick shocks – his sudden recall of the outrage upon his servant, the sound of a trumpet, the sight of Oswald, the sight of Goneril – [Lear] is brought to a stand and to face the realities arrayed against him. This must be made very plain to us. On the one side stand Goneril and Regan and Cornwall in all authority. The perplexed Gloucester stands a little apart. On the other side is Lear, the Fool at his feet, and his one servant, disarmed, freed but a minute since, behind him. Things are at their issue' (Granville-Barker, pp. 289–90). Striking as this conception of the staging is, alternative kinds of blocking are also possible here and at 193.

189 indiscretion want of discernment or judgement. Schmidt compares *Ham.* 5.2.8: 'Our indiscretion sometime serves us well / When our deep plots do pall.'

190 sides 'the sides of the chest, strained by the swellings and passions of the heart' (Hunter).

Will you yet hold? How came my man i'th'stocks?

CORNWALL   I set him there, sir; but his own disorders
Deserved much less advancement.

LEAR   You? Did you?

REGAN   I pray you, father, being weak, seem so.
If till the expiration of your month   195
You will return and sojourn with my sister,
Dismissing half your train, come then to me.
I am now from home and out of that provision
Which shall be needful for your entertainment.

LEAR   Return to her? and fifty men dismissed?   200
No, rather I abjure all roofs and choose
To wage against the enmity o'th'air,
To be a comrade with the wolf and owl,
Necessity's sharp pinch. Return with her?
Why, the hot-blooded France, that dowerless took   205
Our youngest born – I could as well be brought
To knee his throne and, squire-like, pension beg
To keep base life afoot. Return with her?
Persuade me rather to be slave and sumpter
To this detested groom.

GONERILL   At your choice, sir.   210

---

191 Will ... stocks?] *As in* Q; *two lines divided* hold? / How F   191 i'th'] F; it'h Q   192 sir] F, Q; *not in* Q2   202 o'th']
F; of the Q   205–6 Why ... brought] F; *divided* dowerles / Tooke Q   *205 hot-blooded] F *uncorr.*, Pope; hot-bloodied
F *corr.*; hot bloud in Q   207 beg] F; bag Q

192 disorders misconduct.

193 much less advancement Cornwall is sarcastic: he believes Kent deserved much more severe
punishment.

193 You? Did you? Uttered more in contempt
than outrage or shock. 'Gielgud, hands clenched
behind his back, strode up to face Cornwall, spat
You!, passed, rounded on him contemptuously to
finish the line' (Rosenberg, p. 170). But Regan
immediately interrupts that colloquy, reasserting
herself (compare 2.1.119) and thereby turning
Lear's attention back to her and her sister.

199 entertainment reception and care.

201–4 I abjure ... pinch A self-fulfilling prophecy: by the end of the scene Lear does precisely
this.

202–3 To wage ... owl Theobald transposed
these lines, and Oxford follows suit, making
'Necessity's sharp pinch' (204) the object of

'wage'. But 'Necessity's sharp pinch', if anything, should be the subject, not object, of
'wage', which here is used intransitively to signify 'wage war, struggle'. As it stands, however,
the phrase, 'Necessity's sharp pinch', is in apposition to 'To be a comrade with the wolf and
owl', i.e. cohabiting with wild animals is the
result of grim necessity. The lines thus do not
require transposition.

202 enmity o'th'air e.g. storms and in general
the harsh condition of 'houseless poverty' (3.4.26).

204 Necessity's sharp pinch Compare Florio's
Montaigne: 'Necessitie must first pinch you by the
throat' (Muir).

205 hot-blooded passionate.

207 knee kneel before.

207 squire-like like a vassal or servant.

209 sumpter drudge (literally, packhorse).

210 groom i.e. Oswald.

LEAR I prithee, daughter, do not make me mad.
　　　I will not trouble thee, my child. Farewell.
　　　We'll no more meet, no more see one another.
　　　But yet thou art my flesh, my blood, my daughter,
　　　Or rather a disease that's in my flesh,　　　　　　　　　215
　　　Which I must needs call mine. Thou art a boil,
　　　A plague-sore, or embossèd carbuncle
　　　In my corrupted blood. But I'll not chide thee;
　　　Let shame come when it will, I do not call it.
　　　I do not bid the thunder-bearer shoot,　　　　　　　　220
　　　Nor tell tales of thee to high-judging Jove.
　　　Mend when thou canst, be better at thy leisure;
　　　I can be patient, I can stay with Regan,
　　　I and my hundred knights.
REGAN　　　　　　　　　　　　Not altogether so.
　　　I looked not for you yet, nor am provided　　　　　　225
　　　For your fit welcome. Give ear, sir, to my sister,
　　　For those that mingle reason with your passion
　　　Must be content to think you old, and so –
　　　But she knows what she does.
LEAR　　　　　　　　　　　　Is this well spoken?
REGAN I dare avouch it, sir. What, fifty followers?　　　230
　　　Is it not well? What should you need of more?
　　　Yea, or so many, sith that both charge and danger
　　　Speak 'gainst so great a number? How in one house
　　　Should many people under two commands
　　　Hold amity? 'Tis hard, almost impossible.　　　　　　235

---

211 I] F; Now I Q   215 that's in] F; that lies within Q   216 boil] bile Q; Byle F   217–18 A ... thee;] F; *divided* my /
Corrupted Q   217 or] F; an Q   224–7 Not ... passion] F *lineation; lines end* ... yet, / ... welcome, / ... those / ...
passion, Q   224 so] F; so sir Q   225 looked] F; looke Q   226 sir] F, Q; *not in* Q2   228 you] F; you are Q   228 so –]
Rowe; so, Q, F   229 spoken] F; spoken now Q   *230 What,] *Rowe;* what Q, F   233 Speak] F; Speakes Q   233 one] F;
a Q

211–24 I ... knights Lear quickly moves
through several contrasting emotions and attitudes,
from quiet withdrawal and acceptance, to passionate recognition of relationship immediately followed by vigorous rejection, to hard-won self-
control and an attempt, again, to accept the situation and try to make the best of it.
217 embossèd swollen; from French *embosser* 'to
swell, or arise in bunches, hulches, knobs'
(Cotgrave, cited by Furness).
217 carbuncle In medical terminology an
'inflammatory, circumscribed, malignant tumour
... It differs from a boil in having no central core'
(*OED* sv *sb* 3, citing this passage).

218 corrupted i.e. by disease.
220 thunder-bearer Jupiter.
220 shoot i.e. throw thunderbolts.
224 hundred knights Although his train is
diminished (compare 58 above), Lear still thinks
of it as intact.
227 mingle ... passion view your impulsive
behaviour with calm rationality. Indeed, cool rationality characterizes Regan's and Gonerill's speeches
throughout the rest of the scene, culminating in
Lear's appeal, 'O reason not the need', 257 ff.
230 avouch it declare it to be true.
232 sith that since.
232 charge expense.

GONERILL   Why might not you, my lord, receive attendance
　　　　　From those that she calls servants, or from mine?
REGAN   Why not, my lord? If then they chanced to slack ye,
　　　　We could control them. If you will come to me
　　　　(For now I spy a danger) I entreat you   240
　　　　To bring but five and twenty; to no more
　　　　Will I give place or notice.
LEAR   I gave you all.
REGAN 　　　　　　　　And in good time you gave it.
LEAR   Made you my guardians, my depositaries,
　　　　But kept a reservation to be followed   245
　　　　With such a number. What, must I come to you
　　　　With five and twenty? Regan, said you so?
REGAN   And speak't again, my lord. No more with me.
LEAR   Those wicked creatures yet do look well-favoured
　　　　When others are more wicked. Not being the worst   250
　　　　Stands in some rank of praise. [*To Gonerill*] I'll go with
　　　　　thee;
　　　　Thy fifty yet doth double five and twenty,
　　　　And thou art twice her love.
GONERILL 　　　　　　　　　　Hear me, my lord:
　　　　What need you five and twenty? ten? or five?
　　　　To follow in a house where twice so many   255
　　　　Have a command to tend you?
REGAN 　　　　　　　　　　What need one?
LEAR   O reason not the need! Our basest beggars
　　　　Are in the poorest thing superfluous.
　　　　Allow not nature more than nature needs,

---

238 Why ... ye,] *As in* Q; *two lines divided* Lord? / If F   238 ye] F; you Q   *239 control] Q; comptroll F   240 (For ...
danger)] F; For ... danger, Q   249 look] F; seem Q   251 SD] *Hanmer; not in* Q, F   256 need] F; needes Q   257 need!]
need: F; deed, Q   259 needs,] Q; needs: F

238 **slack ye** i.e. lessen their attendance on you.
242 **notice** cognisance, recognition.
243 **I ... all** Compare *King Leir* 2144: 'Ah, cruell *Ragan*, did I giue thee all?' (Muir). Actors at this point often move between the extremes of love and hate, tenderness and rage, gently reproachful pathos and stern obstinacy, astonishment and distraction (Rosenberg, p. 173).
244 **guardians ... depositaries** Synonyms for trustees (of his estate). Muir compares Florio's *Montaigne*, 'depositary and guardian'.
245 **reservation** reserved right; compare 1.1.127.
249 **well-favoured** attractive, handsome.
255 **follow** attend you, be your followers.

257 **O ... need** Ignoring his own earlier attempts to quantify love, Lear appeals to his daughters not to compute his 'need' by rationalist criteria, since it cannot truly be thus calculated. It is beyond practical measures.
257–8 **Our ... superfluous** The little that the lowest and most destitute persons have is (by that way of calculating 'need') not absolutely necessary to keep them alive.
259–60 **Allow ... beast's** Calculated by the lowest common denominators of 'need', human requirements do not differ from animal needs, and in that process human worth becomes downgraded to the level of a beast's.

Man's life is cheap as beast's. Thou art a lady;   260
If only to go warm were gorgeous,
Why nature needs not what thou gorgeous wear'st,
Which scarcely keeps thee warm. But for true need –
You heavens, give me that patience, patience I need.
You see me here, you gods, a poor old man,   265
As full of grief as age, wretched in both;
If it be you that stirs these daughters' hearts
Against their father, fool me not so much
To bear it tamely. Touch me with noble anger,
And let not women's weapons, water drops,   270
Stain my man's cheeks. No, you unnatural hags,
I will have such revenges on you both
That all the world shall – I will do such things –
What they are, yet I know not, but they shall be
The terrors of the earth! You think I'll weep;   275
No, I'll not weep,
                    Storm and tempest
I have full cause of weeping, but this heart
Shall break into a hundred thousand flaws
Or ere I'll weep. O fool, I shall go mad.
                    Exeunt [*Lear, Gloucester, Kent, Gentleman, and Fool*]
CORNWALL   Let us withdraw; 'twill be a storm.   280
REGAN   This house is little. The old man and's people
        Cannot be well bestowed.
GONERILL   'Tis his own blame; hath put himself from rest

---

260 life is] F; life as Q; life's as Q2   262 wear'st] F; wearest Q   263 need –] *Warburton* (*subst.*); need, Q; need:
F   265 you gods,] (you Gods) Q, F   265 man] F; fellow Q   268 so] F; to Q   269 tamely] F; lamely Q   270 And] F;
O Q   273 shall –] F, Q2; shall, Q   *274 are, yet] Q2; are yet Q; are yet, F   275 earth!] earth? F; earth, Q   276–8 No
... flaws] *Jennens's lineation; two lines divided* weeping, / But Q, F   276 SD] *After* weeping (*277*) F; *not in* Q   278 into ...
thousand] F; in a 100. thousand Q; in a thousand Q2   278 flaws] F; flowes Q   *279 SD] *This edn; Exeunt Lear, Leister,
Kent, and Foole* Q; *Exeunt* F   281 and's] F2; an'ds F; and his Q   *283 blame;] *Boswell;* blame Q, F

260–3 Thou ... warm Lear addresses Regan: If
warmth was the only measure of elegance, then you
would not need the elegant apparel you have on,
which hardly keeps you warm. Lear contrasts two
different kinds of 'need' here, one for basic animal
requirements, the other for human dignity and
pride.

263 But for true need This phrase is 'very
important, for it underscores the existence of values
entirely different from demonstrable material needs
– higher needs (his own need, at the moment, is for
symbols of respect and love) which must be imagi-
natively grasped and cannot be mechanically com-
puted' (Heilman, p. 169). Eloquent as Lear's appeal

is, he cannot sustain it, but breaks down into self-
pity, angry, impotent threats, and near incoherence
as he fears approaching insanity.

264 patience See 1.4.217 n.

268 fool ... much i.e. do not make me such a
fool as.

271 you ... hags Lear now turns back to
Gonerill and Regan.

278 flaws fragments.

279 Or ere Before.

282 bestowed accommodated, housed.

283 blame fault.

283 hath he hath.

283 put ... rest deprived himself of repose.

And must needs taste his folly.

REGAN   For his particular, I'll receive him gladly,   285
  But not one follower.

GONERILL   So am I purposed.
  Where is my lord of Gloucester?

CORNWALL   Followed the old man forth.

Enter GLOUCESTER

         He is returned.

GLOUCESTER   The king is in high rage.

CORNWALL   Whither is he going?

GLOUCESTER   He calls to horse, but will I know not whither.   290

CORNWALL   'Tis best to give him way; he leads himself.

GONERILL   My lord, entreat him by no means to stay.

GLOUCESTER   Alack, the night comes on, and the high winds
  Do sorely ruffle; for many miles about
  There's scarce a bush.

REGAN   O sir, to wilful men,   295
  The injuries that they themselves procure
  Must be their schoolmasters. Shut up your doors.
  He is attended with a desperate train,
  And what they may incense him to, being apt
  To have his ear abused, wisdom bids fear.   300

CORNWALL   Shut up your doors, my lord; 'tis a wild night,
  My Regan counsels well: come out o'th'storm.

            Exeunt

---

286 SH] F; *Duke.* Q   **286–7** So ... Gloucester?] F *lineation; one line* Q   **286** purposed] F; puspos'd Q   **288** SH] F; *Reg.* Q   **286–7** So ... Gloucester?] F *lineation; one line* Q   **288** SD] *After 287* Q, F; *at end of line, Capell*   **289–90** CORNWALL Whither ... horse,] F; *not in* Q   **290** but] F; & Q   **291** SH] F; *Re.* Q   **291** best] F; good Q   **293** high] F; bleak Q   **294–5** Do ... bush.] F *lineation; one line* Q   **294** ruffle] F; russel Q   **295** scarce] F; not Q   **301** wild] Q; wil'd F   **302** Regan] F; *Reg* Q   **302** o'th'] F; at'h Q

284 taste experience (the consequences of).

285 For his particular As far as he himself is concerned.

289–91 The king ... himself See Textual Analysis, p. 264 below.

290 will will go.

291 give him way not to obstruct him, give him his head.

291 leads himself i.e. follows no lead or guidance but his own, is headstrong.

294 ruffle rage, bluster; 'ruffle' is in Harsnett (Muir).

295–7 to wilful ... schoolmasters The harm that headstrong men bring on themselves must

teach them a lesson (about how to behave).

298 He ... train Regan assumes that Lear's 'riotous' knights are still with him, or perhaps she is just making excuses for her conduct (Muir).

299–300 being ... abused i.e. Lear being susceptible to misleading stories or lying tales.

300 wisdom bids fear i.e. prudence urges us to take precautions.

301 Shut ... doors Cornwall's repetition of Regan's request, or command (297), indicates Gloucester's hesitation or reluctance to comply, though in the end, perhaps prompted by Cornwall's men, he signals his servants to obey. Compare Rosenberg, p. 182.

3.1 *Storm still. Enter* KENT [*disguised*] *and a* GENTLEMAN, *severally*

KENT   Who's there, besides foul weather?

GENTLEMAN   One minded like the weather, most unquietly.

KENT   I know you. Where's the king?

GENTLEMAN   Contending with the fretful elements;

     Bids the wind blow the earth into the sea,   5

     Or swell the curlèd waters 'bove the main,

     That things might change or cease.

KENT   But who is with him?

GENTLEMAN   None but the fool, who labours to out-jest

     His heart-struck injuries.

KENT   Sir, I do know you,

     And dare upon the warrant of my note   10

     Commend a dear thing to you. There is division,

     Although as yet the face of it is covered

     With mutual cunning, 'twixt Albany and Cornwall,

     Who have – as who have not, that their great stars

     Throned and set high? – servants, who seem no less,   15

Act 3, Scene 1 3.1] *Actus Tertius. Scena Prima.* F; *not in* Q   0 SD] F; *Enter Kent and a Gentleman at seuerall doores.* Q   1 Who's there, besides] F; *Whats here beside* Q   4 elements] F; *element* Q   7 cease.] F *omits eight and a half lines here*   10 note] F; *Arte* Q   12 is] F; *be* Q   14–21 Who … furnishings –] F *substitutes these lines for thirteen lines in* Q (*see p. 253 below*)   14 have – as] have (as *Theobald*; haue, as F   15 high? –] high?) *Theobald*; high? *Rowe*; high; F

Act 3, Scene 1

0 SD *Storm still* At the Globe, thunder was created by rolling an iron ball, or cannon-ball ('a roul'd bullet'), on a sheet of metal, or by drums beating, or by both; lightning was suggested by a squib, or firework, set off. (See Andrew Gurr, *The Shakespearean Stage, 1574–1642*, 2nd edn, 1980, p. 170, and compare Rosenberg, pp. 183–6; Bratton, pp. 26–30.)

   0 SD GENTLEMAN Whether or not this is the same Gentleman who entered with Lear and the Fool in 2.4 is unclear but not of great importance. He has little to say in 2.4, and both Q and F omit an exit for him when Lear, Kent, and the Fool leave (279 SD). Like Kent, he may have become separated from the others in the stormy night. Although Kent recognizes him as trustworthy, i.e. loyal to the king, and he was probably played by the same actor, Oxford regards him as a new character and designates him 'First Gentleman'. Compare Perrett, pp. 198–9.

   4 Contending (1) physically struggling against, (2) competing in violence and anger (Hunter).

   6 main mainland (Onions).

7 things i.e. everything, the world. Compare 3.2.6–9.

   7 cease F lacks eight lines here found in Q: see Textual Analysis, pp. 275–6 below.

   8–9 out-jest … injuries dispel by jests or jokes the injuries (by his daughters) that have struck him to the heart. 'It is the Fool's tragedy that his efforts to cheer up his master serve only to emphasize Lear's folly and its dreadful results' (Kittredge).

   10 note notice, observation.

   11 Commend Entrust.

   11 dear important.

   11 division conflict, a parting of the ways.

   14–21 Who … furnishings On the substitution of these lines in F for Q's, see Textual Analysis, p. 253 below.

   14–15 as who … high i.e. like all those who have been so fortunate as to rise to positions of greatness and power. Presumably, 'throned and set high' is a past participial phrase = 'since they have been throned and set high'.

   15 who … less i.e. who seem to be just servants (but are really spies).

Which are to France the spies and speculations
Intelligent of our state. What hath been seen,
Either in snuffs and packings of the dukes,
Or the hard rein which both of them hath borne
Against the old kind king; or something deeper,   20
Whereof, perchance, these are but furnishings –
GENTLEMAN   I will talk further with you.
KENT   No, do not.
For confirmation that I am much more
Than my out-wall, open this purse and take
What it contains. If you shall see Cordelia –   25
As fear not but you shall – show her this ring,
And she will tell you who that fellow is
That yet you do not know. Fie on this storm!
I will go seek the king.
GENTLEMAN   Give me your hand. Have you no more to say?   30
KENT   Few words, but to effect more than all yet:
That when we have found the king – in which your pain
That way, I'll this – he that first lights on him
Holla the other.

Exeunt

---

*21 furnishings –] *Rowe;* furnishings. F   22 further] F; farther Q   23 am] F; *not in* Q   *24 out-wall,] Q *corr.;* outwall
Q *uncorr.;* out-wall; F   27 that] F; your Q   30 Give . . . say?] *As in* Q; *two lines divided* hand, / Haue F   32 in . . .
pain] F; *not in* Q   33 That way, I'll this – he] That way, Ile this: He F; Ile this way, you that, he Q   33 on him] F; *as
part of 34* Q   34 Holla] F; hollow Q

16 **speculations** observers, spies (abstract for
concrete).
17 **Intelligent of** Bearing or giving information
about.
18 **snuffs** huffs, resentments.
18 **packings** plots, conspiracies. Compare the
verb 'pack' = to plot, scheme, intrigue, and *Shr.*
5.1.121: 'Here's packing . . . to deceive us all!'
(Muir). The word also appears in *King Leir* 1932.
19 **hard rein** An equestrian metaphor, signifying
severe curbing, with a possible pun on 'reign'.
20 **something deeper** This is not disclosed
because Kent's speech is cut off by the Gentleman,
who apparently does not wish to hear any more,
forcing Kent to offer reassurances. In Q, Kent interrupts himself at 21 to shift from internal division to
foreign invasion. Compare Urkowitz, p. 70.
21 **furnishings** extrinsic considerations, or
pretexts.

22 **I . . . you** A 'courteous postponement or dis-
missal of a request' (Delius, cited by Furness). The
Gentleman is being prudent.
24 **out-wall** exterior appearance.
25 **If . . . shall** In F, Kent does not send the
Gentleman to Cordelia, but knowing her approach,
he knows that Lear's followers will meet her.
27 **fellow** A term of address often used for servants, though Schmidt and Muir gloss 'companion', and Furness cites *TN* 3.4.60–78. where the
word is understood in both senses.
30 **Give . . . say** The Gentleman is won over, but
Kent has said enough and, in any case, is now intent
on finding Lear.
31 **to effect** in importance.
32–3 **in which . . . this** i.e. to find the king your
effort (pain) lies that way, mine this way. Kent
motions accordingly.

3.2 *Storm still. Enter* LEAR *and* FOOL

LEAR   Blow, winds, and crack your cheeks! Rage, blow,
You cataracts and hurricanoes, spout
Till you have drenched our steeples, drowned the cocks!
You sulph'rous and thought-executing fires,
Vaunt-couriers of oak-cleaving thunderbolts,   5
Singe my white head; and thou all-shaking thunder,
Strike flat the thick rotundity o'th'world,
Crack nature's moulds, all germens spill at once
That makes ingrateful man.

FOOL   O nuncle, court holy water in a dry house is better than this   10
rain-water out o'door. Good nuncle, in, ask thy daughters
blessing. Here's a night pities neither wise men nor fools.

Act 3, Scene 2 3.2] *Scena Secunda.* F; *not in* Q   0 SD *Storm still.*] F; *not in* Q   2–9 You ... man.] F; *lines end*
... drencht, / ... sulpherous and / ... vaunt-currers to / ... head, / ... flat / ... natures / ... make / ...
man. Q   2 cataracts] F; caterickes Q   2 hurricanoes] Hyrricano's F; Hircanios Q   3 our] F; The Q   *3 drowned]
Q; drown F   4 sulph'rous] F; sulpherous Q   5 Vaunt-couriers of] F; vaunt-currers to Q   7 Strike] F; smite
Q   7 o'th'] F; of the Q   8 moulds] F; Mold Q   9 makes] F; make Q   10–12 O ... fools.] F *lineation; four verse lines
ending* ... house / ... doore, / ... blessing, / ... foole. Q   10 holy water] Q *corr.;* holly water Q *uncorr.;* holy-water
F   11 o'] F; a Q   11 in,] F; in, and Q   *12 wise men] Wisemen F; wise man Q   12 fools] F; foole Q

Act 3, Scene 2

0 SD *Storm still* 'The quality of Lear's resistance
... is determined by his design in the total action.
The Lear who is weak, very cold, already partly
unbalanced must begin to find unexpected
strengths in his ordeal ... The titanic Lears begin
to deteriorate under the erosion within and without
... [A] Lear too old and weak cannot plausibly ride
the storm, a Lear too stalwart cannot be subdued to
the image – even self-image – of a poor, infirm,
weak old man, unless a massive factor of self-pity
is thrown into the equation' (Rosenberg,
pp. 188–9).

1 **crack your cheeks** The winds are personified,
with cheeks ballooned, as in old maps.

2 **cataracts** flood-gates of heaven.

2 **hurricanoes** waterspouts.

3 **drenched ... cocks** Lear demands a second
deluge. Rosenberg, pp. 191–2, notes the sexual
undercurrent that runs through this speech.

3 **cocks** weathercocks.

4 **thought-executing fires** i.e. lightning whose
swiftness exceeds thought (compare *Temp.*
1.2.201–3), or whose fearsomeness extinguishes it.
The lightning flash precedes the actual bolt, or
missile, hurled by the thunder.

5 **Vaunt-couriers** Forerunners. Harsnett uses
the term (Muir).

5 **oak-cleaving thunderbolts** A favourite
Shakespearean image: Muir cites *Temp.* 5.1.44–6,

Cor. 5.3.152–3, *MM* 2.2.115–16.

7–9 **Strike ... man** Delius (cited by Furness)
compares the spherical earth with the 'roundness of
gestation'; the lines continue the image of nature's
orgasm (3 n. above).

8 **Crack ... moulds** Break the forms nature uses
in the process of creation.

8 **germens** seeds; as in *Mac.* 4.1.59. 'Lear wishes
to prevent the birth of any more people, so that the
ungrateful race of man will die out' (Muir).

8 **spill** spill out; hence, destroy.

10 **court holy water** i.e. the flattery of the
court. Compare Cotgrave: '*Eau beniste de Cour.*
Court holy water; complements, faire words,
flattering speeches' (Malone, cited by
Furness). Arthur Kinney, 'Conjectures on the
composition of *King Lear*', *S.Sur.* 33 (1980),
20, cites Iustus Lipsius, *Six Bookes of
Politickes or Civil Doctrine*, trans. William
Jones (1594), 3.8, '*How a Prince ought to behaue
him selfe in hearing counsel*': 'Let him freelie
permit his Counsellers, to speake their minde
boldlie, not louing *this court holy vvater.
Flattery doth more often subuert & ouerthrow
the wealth of a kingdome, then an open enemie
... That Emperour is miserable from vvhom the
troth is hidden*.'

11–12 **ask ... blessing** i.e. ask a blessing from
your daughters. The verb here takes two objects;
compare 5.3.10 (Kittredge).

LEAR   Rumble thy bellyful; spit, fire; spout, rain!
　　　　Nor rain, wind, thunder, fire are my daughters.
　　　　I tax not you, you elements, with unkindness.　　　　　　　15
　　　　I never gave you kingdom, called you children.
　　　　You owe me no subscription. Then let fall
　　　　Your horrible pleasure. Here I stand your slave,
　　　　A poor, infirm, weak, and despised old man;
　　　　But yet I call you servile ministers,　　　　　　　　　　　20
　　　　That will with two pernicious daughters join
　　　　Your high-engendered battles 'gainst a head
　　　　So old and white as this. O, ho! 'tis foul.
FOOL   He that has a house to put 's head in has a good head-piece.
　　　　[*Sings*] The codpiece that will house　　　　　　　　　25
　　　　　　　　Before the head has any,
　　　　The head and he shall louse;
　　　　　　　　So beggars marry many.
　　　　The man that makes his toe

---

15 tax] F; taske Q   17–23 You ... foul.] F; *lines end* ... plesure [*turned under*] / ... weak & / ... seruile / ... ioin'd / ... white / ... foule. Q   17 Then] F; why then Q   21 will] F; haue Q   21 join] F; ioin'd Q   22 battles] F; battel Q   23 ho!] F; *not in* Q   24 put 's] F; put his Q   25 SD] Capell; not in Q, F   25–32 The ... wake.] *Johnson's lineation; four verse lines ending* ... any; / ... many. / ... make, / ... wake. F; *as prose* Q

14 fire Disyllabic.
15 tax charge, accuse.
17 subscription submission, allegiance.
18–23 Here ... as this Lear shifts in these lines from self-pity to defiance to a mixture of both pity and defiance.
20 ministers agents.
22 high-engendered i.e. coming from on high (the heavens).
22 battles battalions, armies.
24 head-piece (1) helmet, head-covering, (2) brain.
25 SD *Sings* Although Hunter, p. 340, finds these lines unsuitable for music and thus does not include Capell's SD, he agrees that 72–5 below are sung and cites the SD from *TN*. The storm is apparently not a consideration to Shakespeare in either case. Compare 72–5 n.
25–32 The codpiece ... wake In the first quatrain the Fool comments on the danger of the sexual appetite overcoming prudence; i.e. reckless fornication leads to forced marriages, beggary, and disease. The second quatrain comments on another foolish inversion of values that eventually leads to misery. Compare the proverb, 'Let not at thy heart what should be at thy heel' (Tilley H317). The Fool alludes to Lear's favouring of Gonerill and Regan over Cordelia, but he also continues the theme of

sexual licence contrasted with real love (see 29 n. below).
25 codpiece (1) fool, (2) euphemism for the penis (as in *MM* 3.2.115). The codpiece (suggested here by 'head-piece') was part of men's clothing worn at the crotch, partly to hide, partly to emphasize the penis and scrotum. Court fools often wore exaggerated versions of the codpiece (compare 38 below). Wiles, p. 190, suggests that the Fool does not wear one but puts his bauble between his legs to mime the lines.
25 house i.e. fornicate.
26 any any house, i.e. adequate provision.
27 louse i.e. become lousy.
28 many The Fool refers to the paradox of 'the Beggarman and his long line of doxies. He "marries" so many because he is poor (the result of an initial imprudence), and not vice versa. The four lines give a kind of condensed Rake's Progress ...' (Danby, p. 111). But 'many' may also refer to lice; or the word order may be inverted for the sake of rhyme: 'many beggars marry after this fashion' (NS).
29 toe Danby, p. 111, considers the toe a symbol of the phallus, paralleling 'codpiece'. The line thus contrasts sexual promiscuity with love ('heart' (30)).

> What he his heart should make,   30
> Shall of a corn cry woe,
> And turn his sleep to wake.
> For there was never yet fair woman but she made mouths
> in a glass.

Enter KENT [*disguised*]

LEAR   No, I will be the pattern of all patience.   35
          I will say nothing.

KENT   Who's there?

FOOL   Marry, here's grace and a codpiece; that's a wise man and a
          fool.

KENT   Alas, sir, are you here? Things that love night   40
          Love not such nights as these. The wrathful skies
          Gallow the very wanderers of the dark
          And make them keep their caves. Since I was man
          Such sheets of fire, such bursts of horrid thunder,
          Such groans of roaring wind and rain I never   45
          Remember to have heard. Man's nature cannot carry
          Th'affliction nor the fear.

LEAR   Let the great gods,
          That keep this dreadful pudder o'er our heads,

---

31 of] F; haue Q   33 but] F, Q *corr.;* hut Q *uncorr.*   34 SD] F; *after 35* Q   *38 wise man] wiseman Q; Wiseman F   40–6 Alas … carry] F *lineation; eight lines ending* … here? / … these, / … of the / … caues, / … fire, / … grones of / … remember / … cary. Q   40 are] F; sit Q   42 wanderers] F; wanderer Q   43 make] F; makes Q   45 never] F; ne're Q   47 Th'] F; The Q   47 fear] F; force Q   47–58 Let … sinning.] F *lineation; eleven lines ending* … dreadful / … now, / … within thee / … Iustice, / … periur'd, and / … incestious, / … couert / … life, / … centers, / … grace, / … sinning. Q   48 pudder] F; Powther Q; Thundering Q2

33–4 For … glass A diversionary tactic by the Fool following his rather pointed satire (Furness); an oblique allusion to the vanity and hypocrisy of Gonerill and Regan (Muir; compare 2.2.32 n.). To 'make mouths in a glass' is to practise smiling or grimacing in a mirror; it can also signal contempt, as in *Ham.* 4.4.50.

38 Marry A common exclamation, derived from 'by the Virgin Mary'.

38 grace and a codpiece An apparent reference to Lear (the king's grace) and the Fool (compare 25 n.), ambiguous because of Lear's foolish behaviour and the Fool's references to him as a fool, as in the previous song. 'This is the dialectic of man, stretched to its limits: man is love and lust, wisdom and folly' (Rosenberg, p. 195).

40 are you here Q's 'sit you here' may reflect the interpretative attitude Lear assumes above as the 'pattern of all patience' (35–6) (compare *TN* 2.4.114–15). F's change lets the emphasis fall on

'here' but does not necessarily require Lear to keep standing (Urkowitz, 'Editorial tradition', pp. 36–7).

42 Gallow Terrify.

42 wanderers … dark wild nocturnal animals.

46–7 Man's … fear Kent's words underscore Lear's titanism. The upheaval in physical nature reflects the upheavals in international relations (conflict with France), the state (division between the dukes), the family, and the individual. According to Kent, the storm is beyond normal human endurance, not only for what it does (causes affliction, i.e. physical buffeting), but for what it means (the 'fear') – the aspect of the storm that Lear concentrates upon in the lines that follow.

46 carry bear, endure.

48 pudder Variant of 'pother' = turmoil, tumult. 'Pother' historically rhymed with 'other', 'smother', 'brother' and was sometimes spelled 'puther', 'pudder' (*OED*).

Find out their enemies now. Tremble, thou wretch,
That hast within thee undivulgèd crimes   50
Unwhipped of justice. Hide thee, thou bloody hand,
Thou perjured and thou simular of virtue
That art incestuous. Caitiff, to pieces shake,
That under covert and convenient seeming
Has practised on man's life. Close pent-up guilts,   55
Rive your concealing continents and cry
These dreadful summoners grace. I am a man
More sinned against than sinning.

KENT   Alack, bare-headed?
Gracious my lord, hard by here is a hovel.
Some friendship will it lend you 'gainst the tempest.   60
Repose you there, while I to this hard house –
More harder than the stones whereof 'tis raised,
Which even but now, demanding after you,
Denied me to come in – return and force
Their scanted courtesy.

LEAR   My wits begin to turn.   65
Come on, my boy. How dost, my boy? Art cold?
I am cold myself. – Where is this straw, my fellow?
The art of our necessities is strange,

---

52 simular] F; simular man Q   53 incestuous] F; incestious Q   53 to] F; in Q   55 Has] F; hast Q   56 concealing continents] F; concealed centers Q   58 than] then F; their Q   58–65 Alack ... courtesy.] F *lineation; as prose* Q   61 while] F; whilst Q   62 harder than] F; hard then is Q   62 stones] F; stone Q   63 you] F; me Q   65 wits begin] F; wit begins Q   68–70 The ... heart] F; *lines end* ... can, / ... poore, / ... heart Q

49 Find ... now The fear caused by the storm will lead guilty creatures (criminals and malefactors) to reveal themselves as enemies of the gods. Compare 46–7 above.

51 of by.

51 bloody hand i.e. murderer (metonymy).

52 simular counterfeiter, pretender. Compare Tyndale's Prologue to Rom. in his New Testament (1526): 'Christ ... calleth them [the Pharisees] ypocrites, that is to safe Simulars' (*OED*).

53 Caitiff Wretch.

54 seeming hypocrisy.

55 practised on plotted against.

55 Close pent-up guilts Crimes kept secret.

56 Rive ... continents Slit open the containers that hide you.

56–7 cry ... grace beg for mercy from these terrible agents of vengeance. A summoner was a minor official who summoned offenders to ecclesiastical courts.

57 grace mercy (Schmidt).

57 I Emphatic (Kittredge). Lear contrasts himself with those murderers, hypocrites, and other 'pent-up guilts'.

59 Gracious my lord My gracious lord; compare 1.1.90.

61 hard pitiless, unyielding.

61 house household.

63 demanding after asking for.

65 My ... turn 'From this point he becomes aware of the sufferings of others' (NS).

66–7 Come ... myself Salvini in the role of Lear took off his cloak here and wrapped it around the shivering Fool, who may be near collapse (Rosenberg, p. 197).

68–9 The art ... precious Poverty (necessity) is an unusual alchemist; it can transform worthless things into precious ones.

And can make vile things precious. Come, your hovel. –
Poor fool and knave, I have one part in my heart   70
That's sorry yet for thee.

FOOL   [*Sings*] He that has and a little tiny wit,
                  With heigh-ho, the wind and the rain,
                  Must make content with his fortunes fit,
                  Though the rain it raineth every day.   75

LEAR   True, boy. – Come, bring us to this hovel.

                              [*Exeunt Lear and Kent*]

FOOL   This is a brave night to cool a courtesan. I'll speak a pro-
       phecy ere I go:
             When priests are more in word than matter;
             When brewers mar their malt with water;   80
             When nobles are their tailors' tutors,
             No heretics burned, but wenches' suitors,
             Then shall the realm of Albion
             Come to great confusion.
             When every case in law is right;   85
             No squire in debt nor no poor knight;
             When slanders do not live in tongues,

---

69 And] F; that Q   69 your] F; you Q   70 in] F; of Q   71 That's sorry] F; That sorrowes Q   72 SD] *Capell; not in* Q,
F   72–5 He . . . day.] F; *as prose* Q   72 and] F; *not in* Q   75 Though] F; for Q   76 boy] F; my good boy Q   76 SD]
Capell; Exit. F; *not in* Q   77–93 FOOL This . . . time.] F; *not in* Q   83–4 Then . . . confusion.] *Pope's lineation; placed here
by NS; as one line following* 90 F (*see Commentary*)

72–5 He . . . day Adapted from Feste's song, *TN*
5.1.387–92. 'The Fool may be referring to Lear, or
to himself' (Muir).

74 Must . . . fit Either (1) must make his happiness fit his fortunes (Kittredge), or (2) must be
content with the fortunes suitable to such a person.

77 This . . . courtesan A pun on 'night' and
'knight' may explain why the comment on the
weather takes this form (Hunter). It would also
partly explain the medieval parody that follows.

77 brave fine.

79–92 When . . . feet These lines and those
immediately preceding and following them were
long suspected of being a non-Shakespearean theatrical interpolation. See Textual Analysis, p. 265
below. Warburton was the first to detect two pro-
phecies (79–84: a satire of England under James I;
85–92: utopia), and to propose the relineation that is
followed here and in NS. Wittreich, echoing
Malone, argues that the lines were deliberately
scrambled (p. 62).

79 When . . . matter i.e. when clergymen talk
more for the sake of talking than to say something.

The pseudo-Chaucerian verse imitated here is cited
in Puttenham's *Arte of English Poesie* (1589) in the
section on merismus or 'the distributor', i.e. amplification (Taylor, 'Date and authorship', p. 383).

81 nobles . . . tutors aristocrats teach their tai-
lors. Compare *Shr.* 4.3.86–95: Petruchio has
instructed and now criticizes a tailor (Kittredge).

82 heretics (1) religious dissenters, (2) lovers.
Compare Donne, 'The Indifferent': 'Poore
Heretiques in love there bee, / Which thinke to
stablish dangerous constancie.'

82 burned A quibble on 'infected with venereal
diseases' (NS).

83–4 Then . . . confusion See collation. If they
were a marginal insertion in copy, the lines may
have confused the compositor, who set them as
one line in the wrong place (NS).

83 Albion An old name for Britain.

85 right (1) just, or (2) genuine (NS). Legal
procedures, then as now, were notoriously complex.

86 nor no Double negatives do not cancel each
other out.

87 live i.e. make a permanent residence in.

Nor cutpurses come not to throngs;
When usurers tell their gold i'th'field,
And bawds and whores do churches build,   90
Then comes the time, who lives to see't,
That going shall be used with feet.
This prophecy Merlin shall make, for I live before his time.

Exit

3.3 *Enter* GLOUCESTER *and* EDMOND

GLOUCESTER Alack, alack, Edmond, I like not this unnatural
dealing. When I desired their leave that I might pity him, they
took from me the use of mine own house, charged me on pain
of perpetual displeasure neither to speak of him, entreat for
him, or any way sustain him.   5
EDMOND Most savage and unnatural!
GLOUCESTER Go to, say you nothing. There is division between
the dukes, and a worse matter than that. I have received a letter
this night – 'tis dangerous to be spoken – I have locked the
letter in my closet. These injuries the king now bears will be   10

Act 3, Scene 3   3.3] *Scaena Tertia.* F; *not in* Q   0 SD] F; *Enter Gloster and the Bastard with lights.* Q   1–5 Alack . . .
him.] F; *six verse lines ending* . . . this, / . . . leaue / . . . from me/ . . . paine / . . . of him, / . . . sustaine him. Q   3 took]
F; tooke me Q   4 perpetual] F; their Q   5 or] F; nor Q   7–17 Go . . . careful.] F; *thirteen verse lines ending* . . . the Dukes,
[*turned over*] / . . . receiued / . . . spoken, / . . . iniuries / . . . home / . . . landed, / . . . him, and / . . . talke / . . . of him / . . .
gon / . . . threatned me, / . . . there is / . . . careful. Q   7 There is] F; ther's a Q   7 between] F; betwixt Q

88 Nor . . . throngs A crowd was an irresistible
target for pickpockets, or cutpurses, as they were
then called, because money was kept in a purse
strung from a girdle.

89 usurers moneylenders, notorious for secrecy.

89 tell count.

90 bawds . . . build i.e. when these low characters are religiously and philanthropically motivated.

92 going . . . feet i.e. normality shall reign and
perversions end.

92 going walking.

93 This . . . time A third prophecy. The Lear
legend antedates Arthurian legend by centuries.

Act 3, Scene 3

0 SD *Enter* . . . EDMOND Q's addition, *with lights*,
requires the actors to enter the Globe stage
carrying torches – a conventional sign to indicate
night scenes and perhaps here to suggest a scene
indoors.

1–2 unnatural dealing i.e. Gonerill's and

Regan's treatment of their father.

2–5 When . . . him By pitying the king,
Gloucester begins to make his move in the conflict
between father and daughters; as a result, his guests
confiscate his house and threaten still worse if he
continues to express compassion for Lear or tries to
help him.

2 pity take pity on, relieve.

6 Most . . . unnatural In the context of the
entire scene, these words are ironic, but they must
be said without deliberate irony.

7 Go to An exclamation: 'Quiet! Enough!'

8 worse matter Possibly the French invasion,
although the suggestion of some vague, ominous
threat is like Kent's 'something deeper'
(3.1.20). Compare also 'strange things toward'
(16 below).

8 a letter See 3.5.8–9. Like Kent, Gloucester is
in communication with Cordelia and the French
forces.

10 closet private room.

revenged home. There is part of a power already footed. We
must incline to the king. I will look him and privily relieve him.
Go you and maintain talk with the duke, that my charity be not
of him perceived. If he ask for me, I am ill and gone to bed. If I
die for it – as no less is threatened me – the king my old master   15
must be relieved. There is strange things toward, Edmond;
pray you be careful.   *Exit*
EDMOND   This courtesy, forbid thee, shall the duke
          Instantly know, and of that letter too.
          This seems a fair deserving, and must draw me   20
          That which my father loses: no less than all.
          The younger rises when the old doth fall.   *Exit*

3.4 *Enter* LEAR, KENT [*disguised*], *and* FOOL

KENT   Here is the place, my lord. Good my lord, enter.
       The tyranny of the open night's too rough
       For nature to endure.
                          Storm still
LEAR   Let me alone.
KENT   Good my lord, enter here.
LEAR   Wilt break my heart?
KENT   I had rather break mine own. Good my lord, enter.   5

---

11 There is] F; Ther's Q   11 footed] F; landed Q   12 look] F; seeke Q   14 bed. If] bed; if *Rowe²*; bed, if F; bed,
though Q   15 for it] F; for't Q   16 There is strange things toward, Edmond;] there is / Some strãge thing toward,
Edmund Q; There . . . toward *Edmund,* F   18–22 This . . . fall.] F *lineation; four verse lines ending . . . know* [*turned under*] /
. . . deseruing / . . . lesse / . . . fall. Q   21 all.] all, Q, F   22 The] F; then Q   22 doth] F; doe Q   Act 3, Scene 4   3.4]
Scena Quarta. F; *not in* Q   1–3 Here . . . endure.] F *lineation; as prose* Q   2 The] F, Q *corr.*; the the Q *uncorr.*   3 SD] F;
not in Q   4 here] F; *not in* Q   5 I . . . enter.] *As in* Q; *two lines divided* owne, / Good F

11 **home** to the full, thoroughly.
11 **footed** landed.
12 **look** i.e. look for.
14 **of** by.
14 **bed** A 'social lie': compare 2.4.81–2.
14–16 **If . . . relieved** Gloucester takes his stand,
aware of the risks, but now fully committed,
morally and otherwise. In assuming the major
initiative in the preservation of Lear, he risks more
than the disguised Kent, and henceforth it is he who
is the suffering servant, 'punished unjustly for his
fidelity to human values' (Warren, 'Diminution', p.
63).
16 **toward** coming, about to happen.
17 SD *Exit* 'With a touch, an embrace,
[Gloucester] goes to face the lightning'
(Rosenberg, p. 200). Edmond watches him leave,
with a knowing smile and even, perhaps, contempt.
18 **courtesy** i.e. to Lear.
18 **forbid** forbidden to.

20 **This . . . deserving** My action bids fair to
merit a good reward.
20–1 **draw . . . all** Edmond calculates correctly:
see 3.5.14.
22 **The . . . fall** Compare Tilley R136: 'The rising
of one man is the falling of another' (NS).

Act 3, Scene 4
0 SD In Trevor Nunn's Royal Shakespeare
Company production (1968), Eric Porter as Lear,
though gaunt and haggard, carried the Fool on stage
in his arms, anticipating the end, when he would
enter carrying Cordelia (Rosenberg, p. 201).
1 **the place** Compare 3.2.59.
2 **open night** night in the open.
3 **For . . . endure** Kent's repeated theme (compare 3.2.46–7). But Lear persists in opposing his
nature against the storm's.
4 **Wilt** Wilt thou.

LEAR   Thou think'st 'tis much that this contentious storm
　　　　Invades us to the skin: so 'tis to thee.
　　　　But where the greater malady is fixed,
　　　　The lesser is scarce felt. Thou'dst shun a bear,
　　　　But if thy flight lay toward the roaring sea,　　　　　　　10
　　　　Thou'dst meet the bear i'th'mouth. When the mind's free,
　　　　The body's delicate. This tempest in my mind
　　　　Doth from my senses take all feeling else,
　　　　Save what beats there: filial ingratitude.
　　　　Is it not as this mouth should tear this hand　　　　　　　15
　　　　For lifting food to't? But I will punish home.
　　　　No, I will weep no more. In such a night
　　　　To shut me out? Pour on, I will endure.
　　　　In such a night as this! O Regan, Gonerill,
　　　　Your old kind father, whose frank heart gave all –　　　　20
　　　　O that way madness lies; let me shun that;
　　　　No more of that.
KENT 　　　　　　　Good my lord, enter here.
LEAR   Prithee, go in thyself, seek thine own ease.
　　　　This tempest will not give me leave to ponder
　　　　On things would hurt me more; but I'll go in.　　　　　　25

---

6 contentious] F; crulentious Q *uncorr.;* tempestious Q *corr.*   *7 skin: so] skin.so F *uncorr.;* skinso F *corr.;* skin, so Q   9 Thou'dst] F; thou wouldst Q2   *10 thy] Q; they F   10 roaring] F; roring Q *corr.;* raging Q *uncorr.,* Q2   11 i'th'] F; it'h Q   *12 body's] bodies Q, F   *12 This] Q *corr.;* the Q *uncorr.,* Q2, F   14 beats] F, Q *corr.;* beares Q *uncorr.,* Q2   14 there: ... ingratitude] there ... ingratitude, F *uncorr.;* there, ... ingratitude F *corr.;* their ... ingratitude Q   16 to't] F, Q; to it Q2   16 home] F; sure Q   17–18 In ... endure.] F; *not in* Q   19–21 O ... that;] F *lineation; three verse lines ending* ... father / ... lies, [*turned over*] / ... that. Q   20 gave] F; gaue you Q   21 lies] Q, F *corr.;* lie F *uncorr.*   22 here] F; *not in* Q   23 thine own] F; thy one Q

8 **greater malady** i.e. his mental torment, as 11–14 explain.

8 **fixed** set, established.

11 **i'th'mouth** i.e. face to face.

11–14 **When ... ingratitude** Compare Montaigne, *Apology for Raymond Sebond,* iv.70: 'our senses are ... many times dulled by the passions of the mind' (Muir).

11 **free** i.e. of pain, undisturbed, untroubled.

12 **delicate** sensitive.

14 **beats** (1) throbs, as of thought, (2) rages, as of a storm (Muir).

15–16 **Is ... to't** Is it not as if my mouth should attack my hand for bringing food to it? The image suggests the absurd rebellion of one part of the body against another (compare *Cor.* 1.1.96 ff.). Lear conceives of the family – himself and his daughters – as an organic whole.

16 **home** thoroughly, to the full.

18 **Pour ... endure** Lear asserts his titanism, his defiance against nature and all it can do to him. On F's addition, see Textual Analysis, p. 265 below.

20 **frank** (1) liberal, bounteous (of giving), (2) open, without guile.

21 **that way** i.e. dwelling upon his foolish generosity and his daughters' ingratitude.

23 **Prithee ... ease** Lear has begun to consider others first, a marked change in his attitude and behaviour.

25 **things ... more** Lear refers to filial ingratitude and his own foolishness. Compare 21 above.

25 **would** that would.

In, boy, go first. You houseless poverty –
Nay, get thee in; I'll pray, and then I'll sleep.

Exit [Fool]

Poor naked wretches, wheresoe'er you are
That bide the pelting of this pitiless storm,
How shall your houseless heads and unfed sides,   30
Your looped and windowed raggedness defend you
From seasons such as these? O I have ta'en
Too little care of this. Take physic, pomp,
Expose thyself to feel what wretches feel,
That thou mayst shake the superflux to them   35
And show the heavens more just.

Enter FOOL

EDGAR [*Within*]   Fathom and half; fathom and half; poor Tom!
FOOL   Come not in here, nuncle! Here's a spirit! Help me, help
  me!

26–7 In ... sleep.] F; *not in* Q   26 poverty –] *Rowe;* pouertie, F   27 SD] *Johnson (subst.); Exit.* F *(after 26); not in*
Q   29 storm] F; night Q   *31 looped] loopt Q; lop'd, F   36 SD] *This edn; Enter Edgar, and Foole.* F; *The Fool runs out
from the hovel. / Theobald (after 39; after 37, Capell); not in* Q   37 EDGAR Fathom ... Tom!] F; *not in* Q   37 SD]
Theobald; not in F

26–7 In, boy ... sleep See Textual Analysis. p.
265 below. The lines, added or restored in F,
underscore Lear's changing attitude and lead
directly and naturally into his prayer, which is
interrupted poignantly by insistent concern for his
Fool.
26 houseless poverty Compare 'Poor naked
wretches' (28 ff.). Here, concrete and abstract are
combined in a typically Shakespearean phrase.
Compare 31 below.
27 I'll pray 'In the night's bleak exposure he
kneels down, like a child at bedtime, to pray'
(Granville-Barker, p. 292). But most editions,
except Oxford, omit a SD.
28–36 Macready deliberately pointed this speech
at Queen Victoria during a performance she
attended (Bratton, p. 143).
29 bide endure.
30 sides Not the sides of the chest, as at 2.4.190,
but the part of the body principally fed by nourish-
ment, as in *Tim.* 4.3.12 (Schmidt).
31 looped ... raggedness More yoking of
concrete and abstract: the ragged clothes of the
poor are full of loopholes and openings
(windows).
32–3 O ... this By assuming responsibility for
the wretched state of his subjects, Lear takes a major
step forward in understanding himself.
33 physic medical treatment, possibly a purge.
33 pomp Abstract for concrete, i.e. rich and

powerful persons accustomed to splendour and
luxury.
34–6 Expose ... just This is the 'physic' Lear
prescribes: the great ones of the earth should subject
themselves to the experiences of the poor (as Lear
himself now does); the action will lead them to
surrender unnecessary possessions ('superflux'),
and by giving them to the poor demonstrate how
heaven can be more just than we realize. Compare
Gloucester's speech, 4.1.62–6, where the same
point is made.
36 SD *Enter* FOOL Q has no SD, while F has both
Edgar and the Fool enter here, though Kent later
calls Edgar (as Poor Tom) to come forth at 42–3. A
line (37) is also missing from Q, which seems (like
the Bedlam's entrance) a response to Lear's prayer
(see Textual Analysis, p. 266 below). Theobald's
emendations suggest a plausible staging of the
scene: the Fool comes running out of the hovel
badly frightened by what he sees there – the hideous
figure of the Bedlam beggar, who utters a despairing
cry from within. His hovel is an imagined place,
entered perhaps from a trap (as in the 1990
Renaissance Theatre Company production) or
from behind curtains upstage centre.
37 Fathom ... half 'Edgar speaks as if he were a
sailor sounding the depth of the water in the hold of
a leaking ship. He is almost "swamped" by the
storm' (Kittredge).
38 spirit supernatural being, demon.

KENT   Give me thy hand. Who's there?   40

FOOL   A spirit, a spirit! He says his name's Poor Tom.

KENT   What art thou that dost grumble there i'th'straw? Come
forth.

[*Enter* EDGAR, *disguised as a madman*]

EDGAR   Away, the foul fiend follows me. Through the sharp
hawthorn blow the winds. Humh! Go to thy bed and warm   45
thee.

LEAR   Didst thou give all to thy daughters? And art thou come to
this?

EDGAR   Who gives anything to Poor Tom, whom the foul fiend
hath led through fire and through flame, through ford and   50
whirlpool, o'er bog and quagmire; that hath laid knives under
his pillow and halters in his pew; set ratsbane by his porridge;
made him proud of heart to ride on a bay trotting-horse over
four-inched bridges, to course his own shadow for a traitor.
Bless thy five wits, Tom's a-cold! O do, de, do, de, do de. Bless   55

41 a spirit] F; *not in* Q   41 name's] F, Q; name is Q2   42 i'th'] F; in the Q   43 SD] *Theobald; not in* Q, F   44 Through]
F; thorough Q   45 blow the winds.] F; blowes the cold wind, Q   45 Humh!] F; *not in* Q   45 bed] F; cold bed
Q   47 Didst thou give] F; Hast thou giuen Q   47 thy] F; thy two Q   *50 through fire] Q; though Fire F   50 through
flame] F; *not in* Q   *50–1 ford and whirlpool] foord, and whirli-poole Q; Sword, and Whirle-poole F   51 hath] F; has
Q   52 porridge] F; pottage Q   *55 Bless] Q; Blisse F   55 O . . . de.] F; *not in* Q   *55 Bless] Q; blisse F

44 **Away** i.e. keep away. As someone followed or
attended by demons, Edgar warns the others off.

44–5 **Through . . . winds** See collation. Hunter
follows Q and inserts 'cold' before 'winds', citing
the same phrase at 89 below. Oxford omits 'cold'
here but with Q inserts it before 'bed' in the next
sentence, following *Shr.* Induction 1.9–10 (see
Textual Companion, p. 535). F's omission of 'cold'
in both places may seem odd (Duthie, p. 148), but
the lines are satisfactory without the adjective; if
anything, they are stronger for the omissions.

45 **Humh** Edgar, half-naked, shivers with cold
(Kittredge).

45–6 **Go . . . thee** See 44–5 n. above. Duthie, p.
149, thinks an actor may have interpolated 'cold'
before 'bed' to make an antithesis. He follows F
both here and earlier, though NS retains Q's 'cold'
before 'winds'.

47–8 **Didst . . . this** Lear's monomania becomes
evident, and his descent into madness is aided by
the image of the Bedlam beggar. 'Immediately after
the *Poor naked wretches* speech [Lear] finds a figure
with whom he can wholly identify himself and
whose role (of madman) he can take over' (Hunter).

49–58 **foul fiend . . . there** As Theobald first
noted, many details of this speech are indebted to
Harsnett's *Declaration*. See also Muir, 'Samuel
Harsnett and *King Lear*', *RES*, n.s., 2 (1951), 17.

Suicide, a result of the sin of despair, was a favourite
temptation of the devil. Compare Marlowe, *Dr
Faustus* 2.2.20–2: 'then swordes and kniues, /
Poyson, gunnes, halters, and invenomd steele /
Are layde before me to dispatch my selfe'
(Steevens, cited by Muir).

50 **ford** 'Sword' in F is an apparent manuscript
misreading (Duthie, p. 178). All the other dangers
are natural phenomena: 'Sword' is exceptional; Q's
'foord' is doubtless right.

51 **that** i.e. he that.

52 **pew** A 'gallery in a house or outside a chamber
window – not a pew in church' (Kittredge; from
Old French *puye*, 'parapet, balustrade, balcony'
(*OED*); compare Cotgrave, *Appuye*: 'An open, and
outstanding terrace, or gallery, set on th'outside
with railes to lean vpon').

52 **porridge** thick soup.

53–4 **ride . . . bridges** i.e. perform a difficult
feat, like walking a tight-rope.

54 **course** chase. Compare the image of a cat
chasing its own tail (NS) and Tilley s281, 'To be
afraid of one's own shadow'.

55 **five wits** These are common wit, imagination,
fantasy, estimation, and memory. They were sometimes confused with the five senses, though not in
Sonnet 141.9–10.

55 **O do . . . de** Sounds of chattering teeth.

thee from whirlwinds, star-blasting, and taking. Do Poor Tom
some charity, whom the foul fiend vexes. There could I have
him now, and there, and there again, and there.

Storm still

LEAR   What, has his daughters brought him to this pass?
  Couldst thou save nothing? Wouldst thou give 'em all?   60

FOOL   Nay, he reserved a blanket, else we had been all shamed.

LEAR   Now all the plagues that in the pendulous air
  Hang fated o'er men's faults, light on thy daughters!

KENT   He hath no daughters, sir.

LEAR   Death, traitor! Nothing could have subdued nature   65
  To such a lowness but his unkind daughters.
  Is it the fashion that discarded fathers
  Should have thus little mercy on their flesh?
  Judicious punishment: 'twas this flesh begot
  Those pelican daughters.   70

EDGAR   Pillicock sat on Pillicock Hill; alow, alow, loo, loo.

FOOL   This cold night will turn us all to fools and madmen.

---

56 star-blasting] F; starre-blusting Q   58 and there again, and there.] F; and and there againe Q   58 SD] F; *not in*
Q   *59 What, has] What, Q; Ha's F   60 Wouldst] F; didst Q   60 'em] F; them Q   63 light] F; fall Q   69 begot] F;
begins next line Q   71 Pillicock Hill] F; pelicocks hill Q   71 alow, alow, loo, loo.] F; a lo lo lo. Q

56 star-blasting In astrology, the adverse influence of malignant stars, which could afflict one with disease.

56 taking The state of becoming infected, blasted.

57–8 There … there 'Edgar makes grabs at different parts of his body as if to catch vermin – or devils' (Kittredge).

59 What, has See collation. On metrical and other grounds, Duthie, pp. 15–16, recommends combining Q and F. Q may have inadvertently omitted 'has'; in correcting Q, the F collator or compositor may have misread the correction as a substitution instead of an addition.

59 pass predicament, extremity (Schmidt).

61 reserved NS suggests an allusion to Lear's 'reservation' of a hundred knights.

62–3 all … faults The idea that infectious plagues were airborne was commonplace, as was the notion of 'star-blasting' (56), the infliction of disease as a punishment for malefactors.

63 fated destined (i.e. to fall).

63 light alight, fall.

65 subdued reduced; accent on the first syllable.

65 nature i.e. human nature.

67–8 Is … flesh Lear refers to Edgar's mortified body (see 2.3.15–16). In his monomania, he insists Edgar must be the victim of ungrateful and cruel daughters, despite Kent's statement (64). Edwin Booth as Lear drew a thorn or spike from Edgar's arm and stuck it in his own (Sprague, cited by NS).

69 Judicious Fitting, well-judged.

69–70 'twas … daughters The bawdry that Lear utters in his madness (e.g. 4.5.108–25) may be traced to this perception.

70 pelican daughters The pelican was proverbial for feeding its young with its own flesh and blood, and the young were proverbial for cruelty to their parents.

71 Pillicock … Hill Edgar's fragment, suggested by 'pelican', may be part of a nursery rhyme: 'Pillycock, Pillycock sat on a hill; / If he's not gone, he sits there still' (Collier, cited by Furness). Compare 'Pillicock' = (1) term of endearment, darling, (2) the penis; 'Pillicock Hill' = female genitals (Partridge).

71 alow … loo Variously explained. Furness suggests the sound of a cockcrow; Kittredge, a wild 'halloo' as if to a hawk; Perrett, a Bedlam's horn; etc., etc.

EDGAR   Take heed o'th'foul fiend, obey thy parents, keep thy
words' justice, swear not, commit not with man's sworn spouse,
set not thy sweet heart on proud array. Tom's a-cold.   75

LEAR   What hast thou been?

EDGAR   A servingman, proud in heart and mind, that curled my
hair, wore gloves in my cap, served the lust of my mistress'
heart, and did the act of darkness with her. Swore as many
oaths as I spake words, and broke them in the sweet face of   80
heaven. One that slept in the contriving of lust and waked to
do it. Wine loved I dearly, dice dearly, and in woman out-
paramoured the Turk. False of heart, light of ear, bloody of
hand; hog in sloth, fox in stealth, wolf in greediness, dog in
madness, lion in prey. Let not the creaking of shoes nor the   85

---

*74 words' justice] *Schmidt 1879;* words Iustice F; words iustly Q; word justly *Pope;* word's justice *Knight*   75 sweet heart] Q; Sweet-heart F   *77 servingman,] Q; Seruingman? F   82 I dearly] F; I deeply Q

---

73 foul fiend Possibly suggested by similar-sounding 'fool' in the preceding line (NS, citing Kökeritz, p. 75, who also notes word-play in *3H6* 5.6.18–20).

73–5 obey ... array A version of five of the Ten Commandments; specifically, to honour one's parents, not to commit false witness, take the Lord's name in vain, commit adultery, or engage in covetousness. Compare also 1 Tim. 2.9: ' ... that they aray them selues in comely apparell, with shame-fastnes and modestie, not with ... golde, or pearles, or costly apparell' (Noble, Shaheen).

73–4 keep ... justice Duthie, p. 150, originally defended the F reading, but in NS favours Q. Muir retains F, but makes 'words' singular possessive. The sense seems to be 'keep the integrity of your utterances', i.e. do not lie or bear false witness. The parody of the Commandments strengthens the F reading. Muir and Shaheen compare the Catechism, 'bee true and iust in all my dealing'.

75 proud array fancy clothes.

77–88 A servingman ... fiend Compare Donne's Elegy IV (*c.* 1595) (Davenport, p. 21).

77 servingman Either (1) servant, or (2) lover; possibly both. The description of a dandified servant as courtier fits Oswald as well.

77 proud in heart Shaheen compares Prov. 16.5: 'All that are proude in heart, are an abomination to the Lord', and 21.4: 'A hautie loke, and a proude heart, which is the light of the wicked, is sinne.' 'Proud' could also signify 'lustful' (Booth, p. 164, n. 19).

77–8 curled my hair Malone (cited by Furness) quotes a long passage from Harsnett, p. 54, in which Master Mainy 'curled his hair' and otherwise demonstrated the sin of pride. The passage continues, as the present one does, with a catalogue of deadly sins represented by devils in the shape of animals, including the dog and the wolf, which Shakespeare may have remembered.

78 wore ... cap i.e. wore the favours of his mistress like a courtly lover or gallant.

81 slept ... lust i.e. dreamt of plotting lascivious deeds.

82 dearly ... dearly See collation. F's repetition appears intentional and emphatic.

82–3 out-paramoured the Turk i.e. had more lovers than the Turkish sultan had in his harem.

83 light of ear 'credulous of evil, ready to receive malicious reports' (Johnson, cited by Furness); i.e. a gossip-monger. Kittredge quotes from *The Schole-House of Women*: 'So light of eare they be and sowre, / That of the better they neuer record, / The worse reherce they word by word.'

84–5 hog ... prey Edgar gives an abbreviated list parodying the Seven Deadly Sins, which were often represented by animals. Compare 77–8 n. above, and Florio, *Second Fruites*, p. 165: 'lyon for surque-dry, goate for letcherie, dragon for crueltie' (cited by Muir).

85 prey preying.

85–6 Let ... silks The sounds a woman makes as she walks. Creaking shoes were fashionable (Kittredge).

rustling of silks betray thy poor heart to woman. Keep thy foot
out of brothels, thy hand out of plackets, thy pen from lender's
books, and defy the foul fiend. Still through the hawthorn
blows the cold wind, says suum, mun, nonny. Dauphin, my boy,
boy, *cessez!* let him trot by.   90

Storm still

LEAR   Thou wert better in a grave than to answer with thy uncovered body this extremity of the skies. Is man no more than
this? Consider him well. Thou ow'st the worm no silk, the beast
no hide, the sheep no wool, the cat no perfume. Ha! Here's
three on's are sophisticated; thou art the thing itself. Unaccom-   95
modated man is no more but such a poor, bare, forked animal
as thou art. Off, off, you lendings! Come, unbutton here.

---

86 rustling] F; ruslngs Q   86 woman] F; women Q   87 brothels] F; brothell Q   87 plackets] F; placket Q   88 books]
F; booke Q   89 says suum, mun, nonny] F; hay no on ny Q   89–90 Dauphin, my boy, boy, *cessez*] *This edn;* Dolphin
my boy, my boy, caese Q; Dolphin my Boy, Boy *Sesey:* F; Dauphin, my boy! Boy, *cessez; Oxford*   90 SD] F; *not in*
Q   91 Thou] F; Why thou Q   91 a] F; thy Q   92 than] then F; but Q   93 ow'st] F; owest Q   94 Ha!] Ha? F; *not in*
Q   97 lendings! Come, unbutton here.] F; leadings, come on be true. Q *uncorr.,* Q2; lendings, come on Q *corr.*

---

87 plackets (1) slits or openings in petticoats,
(2) a euphemism for the female pudendum
(Partridge).

87–8 pen ... books A sure way to fall into
trouble was to borrow from moneylenders.

89 suum, mun, nonny The first two words
suggest the sound of the wind (Knight, cited by
Furness). The third word is used often in ballad
refrains. (Steevens apparently invented a ballad
about a battle in France in which the French king
did not want to risk his son the Dauphin: see
Furness.) Some editions, e.g. NS, conflate emended
Q and F, 'suum, mun, hay nonny nonny', since
Edgar utters the kind of nonsense that could end
in a ballad tag. For 'nonny-nonny' NS quotes *OED*:
'meaningless refrain, formerly often used to cover
indelicate allusions'. Compare *Ham.* 4.5.166, *Ado*
2.3.69.

89–90 Dauphin ... by Unexplained. See collation. Johnson was the first to suggest French *cessez*
for F '*Sesey*', but the reference to the Dauphin of
France is unclear. Johnson thought it referred to a
servant or attendant, others that it is from a ballad
or song, but evidence is absent. John Crow suggested to Muir that 'Dolphin' (Dauphin) could
mean the devil; he quoted a Noah mystery play: 'I
pray to Dolphin, prince of dead, / Scald you all in
his lead.' The identification with the devil derives
from English hatred of the French, and Edgar often
refers to devils or fiends who accompany or torment
him.

91 answer respond, encounter.

92–3 Is ... well Compare Hebrews 2.6: 'What is
man, that thou shouldest bee mindfull of him? or
the sonne of man that thou wouldest consider him?'
(Noble, Shaheen). Nearly the same words appear in
Ps. 8.4. G. C. Taylor cites parallels from
Montaigne's *Apology for Raymond Sebonde*, iii.250,
268; vi.189–90 (in Florio's translation, quoted in
Muir, NS).

94 cat i.e. the civet cat, from whose glands ingredients for perfume are obtained.

95 sophisticated adulterated, artificially altered.

95–6 Unaccommodated Unfurnished with the
trappings of civilization, i.e. unadorned with
clothes.

96 forked two-legged. Compare *2H4* 3.2.311,
where Falstaff describes Justice Shallow as 'a forked
radish'.

97 lendings clothes, i.e. the borrowings mentioned in 93–4. Lear begins tearing off his clothes,
the 'ironic conclusion' to the divestiture begun in
1.1 of everything but the name of king and the
reservation of a hundred knights (Heilman, p. 76).
Now he strips down to 'nothing'.

97 Come ... here Perhaps a delirious command to a groom, but more likely Lear speaking
to himself. Compare 5.3.283. *Hysterica passio* is
evidently afflicting Lear. As he tears off his
clothing, Kent and the Fool try to restrain
him. See collation and compare Clayton, pp.
127–8; Stone, pp. 225–6. Furness suggests
'unbutton here' may be a SD.

FOOL   Prithee, nuncle, be contented; 'tis a naughty night to swim
in. Now a little fire in a wild field were like an old lecher's heart
– a small spark, all the rest on's body cold. Look, here comes a   100
walking fire.

Enter GLOUCESTER *with a torch*

EDGAR   This is the foul Flibbertigibbet; he begins at curfew and
walks till the first cock. He gives the web and the pin, squints
the eye, and makes the harelip; mildews the white wheat, and
hurts the poor creature of earth.   105
[*Chants*] Swithold footed thrice the wold,
         He met the nightmare and her ninefold;

---

98 contented; 'tis] F; content, this is Q   100 on's] F; in Q   101 SD] F (*after 97*); *Enter Gloster.* Q   102 foul] F; foule
fiend Q   102 Flibbertigibbet] F; *Sriberdegibit* Q *uncorr.; fliberdegibek* Q *corr.;* Sirberdegibit Q2   *103 till the] Q; at
F   103 gives] F, Q *corr.;* gins Q *uncorr.,* Q2   103 web and the pin, squints] F; web, the pin– / queues Q *uncorr.;* web, &
the pin, squemes Q *corr.;* web, the pinqueuer Q2   104 harelip] Hare-lippe F; harte lip Q *uncorr.,* Q2; hare lip Q *corr.*   106
SD] *This edn; not in* Q, F; [*Sings*] / *Oxford*   106–10 Swithold . . . thee!] *Capell's lineation; four lines ending* . . . old, / . . .
nine-fold; / . . . -plight, / . . . thee. F; *as prose* Q   106 Swithold] F; swithald Q   *106 wold] *Theobald;* old Q, F   107 He
. . . nightmare] F, Q *corr.;* a nellthu night more Q *uncorr.;* anellthu night More Q2

---

98 naughty wicked.

98 swim Perhaps suggested by Lear's move-
ments and the wet weather.

99 little fire . . . heart As the Fool sees
Gloucester advancing through the field, the comparison is dramatically apt. Accordingly, some editions, e.g. NS, move the SD for Gloucester's
entrance to 99 after 'swim in'.

99 wild uncultivated, not bearing crops (NS).

101 walking fire i.e. someone carrying a torch.
Here the Fool begins his lapse into silence.
Upstaged initially by Edgar as Poor Tom in both
Q and F, the Fool later – in Q – tries to regain his
position, but not in F, as the texts diverge significantly (Kerrigan, p. 226; see Textual Analysis,
p. 267 below).

102 Flibbertigibbet A dancing devil in
Harsnett.

102 curfew 9 p.m.

103 first cock midnight.

103 web . . . pin cataract of the eye. Compare
OED Web *sb* 7.

103 squints i.e. causes to squint. See collation. Q
corr. 'squemes' may be a miscorrection of Q uncorr.
'-queues' for 'squenies' or 'squenes' (Duthie, p.
193); compare 4.5.132. Greg, *Variants*, pp. 165–7,
believes F 'squints' is a sophistication, but other
evidence suggests authorial revision (*Textual
Companion*, p. 536). Muir, who prints 'squinies',
cites Armin's use of 'squiny' as well as 'squened' in
his *Nest of Ninnies* (1608) and 'squeaning' in *The*

Italian Taylor (1609), also cited by Greg.

104 white wheat grain almost ripe for harvest-
ing. Compare John 4.35: 'loke on the regions: for
they are white already vnto haruest' (NS).

105 creature Collective for 'creatures'.

106 Swithold Most editors see 'Swithold' as a
contraction of 'St Withold', mentioned in *The
Troublesome Raigne of Iohn King of England* (1591):
'Sweete S. *Withold* of thy lenitie, defend vs from
extremitie' (1184). The saint, of whom only this is
known, was apparently a protector from harms in
general. Oxford emends to 'Swithune', following
Tate. Swithune, or Swithun (also spelled
Swithin), was a popular English saint famous for
healing and associated with rain (*Textual
Companion*, p. 518, arguing for common *a/u* and
*l/*minim misreadings in Q of 'Swithune' – and presumably *e/d* misreading as well). Q's 'swithald' and
F's '*Swithold*' reinforce each other, however, and
the precedent in *The Troublesome Raigne* is persuasive, since (as *Textual Companion* recognizes) Tate
may have been only simplifying.

106 footed thrice The saint walks over the
downs three times (a magical number).

106 wold upland plain, or downs; Q/F 'old' suggests the dialectal pronunciation.

107 nightmare . . . ninefold The nightmare
was 'a female spirit or monster supposed to beset
people and animals by night, settling upon them
when they are asleep and producing a feeling of
suffocation by its weight' (*OED* Nightmare *sb* 1).

Bid her alight
And her troth plight,
And aroint thee, witch, aroint thee!   110

KENT   How fares your grace?

LEAR   What's he?

KENT   Who's there? What is't you seek?

GLOUCESTER   What are you there? Your names?

EDGAR   Poor Tom, that eats the swimming frog, the toad, the   115
tadpole, the wall-newt, and the water; that in the fury of his
heart, when the foul fiend rages, eats cowdung for salads,
swallows the old rat and the ditch-dog, drinks the green mantle
of the standing pool; who is whipped from tithing to tithing,
and stocked, punished, and imprisoned; who hath had three   120
suits to his back, six shirts to his body,

Horse to ride, and weapon to wear;
But mice and rats and such small deer
Have been Tom's food for seven long year.

Beware my follower. Peace, Smulkin; peace, thou fiend!   125

GLOUCESTER   What, hath your grace no better company?

---

108 alight] a-light F; O light Q, Q2   109 troth plight] Q; troth-plight F   110 aroint] F; arint Q (*both times*)   110 witch]
F, Q *corr.*; with Q *uncorr.*, Q2   116 tadpole] tode pold Q *uncorr.*; tod pole Q *corr.*; Tod-pole F   116 wall-newt] F, Q *corr.*;
wall-wort Q *uncorr.*, Q2   120 stocked, punished,] F; stock-punisht Q   *120 had] Q; *not in* F   122 Horse . . . wear;] F;
part of preceding prose Q   124 Have] F; Hath Q   125 Smulkin] F; snulbug Q

Note the derivation from Anglo-Saxon 'mare' =
incubus, which has nothing to do with 'mare' =
she-horse (Kittredge). But Q corr. 'nine fold' (F
nine-fold) may = 'nine fole' (i.e. 'foal') (Tyrwhitt,
cited by Furness). Excrescent -*d* is common in
Shakespeare, as in 'vilde' for 'vile' (129). Oxford
prints 'foal'. Capell thought the 'nine-fold' referred
to the attendant train of imps or familiars. Nine, as a
multiple of three, is another magic number. NS and
others cite a similar charm to cure the nightmare
from Scot's *Discoverie of Witchcraft* (1584) and
elsewhere.

108 **Bid her alight** i.e. get down off the sleeper's
chest.

109 **troth plight** i.e. promise to do no more
harm.

110 **aroint thee** Command to the demon (or
witch who invoked her) to be gone, as in *Mac.*
1.3.6.

111–13 **How . . . seek?** Kent addresses Lear first,
then Gloucester. Sisson, p. 237, believes the first
query is properly Gloucester's; but since Lear, now
subdued, has just undergone a vigorous struggle,
the question by Kent is appropriate.

116 **wall-newt** wall-lizard.

116 **water** i.e. water-newt.

116–17 **in the fury . . . rages** i.e. when the mad
fit is upon him.

118 **ditch-dog** dead dogs thrown into ditches
(Delius, cited by Furness).

118–19 **green mantle . . . pool** scum from a
stagnant pond. Compare *MV* 1.1.89.

119–20 **whipped . . . imprisoned** Vagabonds
under a statute of 1572 could be punished in these
ways until driven back to wherever they belonged or
whoever would take them in.

119 **tithing** A rural district originally containing
ten households.

120 **stocked** i.e. placed in the stocks.

120–1 **three . . . body** Compare 2.2.14 n. on a
servingman's allowance.

123–4 **mice . . . year** Compare the popular
romance, *Bevis of Hampton*: 'Ratons and myce and
soche smale dere / That was hys mete that seven
yere' (Capell, cited by Kittredge).

123 **deer** game in general.

125 **Smulkin** A minor devil (in mouse's form in
Harsnett, p. 140).

126 **What . . . company** This speech and
Gloucester's next two are directed to Lear.

EDGAR   The Prince of Darkness is a gentleman. Modo he's called,
   and Mahu.

GLOUCESTER   Our flesh and blood, my lord, is grown so vile,
         That it doth hate what gets it.   130

EDGAR   Poor Tom's a-cold.

GLOUCESTER   Go in with me. My duty cannot suffer
         T'obey in all your daughters' hard commands.
         Though their injunction be to bar my doors
         And let this tyrannous night take hold upon you,   135
         Yet have I ventured to come seek you out
         And bring you where both fire and food is ready.

LEAR   First let me talk with this philosopher.
         What is the cause of thunder?

KENT   Good my lord, take his offer; go into th'house.   140

LEAR   I'll talk a word with this same learnèd Theban.
         What is your study?

EDGAR   How to prevent the fiend, and to kill vermin.

LEAR   Let me ask you one word in private.

---

128 Mahu.] F; ma hu – Q   129–30 Our ... it.] *Pope's lineation; as prose* Q, F   129 blood ... vile] F; bloud is growne so vild my Lord, Q   132–7 Go ... ready.] F *lineation; as prose* Q   133 T'] F; to Q   137 fire and food] F; food and fire Q   140 Good ... house.] Q; *two lines divided* offer, / Go F   140 Good my] F; My good Q   140 th'] F; the Q   141–2 I'll ... study?] F *lineation; as prose* Q   141 same] F; most Q

127 Prince ... gentleman Said apparently in reply to Gloucester's question.

127–8 Modo ... Mahu Modu, another name for the devil in Harsnett, was 'a graund Commaunder, Mustermaister over the Captaines of the seaven deadly sinnes', and Maho was 'generall Dictator of hell' (Harsnett, p. 46; compare *ibid.*, p. 166). Edmond Blunden, *Shakespeare's Significances* (cited by Muir), says that Modo may have reminded Shakespeare of a passage in Horace, *Epistles*, 2.1.210–13, which describes the tragic poet and concludes with references to Thebes and Athens (compare 'learned Theban' (141), and 'good Athenian' (164 below)). Harsnett, moreover, quotes and translates from Horace's next epistle on 'Dreames and Magicall affrights'; both epistles are connected by mention of terror and magic (Muir). The passage describing the tragic poet is one 'above all others' in Horace that Shakespeare could be expected to have known (NS).

129 flesh and blood i.e. children. Gloucester's comment may occasion Edgar's cry.

   130 gets begets.

   132 suffer bear, endure.

   133 in all in every respect.

137 bring ... ready Gloucester wants to escort Lear to a more suitable place than Edgar's hovel, possibly a servants' chamber in his castle or a sturdy outbuilding on his estate.

138 philosopher student of natural philosophy, scientist. G. S. Gordon, *Shakespearian Comedy*, 1944, pp. 126–8, says that formerly kings kept philosophers just as they kept a fool and other court officers (Muir, NS). Lear takes Edgar as a member of his court and questions him in the manner of medieval instructional procedures (dialogue or catechism). The cause of thunder was a typical question. Compare 1.5.15 ff., where the Fool parodies the procedure.

139 What ... thunder A stock question, prompted undoubtedly by the storm.

141 learnèd Theban Greek scholar. Compare 127–8 n.

142 study (1) field of research, (2) object of main attention.

143 prevent (1) anticipate, and thus (2) avoid, escape.

143 fiend ... vermin Compare 57–8 n. above.

144 in private Lear and Edgar here converse apart.

KENT   Importune him once more to go, my lord.   145
      His wits begin t'unsettle.

GLOUCESTER   Canst thou blame him?

                Storm still

      His daughters seek his death. Ah, that good Kent,
      He said it would be thus, poor banished man!
      Thou sayst the king grows mad; I'll tell thee, friend,
      I am almost mad myself. I had a son,   150
      Now outlawed from my blood; he sought my life
      But lately, very late. I loved him, friend;
      No father his son dearer. True to tell thee,
      The grief hath crazed my wits. What a night's this!
      I do beseech your grace –

LEAR   O, cry you mercy, sir. –   155
      Noble philosopher, your company.

EDGAR   Tom's a-cold.

GLOUCESTER   In, fellow, there, in t'hovel; keep thee warm.

LEAR   Come, let's in all.

KENT   This way, my lord.

LEAR   With him;
      I will keep still with my philosopher.   160

KENT   Good my lord, soothe him; let him take the fellow.

GLOUCESTER   Take him you on.

KENT   Sirrah, come on. Go along with us.

LEAR   Come, good Athenian.

GLOUCESTER   No words, no words. Hush.   165

145–6 Importune ... t'unsettle] F *lineation; as prose* Q   **145** once more] F; *not in* Q   **146** t'] F; to Q   **146** SD] F; *not in* Q   **147** Ah,] F; O Q   **149** sayst] sayest Q, F   **151** he] F; a Q   **152** friend;] (Friend) F; friend Q   **153** True] F, Q; truth Q2   **154–5** The ... grace –] F *lineation; divided* wits, / What Q   **155** grace –] *Capell* (*subst.*); Grace. Q; grace. F   **155–6** O ... company.] F *lineation; one line* Q   **155–6** mercy, sir. – / Noble] F; mercie noble Q   ***158** in t'] in't Q; into th' F   **159–60** With ... philosopher.] F *lineation; one line* Q   **159–60** him; / I will keep still] F; him I wil keep stil, Q   **161** Good ... fellow.] *As in* Q; *two lines divided* him: / Let F

147 His ... death Perhaps Gloucester interprets 2.4.295–302 to mean this. At 3.6.45, however, after returning from his castle to get help for the king, he says he has heard of 'a plot of death upon him'.

151 outlawed ... blood i.e. disowned and disinherited.

152–3 I loved ... dearer Gloucester's behaviour in 1.2 and 2.1 hardly bears out this statement, but his self-delusion is characteristic.

155–65 I ... Hush Gloucester addresses Lear and tries to lead him away from the Bedlamite. But Lear demurs and wishes to stay with Edgar, whereupon Gloucester again tries to separate them by urging Edgar back into his hovel. Lear insists on keeping with Edgar even as Kent intercedes and also tries to lead him away. Lear, in fact, never enters the hovel (Perrett, p. 260), but at the end of the scene is led elsewhere, taking Edgar and the others with him (160–4).

155 cry you mercy I beg your pardon.

161 soothe humour; used by Harsnett (p. 185) in this sense (Muir).

164 Athenian i.e. philosopher; compare 127–8 n.

EDGAR   Child Roland to the dark tower came.
            His word was still 'Fie, fo, and fum;
            I smell the blood of a British man.'

                                                                Exeunt

3.5 *Enter* CORNWALL *and* EDMOND

CORNWALL   I will have my revenge ere I depart his house.

EDMOND   How, my lord, I may be censured, that nature thus gives
            way to loyalty, something fears me to think of.

CORNWALL   I now perceive it was not altogether your brother's evil
            disposition made him seek his death, but a provoking merit set   5
            a-work by a reprovable badness in himself.

EDMOND   How malicious is my fortune, that I must repent to be
            just! This is the letter which he spoke of, which approves him
            an intelligent party to the advantages of France. O heavens, that
            this treason were not, or not I the detector!   10

CORNWALL   Go with me to the duchess.

EDMOND   If the matter of this paper be certain, you have mighty
            business in hand.

---

166 tower came] F; towne come Q   168 SD] F; *not in* Q   Act 3, Scene 5   3.5] *Scena Quinta.* F; *not in* Q   0 SD
EDMOND] F; *Bastard.* Q   1 his] F; the Q   8 just!] iust? Q, F   8 letter which] F; letter Q   9 heavens,] heauens Q;
Heavens! F   10 this] F; his Q   10 were not,] F; were Q

166–8 Child . . . man 'Tom has the last word.
Silent Fool is usually seen separated inexorably
from his master, following forlornly behind'
(Rosenberg, p. 228; compare Kerrigan, pp. 226–
30). Edgar combines fragments presumably from
two lost ballads: the first line alludes to the exploits
of the epic hero, Roland, famous in the twelfth-
century *Chanson de Roland*. The second and third
lines derive from some version of *Jack the Giant
Killer*. 'British Roland is entering the Giant's
Castle, where his blood (kinship) is in danger of
being smelt (detected)' (NS).
  166 Child Title of candidate for knighthood
(Kittredge).
  166 dark tower Possibly refers to Gloucester's
castle, which is proving quite 'dark'.
  167 word password.
  167–8 Fie . . . man The Giant's speech is 'given,
by an intentional incongruity, to the heroic Child
Rowland' (Muir); the tower may have suggested the
story of the beanstalk (Hunter). It is all very ominous, the apparent nonsense notwithstanding; the
foreboding is borne out in 3.7. In dramatic function,
Edgar's speech parallels the Fool's prophecy at the
end of 3.2.

168 British Instead of 'English', as in the traditional tag; possibly a concession to legendary
history, or to the efforts of James I to unify the
realm.

Act 3, Scene 5
  2 censured judged.
  2–3 nature . . . loyalty Edmond subordinates
the 'natural' loyalty of a child to his father in favour
of loyalty to the duke (from whom he 'naturally'
expects advancement).
  3 something fears somewhat frightens.
  4–6 I now . . . himself The syntax is unclear, but
the sense seems to be: I see now that it was not only
your brother's innate wickedness, but Gloucester's
deserving, which could incite his son's reprehensi-
ble wickedness to kill him.
  5 merit desert (in bad sense) (Schmidt).
  7–8 How . . . just The irony here doubles back
on itself.
  8 approves him proves him to be.
  9 an intelligent party a spy, giving information, intelligence.
  12 this paper Gloucester's letter (8).

CORNWALL True or false, it hath made thee Earl of Gloucester.
Seek out where thy father is, that he may be ready for our   15
apprehension.

EDMOND [*Aside*] If I find him comforting the king, it will stuff his
suspicion more fully. – I will persever in my course of loyalty,
though the conflict be sore between that and my blood.

CORNWALL I will lay trust upon thee, and thou shalt find a dearer   20
father in my love.

Exeunt

3.6 *Enter* KENT [*disguised*] *and* GLOUCESTER

GLOUCESTER Here is better than the open air; take it thankfully. I
will piece out the comfort with what addition I can. I will not be
long from you.

KENT All the power of his wits have given way to his impatience;
the gods reward your kindness!   5

Exit [*Gloucester*]

Enter LEAR, EDGAR [*disguised as a madman*], *and* FOOL

EDGAR Frateretto calls me, and tells me Nero is an angler in the
lake of darkness. Pray, innocent, and beware the foul fiend.

FOOL Prithee, nuncle, tell me whether a madman be a gentleman
or a yeoman.

---

17 SD] *Theobald; not in* Q, F   *20 dearer] Q; deere F   21 SD] F; *Exit.* Q   Act 3, Scene 6   3.6] *Scena Sexta.* F; *not in* Q   0 SD] F; *Enter Gloster and Lear, Kent, Foole, and Tom.* Q   4 to his] F; *to* Q   5 reward] F; deserue Q   5 SD.1] *Capell; Exit* F (*after 3*); *not in* Q   5 SD.2 *Enter … FOOL*] F; *not in* Q (*but see 0 SD*)   6 Frateretto] F; *Fretereto* Q   7 Pray, innocent, and] *Johnson;* pray Innocent, and F; pray innocent Q

16 apprehension arrest.

17 comforting i.e. in legal sense of 'supporting, helping' (Muir).

18 persever The form used by Shakespeare, with the accent on the second syllable (*OED*).

19 blood i.e. filial feeling.

Act 3, Scene 6

2 piece out augment, supplement.

4 have 'wits' influences the plural form.

4 impatience 'lack of self-control; passion' (NS).

5 gods … kindness But what Gloucester gets in 3.7 is cruelly different (Rosenberg, p. 231). Compare 5.3.230.

6 Frateretto Another of the dancing devils in Harsnett (p. 49).

6–7 Nero … darkness After introducing Frateretto and other 'devils of the round, or Morice', Harsnett associates them with 'the Fidler' (p. 49), clearly the Emperor Nero, who fiddled while Rome burned and is imagined condemned to hell for

many crimes against his family and the Empire. Nero's angling, however, comes from Chaucer's *Monk's Tale* (F. E. Budd, 'Shakespeare, Chaucer, and Harsnett', *RES* II (1935), 421–9). Angling in the 'lake of darkness', moreover, may allude not only to the Stygian lake, which Harsnett mentions in the same context, but also to the murder of Agrippina, whose womb Nero 'slitte, to biholde / Wher he conceyved was' (*Monk's Tale*, 485–6). Compare Hamlet's allusion to this crime. *Ham.* 3.2.390–6. The vision of hell is continued in Lear's speech (13–14), where he imagines tortures for Gonerill and Regan.

7 Pray … fiend Perhaps addressed to the Fool, who briefly revives and tries vainly to recapture Lear's attention.

8 madman A possible pun, 'mad' – 'made' (Schmidt, cited by Muir). Kökeritz, pp. 126–7, 164, notes similar puns elsewhere, e.g. *TN* 3.4.52–7 and *TNK* 3.5.72–7 (compare Cercignani, pp. 236–7). A 'made man' is one whose success in life is assured (*OED* Made *ppl a* 7).

LEAR   A king, a king!   10

FOOL   No, he's a yeoman that has a gentleman to his son; for he's a
        mad yeoman that sees his son a gentleman before him.

LEAR   To have a thousand with red burning spits
            Come hizzing in upon 'em!

EDGAR   Bless thy five wits.   15

KENT   O pity! Sir, where is the patience now
            That you so oft have boasted to retain?

EDGAR   [*Aside*] My tears begin to take his part so much
            They mar my counterfeiting.

LEAR   The little dogs and all,   20
            Tray, Blanch, and Sweetheart – see, they bark at me.

EDGAR   Tom will throw his head at them. – Avaunt, you curs!
            Be thy mouth or black or white,
            Tooth that poisons if it bite,
            Mastiff, greyhound, mongrel grim,   25
            Hound or spaniel, brach or him,
            Bobtail tyke or trundle-tail,

11–12 FOOL No . . . him.] F; *not in* Q   13–14 To . . . 'em!] F *lineation; as prose* Q (*continuing 10*)   18 SD] *Rowe; not in* Q,
F   19 They] F; Theile Q   22 Tom . . . curs] *As in* Q; *divided* you / Curres F   23–8 Be . . . wail;] F *lineation* (*except 22–
3*); *three lines ending* . . . bite, / . . . him, / . . . waile, Q   *25–6 mongrel grim, / Hound] *Rowe* (*subst.*); Mongrill, Grim, /
Hound F; mungril, grim-hoūd Q   *26 him,] Q; Hym: F; lym; *Hanmer* (*see Commentary*)   *27 Bobtail tyke] Bobtaile tike
Q; Or Bobtaile tight F   *27 trundle-tail] Q2; trūdletaile Q; Troudle taile F

11–12 FOOL . . . **before him** See Textual
Analysis, p. 266 below. Davenport, p. 21, compares
Joseph Hall's satire on the doting Lolio, a yeoman,
in *Virgidemiae* (1598), Bk IV, sat. ii: 'Old driueling
Lolio drudges all he can, / To make his eldest sonne
a Gentleman . . .' Lolio's son, like Lear's two elder
daughters, is ungrateful.

13 **a thousand** i.e. devils, or demons. Compare
Lear's hundred knights.

14 **hizzing** F's spelling seems a deliberate
attempt at onomatopoeia, i.e. the whizzing sound
of the red-hot weapons (Kittredge).

14 **upon 'em** On F's omission of the mock trial
that follows in Q, see Textual Analysis, pp. 253–4
below.

15 **Bless** . . . **wits** See 3.4.55 n.

20–1 **The little** . . . **me** Lear imagines that even
his lapdogs, possibly bitches as their names suggest,
have turned against him.

22 **throw his head** Unexplained, but the expression (repeated at 29) may mean to shake one's head
wildly or to face menacingly. 'Head' could mean
hair, or the antlers of a deer (Edgar mentions his
'horn' (32)). See also 29 n.

23 **or** . . . **or** either . . . or.

26 **brach bitch.** Compare 1.4.98.

26 **him** i.e. male dog. Hanmer's emendation,
'lym' (=lymmer, a species of bloodhound), generally accepted, is unnecessary. Furthermore,
Blayney's lengthy analysis (in the unpublished second volume of *The Texts of 'King Lear'*) shows that
the philological evidence brought to bear in support
of Hanmer's emendation breaks down. 'Lyam'
means 'leash'; hence, 'lyam-hound' or 'lime-
hound' = 'leash-hound'. According to Hanmer,
'lyam' or 'lym' also means 'leash-hound', which is
about as plausible, Blayney says, as the analogous
claim that 'fox' means 'fox-hound' or that 'cart'
means 'cart-horse'. *OED* errs in citing, out of context, 'lyam' as meaning any kind of dog; in context,
the quotation from 1486 may mean something quite
different, but the entry itself may be wrong.

27 **Bobtail tyke** A small dog with its tail cut short,
or 'bobbed'. Q 'tike' is obviously right; F 'tight' makes
no sense and may be a misreading and miscorrection of
'tike' > 'tite' > 'tight' (Duthie, p. 179).

27 **trundle-tail** A dog with a long, curly tail. F's
'Troudle' is apparently the result of a turned letter,
since 'trondle' is a variant spelling of 'trundle' (Q2).
Compare Duthie, p. 180.

Tom will make him weep and wail;
For with throwing thus my head,
Dogs leap the hatch, and all are fled.   30
Do, de, de, de. *Cessez!* Come, march to wakes and fairs and
market towns. Poor Tom, thy horn is dry.

LEAR Then let them anatomise Regan; see what breeds about her
heart. Is there any cause in nature that makes these hard-
hearts? [*To Edgar*] You, sir, I entertain for one of my hundred,   35
only I do not like the fashion of your garments. You will say
they are Persian; but let them be changed.

KENT Now, good my lord, lie here and rest a while.

LEAR Make no noise, make no noise. Draw the curtains: so, so.

---

28 him] F; them Q   29–30 For ... fled.] F *lineation; as prose* Q   *29 head,] Q; head; F   *30 leap] Q; leapt F   31–2 Do
... dry] *As prose* Q; *two lines divided* Fayres / And F   31 Do, de, de, de] F; loudla doodla Q   *31 Cessez!] *This edn;* sese:
F; Sessey / Johnson; *not in* Q   33–7 Then ... changed.] F; *five verse lines ending* ... her [*turned over*] / ... hardnes, /
... hundred, / ... say, / ... chang'd. Q   *34 makes] Q; make F   34–5 these hard-hearts] F; this hardnes, Q; these hard
hearts *Rowe*   35 SD] *Capell; not in* Q, F   35 entertain] F; entertaine you Q   36 garments. You will] F; garments youle
Q   37 Persian] F; Persian attire Q   38 and rest] F; *not in* Q   39–40 Make ... morning.] *As prose* F; *two verse lines
divided* so, / Weele Q   39 so, so.] so, so, so; F; so, so, so, Q

---

29 throwing ... head Edgar either throws his
horn ('head'), or, putting the horn on his head,
pretends to attack or scare away the dog (Muir).
In Edmond Kean's staging and Macready's, he
threw a straw head-dress at imaginary dogs
(Bratton, p. 229).

30 hatch Lower half of a divided door.

31 Do ... de Compare 3.4.55. Edgar's teeth
chatter again.

31 wakes 'local annual festival of an English
parish observed ... as an occasion for making holi-
day, entertainment of friends, and often for village
sports, dancing, and other amusements' (*OED*
Wake *sb*¹ 4b). Beggars and rogues did well at such
gatherings; compare *WT* 4.3.102: Autolycus 'haunts
wakes, fairs, and bear-baitings'.

32 thy horn is dry Formula for begging drink,
carried in the ox horn beggars wore about their
necks. Perhaps it also means, as Steevens thought,
that Edgar has exhausted his repertoire of Tom
o'Bedlam; in fact, this is his last speech in the scene.

33–4 Then ... heart An acceptable non sequi-
tur, given the context of mad speeches, though
Duthie, p. 8, argues that as it continues the mock
trial in Q, the words retained in F are rendered
pointless after the trial is cut.

33 anatomise dissect. In the theatre, Lear
usually acts out the dissection, plunging a dagger
into the imaginary body, holding up the heart, etc.
(Rosenberg, p. 236). In the Royal Shakespeare
Company production in 1982, directed by Adrian
Noble (who retained the mock trial), Lear here

thrust his dagger into a cushion the Fool held over
his stomach, mortally wounding him. The action
thus accounted for the Fool's disappearance from
the play after 3.6.

33–4 what ... heart i.e. what grows around her
heart (to harden it).

34–5 hard-hearts See collation and *Textual
Companion*, p. 536: 'the compound was current as
a verb and adjective (*OED*), and on the analogy of
hard-head(s) could easily have been understood as
a substantive'. Hard hearts were well known theo-
logical phenomena, caused by a fall from grace
(Hunter); but Lear seeks an anatomical
explanation.

35 entertain engage.

35 my hundred i.e. hundred knights.

37 Persian i.e. gorgeous; but compare 'Theban',
'Athenian' (3.4.141, 164), and next note. Blunden
believed the allusion is to Horace, *Odes*, 1.38:
'Persicos odi, puer, apparatus' ('I dislike Persian
pomp') (NS). A Persian embassy visited England
early in James I's reign (Muir).

37 changed Compare Dan. 6.8: 'Seale the writ-
ing, that it not be changed, according to the lawe of
the Medes and Persians, which altereth not'
(Shaheen). The immutability of Medean and
Persian laws had become proverbial in
Shakespeare's day.

39 Draw ... so, so Lear, exhausted, imagines he
is in a luxurious, canopied bed speaking to his
servant. Perhaps Edgar or Kent and the Fool
mime the action; hence, 'so, so' (Rosenberg, p. 237).

We'll go to supper i'th'morning. [*He sleeps*]   40
FOOL   And I'll go to bed at noon.

Enter GLOUCESTER

GLOUCESTER   Come hither, friend. Where is the king my master?
KENT   Here, sir, but trouble him not; his wits are gone.
GLOUCESTER   Good friend, I prithee take him in thy arms.
I have o'erheard a plot of death upon him.   45
There is a litter ready. Lay him in't
And drive toward Dover, friend, where thou shalt meet
Both welcome and protection. Take up thy master;
If thou shouldst dally half an hour, his life
With thine and all that offer to defend him   50
Stand in assurèd loss. Take up, take up,
And follow me, that will to some provision
Give thee quick conduct. Come, come away.

Exeunt

40 i'th'morning.] F; it'h morning, so, so, so, Q   **40** SD] *Oxford; not in* Q, F   **41** FOOL And . . . noon.] F; *not in* Q   ***41** SD] *As in Capell; after 37* F; *after 40* Q   **42** Come . . . master?] *As in* Q; *two lines divided* Friend: / Where F   **46– 53** There . . . away.] F *lineation; six lines ending* . . . frend / . . . master [*turned under*] / . . . with thine / . . . losse, / . . . prouision / . . . conduct. Q   **46** in't] F, Q; in it Q2   **47** toward] F; towards Q   **51** Take up, take up,] F; Take vp to keepe Q *uncorr.,* Q2; Take vp the King Q *corr.*   **52** me,] F, Q *corr.;* me Q *uncorr.*   **53** conduct.] F *omits four lines here*   **53** come away.] F *omits thirteen and a half lines here*   **53** SD] F; Q *continues scene*

40 We'll ... morning This 'inversion-utterance' (NS) is a characteristic of the Fool (see 41 n.), who has been tutoring Lear to face harsh realities, not curtain them off. Whatever other significance they have, the words may refer, literally, to the lack of food (which Gloucester was supposed to provide), and imply 'We'll eat later.'

41 I'll ... noon The Fool's last line, not in Q, is an 'inversion-statement' (NS, p. xxxii), an appropriate response to Lear's speech. Its underlying significance has been much discussed. It may be proverbial for 'I'll play the fool' (Tilley B197), with a quibble on 'bed' = grave (the Fool, exhausted by events and feeling himself supplanted by Poor Tom, feels his heart breaking). Or Lear's apparent withdrawal from the actual world to the world of hallucination, indicated by the preceding line, culminates here in the Fool's acquiescence in defeat, his 'acceptance of unreality – a purposive pretence that things are other than they are' (Hilda Hulme, *Explorations in Shakespeare's Language*, 1962,

p. 71). Other meanings are possible, including the Fool's intention to abandon his master, since he can no longer help him (Kerrigan, pp. 228–9). In any case, the F addition – if it is one and not a Q oversight – provides the Fool with an appropriate exit line from the play. See Textual Analysis, p. 267 below.

41 SD *Enter* GLOUCESTER See collation. Most editors follow Q and delay Gloucester's entrance. It is unlikely that, given his sense of urgency, Gloucester would stand quietly by for several lines; moreover, he apparently does not see or hear Lear, after whom he enquires (Taylor, 'Censorship', p. 117, n. 48).

45 upon against.

46 litter Evidently, a wheeled vehicle pulled by horses; note 'drive' (47).

52–3 provision ... conduct i.e. Gloucester will quickly lead Kent to where he will find supplies and other necessaries for the trip.

3.7 *Enter* CORNWALL, REGAN, GONERILL, EDMOND, *and Servants*

CORNWALL [*To Gonerill*] Post speedily to my lord your husband;
show him this letter. The army of France is landed. – Seek out
the traitor Gloucester.

[*Exeunt some Servants*]

REGAN   Hang him instantly.

GONERILL   Pluck out his eyes.   5

CORNWALL   Leave him to my displeasure. Edmond, keep you our
sister company. The revenges we are bound to take upon your
traitorous father are not fit for your beholding. Advise the
duke, where you are going, to a most festinate preparation:
we are bound to the like. Our posts shall be swift and intel-   10
ligent betwixt us. Farewell, dear sister; farewell, my lord of
Gloucester.

[*Gonerill and Edmond start to leave*]

Enter OSWALD

How now, where's the king?

Act 3, Scene 7   3.7] *Scena Septima.* F; *not in* Q   0 SD] F; *Enter Cornwall, and Regan, and Gonorill, and Bastard.* Q   1 SD]
Furness; *not in* Q, F   1–3 Post . . . Gloucester.] *As prose* F; *two lines divided letter* [*turned over*] / The Q   3 traitor] F;
vilaine Q   3 SD *Capell* (*subst.*); *not in* Q, F   6–12 Leave . . . Gloucester.] *As prose* F; *six lines of verse ending* . . . company.
[*turned under*] / . . . father, / . . . going [*turned under*] / . . . like, / . . . betwixt vs, / . . . Gloster, Q   7 revenges] F; reuenge
Q   *8 Advise] Q; Advice F   9 festinate] F2; festuant Q, Q2; festiuate F   10 posts] F; post Q   10 intelligent] F;
intelligence Q   12 SD.1] *This edn; not in* Q, F   12 SD.2] F; *Enter Steward.* Q (*after 13*)

Act 3, Scene 7

0 SD Edmond may be dressed in different attire
now, grandly, like the earl he intended to be, though
he will aim still higher. Gonerill and Regan may also
have changed dress to appear more queenly, accent-
uating at the same time a growing competitiveness
between them as much for the new earl as for sole
sovereignty in the kingdom (Rosenberg, p. 240).

1 Post speedily Ride quickly.

2 this letter i.e. the letter Gloucester mentioned
to Edmond, who retrieved it and used it to inform
against him: see 3.3.10; 3.5.8.

5 Pluck out his eyes Editors generally pass over
this line in silence, despite the strange punishment
Gonerill demands, which Cornwall later executes.
Psychoanalytically oriented critics, however, see
blinding, particularly the tearing out of eyes, as a
symbol of castration (N. Holland, *Psychoanalysis
and Shakespeare*, 1966, pp. 217–18). In the Middle
Ages blinding as well as castration was a penalty for
rape (Bridget Lyons, 'The subplot as simplification
in *King Lear*', *Some Facets*, p. 28). Compare
5.3.162–3. That Gonerill is an emasculating female
is evident from her treatment of Albany in 1.4 and

later in 4.2. Blinding as punishment – not for trea-
son, but for adultery – is ironically appropriate for
Gloucester. Compare the homily 'Agaynst
Whoredome, and Adultery' in *Certain Sermons or
Homilies* (1547): 'Emong the Locrensians the adul-
terers had bothe theyr eyes thrust oute' (ed. Ronald
B. Bond, 1987, p. 183). See also J. L. Halio,
'Gloucester's blinding', *SQ* 43 (1992), 221–3.

7 sister i.e. sister-in-law; see 2.2.127 n.

7 bound (1) prepared, ready, (2) obliged, destined (?).

9 festinate preparation hasty preparation (for
war). See collation. A minim misreading results in Q
'festuant' (for 'festinant'? See Stone, p. 182, and
compare Duthie, p. 401, and *Textual Companion*,
p. 519). Either Compositor B similarly misread
copy, or more likely F 'festiuate' is the result of a
turned letter.

10 bound to 'on our way to' (Kittredge).

10 posts messengers.

10–11 intelligent bearing information.

12 Gloucester Edmond: compare 3.5.14. But
Oswald still refers to Edmond's father by that title
(14 below).

OSWALD My lord of Gloucester hath conveyed him hence.
    Some five or six and thirty of his knights,   15
    Hot questrists after him, met him at gate,
    Who, with some other of the lord's dependants,
    Are gone with him toward Dover, where they boast
    To have well-armèd friends.

CORNWALL Get horses for your mistress.   20

                     [*Exit Oswald*]

GONERILL Farewell, sweet lord, and sister.

CORNWALL Edmond, farewell.

              [*Exeunt Gonerill and Edmond*]

[*To Servants*]   Go seek the traitor Gloucester.
    Pinion him like a thief; bring him before us.

              [*Exeunt other Servants*]

    Though well we may not pass upon his life
    Without the form of justice, yet our power   25
    Shall do a curtsy to our wrath, which men
    May blame but not control.

        Enter GLOUCESTER *and Servants*

             Who's there – the traitor?

REGAN Ingrateful fox! 'tis he.

CORNWALL Bind fast his corky arms.

GLOUCESTER What means your graces? Good my friends, consider   30

---

14 hence.] hence, Q; hence F **15–19 Some ... friends.**] F *lineation; as prose* Q **16 questrists**] F; questrits Q ***17 lord's**] *Pope;* Lords Q; Lords, F **18 toward**] F; towards Q **20 SD**] *Staunton; not in* Q, F **22 SD.1**] *Staunton (subst.); Exit Gon. and Bast.* Q *(after 21); Exit* F *(after 21)* **22 SD.2 To Servants**] *Oxford; not in* Q, F **23 SD**] *Capell; not in* Q, F **24 well**] F; *not in* Q **26–7 Shall ... control.**] F *lineation; divided* blame / But Q **26 curtsy**] curt'sie F; curtesie Q ***27 control**] Q; comptroll F **27 SD**] F; *Enter Gloster brought in by two or three,* Q *(after* traytor?) **30–1 What ... friends.**] Q *lineation; three lines ending* ... Graces? / ... Ghests: / ... Friends. F

15 Some ... knights Apparently, Lear's retinue has not yet entirely dissolved, though the play is generally vague about their number, whereabouts, and final disposition. According to Oswald, some three dozen join with Gloucester's men (17) to form a suitable entourage for Lear's trip to Dover, whence they seem to disappear or merge with the forces supporting the king.

16 questrists Probably a Shakespearean coinage = 'questers'; but compare Latin *equestris* = 'equestrian'. Taylor suggests 'questants', as in *AWW* 2.1.16 ('Addenda' to *Division*, p. 488), though Oxford follows F.

23 thief Robbery was then a more heinous crime and punishment more severe than today.

24–5 Though ... justice Cornwall is fully

conscious of the travesty of justice he is about to commit in the ensuing 'trial'.

24 pass upon i.e. pass judgement upon.

25–6 our power ... wrath i.e. our authority will bend to our great anger. As his next clause shows, Cornwall is also conscious that his illegal procedure will excite disapproval; but, hubristically, he believes he can handle the consequences.

26 curtsy i.e. 'do a courtesy to, yield', not the modern word meaning a feminine salutation made by bending the knees and lowering the body.

29 Bind During the next few lines, the servants tie Gloucester to a chair, with apparent reluctance, since Cornwall repeats the command (32).

29 corky 'sapless, dry, and withered' (Muir, citing Harsnett (p. 23), 'an old corkie woman').

You are my guests. Do me no foul play, friends.
CORNWALL   Bind him, I say.
REGAN   Hard, hard! O filthy traitor!
GLOUCESTER   Unmerciful lady as you are, I'm none.
CORNWALL   To this chair bind him. Villain, thou shalt find –
          [*Regan plucks Gloucester's beard*]
GLOUCESTER   By the kind gods, 'tis most ignobly done,   35
          To pluck me by the beard.
REGAN   So white, and such a traitor?
GLOUCESTER   Naughty lady,
          These hairs which thou dost ravish from my chin
          Will quicken and accuse thee. I am your host.
          With robbers' hands my hospitable favours   40
          You should not ruffle thus. What will you do?
CORNWALL   Come, sir, what letters had you late from France?
REGAN   Be simple-answered, for we know the truth.
CORNWALL   And what confederacy have you with the traitors
          Late footed in the kingdom?
REGAN   To whose hands   45
          You have sent the lunatic king. Speak.
GLOUCESTER   I have a letter guessingly set down,
          Which came from one that's of a neutral heart,
          And not from one opposed.
CORNWALL   Cunning.
REGAN   And false.
CORNWALL   Where hast thou sent the king?
GLOUCESTER   To Dover.   50

---

33 lady] Q; Lady, F   33 I'm none.] F; I am true. Q   34 To ... find –] *As in* Q; *two lines divided* him, / Villaine,
F   *34 find –] Q; finde. F   34 SD] *Johnson (subst.); not in* Q, F   35–6 By ... beard.] F *lineation; as prose* Q   37–
8 Naughty ... chin] F; *one line (turned under)* Q   42 Come ... France?] *As in* Q; *two lines divided* Sir. / What F   43
simple-answered] *Hanmer (subst.);* simple answerer Q; simple answer'd F   44–5 And ... kingdom?] *Rowe's lineation; as
prose* Q, F   45–6 To ... Speak.] F *lineation; one line* Q   46 You have sent] F, Q; haue you sent Q2   46 king. Speak.] F;
King speak? Q

32 filthy foul, contemptible.

36 To ... beard This was a gesture of extreme
insult and provocation: compare 75–6 below and
Ham. 2.2.573.

37 Naughty Wicked. The word conveyed a
stronger sense of evil in Shakespeare's time.
Compare 2.4.126.

39 quicken come alive.

40 hospitable favours welcoming features, i.e.
those of a host; compare *1H4* 3.2.136: 'And stain my
favours in a bloody mask'.

41 ruffle treat roughly, disorder violently.

43 simple-answered direct, straightforward in
reply.

45 Late footed Lately landed.

45–6 To ... Speak Q2 inverts 'You have' to
'haue you', making Regan's speech a separate question – a plausible emendation, but not a necessary
one, however consistent with Regan's independent
character (Duthie, p. 402; compare Sisson, p. 237).

47 guessingly set down 'written without certain knowledge' (Muir).

REGAN Wherefore to Dover? Wast thou not charged at peril –
CORNWALL Wherefore to Dover? Let him answer that.
GLOUCESTER I am tied to th'stake, and I must stand the course.
REGAN Wherefore to Dover?
GLOUCESTER Because I would not see thy cruel nails   55
        Pluck out his poor old eyes, nor thy fierce sister
        In his anointed flesh stick boarish fangs.
        The sea, with such a storm as his bare head
        In hell-black night endured, would have buoyed up
        And quenched the stellèd fires.   60
        Yet, poor old heart, he holp the heavens to rain.
        If wolves had at thy gate howled that stern time,
        Thou shouldst have said, 'Good porter, turn the key:
        All cruels else subscribe.' But I shall see

---

51 Wherefore ... peril –] *As in* Q; *two lines divided* Douer? / Was't F **51 peril –] Q; perill. F 52 answer] F; first answere Q 53 I ... course.] *As in* Q; *two lines divided* Stake, / And F 53 to th'] to'th' F; tot'h Q 54 Dover?] F; Douer sir? Q 57 anointed] F, Q *corr.;* aurynted Q *uncorr.*, Q2 57 stick] F; rash Q 58 as his bare] F; of his lou'd Q *uncorr.*, Q2; on his lowd Q *corr.* 59 hell-black night] *Pope;* Hell-blacke-night F; hell blacke night Q   59 buoyed] F; layd Q *uncorr.*, Q2; bod Q *corr.* 60–1 And ... rain.] F *lineation; divided* heart, / Hee Q 60 stellèd] F, Q *corr.;* steeled Q *uncorr.*, Q2 61 holp] F; holpt Q 61 rain] F; rage Q 62 howled] F; heard Q 62 stern] F; dearne Q 64 subscribe] F; subscrib'd Q

---

51 **at peril** at risk (of death).

53 **I ... course** Gloucester uses the image of a bear or bull tied to a post and baited by dogs, a common, cruel entertainment, referred to also in *TN* 3.1.118–20, *Mac.* 5.7.1–2.

53 **course** attack (one of a succession) by dogs.

57 **anointed** At a coronation, the sovereign was anointed with oil in the manner of biblical kings. Compare 1 Sam. 26.9 (Shaheen).

57 **stick** See collation. Although 'rash' (= slash violently) is a more vivid and accurate term for the action of a boar's tusks (Hunter), the F reading is perfectly acceptable. F's 'sticke' for Q's 'rash', like 'sterne' for 'dearne' (62 below), is a sophistication, though not by the F scribe or compositor (Greg, *Editorial Problem*, pp. 99–100). Duthie agrees: 'sticke' is 'an editorial replacement of a difficult word by an easier one', but he does not identify the editor (pp. 17, 194). Muir believes the substitution might be an actor's, though Shakespeare could have made it 'to avoid the thrice repeated "sh"'; he adopts Q anyway.

58–60 **The sea ... fires** In such a storm as the bareheaded king endured in total darkness, the sea itself would have swelled (in rage), reaching and extinguishing the very stars. Compare *Temp.* 1.2.4–5: 'the sea, mounting to th'welkin's cheek, / Dashes the fire out' (NS).

59 **buoyed** risen (like a buoy on a swell).

60 **stellèd** (1) fixed (from *OED* Stell *v* 2 = to fix, place in position), or (2) starry (from Latin *stella* = star; compare *OED*); but either way, shining stars are meant.

61 **holp ... rain** i.e. by his tears.

61 **holp** Obsolete form of 'helped'.

62 **stern** On the preference for Q 'dearne' by many editors, compare Q 'rashe' F 'sticke' (57 above and n.). The present instance may be a simpler (or more complicated) one, since either Q or F may involve only a typographical error. The compartment for the ligature of 'long-s' + 't' was very near that for the 'd' in an English type case. Far from substituting one word for another, the compositor may just have substituted one piece of type for another, though we cannot judge whether it was the Q or the F compositor who was at fault – if indeed a typo was actually involved (McLeod, p. 160). Sisson believes that, as with 'stick' for 'rash', revision occurred in rehearsal or for purposes of euphony; in a sense, he says, 'there is nothing to choose' (p. 238; 'dearne' = dire, dread: compare *Per.* 3 Chorus 15).

63–4 **Good ... subscribe** A famous crux, partly because of the ambiguity in 'cruels' (= cruel creatures or cruel deeds); Q 'subscrib'd' versus F 'subscribe'; and the uncertainty about where the direct address ends. But the main sense seems clear. Gloucester says that on such a night Regan would have pitied wild animals howling outside her gates more than she did her father. Assuming F is correct

The wingèd vengeance overtake such children.   65

CORNWALL   See't shalt thou never. Fellows, hold the chair.
    Upon these eyes of thine I'll set my foot.

GLOUCESTER   He that will think to live till he be old,
    Give me some help! – O cruel! O you gods!

    [*Cornwall puts out one of Gloucester's eyes*]

REGAN   One side will mock another: th'other, too.   70

CORNWALL   If you see vengeance –

SERVANT   Hold your hand, my lord.
    I have served you ever since I was a child,
    But better service have I never done you
    Than now to bid you hold.

REGAN   How now, you dog!

SERVANT   If you did wear a beard upon your chin   75
    I'd shake it on this quarrel. What do you mean?

CORNWALL   My villain!

SERVANT   Nay then, come on, and take the chance of anger.

    [*They draw and fight*]

REGAN   [*To another Servant*] Give me thy sword. A peasant stand up
        thus!

    Kills him

---

67 these] F; those Q   69 you] F; ye Q   69 SD] *Rowe (subst.); not in* Q, F   70 th'other] F; tother Q   *71 vengeance –]
Q; vengeance. F   72 you] F; *not in* Q   73–4 But . . . hold.] F *lineation; one line (turned over)* Q   75–6 If . . . mean?] F
lineation; as prose Q   77 villain!] Villaine? F; villaine. Q; villein! *Oxford*   78 Nay] F; Why Q   *78 SD] *draw and fight* Q
(*after 77*); *not in* F   79 SD.1] *Oxford; not in* Q, F   79 thus!] thus? F; thus. Q   79 SD.2] F; *Shee takes a sword and runs at
him behind.* Q

and direct address ends with 'subscribe', then:
'Good porter, turn the key (and open the gates to
the wolves); all cruel creatures but you yield (to
feelings of sorrow and compassion at a time like
this).' For 'cruels' = cruel creatures, compare 'reso-
lutes', *Ham.* 1.1.98; 'vulgars', *WT* 2.1.94; for 'subscribe' = yield, submit, compare *Tro.* 4.5.105
(Duthie, pp. 152–4, who ends direct address, like
Kittredge, Muir, and Bevington, with 'key'; compare also Furness, Sisson). Stone, p. 197, proposes
the emendation 'ile' (= I'll) for 'else', ending the
direct address with 'key'. He glosses: 'All cruels [=
cruel people or creatures] I'll (= I am, if necessary,
willing to] subscribe [= countenance], but [*sc.* come
what may] I shall see / The winged vengeance
overtake such children.'

65 **wingèd vengeance** 'The vengeance of the
gods, sweeping down upon them like a bird of
prey' (Kittredge). Compare 2.4.154–5.

69 SD *Cornwall . . . eyes* For the various ways

this action has been staged, see Rosenberg, p. 242–
3, and Bratton, p. 157.

75–6 **If . . . quarrel** Compare 36 and n. above.

76 **What do you mean?** NS follows Kittredge,
who assigns these words to Regan (after a conjecture
by Craig) – unnecessarily, since her sense of outrage
(and Cornwall's) is registered strongly enough elsewhere. Some stage business, unrecorded in Q or F,
may prompt the servant's query to Cornwall. Thus,
after 'quarrel' Hunter inserts SD *Cornwall draws his
sword*, but most editors follow Q and have both men
draw at 78.

77 **villain** (1) serf, (2) evil person.

78 **take . . . anger** take the risk (of good or bad
success: Schmidt) that anger brings.

78 SD *They . . . fight* During the swordplay, the
servant fatally wounds Cornwall before Regan is
able to kill him (by running him through from
behind, as Q directs). Compare 94–7.

SERVANT   Oh, I am slain. My lord, you have one eye left   80
    To see some mischief on him. Oh!   [*He dies*]
CORNWALL   Lest it see more, prevent it. Out, vile jelly!
    [*He puts out Gloucester's other eye*]
    Where is thy lustre now?
GLOUCESTER   All dark and comfortless. Where's my son Ed-
    mond?
    Edmond, enkindle all the sparks of nature   85
    To quit this horrid act.
REGAN   Out, treacherous villain!
    Thou call'st on him that hates thee. It was he
    That made the overture of thy treasons to us,
    Who is too good to pity thee.
GLOUCESTER   O, my follies! Then Edgar was abused.   90
    Kind gods, forgive me that, and prosper him.
REGAN   Go thrust him out at gates, and let him smell
    His way to Dover.
            Exit [*a Servant*] *with Gloucester*
    How is't, my lord? How look you?
CORNWALL   I have received a hurt. Follow me, lady.
    [*To Servants*] Turn out that eyeless villain. Throw this
    slave   95
    Upon the dunghill. Regan, I bleed apace.
    Untimely comes this hurt. Give me your arm.
                          Exeunt

80–1 Oh ... Oh!] F *lineation; as prose* Q   80 you have] F; *yet haue you* Q   *81 SD] Q2; *not in* Q, F   82 SD] *Rowe (subst.*);
not in Q, F   84 All ... Edmond?] *As in* Q; *two lines divided* comfortlesse? / *Where's* F   *84 comfortless.] comfortles, Q;
comfortlesse? F   85–6 Edmond ... act.] F *lineation; one line* Q   85 enkindle] F; vnbridle Q   86–9 Out ... thee.] F
lineation; as prose Q   86 treacherous] F; *not in* Q   92–3 Go ... you?] *Capell's lineation; three lines ending* ... smell / ...
Douer. / ... you? F; *as prose* Q   93 SD] *Duthie; Exit with Glouster.* F; *not in* Q   95–7 Turn ... arm.] F *lineation; lines end*
... vpon / ... vntimely / ... arme. Q   95 SD] *Oxford; not in* Q, F   96 dunghill] F; dungell Q   97 SD] F; *Exit.* Q; F *omits
nine lines here*

81 **mischief** injury, harm.
82 **prevent** i.e. I shall prevent.
85 **nature** i.e. filial loyalty and devotion.
86 **quit** repay, requite; as in *Ham.* 5.2.68.
88 **overture** disclosure. The article before the
noun is elided and the second syllable stressed:
'th'ovèrture'.
90 **abused** wronged.
91 **that** i.e. his misjudgement and mistreatment
of Edgar.
92 **smell** Emphatic (Kittredge).
93 SD *Exit ... Gloucester* Although Cornwall
repeats Regan's command two lines later, F is probably right in placing the SD here; Cornwall's repetition is for emphasis.

93 **How ... you** Regan's concern for Cornwall
varies with interpretation. In some productions,
intent on Edmond, she ignores Cornwall's request
for her arm (97) and walks coolly off. But the
language here suggests more than a modicum of
compassion for her husband.
93 **How look you** i.e. how are you feeling?
96 **dunghill** manure pile. The rebellious servant
receives ignominious treatment, denied the rites of
burial and cast unburied upon offal.
97 **Untimely** i.e. because of the invasion and
other problems.
97 SD *Exeunt* In modern stage productions, the
interval usually occurs here. On F's omission of
nine lines, see Textual Analysis, pp. 254–5.

4.1 *Enter* EDGAR [*disguised as a madman*]

EDGAR   Yet better thus, and known to be condemned,
        Than still condemned and flattered. To be worst,
        The low'st and most dejected thing of fortune,
        Stands still in esperance, lives not in fear.
        The lamentable change is from the best;   5
        The worst returns to laughter. Welcome, then,
        Thou unsubstantial air that I embrace:
        The wretch that thou hast blown unto the worst
        Owes nothing to thy blasts.

Enter GLOUCESTER *and an* OLD MAN

                  But who comes here?
        My father, parti-eyed? World, world, O world!   10
        But that thy strange mutations make us hate thee,
        Life would not yield to age.

Act 4, Scene 1   4.1] *Actus Quartus. Scena Prima.* F; *not in* Q   *2 flattered. To be worst,] *Pope;* flatter'd, to be worst: F;
flattered to be worst, Q   3 low'st] *Oxford;* lowest Q, F   4 esperance] F; experience Q   6–9 Welcome ... blasts.] F; *not
in* Q   9 SD] F; *Enter Glost. led by an old man.* Q (*after* age, *12*)   9–10 But ... world!] *Pope's lineation;* F *begins new line with*
But *and divides* led? / World; *one line* Q   9 But who comes] F; Who's Q   *10 parti-eyed] *Oxford* (*Davenport conj.*); parti,
eyd Q *corr.;* poorlie,leed Q *uncorr.;* poorely led? Q2, F

Act 4, Scene 1

0 SD *Enter* EDGAR Edgar has become detached
from Lear and his entourage, left behind deliberately, perhaps, since he is ignored at the end of 3.6.
In the fictional narrative, it is the next morning
(compare 32 below).

1–4 Yet ... fear Edgar says it is better to know
one's condemnation openly than to suffer it under
the false guise of flattery. When one is at the worst,
i.e. the very bottom of Fortune's wheel, one lives
always in hope, not fear (of falling further). See
collation. Pope's punctuation helps clarify the
sense and is not inconsistent with F (compare
Sisson, pp. 238–9). 'To be worst' is most likely in
apposition to 'The low'st'. Perrett, however,
defends F punctuation (see Muir).

1 thus i.e. a Bedlam beggar.

3 dejected cast down.

4 esperance hope.

6 The worst ... laughter Compare Dent, p.
228, T216: 'When things are at the worst they will
mend.'

6 laughter happiness, good times.

6–9 Welcome ... blasts See Textual Analysis,
p. 267 below.

9 Owes ... blasts i.e. has nothing left to be

swept away and therefore can embrace you freely.

10 parti-eyed 'with his eyes "motley" or parti-
coloured, i.e. bleeding' (Riverside). A major crux: see
collation. Q corr. may reflect copy. Either (1) the
reviser or collator, working from an exemplar of Q
with sheet H in the uncorrected state, corrected
only the spelling he saw there; or (2) Q2, deriving
from Q uncorr., directly influenced F, especially if
the playhouse manuscript was illegible (see Greg,
Variants, p. 169; Textual Analysis, p. 59 above). F
makes sufficient, if feeble, sense; but many recent
editions, e.g. Hunter, Riverside, adopt emended Q
corr., whose comma might have been meant for a
hyphen, as sometimes happens in texts of foul-papers
provenance, or a hyphen might have been misunderstood as a comma by the Q compositor or corrector
(Davenport, p. 21; compare *Textual Companion*, pp.
519, 536.) Compare *LLL* 5.2.766: 'parti-coated presence of loose love'; *MV* 1.3.88: 'parti-coloured
lambs'. From the description of the Paphlagonian
king and his son in Sidney's *Arcadia*, Muir conjectures 'poorly 'rayd' but follows F.

10–12 world ... age i.e. life would not willingly
submit to old age (and death) except that the
world's changes and vicissitudes make us welcome
release from them.

OLD MAN   O my good lord,
    I have been your tenant and your father's tenant
    These fourscore –
GLOUCESTER   Away, get thee away; good friend, be gone.   15
    Thy comforts can do me no good at all;
    Thee they may hurt.
OLD MAN   You cannot see your way.
GLOUCESTER   I have no way, and therefore want no eyes:
    I stumbled when I saw. Full oft 'tis seen,
    Our means secure us, and our mere defects   20
    Prove our commodities. Oh, dear son Edgar,
    The food of thy abusèd father's wrath:
    Might I but live to see thee in my touch,
    I'd say I had eyes again.
OLD MAN   How now? Who's there?
EDGAR   [*Aside*] O gods! Who is't can say 'I am at the worst'?   25
    I am worse than e'er I was.
OLD MAN   'Tis poor mad Tom.
EDGAR   [*Aside*] And worse I may be yet. The worst is not
    So long as we can say 'This is the worst.'
OLD MAN   Fellow, where goest?
GLOUCESTER   Is it a beggarman?
OLD MAN   Madman and beggar too.   30
GLOUCESTER   He has some reason, else he could not beg.
    I'th'last night's storm I such a fellow saw,

12–14 O … fourscore –] *Johnson's lineation; two lines divided* Tenant, / And F; *as prose* Q   *14 These fourscore –] this forescore – Q; these fourscore years. F   17 You] F; Alack sir, you Q   21 Oh] F; ah Q   25, 27, 37, 52, 54 SD] *Johnson; not in* Q, F   28 So] F; As Q   30 Madman] F; Mad man Q   31 He] F; A Q   32 I'th'] F; In the Q

14 **fourscore** – See collation. Compositor B, who set these lines in F, appears guilty of sophistication, completing a sentence meant to be interrupted, as Q indicates.

17 **Thee … hurt** Gloucester is concerned for the Old Man's safety if he should be found aiding the proclaimed traitor. Compare 4.4.39–40.

18–19 **I have … saw** 'Gloucester here summarizes his whole career' (Heilman, p. 44). When he had eyes, he could not see what he most needed to see and understand, and thus he erred; blind and knowing what he knows, his actions are now without purpose. Colie (pp. 131–2) compares Isa. 59.10, Matt. 13.13, and Job 5.14.

20–1 **Our means … commodities** i.e. our

assets, or advantages, give us a false sense of security (overconfidence), whereas our very lacks, or deficiencies, turn out to be advantages. Compare *Mac.* 3.5.32–3: 'And you all know, security / Is mortals' chiefest enemy.' Dent, p. 244, compares W152: 'He that is secure is not safe', and *R2* 2.1.265–6.

22 **abusèd** deceived.

23 **to see … touch** i.e. to recognize by touching you. Compare 4.5.143. Kittredge paraphrases more freely: 'To hold thee in my embrace'.

25–6 **Who is't … was** Compare 1–9 above. Edgar's shock is an object lesson to him against false optimism, as his next speech explicitly states.

31 **reason** rational capacity, sanity.

Which made me think a man a worm. My son
Came then into my mind, and yet my mind
Was then scarce friends with him. I have heard more
    since.   35
As flies to wanton boys are we to th'gods;
They kill us for their sport.
EDGAR   [*Aside*]   How should this be?
Bad is the trade that must play fool to sorrow,
Ang'ring itself and others. – Bless thee, master.
GLOUCESTER   Is that the naked fellow?
OLD MAN   Ay, my lord.   40
GLOUCESTER   Get thee away. If for my sake
Thou wilt o'ertake us hence a mile or twain
I'th'way toward Dover, do it for ancient love,
And bring some covering for this naked soul,
Which I'll entreat to lead me.   45
OLD MAN   Alack, sir, he is mad.
GLOUCESTER   'Tis the time's plague when madmen lead the
    blind.
Do as I bid thee; or rather do thy pleasure.

---

35 Was … since.] *As in* Q; *two lines divided* him. / I F   36 flies to] F; flies are toth' Q   37 kill] F; bitt Q   37–9 How … master.] F *lineation; as prose* Q   38 fool] F; the foole Q   39 others. – Bless] *Theobald;* others, blesse Q; others. Blesse F   41 Get thee away] F; Then prethee get thee gon Q   42 hence] F; here Q   43 I'th'] F; Ith' Q   43 toward] F, Q; to Q2   45 Which] F; Who Q   47 'Tis … blind.] *As in* Q; *two lines divided* plague, / When F

33 a man a worm Compare Job 25.6: 'How much more man, a worme, euen the sonne of man, which is but a worme?' (cited by Kittredge and others. Shaheen compares Ps. 22.6: 'But I am a worme, & not a man').

36–7 As flies … sport Often mistakenly believed to sum up the basic philosophy or 'message' of the play, these lines represent, rather, Gloucester's despairing viewpoint at this stage in his development. Edgar will try to bring him out of it, as he explains later (4.5.33–4). Here, Gloucester, deeply cynical, believes human beings are of no greater significance or importance to the gods than insects are to sportive children, who enjoy killing them for fun. Shakespeare may have recalled Plangus's lament in Sidney's *Arcadia*, Bk 11, ch. 12, where human beings are called 'Balles to the starres, and thralles to Fortunes raigne'. Montaigne uses a similar expression: 'The gods perdie doe reckon and racket us men as their tennis-balles' (Florio's translation, cited by Muir). Compare the fly-killing episode in *Tit.* 3.2.52 ff.

37 How … be Edgar is astonished by his father's physical or mental condition, or both.

38–9 Bad … others Considering his father's real misery, Edgar deplores the role he must resume, one that upsets both himself and others. NS regards this speech as Shakespeare's apology to the audience, as well as Edgar's to himself, and compares the Fool and Lear.

41 Get thee away See collation. Although Q offers a metrically regular line, F repeats the earlier command (15) and is no more abrupt here than there or at 49 (but compare Duthie, p. 180, who adopts Q). Werstine, p. 283, notes Compositor B's omission of line beginnings elsewhere and thinks he may have done so here, though conflation produces a metrically difficult line. Oxford considers the tetrameter acceptable and follows F (*Textual Companion*, p. 536).

47 'Tis … blind It is the curse of our time when rulers (madmen) lead ignorant (blind) subjects. Gloucester makes a kind of parable out of his situation (Kittredge).

48 Do … pleasure Gloucester alters his command, realizing it is no longer appropriate for him to order anyone to do anything.

Above the rest, be gone.

OLD MAN   I'll bring him the best 'parel that I have,   50
　　　　　Come on't what will.   *Exit*

GLOUCESTER   Sirrah, naked fellow.

EDGAR   Poor Tom's a-cold. [*Aside*] I cannot daub it further.

GLOUCESTER   Come hither, fellow.

EDGAR   [*Aside*] And yet I must. – Bless thy sweet eyes, they bleed.

GLOUCESTER   Know'st thou the way to Dover?   55

EDGAR   Both stile and gate, horseway and footpath. Poor Tom hath
　　been scared out of his good wits. Bless thee, goodman's son,
　　from the foul fiend.

GLOUCESTER   Here, take this purse, thou whom the heavens'
　　　　　plagues
　　Have humbled to all strokes. That I am wretched   60
　　Makes thee the happier. Heavens deal so still.
　　Let the superfluous and lust-dieted man
　　That slaves your ordinance, that will not see
　　Because he does not feel, feel your power quickly.

---

50 'parel] *Rowe;* Parrell Q, F   50 have,] Q2; haue Q, F   51 SD] F; *not in* Q   *52 a-cold] *Rowe;* a cold Q, F   52 daub] F;
dance Q   52 further] F; farther Q   54 And … bleed.] *Capell's lineation; two lines divided* must: / Blesse F   54 And yet
I must.] F; *not in* Q   54 must. – Bless] Capell (*subst.*); must: / Blesse F   56–8 Both … fiend.] *As prose* F; *three verse lines
ending* … footpath, / … wits, / … fiend, Q   *57 scared] scard Q; scarr'd F   57 thee, goodman's son,] thee good mans
sonne, F; the good man Q   58 fiend.] F *omits five lines here*   58 heavens'] heauens Q; heau'ns F   60–1 Have … still] F
lineation; divided thee [*turned under*] / The Q   63 slaves] F; stands Q   64 does] F, Q; doth Q2

49 **Above the rest** Above all.
50 **'parel** apparel. Compare Marlowe, *Jew of
Malta* 4.4: 'Here's goodly 'parrell, is here not?'
(Muir; see Abbott 460, for dropped prefixes
elsewhere.)
51 **Come** … **will** i.e. regardless of what happens
as a result.
52 **daub it further** dissemble any longer.
Compare Old French *dauber*, Latin *dealbare*, 'to
whiten over, whitewash, plaster'; *R3* 3.5.29: 'So
smooth he daub'd his vice with show of virtue';
and 2.2.57 above.
54 **And** … **must** See Textual Analysis, pp.
267–8 below.
55 **Dover** Gloucester is thinking of Dover as a
suitable place for suicide (68–73), not as the place
where he has sent Lear to meet the other 'traitors'.
Perhaps Dover was suggested by the interrogation
in 3.7: 'in his half-crazed state he has an irrational
urge to end his life there' (Muir, p. xlix). But not
only the exigencies of the plot require the meeting
of all principal characters at Dover; the source in
Sidney's *Arcadia* also included the desire of the
Paphlagonian king to jump off a high rock
(Moberly, cited by Furness; compare Bullough, p.
403).

56 **Both** … **footpath** 'Each kind of path has its
appropriate obstacle – the stile for the footpath, the
gate for the horse-way (bridle path)' (Hunter).
60 **humbled** … **strokes** i.e. made you susceptible to every misfortune.
61 **Heavens** i.e. may the heavens.
62–6 **Let** … **enough** Compare 3.4.33–6, where
Lear expresses similar sentiments.
62 **superfluous** i.e. having too much, more than
enough (hypallage, or transferred epithet: see
Joseph, p. 56).
62 **lust-dieted** i.e. fed by pleasures.
63 **slaves your ordinance** 'makes your law sub-
servient to his own desires' (Riverside). All men are
commanded to help one another; the rich are especially enjoined to help the poor, not to ignore or
exploit them. Compare the parable of Dives the rich
man and Lazarus the beggar in Luke 16.19–31 and
the marginal gloss at verse 19 in the Geneva Bible:
'By this storie is declared what punishment thei shal
haue, which liue deliciously & neglect the poore.'
Compare also Mark 10.21.
64 **feel, feel** (1) sympathize, (2) experience.
64 **quickly** A triple pun: (1) very soon, (2) while
he is still alive, and (3) sharply, piercingly (NS).

So distribution should undo excess,   65
And each man have enough. Dost thou know Dover?
EDGAR   Ay, master.
GLOUCESTER   There is a cliff whose high and bending head
Looks fearfully in the confinèd deep.
Bring me but to the very brim of it,   70
And I'll repair the misery thou dost bear
With something rich about me. From that place
I shall no leading need.
EDGAR   Give me thy arm.
Poor Tom shall lead thee.

Exeunt

4.2 *Enter* GONERILL [*with*] EDMOND, *and* OSWALD, [*severally*]

GONERILL   Welcome, my lord. I marvel our mild husband
Not met us on the way. – Now, where's your master?
OSWALD   Madam, within; but never man so changed.
I told him of the army that was landed;
He smiled at it. I told him you were coming;   5
His answer was, 'The worse'. Of Gloucester's treachery,
And of the loyal service of his son
When I informed him, then he called me sot,
And told me I had turned the wrong side out.
What most he should dislike seems pleasant to him;   10
What like, offensive.
GONERILL   [*To Edmond*] Then shall you go no further.

---

65 undo] F; vnder Q   69 fearfully] F; firmely Q   72–3 With ... need.] F *lineation; divided* me, / From Q   73–4 Give
... thee.] F *lineation; one line* Q   74 SD] F; *not in* Q   Act 4, Scene 2   4.2] *Scena Secunda.* F; *not in* Q   0 SD] *This edn;*
Enter Gonerill, Bastard, and Steward. F; *Enter Gonorill and Bastard* Q (*which places Steward's entrance after* 2)   3–11 Madam
... offensive.] F *lineation; as prose* Q   10 most he should dislike] F; hee should most desire Q   12 SD] *Hanmer; not*
in Q; F

65 So ... excess Thus (heaven's intervention
having punished the rich for insensitivity to the
poor), excesses will be eliminated by a redistribu-
tion of wealth.
65 distribution (1) administration (of justice),
(2) sharing out (NS, citing *Cor.* 3.3.99).
68–9 a cliff ... deep The cliff itself becomes the
image of someone who, bending over its edge and
looking down at the straits far below, is stricken
with fear at the sight.
69 in into.
69 confinèd deep 'pent in straits' (Capell, cited
by Furness). Dover is the closest point in Britain to
France on the other side of the Channel.

Act 4, Scene 2
1 Welcome, my lord Gonerill welcomes
Edmond to her castle, although they arrive
together.
4 the army i.e. the French forces. Compare
3.7.2.
8 sot fool.
9 turned ... out A clothing metaphor: Oswald
has inverted the treachery and treason.
11 What like i.e. what he should like.

It is the cowish terror of his spirit
That dares not undertake. He'll not feel wrongs
Which tie him to an answer. Our wishes on the way   15
May prove effects. Back, Edmond, to my brother.
Hasten his musters and conduct his powers.
I must change names at home and give the distaff
Into my husband's hands. This trusty servant
Shall pass between us. Ere long you are like to hear   20
(If you dare venture in your own behalf)
A mistress's command. Wear this; spare speech.
Decline your head. This kiss, if it durst speak,
Would stretch thy spirits up into the air.
Conceive, and fare thee well.   25

EDMOND   Yours in the ranks of death.

GONERILL   My most dear Gloucester.

Exit [Edmond]

---

13 terror] F; curre Q *uncorr.*, Q2; terrer Q *corr.*   16 Edmond] F; *Edgar* Q   18 names] F; armes Q   21 (If ... behalf)] F; If ... behalfe Q   22 command] F, Q *corr.*; coward Q *uncorr.*, Q2   22 this; spare] F; this spare Q *uncorr.*, Q2; this, spare Q *corr.*   25 fare thee] F; far you Q; farye Q2   26–8 My ... due] F *lineation; one line* Q, *which omits 27*   26 dear] F; deere Q *uncorr.*; deer Q *corr.*   26 SD] *As in Rowe; Exit.* F (*after* death.); *not in* Q

13 cowish cowardly.

14 undertake take responsibility (for some enterprise).

14–15 He'll ... answer He will not notice injuries which would require him to respond manfully.

15–16 Our ... effects Our desires as we travelled here together may be fulfilled. Gonerill hopes that Edmond will supplant Albany as her husband; ever the opportunist, Edmond has apparently encouraged that hope. Neither one knows yet of Cornwall's death: see 39 ff. below, especially 52–5.

16 effects realized facts, fulfilments.

16 brother brother-in-law.

17 musters levies of troops.

17 conduct escort, guide, accompany (compare *OED* sv *v* 1); *not* 'to lead as a commander' (Schmidt).

18 change exchange.

18 names titles (i.e. wife and husband). Compare *1H4* 3.4.64, *Temp.* 2.1.150 (Onions). Many modern editors adopt Q's 'armes' = weapons, or possibly = insignia (Craig, cited by Duthie). F's 'names' may be a misreading, as Jackson believes (p. 323). F. E. Budd, 'Shakespeare, Chaucer, and Harsnett', *RES* (1935), 427, notes a close parallel from Chaucer's *Monk's Tale*, where the Host recalls his wife's reproach: 'I wol have thy knyf, / And thou shalt have my distaf and go spinne' (B.3096–7). Though he adopts Q, Duthie considers F

defensible: 'Goneril says that she must adopt the name of man and her husband the name of woman, and then goes on to refer to an exchange of symbols of husband and wife – she will give Albany the distaff and (this is implied) take from him the sword' (p. 181).

18 distaff 'cleft stick on which wool or flax was formerly wound; (used as the type for woman's work) wifely duties' (Onions). Compare *Cym.* 5.3.34.

20 like likely.

22 mistress's command (1) liege's, or (2) lover's order, presumably to get rid of Albany.

22 Wear this Gonerill here gives Edmond a favour to wear, such as a chain or scarf; but she may simply refer to a kiss.

23 Decline your head i.e. so that she can put the favour around his neck or kiss him.

24 Would ... air This speech and the lines that follow contain several sexual innuendos (Heilman, p. 318, n. 15; Muir and Hunter agree). For 'stretch' and 'spirits' see Rubenstein.

25 Conceive Compare 1.1.10–11.

26–9 Yours ... body See collation. In Q not only is 27 missing, but so is Edmond's exit. Gonerill's entire speech is thus directed in Q to her lover, not to herself as in F.

26 Yours ... death Muir and others find a sexual pun on 'death' = orgasm, and compare 4.5.189. In other respects, the speech is prophetic (Rosenberg, p. 251).

> Oh, the difference of man and man.
> To thee a woman's services are due;
> My fool usurps my body.

OSWALD   Madam, here comes my lord.   [*Exit*]   30

Enter ALBANY

GONERILL   I have been worth the whistle.

ALBANY   O Gonerill,
> You are not worth the dust which the rude wind
> Blows in your face.

GONERILL   Milk-livered man,
> That bear'st a cheek for blows, a head for wrongs;
> Who hast not in thy brows an eye discerning   35
> Thine honour from thy suffering –

ALBANY   See thyself, devil:

---

28 a] F, Q *corr.; not in* Q *uncorr.,* Q2   **29** My ... body.] F; My foote vsurps my body. Q *uncorr.;* A foole vsurps my bed. Q *corr.;* My foote vsurps my head. Q2   ***30** SD.1   *Exit*] *Exit Stew.* Q; *not in* F   **30** SD.2 *Enter* ALBANY] F; *not in* Q   **31** whistle.] F, Q *uncorr.;* whistling. Q *corr.*   **31–2** O ... wind] F *lineation; one line (turned under)* Q   **33** face.] F *omits twenty lines here*   **34** bear'st] F; bearest Q   **35–6** Who ... suffering –] F *lineation; divided* honour, / From Q, *which continues with six lines not in* F   ***35** eye discerning] *Rowe*; eye-discerning F; eye deseruing Q   ***36** suffering –] *Oxford*; suffering, Q; suffering. F   **36–8** See ... woman.] F *lineation; as prose* Q

28 a woman's services 'the service that a woman naturally gives to a *real* man' (Hunter).

29 My ... body Though Albany is Gonerill's husband, she thinks him a 'fool' who does not deserve possession of her body (which Edmond, a real man, does). Thomas Clayton makes a good case for Q uncorr. 'My foote vsurps my body' as the original manuscript reading, miscorrected in Q corr. and further in Q2 ('Old light on the text of *King Lear*', *MP* 78 (1981), 347–67). F can be defended, but compare Greg, who concludes that 'My foole vsurps my bed' was what the copy for Q actually contained (*Variants*, pp. 170 ff.).

30 SD.1 F omits Q's *Exit Stew.* The omission is more likely an error by Compositor B, who needed to insert *Enter Albany* at this point and may have mistaken the added SD for a substitution (NS). Albany's entrance is missing in Q, but *Enter the Duke of Albany* appears in Q2 after Gonerill's speech (31).

31 worth the whistle i.e. worth finding, seeking out. See collation. The usual proverbial form may have led to miscorrection in Q corr. (Greg, *Variants*, p. 172; Duthie, p. 406; and Muir). Compare Heywood's *Proverbs*: 'It is a poore dogge that is not woorth the whystlyng' (Steevens, cited by Furness), and Tilley W311. In NS, Duthie adopts Q corr. and proposes the quibble: (1) entice, allure (*OED v* 7a *fig.*), (2) wait for (*OED v* 9).

32–3 You ... face Albany compounds Gonerill's sarcasm and plays on 'worth the whistle'. For the marked change in his attitude, compare 1.4.266 ff.

32 rude (1) harsh, rough (Schmidt), (2) uncivil (compare *TGV* 5.4.60: 'Ruffian! Let go that rude uncivil touch').

33 face For F omissions here, see Textual Analysis, p. 255 below.

33 Milk-livered White-livered, i.e. cowardly. Cowardice was believed to be caused by lack of blood in the liver (Kittredge). Compare 2.2.15.

34 That ... blows Compare Matthew 5.39 and Luke 6.29 on turning the other cheek (Shaheen).

35–6 eye ... suffering i.e. you cannot see the difference between what can be honourably borne and what should be resented (Muir). Compare Hamlet's dilemma, *Ham.* 3.1.55–9.

36 See ... devil In Q, Gonerill's speech continues for six more lines and comes to a proper conclusion (see Textual Analysis, p. 268 below). In F, Albany abruptly and vehemently breaks into the middle of her speech, holding up to her, perhaps, the mirror she carries by her side (see 2.2.32 n.). Shakespeare may be alluding to Renaissance iconography, in which the devil is sometimes portrayed standing behind the figure of Lady Vanity, his face rather than hers reflected in the mirror she gazes into (Meagher, p. 254).

Proper deformity shows not in the fiend
So horrid as in woman.

GONERILL   O vain fool!

Enter a MESSENGER

MESSENGER   O my good lord, the Duke of Cornwall's dead,
Slain by his servant going to put out   40
The other eye of Gloucester.

ALBANY   Gloucester's eyes?

MESSENGER   A servant that he bred, thrilled with remorse,
Opposed against the act, bending his sword
To his great master; who, thereat enraged,
Flew on him and amongst them felled him dead,   45
But not without that harmful stroke which since
Hath plucked him after.

ALBANY   This shows you are above,
You justicers, that these our nether crimes
So speedily can venge. But O, poor Gloucester!
Lost he his other eye?

MESSENGER   Both, both, my lord.   50
This letter, madam, craves a speedy answer:
'Tis from your sister.

GONERILL   [*Aside*]   One way I like this well;

---

*37 shows] shewes Q *corr.;* seemes Q *uncorr.,* F   38 fool!] F *omits seven lines here*   38 SD] F; *Enter a Gentleman* Q   39 SH] F; *Gent.* Q (*as throughout scene*)   39–41 O ... Gloucester] F *lineation; as prose* Q   *41 eyes?] Q; eyes. F   42 thrilled] F; thrald Q   *44 thereat enraged] Q; threat–enrag'd F   47–50 This ... eye?] F *lineation; three lines ending ...* Iustisers, / ... venge. / ... eye. Q   *48 You justicers] Q *corr.;* your Iustices Q *uncorr.,* Q2; You Iustices F   50–1 Both ... answer:] F *lineation; one line (turned over)* Q   52 SD] *Johnson; not in* Q, F

37–8 Proper ... woman The deformity of devils is appropriate to demons and therefore not so horrid in them as in women (whose faces should reflect more suitable feelings and attitudes). Muir compares *King Leir* 2582: 'Thou fiend in likenesse of a humane creature'.

38 O vain fool 'vain' = silly; but the epithet may reflect back upon Gonerill ironically if she is a representation of Lady Vanity (see 2.2.32 n., and Meagher, pp. 250–3).

42 bred brought up (*OED* Breed *v* 10b).

42 thrilled pierced, suddenly moved.

42 remorse compassion, pity.

43 bending directing.

44 To Against.

44 thereat enraged See collation. Q is preferable here. As Oxford observes, 'F1 could as easily result from Compositor B omitting a single type as from a

misreading of, or in, the manuscript' (*Textual Companion*, p. 537).

45 felled he felled. Compare Abbott 399 on ellipses. The Messenger implies a struggle among several of those present but does not mention Regan's attack.

47 plucked him after i.e. pulled him after his servant (into death).

48 justicers (divine) judges. See collation. Q corr. is 'unquestionably correct' and is supported by 'justicer' elsewhere in Q (Greg, *Variants*, p. 175; see Appendix, p. 281 below, xii, line 36).

48 nether earthly.

49 venge avenge.

52 One ... well In so far as Cornwall's death removes an obstacle to Gonerill's taking over the whole kingdom, she is pleased at the news.

But being widow, and my Gloucester with her,
May all the building in my fancy pluck
Upon my hateful life. Another way   55
The news is not so tart. – I'll read, and answer.   *Exit*

ALBANY   Where was his son when they did take his eyes?

MESSENGER   Come with my lady hither.

ALBANY   He is not here.

MESSENGER   No, my good lord; I met him back again.

ALBANY   Knows he the wickedness?   60

MESSENGER   Ay, my good lord; 'twas he informed against him
     And quit the house on purpose that their punishment
     Might have the freer course.

ALBANY   Gloucester, I live
     To thank thee for the love thou showed'st the king,
     And to revenge thine eyes. – Come hither, friend.   65
     Tell me what more thou know'st.

                                                   Exeunt

4.3 *Enter with drum and colours,* CORDELIA, GENTLEMAN, *and Soldiers*

CORDELIA   Alack, 'tis he: why, he was met even now,
     As mad as the vexed sea, singing aloud,

---

54 in] F; on Q   55–6 Upon … answer.] F *lineation; divided* tooke, / Ile Q   *56 tart. –] *Capell* (*subst.*); tart. F; tooke,
Q   *56 SD] Q; *not in* F   57 Where … eyes?] *As in* Q; *two lines divided* Sonne, / When F   63–4 Gloucester … king,] F
lineation; one line (turned over) Q   64 showed'st] shewedst Q; shew'dst F   65 thine] F; thy Q   65 eyes. –] *Capell;* eyes,
Q; eyes. F   66 know'st] F; knowest Q   66 SD] F; *Exit.* Q; F *omits a full scene here. See p. 77 above*   Act 4,
Scene 3   4.3] *Scena Tertia.* F; *not in* Q   0 SD] F; *Enter Cordelia, Doctor and others.* Q   *1 why,] why Q, F   2 vexed]
F; vent Q   *3 fumitor] *Oxford;* femiter Q; Fenitar F; fumiterr *Theobald;* fumitory *Hanmer*

---

53 my Gloucester Gonerill's possessiveness is
patent.
54–5 May … life The dream that Gonerill's
imagination has constructed (of marrying Edmond)
may be demolished (if Regan takes her place); then
life (with Albany) will remain hateful to her.
55–6 Another way … tart An apparent redundancy, as she reverts to her attitude in 52.
59 back i.e. on his way back.
66 SD *Exeunt* F omits an entire scene following
4.2, probably to shorten the play in performance.
See Doran, p. 70, Duthie, p. 8, and Textual
Analysis, p. 255 below.

Act 4, Scene 3
0 SD *Enter … CORDELIA* Cordelia's reappearance in the play in F differs significantly from her
reappearance in Q (Warren, 'Diminution', p. 67).
Here, she is at the head of an army, and although

she voices the humane concerns the Gentleman
attributes to her in Q's Scene 3, she is much more
the active exponent of her father's rights. In Q,
'Monsieur La Far' was named the leader of the
French army after the King of France suddenly
had to return home; in F, Cordelia leads the
French, and there is no mention of either her husband or his proxy (Goldring, p. 149; compare
Urkowitz, p. 94).
0 SD GENTLEMAN See collation and compare
4.6.0 SD. Taylor ('War', p. 30) suggests that the
scene in Q is intimate rather than military, more
suitable for a doctor's presence than a military setting, where Shakespeare has surgeons rather than
doctors appear – a nice distinction.
1 he i.e. Lear, of whom they have been just
speaking.
2 vexed turbulent; compare *Ham.* 4.1.7: 'Mad as
the sea and wind when both contend'.

Crowned with rank fumitor and furrow-weeds,
With burdocks, hemlock, nettles, cuckoo-flowers,
Darnel, and all the idle weeds that grow   5
In our sustaining corn. A century send forth.
Search every acre in the high-grown field,
And bring him to our eye.

                                        [*Exit an Officer*]
                    What can man's wisdom
In the restoring his bereavèd sense?
He that helps him take all my outward worth.   10
GENTLEMAN   There is means, madam.
Our foster-nurse of nature is repose,
The which he lacks. That to provoke in him
Are many simples operative, whose power
Will close the eye of anguish.
CORDELIA   All blest secrets,   15
All you unpublished virtues of the earth,

---

*3 fumitor] *Oxford;* femiter Q; Fenitar F; fumiterr *Theobald;* fumitory *Hanmer*   *4 burdocks] *Hanmer;* hor-docks Q; Hardokes F, F2; Hardocks F3–4; bur-docks *Capell*   6 century send] Centery send F; centurie is sent Q   8 SD] *Malone (following Capell);* not in Q, F   8 wisdom] F, Q; wisedom do Q2   9–10 In ... worth.] *Pope's lineation; divided* him / Take Q, F   9 sense?] Q2; sence, Q; Sense; F   10 helps] F; can helpe Q   11 SH] F; *Doct.* Q   15–16 All ... earth] F *lineation; one line* Q

---

3 fumitor fumitory, a weed (compare Old French *fumeterre,* medieval Latin *fumus terrae,* 'smoke of the earth', so-called because it springs from the earth in great quantity like smoke: see *OED*). *H5* 5.2.45 similarly lists 'rank femetary' along with darnel and hemlock. F's 'Fenitar' may derive from a minim misreading; Q 'femiter' may reflect Shakespeare's spelling (NS).

3 furrow-weeds i.e. weeds growing in ploughed land.

4 burdocks 'coarse weedy plant ... bearing prickly flower-heads called burs, and large leaves like those of the dock' (*OED*). See collation. Q's 'hor-docks' is probably the result of misreading copy, an error compounded in F 'Hardokes' by the collator and/or compositor (see Stone, pp. 56, 101, 209; *Textual Companion,* p. 521).

4 cuckoo-flowers Variously identified as ragged robin, ladies' smocks, and bedlam cowslip. Ladies' smocks, or *Cardimine pratensis,* was used as long ago as the ancient Greeks and Romans and as recently as the last century for treating mental diseases (Muir).

5 Darnel Any troublesome weed (Furness); tares.

5 idle i.e. useless.

6 sustaining life-supporting, in contrast to 'idle weeds'.

6 century A hundred soldiers. The number may

faintly suggest the restoration of Lear's train (Perrett, p. 201).

7 high-grown field 'It is now, for symbolic purposes, high summer at Dover. The height of Lear's escape into "natural" chaos is supported by a natural riot of vegetation' (Hunter).

8 What ... wisdom i.e. what can human knowledge accomplish.

10 worth wealth.

12 Our ... nature i.e. what naturally nourishes and helps us. Shakespeare opposes a natural remedy – repose – to quack cures, such as scourging, charms, bleeding, scalp-shaving, etc., used by contemporary physicians (A. E. Kellogg, *Shakespeare's Delineation of Insanity, Imbecility, and Suicide,* 1866, cited by Furness).

13 provoke induce.

14 simples operative effective medicinal herbs. Compare 'simples' in *Rom.* 5.1.40.

15–16 All blest ... earth Cordelia invokes the assistance of natural, or white, magic, dependent here on herbs and plants for its effectiveness. Compare Giambattista della Porta, *Magiae naturalis* (Naples, 1589); English trans., London, 1658: Bk 8, ch. 1, 'Of Medicines which cause sleep', pp. 217–18.

16 unpublished ... earth i.e. secret, powerful herbs.

Spring with my tears; be aidant and remediate
In the good man's distress. – Seek, seek for him,
Lest his ungoverned rage dissolve the life
That wants the means to lead it.

Enter MESSENGER

MESSENGER   News, madam.   20
         The British powers are marching hitherward.
CORDELIA   'Tis known before. Our preparation stands
         In expectation of them. – O dear father,
         It is thy business that I go about:
         Therefore great France   25
         My mourning and importuned tears hath pitied.
         No blown ambition doth our arms incite,
         But love, dear love, and our aged father's right.
         Soon may I hear and see him.

                                                Exeunt

4.4 *Enter* REGAN *and* OSWALD

REGAN   But are my brother's powers set forth?
OSWALD   Ay, madam.
REGAN   Himself in person there?
OSWALD   Madam, with much ado.
         Your sister is the better soldier.   5

---

*18 good man's distress. –] *Capell* (*subst.*); good mans distresse, Q; Goodmans desires: F   **20–1** News ... hitherward.] F
lineation; one line (*turned under*) Q   **23** them. –] *Capell;* them, Q; them. F   **24–5** It ... France] *Johnson's lineation; one line*
Q, F   **26** importuned] F; important Q   **27** incite] F; in sight Q   **28** right.] right, Q; Rite: F   **29** SD] F; *Exit.* Q   Act 4,
Scene 4   **4.4**] *Scena Quarta.* F; *not in* Q   **3** there] F; *not in* Q   **4–5** Madam ... soldier.] F *lineation; one line* Q   **5** sister
is] F, Q; sister's Q2

17 Spring ... tears Cordelia figuratively and
literally waters the plants with her tears to encourage growth.
  17 aidant and remediate helpful and remedial.
Shakespeare may have coined 'remediate' to avoid
the jingle with 'aidant' that 'remediant' would cause
(Muir; compare Wright, cited by Furness).
  18 good man's distress See collation. F's error
cannot derive from Q; Compositor B misread manuscript copy (see Textual Analysis, p. 57 above, and
compare Stone, pp. 101, 222).
  19–20 Lest ... it Cordelia is afraid that in his
madness Lear will kill himself.
  19 rage madness, frenzy.
  20 wants the means lacks sanity, reason.
  22 preparation forces ready to fight; as in *Oth.*
1.3.14.
  23–4 O ... about Compare Luke 2.49: 'knewe
ye not that I must go about my fathers business?'

25 France i.e. the King of France.
  26 importuned importunate, solicitous. Q's
'important' means the same, though it may be a
misreading of 'importund' (Duthie, p. 410) or
'importune' (also meaning importunate: Muir).
  27–8 No ... right Cordelia here proclaims her
reasons for coming to England – not the seizure of
political power for herself, but filial devotion and
the wish to restore her father's rights.
  27 blown puffed up, inflated. Compare 1 Cor.
13.4–5: 'Loue suffreth long: it is bountiful ... it is
not puffed vp: / It disdaineth not: it seketh not her
owne things ...' (Muir).

Act 4, Scene 4
  4 with much ado It has apparently required
considerable effort from Gonerill to get Albany,
uncertain where his duty lay, to take command of
his army and march on.

REGAN   Lord Edmond spake not with your lord at home?
OSWALD   No, madam.
REGAN   What might import my sister's letter to him?
OSWALD   I know not, lady.
REGAN   Faith, he is posted hence on serious matter.   10
          It was great ignorance, Gloucester's eyes being out,
          To let him live. Where he arrives he moves
          All hearts against us. Edmond, I think, is gone,
          In pity of his misery, to dispatch
          His 'nighted life, moreover to descry   15
          The strength o'th'enemy.
OSWALD   I must needs after him, madam, with my letter.
REGAN   Our troops set forth tomorrow. Stay with us.
          The ways are dangerous.
OSWALD   I may not, madam.
          My lady charged my duty in this business.   20
REGAN   Why should she write to Edmond? Might not you
          Transport her purposes by word? Belike –
          Some things – I know not what. I'll love thee much:
          Let me unseal the letter.
OSWALD   Madam, I had rather –
REGAN   I know your lady does not love her husband.   25
          I am sure of that; and at her late being here

---

6 lord] F; Lady Q   6 home?] F; home. Q   8 letter] F; letters Q   13 Edmond] F; and now Q   14–16 In . . . enemy.] F
lineation; two lines divided life, / Moreouer Q   16 o'th'enemy.] F; at'h army. Q; of the Army. Q2   17 madam] F; *not in*
Q   17 letter] F; letters Q   18 troops set] F; troope sets Q   19–20 I . . . business.] F *lineation; as prose* Q   21–2 Why . . .
Belike –] *As in* Q; *divided:* Edmond? / Might F   *22 Belike –] *Oxford*; belike Q; Belike, F   *23 Some things –]
Something – *Pope*; Some things, F; Some thing, Q; Something Q2   23 much:] *Oxford*; much, Q; much F   24 I had]
F; I'de Q

6–8 Lord . . . him Regan is curious about
Edmond's sudden departure and the reason
Gonerill so swiftly sent a letter after him.

6 lord See collation. Copy for Q probably had
'L.', which the compositor mistook for an abbrevia-
tion of 'Lady' (Duthie, p. 411; Stone, p. 38).

8 import signify.

10 Faith In faith (a common oath).

11–12 It . . . live Compare 3.7.4. Regan initially
counselled death, which was practical, but
Gonerill's sadism better suited Cornwall's tempera-
ment and then excited Regan (King).

11 ignorance folly.

15 'nighted benighted; literally, because he is
blind, but Regan may also contemptuously imply
the figurative sense.

17 after See collation. 'Madam' was possibly
meant to replace rather than follow 'him', but the

correction was misunderstood and the line
remained unmetrical (*Textual Companion*, p. 537).

18–19 Stay . . . dangerous Regan's motive in
cajoling Oswald is related to her suspicion concerning the relationship between her sister and
Edmond. Compare 23–4 and n.

20 charged . . . business i.e. laid particular
stress upon me to carry out her orders.

22–3 Belike . . . what Regan is momentarily
unsure how to proceed, as her suspicions mount
regarding Gonerill and Edmond.

22 Belike Probably.

23–4 I'll . . . letter In the theatre these lines are
often accompanied by significant gestures, as
Regan attempts to seduce Oswald, caressing –
even kissing – him while reaching for the letter he
carries on his person (Rosenberg, p. 261).

        She gave strange oeilliads and most speaking looks

        To noble Edmond. I know you are of her bosom.

OSWALD I, madam?

REGAN I speak in understanding. Y'are, I know't.   30

        Therefore I do advise you take this note:

        My lord is dead; Edmond and I have talked;

        And more convenient is he for my hand

        Than for your lady's. You may gather more.

        If you do find him, pray you give him this;   35

        And when your mistress hears thus much from you,

        I pray desire her call her wisdom to her.

        So, fare you well.

        If you do chance to hear of that blind traitor,

        Preferment falls on him that cuts him off.   40

OSWALD Would I could meet him, madam, I should show

        What party I do follow.

REGAN   Fare thee well.

                             Exeunt

4.5 *Enter* GLOUCESTER *and* EDGAR [*dressed like a peasant*]

GLOUCESTER When shall I come to th'top of that same hill?

EDGAR You do climb up it now. Look how we labour.

---

27 oeilliads] Eliads F; Iliads F2–4; aliads Q; oeilliads *Rowe*   29 madam?] F; Madam. Q   30 Y'are] F; for Q   *34 lady's] *Rowe;* Ladies Q, F   37–8 I . . . well.] F *lineation; one line* Q   38 fare you well] F; farewell Q   *41 him] Q; *not in* F   41 should show] should shew F; would shew Q   42 party] F; Lady Q   42 SD] F; *Exit.* Q   **Act 4, Scene 5** 4.5] *Scena Quinta.* F; *not in* Q   0 SD] *Theobald; Enter Gloucester, and Edgar.* F; *Enter Gloster and Edmund.* Q   1 I] F; we Q   2 up it now.] F; it vpnow, Q; it vp it now, Q2   2 labour.] F; labour? Q

---

27 oeilliads amorous glances (*OED*, Onions); compare *Wiv.* 1.3.61, and Cotgrave: *Oeilliade*, 'An amorous looke, affectionate winke, wanton aspect, lustfull iert [= jerk], or passionate cast, of the eye; a Sheepes eye'. *OED* and Muir cite Greene, *Disputation between a He and a She Cony-Catcher* (1592); 'amorous glaunces, smirking oeyliads'. Q's 'aliad' involves *a/e* misreading.

27 speaking looks Muir compares the phrase in Florio's *Montaigne*, iii.211.

28 of her bosom (1) in her confidence, (2) sexually intimate. Compare 5.1.11 n. and *R3* 1.2.124, Richard III to Lady Anne: 'So I might live one hour in your sweet bosom' (NS; Partridge, p. 77).

30 understanding knowledge (Schmidt).

31 take this note i.e. note this carefully.

32 talked i.e. come to an understanding (Kittredge).

33 convenient suitable, fitting.

34 You . . . more You may infer more from what I have said.

35 give him this Precisely what Regan gives Oswald for Edmond is not clear. It may be a ring or other token rather than a note, since Edgar reads only one letter after rifling Oswald's pockets (4.5.250–8). Compare Furness, Muir, Hunter.

36 thus much i.e. what I have told you.

37 I pray . . . to her Compare *Wiv.* 3.3.118. The image is the summoning of a subordinate. The repetition of 'her' propels the irony of this line into sarcasm, which Regan hardly expects Oswald to repeat (King).

Act 4, Scene 5

0 SD *dressed like a peasant* The Old Man in 4.1 has apparently kept his word and given Edgar new apparel. See 4.1.50 and 222 below.

1 that same hill Compare 4.1.68–70.

2 You . . . labour Edgar's deception throughout this scene may seem cruel, his explanation and

GLOUCESTER   Methinks the ground is even.
EDGAR   Horrible steep.
      Hark, do you hear the sea?
GLOUCESTER   No, truly.
EDGAR   Why, then your other senses grow imperfect   5
      By your eyes' anguish.
GLOUCESTER   So may it be indeed.
      Methinks thy voice is altered, and thou speak'st
      In better phrase and matter than thou didst.
EDGAR   Y'are much deceived. In nothing am I changed
      But in my garments.
GLOUCESTER   Methinks y'are better spoken.   10
EDGAR   Come on, sir, here's the place. Stand still. How fearful
      And dizzy 'tis to cast one's eyes so low.
      The crows and choughs that wing the midway air
      Show scarce so gross as beetles. Half-way down
      Hangs one that gathers samphire, dreadful trade!   15
      Methinks he seems no bigger than his head.
      The fishermen that walk upon the beach
      Appear like mice, and yon tall anchoring barque
      Diminished to her cock; her cock, a buoy
      Almost too small for sight. The murmuring surge,   20
      That on th'unnumbered idle pebble chafes,
      Cannot be heard so high. I'll look no more,

3–4 Horrible . . . sea?] F *lineation; one line* Q   7 speak'st] F; speakest Q   8 In] F; With Q   11 Come . . . fearful] *As in* Q;
two lines divided Sir, / Heere's F   14 Show] Shew Q, F   *17 walk] Q; walk'd F   *18 yon] Q; yond F   21 th'] F; the
Q   21 pebble] F; peeble Q   21 chafes] F; chaffes Q   22 so] F; its so Q

defence at 33–4 notwithstanding. Especially cruel is
the attempt to rob Gloucester of confidence in the
senses he still retains.
  6 anguish extreme pain; this may include both
physical and mental pain. Compare Florio's
Montaigne, iv.70: 'Our senses are not onely altered,
but many times dulled, by the passions of the mind'
(Muir).
  7–8 Methinks . . . didst Gloucester's observation is accurate. Edgar has dropped mad Tom's
idiom and manner, and his tone of voice is
accordingly different. He now speaks in blank
verse.
  11–24 How . . . headlong Muir again compares
Florio's *Montaigne*, iv.67–8, on the effect of dizzy-
ing heights. The details of the description, which
Addison admired and to which Dr Johnson
objected, are precisely what make the passage moving and persuasive, particularly to eyeless
Gloucester. See Furness.

13 choughs jackdaws, or possibly the Cornish
chough or red-legged crow (Onions, cited by NS;
pronounced 'chuffs'). Compare 'russet-pated
choughs', *MND* 3.2.21.
  14 gross large.
  15 samphire St Peter's herb, or *herbe de Saint
Pierre*, an aromatic plant growing along sea-cliffs,
used in pickling and gathered by men suspended by
ropes.
  18 yon See collation. Again at 114 and 145, F has
'yond' for Q's 'yon', a recurrent Folio mannerism
that apparently reflects its modernizing tendency
rather than a concern for accuracy (Hunter).
  19 cock A small ship's-boat, cockboat.
  21 unnumbered innumerable.
  21 idle useless, barren.
  21 pebble Collective plural.

Lest my brain turn and the deficient sight
Topple down headlong.

GLOUCESTER   Set me where you stand.

EDGAR   Give me your hand. You are now within a foot   25
Of th'extreme verge. For all beneath the moon
Would I not leap upright.

GLOUCESTER   Let go my hand.
Here, friend, 's another purse: in it, a jewel
Well worth a poor man's taking. Fairies and gods
Prosper it with thee. Go thou further off.   30
Bid me farewell, and let me hear thee going.

EDGAR   Now fare ye well, good sir.

GLOUCESTER   With all my heart.

EDGAR   [*Aside*] Why I do trifle thus with his despair
Is done to cure it.

GLOUCESTER [*Kneels*]   O you mighty gods!
This world I do renounce, and in your sights   35
Shake patiently my great affliction off.
If I could bear it longer and not fall
To quarrel with your great opposeless wills,
My snuff and loathèd part of nature should
Burn itself out. If Edgar live, O bless him.   40
Now, fellow, fare thee well.

EDGAR   Gone, sir; farewell.
[*Gloucester throws himself forward and falls*]

25-7 Give . . . upright.] *As in* Q; *lines end* . . . hand: / . . . Verge: / . . . vpright. F   **30** further] F; farther Q   **32** ye] F; you Q   **33** SD] *Capell; not in* Q, F   **33-4** Why . . . it.] F *lineation; one line (turned over)* Q   **34** Is] F, Q; 'tis Q2   *34 SD] *He kneeles.* Q (*after* Gods,); *not in* F   **39** snuff] F; snurff Q   **40** him] F; *not in* Q   **41-8** Gone . . . sir?] F *lineation; as prose* Q   **41** SD] *Capell; He fals.* Q (*after* thee well); *not in* F

23 **turn** spin, become giddy.

23 **deficient** failing, defective.

24 **Topple** i.e. topple me.

27 **leap upright** Having been pulled along, wearily climbing the 'hill' (1–2), Gloucester is in a crouching position. Edgar warns that to straighten or jump up suddenly could result in loss of balance and prove fatal.

28 **another purse** Compare 4.1.59, 72.

29-30 **Fairies . . . thee** Gloucester alludes to the superstition that fairies who guard hidden treasure can make it multiply miraculously in the possession of the discoverer (Kittredge). Compare *WT* 3.3.123.

36 **patiently** Gloucester, of course, is anything

but 'patient'. Compare 38 n.

38 **opposeless** Unaware of his futility as well as inconsistency, Gloucester opposes ('quarrels with') the gods by attempting suicide while at the same time asserting that their wills cannot be resisted (opposed).

39 **snuff** candle-end or smouldering wick.

39 **loathèd . . . nature** the fag end of life, characterized by senility and therefore disgusting.

40 **Burn itself out** i.e. end naturally.

41 SD *Gloucester . . . falls* Gloucester doubtless waits till he hears Edgar say he is gone before he throws himself forward. Q places the SD *He fals* after Gloucester's speech, where there is ample space, rather than in the midst of Edgar's speech. Why F

> [*Aside*] And yet I know not how conceit may rob
> The treasury of life, when life itself
> Yields to the theft. Had he been where he thought,
> By this had thought been past. – Alive or dead?   45
> Ho, you sir, friend! Hear you, sir? Speak!
> [*Aside*] Thus might he pass indeed. Yet he revives. –
> What are you, sir?

GLOUCESTER   Away, and let me die.

EDGAR   Hadst thou been aught but gossamer, feathers, air,
> So many fathom down precipitating,   50
> Thou'dst shivered like an egg. But thou dost breathe,
> Hast heavy substance, bleed'st not, speak'st, art sound.
> Ten masts at each make not the altitude
> Which thou hast perpendicularly fell.
> Thy life's a miracle. Speak yet again.   55

GLOUCESTER   But have I fall'n or no?

EDGAR   From the dread summit of this chalky bourn.
> Look up a-height: the shrill-gorged lark so far
> Cannot be seen or heard; do but look up.

---

42 SD] *Capell; not in* Q, F   42 may] F; my Q   45 had thought] F, Q; thought had Q2   45 past. –] *Theobald;* past, Q; past. F   *46 Ho … Speak!] *This edn;* Hoa, you Sir: Friend, heare you Sir, speake: F; ho you sir, heare you sir, speak Q   47 SD] *Capell; not in* Q, F   49 Hadst … air,] *As in* Q; *two lines divided* ought / But F   49 gossamer] gosmore Q; Gozemore F; goss'mer *Pope*   50 So … precipitating,] Q; (So … precipitating) F   51 Thou'dst] F; Thou hadst Q   52 speak'st] F; speakest Q   56 fall'n] falne F; fallen Q   56 no?] F; no l Q   57 summit] Somnet F; sommons Q; summons Q2   *58 a-height] *Warburton;* a hight Q; a height F   59 up.] F; vp? Q

lacks the SD is unclear, unless Compositor B simply overlooked it. On staging-techniques, see Bratton, pp. 175–7; Derek Peat, '*King Lear* and the tension of uncertainty', *S.Sur.* 33 (1980), 46–9; and pp. 28–9 above.

42–4 And yet … theft Edgar takes a calculated risk: the illusion ('conceit') of a death leap may have the same effect as the reality, especially when death is willed. But see W. Schleiner's discussion of 'cure by imagination' in *Melancholy, Genius, and Utopia in the Renaissance*, Wiesbaden, 1991, pp. 274–86.

43 treasury treasure; as in *2H6* 1.3.131.

45–6 Alive … Speak Edgar changes his tone of voice to suggest still another character as he moves into the next phase of ministering to Gloucester, who has apparently fainted but may appear to be dead.

47 pass die.

49 gossamer Disyllabic; compare Q, F spellings in collation.

50 fathom Plural.

53 at each i.e. end to end, one on top of the other. Stone conjectures that 'alenth' (= 'alength') stood in the copy, and Oxford adopts 'a-length'. But none of the early quartos and Folios emend, so the expression was probably understood as it stands.

55 Thy … miracle The theme of Edgar's ministrations to his father; compare 72–7.

57 summit F 'Somnet', a variant but erroneous spelling of 'summit' (*OED*), probably derives from Shakespeare's hand: see Duthie, p. 412.

57 bourn boundary; i.e. cliff bordering on the sea.

58 a-height on high; compare *R3* 4.4.86: 'One heaued a high, to be hurld downe belowe' (*William Shakespeare: The Complete Works (Original-Spelling Edition)*, ed. Stanley Wells and Gary Taylor, 1986).

58 shrill-gorged shrilly voiced.

GLOUCESTER   Alack, I have no eyes.   60
              Is wretchedness deprived that benefit
              To end itself by death? 'Twas yet some comfort
              When misery could beguile the tyrant's rage
              And frustrate his proud will.

EDGAR   Give me your arm.
              Up; so. How is't? Feel you your legs? You stand.   65

GLOUCESTER   Too well, too well.

EDGAR   This is above all strangeness.
              Upon the crown o'th'cliff what thing was that
              Which parted from you?

GLOUCESTER   A poor unfortunate beggar.

EDGAR   As I stood here below, methought his eyes
              Were two full moons. He had a thousand noses,   70
              Horns whelked and waved like the enragèd sea.
              It was some fiend. Therefore, thou happy father,
              Think that the clearest gods, who make them honours
              Of men's impossibilities, have preserved thee.

GLOUCESTER   I do remember now. Henceforth I'll bear   75
              Affliction till it do cry out itself
              'Enough, enough', and die. That thing you speak of,
              I took it for a man. Often 'twould say
              'The fiend, the fiend!' He led me to that place.

EDGAR   Bear free and patient thoughts.

---

*63 tyrant's] tyrants Q; Tyranrs F   65 is't?] F; *not in* Q   *66 strangeness.] strangenes Q; strangenesse: Q2; strangenesse, F   *67 o'th'cliff] of the cliffe what Q; o'th'Cliffe. What F   68 beggar] F; bagger Q   69 methought] F; me thoughts Q   70 He] F; a Q   71 whelked] *Hanmer (subst.);* welk't Q; welkt Q2; wealk'd F   71 enragèd] F; enridged Q   73 make them] F; made their Q   78 'twould] F; would it Q; would he Q2   79 fiend!] fiend, Q; Fiend, F   80 Bear] F; Bare Q

63 **beguile** deceive, cheat.

63 **tyrant's rage** Gloucester alludes to the traditional defence of suicide among the Romans, particularly the Stoics under emperors like Nero or Domitian (Hunter).

69–72 Compare *Ham.* 1.4.69–78: Horatio warns Hamlet that a demon might drive him to insanity and to suicide by jumping off a cliff (Kittredge).

71 **whelked** convoluted, twisted.

71 **enragèd** Although most editors prefer Q's 'enridged' and regard F's 'enraged' as a 'vulgarisation' (Hunter; compare Duthie, p. 182), F is acceptable. Moreover, Shakespeare describes the 'enraged' sea many times elsewhere and could as easily be responsible for F's adjective as Q's (*Textual Companion*, p. 537).

72 **father** i.e. old man.

73 **clearest** brightest, purest, most glorious (Schmidt; cited by Furness, Muir).

73–4 **who ... impossibilities** i.e. who acquire honour and reverence by performing miracles. Compare Luke 18.27: 'The things which are vnpossible with me[n], are possible with God' (Furness; Shaheen cites Matt. 19.26 as well). Compare also 'Man's extremity is God's opportunity' (Kittredge; Tilley M471).

75 **I ... now** It is not clear what Gloucester refers to – the patience he earlier rejected (35–40), or Tom o'Bedlam.

75–7 **Henceforth ... die** i.e. from now on I shall bear affliction patiently until it wearies itself out and stops.

80 **free** not guilty or troubled.

Enter LEAR, [*mad*]

                                      But who comes here?   80
        The safer sense will ne'er accommodate
        His master thus.
LEAR   No, they cannot touch me for crying. I am the king himself.
EDGAR   O thou side-piercing sight!
LEAR   Nature's above art in that respect. There's your press-   85
    money. That fellow handles his bow like a crow-keeper. Draw
    me a clothier's yard. Look, look, a mouse! Peace, peace, this
    piece of toasted cheese will do't. There's my gauntlet. I'll prove

---

80 SD] Q (subst., following 82); Enter Lear. F   81–2 The … thus.] F lineation; one line Q   81 ne'er] F; neare Q   83 crying] F; coyning Q   85 Nature's] F; Nature is Q   87 piece of] F; not in Q   88 do't] F; do it Q

80 SD *Enter* LEAR, *mad* Many editions expand Q's SD with a description of Lear fantastically dressed, crowned with weeds and flowers, etc. For various theatrical representations, see Rosenberg, pp. 267–8; Bratton, pp. 177–9. A change of garments here and in the next scene is appropriate to Lear's changed condition. Obviously, to have the Fool accompany him in this state would be both superfluous and distracting: another reason to terminate his role in Act 3. Compare 3.6.41 n.

81–2 The safer … thus i.e. no one in his right mind would be dressed like this.

81 safer sounder, saner (Onions). Compare *MM* 1.1.72; *Oth.* 4.1.269: 'Are his wits safe? Is he not light of brain?'

81 accommodate Compare 3.4.95–6, where Lear refers to 'unaccommodated man' in a different sense.

82 His Its.

83 touch … crying See collation. If the reading 'crying' is preferred, then 'touch' = (1) lay hands on, or (2) rebuke, censure, accuse. M. Warren sees an allusion to the special sense of laying the hand upon (a diseased person) for the cure of the 'king's evil', or scrofula (*OED* Touch v 2b) ('*King Lear*, IV.iv.83: the case for "crying"', *SQ* 35 (1984), 320). If the chosen reading is 'coining', this would constrict the meaning of 'touch'. Since 'coining' means minting coins (a royal prerogative), Lear would then be understood as saying, 'since I am the king, I cannot be arrested ("touched") for forgery'. See Rosenberg, pp. 267–8, who also defends F's 'crying'.

84 side-piercing i.e. heart-rending (Schmidt), with a possible allusion to Christ on the cross. Compare John 19.34; in the Geneva Bible the column heading reads 'Christs side perced'.

85 Nature's … respect A king is born, not made, and cannot lose his natural rights (Schmidt 1879, cited by Furness). But Lear may also allude to the natural propensity for emotional outlet. The relation between art and nature was frequently discussed, as in *WT* 4.4.87–103. The disjointed sentences in this speech and elsewhere suggest Lear's disordered mental state, although a submerged thread of sense often connects his utterance.

85–6 press-money Payment for enlistment or impressment into the king's army. Lear distributes his coins, real or imagined, to Gloucester and Edgar, or to soldiers he imagines standing by.

86 That fellow i.e. one of Lear's imaginary soldiers.

86 crow-keeper scarecrow, or a farm-boy assigned to keep crows off a field; here, an inept archer. *OED* cites *Dick of Devon* (1626), 2.4: 'Sure these can be no Crowkeepers nor birdscarers.' Compare *Rom.* 1.4.6.

87 clothier's yard i.e. full length of the arrow (36 inches).

87 mouse Perhaps imagined, through association with 'crow-keeper', though actual fieldmice were abundant then as now.

87 Peace, peace Addressed to the soldiers Lear imagines are startled into action.

88 do't i.e. catch the mouse.

88 gauntlet i.e. challenge (literally, a thrown glove).

88–9 I'll … giant I'll make good my cause against anyone, even a giant (let alone a mouse). Lear imagines himself as a mighty champion.

it on a giant. Bring up the brown bills. O well flown bird: i'th'
clout, i'th'clout! Hewgh! Give the word.   90

EDGAR   Sweet marjoram.

LEAR   Pass.

GLOUCESTER   I know that voice.

LEAR   Ha! Gonerill with a white beard? They flattered me like a
dog and told me I had the white hairs in my beard ere the black   95
ones were there. To say 'ay' and 'no' to everything that I said
'ay' and 'no' to was no good divinity. When the rain came to
wet me once and the wind to make me chatter, when the
thunder would not peace at my bidding, there I found 'em,
there I smelt 'em out. Go to, they are not men o'their words.   100
They told me I was everything; 'tis a lie, I am not ague-proof.

GLOUCESTER   The trick of that voice I do well remember.
      Is't not the king?

---

90 i'th'clout ... Hewgh!] F; in the ayre, hagh, Q   94 Ha! ... beard?] F; Ha *Gonorill*, ha *Regan*, Q   95 the white] F; white
Q   *96–7 To say ... was] *Oxford;* to say I and no, to euery thing I saide, I and no toe, was Q; to say I and no to all I
saide: I and no too was Q2; To say I, and no, to euery thing that I said: I, and no too, was F   99 'em] F; them Q *(both
times)*   100 o'] F; of Q   101 ague-proof] F; argue-proofe Q   102–5 The ... cause?] F *lineation; as prose* Q

89 **brown bills** Halberds painted brown to prevent rust. Having assembled his archers, Lear
orders up his billmen.

89 **O ... bird** Falconer's cry of approval when his
falcon was successful (Steevens, cited by Furness);
but Lear may refer to the feathered arrow he imagines shot off.

90 **clout** Centre of target or mark, as in *LLL*
4.1.134.

90 **Hewgh** Whistling sound to indicate (1) sound
of the arrow through the air, or (2) cry of astonishment (NS).

90 **word** password.

91 **Sweet marjoram** Edgar humours Lear with
this fanciful password, which may allude to the
wildflowers bedecking Lear and/or to 'a blessed
remedy for diseases of the brain' (Blunden, cited
by Muir).

94 **Gonerill ... beard** Lear takes Gloucester for
Gonerill in disguise (Kittredge), or he asks how she
could be so inhuman to her aged father (Halliwell,
cited by Furness). Either way, Lear is prompted by
the sight of white-bearded Gloucester, as F's alteration of Q indicates (see collation and R. Warren, p.
50). Hunter adds a SD *He kneels* after 93, so that
Gloucester's obsequious or flattering attitude
reminds Lear of Gonerill. But the hag image is
more complex, suggesting transsexuality

(Rosenberg, p. 270), a demon witch, the inversion
of child and parent, etc. Also: Gloucester was to
Edgar what Gonerill was to Lear, as Edgar says in Q
(see Appendix, p. 280 below, xiv, 9), and both are
lechers (King).

94–6 **They ... there** Another abrupt mental
shift, prompted perhaps by recollection of
Gonerill's flattery in 1.1. The image of the fawning
dog is typically Shakespearean (Spurgeon, p. 195).
Lear complains of the world's flattery that praises
prematurely a king's ripe wisdom. A white beard
symbolizes the wisdom of age, which 'they' said he
had before he was old enough to grow any beard.

97 **no good divinity** bad theology. Several
biblical verses are possible sources or analogues.
Compare Matt. 5.37: 'But let your communication be, Yea, yea: Nay, nay. For whatsoeuer is
more the[n] these, commeth of euil.' Compare
also Matt. 5.36: 'Nether shalt thou sweare by
thine head, because thou canst not make one
heere white or blacke' (Hunter), and James
5.12, 2 Cor. 1.18–19.

97–100 **When ... out** Lear recalls the storm.
Compare *AYLI* 2.1.6–12 (NS).

101 **ague-proof** immune to severe chill. J. C.
Maxwell cites Florio's *Montaigne*, i.42: 'Doth the
ague ... spare him [the king] more than us?' (NS).

102 **trick** peculiar characteristic.

LEAR   Ay, every inch a king.
When I do stare, see how the subject quakes.
I pardon that man's life. What was thy cause?   105
Adultery?
Thou shalt not die. Die for adultery? No,
The wren goes to't, and the small gilded fly
Does lecher in my sight.
Let copulation thrive: for Gloucester's bastard son   110
Was kinder to his father than my daughters
Got 'tween the lawful sheets.
To't, luxury, pell-mell, for I lack soldiers.
Behold yon simp'ring dame,
Whose face between her forks presages snow,   115
That minces virtue, and does shake the head
To hear of pleasure's name.
The fitchew nor the soilèd horse goes to't
With a more riotous appetite.

---

103 every] F; euer Q   106–8 Adultery ... fly] *Capell's lineation; two lines divided* for Adultery? / No, F; *as prose*
Q   107 die. Die] dye: dye F; die Q   108 to't] F; toot Q   109–12 Does ... sheets.] *Johnson's lineation; three lines ending*
... thriue: / ... Father, / ... sheets. F; *as prose* Q   109 Does] F; doe Q   113 lack] F, Q; want Q2   114–22 Behold ...
inherit;] *Capell's lineation; as prose* Q, F   *114 yon] Q; yond F   115 presages] F; presageth Q   116 does] F; do
Q   117 To] F; *not in* Q   118 The] F; to Q   118 to't] F; toot Q

103 **Ay ... king** Spoken with various emphasis
and intonation, from regal reassertion to dreamy
recollection of bygone glory (Rosenberg, pp. 271–
2; Bratton, pp. 178–81).
104–23 **When ... fiend's** Prompted by
Gloucester's appearance, Lear begins a disquisition
on adultery that combines sense and nonsense and
varies the idiom of the absent Fool. Hunter notes
the progression from 'natural' or illicit sexuality
(adultery, copulation) to more violent representations of animal lust (pell-mell luxury, riotous appetite, centaurs). Lear's vision also includes the
breakdown of normal safeguards (the king, lawful
sheets, gods), culminating in unrestrained animal
behaviour and damnation (124–5). The lineation
reflects either Shakespeare's unrevised, roughed-
out version of the speech, or (more probably) irregular verse, ending as prose and meant to accord
with Lear's state of mind (Duthie, pp. 413–14).
104 **the subject** Collective, as in *MM* 3.2.136.
Here = 'my people' (NS).
105 **cause** offence, charge. Compare *Oth.* 5.2.1
(NS).
107 **Thou ... adultery** Compare *Lev.* 20.10 and
John 8.4–5, where death is the penalty for adultery
(Noble, Shaheen).

109 **lecher** fornicate.
113 **luxury** lechery, lust.
113 **pell-mell** i.e. promiscuously, randomly, like
men plunging headlong into battle; hence, the association with soldiers (NS).
113 **I lack soldiers** Promiscuity will help fill the
ranks of the king's army (Hunter).
114–23 Both Q and F print these lines as prose,
but Johnson relined them as verse following the
example of 103–13. (See 104–23 n. above.)
115 **Whose ... forks** Usually taken to refer to
the pudendum ('forks' = legs; compare 3.4.96). But
H. C. Hart suggests that 'forks' may refer to instruments for holding up women's hair; compare
Stubbes, *Anatomy of Abuses*, on women's hair
'vnderpropped with forks, wyers, and I can not tel
what' (Muir).
115 **presages snow** forecasts chastity, frigidity.
116 **minces virtue** coyly affects virtue, chastity.
116–17 **shake ... name** Compare Florio's
Montaigne, iv.131: 'Wee haue taught Ladies to
blush, onely by hearing that named, which they
nothing feare to doe' (Muir).
118 **fitchew** (1) polecat, (2) prostitute.
118 **soilèd** 'Fed with fresh-cut green fodder'
(Onions); hence, frisky.

Down from the waist they're centaurs, 120
Though women all above.
But to the girdle do the gods inherit;
Beneath is all the fiend's.
There's hell, there's darkness, there is the sulphurous pit,
burning, scalding, stench, consumption. Fie, fie, fie; pah, pah! 125
Give me an ounce of civet, good apothecary, sweeten
my imagination: there's money for thee.

GLOUCESTER O, let me kiss that hand!

LEAR Let me wipe it first; it smells of mortality.

GLOUCESTER O ruined piece of nature! This great world 130
Shall so wear out to naught. Dost thou know me?

LEAR I remember thine eyes well enough. Dost thou squiny at me?
No, do thy worst, blind Cupid, I'll not love.

---

*120 they're] th'are Q; they are F   123–4 Beneath ... pit] *Globe's lineation; as prose* Q, F   124 there is] F; ther's Q   124 sulphurous] F; sulphury Q   125 consumption] F; consumation Q   *126 civet,] Q; Ciuet; F   126 sweeten] F; to sweeten Q   129 Let ... mortality.] *As in* Q; *two lines divided* first, / It F   129 Let me] F; Here Q   130–1 O ... me?] *Rowe's lineation; lines end ... world; / ... naught. / ... me?* F; *as prose* Q   131 Shall] F; should Q   131 Dost thou] F; do you Q   132–4 I ... it] *Muir's lineation; as prose* Q, F   132 thine] F; thy Q   132 at] F; on Q

120 **centaurs** Half human, half horse, the centaur was notorious for riot and lechery. In an infamous battle, mentioned in *MND* 5.1.44, centaurs attempted to carry off Hippodamia, bride of Theseus's friend Pirithous (Ovid, *Metamorphoses*, 12.210 ff.; summarized in North's Plutarch, *The Life of Theseus*).

122–3 **But ... fiend's** Much Renaissance thought was preoccupied with humanity's double nature. Compare C. Carlile, *A Discourse of Peters life* (1580): 'Serverus said that a woman was the worke of the devil, and the upper part of a man of God, but from the navell downe of sathan: and therefore they that marrie doe fulfill the works of the devill' (Dent, p. 31). Exorcists hunted the devil through various parts of the woman's body; the girdle of a martyred saint, moreover, was allegedly used 'to confine the chief fiend to the lower part of the woman's body, her "hell"'' (M. C. Bradbrook, *Shakespeare: The Poet in his World*, 1978, p. 196). Compare Virgil's description of Scylla: a fair virgin to the waist, a sea-monster below (*Aeneid*, 3.426–8).

122 **girdle** waist.

122 **inherit** possess, govern.

124–5 **hell ... consumption** 'The obvious sexual references point to a climax of hysterical disgust at female sexuality' (Hunter).

124 **hell** (1) place of damnation, (2) slang for female genitals (Riverside).

125 **consumption** destruction.

125 **Fie ... pah** 'The monosyllables are, of course, not voiced as such: they are inarticulate sounds of physical disgust that may be accompanied

by grimace, spitting, vomiting' (Rosenberg, p. 274).

126–7 **Give ... thee** Lear now addresses Gloucester as an apothecary from whom he buys perfume to 'sweeten' his imagination, which engendered his foul vision of hell. Compare Marston, *The Fawne* (1606), 2.1: 'Sweeten your imaginations, with thoughts of – ah why women are the most giddie, uncertaine motions under heaven ... onely meere chancefull appetite swayes them' (Muir).

126 **ounce** (1) one sixteenth of a pound (weight), (2) lynx (King).

126 **civet** Perfume made from the anal glands of civet cats. The association is suggested by Gloucester's bandages: civet cats have reddish eyes (King). NS suspects irony and compares *AYLI* 3.2.64–8.

130 **piece** masterpiece (probably, in view of Lear's former majesty); compare *Ant.* 5.2.98–9: 't'imagine / An Antony were nature's piece 'gainst fancy' (Schmidt 1879, cited by Furness).

130–1 **This ... naught** The universe will, like Lear, disintegrate into ruin.

132 **I ... enough** Lear is bitterly tendentious. His 'remembering' focuses on the absent organs and forces attention on them.

132 **squiny** squint. Compare 3.4.103 n.

133 **blind Cupid** 'Love is blind' is proverbial (Tilley L506; *MV* 2.6.36–7). But 'blind Cupid' also adorned the sign of a brothel, as Benedick indicates in *Ado* 1.1.253–4. Gloucester, as Edmond's father, his eye-sockets bandaged, reminds Lear of brothel love. In Sidney's *Arcadia*, Bk II, ch. 14, Cupid is 'an old false knaue', half man, half beast (Muir).

Read thou this challenge; mark but the penning of it.

GLOUCESTER   Were all thy letters suns, I could not see.   135

EDGAR   [*Aside*] I would not take this from report; it is,
    And my heart breaks at it.

LEAR   Read.

GLOUCESTER   What – with the case of eyes?

LEAR   O ho, are you there with me? No eyes in your head, nor no   140
    money in your purse? Your eyes are in a heavy case, your purse in a
    light; yet you see how this world goes.

GLOUCESTER   I see it feelingly.

LEAR   What, art mad? A man may see how this world goes with no
    eyes; look with thine ears. See how yon justice rails upon yon   145
    simple thief. Hark in thine ear: change places, and handy-
    dandy, which is the justice, which is the thief? Thou hast seen
    a farmer's dog bark at a beggar?

GLOUCESTER   Ay, sir.

LEAR   And the creature run from the cur? There thou mightst   150
    behold the great image of authority. A dog's obeyed in office.

---

134 this] F; that Q   134 but] F; *not in* Q   134 of it] F; oft Q   135 thy] F; the Q   135 see.] F; see one. Q   136 SD]
Hanmer; not in Q, F   136–7 I . . . it.] *Theobald's lineation; divided* report, / It F; *as prose* Q   *139 What –] *Oxford;* What!
Q; What, Q2; What F   144 this] F; the Q   145 thine] F; thy Q   *145 yon] Q; yond F   *145 yon] Q; yond F   *146
thine] F; thy Q   146 change places, and] F; *not in* Q   147 justice] F; theefe Q   147 thief?] F; Iustice, Q   *150 cur?
There] *Theobald;* Cur: there F; cur, ther: Q   151 dog's obeyed] F; dogge, so bade Q; dogge, so bad Q2

134 this challenge Compare 88 above.
Whether Lear actually holds a piece of paper
(the proclamation for Gloucester's death,
as Staunton believed), or imagines one, is
uncertain, but irrelevant where unseeing
Gloucester is concerned. Compare 1.2.27 ff.
(Cavell).

   134 penning style (Schmidt).

   136 take this believe this spectacle.

   139 case of eyes eye-sockets.

   140 are . . . me (1) is that your meaning? (2) are
we both blind, i.e. are we both victims of impercep-
tiveness? (Rosenberg, p. 275).

   141 heavy case sad predicament; with quibbles
on 'heavy' and 'case'.

   142 see (1) understand, (2) view.

   143 feelingly (1) deeply, keenly, (2) with my
sense of touch.

   144 What, art mad Taking Gloucester's 'feelingly' in sense (2), Lear is outraged that he should
complain of blindness, i.e. impaired perception,
since all senses are equally valid – and invalid.

   145–6 See . . . thief An example of looking with
ears.

   146 simple Either (1) humble, ordinary, or (2)
weak-witted.

   146–7 handy-dandy A child's guessing game in
which an object is concealed in one hand; here =
'take your choice', the difference between justice
and thief is insignificant or indistinguishable, more
a matter of luck or chance than anything else. Dent,
p. 227, quotes Barclay's *Mirrour of good Maners* (*c.*
1523), 34 (8–14): 'What difference betwene a great
thief and a small . . . The small thief is judged, oft
time the great is Judge'; compare *MM* 2.1.19–23,
2.2.175–6. Florio's *Montaigne*, vi.85, has several
references to guilty judges, including an adulterer
passing sentence on another (Muir).

   151 A . . . office i.e. response to authority is
governed by role or status, not intrinsic worth or
right; 'dog's' is emphatic. Compare Florio's
Montaigne, iii.210: 'there are Nations, who
receive and admit a Dogge to be their King'
(Muir).

Thou rascal beadle, hold thy bloody hand.
Why dost thou lash that whore? Strip thy own back.
Thou hotly lusts to use her in that kind
For which thou whip'st her. The usurer hangs the
          cozener.   155
Through tattered clothes great vices do appear:
Robes and furred gowns hide all. Plate sin with gold,
And the strong lance of justice hurtless breaks;
Arm it in rags, a pygmy's straw does pierce it.
None does offend, none, I say none. I'll able 'em.   160
Take that of me, my friend, who have the power
To seal th'accuser's lips. Get thee glass eyes,

152–5 Thou . . . cozener.] *Pope's lineation; as prose* Q, F   153 thy] F; thine Q   154 Thou] F; thy bloud Q   155 cozener] F; cosioner Q   156–63 Through . . . seem] *Rowe's lineation; as prose* Q, F   156 Through] Q; Thorough F   156 tattered clothes] F; tottered raggs, Q   156 great] F; smal Q   157 furred gowns hide] F; furd-gownes hides Q   157–62 Plate . . . lips.] F; *not in* Q   *157 Plate sin] *Theobald;* Place sinnes F

152–5 Thou . . . her Compare John 8.7 on the woman taken in adultery, and Rom. 2.1 on hypocrisy: 'Therefore thou art inexcusable, o ma[n], whosoeuer thou art that iudgest: for in that thou iudgest another, thou co[n]demnest thy self: for thou that iudgest, doest the same things' (NS, p. xxxvi).

152 beadle A minor parish officer who whipped whores and other offenders.

154 kind manner.

155 The usurer . . . cozener Compare 'The great thieves hang the little ones' (Tilley T119), and 146–7 n. above. 'In this period usurers or capitalists were acquiring respectability and were being appointed to offices such as that of magistrate, against the protests of preachers and poets' (Hunter). Usury had become legal in 1571.

155 usurer moneylender.

155 cozener cheater.

156 Through F 'thorough' is probably the result of a page-break, which required splitting the word (*Textual Companion*, p. 537).

156 great See collation. Although Duthie, p. 183, prefers Q's 'smal', Maxwell argues that F restores the Shakespearean phrasing for Q's cliché; he compares similar Q/F alterations elsewhere, e.g. 'houres'/'yeares', 2.2.51 (NS). Compare Furness: 'When looked at through tattered clothes, all vices are great'; Hunter: 'it is not the smallness of their vices that distinguishes the poor, but the exposure to which they are subject'.

157 Robes . . . all i.e. judges and magistrates get away with crimes which the poor cannot. Robes and gowns are used both literally and metaphorically. Compare the furred gowns of usurers, *MM* 3.2.7–8, and 155 n. above.

157–62 Plate . . . lips See Textual Analysis, pp. 268–9 below.

157 Plate sin Cover sin in armour plate. F 'Place' derives from easy *t*/*c* misreading; a singular noun, moreover, is required as the antecedent of 'it' (159). Copy for F probably read 'sinne' (NS; Duthie, p. 415). The imagery here and in the two lines following is from jousting: compare *R2* 1.3.1 ff., especially 26–30, where 'plated in habiliments of war' occurs.

159 pygmy's straw i.e. a weak weapon. In the pseudo-Homeric epic *The Battle of the Frogs and Mice* the frogs carried rushes for spears (Hunter).

160 None . . . able 'em Again, Shakespeare alludes to the woman taken in adultery, John 8.7, the passage in scripture that also influenced Montaigne (Muir; compare 152–5 n. above). If everyone sins, then no one does. As king, Lear can vouch for ('able') everyone and exempt them from punishment. Lear 'needs to forgive so as to forgive himself, too; needs to obviate the compulsion to punish' (Rosenberg, p. 277).

161 Take . . . me Lear offers Gloucester an imaginary pardon (Kittredge), information (Muir), guarantee of immunity (Harbage, Bevington), or imaginary money (NS): the context permits any of these interpretations.

161 power i.e. either as king or as briber.

162–4 Get . . . not Lear returns to harping upon blindness and false perception. The 'scurvy politician' (= vile machiavel or schemer, as in *1H4* 1.3.241) pretends to perceptions he does not and cannot have. Lear's fierce attack sets Gloucester weeping.

162 glass eyes spectacles (Onions).

And, like a scurvy politician, seem
To see the things thou dost not. Now, now, now, now.
Pull off my boots. Harder, harder! So.   165

EDGAR   [*Aside*] O matter and impertinency mixed,
Reason in madness.

LEAR   If thou wilt weep my fortunes, take my eyes.
I know thee well enough; thy name is Gloucester.
Thou must be patient. We came crying hither.   170
Thou know'st the first time that we smell the air
We wawl and cry. I will preach to thee: mark.

GLOUCESTER   Alack, alack the day.

LEAR   When we are born, we cry that we are come
To this great stage of fools. This' a good block.   175
It were a delicate stratagem to shoe

164–5 To ... So.] *Capell's lineation; as prose* Q, F   164 dost] F; doest Q   164 Now ... now.] F; no now Q   166 SD] *Capell; not in* Q, F   166–7 O ... madness.] F; *one line* Q   166 impertinency mixed,] F; impertinencie mixt Q; impertinency, mixt Q2   168–72 If ... mark.] F *lineation; as prose* Q   168 fortunes.] F; fortune Q   171 know'st] F; knowest Q   172 wawl] F; wayl Q   172 mark] F; mark me Q   174–9 When ... kill!] F *lineation; as prose* Q   *175 This'] *Singer;* this Q; This F   176 shoe] shoo F; shoot Q

164 Now ... now Lear's tone changes as Gloucester weeps, and he tries to comfort the blind old man. See collation. Blayney conjectures that Q's 'No now' marks a lacuna, 'teares' being omitted (cited by *Textual Companion*, p. 522). But the emendation, however attractive, is unnecessary, as Q2 punctuation, 'No, now', shows that Q can make sense as well as F. Alternatively, the *w* may have been indistinct in Q's copy, as elsewhere (Duthie, p. 399).

165 Pull ... So Lear commands Gloucester to pull off his boots, a reminiscence perhaps of his return from hunting in 1.4, though he may in fact be barefoot. 'So' may express (imagined) relief at being rid of the uncomfortable gear.

166 matter and impertinency i.e. sense and nonsense.

167 Reason in madness Compare *Ham.* 2.2.205–6; 4.5.174, 178.

168–75 If ... fools Lear's tenderness towards Gloucester reaches its apogee as he recognizes his old retainer and preaches patience to him, the virtue he had vainly tried to practise himself during his initial distress.

170–2 We ... cry Compare Wisdom 7.6; also 7.3: 'When I was borne, I receyued the common ayre ... crying and weeping at the first as all other doe' (Noble, Shaheen). Muir cites Plangus's lament in Sidney's *Arcadia*, Bk II, ch. 12, and Florio's *Montaigne*, i.107: 'So wept we, and so much did it cost us to enter into this life.' The thought is proverbial: 'We weeping come into the world, and

weeping hence we go' (Tilley w889); compare 5.2.9–11.

172 wawl wail.

175 this ... fools Shakespeare frequently compares the world to a stage, as in *AYLI* 2.7.136–66. Compare also Tilley, w882, 896.

175 This' This is.

175 block The association with 'felt' (177) suggests a hat. It may be Lear's, which he removes at 172 to begin his sermon – either the crown of weeds and wildflowers he has made (4.3.3–5), an actual hat bedecked with flora, or an imaginary one; or it may be Edgar's or Gloucester's. On the other hand, 'A troop of horse' (177) suggests a mounting-block; in some productions, Lear has mounted a stump to begin preaching (Furness); 'stage' (175) = scaffold, or a boulder or tree-stump that Lear mistakes and quibbles on (Muir). The associations are not mutually exclusive, and Lear's mind rapidly shifts from one association to another.

176–7 a delicate ... felt Lord Herbert of Cherbury's *Life of Henry VIII* describes a joust in which horses were shod this way to prevent sliding (Malone, cited by Furness); here the stratagem is for a sneak attack.

176 delicate finely skilful, ingenious (Onions). Compare *Oth.* 4.1.187: 'So delicate with her needle'.

176 shoe See collation. Q 'shoot' probably derives from *t*/*e* misreading; Q copy may have had 'shooe' (Duthie, p. 415).

A troop of horse with felt. I'll put't in proof,
And when I have stol'n upon these son-in-laws,
Then kill, kill, kill, kill, kill, kill!

Enter a GENTLEMAN [*with Attendants*]

GENTLEMAN   O here he is: lay hand upon him. Sir,   180
    Your most dear daughter –
LEAR   No rescue? What, a prisoner? I am even
    The natural fool of fortune. Use me well.
    You shall have ransom. Let me have surgeons,
    I am cut to th'brains.
GENTLEMAN   You shall have anything.   185
LEAR   No seconds? All myself?
    Why, this would make a man a man of salt,

---

177 felt.] F; fell, Q   177 I'll ... proof,] F; *not in* Q   178 stol'n] F; stole Q   178 son-in-laws] Son in Lawes F, Q; sonnes in law Q2   *179 SD] *Rowe; Enter three Gentlemen.* Q; *Enter a Gentleman.* F   180–1 O ... daughter –] *lineation; one line* Q   180 hand] F; hands Q   *180 him. Sir,] *Johnson;* him, Sir. F; him sirs, Q; him sirs. Q2   181 Your most dear daughter –] F; your most deere Q; *not in* Q2   182–5 No ... brains.] F *lineation; as prose* Q   182 even] F; eene Q   184 ransom] F, Q; a ransom Q2   184 surgeons] F; a churgion Q   185 to th'] F; to the Q   186–91 No ... that?] F; *two prose speeches in* Q, *which gives second* SH *before* I will die ... , *where* Q2 *inserts:* Gent. Good Sir. (*not in* Q, F)   187 a man a man] F; a man Q

---

177 felt Q 'fell' probably derives from *l*/*t* misreading (Duthie, p. 415).

177 I'll ... proof I'll put it to the test, try the experiment.

178 son-in-laws A possible colloquial plural (Doran, p. 97).

179 SD GENTLEMAN *with Attendants* See collation. Obviously, more than one person enters since a Gentleman stays behind to talk with Edgar (195 ff.). The stage business that follows is complicated. Lear has no way of knowing that the Gentleman means him no harm. He attempts to escape, especially as the Gentleman orders the others to 'lay hand upon him' (180). They hold him so gently that he easily breaks free, or they release their hold momentarily to kneel when he says 'I am a king' (190). Lear does not hear what the Gentleman says until 192, and then may not credit him; hence his flight, forcing pursuit.

180 him. Sir See collation. Since it is unlikely that the Gentleman would address Lear without a vocative, Johnson's emendation of the punctuation (anticipated by Rowe) appears correct.

183 natural (1) born (as in *3H6* 1.1.82), (2) idiot.

183 fool of fortune Compare *Rom.* 3.1.136: 'O, I am fortune's fool!' Note Lear's irony: just a moment

ago he was leading a charge against the 'son-in-laws'; now he is a prisoner (Hunter).

183–4 Use ... ransom A royal prisoner was worth much in ransom and was accordingly well treated (NS).

184 surgeons Trisyllabic. Abbott 479 scans the line: 'Yóu shall have ránsom. Lét me have súrgeóns.'

185 cut to th'brains Literally and figuratively: Lear imagines a head wound and feels a psychic one.

186–91 No ... that See collation and Textual Analysis, pp. 255–6 below. F omits an inessential half-line ('I and laying Autums dust'), but prints 188–91 as three lines. Modern editions that conflate Q and F also retain metrical anomalies. By conflating Q2 and F, and by various linebreaks, Furness, Riverside, and Halio come closer to providing regular scansion. Rearranging F, Oxford (followed here) provides nearly regular lineation, except for (1) an apparently excrescent 'What?' (189), found in both Q and F, and (2) a half-line (191). Compare Taylor, 'Date and authorship', pp. 363–4; Duthie, pp. 415–16.

186 seconds supporters. Lear's sense of isolation is acute.

187 a man a man By adding 'a man', F corrects both sense and metre.

187 salt i.e. tears. Lear remains preoccupied with weeping.

To use his eyes for garden water-pots.
I will die bravely, like a smug bridegroom. What?
I will be jovial. Come, come, I am a king.   190
Masters, know you that?
GENTLEMAN   You are a royal one, and we obey you.
LEAR   Then there's life in't. Come, and you get it, you shall get it by
running. Sa, sa, sa, sa!

Exit [running, Attendants following]

GENTLEMAN   A sight most pitiful in the meanest wretch,   195
Past speaking of in a king. Thou hast a daughter
Who redeems nature from the general curse
Which twain have brought her to.
EDGAR   Hail, gentle sir.
GENTLEMAN   Sir, speed you: what's your will?
EDGAR   Do you hear aught, sir, of a battle toward?   200
GENTLEMAN   Most sure and vulgar: everyone hears that,
Which can distinguish sound.
EDGAR   But, by your favour,
How near's the other army?

188–91 To … that?] *Furness's lineation; three lines ending* … brauely, / … Iouiall: / … that? F; *as prose* Q   188 water-pots.] F; waterpots, I and laying Autums dust. Q; water-pottes, I and laying Autumnes dust. Q2   *Gent.* Good Sir. Q2   189 smug] F; *not in* Q   191 Masters] F; my maisters Q   191 that?] F; that. Q   193–4 Then … running.] *As in* Q; *two verse lines divided* get it, / You F   193 Come,] F; nay Q   193 by] F; with Q   194 Sa … sa!] F; *not in* Q   194 SD] *Capell* (*subst.*); *Exit King running.* Q; *Exit.* F   195–8 A sight … to.] F *lineation; as prose* Q   196 a daughter] F; one daughter Q   198 have] F; hath Q   200 sir,] (Sir) F; *not in* Q   200 toward?] Q2; toward. Q, F   201–2 Most … sound.] *As in* Q; *divided* heares / That Q2; vulgar: / Euery F   201 everyone] F, Q; euery ones Q2   201 hears that] F, Q; heares Q2   202 Which] F; That Q   202 sound] F; sence Q   202–3 But … army?] F *lineation; one line* Q

189 **die** (1) end my life, (2) reach sexual climax. Compare *Ant.* 4.14.99–101: 'but I will be / A bridegroom in my death, and run into't / As to a lover's bed' (NS).
189 **bravely** (1) courageously, (2) handsomely, in fine attire (as Lear regards his fantastic garb).
189 **smug** neat, trim, spruce.
190 **jovial** (1) majestic, Jove-like (*OED* sv *adj* 1), (2) merry, convivial (*OED* sv *adj* 6). Compare *Mac.* 3.2.28.
193 **there's life in't** 'The case is not yet desperate' (Johnson, cited by Furness); i.e. Lear still commands some shreds of respect as king.
193 **and** if.
193 **it** i.e. the ransom (NS).
194 **Sa … sa** An old hunting cry (French *ça, ça!*) to urge dogs forward in the chase (Kittredge).
195–8 **A sight … to** The Gentleman's speech is choric, spoken to the audience rather than to anyone on stage; although the second sentence uses direct

address, it is a comment upon Lear's situation, not spoken to him.
196 **speaking of** Oxford deletes 'of', which it regards as inessential as well as hypermetrical, an 'easy compositorial interpolation' (*Textual Companion*, p. 523). But the Gentleman's speech, prose in Q, is otherwise irregular and requires elisions – e.g. 'pit'ful', 'gen'ral' – to scan.
197 **nature** i.e. human nature.
197 **general** universal; with connotations of original sin.
198 **twain** i.e. Gonerill and Regan. Danby, p. 125, sees an indirect allusion to Adam and Eve.
198 **her** i.e. human nature.
199 **speed you** (God) prosper you, give you success.
200 **toward** impending.
201 **vulgar** i.e. a matter of common knowledge (Kittredge).
203 **other army** i.e. the army of Gonerill and Regan.

GENTLEMAN   Near and on speedy foot: the main descry
          Stands on the hourly thought.

EDGAR   I thank you, sir. That's all.   205

GENTLEMAN   Though that the queen on special cause is here,
          Her army is moved on.

EDGAR   I thank you, sir.

                                        Exit [Gentleman]

GLOUCESTER   You ever gentle gods, take my breath from me.
          Let not my worser spirit tempt me again
          To die before you please.

EDGAR   Well pray you, father.   210

GLOUCESTER   Now, good sir, what are you?

EDGAR   A most poor man, made tame to fortune's blows,
          Who by the art of known and feeling sorrows
          Am pregnant to good pity. Give me your hand;
          I'll lead you to some biding.

GLOUCESTER   Hearty thanks;   215
          The bounty and the benison of heaven
          To boot, and boot.

                        Enter OSWALD

OSWALD   A proclaimed prize! most happy!
          That eyeless head of thine was first framed flesh
          To raise my fortunes. Thou old, unhappy traitor,

---

204 speedy foot:] F; speed fort Q   204 descry] F; descryes, Q   205 Stands] F; Standst Q   205 thought] F; thoughts
Q   *207 SD] *Johnson; Exit.* Q; *Exit.* F (*after* moved on.)   212 tame to] F; lame by Q   215–17 Hearty ... boot.] F
lineation; as prose Q   216 bounty] F, Q *corr.;* bornet Q *uncorr.*   216 the benison] F, Q *corr.* (the benizon); beniz Q
uncorr.   216–17 heaven / To boot, and boot.] F; heauen to saue thee. Q *uncorr.;* heauen, to boot, to boot. Q *corr.,*
Q2   217–21 A proclaimed ... thee.] F *lineation; as prose* Q   217 happy!] happy, Q; happie F; happy: F2–4   218 first] F;
not in Q *uncorr.*   219 old] F; most Q

---

204 **on speedy foot** marching rapidly.
  204–5 **the main ... thought** Most editors
accept Johnson: 'The main body is expected to be
descried every hour.' But Stone, pp. 47, 210,
objects that this paraphrase depends upon unwar-
rantable glosses and says a line or two may be missing between 204 and 205.
  205 **Stands on** Rests on, depends on
(Kittredge); compare 5.1.58.
  206 **Though that** Though.
  208 **take ... me** i.e. take my life before I am
tempted to suicide again.
  209 **worser spirit** evil side of my nature; with an
allusion perhaps to 'evil angel'.
  210 **father** old man; as at 72 above.
  212 **tame** yielding, submissive; the image is of a
whip used for taming animals (King).
  213 **art** instruction, lesson.

213 **known ... sorrows** Either (1) misfortunes
experienced and sympathized with, or (2) sorrows I have known by feeling them (hendiadys)
(King).
  214 **pregnant to** 'ready, by intervention of sorrow, to give birth to pity' (King); receptive to
(Onions). Compare *TN* 3.1.88–9: 'My matter hath
no voice, lady, except to your own most pregnant
and vouchsafed ear.'
  215 **biding** abode, dwelling.
  216 **benison** blessing.
  217 **To boot, and boot** Gloucester plays on
noun and verb: 'in addition' (*OED* Boot *sb*[1] 1) and
'(may it) profit (you)' (*OED* Boot *v*[1] 3). Oswald may
interrupt before Gloucester reaches his verb (King).
Compare NS; Greg, *Variants*, p. 176; *Textual
Companion*, p. 537.
  217 **happy** opportune; compare 2.3.2.

Briefly thyself remember: the sword is out   220
That must destroy thee.

GLOUCESTER   Now let thy friendly hand
Put strength enough to't.

OSWALD   Wherefore, bold peasant,
Dar'st thou support a published traitor? Hence,
Lest that th'infection of his fortune take
Like hold on thee. Let go his arm.   225

EDGAR   Chill not let go, zir, without vurther 'casion.

OSWALD   Let go slave, or thou di'st.

EDGAR   Good gentleman, go your gait, and let poor volk pass. And
chud ha' been zwaggered out of my life, 'twould not ha' been
zo long as 'tis by a vortnight. Nay, come not near th'old man.   230
Keep out, che vor'ye, or I s' try whether your costard or my
ballow be the harder; chill be plain with you.

221–2 Now ... to't.] F *lineation; one line* Q   222–5 Wherefore ... arm.] F *lineation; as prose* Q   223 Dar'st] F*;* durst Q   224 that th'] F*;* the Q   226 Chill ... 'casion.] *As in* Q*; two lines divided* Zir, / Without F   226 zir] F*;* sir Q   226 vurther 'casion] F*;* cagion Q   227 di'st] F*;* diest Q   228 and] F*; not in* Q   229 ha'] F*;* haue Q (*both times*)   229 zwaggered] F*;* swagger'd Q   229 'twould] F*;* it would Q   230 zo] F*;* so Q   230 as 'tis] F*; not in* Q   230 vortnight] F*;* fortnight Q *uncorr.*   230 th'] F*;* the Q   *231 out,] Q *uncorr.;* out Q *corr.,* F   231 che vor'ye] F*;* cheuore ye Q   231 I s'] ice F*;* ile Q   231 whether] Q*;* whither F   231 costard] F*;* coster Q *uncorr.;* costerd Q *corr.*   232 ballow] F*;* battero Q *uncorr.;* bat Q *corr.,* Q2   232 chill] F*;* ile Q

220 Briefly thyself remember i.e. quickly confess your sins and pray for forgiveness. Even Oswald is loath to kill someone without giving the victim an opportunity to prepare his soul for death. Compare analogous situations in *Ham.* 3.3.73–86; *Oth.* 5.2.26–32.

221 friendly i.e. because Gloucester wants to die.

222–3 Wherefore ... traitor Johnson and later editors insert a SD here, e.g. *Edgar interposes*, as the dialogue suggests. Oswald's epithet indicates Edgar's changed habit and perhaps gives him a cue for speaking in dialect. Oswald is more aggressive here than he was to Kent in 2.2, probably because he feels superior to a mere peasant with no schooling in weaponry, and because he anticipates a reward for killing Gloucester (4.4.40) (King).

223 published proclaimed.

226–34 Chill ... foins Edgar's dialect is borrowed mainly from Somersetshire, but Elizabethan dramatists were no dialectologists: their purpose was simply to write dialect that sounded rustic enough to be funny or otherwise suit the dramatic occasion. Q2 and F introduce many more dialectal spellings than Q, elaborating the indications of dialect typical of Jaggard's printing-house (*Textual Companion*, p. 537)*;* but from a philological standpoint the passage is merely a patchwork of current colloquialisms and conventional stage dialect (Kökeritz, pp. 37–9; compare Kittredge). This

dialect is identical with the Devonshire dialect in *The London Prodigal* (1605), performed by the King's Men (Muir).

226 Chill I will.

226 'casion occasion, cause. Oxford adopts Q's 'cagion', suspecting compositorial substitution of the common for the unusual form (*Textual Companion*, p. 537). But possibly F was altered to make the speech more comprehensible.

228 go your gait get along, go your way.

228 volk F is probably an unintentional normalization of Q 'voke' (*Textual Companion*, p. 537), but the pronunciation is not affected (compare Kökeritz, p. 310).

228–30 And chud ... vortnight i.e. if I could have been killed by boasting (swaggering), I would not have lasted a fortnight.

231 che vor'ye I warrant you (Kökeritz, 'Elizabethan *Che vor ye* "I warrant you"', *MLN* 57 (1942), 98 ff.).

231 costard Slang for 'head' (literally, a large apple).

231 ballow cudgel (Onions). See collation. Oxford prints 'baton', assuming a misreading in F similar to that which led to Q uncorr. 'battero' (*Textual Companion*, p. 538; compare Greg, *Variants*, pp. 176–7). But Wright, *English Dialect Dictionary* (cited by Muir, Kökeritz) records later use in Nottingham and elsewhere.

OSWALD   Out, dunghill!

[They fight]

EDGAR   Chill pick your teeth, zir: come, no matter vor your foins.

OSWALD   Slave, thou hast slain me. Villain, take my purse.   235
          If ever thou wilt thrive, bury my body,
          And give the letters which thou find'st about me
          To Edmond, Earl of Gloucester: seek him out
          Upon the English party. O untimely death, death.

[He dies]

EDGAR   I know thee well – a serviceable villain,   240
          As duteous to the vices of thy mistress
          As badness would desire.

GLOUCESTER   What, is he dead?

EDGAR   Sit you down, father; rest you.
          Let's see these pockets. The letters that he speaks of
          May be my friends. He's dead. I am only sorry   245
          He had no other deathsman. Let us see.
          Leave, gentle wax; and manners, blame us not:
          To know our enemies' minds, we rip their hearts;
          Their papers is more lawful.

Reads the letter

---

*233 SD] Q; not in F   234 zir] F; sir Q   234 vor] F; for Q   238–9 out / Upon the] F; out vpon / The Q *uncorr.;* out, vpon / The Q *corr.*   239 English] F; British Q *uncorr.;* Brittish Q *corr.*   239 death,] F; death! Q   *239 SD] Q; not in F   241–2 As duteous . . desire.] F *lineation; one line (turned under)* Q   243–7 Sit . . . . not:] F *lineation: four verse lines ending . . . pockets / . . . friends, / . . . deathsmā / . . . not* Q   243–4 you. / Let's] F; you lets Q *uncorr.;* you, lets Q *corr.*   244 these] F; his Q   244 The] F; These Q   244–5 of / May] F; of may Q *uncorr.;* of,may Q *corr.*   245 sorry] F; sorrow Q   *247 wax; and manners,] Capell (subst.);* waxe, and manners Q; waxe, and manners: F   *247 not:] Pope; not Q, F   248 minds, we] F; minds wee'd Q *uncorr.;* minds,wee'd Q *corr.*   249 SD] F; *not in* Q *uncorr.;* A letter. Q *corr.*

233 Out Out upon you! (Kittredge).

234 pick your teeth i.e. with his ballow (231), a 'Rabelaisian toothpick' (King), or possibly during the fight Edgar manages to get Oswald's dagger, with which he promises to pick the steward's teeth (Hunter); a proverbial threat (Tilley T424.1; Dent, p. 235).

234 foins sword-thrusts. Oswald is apparently fencing like a courtier. Compare Mercutio's description of Tybalt's fencing, *Rom.* 2.4.20–6 (NS).

237 letters letter; as at 244. See 1.5.1 n.

239 English See collation. Greg, *Variants*, p. 177, and Duthie, pp. 158–9, both believe this is the original Shakespearean reading. Greg speculates that Q 'British' resulted from an actor correcting the anachronism, but this hypothesis assumes memorial reconstruction. Compare 3.4.168: Shakespeare of course could be inconsistent, and the fact that he wrote 'British' there (as an apparent compliment to James) does not mean he could not have written 'English' here, even when revising

(Duthie; compare Stone, p. 116, n.7).

239 death, death Some editors, e.g. Bevington, break the line after the first 'death', making the second a separate line. But this division solves nothing metrically; both lines remain irregular. The odd exclamation may be an actor's interpolation; if so, the line should end 'untimely –' (NS).

240–2 I know . . . desire A further hint that Oswald has been more than a mere steward; compare 2.2.16–19, 3.4.77–82, and nn.

240 serviceable '(obsequiously) diligent in service' (NS); Kent calls him a 'superserviceable, finical rogue' (2.2.16).

245 my friends i.e may be useful.

246 deathsman executioner.

247 Leave . . . not Edgar opens the sealed letter. Compare Tilley B637, 'The breaking open of letters is the basest kind of burglary', and Malvolio's 'By your leave, wax', *TN* 2.5.91 (NS).

247 Leave i.e. by your leave, allow me.

249 Their papers i.e. to rip open their letters.

'Let our reciprocal vows be remembered. You have many   250
opportunities to cut him off. If your will want not, time and
place will be fruitfully offered. There is nothing done, if he
return the conqueror; then am I the prisoner, and his bed my
gaol, from the loathed warmth whereof, deliver me, and supply
the place for your labour.   255

Your (wife, so I would say)

affectionate servant,

Gonerill.'

O indistinguished space of woman's will,
A plot upon her virtuous husband's life –   260
And the exchange my brother! Here in the sands
Thee I'll rake up, the post unsanctified
Of murderous lechers; and in the mature time
With this ungracious paper strike the sight
Of the death-practised duke. For him 'tis well   265
That of thy death and business I can tell.

[*Exit, dragging out the body*]

GLOUCESTER   The king is mad. How stiff is my vile sense,

250–7 Let . . . servant,] *As in* Q; *italics in* F   250 our] F; your Q   *252 done, if] done, If Q; done: If Q2; done. If F   *253 conqueror; then] *Furness;* conquerour, then Q; Conqueror, then F; conqueror. Then *Pope*   254 gaol] F; iayle Q *corr.;* gayle Q *uncorr.*   255–6 labour. / Your] F; labour, your Q   256 (wife, so . . . say)] F; wife (so . . . say) your Q   257 servant,] Seruant. F; seruant and for you her owne for *Venter,* Q   259 O] Oh F; *Edg.* O Q   259 indistinguished] Indistinguisht Q; indinguish'd F   259 will] F; wit Q   266 thy] F, Q; his Q2   266 SD] *Capell* (*subst.*); *not in* Q, F   267 The . . . sense,] *As in* Q; *two lines divided* mad. / How F

250 **reciprocal vows** Compare 4.2.20–6. Muir, p. 250, lists 'reciprocal' among the words in Florio's *Montaigne* not used by Shakespeare before 1603.

251 **him** i.e. Albany.

251 **will** (1) intention, purpose, (2) carnal desire, lust.

251 **want** lack.

252 **fruitfully** abundantly.

252–3 **There . . . conqueror** i.e. nothing important will have been accomplished if we win and Albany returns (and the sexual activity you and I anticipate is forestalled). See collation: Duthie, p. 184, comments that F's full stop after 'done' may have been influenced by Q's 'If', the capital an aberration which probably misled the collator.

255 **for your labour** (1) as a recompense for your work, (2) as a place for your (amorous) activity (Hunter).

257 **servant** lover. See collation, and Textual Analysis, pp. 256–7 below.

259 **O . . . will** 'O woman's lust, how limitless is thy range!' (Kittredge).

259 **indistinguished** indefinable, undiscernible (because vast).

262 **rake up** cover up, bury.

263 **mature time** when the time is right, at the proper occasion. The first syllable of 'mature' is accented.

264 **ungracious** i.e. because evil.

264 **strike** blast.

265 **death-practised** i.e. whose death has been plotted.

266 SD *Exit . . . body* Capell's SD is necessary: unless Edgar drags off the body here, two 'gross improbabilities' arise: (1) Edgar drags off the body as he simultaneously leads his blind father by the hand – a 'very clumsy exit, at best'; (2) Edgar's speech (273–5) uncharacteristically ignores Gloucester's lapse into gloominess (Urkowitz, pp. 158–9).

267 **stiff** unbending, obstinate.

267 **sense** 'mental power, faculty of thinking and feeling' (Schmidt); compare Sonnet 112.8: 'my steel'd sense'.

That I stand up and have ingenious feeling
Of my huge sorrows! Better I were distract,
So should my thoughts be severed from my griefs,   270
            Drum afar off
And woes by wrong imaginations lose
The knowledge of themselves.

                    [*Enter* EDGAR]

EDGAR   Give me your hand.
Far off methinks I hear the beaten drum.
Come, father, I'll bestow you with a friend.

                                        Exeunt

4.6 *Enter* CORDELIA, KENT [*disguised*], *and* GENTLEMAN

CORDELIA   O thou good Kent, how shall I live and work
            To match thy goodness? My life will be too short,
            And every measure fail me.
KENT   To be acknowledged, madam, is o'erpaid.

---

269 sorrows!] Sorrowes? F; sorowes, Q   270 severed] F; fenced Q   270 SD] F; *A drumme a farre off.* Q (*after* themselues 272)   272 SD] *Capell* (*subst.*); *not in* Q, F   272–3 Give . . . drum.] F *lineation; one line* (*turned under*) *in* Q   274 SD] F; *Exit.* Q   *Act* 4, *Scene* 6 4.6] *Scæna Septima.* F (*see Commentary*); *not in* Q   0 SD] F; *Enter Cordelia, Kent, and Doctor.* Q   1–3 O . . . me.] *Rowe's lineation; two lines divided* thy goodnes, [*turned over*] / My Q; *five lines ending* . . . Kent, / . . . worke / . . . goodnesse? / . . . short, / . . . me. F

---

268 ingenious intelligent, sensitive (Onions)*;* in antithesis to 'mad'. But the word already had the meaning 'inventive, skilful' and thus 'suggests a clever inner destructive force contriving to remind Gloucester of, and intensify, his misery' (Rosenberg, p. 282).

269 distract mad.

270–2 So . . . themselves Thinking it would bring him relief, Gloucester longs for madness, a world of illusions ('wrong imaginations') divorced from the reality of his sorrows and their causes.

274 bestow lodge; compare *Mac.* 3.1.29.

274 a friend The mysterious friend never appears; perhaps Edgar and Gloucester never reach him, or are overtaken by events (King). Compare 5.2.1–2.

Act 4, Scene 6
4.6 F, which omits a scene after 4.2, incorrectly numbers this '*Scæna Septima*'. Possibly, after the long preceding scene, the collator forgot to alter the scene number as he had done for the three previous scenes. On the other hand, the F compositors suspended work on *Lear* at precisely the page on which

this scene begins (signature ss), and did not resume composition until the last pages of *Rom.* (which had been interrupted by problems involving *Tro.*) and all of *Tim.* were set. Conceivably, when he returned to *King Lear*, Compositor E forgot to continue altering scene numbers which Compositor B had begun. Compare Hinman, II, 281, 293–5; Doran, p. 70; Duthie, p. 418; Taylor, 'Date and authorship', pp. 417–18; Greg, *SFF*, p. 388.

0 SD *Enter* . . . GENTLEMAN See collation, and Appendix, p. 284 below, xx, 0 SD n. Rosenberg suggests, p. 283, that some hint of French costumes or décor in Cordelia's camp prompts Lear's question (75).

2 My . . . short Dramatic irony (King).

3 measure 'that by which extent or quantity is ascertained' (Schmidt)*;* compare *Ant.* 1.1.1–2: 'this dotage of our general's / O'erflows the measure'. Every attempt at recompense will fail, Cordelia says, because Kent's goodness is immeasurable.

4 To . . . o'erpaid Recognition for his loyal service is all the recompense Kent wishes. But compare 9 below and n.

All my reports go with the modest truth,   5
Nor more, nor clipped, but so.
CORDELIA   Be better suited:
These weeds are memories of those worser hours.
I prithee, put them off.
KENT   Pardon, dear madam.
Yet to be known shortens my made intent.
My boon I make it that you know me not   10
Till time and I think meet.
CORDELIA   Then be't so, my good lord. – How does the king?
GENTLEMAN   Madam, sleeps still.
CORDELIA   O you kind gods,
Cure this great breach in his abusèd nature;   15
Th'untuned and jarring senses O wind up
Of this child-changèd father!
GENTLEMAN   So please your majesty,
That we may wake the king? He hath slept long.
CORDELIA   Be governed by your knowledge, and proceed   20
I'th'sway of your own will. Is he arrayed?

Enter LEAR [*asleep*] *in a chair carried by servants*

6–8 Be ... off.] F *lineation; two lines divided* those / Worser Q   8 Pardon] F; Pardon me Q   12 Then ... king?] *As in* Q; *two lines divided* Lord: / How F   13 SH] F; *Doct.* Q (*throughout scene*)   14–15 O ... nature;] F *lineation; one line* (*turned over*) Q   14 gods,] Gods Q; Gods! F   16 Th'] F; The Q   16 jarring] F; hurrying Q   18–19 So ... long.] F; *divided* king, / He Q   19 That] F, Q; *not in* Q2   *19 king?] *Hanmer*; King, F, Q; King Q2   *19 long.] Q; long? F   21 SD] F (*subst.*); *not in* Q

5–6 All ... so Either (1) everything I have said about what has happened is accurate and unadorned, or (2) may everything said about me be told simply and accurately.
5 go with accord with.
6 Nor ... clipped Neither exaggerated nor understated.
6 suited dressed. Kent still wears servant's clothes.
7 weeds clothes.
7 memories reminders.
9 Yet ... intent To be revealed now would be premature and so contrary to my plan. Kent wants Lear to make the connection with Caius, which he fails to do (5.3.256–64). Whatever Kent's purpose in maintaining his disguise, Shakespeare's is clear: he does not want 'to spoil Lear's reconciliation with Cordelia, by adding to it a recognition of Kent' (Granville-Barker, p. 308).
9 made formed.
10 My boon ... it The favour I request is.
11 meet suitable, appropriate. Like Edgar, Kent respects 'ripeness' (5.2.11), and may also misjudge:

compare 5.3.183.
15 breach i.e. wound.
16 Th'untuned ... senses Shakespeare often uses the metaphor of discord in music to portray mental disorder, as in *Ham.* 3.1.157–8. Hendiadys: 'jarring' because 'untuned' (King).
16 wind up i.e. tune by tightening the strings.
17 child-changèd i.e. changed by his children (Malone, cited by Furness); compare 'carecrazed mother', *R3* 3.7.184.
18 majesty Cordelia is Queen of France.
21 I'th' ... will As your desire directs you, i.e. as you see fit.
21 arrayed i.e. clothed in his royal robes (NS, citing Granville-Barker, p. 298). But often he is dressed 'in a purity of white' (Rosenberg, p. 284). Compare 23 n. below.
21 SD chair The chair may suggest or even be a throne, as in Trevor Nunn's 1968 RSC production, which made this entrance parallel Lear's in 1.1 (Taylor, 'Date and authorship', p. 412; compare Bratton, p. 189).

GENTLEMAN   Ay, madam: in the heaviness of sleep
          We put fresh garments on him.
          Be by, good madam, when we do awake him;
          I doubt not of his temperance.   25

CORDELIA   O my dear father, restoration hang
          Thy medicine on my lips, and let this kiss
          Repair those violent harms that my two sisters
          Have in thy reverence made.

KENT   Kind and dear princess!

CORDELIA   Had you not been their father, these white flakes   30
          Did challenge pity of them. Was this a face
          To be opposed against the warring winds?
          Mine enemy's dog,
          Though he had bit me, should have stood that night
          Against my fire. And wast thou fain, poor father,   35
          To hovel thee with swine and rogues forlorn
          In short and musty straw? Alack, alack,
          'Tis wonder that thy life and wits at once
          Had not concluded all. He wakes. Speak to him.

22 of] F; of his Q   24 Be by, good madam] F; *Gent.* Good madam be by, Q; *Kent.* Good Madam be by Q2   *25 not] Q;
not in F   25 temperance] F *omits one and a half lines here*   26–8 O ... sisters] F *lineation; two lines divided* lips, / And
Q   31 Did challenge] F; Had challengd Q   32 opposed] F; exposd Q   *32 warring] Q, *Oxford;* iarring F   32 winds?]
F *omits three and a half lines here*   33–5 Mine ... father,] *This edn (following* Q); *lines end* ... bit me. / ... fire, / ... Father)
F   33 enemy's] F; iniurious Q

23 **fresh garments** As elsewhere in Shakespeare, change of clothing signals a change in character or disposition, especially after significant absence. Compare *Cor.* 4.4.0 SD; Heilman, p. 82.

25 **not** See collation. Rhythm, metre, and sense argue that Q is correct. Compositor E apparently omitted 'not' accidentally, as at 1.1.287. Compare Duthie, p. 185; *Textual Companion*, p. 538.

25 **temperance** self-control. F omits a line and a half here: see Textual Analysis, p. 257 below.

26 **restoration** Perhaps personified as a goddess.

29 **reverence** condition of being respected or venerated (Onions).

30 **flakes** thin or delicate hair. Compare Lyly, *Midas* (1592), 3.2: 'your mustachoes ... hanging downe to your mouth like goates flakes' (Kittredge).

31 **challenge** demand.

32 **warring** See collation. F 'iarring' could be Compositor E's misreading of 'warring' combined with a recollection of 'iarring' (16). Compare Sisson, p. 243; Duthie, 185; *Textual Companion*, p. 538.

32 **winds** F omits three and a half lines here: see Textual Analysis, p. 257 below.

33–5 **Mine ... fire** Compare 3.7.62–4.

33 **Mine enemy's dog** The irregular line results from cutting three and a half inessential though eloquent lines.

36 **To hovel ... forlorn** See 3.6.0 SD n. Shaheen compares the parable of the Prodigal Son in Luke 15, an analogue or source developed by Susan Snyder, '*King Lear* and the Prodigal Son', *SQ* 17 (1966), 361–9.

36 **rogues forlorn** outcast vagabonds. This reference justified Grigori Kozintsev's setting for 3.6 in his film, which shows the room Lear enters inhabited by poor, ragged vagrants.

37 **short** Because broken up by constant use as bedding (Kittredge). It would give less comfort and warmth than long, dry straw.

39 **all** i.e. all together, entirely.

39 **He wakes** These words signal the moment of greatest emotional tension in the play. How will Lear react to Cordelia? All eyes are fixed on him in silent expectation as slowly, very slowly he awakens and gains comprehension. (Compare Rosenberg, pp. 284–6, and E. A. J. Honigmann, *Myriad-Minded Shakespeare*, 1989, p. 86, where a parallel is drawn with Gloucester's reawakening after his attempted suicide in 4.5.)

GENTLEMAN   Madam, do you; 'tis fittest.   40

CORDELIA   How does my royal lord? How fares your majesty?

LEAR   You do me wrong to take me out o'th'grave.

    Thou art a soul in bliss, but I am bound

    Upon a wheel of fire, that mine own tears

    Do scald like molten lead.

CORDELIA   Sir, do you know me?   45

LEAR   You are a spirit, I know. Where did you die?

CORDELIA   Still, still far wide.

GENTLEMAN   He's scarce awake. Let him alone a while.

LEAR   Where have I been? Where am I? Fair daylight?

    I am mightily abused. I should ev'n die with pity   50

    To see another thus. I know not what to say.

    I will not swear these are my hands. Let's see:

    I feel this pin prick. Would I were assured

    Of my condition.

CORDELIA   O look upon me, sir,

---

41 How ... majesty?] *As in* Q; *two lines divided* Lord? / How F   42 o'th'] F; ath Q   *45 scald] Q; scal'd F   45 Sir, do you know] F; Sir know Q   46 You are] F; Yar Q; Y'are Q2   *46 spirit,] *Theobald*; spirit Q, F   46 Where] F; when Q2   48 He's ... while.] *As in* Q; *two lines divided* awake, / Let F   49 Where ... daylight?] *As in* Q; *two lines divided* bin? / Where F   50 ev'n] F; ene Q   53–4 I ... condition.] F *lineation; one line* Q   54–6 O ... kneel.] F *lineation; as prose* Q

---

42 do ... grave (1) commit a sacrilege by opening my grave, (2) hurt me by restoring me to life, (3) injure me by subjecting me to shame, (4) afflict me by bringing me out of the grave into consciousness of the afterlife (King).

44 wheel of fire This image is complex and syncretic, alluding to pagan, Christian, and other symbols not only of torture and suffering, but also of energy (Elton, pp. 236–8). Lear thinks he is damned and Cordelia is an angel in heaven: in this context, Ixion's wheel, which was sometimes placed in the heavens (Elton cites Christopher Middleton's *Historie of Heaven* (1596)), is especially relevant. There are other references to the sun (e.g. 1.1.103), and wheel images appear elsewhere (e.g. 2.2.156, 2.4.65–6, 5.3.164). For further discussion of the image's archetypal aspects, especially Jung's studies of the mandala, or magic circle, see James Kirsch, *Shakespeare's Royal Self*, 1966, pp. 283–6. Kirsch says the wheel of fire image could be understood as Lear's 'horoscope, that is, his fundamental constitution; his Self is set on fire by his wild affects' (p. 285).

44 that so that.

44–5 mine ... lead i.e. his tears, provoked by shame and guilt as well as suffering, are heated by the fire so that they scald.

46 Where See collation. NS and other editions

(e.g. Kittredge, Riverside) adopt Q2 'when'. Conceivably, copy for Q had 'when', which was misread as 'wher'. But Q/F 'where' makes no less sense, in context, than 'when'; hence the reviser or collator could easily have accepted it. Compare Duthie, p. 419, whose argument for Q/F Dover Wilson rejects in NS.

47 wide i.e. of the mark; hence, astray, mistaken. Compare *Tro*. 3.1.88: 'no such matter, you are wide'.

50 abused Lear could mean that he is (1) deluded, deceived, (2) taken advantage of, (3) ill-used, wronged, (4) misrepresented – or some combination of these senses (see *OED* Abuse v 4b, 2, 5, 3). Lear is in 'a strange mist of uncertainty' (Johnson, cited by Furness). Compare 'abusèd nature' (15), where the sense 'mistreated' is uppermost, and later (76), where 'wrong' or 'deceive' is meant. In 'do not mock me' (56) Lear fears he is being ill-used or misrepresented (as loving father or king).

53 pin prick Lear takes a brooch or some other ornament from his costume to test himself.

54–6 O look ... kneel After 'sir' or during the next line, Cordelia kneels to receive her father's blessing, whereupon Lear rises from his chair and starts to kneel before her. The business is borrowed and modified from *King Leir* (2298–2304), where the kneeling is excessive and involves other

<table>
<tr><td></td><td>And hold your hand in benediction o'er me.</td><td>55</td></tr>
<tr><td></td><td>You must not kneel.</td><td></td></tr>
</table>

LEAR   Pray do not mock me:
I am a very foolish, fond old man,
Fourscore and upward,
Not an hour more nor less; and to deal plainly,
I fear I am not in my perfect mind.   60
Methinks I should know you and know this man;
Yet I am doubtful: for I am mainly ignorant
What place this is, and all the skill I have
Remembers not these garments, nor I know not
Where I did lodge last night. Do not laugh at me,   65
For, as I am a man, I think this lady
To be my child Cordelia.

CORDELIA   And so I am: I am.

LEAR   Be your tears wet? Yes, faith. I pray, weep not.
If you have poison for me, I will drink it.   70
I know you do not love me; for your sisters
Have, as I do remember, done me wrong.
You have some cause; they have not.

CORDELIA   No cause, no cause.

LEAR   Am I in France?

KENT   In your own kingdom, sir.   75

---

55 your hand] F *corr.;* yours hand F *uncorr.;* your hands Q   56 You] F; no sir you Q   56 me] F; *not in* Q   58 Fourscore and upward,] F; Q *combines in one line with* and to deale plainly   59 Not an hour more nor less] F; *not in* Q   60 in ... mind.] F, Q; perfect in my minde. Q2   65 Do not] F, Q; Do no Q2   68 am: I am.] F; am. Q   69 Be ... not.] *As in* Q; *two lines divided* wet? / Yes F

characters as well. 'Shakespeare compresses the moment, as he does the scene, to save sentiment from sentimentality' (Rosenberg, p. 288).

56 mock Because of the next lines, the sense 'ridicule' is usually understood; but Shakespeare also uses 'mock' in the sense 'defy; set at nought' (*OED* sv *v* IC, citing *MV* 2.1.30 and *Ant.* 3.13.184), which the preceding line prompts; hence, the meanings combine.

57 fond silly (because in his dotage).

58–9 Fourscore ... less Lear is still 'far wide', as he himself recognizes (60); therefore, even his attempt to state his age is confused. He may well be an octogenarian, and is usually so portrayed. The F addition, 'Not ... less', renders the lines irregular, but there is no reason to suspect they are inauthentic. See Textual Analysis, p. 269 below, and compare the debate in Furness.

58 upward more; compare *Wiv.* 3.1.56. 'Not ... less' (59) contradicts this (King).

61 this man i.e. Kent, as Caius.

62 mainly entirely (Onions).

65 Do ... me Lear misinterprets the smiles of Cordelia, Kent, and the Gentleman; they are smiles of compassion and understanding, not derision.

68 I am: I am Perhaps the second 'I am' was inserted to pad out the half-line to join with the preceding half-line (Stone, p. 63). Moreover, throughout this column of printing in F, Compositor E seems to be stretching copy. But the insertion, for all that, may be authentic and is certainly expressive. F's colon indicates a longer pause than the comma usually substituted in modern editions; therefore, it is retained.

75 France Lear recalls that the King of France married Cordelia.

LEAR   Do not abuse me.
GENTLEMAN   Be comforted, good madam. The great rage
    You see is killed in him. Desire him to go in.
    Trouble him no more till further settling.
CORDELIA   Will't please your highness walk?   80
LEAR   You must bear with me. Pray you now, forget
    And forgive. I am old and foolish.

                                     Exeunt

5.1   *Enter with drum and colours,* EDMOND, REGAN, *Officers and Soldiers*

EDMOND   [*To an Officer*] Know of the duke if his last purpose hold,
    Or whether since he is advised by aught
    To change the course. He's full of alteration
    And self-reproving. Bring his constant pleasure.

                                  [*Exit Officer*]

REGAN   Our sister's man is certainly miscarried.   5
EDMOND   'Tis to be doubted, madam.
REGAN   Now, sweet lord,
    You know the goodness I intend upon you.
    Tell me but truly, but then speak the truth,

---

76 me.] F; me? Q   **77–9** Be . . . settling.] F *lineation; as prose* Q   **78** killed] F; cured Q   **78** him.] F *omits one and a half lines here*   **80** Will't] *Rowe;* Wilt Q, F   **81–2** You . . . foolish.] *Oxford's lineation; three lines ending . . . *me: / *. . .* forgiue, / *. . .* foolish. F; *as prose* Q   **81** Pray you] F; pray Q   **82** SD] F *ends scene here, omitting a dozen lines found in* Q; *Exeunt. Manet Kent and Gent.* Q   **Act 5, Scene 1**   **5.1**] *Actus Quintus. Scena Prima.* F; *not in* Q   **0** SD] *After* F; *Enter Edmond, Regan, and their powers.* Q   **0** SD *Officers*] *This edn; Gentlemen* F   **1** SD] *This edn (Capell subst.); not in* Q, F; (*To a Gentleman*) *Duthie*   **3** He's] F, Q *uncorr.;* hee's Q *corr.;* he is Q2   **3** alteration] F, Q *corr.;* abdication Q *uncorr.*   **4** SD] *This edn (Capell subst.); not in* Q, F; *Exit Gentleman. / Duthie*

---

76 abuse (1) dupe, deceive, (2) mistreat, wrong. The past is coming back to him, with pain.

77 Be comforted Cordelia is overcome momentarily with emotion.

77 rage madness, frenzy.

78 in him F omits a line and a half here; see Textual Analysis, pp. 257–8 below.

79 further settling i.e. until his wits have settled more.

80 walk withdraw.

82 foolish F omits the dialogue between Kent and the Gentleman that concludes the scene in Q. See Textual Analysis, p. 258 below.

Act 5, Scene 1

0 SD *drum and colours* This is a standard military entrance, with flags flying and drum beating.

0 SD *Officers* See collation. Officers were called 'Gentlemen' in Shakespeare's day, as F designates them.

1 his last purpose i.e. most recent intention (to fight with us against Cordelia and her army).

2 advised by aught persuaded by anything.

3 alteration vacillation. See collation. Not everyone accepts Greg's judgement (*Variants*, p. 177) that F is 'certainly correct'. Stone, p. 291, and Taylor, 'Date and authorship', p. 459, prefer Q uncorr. 'abdication' as the more pointed reading, which Oxford prints and which Rosenberg says 'has more energy, and is curiously prophetic' (p. 292).

4 constant pleasure i.e. fixed resolution.

5 sister's man i.e. Oswald.

6 doubted feared.

7 intend upon i.e. mean to confer upon.

8 Tell ... truth Regan is suspicious that Edmond will equivocate or extenuate his position. In Q she remains uncertain and unconvinced by Edmond's protestations (see below).

Do you not love my sister?

EDMOND   In honoured love.

REGAN   But have you never found my brother's way   10
      To the forfended place?

EDMOND   No, by mine honour, madam.

REGAN   I never shall endure her. Dear my lord,
      Be not familiar with her.

EDMOND   Fear me not.
      She and the duke her husband –

Enter with drum and colours, ALBANY, GONERILL, *Soldiers*

ALBANY   Our very loving sister, well bemet.   15
      Sir, this I heard: the king is come to his daughter,
      With others whom the rigour of our state
      Forced to cry out.

REGAN   Why is this reasoned?

GONERILL   Combine together 'gainst the enemy;
      For these domestic and particular broils   20
      Are not the question here.

ALBANY   Let's then determine with th'ancient of war

---

9 In] F; I, Q; I Q2   *11 forfended] Q; fore-fended F   11 place?] F *omits two and half lines here*   12–13 I . . . her.] F *lineation; one line (turned over) in* Q   13–14 Fear . . . husband –] *Capell's lineation; one line in* Q, F   *13 me] Q; *not in* F   *14 husband –] *Rowe;* husband. Q, F; F *omits a line and a half here*   14 SD] F; *Enter Albany and Gonorill with troupes* Q   16 Sir,] F; For Q   16 heard] F; heare Q   18 out.] F *omits five lines here*   20 and particular broils] F; *d*ore particulars Q; *d*oore particulars Q2   21 the] F; to Q   22–3 Let's . . . proceeding.] F *lineation; as prose in* Q; *divided* determine / With Q2   22 Let's] F; Let vs Q   22 th'ancient] F; the auntient Q; th'ensign *Oxford*

9 honoured i.e. honourable.
10 brother i.e. Albany.
11 forfended place forbidden place, i.e. Gonerill's bed or 'bosom', as Q emphasizes. Regan suspects her sister and Edmond of adultery, with reason (compare 4.2.15–29, 4.4.25–8, and nn.).
11 place F omits three lines here. For this cut and those a few lines later, see Textual Analysis, pp. 258–9 below.
12 I . . . her i.e. I can't stand her. The antagonism between Gonerill and Regan, which was carefully concealed in 1.1 and 2.4, is now broken wide open by their rivalry for Edmond.
13 me Apparently accidentally omitted by Compositor E.
14 She . . . husband – Many editors take the line as an announcement or exclamation, but Rowe and others see the speech dramatically interrupted by the entrance of the persons discussed. F omits one

and a half lines here.
16 the king Albany, alone among those present, still refers to Lear as 'king'.
17 rigour . . . state harshness of our government.
18 cry out i.e. protest in pain. F omits five lines here.
18 Why . . . reasoned i.e. why are you going into all that? In its new context Regan's question takes on new meaning. See Textual Analysis, pp. 258–9 below.
19–21 Combine . . . here Gonerill efficiently and swiftly focuses on the immediate problem and gets things moving. Compare 4.2.16–17.
19 Combine together i.e. unite Albany's army and Regan's.
20 domestic internal.
20 particular broils private quarrels.
22 th'ancient of war senior officers.

On our proceeding.

REGAN   Sister, you'll go with us?

GONERILL   No.

REGAN   'Tis most convenient. Pray, go with us.   25

GONERILL   [*Aside*] O ho, I know the riddle. – I will go.

Enter EDGAR [*dressed like a peasant*]

EDGAR   If e'er your grace had speech with man so poor,
        Hear me one word.

ALBANY   [*To the others*]   I'll overtake you.

                                    Exeunt both the armies
                            Speak.

EDGAR   Before you fight the battle, ope this letter.
        If you have victory, let the trumpet sound   30
        For him that brought it. Wretched though I seem,
        I can produce a champion that will prove
        What is avouchèd there. If you miscarry,
        Your business of the world hath so an end,
        And machination ceases. Fortune love you.   35

ALBANY Stay till I have read the letter.

EDGAR   I was forbid it.
        When time shall serve, let but the herald cry,
        And I'll appear again.   *Exit*

23 proceeding] F; proceedings Q   25 Pray] F; pray you Q   26 SD.1] Capell; not in Q, F   26 riddle. –] Capell (subst.);
riddle, Q; Riddle. F   27 man] F, Q; one Q2   28 SD.1] Oxford; not in Q, F   28 SD.2 Exeunt ... armies] F (after 26);
Exeunt. Q (after word.); Exit. Q2 (after 26); Exeunt all but Albany and Edgar. / Cam.   35 And ... ceases.] F; not in
Q   *35 love] Q; loues F   36–8 I ... again.] F lineation; as prose Q

23 proceeding i.e. battle plan. Albany apparently addresses Edmond, but unlike Q, F does not include a response; indeed, Edmond remains silent throughout this part of the dialogue. See Textual Analysis, pp. 258–9 below.

23 Sister ... us Regan tries to steer Gonerill away from the others, especially Edmond, with whom she does not trust her for a moment. Or perhaps she does not want Gonerill to participate in the council of war, close to Edmond (Muir).

23, 25 us The royal plural (compare 5.3.55–7), or herself and her troops.

25 convenient (1) expedient, (2) seemly (NS).

26 I ... riddle i.e. I get your drift, insinuation. Here, Gonerill may recognize Regan's priority with Edmond and plan to kill her (Rosenberg, p. 293).

26 SD.2 Enter EDGAR Edgar is still dressed as a peasant, though his speech is correct. He intercepts Albany as he is leaving with the others.

29 this letter i.e. the letter Oswald carried (4.5.250–8).

32 champion In chivalry, someone who undertakes a cause in single combat.

33 avouchèd asserted, declared.

33 miscarry lose the battle and die.

35 And ... ceases See collation. The Q compositor, who set Albany's response on the same line with 'Fortune loue you', may have dropped a clause to save space.

35 machination intrigue. Compare 50–4 below.

35 love See collation. An easy compositorial error: 'The sense shows that Q is right' (Duthie, p. 186).

ALBANY   Why, fare thee well. I will o'erlook thy paper.

Enter EDMOND

EDMOND   The enemy's in view; draw up your powers.   40
Here is the guess of their true strength and forces
By diligent discovery; but your haste
Is now urged on you.
ALBANY   We will greet the time.   *Exit*
EDMOND   To both these sisters have I sworn my love,
Each jealous of the other as the stung   45
Are of the adder. Which of them shall I take?
Both? one? or neither? Neither can be enjoyed
If both remain alive. To take the widow
Exasperates, makes mad her sister Gonerill,
And hardly shall I carry out my side,   50
Her husband being alive. Now then, we'll use
His countenance for the battle, which being done,
Let her who would be rid of him devise
His speedy taking off. As for the mercy
Which he intends to Lear and to Cordelia,   55
The battle done, and they within our power,

---

39 o'erlook] ore-looke Q, F; looke ore Q2   **39** thy] F; the Q   **41** Here] F; Hard Q   **41** guess] F; quesse Q   **41** true] F; great Q   **42–3** By ... you.] F *lineation; one line* Q   **44** sisters] F; sister Q   **45–7** Each ... enjoyed] F *lineation; two lines divided* Adder, / Which [inioy'd *turned under*] Q   **45** stung] F; sting Q   **53** who] F; that Q   **54** the] F; his Q   **55** intends] F; entends Q; extends Q2

39 o'erlook look over, read. The text does not indicate whether Albany reads the letter or any part of it before Edmond enters. If he does, a new tension develops between him and Edmond, motivating his terse response at 43 (Rosenberg, p. 293; compare Urkowitz, p. 103, who argues that Edmond should rush in with his letter, or paper, before Albany has a chance to read the letter Edgar gives him).

39 SD *Enter* EDMOND Fully accoutred for battle, Edmond enters amidst growing sounds of war. Presumably, he has met with 'th'ancient of war' (22) while Albany conversed with Edgar.

41–2 Here ... discovery Edmond offers Albany a written estimate of the enemy's army and its disposition. Again, the text fails to show whether Albany accepts it or not.

42 discovery spying, reconnaissance.

43 We ... time Unlike Edmond, who is eager for battle, but like Kent and Edgar, with whom he

shows increasing affinities, Albany understands 'ripeness'.

43 greet embrace, welcome.

45 jealous suspicious.

47–8 Both ... alive Edmond's hubris does not long permit him to think he can enjoy *both* sisters; if he is to enjoy either, then one must die.

50 carry ... side make my game, achieve my goal (i.e. to become king: Edmond's ambitions have grown). But compare 'fulfil my side of the bargain with Goneril – satisfy her lust in return for advancement' (Muir).

52 countenance authority, support.

54 taking off murder.

54–5 mercy ... Cordelia Till now, Albany has nowhere explicitly mentioned his intention regarding Lear and Cordelia, let alone revealed it to Edmond. Shakespeare introduces the information here partly to develop Albany's character, and to prepare for Edmond's treachery after the battle.

> Shall never see his pardon; for my state
> Stands on me to defend, not to debate.   *Exit*

5.2 *Alarum within. Enter with drum and colours,* LEAR, CORDELIA,
and Soldiers, over the stage, and exeunt

Enter EDGAR [*dressed like a peasant*] *and* GLOUCESTER

EDGAR   Here, father, take the shadow of this tree
> For your good host; pray that the right may thrive.
> If ever I return to you again
> I'll bring you comfort.
GLOUCESTER   Grace go with you, sir.

Exit [*Edgar*]

Alarum and retreat within. Enter EDGAR

EDGAR   Away, old man! Give me thy hand; away!   5
> King Lear hath lost, he and his daughter ta'en.
> Give me thy hand. Come on.
GLOUCESTER   No further, sir; a man may rot even here.
EDGAR   What, in ill thoughts again? Men must endure

Act 5, Scene 2   5.2] *Scena Secunda.* F; *not in* Q   0 SD] F; *Alarum. Enter the powers of France ouer the stage, Cordelia with her father in her hand. / Enter Edgar and Gloster.* Q   1 tree] F; bush Q   3–4 If ... comfort.] F *lineation; one line* Q   4 SD.1 *Exit Edgar*] Pope; *Exit.* Q (*after* comfort), F   4 SD.2 *within*] F; *not in* Q   4 SD.2 *Enter* EDGAR] F; *not in* Q   8 further] F; farther Q   9 What ... endure] *As in* Q; *two lines divided* againe? / Men F

57 Shall i.e. they shall.
57 state situation, position.
58 Stands on Rests, depends on.

Act 5, Scene 2
0 SD.1–2 *Alarum ... stage* Having shown the British side, Shakespeare now has Cordelia's army march with her father over the stage amidst sounds of battle. This, again, is a standard military entrance, but significantly altered from Q (see collation). Lear's strength and defiance are suggested, not his weakness and infirmity; regally attired, he may also carry a sword. After the army departs, Edgar leads Gloucester on, while the battle occurs off stage.
1 father Compare 4.5.72 n., 243, 274. Although Edgar has not yet revealed himself to Gloucester, he favours this term of address.
2 good host i.e. one who gives shelter.
4 SD.2 *Alarum and retreat* Trumpet calls. Gloucester is left alone on stage during the course of the battle which, though brief, is long enough to let the image of the solitary, blind, tormented old man, early victim of the struggle, impress itself upon the audience. Some modern productions

present the clash of arms on stage or mime the battle balletically (Rosenberg, p. 296; Bratton, p. 197). But a stage empty except for this solitary figure is clearly Shakespeare's intention, i.e. he preferred to minimize the battle and concentrate on larger issues. Compare Granville-Barker, pp. 298–9.
8 a man may rot Gloucester lapses into despair ('ill thoughts') again.
9–11 Men ... all Compare *Ham.* 5.2.219–22. Edgar's counsel was proverbial in the Renaissance and combined both pagan (especially Stoic) and Judaeo-Christian attitudes (compare Eccles. 3.1–8: 'All things haue their time') (Elton, pp. 100–5). Shakespeare uses the concepts of 'endurance' and 'ripeness' here very precisely. In essence, Edgar tells Gloucester (as Hamlet tells Horatio) that Providence or the gods control our lives; hence, we must endure the time of our death even as, perforce, we endure the time of our birth. Providence, or the gods, not man, determines when the time is 'ripe', an idea which has little to do with modern theories of maturation or development. Cordelia is hardly 'ripe' for death in any other sense (compare Berlin, p. 91).

Their going hence even as their coming hither: 10
Ripeness is all. Come on.

GLOUCESTER   And that's true too.

                                                  Exeunt

5.3 *Enter in conquest with drum and colours* EDMOND; LEAR *and*
CORDELIA, *as prisoners; Soldiers;* CAPTAIN

EDMOND   Some officers take them away: good guard,
        Until their greater pleasures first be known
        That are to censure them.

CORDELIA   We are not the first
        Who with best meaning have incurred the worst.
        For thee, oppressèd king, I am cast down,   5
        Myself could else outfrown false fortune's frown.
        Shall we not see these daughters and these sisters?

LEAR   No, no, no, no! Come, let's away to prison.
        We two alone will sing like birds i'th'cage.
        When thou dost ask me blessing, I'll kneel down   10
        And ask of thee forgiveness: so we'll live,
        And pray, and sing, and tell old tales, and laugh
        At gilded butterflies, and hear poor rogues
        Talk of court news, and we'll talk with them too –
        Who loses and who wins; who's in, who's out –   15

---

11 all.] *Johnson;* all Q, F   11 GLOUCESTER And . . . too.] F; *not in* Q   11 SD] F; *not in* Q; *Exit.* Q2   Act 5, Scene 3   5.3]
Scena Tertia. F; *not in* Q   0 SD] F; *Enter Edmond, with Lear and Cordelia prisoners.* Q   2 first] F; best Q   3–5 We . . .
down,] F *lineation; two lines divided* incurd [*turned over*] /The worst Q   5 I am] F; am I Q   8 No, no, no, no] F; No,
no Q   9 i'th'] F; it'h Q   12 and sing] F; *not in* Q2   *13 hear poor rogues] Q; heere (poore Rogues) F   15 who's in,
who's] F; whose in, whose Q

---

11 And . . . too Appearing only in F, these words
(which fill out the pentameter line) have been
attacked as a vacuous 'stopgap' (Stone, pp. 69–70),
and defended as emblematic of the play's complementarity (Peat, p. 44; compare Urkowitz, p. 44).

Act 5, Scene 3

0 SD *Enter . . .* CAPTAIN See collation. Unlike Q,
F builds up the image of victorious Edmond, who
reaches the summit of his success and, from the
beginning of the scene, commands a much larger
share of audience attention – until the entrance of
Albany (38) (Taylor, 'War', pp. 32–3).

1 **good guard** i.e. let them have careful guard.

2 **their greater pleasures** the wishes of those of
higher rank.

3 **censure** judge.

4 **best meaning** i.e. rescuing Lear and restoring
him to his throne.

5 **cast down** i.e. by Fortune; humbled. The
figurative sense, dejected, is improbable at this
date (Brockbank, p. 5 n.).

9 **cage** (1) birdcage, (2) prison (Muir).

10–11 **When . . . forgiveness** A reminiscence,
perhaps, of the kneeling in *King Leir* (2298–2304).
Compare 4.6.54–6 and n.

12 **old tales** folktales; as in *AYLI* 1.2.120, *WT*
5.2.61.

13 **gilded butterflies** (1) gaily coloured butterflies, (2) lavishly adorned courtiers. Compare
Marston, *Antonio and Mellida* 4.1.49: 'Troopes of
pide butterflies, that flutter still / In greatnesse
summer, that confinne a prince' (Craig, cited by
Muir).

13 **poor rogues** wretched creatures (Kittredge).
F punctuation mistakenly assumes that 'Talk' in
the next line is a noun.

> And take upon 's the mystery of things,
> As if we were God's spies; and we'll wear out
> In a walled prison packs and sects of great ones
> That ebb and flow by th'moon.

EDMOND   Take them away.

LEAR   Upon such sacrifices, my Cordelia,   20
> The gods themselves throw incense. Have I caught thee?
> He that parts us shall bring a brand from heaven
> And fire us hence like foxes. Wipe thine eyes.
> The goodyears shall devour them, flesh and fell,
> Ere they shall make us weep. We'll see 'em starved first.   25
> Come.

Ex[eunt Lear and Cordelia, guarded]

---

21 The . . . thee?] *As in* Q*; two lines divided* Incense. / Haue F   *24 goodyears] good yeares F*;* good Q   24 them] F*;* em Q   24 flesh] F*;* fleach Q   25–6 Ere . . . Come.] *Pope's lineation; two lines divided* weepe? / Weele F*; one line* (come *turned under*) Q   25 'em] F3*;* vm Q*;* em Q2*;* e'm F, F2   26 Come.] F, Q*; not in* Q2   26 SD] *Theobald; Exit.* F, Q2*; not in* Q

16 take . . . things assume the responsibility of understanding and explaining the hidden workings of the world.

17 God's spies Either (1) spies commissioned and enabled by God to pry into even the most deeply hidden secrets (Heath, cited by Furness), or (2) 'detached observers surveying the deeds of mankind from an eternal vantage point' (Bevington). Though both capitalize, neither F nor Q uses an apostrophe in 'Gods'. Perrett, pp. 250–1, argues for the plural possessive in this pagan setting, but this is 'surely pedantry' (NS).

17 wear out outlast, outlive (*OED* Wear *v* 9).

18 packs and sects cliques and parties (Muir).

19 That ebb . . . moon As the changeable moon governs the ever-shifting tides, so power and position at court shift, too. In prison, Lear believes, he and Cordelia will be insulated from such vicissitudes.

20 such sacrifices Either (1) their renunciation of the world (Bradley, pp. 289–90), or (2) Cordelia's sacrifice for Lear (Kittredge). Muir notes the suggestion of human sacrifice, which looks forward to the murder of Cordelia, and echoes the Old Testament stories underlying Lear's speech, e.g. Jephthah's daughter, who was sacrificed; Samson and the foxes; etc. Brockbank (p. 13) compares Heb. 13.16: 'To do good, & to distribute forget not: for with suche sacrifices God is pleased', which the Geneva Bible glosses: 'Thanksgiuing & doing good are our onlie sacrifices which please God.'

21 The gods . . . incense Lear imagines gods as priests performing a ritual.

21 Have . . . thee Lear still cannot believe his luck and holds Cordelia ever more tightly. Compare the second song from Sidney's *Astrophel and Stella* (1591): 'Have I caught thee, my heavenly jewel?', which Falstaff quotes, *Wiv.* 3.3.43 (Brockbank, pp. 15–16).

22–3 He . . . foxes i.e. it will take divine assistance to separate us again. Shaheen cites Judges 15.4–5, but the story of Samson and the foxes is only obliquely relevant here, as it concerns Samson's revenge on the Philistines for causing a breach between him and his wife. Compare Harsnett, p. 97: 'to fire him out of his hold, as men smoke out a Foxe out of his burrow' (Kittredge).

24 goodyears malefic powers (*OED*); specifically, the plague or pox: see F. Rubenstein, 'They were not such good years', *SQ* 40 (1989), 70–4. An allusion to Pharaoh's dream (Gen. 41.1–36) seems remote; compare Taylor, 'Addenda' to *Division*, p. 489, who argues for the singular, which Oxford adopts.

24 fell skin; 'flesh and fell' = altogether (Onions).

25 Ere . . . weep Compare 2.4.268–71.

26 SD *Exeunt* Taylor argues ('War', p. 33) that only Edmond and the Captain remain; everyone else goes off with Lear and Cordelia. Moreover, Albany later says (96–8) that Edmond's army has been discharged. But it is not necessary to clear the stage entirely for Edmond and the Captain to talk apart, and the drummer is needed later for the concluding dead march. Oxford has the drummer re-enter with Albany, Gonerill, and Regan (38 SD.2), accompanied by a 'trumpeter', although F calls only for a *Flourish*.

EDMOND   Come hither, captain. Hark.
         Take thou this note. Go follow them to prison.
         One step I have advanced thee; if thou dost
         As this instructs thee, thou dost make thy way   30
         To noble fortunes. Know thou this: that men
         Are as the time is; to be tender-minded
         Does not become a sword. Thy great employment
         Will not bear question: either say thou'lt do't,
         Or thrive by other means.
CAPTAIN   I'll do't, my lord.   35
EDMOND   About it, and write 'happy' when th'hast done.
         Mark, I say, instantly, and carry it so
         As I have set it down.

                                            Exit Captain

Flourish. Enter ALBANY, GONERILL, REGAN, [*Officers,*] *Soldiers*

ALBANY   Sir, you have showed today your valiant strain,
         And fortune led you well. You have the captives   40
         Who were the opposites of this day's strife.
         I do require them of you, so to use them
         As we shall find their merits and our safety
         May equally determine.
EDMOND   Sir, I thought it fit
         To send the old and miserable king   45
         To some retention and appointed guard,

---

29 One] F, Q *corr.*; And Q *uncorr.*   34 thou'lt] F; thout Q   36 th'hast] F; thou hast Q   38 down.] F *omits two lines here*   38 SD.1 *Exit Captain*] F; *not in* Q   38 SD.2 *Flourish . . . Soldiers*] F (*subst.*); *Enter Duke, the two Ladies, and others.* Q   38 SD.2 *Officers*] *This edn; not in* Q, F   39 showed] shew'd F; shewed Q; shewne Q2   40 well. You] well: you Q2, F; well you Q *uncorr.*; well, you Q *corr.*   41 Who] F; That Q   42 I] F; We Q   42 require them] F; require then Q   *45–6 To . . . guard,] *As in* Q2; *one line* Q *corr.* (*pointed* guard *turned under*); *one line* F, Q *uncorr.* (*which omit* and appointed guard)   45 send] F; saue Q *uncorr.*

28 **this note** Lear and Cordelia's death warrant, signed by Gonerill and Edmond: compare 226–9.
31 **noble fortunes** i.e. further advancement to nobility.
31–2 **men . . . is** A counsel of expediency, consistent with Edmond's philosophy.
33 **a sword** i.e. soldiers in wartime.
34 **question** discussion.
35 **my lord** F omits two lines here: see Textual Analysis, p. 259 below.
36 **write 'happy'** count yourself fortunate.
37 **Mark** Attend.
37–8 **carry . . . down** manage it as I have

indicated, i.e. as if Cordelia had slain herself (compare 227–9).
39 **strain** Either (1) quality, or (2) lineage (compare *JC* 5.1.59).
41 **opposites** opponents (compare 143 below).
43 **merits** deserts.
46 **To . . . guard** See collation, and Textual Analysis, p. 57 above, n. 3. This line appears out of sequence and should possibly precede 45. Compare Halio, p. 164; Taylor, 'Date and authorship', pp. 361–2.
46 **retention** detention, imprisonment.

Whose age had charms in it, whose title more,
To pluck the common bosom on his side
And turn our impressed lances in our eyes
Which do command them. With him I sent the queen: 50
My reason all the same, and they are ready
Tomorrow, or at further space, t'appear
Where you shall hold your session.

ALBANY   Sir, by your patience,
I hold you but a subject of this war,
Not as a brother.

REGAN   That's as we list to grace him. 55
Methinks our pleasure might have been demanded
Ere you had spoke so far. He led our powers,
Bore the commission of my place and person,
The which immediacy may well stand up
And call itself your brother.

GONERILL   Not so hot. 60
In his own grace he doth exalt himself
More than in your addition.

REGAN   In my rights,
By me invested, he compeers the best.

ALBANY   That were the most if he should husband you.

REGAN   Jesters do oft prove prophets.

---

47 had] F; has Q   47 more,] F, Q *corr.*; more Q *uncorr.*   48 common bosom] F, Q *corr.*; coren bossom Q *uncorr.*; common blossomes Q2   48 on] F; of Q   51–2 My ... t'appear] F *lineation; lines end ... to morrow, / ... shall hold* Q (*see* 5.3.53 *n.*)   52 t'] to Q   53 session.] F *omits five lines here*   54–5 I ... brother.] F *lineation; one line* Q   56 might] F; should Q   59 immediacy] F; imediate Q   60–2 Not ... addition.] F *lineation; as prose* Q   62 addition] F; aduancement Q   62–3 In ... best.] F *lineation; one line* Q   62 rights] F; right Q   64 SH] F; *Gon.* Q

---

47 **Whose** Its antecedent is 'king' (45).

47 **title** (1) kingship, (2) legal right to possession of the land (Hunter).

48 **common bosom** hearts of the people.

48 **on** onto.

49–50 **turn ... them** turn our forces against us, their leaders; literally, turn the weapons of our conscripted pikemen into our own eyes (with a reminiscence of Gloucester's blinding?).

53 **session** sitting of a court of justice. F omits four and half lines here: see Textual Analysis, p. 259 below.

53 **by your patience** i.e. pardon me.

54 **subject of** i.e. subordinate in.

55 **brother** equal.

55 **we list** I choose, please. Regan uses the royal plural; compare 5.1.23–5.

58 **Bore ... person** Carried the authority of my

position and represented me personally.

59 **immediacy** direct connection; compare *Ham.* 1.2.109.

61 **grace** merit and honour (Kittredge); compare 55.

62 **your addition** i.e. the title or position you have bestowed.

63 **compeers** equals.

64 **That ... you** i.e. he would be most fully invested with your rights (and Albany's equal) if he were your husband. See collation: Q gives this line to Gonerill, but the compositor very likely erred in assuming that the Regan/Gonerill alternation continued (Duthie, pp. 85, 161). Albany interrupts again later (76); the interruption here makes good dramatic sense.

65 **Jesters ... prophets** Compare 'There is many a true word spoken in jest' (Tilley W772).

GONERILL   Holla, holla!   65
    That eye that told you so, looked but asquint.

REGAN Lady, I am not well, else I should answer
    From a full-flowing stomach. [*To Edmond*] General,
    Take thou my soldiers, prisoners, patrimony.
    Dispose of them, of me; the walls is thine.   70
    Witness the world that I create thee here
    My lord and master.

GONERILL   Mean you to enjoy him?

ALBANY The let-alone lies not in your good will.

EDMOND Nor in thine, lord.

ALBANY   Half-blooded fellow, yes.

REGAN [*To Edmond*] Let the drum strike, and prove my title thine.   75

ALBANY Stay yet, hear reason. Edmond, I arrest thee
    On capital treason, and in thy attaint
    This gilded serpent. For your claim, fair sister,
    I bar it in the interest of my wife.
    'Tis she is subcontracted to this lord,   80
    And I, her husband, contradict your banns.

65–6 Holla ... asquint.] F *lineation; one line* Q   65 Holla, holla!] *Theobald;* Hola, hola, Q, F   *66 asquint] a squint Q, F; a-squint *Rowe*   68 full-flowing] *Theobald;* full flowing Q, F   68 SD] *Oxford; not in* Q, F; – General, *Capell*   70 Dispose ... thine.] F; *not in* Q   72 him?] F; him then? Q   *73 let-alone] *Capell;* let alone Q, F   75 SH] F; *Bast.* Q   75 SD] *Malone; not in* Q, F   75 thine] F; good Q   *77 thy attaint] thine attaint Q; thy arrest F   *78 sister,] sister Q; Sisters, F   79 bar] *Rowe;* bare Q, F   80 this] F, Q; her Q2   81 your] F; the Q   81 banns] Banes F, Q; bans *Malone*

66 That ... asquint Gonerill alludes to the proverb, 'Love, being jealous, makes a good eye look asquint' (Tilley L498; Dent, p. 159, cites Florio, *Second Fruites*, 6.83: 'To much loue makes a sound eye oftentimes to see a misse').

68 full-flowing stomach i.e. a full tide of anger, resentment.

70 walls i.e. of the heart or person (typically conceived as a fortress besieged by a lover). On F's additional line, see Textual Analysis, p. 269 below.

73 let-alone (1) permission, (2) hindrance (NS).

74 Half-blooded Not only is Edmond a bastard, but his parenting was mixed, i.e. only one parent had noble blood.

75 Let ... thine See collation. F alters not only the speech ascription, but the final word in the line. Instead of Edmond boldly defying Albany, Regan orders the drum to beat, so that the world will witness her action (69–72), and invites Edmond to establish his right to her title, putting the matter to

trial by combat if necessary. Compare Urkowitz, p. 109; Stone, p. 229.

76 thee To underscore his contempt, Albany henceforward uses the second-person familiar pronoun in addressing Edmond.

77 attaint (1) impeachment, (2) dishonour. Most modern editors agree that F 'arrest' is a mistaken repetition from the preceding line and Q is correct here. But compare Furness and Duthie, pp. 186–8.

78 gilded serpent i.e. Gonerill, 'gilded' because beautifully accoutred (and brilliantly: King).

79 I ... wife With heavy irony, Albany as Gonerill's husband moves to protect his wife's 'interest', or rights.

80 subcontracted has a subsidiary or secondary contract (subsidiary, that is, to her marriage contract with Albany).

81 contradict your banns i.e. oppose the declaration of your intention to marry.

> If you will marry, make your love to me,
> My lady is bespoke.

GONERILL   An interlude!

ALBANY   Thou art armed, Gloucester; let the trumpet sound.
If none appear to prove upon thy person   85
Thy heinous, manifest, and many treasons,
There is my pledge!
                    [*Throws down a glove*]
                              I'll make it on thy heart,
Ere I taste bread, thou art in nothing less
Than I have here proclaimed thee.

REGAN   Sick, O sick!

GONERILL   [*Aside*] If not, I'll ne'er trust medicine.   90

EDMOND   There's my exchange!
                    [*Throws down a glove*]
                              What in the world he is
That names me traitor, villain-like he lies.
Call by the trumpet: he that dares, approach;
On him, on you – who not? – I will maintain
My truth and honour firmly.

ALBANY   A herald, ho!   95

Enter a HERALD

Trust to thy single virtue, for thy soldiers,

---

*82 love] Q; loues F   **83** GONERILL An interlude!] F; *not in* Q   **84** Thou … sound.] *Rowe's lineation; two lines divided*
Gloster, / Let F; Q *combines* My … bespoke. *(83) with* Thou … Gloster, / *in one line and omits* SH *and* Let … sound   **84**
trumpet] F2; Trmpet F   **85** person] F; head Q   **87** SD] *Malone (subst.); not in* Q, F   **87** make] F; proue Q   **90** SD]
Rowe; not in Q, F   **90** medicine] F; poyson Q   **91** SD] *Malone (subst.); not in* Q, F   ***91** he is] Q; hes F   **93** the] F; thy
Q   ***93** dares, approach;] *Oxford;* dares approach; F; dares approach, Q   ***94** you – who not? –] *Furness;* you, who
not, Q, F; you, (who not?) *Theobald*   **95** ho!] ho. F; ho. *Bast.* A Herald ho, a Herald. Q   **95** SD] *As in Theobald; after*
firmely. F; *not in* Q

82 If … me Albany sarcastically advises Regan
to direct her matrimonial intentions to him, as
Edmond has spoken for Gonerill.

82 love See collation. Q appears correct. Faulty
plurals (characteristic of Compositor E) occur elsewhere in F, e.g. 'Sisters' (78).

83 An interlude What a farce! (Kittredge).
Interludes were brief plays, usually comic, performed in the intervals of festivities; they are so
called in *MND* 1.2.6, *TN* 5.1.372. On F's addition
here, see Textual Analysis, p. 270 below.

84 let … sound See Textual Analysis, p. 270
below, and compare Taylor, 'War', p. 33.

87 pledge gage.

87 make it i.e. make it good.

88 in nothing in no single detail.

90 medicine poison. See collation. In F
Gonerill's humour is grimmer.

91 What … is i.e. whoever and of whatsoever
rank he is (compare Abbott 254).

95–107 A herald … Again See collation. In Q,
Edmond insistently repeats the call for a herald, and
it is he, not the Herald, who orders the second and
third trumpet calls (106–7). Q has a Captain (not in
F) order the first trumpet call. F's alterations show
Albany still very much in charge. (See Textual
Analysis, pp. 64–5 above, on recasting; Sisson, pp.
243–4, who supports F; Duthie, pp. 188–9.)

96 virtue strength, valour (compare Latin
virtus).

All levied in my name, have in my name
Took their discharge.

REGAN   My sickness grows upon me.

ALBANY   She is not well. Convey her to my tent.

> [*Exit Regan, led by an Officer*]

Come hither, herald. Let the trumpet sound,   100
And read out this.

> *A trumpet sounds*

HERALD   *Reads* 'If any man of quality or degree within the lists of
the army will maintain upon Edmond, supposed Earl of
Gloucester, that he is a manifold traitor, let him appear by the
third sound of the trumpet. He is bold in his defence.'   105

> *First trumpet*

Again.

> *Second trumpet*

Again.

> *Third trumpet*

> *Trumpet answers within. Enter* EDGAR, *armed*

ALBANY   Ask him his purposes, why he appears
Upon this call o'th'trumpet.

HERALD   What are you?
Your name, your quality, and why you answer   110
This present summons?

EDGAR   Know, my name is lost,
By treason's tooth bare-gnawn and canker-bit.

97–8 All ... discharge.] F *lineation; one line* (discharge *turned under*) Q   98 My] F; This Q   99 SD] *This edn (after Theobald); not in* Q, F   100 hither] F; hether Q   100 trumpet] Q; Trumper F   101 this.] F; this. *Cap.* Sound trumpet? Q   101 SD] F; *not in* Q   102 SD] F; *not in* Q   102–5 'If ... defence.'] *As in* Q (*quotation marks added*); *in italics* F   102 within the lists] F; in the hoast Q   104 he is] F; he's Q   104 by] F; at Q   105 SD] F; *not in* Q, *which inserts* / *Bast.* Sound? *on new line*   106 Again.] *Her.* Againe. F; Againe? Q   106 SD] F; *not in* Q   107 Again.] *Her.* Againe. F; *not in* Q   107 SD.1] F; *not in* Q   107 SD.2 *Trumpet ... armed*] F; *Enter Edgar at the third sound, a trumpet before him.* Q   109 o'th'] F; oth' Q   109–11 What ... summons?] F *lineation; two lines divided* qualitie? / *And* Q   110 name, your] F; name and Q   111–14 Know ... cope.] F *lineation; three lines ending* ... tooth. / ... mou't / ... cope with all. Q   111 Know,] F; O know Q   111 lost,] lost Q, F; lost; *Theobald*   *112 tooth] *Theobald;* tooth. Q; tooth: Q2, F

---

102 degree rank.

102 lists Either (1) palisades, boundaries (*OED* List *sb*³ 10), or (2) rolls, catalogue (*OED* List *sb*⁶; compare *Ham.* 1.2.32).

107 SD.2 *Enter ... armed* Edgar is in combat armour, his beaver down barring recognition. In Q, Edgar enters with *a trumpet before him*, apparently the trumpet that answered the third call, though it has no other function except possibly to respond to Edmond's command (140). Neither Q

nor F, however – nor most modern editions – provide an entrance for the trumpeter who sounds the calls at 105–7, and who must enter with either Albany (38 SD) or the Herald (95 SD). Compare 26 SD n. above. Whereas in Q no trumpet answers and Edgar enters *at* the third sound, F's staging seems calculated to increase suspense (Peat, p. 50).

112 canker-bit i.e. destroyed (literally, eaten by worms; as in Sonnets 70.7, 99.13).

                    Yet am I noble as the adversary
                    I come to cope.

ALBANY   Which is that adversary?

EDGAR   What's he that speaks for Edmond, Earl of Gloucester?   115

EDMOND   Himself. What sayst thou to him?

EDGAR   Draw thy sword,
                    That if my speech offend a noble heart
                    Thy arm may do thee justice. Here is mine.
                    Behold, it is the privilege of mine honour,
                    My oath, and my profession. I protest,   120
                    Maugre thy strength, place, youth, and eminence,
                    Despite thy victor-sword and fire-new fortune,
                    Thy valour and thy heart, thou art a traitor:
                    False to thy gods, thy brother, and thy father,
                    Conspirant 'gainst this high illustrious prince,   125
                    And from th'extremest upward of thy head
                    To the descent and dust below thy foot,
                    A most toad-spotted traitor. Say thou no,
                    This sword, this arm, and my best spirits are bent
                    To prove upon thy heart, whereto I speak,   130
                    Thou liest.

EDMOND   In wisdom I should ask thy name,
                    But since thy outside looks so fair and warlike,

---

113 Yet am I noble as] F; yet are I mou't / Where is Q; Where is Q2   114 cope] F; cope with all Q   114 Which] F, Q; What Q2   116 sayst] F; saiest Q   117–18 That . . . mine.] F *lineation; divided* arme / May Q   *119 Behold . . . honour,] F *lineation; divided* spirits, / As in Pope; Behold it is the priuiledge of my tongue, Q; Behold it is my priuiledge, / The priuiledge of mine Honours, F   *119 honour] *Oxford;* Honours F; tongue Q   120 and my] F, Q; and Q2   121 Maugre] F; Maugure Q   121 place, youth,] F; youth, place Q   *122 Despite] Q; Despise F   122 victor-sword] F; victor, sword Q   122 fire-new] *Rowe;* fire new Q, F   122 fortune] F; fortun'd Q   124 thy gods] F, Q; the gods Q2   125 Conspirant] F; Conspicuate Q   126 th'extremest] F; the'xtremest Q   127 below thy foot] F; beneath thy feet Q   129–31 This . . . liest] F *lineation; two lines divided* spirits, / As bent Q   129 are] F; As Q; Is Q2

---

114 **cope** cope with, encounter.

115 **What's** Who is (Abbott 254; compare *H5* 4.3.18).

118 **Here is mine** Edgar draws his sword.

119 **Behold . . . honour** See collation. Either the compositor (Duthie, p. 422) or the collator (*Textual Companion*, p. 538) is responsible for unnecessary duplication in F.

119 **it** 'i.e. the drawing of a sword against an adversary, and the challenge of him to single combat' (NS).

119 **honour** personal integrity. While executing the change from Q 'my tongue', Compositor E (typically) pluralized the noun, thereby further altering the sense (*Textual Companion*, p. 538).

120 **oath . . . profession** i.e. as a knight.

121 **Maugre** In spite of.

122 **fire-new** i.e. brand new, freshly minted.

126–7 **from . . . foot** i.e. from top to toe.

127 **descent** lowest part, i.e. the sole.

128 **toad-spotted** i.e. stained or marked with infamy as a toad is with (supposedly) venomous spots.

131 **In wisdom . . . name** In chivalry, one was not bound to fight a social inferior. Edmond rejects prudence ('wisdom'), revealing his 'sentimental side' in accepting the old code of honour Edgar represents (Heilman, pp. 244–7). Compare 141–4 and 155–6 n. below.

And that thy tongue some say of breeding breathes,
What safe and nicely I might well delay
By rule of knighthood, I disdain and spurn.   135
Back do I toss these treasons to thy head,
With the hell-hated lie o'erwhelm thy heart,
Which, for they yet glance by and scarcely bruise,
This sword of mine shall give them instant way
Where they shall rest for ever. Trumpets, speak!   140
          Alarums. [They] fight. [Edmond falls]

ALBANY   Save him, save him.

GONERILL   This is practice, Gloucester;
By th'law of war thou wast not bound to answer
An unknown opposite. Thou art not vanquished,
But cozened and beguiled.

ALBANY   Shut your mouth, dame,

---

133 tongue] F; being Q   *133 some say] Q; (some say) F   134 What ... delay] F; not in Q   135 rule] F; right Q   136 Back ... head] F, Q; not in Q2   136 Back] F; Heere Q   136 these] F; those Q   137 hell-hated lie] F; hell hatedly Q   137 o'erwhelm] ore-whelme F; oreturnd Q   *138 scarcely] Q; scarely F   140 SD] Capell; Alarums. Fights. F (after saue him.); not in Q   141 SH ALBANY] Q, F; ALL Oxford (conj. van Dam, Blayney)   141–4 This ... beguiled.] F lineation; three lines ending ... armes / ... opposite, / ... beguild. Q   141 practice] F; meere practise Q   142 th'] F; the Q   142 war] F; armes Q   142 wast] F; art Q   142 answer] F, Q; offer Q2   144 cozened] F; cousned Q   144–7 Shut ... it.] F lineation; as prose Q   144 Shut] F; Stop Q

133 tongue See collation. Q 'being' is probably a misreading of 'tong' (Duthie, p. 423).
133 say Aphetic form of 'assay' = proof, sample (Onions); hence, 'smack', 'air'. The F collator or compositor mistook the noun for a verb and, treating the expression as parenthetical, inserted brackets. Compare Duthie, pp. 195–6.
134 What ... delay See Textual Analysis, p. 270 below, on line missing in Q.
134 safe and nicely legally and punctiliously.
135 rule See collation. Q 'right' may derive from misreading 'rit' for 'rule' in copy (compare Duthie, p. 423); or F may have altered Q (as often in this passage) to avoid the internal rhyme, 'right' – 'knighthood'.
137 hell-hated lie lie as hateful as hell. Q 'hell hatedly' derives from the compositor mistaking 'ly' (= 'lie') for an adverbial suffix (Duthie, p. 423).
138 Which i.e. those treasons (136). 'Which' is also the object of the verb in the next line, where 'them' is grammatically redundant (Kittredge).
138 for because.
138 bruise i.e. you.
139 instant way immediate passage.
140 Where ... for ever i.e. in you.
140 SD A realistic duel must involve a fight, not just swordplay (Rosenberg, p. 305; compare

Bratton, p. 205).
141 Save him Albany apparently calls out to save Edmond from a *coup de grâce*, because he wants Edmond's confession (Johnson). Or he may be calling out to soldiers to save Edgar, momentarily in danger, as Gonerill with murder in her eyes accuses him of 'practice'. Blayney, following van Dam (see collation), regards Q/F *Alb.* as a misreading of *All*, which could also make sense dramatically.
143 opposite opponent; as at 41 above.
144 cozened cheated, duped.
144–51 Shut ... her See collation. To Duthie, p. 43, the Q/F variants here were evidence of memorial reconstruction, but to more recent scholars they reveal differences in dramatic intention: e.g. in Q, Albany acts more straightforwardly throughout the passage; in F, his actions are more disjointed, hesitant, consistent with his 'pattern of delay' later in this scene (Urkowitz, pp. 111–15). Gonerill's final exit similarly shows 'a very clear differentiation': in Q, she leaves the stage defeated and shamefaced; in F, she is challenged but strong and defiant (McLeod, pp. 187–8). Speech headings and address have also aroused comment, as indicated below. On recasting speeches, see Textual Analysis, pp. 64–5 above.

Or with this paper shall I stop it. – Hold, sir.　　　　145
Thou worse than any name, read thine own evil. –
No tearing, lady. I perceive you know it.

GONERILL　Say if I do; the laws are mine, not thine.
Who can arraign me for't?　　　　　　　　*Exit*

ALBANY　　　　　　　　　　Most monstrous! O,
Know'st thou this paper?

EDMOND　　　　　　　　　　Ask me not what I know.　　　150

ALBANY　Go after her, she's desperate, govern her.

　　　　　　　　　　　　　　　[*Exit an Officer*]

EDMOND　What you have charged me with, that have I done,
And more, much more; the time will bring it out.
'Tis past, and so am I. But what art thou
That hast this fortune on me? If thou'rt noble,　　155
I do forgive thee.

---

145 stop] F; stople Q　145 – Hold, sir.] hold Sir, F; *not in* Q　146 name] F; thing Q　147 No] F; nay no Q　147 know
it] F; know't Q　148–9 Say . . . for't] F *lineation; one line* (me for't. *turned under*) Q　149 can] F; shal Q　149 SD] F; *Exit.*
Gonerill. Q (*after 150*)　149–50 Most . . . paper?] Capell's *lineation; one line* Q, F　149 O,] F; *not in* Q　150 SH] F; *Gon.* Q
(*see Commentary*)　151 SD] Capell; *not in* Q, F　152 What . . . done,] *As in* Q; *two lines divided* with, / That F　155
thou'rt] F; thou bee'st Q

145 **this paper** i.e. the letter Edgar has given him
(5.1.29).
145 **Hold, sir** These words, not in Q, show who
is addressed. 'Hold' = take, receive (often with the
implication of wait or desist: see Schmidt, and
compare *TN* 3.3.38, *Mac.* 2.1.4).
146 **Thou** . . . **evil** Albany addresses Edmond,
not Gonerill, since he does not use the familiar
pronoun for her, as he now consistently does for
Edmond. Only once (4.2.36), after she uses the
familiar pronoun to him, does Albany address her
thus (Urkowitz, p. 111).
146 **thine own evil** Edmond is thoroughly
implicated in Gonerill's letter, which explicitly
mentions their 'reciprocal vows' (4.5.250), although
Gonerill takes the initiative in urging the further
evil of Albany's murder.
147 **No tearing** Gonerill tries to tear the letter
out of Albany's hands as he gives it to Edmond.
Compare a similar incident in *King Leir* (2586).
148–9 **the laws** . . . **for't** Gonerill refers to her
position as queen and to Albany as merely consort.
The sovereign had no peer and therefore could not
be tried: see *R2* 1.2.37–41, 3.2.54–7.
149 SD See collation. Q delays Gonerill's exit
until after 'Ask me not what I know' (150), which
it assigns to her, not Edmond. In F she exits

defiantly asserting her superiority over Albany and
law (McLeod, p. 187).
150 **Know'st** . . . **paper** In F, Albany's address to
Edmond is clear, whereas in Q, with Gonerill still
on stage, it is ambiguous and even contradictory:
Albany has already indicated that Gonerill recognizes the letter (147). Compare Furness.
150 SH EDMOND Q assigns this speech to
Gonerill, who then exits vanquished, implying her
guilt (McLeod, p. 188). In assigning the line to
Edmond, F resolves any ambiguity and contradic-
tion (see previous note). Edmond's response is not
necessarily defiant, but may be 'a resigned admis-
sion' of guilt, delivered sombrely, i.e. 'You need not
ask' (Urkowitz, p. 114). Perhaps the Q compositor
mistakenly continued the Albany/Gonerill alternation; moreover, Gonerill's name after her exit in Q
would be redundant if the speech were hers (Halio,
p. 164; compare Duthie, pp. 189–90, and Muir,
who follow Q).
151 **Go** . . . **govern her** Somewhat belatedly,
Albany recognizes Gonerill's despair and shows
justified concern; this is consistent with his emer-
ging pattern of delayed response.
155–6 **If** . . . **thee** Edmond implicitly repudiates
his stance in 1.2 and reverts to traditional concepts
of nobility and breeding (Hunter).

EDGAR   Let's exchange charity.
          I am no less in blood than thou art, Edmond.
          If more, the more th'hast wronged me.
          My name is Edgar, and thy father's son.
          The gods are just, and of our pleasant vices   160
          Make instruments to plague us.
          The dark and vicious place where thee he got
          Cost him his eyes.
EDMOND   Th'hast spoken right; 'tis true.
          The wheel is come full circle; I am here.
ALBANY   Methought thy very gait did prophesy   165
          A royal nobleness. I must embrace thee.
          Let sorrow split my heart if ever I
          Did hate thee or thy father.
EDGAR   Worthy prince, I know't.
ALBANY   Where have you hid yourself?   170
          How have you known the miseries of your father?
EDGAR   By nursing them, my lord. List a brief tale,
          And when 'tis told, O that my heart would burst!

---

157 art,] F4; art Q, F   158 th'hast] F; thou hast Q   160 vices] F; vertues Q   161–3 Make . . . eyes.] F *lineation; two lines divided* vitious / Place Q   161 plague] F; scourge Q   162 thee he] F, Q; he thee Q2   163–4 Th'hast . . . here.] F *lineation; as prose* Q   163 Th'hast] F; Thou hast Q   163 right; 'tis true] F; truth Q   164 circle] F; circled Q   167–8 Let . . . father.] F *lineation; one line* Q   167–8 ever I / Did] F; I did euer Q   169 know't] F, Q; know it Q2   172–80 By . . . rings,] F *lineation; nine lines ending* . . . Lord, / . . . told / . . . proclamation / . . . neere, / . . . death, / . . . once. / . . . rags / . . . disdain'd / . . . rings, Q

---

156 **Let's exchange charity** Edgar's fierceness apparently abates, although his character 'has too much validity to be merely humble and gentle', and his speech reflects a 'bitter morality' that offers Edmond no solace (Rosenberg, p. 307).

158 **If more** i.e. since Edmond is 'half-blooded' (74).

159 **My . . . son** Edgar removes his helmet.

160–1 **The gods . . . us** Compare Wisdom 11. [13]: 'wherewith a man sinneth, by the same also shal he be punished', and Jer. 2.19: 'Thine owne wickednes shal correct thee, and thy turnings backe shal reproue thee' (Noble).

160 **pleasant** pleasure-giving.

162–3 **The dark . . . eyes** Edgar applies his statement of compensatory justice to the specific instance: the sinful fornication that bred Edmond led to events culminating in Gloucester's blinding.

162 **dark** (1) dim, unlit, (2) morally benighted.

162 **vicious place** Compare 'forfended place' (5.1.11) (King).

162 **got** begot.

164 **The wheel . . . here** More is suggested than

Fortune's wheel, which has returned Edmond to the bottom whence he began. Events have circled back so that he, who was the initiator and beneficiary of much evil, is now its victim. Compare Bradley, p. 15: 'That men may start a course of events but can neither calculate nor control it, is a *tragic* fact.'

165–6 **Methought . . . nobleness** Albany addresses Edgar, whose demeanour and very manner of walking, he says, suggest something kingly. Albany's specific terms, 'royal nobleness', are themselves prophetic: compare 293–4 below.

166 **royal** (1) dignified, (2) regal, kingly.

167 **sorrow . . . heart** Compare *R3* 1.3.299. where Queen Margaret uses the same expression.

169 **Worthy** Noble.

172 **List** Listen to.

173 **O that . . . burst** Emotionally overtaxed by now, Edgar uncharacteristically, like his father, yearns for death. But his work is not yet finished. (At 4.1.10–12, he said the opposite; see Rosenberg, p. 307, on Edgar's inconsistencies.)

> The bloody proclamation to escape
> That followed me so near (O, our lives' sweetness,   175
> That we the pain of death would hourly die
> Rather than die at once!) taught me to shift
> Into a madman's rags, t'assume a semblance
> That very dogs disdained; and in this habit
> Met I my father with his bleeding rings,   180
> Their precious stones new-lost; became his guide,
> Led him, begged for him, saved him from despair,
> Never – O fault! – revealed myself unto him
> Until some half hour past, when I was armed.
> Not sure, though hoping of this good success,   185
> I asked his blessing, and from first to last
> Told him our pilgrimage; but his flawed heart –
> Alack, too weak the conflict to support –
> 'Twixt two extremes of passion, joy and grief,
> Burst smilingly.

EDMOND   This speech of yours hath moved me,   190
> And shall perchance do good. But speak you on,
> You look as you had something more to say.

ALBANY   If there be more, more woeful, hold it in,
> For I am almost ready to dissolve,
> Hearing of this.   195

---

176 we] F; with Q   178 madman's] mad-mans Q, F   178 t'assume] F; To assume Q   181 Their] F; The Q   *182
despair,] Q; dispaire. F   183 fault] F; Father Q   187 our] F; my Q   194–5 For ... this.] F *lineation; one line*
Q   195 this.] F *omits eighteen lines here*

174 **bloody proclamation** Compare 2.1.55–7,
2.3.1–5.

175–7 **O, our ... once** i.e. life is so precious to us
that we prefer to prolong it, suffering agonies
repeatedly, rather than to die quickly and be done.
Compare *Cym.* 5.1.25–7.

177 **shift** change.

180 **rings** i.e. eye-sockets. The next line continues the metaphor.

183 **O fault** Edgar now realizes he was wrong to
delay reconciliation with his father. 'In effect,
Edgar's way and time of telling killed his father'
(Rosenberg, p. 308).

185 **success** outcome; i.e. victory in the duel.

187–90 **his flawed ... smilingly** In Sidney's
Arcadia, Bk II, ch. 10, the blind Paphlagonian king
dies similarly of a broken heart, 'with many teares
(both of ioy and sorrow)'.

187 **flawed** cracked, i.e. damaged by suffering.

190 **Burst smilingly** Gloucester's dying smile
suggests not only joyful reunion with Edgar, but
gladness that death has come to him at last.
Gloucester's death prepares in some ways for
Lear's, brought closer in F by substantial cutting
after 195 (Clayton, p. 137; compare 196–201 n.
below).

190–2 **This ... say** Edmond 'becomes huma-
nised' in the course of *King Lear*, discovering the
limitations and passions that being human involves,
as this speech and others in the scene reveal
(Reibetanz, p. 59).

191 **shall ... good** Compare 217–25 below.

193 **hold it in** As if taking a cue from Albany, F
cuts seventeen lines following this speech: see
Textual Analysis, pp. 259–60 below.

194 **dissolve** i.e. in tears.

Enter a GENTLEMAN [*with a bloody knife*]

GENTLEMAN   Help, help, O help!
EDGAR   What kind of help?
ALBANY   Speak, man.
EDGAR   What means this bloody knife?
GENTLEMAN   'Tis hot, it smokes.
        It came even from the heart of – O, she's dead.
ALBANY   Who dead? Speak, man.
GENTLEMAN   Your lady, sir, your lady; and her sister   200
        By her is poisoned: she confesses it.
EDMOND   I was contracted to them both; all three
        Now marry in an instant.
EDGAR   Here comes Kent.

Enter KENT [*as himself*]

ALBANY   Produce the bodies, be they alive or dead.
        Gonerill's and Regan's bodies brought out
        This judgement of the heavens, that makes us tremble,   205

195 SD] *Enter one with a bloudie knife,* Q; *Enter a Gentleman.* F   196 O help!] F; *not in* Q   196 SH EDGAR] F; *Alb.*
Q   196 ALBANY Speak, man.] F; *not in* Q   197 SH EDGAR] F; *not in* Q, *which continues speech as part of previous
line*   197 this] F; *that* Q   197–8 'Tis ... dead.] *Steevens's lineation (Capell subst.); one line* Q, *which omits* O she's dead;
as prose F   197 'Tis] F; *Its* Q   199 dead? Speak, man.] F; *man, speake?* Q   201 confesses] F; *hath confest* Q; *has confest*
Q2   203 EDGAR Here comes Kent.] F; *after pity 206* Q   203 Kent.] F; *Kent sir.* Q   203 SD] *Oxford (subst.); Enter
Kent* Q, Q2, F (*after 207* Q; *after pity 206* Q2)   204 the] F; *their* Q   204 SD] F; *The bodies of Gonerill and Regan are brought
in.* Q (*after 212; see Commentary*)   205 judgement] F; *Iustice* Q   205 tremble,] Q; *tremble.* F

196–201 Help ... it See collation. Revision of
this sequence in F gives Edgar two speeches. By
sharing the interrogation with Albany, he begins
taking over responsibility for events (compare
Textual Analysis, p. 63–4 above; Urkowitz, pp.
116–17; and 222–5 below). Doran, pp. 53–4, 72,
believed Shakespeare was responsible for the revision, as for the deletion of the lines following 195.
The episode was modified by all eighteenth- and
nineteenth-century actor-editors, who often cut it
completely (Bratton, p. 209).
   197 smokes steams. 'Fresh blood commonly
"smokes" in Sh[akespeare]' (NS). The line is one
of the most difficult for a modern audience to take
seriously, unless very carefully controlled and
modulated (Rosenberg, p. 309).
   198 It ... dead The line generates deliberate
tension and suspense. Regan's death is expected,
but by poison. Gonerill and Cordelia are other
possible victims, but which one, and why?
   200 Your lady Edmond's prophecy (4.2.26) is
fulfilled.
   203 marry unite; with a pun on sex and death
(Rosenberg, p. 309, who compares 4.5.189).

203 EDGAR ... Kent See collation. In Q, Edgar's
line and Kent's entrance occur in the middle of
Albany's speech. In F, Kent 'comes slowly down
the stage while Albany is speaking' (Muir) – a more
effective entrance. Moreover, in F's lineation the
metre improves.
   203 SD Enter KENT Kent now drops his disguise
as Caius. He was last seen in 4.6 and may be imagined as having become separated from Lear and
Cordelia during the battle.
   204 SD Gonerill's ... out See collation. Muir
believes Q is right, allowing time for Albany's
order to be obeyed. But Q's SD occurs at an awkward
moment; in F, only a brief pause is needed, and
'This judgement of the heavens' (205) becomes
immediately visual. The business is unfortunately
often cut, destroying the tragic reprise of 1.1 when
Lear enters (Bratton, p. 209; compare Granville-
Barker, p. 277).
   205–6 This judgement ... pity i.e. this divine
retribution is terrible (in swiftness and finality), but
it does not evoke sorrow or compassion (since the
victims deserved their fate).

> Touches us not with pity. – O, is this he?
> [*To Kent*] The time will not allow the compliment
> Which very manners urges.

KENT   I am come
>   To bid my king and master aye good night.
>   Is he not here?

ALBANY   Great thing of us forgot!   210
>   Speak, Edmond; where's the king, and where's Cordelia?
>   Seest thou this object, Kent?

KENT   Alack, why thus?

EDMOND   Yet Edmond was beloved.
>   The one the other poisoned for my sake,
>   And after slew herself.   215

ALBANY   Even so. – Cover their faces.

EDMOND   I pant for life. Some good I mean to do,
>   Despite of mine own nature. Quickly send –
>   Be brief in it – to th'castle; for my writ
>   Is on the life of Lear and on Cordelia.   220
>   Nay, send in time.

ALBANY   Run, run, O run!

EDGAR   To who, my lord? – Who has the office? Send
>   Thy token of reprieve.

---

206 us] F, Q; *not in* Q2   206–8 O ... urges.] F *lineation; two lines divided* allow / The *and with* SH *Alb.* / *before* O (*see 5.3.203 n.*) Q   206 is this] F; 'tis Q   207 SD] *Hanmer; not in* Q, F   208 Which] F; that Q   208–9 I ... night.] F *lineation; one line* Q   210–12 Great ... Kent?] F, Q *lineation; as prose* Q2   210 thing] F, Q; things Q2   213–15 Yet ... herself.] F, Q *lineation; as prose* Q2   217–21 I ... time.] F, Q *lineation; as prose* Q2   218 mine] F; my Q   219 Be brief in it – to th'] F; Be briefe, int toth' Q; bee briefe, into the Q2   222–3 To ... reprieve.] *As in* Q; *divided* Office? / Send F, Q2   222 has] F; hath Q

206 O ... he Albany finally sees Kent.

207–8 The time ... urges Events do not permit the ceremony of greeting which mere courtesy demands.

208–9 I am ... night Kent is not interested in ceremony; he is concerned only to see Lear.

210 Great ... forgot Events before and after the battle have distracted Albany from concern for Lear and Cordelia. Kent's reminder, however, does not lead to immediate action. Albany questions Edmond, but then directs Kent's gaze to the bodies of Gonerill and Regan which, in Q, are brought out here. In F, something else apparently motivates Albany's interrupted response, 'some sudden eruption of concern within himself' (Urkowitz, p. 119), or 'involvement with his own repressed feeling' of love for Gonerill (Rosenberg, p. 309). But Shakespeare may simply have made a characteristic minor slip, one scarcely noticed in the theatre.

Whatever the case, Albany reveals an inability from here on to take effective and timely action, which justifies his relinquishment of the throne at the end. (Compare 144–51 n. and 151 n.above.)

212 this object i.e. the bodies of Gonerill and Regan; 'object' = sight, spectacle.

213–16 Yet Edmond ... faces Edmond's boast there as at 202–3 deeply wounds Albany, who utters a terse 'Even so'. Then, before ordering their faces covered, 'Reminded of his great love, great hurt, he takes one last look' (Rosenberg, p. 310).

215 after afterwards, later.

219 Be brief i.e. don't waste time.

220 on against.

221–3 Run ... reprieve Albany's exhortation to Edgar shows turmoil and confusion; it remains for the younger man again to take charge and get from Edmond the important details.

EDMOND   Well thought on. Take my sword. The captain,
           Give it the captain.

EDGAR   Haste thee for thy life.   225

                                              [*Exit an Officer*]

EDMOND   He hath commission from thy wife and me
           To hang Cordelia in the prison and
           To lay the blame upon her own despair,
           That she fordid herself.

ALBANY   The gods defend her. Bear him hence a while.   230

                                              [*Edmond is borne off*]

Enter LEAR *with* CORDELIA *in his arms* [*and the* OFFICER *following*]

LEAR   Howl, howl, howl, howl! O, you are men of stones.
         Had I your tongues and eyes, I'd use them so,

224–5 Well . . . captain.] F, Q *lineation; one line* Q2   *224 sword. The captain,] *Oxford;* sword the Captaine Q; sword, Q2,
F   225 SH] F; *Duke.* Q; *Alb.* Q2   225 SD] *This edn; Exit the Gentleman / Oxford; not in* Q, F   226–8 He . . . despair] *As
verse* F, Q; *as prose* Q2   227–8 To . . . despair] F; *divided* lay / The Q   229 That . . . herself.] F, Q; *not in* Q2   230
SD.1 *Edmond . . . off*] *Theobald; not in* Q, F   230 SD.2 *and the* OFFICER *following*] *This edn; not in* Q, F   *231 Howl . . .
howl!] *As in* Q; F *omits one* howle   *231 you] Q; your F   232 I'd] F; I would Q

224 **The captain** See collation. Like Q2, F omits
these words, which Duthie, p. 424, believes the Q
compositor erred in setting up too soon and then
repeated in their proper place. More likely,
Compositor E was influenced by Q2, whose compositor tried to correct the syntax, save space (making
224–5 one line), and avoid what seemed to him an
awkward and unnecessary repetition. Edmond's
gasping repetition, however, is dramatically effective and helps make the next line metrically complete, though half an iamb in 224 is sacrificed.

225 SH EDGAR Q assigns this speech to Albany,
rightly according to Sisson, p. 244, and to Duthie,
p. 191, who argues (1) that Edmond gives Edgar his
sword, and (2) that Albany earlier bade him run to
the castle. But F revises or corrects Q, allowing
Edgar (who sends an officer with Edmond's
sword) more authority. Compare 221–3 n.;
Hunter; and 249 below, where the officer, not
Edgar, confirms Lear's boast.

228 **To lay . . . despair** In the sources, e.g.
Geoffrey of Monmouth, Cordeilla does commit
suicide years later. See p. 9 above.

229 **fordid** killed.

230 **Bear . . . while** Edmond no longer matters
(compare 269 below). He is borne off through one
door as Lear enters through another.

230 SD.2 *Enter . . . arms* This image, often
regarded as an inverted or secular pietà, is properly
not a 'prefiguration' but 'a representative event of
human history' (Brockbank, p. 14). Both Q and F

leave open the question of Cordelia's physical
state, although many editors prejudice readers by
following Rowe and inserting *dead* after CORDELIA.
The ambiguity of Cordelia's state is crucial, as
throughout the scene 'the audience continue to
alternate between hope and despair' (Peat, pp. 49,
51; compare E. A. J. Honigmann, *Myriad-Minded
Shakespeare*, 1989, pp. 90–2).

230 SD.2 *and . . . following* After repeated delays
in the reprieve, the officer has arrived too late. He
re-enters, trailing behind Lear (compare *Textual
Companion*, p. 539).

231 **Howl . . . howl** See collation. Compositor E
may have dropped the fourth 'howl' because the
line was too long for his stick. The fourth 'howl'
syllabically fills out the metre. In actual stage practice, however, 'howl' is not usually articulated as a
word but rather as 'a voiced pain, often an animal
ululation' (Rosenberg, p. 312; compare Bratton, p.
209).

231 **stones** i.e. insensitive as statues. The
onlookers are all stunned into frozen silence and
grief; in fact, the 'howls' are sometimes taken as
demands that they cry out (Rosenberg, p. 312).
Hunter believes the overall imagery is of a funerary
chapel or pantheon of statues. (Perhaps Compositor
E created another false plural, but elsewhere
Shakespeare uses similar plurals, e.g. *R3* 3.7.224:
'I am not made of stones.')

232 **eyes** i.e. used for weeping along with wailing;
or perhaps for lightning looks.

That heaven's vault should crack. She's gone for ever.
I know when one is dead and when one lives.
She's dead as earth.

                    [*He lays her down*]
                    Lend me a looking-glass;   235
If that her breath will mist or stain the stone,
Why then she lives.

KENT   Is this the promised end?

EDGAR   Or image of that horror?

ALBANY   Fall and cease.

LEAR   This feather stirs, she lives: if it be so,
It is a chance which does redeem all sorrows   240
That ever I have felt.

KENT   O my good master!

LEAR   Prithee, away.

EDGAR   'Tis noble Kent, your friend.

LEAR   A plague upon you murderers, traitors all.
I might have saved her; now she's gone for ever.

---

235 SD] *Oxford; not in* Q, F   236–7 If . . . lives] F, Q *lineation; one line* Q2   237 Why then she] F, Q; she then Q2
239–41 This . . . felt.] F, Q *lineation; as prose* Q2   239 stirs, she lives:] F; stirs she liues, Q; stirs; She lives!
Capell   241 O] F; A Q   243–8 A . . . thee.] F, Q *lineation; as prose* Q2   243 you murderers] F; your murderous Q;
you murdrous Q2

---

233 heaven's . . . crack Compare 3.2.1–9.

235–7 She's dead . . . lives Lear's oscillation
between belief that Cordelia is dead and hope that
she is not has led to controversy concerning whether
he is finally deluded or not. 'The tension here, and it
is the underlying tension in Lear until his death, lies
between an absolute knowledge that Cordelia is
dead, and an absolute inability to accept it'
(Stampfer, p. 2). Compare also 284–5 n. below.

235 Lend me a looking-glass The stage business from here through the next fifteen lines is
complicated and subject to various interpretation.
Someone may actually give Lear a glass (perhaps
one that Gonerill wears), or he hallucinates having
one about him. If he has a glass, why does he refer to
a feather four lines later, and where does it come
from? Again, he may fantasize or pluck a feather
from his garment or a plume from someone's helmet, as he earnestly tries to discover or restore some
sign of life, however faint. Much depends on how
the actor interprets Lear's state of mind and the
fluctuating madness that still afflicts him, understandably, given the shock of Cordelia's hanging.
Compare Meagher, pp. 248–9, 254–7; Rosenberg,
p. 314; Stampfer, pp. 2–3.

236 stone 'mirror of polished stone or crystal'
(Onions). Compare Webster, *The White Devil*

(1612), 5.2.38–40: 'Fetch a looking glasse, see if
his breath will not stain it; or pull out some feathers
from my pillow, and lay them to his lippes'
(Steevens). Webster   doubtless   recalled
Shakespeare's scene and was more explicit about
the feather.

237 promised end (1) Judgement Day, the end
of the world, (2) what Lear promised himself when
he divided his kingdom (Hunter), (3) the outcome
promised by what has occurred.

238 Or image . . . horror Edgar understands
Kent's question in sense (1); 'image' = likeness,
representation.

238 Fall and cease Vocatives: either (1) let
judgement come and all things end, or (2) may
Lear fall and cease to be (rather than continue living
a wretched existence) (Steevens).

239 This . . . lives Although most early editors
adopt F's punctuation, as here, Capell takes the first
clause as simply declarative and the second as a
joyous exclamation. Many editions (e.g. NS) follow.
But the line, which parallels 236–7, carries an
implied 'if' at the beginning. Lear's uncertainty
continues in the next lines, as he toils over
Cordelia's body.

Cordelia, Cordelia, stay a little. Ha?   245
What is't thou sayst? – Her voice was ever soft,
Gentle, and low, an excellent thing in woman. –
I killed the slave that was a-hanging thee.

OFFICER   'Tis true, my lords, he did.

LEAR   Did I not, fellow?
I have seen the day with my good biting falchion   250
I would have made them skip. I am old now,
And these same crosses spoil me. [*To Kent*] Who are you?
Mine eyes are not o'th'best, I'll tell you straight.

KENT   If fortune brag of two she loved and hated,
One of them we behold.   255

LEAR   This' a dull sight. Are you not Kent?

KENT   The same,
Your servant Kent. Where is your servant Caius?

LEAR   He's a good fellow, I can tell you that.
He'll strike, and quickly too. He's dead and rotten.

KENT   No, my good lord, I am the very man –   260

LEAR   I'll see that straight.

KENT   That from your first of difference and decay
Have followed your sad steps.

---

246 sayst] F, Q2; sayest Q   247 woman] F; women Q   *249 SH OFFICER] *Capell; Gent.* F; *Cap.* Q   249 my lords,] Q;
(my Lords) F   249–53 Did … straight.] F *lineation; as prose* Q2   249–51 Did … now,] *Lines end* … day, / … would /
… now, Q   250 have] F, Q; ha Q2   250 with my good] F, Q; that with my Q   *251 them] Q; him F   252 SD] *Oxford;
not in* Q, F   253 o'th'] F; othe Q   254 brag] F; bragd Q   254 and] F; or Q   256 This' … sight] F; *not in*
Q   *256 This'] *Schmidt 1879 (conj. S. Walker);* This is F   256 you not] F; not you Q   256–7 The … Caius?]
Capell's lineation; divided: Kent, / *Where* F; *one line* Q   258 you] F; *not in* Q   *260 man –*] *Pope;* man. Q, F   262
first] F; life Q

245 **Cordelia … little** The eloquence and
poignancy of this simple utterance are unsurpassed.

249 SH OFFICER See collation and compare 5.1.0
SD and 5.3.225 SD, 230 SD.2.

250–1 **I have … skip** Compare *Wiv.* 2.1.227–9,
Oth. 5.2.261–4.

250 **falchion** A hooked, or curved, sword.

251 **them** See collation: Q makes better sense.
Lear is speaking of his enemies generally, not
Cordelia's executioner (Duthie, p. 191). An easy
compositorial error.

252 **crosses** vexations, thwartings.

252 **spoil me** 'i.e. as a swordsman' (Muir).

253 **straight** straightaway.

254–5 **If … behold** Kent and Lear are looking at
each other; hence, 'the two objects of fortune's love
and her hate are, – himself, and his master …: of
these two, says the speaker, you (the person spoke

to) "behold" one, and I another' (Capell, cited by
Furness, NS).

256 **This'** This is.

256 **dull sight** Either (1) melancholy spectacle
(referring to Cordelia's body), or (2) poor eyesight
(Booth, pp. 31–2; compare 253 above).

256 **Are … Kent** Eyesight failing, Lear peers at
Kent and is briefly diverted from Cordelia. Failing
eyesight was a symptom of approaching death
(Bucknill, cited by Hoeniger (p. 96)).

257 **Where … Caius** Kent earnestly wants Lear
to make the connection. Compare 4.6.9 n.

261 **I'll … straight** I'll attend to that in a
moment's time. Lear is still preoccupied with
Cordelia. His 'welcome' (263) is similarly
peremptory.

262 **your … decay** the beginning of your change
and decline (of fortunes).

LEAR   You're welcome hither.

KENT   Nor no man else. All's cheerless, dark, and deadly.
      Your eldest daughters have fordone themselves   265
      And desperately are dead.

LEAR   Ay, so I think.

ALBANY   He knows not what he says, and vain is it
      That we present us to him.

Enter a MESSENGER

EDGAR   Very bootless.

MESSENGER   Edmond is dead, my lord.

ALBANY   That's but a trifle here.
      You lords and noble friends, know our intent.   270
      What comfort to this great decay may come
      Shall be applied. For us, we will resign
      During the life of this old majesty
      To him our absolute power; [*To Edgar and Kent*] you, to
          your rights,
      With boot, and such addition as your honours   275
      Have more than merited. All friends shall taste
      The wages of their virtue, and all foes
      The cup of their deservings. O see, see!

263 You're] *Pope;* You'r Q; Your are F   264 Nor … deadly.] *As in* Q; *two lines divided* else: / All's F   265 fordone] fore-done F; foredoome Q; foredoom'd Q2   266 Ay … think.] F; So thinke I to. Q   267 says] F; sees Q   267 is it] F; it is Q   268 SD] F; *Enter Captaine.* Q (*after* bootlesse)   269–78 That's … see!] F *lineation (except 276–7); as prose* Q   271 great] F; *not in* Q   274 SD] *Malone; not in* Q, F   275 honours] F; honor Q   276–7 Have … foes] *Pope's lineation; divided* shall / Taste F

263 **You're** See collation. F's sophistication has gone awry; Q's 'you'r' is metrically superior. Compare Duthie, p. 379, and 231 above.

264 **Nor … else** i.e. no one else deserves your welcome if I don't. On double negatives, see Abbott 406. Some editors follow Rowe and continue from Kent's preceding lines: 'I am the very man … and no one else.' Booth believes the reference is 'unfixed and multiple … a vague and syntactically unattached comment on the general scene' (p. 32).

265 **fordone** killed. Q 'foredoome' may be a misreading of 'foredoone' (Duthie, p. 425), or possibly 'foredoomd'.

266 **desperately** in despair.

266 **Ay … think** Although the bodies of Gonerill and Regan are on stage (204 SD), Lear, intent on Cordelia, has paid no attention to them. He may glance at them here before falling silent, tranced perhaps, certainly bemused (compare 278 n.).

268 **bootless** useless.

270 **know our intent** Again, the wheel comes

full circle. Compare 1.1.32 ff. (NS).

270 **our** Albany uses the royal plural appropriately throughout this speech.

271 **great decay** i.e. Lear, whose physical and mental decline is increasingly apparent. Compare 'noble ruin', i.e. Antony, *Ant.* 3.10.18 (NS).

275 **boot** something additional.

275 **addition** title; quibbling on 'boot'.

275 **honours** i.e. honourable deeds, conduct.

276–8 **All … deservings** Albany's peroration appears suitable for the end of a tragedy (compare *Mac.* 5.9.26–41). But Shakespeare has more. Compare J. K. Walton, 'Lear's last speech', *S.Sur.* 13 (1960), 17, and John Shaw, '*King Lear*: the final lines', *Essays in Criticism*, 16 (1966), 262–3.

278 **O see, see** Some piece of stage business refocuses everyone's attention on Lear. Perhaps, having momentarily fallen into a tranced or tranquil state (266 n.), he awakens abruptly and, rocking Cordelia in his arms, has begun speaking to her.

LEAR   And my poor fool is hanged. No, no, no life?
            Why should a dog, a horse, a rat have life,   280
            And thou no breath at all? Thou'lt come no more,
            Never, never, never, never, never.
            Pray you, undo this button. Thank you, sir.
            Do you see this? Look on her! Look, her lips.
            Look there, look there.   *He dies*
EDGAR   He faints. My lord, my lord!   285
KENT   Break, heart, I prithee break.
EDGAR   Look up, my lord.
KENT   Vex not his ghost. O, let him pass. He hates him
            That would upon the rack of this tough world
            Stretch him out longer.
EDGAR   He is gone indeed.
KENT   The wonder is he hath endured so long.   290
            He but usurped his life.
ALBANY   Bear them from hence. Our present business
            Is general woe. Friends of my soul, you twain
            Rule in this realm and the gored state sustain.

279–83 And ... sir.] F *lineation; as prose* Q   279 No, no, no] F; no, no Q   280 have] F; of Q   281 Thou'lt] F; O thou
wilt Q   282 Never ... never.] F; neuer, neuer, neuer, Q   283 Pray you] F, Q; pray Q2   283 sir.] F; sir, O, o, o. Q; sir,
O, o, o, o. Q2   284–5 Do ... there.] F; *not in* Q   284 this? Look] F *corr.*; this, looke F *uncorr.*   *284 her!] her?
F   285 SD] F; *not in* Q   286 SH KENT] F; *Lear.* Q   287–9 Vex ... longer.] F *lineation; lines end* ... passe, / ... wracke, /
... longer. Q   287 hates him] F, Q; hates him much Q2   289 He] F; O he Q   293 Is] F; Is to Q   294 realm] F;
kingdome Q   294 gored] F, Q; good Q2

279 And ... hanged Lear appears to be in mid
sentence. Since 'fool' was a common term of
endearment, most commentators believe Lear
refers to Cordelia (see Furness). But his term inevi-
tably recalls the Fool, last seen in 3.6, whom he also
loved. Moreover, the actor who played Cordelia
probably doubled as the Fool. (See p. 13 above,
and compare Bradley, p. 314; Rosenberg, p. 318,
Booth, pp. 32–3).

283 Pray ... button Compare 3.4.97 n.
Although Lear may ask help to undo Cordelia's
button, most commentators believe he is suffering
a final attack of the 'mother' and wants the button at
his own throat loosened. Kent obliges. (Q follows
with death groans.)

284–5 Do ... there In 1.1, Lear, egocentric,
demanded that everyone's attention be focused
upon himself, as he asked his daughters publicly
to declare their love. Here, finally, he directs attention not to himself, but to the Other, to Cordelia,
now more precious to him than his own life.

285–6 He ... lord Edgar rushes to assist Lear,
trying to revive him, until he gives up at 289.

286 SH KENT See collation, and Textual
Analysis, p. 81 above. 'What Shakespeare has
done in revising is to transfer Lear's ultimate
Quarto line ... to Kent, thus utterly altering action,
character, context, and significance' (Clayton, p.
135). Bradley, p. 309, suggests that Kent refers to
his own heart.

287 ghost i.e. departing spirit. Medieval and
Renaissance iconography typically depicts the spirit
of a person departing at the point of death.

288 rack A torture machine upon which the
victim was bound and stretched, forcing his limbs
to become dislocated. Hunter believes 'tough' suggests 'rack' = the body, which encloses the spirit
while a person lives. Lear's corporeal strength was
great: compare 248–51.

289 longer (1) for a longer time, (2) with his body
stretched further on the rack (Muir).

291 usurped stole (*OED* Usurp *v* 3).

294 gored bleeding, wounded.

KENT　I have a journey, sir, shortly to go: 295

　　　　My master calls me; I must not say no.

EDGAR　The weight of this sad time we must obey,

　　　　Speak what we feel, not what we ought to say.

　　　　The oldest hath borne most; we that are young

　　　　Shall never see so much, nor live so long. 300

　　　　　　　　　　Exeunt with a dead march

---

296 calls me;] F; cals, and Q　**297** SH] F; *Duke.* Q　**299** hath] F; haue Q

297 SH EDGAR See collation. Albany, the survivor with highest rank, would ordinarily utter the concluding lines. But Edgar owes him a reply, and the speech otherwise suits the younger man, especially as F alters his role: see Textual Analysis, p. 65.

297 weight heavy burden (sadness was 'heavy').

297 obey submit to, comply with.

298 we Perhaps the royal plural, as Edgar puts on the crown (Rosenberg, p. 323). Alternatively, the pronoun may include Albany, whose 'design of uncertainty' implies youth.

300 SD *dead march* 'A piece of solemn music played at a funeral procession, *esp.* at a military funeral; a funeral march' (*OED* Dead *adj* D.2).

TEXTUAL ANALYSIS, PART 2

Q has approximately 300 lines not in F, and F has about 100 lines not in Q. First, the longer Q passages omitted from F are here examined in detail (a) to determine what range of reasons there might have been for cutting them; (b) to trace connections between passages which might suggest comprehensive revision; and (c) to weigh the advantages and disadvantages of restoring them to the present modernized, Folio-based text. So that readers may consult the materials fully, all Q-only passages are presented (in edited form) in an Appendix, pp. 273–89 below. In the analyses that follow, most passages are shown in slightly reduced photo-facsimile; but for longer passages, especially those that do not involve complex bibliographical problems, the reader must refer to the Appendix. Analyses of F-only passages follow the section of Q-only passages.

Q-Only Passages

A number of these passages have been discussed in Part 1 of the Textual Analysis (pp. 50–78 above), but others require analysis, sometimes in conjunction with those previously considered. The lines in question are enclosed by square brackets in the facsimile reproductions.

(i) After 1.2.85:

> *Glost.* He cannot be such a monster.
> [*Bast.* Nor is not sure.
> *Glost.* To his father, that so tenderly and intirely loues him,
> heauen and earth!]*Edmund* seeke him out, wind mee into him, I
> pray you frame your busines after your own wisedome, I would
> vnstate my selfe to be in a due resolution.

The omission from F appears deliberate, not accidental on the part of Compositor B, who set the passage. Theatrical cuts this early in the text are rare, and the column that B was setting on signature qq3^v shows signs of crowding later on. On the other hand, the lines are not indispensable; moreover, another cut of several lines (complemented by a Folio addition, lines 96–100) occurs at 125. In view of these other alterations suggesting revision, the lines here may have been deleted by a reviser.

(ii)   After 1.2.125:

> *Edg.* Doe you bufie your felfe about that?
> *Baf.* I promife you the effects he writ of, fucceed vnhappily,
> [as of vnnaturalneffe betweene the child and the parent, death,
> dearth, diffolutions of ancient amities, diuifions in ftate, mena-
>
> ces and maledictions againft King and nobles, needles diffiden-
> ces, banifhment of friёds, diffipation of Cohorts, nuptial breach-
> es, and I know not what.
> *Edg.* How long haue you beene a fectary Aftronomicall?
> *Baf.* Come, come, when faw you my father laft?
> *Edg.* Why, the night gon by.

Since these lines essentially repeat Gloucester's speech 96 ff., added in F, they are unnecessary here. Folio lineation, moreover, suggests that a cut has been made:

> *Edg.* Do you bufie your felfe with that?
> *Baft.* I promife you, the effects he writes of, fucceede
> vnhappily.
> When faw you my Father laft?
> *Edg.* The night gone by.

(iii)   After 1.3.16:

> *Gon.* Put on what wearie negligence you pleafe, you and your
> fellow feruants, i'de haue it come in queftion, if he diflike it, let
> him to our fifter, whofe mind and mine I know in that are one,
> [not to be ouerruld; idle old man that ftill would manage thofe
> authorities that hee hath giuen away, now by my life old fooles
> are babes again, & muft be vs'd with checkes as flatteries, when
> they are feene abufd] remember what I tell you.
> *Gent.* Very well Madam.
> *Gon.* And let his Knights haue colder looks among you, what
> growes of it no matter, aduife your fellowes fo, I would breed
> from hence occafions, and I fhall. that I may fpeake, ile write
> ftraight to my fifter to hould my very courfe, goe prepare for
> dinner.   *Exit.*

Two cuts in this passage are complemented by additions in the following scene. These alterations and others affect Gonerill's character in ways described above (p. 63); furthermore, local alterations, e.g. F 'Remember what I have said' (17) for Q 'remember what I tell you', also point to a revising hand.

(iv)   After 1.4.119 (see Textual Analysis, Part 1, pp. 68–9 above).

E. K. Chambers (1: 467) suggests that censorship as well as theatrical abridgement may be responsible for the F omission. The overt satirical reference to monopolies was dangerous under James I, especially in the bawdy context the Fool describes, and censorship or the threat of it may have intervened. But after developing the argument for censorship at length, Taylor ('Censorship', pp. 101–9) concedes that the passage as abbreviated in F 'makes good dramatic sense' and does not argue for restoration of Q's lines, as he does for 'Fut' at 1.2.115 ('Censorship', p. 110). If censorship was imposed, Shakespeare could have recast the passage, but evidently he or his fellows found it was better left out. Compare Kerrigan, pp. 218–19, who notes revisions elsewhere, such as the reassigned speech headings at 91 and 189, and changes in the Fool's psychology. For Compositor E's failure to delete the first three lines of the passage, see above, pp. 68–9.

(v) After 1.4.190 (see Textual Analysis, Part 1, p. 64 above).

As Urkowitz notes ('Editorial tradition', p. 34), Capell was the first to suggest that Shakespeare was responsible for revising this passage, a position supported by, for example, Kerrigan, p. 220. He argues that F's assignment of 190 to the Fool complements the cut and highlights 'Lear's shadow'. Although Q is good, F is better: 'it opens a gap between "Lear's shadow" and "Your name …" which is both painful and unignorable. The poetic space can scarcely be played across. Within it, the Fool's words resonate.'

(vi) After 2.2.128:

```
   Glost. Let me beseech your Grace not to doe so,
[ His fault is much, and the good King his maister
  VVill check him for't, your purpose low correction
  Is such, as basest and temnest wretches for pilfrings
  And most common trespasses are punisht with,]
  The King must take it ill, that hee's so slightly valued
  In his messenger, should haue him thus restrained.
      Duke. Ile answer that.
      Reg. My sister may receiue it much more worse,
  To haue her Gentlemen abus'd, assalted
[ For following her affaires, put in his legges,]
  Come my good Lord away?
```

Duthie, p. 174, believes that the first cut of four and a half lines is deliberate, and the patch (with appropriate relineation) is expert (compare Stone, p. 235). Revision appears to be at work here. The lines are not essential to the action, although they spell out the situation in fuller detail and show Gloucester pleading more earnestly. F also lacks a line after 133, which Duthie, p. 175, calls a compositor error. Since F otherwise alters Q, giving the next half-line to Cornwall (instead of continuing it as part of Regan's speech) and dropping 'good' from the term of address, the changes again seem to indicate revision.

(vii) After 2.4.17:

Q: *Kent.* It is both he and fhee, your fonne & daugter.
    Lear. No.   *Kent.* Yes.
    Lear. No I fay,   *Kent.* I fay yea.
  [*Lear.* No no,they would not. *Kent.* Yes they haue.]
    Lear. By *Iupiter* I fweare no,they durft not do't,
They would not, could not do't,tis worfe then murder,

F: *Kent.* It is both he and fhe,
   Your Son,and Daughter.
     Lear. No.
     Kent. Yes.
     Lear. No I fay.
     Kent. I fay yea.
     Lear. By *Iupiter* I fweare no,

  [*Kent.* By *Iuno*,I fweare I,]
    Lear. They durft not do't:
They could not,would not do't : 'tis worfe then murther,

F omits two brief speeches and adds one – Kent's oath, introduced to parallel Lear's. Evidently the cut was made to allow for the addition, although some editors (e.g. Duthie, Muir) have found the speeches so impressive that they conflate. But, as Michael Warren says, conflation has no authority – unless, of course, we assume the collator accidentally skipped Q's crowded line. But within the puerile, see-saw argument between Lear and Kent, effective for three interchanges in either Q or F, a fourth seems tedious and unnecessary. Finally, if F's additional line was accidentally omitted by the Q compositor as well, a remarkable coincidence of errors results – possible, but unlikely.

(viii) After 3.1.7:

  Gent. Contending with the fretfull element,
Bids the wind blow the earth into the fea,
Or fwell the curled waters boue the maine   (haire,
That things might change or ceafe, fteares his white
Which the impetuous blafts with eyles rage
Catch in their furie,and make nothing of,
Striues in his little world of man to outfcorne,
The too and fro confli333ting wind and raine,
This night wherin the cub-drawne Beare would couch,
The Lyon,and the belly pinched Wolfe
Keepe their furre dry, vnbonneted he runnes,
And bids what will take all.]

The eight and a half lines missing from F represent theatrical abridgement, reducing the prominence Q gives the Gentleman. Moreover, the action he describes occurs in the immediately following scene. Duthie, p. 8, compares it to the cut at 5.3.195.

(ix)   After 3.1.13:

Q: *Kent*, Sir I doe know you,
       And dare vpon the warrant of my Arte,
       Commend a deare thing to you, there is diuifion,.
       Although as yet the face of it be couer'd,
       With mutuall cunning, twixt *Albany* and *Cornwall*
       But true it is, from *France* there comes a power
       Into this fcattered kingdome, who alreadie wife in our
       Haue fecret feet in fome of our beft Ports, (negligéce,
       And are at point to fhew their open banner.
       Now to you, if on my credit you dare build fo farre,
       To make your fpeed to Douer, you fhall find
       Some that will thanke you, making iuft report
       Of how vnnaturall and bemadding forrow
       The King hath caufe to plaine,
       I am a Gentleman of blood and breeding,
       And from fome knowledge and affurance,
       Offer this office to you.
           Gent. I will talke farther with you.
           Kent, No doe not,

F: *Kent*. Sir, I do know you,
       And dare vpon the warrant of my note
       Commend a deere thing to you. There is diuifion
       (Although as yet the face of it is couer'd
       With mutuall cunning) 'twixt Albany, and Cornwall:
       Who haue, as who haue not, that their great Starres
       Thron'd and fet high; Seruants, who feeme no leffe,
       Which are to France the Spies and Speculations
       Intelligent of our State. What hath bin feene,
       Either in fnuffes, and packings of the Dukes.
       Or the hard Reine which both of them hath borne
       Againft the old kinde King; or fomething deeper,
       Whereof (perchance) thefe are but furnifhings.
           Gent. I will talke further with you.
           Kent. No, do not:

Here is an instance (compare vii above) not of simple abridgement but of substitution (see p. 64). Both sets of lines are Shakespearean, although the Folio lines are in a style more typical of Shakespeare's later work. Combining the passages, however, not only gives Kent an inordinately long speech but, as Urkowitz notes, introduces difficulties not found in either Q or F. For example, in Q, France does not know of the king's mistreatment by his daughters and needs to be told, so Kent sends the Gentleman to Dover with the news; in F, France already knows, and Kent does not need to (and therefore does not) send the Gentleman to Dover; in the composite text, France has the news, and Kent sends the Gentleman to Dover with it anyway. Finally, although they include mention of French spies, the Folio lines eliminate a reference to French invasion and thus form part of a pattern of cuts that downplay this aspect of the plot (see above, pp. 66–7; on fragmented syntax, see Commentary notes to 3.1.14–15 and 20).

(x)   After 3.6.14 (see Appendix, pp. 277–9 below, xii).

The omission of the 'mock trial' episode in F has aroused considerable controversy. Some scholars have argued for authorial revision, though the effect or rather the value of the cut in dramatic terms is debatable. For example, Roger Warren maintains that the omission of Lear's mad trial of Gonerill and Regan not only tightens the dramatic structure, but avoids duplication of Lear's mock justice in Act 4. Moreover, cutting the mad trial in 3.6 hurries the action forward to the 'thing itself', that is, the insane enactment of justice that immediately follows in 3.7, the trial and sentencing of Gloucester. But these putative gains may not be worth the loss of what, in the theatre, is a most impressive piece of drama. The parallel with events in 3.7 is sharp: the madness in 3.6 contrasts with the diabolical cruelty in 3.7. Furthermore, the quarto version of 3.6 completes Lear's descent into madness; the king does not appear again until much later in Act 4. Without appreciably shortening performance time (35 lines), removing the mock trial foreshortens a process that Lear has been struggling to contain since the end of Act 1. If Shakespeare was responsible for this cut, he may have had reason, as Warren argues, for his alterations. But authors – even Shakespeare – are not always the best judges of their own work, and theatre directors (who are notorious for making alterations of their own, regardless of whose play it is) seldom cut the mock trial in 3.6.

(xi)   After 3.6.53 (see Appendix, pp. 279–80 below, xiii–xiv).

Better arguments can be made for cuts at the end of 3.6 – Kent's meditation on the sleeping king and Edgar's soliloquy – than for the omission of the mock trial. The argument for swiftly juxtaposing events in 3.6 with those in 3.7 is more pertinent here; moreover, the sense of urgency in Gloucester's begging the group to flee is enhanced. The effect of the Fool's last line, 'And I'll go to bed at noon', added in F, is not diluted by Kent's urging him to help carry Lear off. On the contrary, by ignoring the Fool, Kent and the others allow him to remain isolated and alone, overwhelmed by everything that has happened and now utterly spent.

   Edgar's sententious closing soliloquy is also, in a more obvious sense, dispensable. As Granville-Barker says, the lines lower the dramatic tension and thus may adversely affect the following scene of Gloucester's blinding. The soliloquy is better postponed to the beginning of Act 4, especially if an act-interval comes at that point. Michael Warren has shown, moreover, that the omission of these lines paradoxically enhances Edgar's role, giving his opening soliloquy in 4.1, expanded in F, greater prominence. This prominence gains further by the deletion of the servants' dialogue at the end of 3.7. Indeed, Warren shows how other alterations in F affecting Edgar's role significantly change it in ways that traditionally conflated editions obscure ('Albany and Edgar', pp. 103–4; compare xxiv, pp. 259–60 below, on the cut at 5.3.195). Furthermore, there appears to be in F a consistent pattern in reducing the passages of moral commentary found in Q. Altogether, these alterations suggest revision as well as theatrical abridgement.

(xii)   After 3.7.97 (see Appendix, p. 280 below, xv).

F's omission of the servants' dialogue (nine lines) reduces the number of minor speaking parts, hurries the action to the next scene, and, like the omission of Edgar's soliloquy in 3.6, eliminates reflective commentary (see Doran, pp. 71, 77; Stone, p. 236). Moreover, as Urkowitz notes, p. 51, the servant's plan (to get Tom o'Bedlam to help Gloucester) conflicts with what actually happens in 4.1: the Old Man enters leading the earl, and the meeting with Poor Tom is accidental and in many ways ironic. If an interval was inserted at this point between Acts 3 and 4, the effect achieved in Q of juxtaposing Edgar's entrance and the compassion of the servants would be nullified, as Williams says; hence, the loss of their dialogue is of less consequence. But Granville-Barker, p. 331, regards the piece of dialogue as 'significant' and worth retaining.

(xiii) After 4.1.58:

> *Edg.* Both ftile and gate, horfe-way, and foot-path,
> Poore *Tom* hath beene fcard out of his good wits,
> Bleffe the good man from the foule fiend,
> [Fiue fiends haue beene in poore *Tom* at once,
>   Of luft, as *Obidicut, Hobbididence* Prince of dumbnes,
>   *Mahu* of ftealing, *Modo* of murder, *Stiberdigebit* of
>   Mobing, & *Mobing* who fince poffeffes chamber maids
> And waiting women, fo, bleffe thee maifter.]

Edgar's identity as Poor Tom is by now well established and does not require further ravings of the kind extensively presented in Act 3; or, as Stone says, 'the reviser probably felt there was more in this speech than was dramatically justified' (p. 236).

(xiv) After 4.2.33 (see Appendix, pp. 281–3 below, xvii–xix).

Theatrical abridgement may have prompted the extensive cuts from Albany's and Gonerill's quarrel in this scene, but combined with the cuts, additions, and alterations elsewhere (see above, pp. 63–4), they seriously affect the ethos of these characters and suggest authorial revision. Several local emendations in the Folio text, especially at the entrance of Albany, tend to confirm this view.

(xv) After Act 4, Scene 2 (see Appendix, pp. 284–6 below, xx).

Theatrical abridgement again probably occasioned an extensive cut (56 lines) of expository but inessential material – an entire scene (see above, p. 66, and compare Doran, p. 70; Duthie, p. 8). The cut, however, along with other cuts in Acts 4 and 5, reduces the role of Kent and helps bring Edgar and Cordelia into greater prominence (Warren, 'Diminution', pp. 66–8). It also reduces the amount of moral commentary found in Q. Removing the scene resolves several dramatic problems, such as questions regarding Lear's actual whereabouts and his attitude towards Cordelia (Urkowitz, pp. 53–4). Compare Granville-Barker, p. 332: 'I could better believe that Shakespeare cut [the scene] than wrote it.'

(xvi) After 4.5.188:

Q: *Lear.* No feconds, all my felfe, why this would make a man
of falt to vfe his eyes for garden waterpots, I and laying Autumns
duft.
>   *Lear.* I will die brauely like a bridegroome, what ? I will be
> Iouiall, come, come, I am a King my maifters, know you that.
>   *Gent.* You are a royall one, and we obey you.
>   *Lear.* Then theres life int, nay and you get it you fhall get it
> with running.   *Exit King running.*

Q2:   *Lear.* No feconds, all my felfe : why this would make a man
       of falt to vfe his eyes for garden water-pottes, I and laying Au-
       tumnes duft.   *Gent.* Good Sir.
          Lear. I will dye brauely like a Bridegroome. What, I will bee
       iouiall : Come, come, I am a King my mafters, know you that ?
          Gent. You are a royall one, and we obey you.
          Lear. Then theres life int, nay if you get it you fhall get it
       with running.   *Exit King running.*

F: *Lear.* No Seconds ? All my felfe?
       Why, this would make a man, a man of Salt
       To vfe his eyes for Garden water-pots. I wil die brauely,
       Like a fmugge Bridegroome. What ? I will be Iouiall :
       Come, come, I am a King, Mafters, know you that ?
          Gent. You are a Royall one, and we obey you.
          Lear. Then there's life in't. Come, and you get it,
       You fhall get it by running : Sa, fa, fa, fa.   *Exit.*

At first, Greg rejected Daniel's conjecture that the anomalous Q2 insertion may
derive from a variant, corrected state of sheet 1 (no longer extant) in the exemplar of
Q that served as copy for Q2 (*Variants*, pp. 188–90). Later he reluctantly reconsidered the possibility (Postscript, in *ibid.*, p. 192). Whether or not the Gentleman's
speech originally stood in the copy for Q remains uncertain, since a press-corrector,
seeing the error in two consecutive speeches by Lear, could have added it independently of copy; or the Q2 compositor could have added it (for the same reason). But
either of these hypotheses seems less likely than that it was in the original manuscript. F was not here influenced by Q2. Working on an exemplar of Q with
uncorrected sheet 1, the F reviser or collator solved the problem of Lear's consecutive speeches by fusing them, but left the lines metrically irregular. (See
Commentary 4.5.186–91 and compare Taylor, 'Date and authorship', pp. 363–4,
and Duthie, pp. 415–16.) Stone, p. 236, believes the reviser omitted the line after
188 because he found it obscure.

(xvii) After 4.5.257:

Q: your labour, your wite (fo I would fay) your affectionate feruant
      [and for you her owne for *Venter*] *Gonorill.*
         Edg. O Indiftinguifht fpace of womans wit,

Q2:   *And fupply the place for your labour.*
             Your wife (fo I would fay) & your affectionate feruant,
                                                                Gonorill.

      Edg. O vndiftinguifht fpace of womans wit,

F: *ply the place for your Labour.*
                    Your (Wife, so I would say) affectio-
                          nate Servant . Gonerill.
          Oh indinguifh'd fpace of Womans will,

Both Q2 and F omit Q's words 'and for you her owne for *Venter*', perhaps because they were incomprehensible (Stone, pp. 132, 146). Duthie, p. 416, regards Q's words as an actor's mangled interpolation; citing 4.2.20, Muir thinks the words may conceal sense; Halio, p. 162, suspects that a word such as 'life' may have dropped out after 'owne' in Q. Unlike xvi above, the passage appears on variant sheet K but is found in all extant copies of Q. The different emendations in Q2 and F suggest that both the Q2 editor or compositor and the F reviser or collator independently deleted the nonsense line.

(xviii) After 4.6.25:

Gent. Good madam be by, when we do awake him
I doubt not of his temperance.
[*Cord.* Very well.
[*Doct.* Pleafe you draw neere, louder the muficke there,]
   Cor. O my deer father reftoratiõ hang thy medicin on my lips,
And let this kis repaire thofe violent harmes that my two fifters
Haue in thy reuerence made.
   Kent. Klnd and deere Princeffe,
Cord. Had you not bene their father thefe white flakes,
Had challengd pitie of them, was this a face

To be expofd againft the warring winds,
[To ftand againft the deepe dread bolted thunder,
In the moft terrible and nimble ftroke
Of quick croffe lightning to watch poore *Per du,*
With this thin helmdmine iniurious dogge,
Though he had bit me, fhould haue ftood that night
Againft my fire, and waft thou faine poore father,

The first cut may have been prompted by changed playhouse conditions (see above, pp. 67–8). However, music in Shakespeare often accompanies scenes of restored harmony, as in *MND* 5.1.395–400, *MV* 5.1.55 ff., *WT* 5.3.98. Perhaps on reflection Shakespeare now preferred silence at Lear's awakening (Taylor, 'Date and authorship', p. 413). The second cut of three and a half inessential though eloquent lines results in an irregular line caused, as Stone thinks, by a reviser's oversight and the copyist's subsequent attempt to avoid an obviously short line (p. 118, n. 10; see the play-text, p. 221 above).

(xix) After 4.6.78:

   Doct. Be comforted good Madame, the great rage you fee is
cured in him, and yet it is danger to make him euen ore the time
hee has loft, defire him to goe in, trouble him no more till further fetling.   *Cord.* Wilt pleafe your highnes walke?

Duthie, pp. 419–20, suspects that the F compositor (B) is responsible for dropping these lines through eye-skip or faulty comprehension (compare Stone, p. 236). But considerable cutting follows afterwards (see below) and the alteration F 'killed' for Q 'cured' suggests revision, although the verse lines in F (see the play-text, p. 224 above) remain irregular.

(xx) After 4.6.82 (see Appendix, p. 287 below, xxiv).

F omits a dozen lines of dialogue here between Kent and the Gentleman, a cut 'precisely analogous' to those at the end of 3.6 and 3.7 (Stone, p. 237). The dialogue is about Cornwall's death, Kent's supposed whereabouts (he is still in disguise), and the impending battle between Cordelia's army and her sisters'. Urkowitz, pp. 54–5, notes how the elimination of these lines juxtaposes more sharply contrasting stage pictures: the 'gentle pageant of physical and familial restoration' that ends 4.6 and 'the harsh conjunction of authority and violence' that begins 5.1. But again, if an interval was inserted between the acts, this effect would be lost, or at least diminished. The deletion, however, obviates a potential inconsistency: Cordelia addresses Kent at the beginning of the scene in the presence of the Gentleman, who in the missing lines apparently does not know whom he is addressing.

(xxi) After 5.1.11:

> *Reg.* But haue you neuer found my brothers way,
> To the forfended place?   [*Bast.* That thought abufes you.
>   *Reg.* I am doubtfull that you haue beene coniunct and bo-
> fom'd with hir,as far as we call hirs.]
>   *Bast.* No by mine honour Madam.   (with her.
>   *Reg.* I neuer fhall indure hir, deere my Lord bee not familiar
>   *Bast.* Feare me not, fhee and the Duke her husband.
>   *Enter Albany and Gonorill with troupes.*
> [*Gono.* I had rather loofe the battaile, then that fifter fhould
> loofen him and mee.]
>   *Alb.* Our very louing fifter well be-met
> For this I heare the King is come to his daughter
> With others,whome the rigour of our ftate
> Forft to crie out,[where I could not be honeft
> I neuer yet was valiant, for this bufines
> It touches vs, as France inuades our land
> Not bolds the King, with others whome I feare,
> Moft iuft and heauy caufes make oppofe.
>   *Bast.* Sir you fpeake nobly.]   *Reg.* Why is this reafon'd?
>   *Gono.* Combine togither gainft the enemy,
> For thefe domeftique dore particulars
> Are not to queftion here.
>   *Alb.* Let vs then determine with the auntient of warre on our
> proceedings.   [*Bast.* I fhall attend you prefently at your tent.]
>   *Reg.* Sifter you I goe with vs?   *Gon.* No.
>   *Reg.* Tis moft conuenient, pray you goe with vs.
>   K 3   *Gon.*

Stone, p. 237, regards these cuts as 'deliberate pruning', as in 2.2 and 4.2, although he
recognizes that the last one may be the result of copyist or compositor error. The most
significant cut is the longest one, where Albany says he will fight because the French
invade, not because he opposes Lear. Without these lines, Albany in F appears less
sure of his stance – a weakening of his character that correlates with cuts earlier in Act
4 (see above). When Regan interrupts him impatiently, her line means something
different in F from what it means in Q, where she questions why Albany is moralizing
over a decision already made; in F, she asks why he is raising a new issue (Urkowitz, p.
99). The earlier cuts remove some slackness and gratuitous comment from the
dialogue.

(xxii) After 5.3.35:

> *Baſt.* About it, and write happy when thou haſt don,
> Marke I ſay inſtantly, and carie it ſo
> As I haue ſet it downe.
> *Cap.* [I cannot draw a cart, nor eate dride oats,
> If it bee mans workĝile do't.

The Captain's lines are a distracting and unnecessary bit of grim humour. Compare
Stone, p. 237.

(xxiii) After 5.3.53:

> *Baſt.* Sir I thought it fit,
> To ſend the old and miſerable King to ſome retention, and ap-
> Whoſe age has charmes in it, whoſe title more.   (pointed guard,
> To pluck the common boſſome of his ſide,
> And turne our impreſt launces in our eyes
> Which doe commaund them, with him I ſent the queen
> My reaſon, all the ſame and they are readie to morrow,
> Or at further ſpace, to appeare where you ſhall hold
> Your ſeſſion at this time, wee ſweat and bleed,
> The friend hath loſt his friend and the beſt quarrels
> In the heat are curſt, by thoſe that feele their ſharp nes,
> The queſtion of *Cordelia* and her father
> Requires a fitter place.]
> *Alb.* Sir by your patience,
> I hold you but a ſubiect of this warre, not as a brother.

Edmond's speech in F (properly lined: see the play-text, pp. 232–3 above) is sufficient
to justify his action; in Q, the speech continues beyond the point of impertinence.
Albany's response is appropriate with or without the deleted lines, which are largely
reflective and sententious. Compare Urkowitz, p. 107; Stone, p. 238.

(xxiv) After 5.3.195 (see Appendix, p. 289 below, xxxi).

F's omission of Edgar's seventeen lines describing his meeting with Kent does more than
reduce the inexplicable delay between Edmond's announced intention to do some good
and the actual attempt to save Lear and Cordelia. It also modifies the role of Edgar as 'the

immature, indulgent man displaying his heroic tale of woe' in the face of Albany's desire not to hear anything 'more woeful'. Edgar thus emerges as a man worthier of the responsibility that becomes his at the close, certainly as F fashions it (Warren, 'Albany and Edgar', p. 104). The omission of these lines, moreover, more sharply juxtaposes the pathos of Gloucester's death with the deaths of Gonerill and Regan. Theatrical abridgement may have been a major motive in the cut, but artistic considerations were clearly involved as well.

F-Only Passages

F-only passages are essentially of two kinds: (1) passages restored to the text that were accidentally omitted from Q; (2) passages that could not have been accidentally omitted from Q and must have been added by a reviser. The first kind would have appeared in the original prompt-book along with a number of alternative manuscript readings (Doran, pp. 38–52); the other kind might have appeared there, if revision was early, or in the second playhouse manuscript (the result of collation with revised Q), if revision came later. Accidental omissions in Q usually involve passages of a line or two; more extensive F-only passages are most likely additions to the original text. In the passages reproduced below, F-only lines are marked by brackets.

(xxv) After 1.1.36 (see above, p. 62).

(xxvi) After 1.1.59:

> *Lear.*Of all thefe bounds euen from this Line,to this,
> With fhadowie Forreſts,and with Champains rich'd
> With plenteous Riuers,and wide-skirted Meades
> We make thee Lady. To thine and *Albanies* iſſues
> Be this perpetuall. What fayes our fecond Daughter?

These words may have stood in the original manuscript but the Q compositor accidentally skipped from 'and' in 59 to 'and' in 60 (Doran, p. 57). Revisions at the beginning of the play, however, tend to be more frequent and fussy than they are elsewhere, and this could be a genuine addition (Stone, p. 239).

(xxvii) After 1.1.82:

> Q: Then that confirm'd on *Gonorill*,but now our ioy,
> Although the laſt,not leaſt in our deere loue,
> What can you fay to win a third, more opulent
> Then your ſiſters.
> *Cord.* Nothing my Lord.   (againe.
> *Lear.* How, nothing can come of nothing, ſpeake
> *Cord.* Vnhappie that I am, I cannot heaue my heart into my
> mouth,I loue your Maieſtie according to my bond,nor more nor
> leſſe.
> *Lear.* Goe to,goe to,mend your fpeech a little,
> Leaſt it may mar your fortunes,

F: Then that conferr'd on *Generill.* Now our Ioy,
    Although our laſt and leaſt ; to whoſe yong loueſ
    The Vines of France, and Milke of Burgundie,
    Striue to be intereſt. What can you ſay, to draw
    A third, more opilent then your Siſters? ſpeake.
        Cor. Nothing my Lord.
        Lear. Nothing ?

        Cor. Nothing.
        Lear. Nothing will come of nothing, ſpeake againe.
        Cor. Vnhappie that I am, I cannot heaue
    My heart into my mouth: I loue your Maieſty
    According to my bond, no more nor leſſe.
        Lear. How, how *(Cordelia?* Mend your ſpeech a little,
    Leaſt you may marre your Fortunes.

Besides additions, other alterations in F clearly indicate revision here. The additions
not only make Cordelia's response emphatic, they provide the actor playing Lear with
space for further reaction.

(xxviii) 1.2.96–100:

Glou. Theſe late Eclipſes in the Sun and Moone portend no good to vs : though the wiſedome of Nature can
reaſon it thus, and thus, yet Nature finds it ſelfe ſcourg'd
by the ſequent effects. Loue cooles, friendſhip falls off,
Brothers diuide. In Cities, mutinies ; in Countries, diſ-
cord ; in Pallaces, Treaſon ; and the Bond crack'd, 'twixt
Sonne and Father.[This villaine of mine comes vnder the
prediction; there's Son againſt Father, the King fals from
byas of Nature, there's Father againſt Childe. We haue
ſeene the beſt of our time. Machinations, hollowneſſe,
treacherie, and all ruinous diſorders follow vs diſquietly
to our Graues.] Find out this Villain, *Edmond,* it ſhall loſe
thee nothing, do it careſully : and the Noble & true-har-
ted Kent baniſh'd ; his offence, honeſty. 'Tis ſtrange. *Exit*

An unlikely though not impossible accidental omission from Q (Doran, p. 58), these
lines complement the cut later on at 1.2.125. See above, p. 249; Stone, p. 239; and
Taylor, 'Censorship', pp. 81–8.

(xxix) 1.2.139–44:

Q: *Edg.* Some villaine hath done me wrong.
        Baſt. Thats my feare brother, I aduiſe you to the beſt, goe
    arm'd, I am no honeſt man if there bee any good meaning to-

    wards you, I haue told you what I haue ſeene & heard, but faint-
    ly, nothing like the image and horror of it, pray you away !

F: *Edg.* Some.Villaine hath done me wrong.

    Edm. That's my feare; [I pray you haue a continent
forbearance till the speed of his rage goes flower : and as
I say, retire with me to my lodging, from whence I will
fitly bring you to heare my Lord speake : pray ye goe,
there's my key : if you do stirre abroad, goe arm'd.

    [*Edg.* Arm'd, Brother?

    Edm.] Brother, I aduise you to the best, I am no honest
man, if ther be any good meaning toward you: I haue told
you what I haue seene, and heard : But faintly. Nothing
like the image, and horror of it, pray you away.

Stone, p. 240, and Doran, p. 63, agree that the omission from Q of the bracketed lines
could hardly have been accidental. The different position of 'goe arm'd' in Q and F
indicates a deliberate interpolation of matter not originally in Q.

(xxx) 1.4.217:

               Enter Albany.

    Lear. Woe, that too late repents :
Is it your will, speake Sir ? Prepare my Horses.
Ingratitude ! thou Marble-hearted Fiend,
More hideous when thou shew'st thee in a Child,
Then the Sea-monster.

    [*Alb.* Pray Sir be patient.

    Lear.] Detested Kite, thou lyest.
My Traine are men of choice, and rarest parts,
That all particulars of dutie know,
And in the most exact regard, support
The worships of their name. O most small fault,

Besides several local corrections and changing Q's prose to verse, F interpolates
Albany's speech, which 'punctuates' Lear's tirade (Urkowitz, p. 44) and gives the
duke something to say soon after his entrance (Stone, p. 240). See also pp. 63–4
above.

(xxxi) 1.4.229:

And added to the gall. O *Lear*, *Lear*, *Lear*!
Beate at this gate that let thy Folly in,
And thy deere Iudgement out. Go, go, my people.

    Alb. My Lord, I am guiltlesse, as I am ignorant
[Of what hath moued you.]

    Lear. It may be so, my Lord.

Albany's additional half-line completes his meaning and was probably omitted accidentally by the Q compositor, who printed almost the entire scene as prose and omitted
the third '*Lear*' in 225 as well.

(xxxii) 1.4.276–87 (see the play-text, p. 123 above).

Duthie, p. 378, believes that Gonerill's speech was cut in Q to shorten the play in performance and restored in F (compare Stone, pp. 76–80). But others, e.g. McLeod, find the F-only lines consistent with changes elsewhere in Gonerill's speeches (see above, p. 250). Other alterations also strongly suggest revision here; for example, Gonerill's interruption of her husband and her summons to Oswald (281–2) are changed from Q and result in metrical irregularity (see collation, and Doran, pp. 65–6).

(xxxiii) 2.4.19 (see above, p. 252).

(xxxiv) 2.4.43–51:

```
Your Sonne and Daughter found this trespasse worth
The shame which heere it suffers.                     (way,
    [Foole. Winters not gon yet,if the wil'd Geese fly that
Fathers that weare rags, do make their Children blind,

But Fathers that beare bags,shall see their children kind.
Fortune that arrant whore,nere turns the key toth' poore.
But for all this thou shalt haue as many Dolors for thy
Daughters,as thou canst tell in a yeare,]
    Lear. Oh how this Mother swels vp toward my heart!
Historica passio,downe thou climing sorrow,
```

Stone, p. 241, says the Fool's lines are an obvious theatrical interpolation not in the style of the reviser and added as an afterthought. He suggests that F's faulty lineation is the result of the lines' being written sideways in the margin of the prompt-book, as an addition of such length would be. Doran, p. 66, and others find the lines consistent with Shakespeare's style for the Fool; but if the reference to 'wild geese' is an allusion to the Wildgoose family (see p. 8 above), then the addition was probably early. The Folio lineation, obviously crowded, may result from faulty casting-off of copy for signature rr1[r], set by Compositor E. Taylor, 'Date and authorship', p. 396, and Kerrigan, p. 220, argue for both authenticity and dramatic aptness; Granville-Barker remarks that the Fool's song alters the dramatic effect as Lear 'stands speech-less, his agony upon him' (p. 329).

(xxxv) After 2.4.90:

```
Q: why Glofter,Glofter, id'e speake with the Duke of Cornewal,and
      his wife.
         Glof. I my good Lord.
         Lear. The King would speak with Cornewal,the deare father
      Would with his daughter speake,commands her seruice,
      Fierie Duke, tell the hot Duke that Lear,
      No but not yet may be he is not well,
```

F: Fiery? What quality ? Why *Closter. Closter*,
   I'ld speake with the Duke of *Cornewall*, and his wife.
   [*Glo*. Well my good Lord, I haue inform'd them so.
   Lear. Inform'd them ? Do'ft thou vnderstand me man.]
   Glo. I my good Lord.
   Lear. The King would speake with *Cornwall*,
   The deere Father
   Would with his Daughter speake, commands, tends, fer-
   [Are they inform'd of this? My breath and blood;] (uice,
   Fiery? The fiery Duke, tell the hot Duke that ———
   No, but not yet, may be he is not well,

Besides the additional lines, the passage shows other signs of revision. According to Stone, p. 241, the reviser must have thought Gloucester's behaviour in Q needed verbal extenuation. The additional lines 91–2 are complemented by the further addition at 96. On the other variants here, see Commentary.

(xxxvi) 2.4.132–7 (see the play-text, p. 150 above).

Since Regan speaks in convoluted syntax, amplification of her meaning was probably felt to be necessary for Lear's benefit (and for that of the audience), as Stone suggests, p. 242, although he does not believe the addition is Shakespeare's. But in discerning a professional rivalry between the original author and a reviser, Stone may miss the rhetorical and dramatic point of the passage, which is developed more fully by the addition.

(xxxvii) 2.4.289–90:

Q: *Duke*. So am I puspos'd, where is my Lord of *Closter*?   *Enter Glo*
   Reg. Followed the old man forth, he is return'd.
   Glo. The King is in high rage, & wil I know not whe-
   Re. Tis good to giue him way, he leads himselfe.(ther.
   Gon. My Lord, intreat him by no meanes to stay.
   Glo. Alack the night comes on, and the bleak winds

F: *Enter Glofter*.
   Corn. Foilowed the old man forth, he is return'd.
   Glo. The King is in high rage.
   [*Corn*. Whether is he going ?
   Glo. He cals to Horse, but will I know not whether.
   Corn. 'Tis best to giue him way, he leads himselfe.
   Gon. My Lord, entreate him by no meanes to stay.
   Glo. Alacke the night comes on, and the high windes

Again, besides the added lines, other signs of revision appear here, such as reassigned speech headings and local emendations. A reviser may have noticed the hypermetrical line in Q and made two regular lines using interpolated matter, as Stone thinks, p. 242; on the other hand, the hypermetrical line could have been the result of an accidental omission that F either recovers or substitutes for.

(xxxviii) 3.1.14–21 (see p. 253 above).

(xxxix) 3.2.77–93 (see the play-text, pp. 165–6 above).

Like the Fool's additional lines in 2.4 (xxiv above), 'Merlin's Prophecy' is sometimes
considered spurious. For long it was regarded as an interpolation by the actor who
played the Fool, a bit of irrelevant nonsense, food for the groundlings, as Cowden Clarke
suggested (cited by Furness, p. 179). More recently, however, the lines have been
defended as not only Shakespearean, but relevant to both the dramatic context and
the Fool's changed character in F (Kerrigan, pp. 221–6). They parody some pseudo-
Chaucerian verses found in Thynne's edition of Chaucer (1532) cited by Puttenham, in
slightly different form, in *The Arte of English Poesie* (1589), which Shakespeare was
apparently reading at about the time he wrote *The Winter's Tale* (Taylor, 'Date and
authorship', pp. 382–6). The addition reflects this later source and, while not indispensable, adds to the ironic use of prophecy found elsewhere in the play.

(xl) 3.4.17–18:

Q: Is it not as this mouth fhould teare this hand
    For lifting food to't, but I will punifh fure,
    No I will weepe no more, in fuch a night as this !
    O *Regan, Gonorill,*your old kind father   (lies,
    Whofe franke heart gaue you all, O that way madnes
    Let me fhun that, no more of that.

F: Is it not as this mouth fh ould teare this hand
     For lifting food too't ? But I will pun fh home;
     No, I will weepe no more; in fuch a night,

     To fhut me out ? Poure on, I will endure:]
     In fuch a night as this ? O *Regan, Gonerill,*
     Your old kind Father, whofe tranke heart gaue all,
     O that way madneffe lies, let me fhun that :
     No more of that.

Probably the lines not found in Q are the result of compositor eye-skip, caused by the
repetition of 'in such a night' and making Q's lines irregular. Stone, however,
suspects revision, since Lear cannot know at this point that he has, in fact, been
'shut out' of Gloucester's castle (p. 243), and other indications of revision appear
here and elsewhere in the scene (see xli–xlii below).

(xli) 3.4.26–7:

   Kent. Good my Lord enter here.
      Lear. Prythee go in thy felfe, feeke thine owne eafe,
   This tempeft will not giue me leaue to ponder
   On things would hurt me more, but Ile goe in,
   [In Boy, go firft. You houfeleffe pouertie,   *Exit.*
   Nay get thee in; Ile pray, and then Ile fleepe.]
   Poore naked wretches, where fo ere you are
   That bide the pelting of this pittileffe ftorme,
   How fhall your Houfe-leffe heads, and vnfed fides,

While the lines not in Q may again be the result of accidental omission, eye-skip is less likely here. Both Stone, p. 244, and Urkowitz, p. 44, see a reviser's hand at work. The '*Exit*' added in F may be the book-keeper's notation.

(xlii) 3.4.37:

> Your lop'd,and window'd raggedneſſe defend you
> From ſeaſons ſuch as theſe ? O I haue tane
> Too little care of this : Take Phyſicke, Pompe,
> Expoſe thy ſelfe to feele what wretches feele,
> That thou maiſt ſhake the ſuperflux to them,
> And ſhew the Heauens more iuſt.
>
> *Enter Edgar, and Foole.*
>
> *Edg.* Fathom,and halfe,Fathom and halfe;poore *Tom.*
>   *Foole.* Come not in heere Nuncle,here's a ſpirit,helpe
> me,helpe me.
>   *Kent.* Giue me thy hand,who's there ?

Edgar's interpolated scream dramatically motivates the Fool's terrified re-entrance. F also adds a stage direction, although Edgar's actual emergence follows the Fool's a few lines later (see Commentary).

(xliii) 3.6.11–12:

> *Foole.* Prythee Nunkle tell me,whether a madman be
> a Gentleman,or a Yeoman.
>   *Lear.* A King,a King.
>   [*Foole.* No, he's a Yeoman, that ha's a Gentleman to
> his Sonne : for hee's a mad Yeoman that ſees his Sonne a
> Gentleman before him.
>   *Lear.*] To haue a thouſand with red burning ſpits
> Come hizzing in vpon 'em.

Doran, p. 67, supposes that the F-only lines are original and that the Q compositor had difficulty with the passage and deliberately omitted it. Stone, p. 67, and Kerrigan, pp. 227–30, consider the passage evidence of revision, Lear's response to the Fool's question having apparently been regarded as insufficient by the reviser. Kerrigan is sure the lines are Shakespeare's and allude to the dramatist's father, John, a yeoman, for whom his son obtained a grant from the College of Arms in 1596. In 1602, however, after John Shakespeare's death, the grant was challenged by York Herald Ralph Brooke, and possibly William had to justify his own claim (through his father) to the title 'gentleman' when he was writing or revising his play. But no evidence has been found to this effect and, as Kerrigan says, what happened to Brooke's complaint is not known. If the reviser intended a personal allusion, then (like xxxiv above) the addition – if it was one – was probably early.

(xliv) 3.6.41:

Q: *Lear*. Make no noife,make no noife,draw the curtains,fo,fo,fo,
    Weele go to fupper it'h morning,fo,fo,fo,   *Enter Glofter.*
        Glof. Come hither friend, where is the King my maifter.

F: *Enter Glofter.*
        Kent. Now good my Lord,lye heere,and reft awhile.
        Lear. Make no noife,make no noife, draw the Cur-
    taines : fo,fo,wee'l go to Supper i'th'morning.
        [*Foole*. And Ile go to bed at noone.]
        Glon. Come hither Friend :
    Where is the King my Mafter?

Taylor speculates that the Fool's last, cryptic line was an early addition, perhaps inserted in the original prompt-book. By the time rehearsals began, Shakespeare knew that the Fool's role ended here and may have decided to give him a suitable concluding line ('Date and authorship', p. 405). Other alterations, further evidence of revision, surround the line, which is susceptible to several interpretations (see Commentary). Stone, pp. 244–5, and Kerrigan, pp. 228–9, accept the line as an interpolation, though Stone questions its authenticity.

(xlv) 4.1.6–9:

                          Enter Edgar.
        Edg. Yet better thus,and knowne to be contemn'd,
    Then ftill contemn'd and flatter'd, to be worft :
    The loweft, and moft deiected thing of Fortune,
    Stands ftill in efperance, liues not in feare :
    The lamentable change is from the beft,
    The worft returnes to laughter. [Welcome then,
    Thou vnfubftantiall ayre that I embrace :
    The Wretch that thou haft blowne vnto the worft,
    Owes nothing to thy blafts,]
            Enter Gloufter,and an Oldman.

The lines at first appear more like a deliberate cut in Q than an addition to F (Stone, p. 245). But they complement the omission of Edgar's lines at the end of 3.6 (see above, p. 254), improve the metre, and make Edgar more vulnerable to the shock of seeing his newly blinded father.

(xlvi) 4.1.54:

        Glon. Sirrah, naked feilow.
        Idg. Poore Tom's a cold.. I cannot daub it further.
        Glon. Come hither fellow.
    [*Edg*. And yet I muft :]
    Bleffe thy fweete eyes, they bleede.
        Glon. Know'ft thou the way to Douer?

Edgar's half-line completes the sense of 'I cannot daub it further' and regularizes the line metrically. Its omission in Q may be accidental, or its appearance in F may be a consequence of the correction 'daub' for Q 'dance'. Note also the cut after 58 (see above, p. 254).

(xlvii) 4.2.27:

Q: *Baſt*. Yours in the ranks of death.   (are dew
    Gon. My moſt deer *Gloſter*, to thee a womans ſeruices
A foole vſurps my bed.
    Stew. Madam, here comes my Lord.   *Exit Stew*.
    Gon. I haue beene worth the whiftling. (rude wind
    Alb. O *Gonoril*, you are not worth the duſt which the

F: *Baſt*. Yours in the rankes of death.   *Exit*.
    Gon. My moſt deere Gloſter.

   ⌈Oh, the difference of man, and man,⌉
    To thee a Womans feruices are due,
    My Foole vſurpes my body.
      Stew. Madam, here come's my Lord.
            Enter Albany.
    Gon. I haue beene worth the whiftle.
    Alb. Oh *Gonerill*,
You are not worth the duſt which the rude winde

Gonerill's added line appears to be part of extensive Folio correction and revision in this scene (see above, p. 255, and Commentary). In Q, Gonerill's line is unnecessary, since she apparently addresses Edmond (whose exit is missing); but in F, Edmond leaves, and Gonerill comments to herself. Compare Stone, p. 245; Taylor, 'Date and authorship', p. 379.

(xlviii) 4.5.157–62:

rough tatter'd cloathes great Vices do appeare: Robes,
and Furr'd gownes hide all. ⌈Place finnes with Gold, and
the ſtrong Lance of Iuſtice, hurtleſſe breakes: Arme it in
ragges, a Pigmies ſtraw do's pierce it. None do's offend,
none, I ſay none, Ile able 'em; take that of me my Friend,
who haue the power to ſeale th'accuſers lips,⌉ Get thee
glaſſe-eyes, and like a ſcuruy Politician, ſeeme to ſee the
things thou doſt not. Now, now, now, now. Pull off my

Stone, pp. 68, 122, and Doran, p. 68, agree that the F-only lines are an interpolation, since 'Get thee glasse eyes' naturally follows from 'hide all'. Chambers, 1: 467, believes the lines were cut from Q because of censorship, but censorship would hardly affect foul papers. Roger Warren, p. 52, cites these lines as complementing the omission of the mock trial in 3.6. The passage shows other signs of correction and revision (see collation). Stone, pp. 123–5, sees an allusion in the lines to the Overbury affair (1613–16), but Taylor rejects the allusion on grounds that the lines are too general and commonplace; he compares *Ham.* 3.3.57–60 ('Date and authorship', p. 403).

(xlix) 4.6.59:

Q: *Lear*. Pray doe not mocke,
  I am a very foolifh fond old man,
  Fourefcore and vpward,and to deale plainly
  I feare I am not in my perfeſt mind,
  Mee chinks I fhould know you,and know this man;

F: *Lear*. Pray do not mocke me:
  I am a very foolifh fond old man,
  Fourefcore and vpward,
  [Not an houre more,nor leffe:]
  And to deale plainely,
  I feare I am not in my perfeſt mind.
  Me thinkes i fhould know you,and know this man,

Lear's nonsense line seems more like an interpolation than an accidental omission from Q. Compare the later augmentation at 68, Cordelia's 'I am: I am'.

(l) 5.2.11:

  Glo. No further Sir,a man may rot euen heere.
  Edg. What in ill thoughts againe?
Men muſt endure
Their going hence,euen as their comming hither,
Ripeneffe is all come on.
  [*Glo.* And that's true too.]   *Exeunt.*

Gloucester's final half-line may have been dropped by the Q compositor, whose page (K4ʳ) shows signs of crowding; or it may have been added in F by a reviser concerned to fill out the line (Stone, p. 247) and/or intent upon augmenting the play's 'complementarity': see Commentary.

(li) 5.3.70:

  Rega. Lady I am not well,elfe I fhould anfwere
From a full flowing ftomack. Generall,
  Take thou my Souldiers,prifoners,patrimony,
  [Difpofe of them, of me,the walls is thine:]
  Witneffe the world,that I create thee heere
My Lord,and Mafter.

'Very possibly an accidental omission from Q' (Stone, p. 246).

(lii) 5.3.83–4:

Q: And I her husband contradict the banes,
   If you will mary, make your loue to me,
   My Lady is befpoke, thou art arm'd *Glofter,*
   If none appeare to proue vpon thy head,
   Thy hainous, manifeft, and many treafons,
   There is my pledge, ile proue it on thy heart

F: And I her husband contradict your Banes.
   If you will marry, make your loues to me,
   My Lady is befpoke.
       Gon. An enterlude.]
       Alb. Thou art armed *Glefter,*
   [Let the Trumpet found :]
   If none appeare to proue vpon thy perfon,
   Thy heynous, manifeft, and many Treafons,
   There is my pledge : Ile make it on thy heart

F's additions are obviously interpolated. Gonerill's half-line provides 'dramatic punctuation' (compare xxxi, p. 262 above, 1.4.217; and Stone, p. 246). The addition to
Albany's speech underscores the duke's eagerness for confrontation with Edmond
(compare Urkowitz, pp. 109–11). The passage contains other indications of revision
(e.g. F 'person' / Q 'head'; F 'make' / Q 'prove'), which appear throughout the scene.

(liii) 5.3.134:

Q: *Baft.* In wifdome I fholud aske thy name,
   But fince thy outfide lookes fo faire and warlike,
   And that thy being fome fay of breeding breathes,
   By right of knighthood, I difdaine and fpurne
   Heere do I toffe thofe treafons to thy head.
   With the hell hatedly, oreturnd thy heart,

F: *Baft.* In wifedome I fhould aske thy name,
   But fince thy out-fide lookes fo faire and Warlike,
   And that thy tongue (fome fay) of breeding breathes,
   [What fafe, and nicely I might well delay,]
   By rule of Knight-hood, I difdaine and fpurne:
   Backe do I toffe thefe Treafons to thy head,
   With the hell-hated Lye, ore-whelme thy heart,

Stone, pp. 68–9, believes F's additional line and other alterations are the result of a
misprint in Q at the beginning of 135, 'By' for 'My'. Failing to detect the error (after
substituting 'tongue' for 'being' at 133), the reviser recognized that 'disdaine and
spurne' required an object; hence, he added a new line and changed 'right' to 'rule' to
make the phrase more idiomatic. Alterations in other lines also show revision as well as
correction.

(liv) 5.3.256:

Q: *Kent.* If Fortune bragd of two fhe loued or hated,
   One of them we behold.   *Lear.* Are not you *Kent?*
    Kent. The fame your feruant *Kent*, where is your feruant *Caius,*
     Lear. Hees a good fellow, I can tell that,
Heele ftrike and quickly too, hees dead and rotten.

F: *Kent.* If Fortune brag of two, fhe lou'd and hated,
   One of them we behold.
     Lear. [This is a dull fight] are you not *Kent* ?
    Kent. The fame : your Seruant *Kent,*
  Where is your Seruant *Caius* ?
     Lear. He's a good fellow, I can tell you that,
He'le ftrike and quickly too, he's dead and rotten.

Lear's added half-line helps improve the metre. The Q compositor, nearing the end of his copy and obviously crowding his text (as the last three pages of Q reveal), may have omitted the speech deliberately. Compare Stone, p. 247.

(lv) 5.3.284–5 (see above, p. 65).

The additions together with other alterations undoubtedly indicate revision, an attempt to improve dramatically the play's final moments (Stone, p. 247). Certainly they change the ending, as Clayton notes, pp. 129, 133–7.

Conclusions

The weight of the evidence clearly indicates that F represents a revised text of *King Lear*, with Q reflecting a version of the original. Only a few, short omissions from Q and F can be attributed to compositor errors. In revising, very likely more than one motive and possibly more than one hand were involved over the period of time (seventeen years) that separates the date of first composition from the date of publication of the Folio text. Several of the largest omissions from the Q text – those after 3.6.13, 3.7.97, 4.6.82, 5.3.195, and a whole scene in Act 4 – may be the result of theatrical shortening, but it is by no means clear that Shakespeare did not have any responsibility for them. The remaining cuts often involve other alterations that point to a reviser's hand at work. Similarly, the F additions are usually, though not always, the result of deliberate interpolation, not accidental omission from Q. On stylistic grounds, Shakespeare remains the leading candidate for the authorship of the additions, which often mesh well with other changes in the Q text. Although Stone has proposed Philip Massinger as the reviser, Foster and Taylor have argued that he was not (his involvement with the King's Men as a reviser of old plays notwithstanding) and that Shakespeare was.

    The Folio text, then, presents a version of *King Lear* that was performed in the early seventeenth century, first at the Globe and at court, and afterwards at the Blackfriars and probably again at court in revised form (or forms). The instability not only of Shakespeare's texts, but of any play-text, is notorious. Since one aim of this edition (as of the New Cambridge Shakespeare in general) is to emphasize Shakespeare's plays as *plays*, that is, scripts for performance, the choice of F as the copy-text for *King Lear* is both logical and appropriate. But as no definitive, 'final' text of the play does or can exist, what Shakespeare wrote in both Q and F is preserved. Unlike traditionally conflated texts, however, this edition removes Q-only passages from the text proper and presents them in an Appendix. By consulting those passages and taking careful note through the collation of the Folio additions and other alterations, the reader may reconstruct the quarto, whereas the main body of the text presents an acting version of *King Lear* that Shakespeare may have seen performed on one of the stages he was familiar with. The reader should thus not become confused about a text − Q + F − that is neither Shakespeare's nor the King's Men's, but a construct of modern conflating editors in the tradition of Alexander Pope and his contemporaries.

APPENDIX:
PASSAGES UNIQUE TO THE FIRST QUARTO

(i) After 1.2.85 ('such a monster') Q reads:

EDMOND   Nor is not, sure.
GLOUCESTER   To his father, that so tenderly and entirely loves him. Heaven and earth!

1 EDMOND ... **sure** Edmond interrupts
Gloucester in mid sentence with an emphatic double negative.

(ii) After 1.2.125–6 ('I promise you, the effects he writes of succeed unhappily') Q reads:

       as of unnaturalness between the child and the parent, death,
       dearth, dissolutions of ancient amities, divisions in state,
       menaces and maledictions against king and nobles, needless
       diffidences, banishment of friends, dissipation of cohorts,
       nuptial breaches, and I know not what.
EDGAR   How long have you been a sectary astronomical?   5
EDMOND   Come, come,

2 amities] Q; armies Q2

3 **diffidences** distrusts, doubts.
3 **dissipation of cohorts** dispersal of military
companies. NS suggests desertion and disease, 'a
common fate of military bands' at that time, but
Shakespeare is doubtless anticipating the dissolu-
tion of Lear's hundred knights, just as 'nuptial
breaches' anticipates Gonerill's adultery with
Edmond.
5 **sectary astronomical** believer in astrology, or
student of it; 'sectary' appears in Florio's *Montaigne*
(Muir).

(iii) After 1.3.16 Q reads (as prose):

       Not to be overruled. Idle old man,
       That still would manage those authorities
       That he hath given away! Now, by my life,
       Old fools are babes again, and must be used
       With checks as flatteries when they are seen abused.   5

1–5 Not ... abused] *Theobald's lineation; as prose* Q

1 **Idle** Silly, foolish.
4 **Old ... again** Compare Tilley M570: 'Old men
are twice children.'
4–5 **used ... abused** i.e. we must use rebukes as
well as soothing words ('flatteries') with foolish old
men when they are deluded ('abused'; compare
4.6.50).

(iv) After 1.3.20 Q reads (as prose):

> I would breed from hence occasions, and I shall,
> That I may speak.

1–2 I . . . speak] *Capell's lineation; as prose* Q

1 **occasions** opportunities.

(v) After 1.4.117 Q reads (with first three lines also in F):

FOOL   Dost thou know the difference, my boy, between a bitter fool and a sweet
     one?
LEAR   No, lad; teach me.
FOOL   That lord that counselled thee
          To give away thy land,   5
       Come place him here by me,
          Do thou for him stand;
       The sweet and bitter fool
          Will presently appear,
       The one in motley here,   10
          The other found out there.
LEAR   Dost thou call me fool, boy?
FOOL   All thy other titles thou hast given away; that thou wast born with.
KENT   This is not altogether fool, my lord.
FOOL   No, faith; lords and great men will not let me. If I had a monopoly out, they   15
     would have part on't; and ladies too – they will not let me have all the fool to
     myself; they'll be snatching.

*1 thou] F; *not in* Q   *2 one] F; fool Q   4–11 That . . . there] *Capell's lineation; four lines ending* . . . land, / . . . stand, /
. . . appeare, / . . . there. Q   16 on't; and ladies] *Capell* (*subst.*); an't, and Ladies Q *corr.*; an't, and lodes Q *uncorr.*; on't, and
lodes Q2   16 all the] Q; all Q2

1–3 **Dost . . . me** These lines appear in F, but
were probably intended to be cut along with the rest
of this passage, with which they are clearly connected. See Textual Analysis, p. 68 above.
  1 **my boy** The Fool's term for Lear that Lear has
just used for him (1.4.116).
  4 **That lord** In *King Leir*, Skalliger advised the
king, but no one advised Lear, who was apparently
his own counsel (the implied point of 7).
  4 **thee** Wiles, p. 191, says that the Fool here
addresses his bauble, or *marotte*, and elsewhere
uses his bauble thus to avoid directly addressing
the king, as at 1.4.117.
  6–7 **Come . . . stand** The Fool is stage-directing,
moving characters around and using gestures. He
has Lear stand for the counsellor.
  10 **The one** i.e. the sweet fool; the Fool indicates
himself.
  11 **The other** i.e. the bitter fool.
  11 **found out** discovered.
  11 **there** The Fool points to Lear. Some editions,

e.g. NS, place a dash before 'there' to make the
emphasis clearer. 'In early 1606, it would have
been hard not to see the Fool's jibe at Lear as
a reflection of King James's own royal fool [Archie
Armstrong] commenting on the folly of James himself' (Taylor, 'Censorship', p. 105).
  13 **that . . . with** either (1) you are a born fool, or
(2) folly is a universal human characteristic, i.e.
something you can't give away (compare Hunter).
  14 **altogether** entirely; but the Fool quibbles on
the sense 'only', i.e. having all there is (Kittredge).
  15 **out** officially granted. Like the slur implied at
11, this was also a possible cause for censorship:
James I was notorious for awarding monopolies to
court favourites.
  16 **on't** i.e. of it.
  16–17 **ladies . . . snatching** The Fool refers to
his bauble, used to suggest a phallus. The indecent
behaviour of court ladies was another sensitive
issue.

(vi) After 1.4.190 Q reads (continuing 'Lear's shadow' as part of Lear's speech: see above, pp. 64–5):

LEAR   I would learn that, for by the marks of sovereignty, knowledge, and reason, I
         should be false persuaded I had daughters.
FOOL   Which they will make an obedient father.

*1 SH] *Steevens; not in* Q   *3 they] Q3; they, Q, Q2

1 **that** i.e. who I am.
1–2 **for … daughters** i.e. every indication – the outward signs of majesty (e.g. my crown), as well as the information I have and my own reason – tells me that I have daughters. But that cannot be, since no daughters would behave this way towards me.
3 **Which** Whom. Compare Abbott 265 and 266, and 3.1.16.

(vii) After 2.2.128 ('not to do so') Q reads:

    His fault is much, and the good king, his master,
    Will check him for't. Your purposed low correction
    Is such as basest and contemned'st wretches
    For pilferings and most common trespasses
    Are punished with.   5

3–4 Is … trespasses] *Pope's lineation; divided …* pilfrings / And Q   3 basest] Q *corr.;* belest Q *uncorr.*   *3 contemned'st] *Capell;* contaned Q *uncorr.;* temnest Q *corr.,* Q2

2 **check** rebuke. Compare (iii) above.
3 **contemned'st** most despised. Stone, p. 201, believes 'conte[m]ned' stood in Q copy. Greg thinks the press-corrector crossed out 'taned' in Q uncorr. 'contaned' and wrote 'temnest' in the margin, meaning the compositor to correct that half of the word only. Instead, he altered the entire word to Q corr. 'temnest' (*Variants*, p. 159). While agreeing that this probably happened, Blayney (pp. 247–8) says that the proofreader's intention may not have been correct and proposes (like Stone) the emendation 'contemned', which Oxford accepts (in *The History of King Lear*).
4 **pilferings** petty thefts.

(viii) After 2.2.133 ('abused, assaulted') Q reads:

    For following her affairs. – Put in his legs.

(ix) After 2.4.17 ('I say, yea.') Q reads:

LEAR   No, no, they would not.
KENT   Yes, they have.

(x) After 3.1.7 ('That things might change or cease;') Q reads:

                tears his white hair,
      Which the impetuous blasts with eyeless rage

2 **eyeless** blind, undiscriminating.

Catch in their fury and make nothing of;
Strives in his little world of man to outstorm
The to-and-fro-conflicting wind and rain.   5
This night, wherein the cubdrawn bear would couch,
The lion and the belly-pinchèd wolf
Keep their fur dry, unbonnetted he runs,
And bids what will take all.

---

*4 outstorm] out-storm Muir (conj. Steevens); outscorne Q   5 to-and-fro-conflicting] Hyphenated Capell   7 belly-pinchèd] Hyphenated Pope   8 fur] furre Q corr.; surre Q uncorr., Q2

---

3 make nothing of disperse, make it disappear into nothingness.
4 little world of man i.e. the microcosm. Compare *Mac.* 1.3.140.
4 outstorm Steevens first proposed the emendation (an easy *t/c* misreading) and compared *A Lover's Complaint*, 7: 'Storming her world with sorrows wind and rain' (cited by Furness).
5 to-and-fro-conflicting i.e. wildly buffeting.
6 cubdrawn sucked dry by cubs, therefore ravenous. Kittredge compares *Arden of Feversham* 2.2.118–20: 'Such mercy as the staruen Lyones, / When she is dry suckt of her eager young, / Showes to the prey that next encounters her'. The image of

the udder-drawn lioness appears also in *AYLI* 4.3.114.
6 couch lie down (and not be out hunting). Compare the animals in Job's storm, Job 37.8: 'the beasts go into the denne, and remaine in their places' (Colie, p. 130).
8 unbonneted hatless ('a stronger idea then than now: totally abandoning self-respect as well as self-protection': Hunter). Compare xxii below.
9 bids ... all A cry of desperation: let it all go, the whole world (compare 3.2.1–9). 'Take all!' was the gambler's cry when staking everything on a last throw of the dice; but compare *Ant.* 4.2.8.

(xi)   After 3.1.21 ('but furnishings –') Q reads:

But true it is, from France there comes a power
Into this scattered kingdom, who already,
Wise in our negligence, have secret feet
In some of our best ports, and are at point
To show their open banner. Now to you: 5
If on my credit you dare build so far
To make your speed to Dover, you shall find
Some that will thank you making just report

2–6 Into ... far] Pope's lineation; lines end ... negligêce, [turned under] / ... Ports, / ... banner, / ... farre, Q

The consistent though not perfect elimination in F of references to France as the invading power has led critics, e.g. Greg ('Time, place and politics in *King Lear*', *MLR*, 35 (1940), 431–46) and Doran, pp. 73–6, to suspect censorship. Taylor seriously questions that explanation ('Censorship', pp. 80–1). If censorship was not an issue, then motivation on dramatic and/or thematic grounds must explain F's alteration here and elsewhere. Shakespeare de-emphasizes invasion by a foreign power in favour of Lear's rescue by his youngest daughter, Cordelia, whom he had rejected and cast out. Love, not politics, thus becomes central. See also Textual Analysis, pp. 66–7 above.

1 power army.
2 scattered divided, broken up.
2 who i.e. the French.
3 Wise in our negligence Informed of our neglect (in making adequate defences).
3 have secret feet i.e. have secretly gained footholds.
4 at point in (armed) readiness. Compare 1.4.278.
6 my credit belief in me.
7 To As to.
8 making i.e. for making.
8 just accurate

Of how unnatural and bemadding sorrow
The king hath cause to plain.   10
I am a gentleman of blood and breeding,
And from some knowledge and assurance offer
This office to you.

12–13 And . . . you] *Jennens's lineation; divided . . .* assurance, / Offer Q

9 **bemadding** maddening.
10 **plain** complain.
13 **office** duty, commission.

(xii) After 3.6.14 ('Come hizzing in upon 'em') Q reads:

EDGAR   The foul fiend bites my back.

FOOL   He's mad that trusts in the tameness of a wolf, a horse's health, a boy's love, or
a whore's oath.

LEAR   It shall be done; I will arraign them straight.
[*To Edgar*] Come, sit thou here, most learnèd justicer.   5
[*To the Fool*] Thou, sapient sir, sit here. – No, you she-foxes –

EDGAR   Look where he stands and glares! Want'st thou eyes at trial, madam?
[*Sings*] Come o'er the bourn, Bessy, to me.

FOOL   [*Sings*]   Her boat hath a leak
And she must not speak   10
Why she dares not come over to thee.

2 health] Q; heels *Warburton*   5 SD] *Capell; not in* Q   5 justicer] *Theobald;* Iustice Q   6 SD] *Capell; not in* Q   6 No] Q;
now Q2   7 Want'st] wantst Q2; wanst Q   7 eyes at trial, madam?] eies at tri- / all madam, Q2; eyes, at tral madam Q;
eyes at troll-madam? *Oxford*   8 SD] *Hunter (conj. Staunton); not in* Q   8 Come . . . me] *As verse, Capell; as prose, continuing
from 1* Q   *8 **bourn**] boorne *Capell;* broome Q   9 SD] *Cam.; not in* Q   9–10 Her . . . speak] *Capell's lineation; one
line* Q

On F's omission of the 'mock trial', see Textual
Analysis, pp. 253–4 above.
   1 **foul . . . back** Compare 3.4.144. Tom imagines
a lousy devil.
   2 **tameness of a wolf** D. R. Klinck offers evidence that this phrase, like the ones that follow, is
proverbial (*N&Q*, n.s., 24 (1977), 113–14).
   2 **horse's health** Horses are notoriously given to
disease. Warburton's conjectured emendation,
'heels' for 'health', is supported by the proverb,
'Trust not a horse's heels nor a dog's tooth'
(Tilley H711), and by two citations that include
analogues to 'whore's oath' (Dent, pp. 31, 140).
   2 **boy's love** Compare 'Love of lads and fire of
chats [= small twigs, kindling] is soon in and soon
out' (Tilley L526; Dent, p. 161).
   4 **straight** straightaway. Compare 1.3.21.
   5 **justicer** judge. Theobald's emendation is generally accepted as improving the metre and is supported by 36 below, and by 4.2.48.
   6 **No** Duthie accepts Q2 'Now' as 'obviously the
required reading' (p. 399). But there is nothing

obvious about it, and many editions, e.g. Hunter,
Oxford, retain Q.
   7 **he** i.e. more likely an imagined 'fiend' than
Lear. But compare 15 below.
   7 **Want'st . . . madam** i.e. do you lack spectators
at (your) trial, madam? Explaining Oxford's emendation, 'eyes at troll-madam', Taylor compares *WT*
4.3.87, 'troll-my-dames', from the French game
'trou-madame' (similar to bagatelle) played by
ladies ('Addenda' to *Division*, pp. 486–8).
   8 **Come . . . me** Edgar's fragment, which the
Fool picks up, is from an old song recorded in W.
Wager's *The Longer Thou Livest, the More Fool
Thou Art* (*c.* 1559). Malone (cited by Furness)
notes that 'Bessy' and 'poor Tom' may have been
vagabond companions.
   8 **bourn** burn, brook.
   9–11 **Her . . . thee** These are not the words of the
old song, but the Fool's bawdy improvisation (compare Partridge, pp. 76, 139–40, and *Temp.*
1.1.46–8).

EDGAR   The foul fiend haunts poor Tom in the voice of a nightingale. Hoppedance
cries in Tom's belly for two white herring. Croak not, black angel! I have no food
for thee.

KENT   How do you, sir? Stand you not so amazed.   15
Will you lie down and rest upon the cushions?

LEAR   I'll see their trial first. – Bring in their evidence.
[*To Edgar*] Thou robèd man of justice, take thy place.
[*To the Fool*] And thou, his yoke-fellow of equity,
Bench by his side. [*To Kent*] You are o'th'commission;   20
Sit you too.

EDGAR   Let us deal justly.
Sleepest or wakest thou, jolly shepherd?
Thy sheep be in the corn;
And for one blast of thy minikin mouth   25
Thy sheep shall take no harm.
Purr, the cat, is grey.

LEAR   Arraign her first; 'tis Gonerill. I here take my oath before this honourable
assembly, she kicked the poor king her father.

FOOL   Come hither, mistress. Is your name Gonerill?   30

LEAR   She cannot deny it.

15–16 How ... cushions] *Theobald's lineation; as prose* Q   *16 cushions] Q2; cushings Q   17–21 I'll ... too] *Pope's lineation; as prose* Q   18 SD] *Capell; not in* Q   18 robèd] *Pope;* robbed Q   19 SD] *Capell; not in* Q   20 SD] *Capell; not in* Q   20 o'th'] o'th Q2; ot'h Q   22–6 Let ... harm] *Theobald's lineation; all as prose* Q   *27 cat,] *This edn;* cat Q   *29 she] Q2; *not in* Q

---

12 **The foul ... nightingale** This is Tom's witty response to the Fool. Rosenberg, p. 233, notes the growing rivalry between the Fool and Edgar and suggests a pun, 'foul' – 'fool'; compare 3.4.73 n.

12   **Hoppedance** 'Hoberdidance' or 'Haberdidance' in Harsnett, pp. 49, 140, 180.

13 **white herring** fresh, unsmoked herring (Kittredge).

13 **Croak not** Poor Tom is hungry, and his belly rumbles. Exorcists 'would make a wonderful matter' of such 'croaking' (usually caused by fasting), saying 'it was the deuill ... that spake with the voyce of a Toade' (Harsnett, pp. 194–5).

13 **black angel** i.e. the fiend in his belly.

15 **amazed** 'A very strong word, indicating a state of utter confusion' (Kittredge, who compares *Ham.* 2.2.565–6). Lear is dumb-founded, or perhaps tranced; compare 5.3.278 n.

16 **cushions** Duthie, p. 80, suspects that Q 'cushings', like Q 'Aurigular' (1.2.82), may reflect popular pronunciation.

17 **their evidence** i.e. witnesses to testify against them.

18 **robèd ... justice** Lear takes Edgar's blanket for judicial robes, imagining him as the Chief Justice, who presided over the Court of King's Bench (compare NS).

18 **take thy place** Lear stage-directs, arranging

Edgar, the Fool, and Kent to sit as a judicial panel, or 'commission' (20), to hear the trial.

19 **yoke-fellow** partner; i.e. the Lord Chancellor, who presided over the Courts of Equity (NS). At exceptional trials, e.g. of Mary Stuart, the Courts of Justice and of Equity were combined, as Lear imagines them here (Hunter).

20 **Bench** Sit on the bench (compare Abbott 290).

22 **Let ... justly** Edgar begins sagaciously but quickly resumes his mad act.

23–6 **Sleepest ... harm** This pastoral ditty has not been traced. Its modern analogue is 'Little Boy Blue' (Hunter). Whether or not Edgar sings it is unclear. Does he compete with the Fool in singing, too? Oxford and Bevington add SD *Sings*, following Capell, but Hunter does not. Compare 8 n.

25 **minikin** Either (1) dainty, sprightly (*OED* sv *adj* 1a), or (2) shrill (*OED* sv *adj* 2).

27 **Purr** An apt name for a familiar in the form of a cat; compare *Mac.* 1.1.8, 'I come, Graymalkin', and 4.1.1 'Purre' is the name of a 'fat devil' in Harsnett, p. 50.

29 **she** Accidentally omitted by Q compositor (Duthie, p. 400).

30 **Come ... Gonerill** The Fool picks up a stool and addresses it.

FOOL   Cry you mercy, I took you for a joint-stool.
LEAR   And here's another whose warped looks proclaim
              What store her heart is made on. – Stop her there!
              Arms, arms, sword, fire! Corruption in the place!   35
              False justicer, why hast thou let her 'scape?

---

*32 joint-stool] *Pope;* ioyne stoole Q; ioynt stoole Q2   *34 on] *Capell;* an Q

---

32 I . . . joint-stool A jocose apology for over-looking someone, as in Lyly's *Mother Bombie* 4.2.28 (compare Tilley M897). 'The Fool takes professional delight in this opportunity to give the worn-out phrase a point; for, in this case, the stool is there and Goneril is not' (Kittredge). But the Fool's joke also underscores the reality of the hallucination for Lear. As Granville-Barker suggested, the real and the imagined must carry equal value, so that what Lear feels intensely the audience also feels (Rosenberg, p. 234).
    32 joint-stool A stool with fitted legs (as against a carpenter's rougher work). Duthie, p. 400, says Q 'ioyne' for 'ioynt' may be *t/e* misreading (compare Q2 'ioynt stoole'), but 'ioyne-stool' is an accepted seventeenth-century variant spelling (*OED*).

33 here's another Lear points to or grasps another piece of furniture. In the Granada television production, Olivier caught a hen, which then escaped, giving point to his later outcries (Bratton, p. 153). But note the pun on 'warped'.
    33 warped (1) (of wood) twisted, (2) (of the face) distorted by evil passions (Kittredge).
    34 store material, stuff.
    34 Stop her there Mischievously trying to gain attention, the Fool may snatch the object away from Lear and hide it; or perhaps Lear drops it and the Fool takes it away. But the whole episode may be purely Lear's hallucination, evoking Edgar's 'Bless thy five wits' (3.6.15). Compare Rosenberg, pp. 234–5.

(xiii) After 3.6.53 ('Give thee quick conduct') Q reads:

KENT   Oppressed nature sleeps.
              This rest might yet have balmed thy broken sinews
              Which, if convenience will not allow,
              Stand in hard cure. – Come, help to bear thy master;
              Thou must not stay behind.   5

3–5 Which . . . behind] *Theobald's lineation; divided . . .* cure, / Come Q   4 cure. –] *This edn;* SD *To* Fool *Theobald*

---

2 balmed . . . sinews soothed your shattered nerves. For the analogy of nerves to 'sinews', Muir quotes from 'The Senses' in Sir John Davies's *Nosce Teipsum* (1599): 'Lastly, the feeling power which is life's root, / Through every living power itself doth shed / By sinews, which extend from head to foot, / And like a net, all o'er the body spread.'
    4 Stand in hard cure i.e. will be difficult to heal.
    4–5 Come . . . behind Kent addresses the Fool who, exhausted, lags behind and may even be dying, as he does not appear again. See 3.6.41 n.

(xiv) After 3.6.53 ('Come, come away') Q reads:

EDGAR   When we our betters see bearing our woes,
              We scarcely think our miseries our foes.
              Who alone suffers, suffers most i'th'mind,

1–2 When . . . foes] Q2 *lineation; as prose* Q   *3 suffers, suffers most] *Theobald;* suffers suffers, most Q; suffers, most Q2

---

1 our woes i.e. miseries like ours.
    3 Who . . . mind i.e. anguish is exacerbated mentally by isolation. NS compares *Lucrece*, 790:

'Fellowship in woe doth woe assuage', and Tilley C571 ('It is good to have company in misery').

Leaving free things and happy shows behind.
But then the mind much sufferance doth o'erskip,   5
When grief hath mates, and bearing, fellowship.
How light and portable my pain seems now,
When that which makes me bend makes the king bow.
He childed as I fathered. Tom, away!
Mark the high noises, and thyself bewray   10
When false opinion, whose wrong thoughts defile thee,
In thy just reproof repeals and reconciles thee.
What will hap more tonight, safe 'scape the king!
Lurk, lurk!

4 free i.e. free from trouble or suffering; carefree.
4 happy shows joyous sights.
5 sufferance suffering.
6 bearing suffering, endurance (syllepsis).
7 portable bearable.
9 He ... fathered His experience of children is the same as mine of my father.
10 high noises rumours or events among the mighty. Compare 'noises'= rumours, *Tro.* 1.2.12; 'high' = mighty, *Ant.* 1.2.189–90.

10 bewray reveal.
12 In ... reproof i.e. when the charges against you have been justly disproved or refuted; 'reproof' = disproof, refutation (compare *Cor.* 2.2.33).
12 repeals calls back into favour or honour (Onions).
12 reconciles i.e. to your former standing (with your father).
13 What ... more Whatever else will happen.
13 safe ... king may the king escape safely.
14 Lurk Lie hidden and in wait (Schmidt).

(xv) After 3.7.97 Q reads:

SECOND SERVANT   I'll never care what wickedness I do,
        If this man come to good.
THIRD SERVANT   If she live long
        And in the end meet the old course of death,
        Women will all turn monsters.
SECOND SERVANT   Let's follow the old earl and get the Bedlam   5
        To lead him where he would; his roguish madness
        Allows itself to anything.
THIRD SERVANT   Go thou. I'll fetch some flax and whites of eggs
        To apply to his bleeding face. Now, heaven help him!

                                                                        Exeunt

1 SH] *Capell; Seruant* Q   2, 8 SH] *Capell; 2 Ser.* Q   2–4 If she ... monsters] *Theobald's lineation; as prose* Q   5 SH] *Capell;*
1 *Ser.* Q   *6 roguish] Q *uncorr.; not in* Q *corr.*   8–9 Go ... him] *Theobald's lineation; as prose* Q   9 SD *Exeunt*] *Exit* Q;
Exeunt severally / Theobald

1 SH SECOND Capell renumbered the servants to account for the one who died.
2 this man Cornwall.
2 she Regan.
3 meet ... death i.e. die a natural death.
4 Women ... monsters i.e. because they will not fear retribution.
5 the Bedlam Poor Tom.
6 roguish characteristic of vagrants (*OED* sv *adj* 1). Q corr.'s omission is probably an accident. Perhaps the corrector, intending an alteration,

crossed the word out and forgot to insert his emendation (Greg, *Variants*, p. 169). Compare Blayney, p. 250, who suggests that a deletion symbol, or what looked like one, somehow got into the Q uncorr. margin, resulting in false correction.
7 Allows ... anything i.e. lets him do anything.
8 flax ... eggs Sixteenth- and seventeenth-century medical books recommend this treatment for injured eyes.

(xvi)   After 4.1.58 Q reads:

> Five fiends have been in poor Tom at once: of lust, as Obidicut; Hob
> bididence, prince of dumbness; Mahu, of stealing; Modo, of murder;
> Flibbertigibbet, of mopping and mowing, who since possesses chambermaids
> and waiting-women. So, bless thee, master!

1–4 Five ... master] *Pope; as verse, lines ending ... once, / ... dumbnes, / ... Stiberdigebit of / ... chambermaids / ...* maister. Q   **2** Flibbertigibbet] *Pope; Stiberdigebit* Q   **3** mopping and mowing] *Theobald;* Mobing, & *Mohing* Q

The passage derives directly from Harsnett and was cut not only to shorten the play, but to remove the allusion to chambermaids, since the joke had probably been forgotten (Johnson).

1 Five fiends On multiple possession by devils, compare Harsnett, p. 141, where Maynie recalls the 'Maister-deuils' who were made to depart from him, taking the form of the Seven Deadly Sins.

1 of lust i.e. prince of lust (syllepsis). All the devils named are 'princes', not only Hobbididence.

1 as namely.

1 Obidicut 'The Prince of hel ... Hoberdicut' (Harsnett, p. 119).

2–3 Flibbertigibbet ... mowing A 'flibber-tigibbet' is a flirt or frivolous creature (*OED* sv 1),

hence a good name for a demon that prompts affectations, such as grimacing and making faces ('mopping and mowing') (Kittredge). Harsnett, p. 136, uses the term 'mop and mow like an ape' in context with 'make antike faces, grinne'. The compositor got the spelling of 'Flibbertigibbet' wrong and has taken mowing (Q '*Mohing*') for another devil. Compare NS and Duthie, p. 404, who suspects that Q 'Mobing' may be a misreading for 'moking' (= mocking), which Oxford adopts. Compare also *Temp.* 3.3.82 SD, 4.1.47.

3 since i.e. since he left me.

3 possesses chambermaids In Harsnett, Sarah and Friswood Williams and Anne Smith, chambermaids, submitted to exorcism.

(xvii)   After 4.2.33 ('Blows in your face') Q reads:

> I fear your disposition:
> That nature which condemns its origin
> Cannot be bordered certain in itself.
> She that herself will sliver and disbranch
> From her material sap, perforce must wither   5
> And come to deadly use.

GONERILL   No more, the text is foolish.

ALBANY   Wisdom and goodness to the vile seem vile;
            Filths savour but themselves. What have you done?

2 its] Q3; it Q *uncorr.,* Q2; ith Q *corr.*

1 fear have fears concerning (Muir).

2 its Greg, *Variants*, pp. 172–3, believes that Q uncorr. 'it' is right, and Q corr. 'ith' wrong, but that the corrector's intention is unclear. Stone, p. 213, agrees that Q uncorr. is right and compares the genetive 'it' at 1.4.176. He does not press the comparison; the Fool there, after all, is using baby-talk. Thus it seems best to modernize the genetive.

3 Cannot ... itself Cannot be certain of itself, i.e. know itself and its boundaries (hence, may be uncontrollable).

4–6 She ... use That woman who will detach herself from the nourishing substance of her life and

being must necessarily degenerate and die. The image is of a branch broken off from its trunk that dries up and is used for firewood. Shaheen compares *King Leir* 1242–6, and especially John 15.6: 'If a man abide not in me, he is cast forth as a branche, and withereth: and men gather them, and cast them into the fire, and they burne.'

5 material substantial, essential.

6 come ... use Muir, Hunter compare Hebrews 6.8; NS suspects a hint of hell-fire.

6 text (1) commentary, (2) passage of scripture; perhaps Gonerill anachronistically recognizes the biblical allusion.

8 savour relish.

Tigers, not daughters, what have you performed?
A father, and a gracious agèd man,   10
Whose reverence even the head-lugged bear would lick,
Most barbarous, most degenerate, have you madded.
Could my good brother suffer you to do it?
A man, a prince, by him so benefited?
If that the heavens do not their visible spirits   15
Send quickly down to tame these vilde offences,
It will come.
Humanity must perforce prey on itself
Like monsters of the deep.

---

11 even] Q; *not in* Q2   14 benefited] Q *corr.;* beneflicted Q *uncorr.,* Q2; benefacted *Oxford*   16–17 Send ... come]
Malone's lineation; one line (come *turned over*) Q   ***16** these] *Jennens* (*conj. Heath*); the Q *uncorr.,* Q2; this Q *corr.*   16
vilde] Q2; vild Q; vile *Pope*   18–19 Humanity ... deep] *Pope's lineation; one line* (the deepe. *turned under*)
Q   18 Humanity] Q *corr.;* Humanly Q *uncorr.,* Q2

11   **head-lugged** i.e. ill-tempered (because tugged along by the head; compare *1H4* 1.2.74).
12   **madded** maddened.
13   **brother** i.e. brother-in-law (= Cornwall).
14   **benefited** Taylor believes Q uncorr. 'beniflicted' is a mistake for 'benefacted', not the more common and obvious 'benefited', which became the correction ('Four new readings in *King Lear*', *N&Q* 29 (1982), 121–2).
15   **visible spirits** supernatural beings in visible form: Albany speaks apocalyptically of 'lightning and thunderbolt' (NS).
16   **these** Q corr. 'this' (from 'thes' = these) may have been intended as a correction for Q uncorr. 'the', but as in the false correction 'ith' (2 above) something has gone awry. Compare Greg, *Variants*, p. 173; *Textual Companion*, p. 520.
16   **vilde** The old spelling of 'vile', adopted here for the sake of the pun on 'wild', playing off 'tame' (Muir).

17   **It will come** Either 'It' is a pronoun, with divine retribution as an implied antecedent; or an expletive = it will come to this, that (Greg, *Variants*, p. 173). Although the short, elliptical line induces a pause emphasizing Albany's conclusion, the words are in an extremely crowded, turned-over line; the orthography, as well as syntax and metrical irregularity, thus suggests possible textual disruption.
18–19   **Humanity ... deep** Greg (*Variants*, p. 173) compares Shakespeare's lines in *Sir Thomas More* 84–7: 'For other ruffians ... / Would shark on you, and men like revenous fishes / Would feed on one another.' Compare also *Tro.* 1.3.121–4: 'And appetite, an universal wolf / (So doubly seconded with will and power), / Must make perforce an universal prey, / And last eat up himself.' The concept was widespread and can be traced back to Hesiod, *Works and Days*, 1.434–7, and Theodoretus; it appeared also in Renaissance iconography (Muir).

(xviii)   After 4.2.36 ('from thy suffering') Q reads:

that not know'st
Fools do those villains pity who are punished
Ere they have done their mischief. Where's thy drum?
France spreads his banners in our noiseless land,

1–4 that ... land] *Theobald's lineation; lines end* ... pitty / ... mischiefe, / ... land, Q   2 those] Q; these Q2   4 noiseless] Q *corr.,* Q2; noystles Q *uncorr.*

2–3   **Fools ... mischief** Compare 1.4.282.–4. Gonerill condemns soft-hearted fools who do not see the value of preventive punishment. She
apparently refers to Lear, not Gloucester, since it is of her father, who has done no 'mischief' yet, that Albany has been speaking.

With plumèd helm thy flaxen biggin threats,   5
Whilst thou, a moral fool, sits still and cries
'Alack, why does he so?'

5 thy] Q; his *Duthie* (*conj. Greg*)   *5 flaxen] *Oxford;* slayer Q *uncorr.;* slaier Q2; state Q *corr., Jennens*   *5 biggin] *Oxford* (*conj. Stone*); begin Q *uncorr.;* begins Q *corr.,* Q2, *Jennens*   *5 threats] Q *uncorr.;* thereat Q *corr.;* threats Q2; to threat *Jennens*   6 Whilst] Q *corr.;* Whil's Q *uncorr.,* Q2; Whiles *Oxford*

5 flaxen biggin threats An unsolved crux for many years; no plausible alternative was found to Jennens's universally accepted emendation, 'state begins to threat', which cannot be defended on the evidence (Greg, *Variants,* p. 174). Stone, p. 184, however proposed 'slyre' (= fine linen or lawn) and 'biggin' (= a cap or hood for the head, a nightcap; sometimes spelled 'begin'), but was uncomfortable with 'slyre', a Scottish word.

Taylor ('Addenda' to *Division,* p. 488) then proposed 'flaxen' for Q uncorr. 'slayer' instead of 'slyre' or Q corr.'s 'state'. The emendation, which makes sense and is palaeo-graphically sound, alters Q uncorr. minimally. The comparison between the King of France with his plumèd helm and Albany in his nightcap is deliberately ludicrous. Compare *2H4* 4.5.27.
6 moral i.e. moralizing.

(xix) After 4.2.38 ('O vain fool!') Q reads:

ALBANY   Thou changèd and self-covered thing, for shame
                  Be-monster not thy feature. Were't my fitness
                  To let these hands obey my blood,
                  They are apt enough to dislocate and tear
                  Thy flesh and bones. Howe'er thou art a fiend,   5
                  A woman's shape doth shield thee.

GONERILL   Marry, your manhood! Mew!
                                 Enter a GENTLEMAN
ALBANY   What news?

*4 dislocate] Q3; dislecate Q, Q2   *7 manhood! Mew!] *N.S;* manhood – Mew! *Cam.* (*conj. Daniel*); manhood mew—Q *corr.;* manhood now—Q *uncorr.;* man-hood now—Q3   7 SD] Q (*after 8*); Messenger F

1 changèd transformed, i.e. from woman to monster.
1 self-covered hidden from one's true form or self, disguised; i.e. the devil in woman's form. Compare 5–6 below.
2 Be-monster . . . feature i.e. don't make your appearance hideous (by revealing your true nature). Gonerill's features, distorted with anger and contempt, make her look diabolical.
2 Were't my fitness If it were fitting for me (as a man).
3 blood emotion, passion.
4 apt ready.
4–5 dislocate . . . bones An example of chiasmus, the rhetorical figure in which the order of words in one of two parallel elements is inverted

in the other. 'Albany maddens at the terrible impulses crowding him' (Rosenberg, p. 255).
5 Howe'er However much, although.
7 Marry . . . Mew Greg does not doubt the correctness of Q corr.'s 'excellent emendation' (*Variants,* p. 175); Stone does (p. 213). Both Q uncorr. and Q corr. make sense, differing only in the degree of contempt Gonerill expresses. Q corr. is stronger, consistent with Q's version of Gonerill; moreover, why would the corrector alter Q uncorr. if 'mew' were not a bona fide correction from copy?
7 Marry An oath, literally 'By the Virgin Mary!'
7 Mew Imitating mockingly the sound of a cat. Compare *1H4* 3.1.127.

(xx) After 4.2, Q adds a scene:

Enter KENT *and a* GENTLEMAN

KENT Why the King of France is so suddenly gone back, know you no reason?

GENTLEMAN Something he left imperfect in the state which since his coming forth
    is thought of, which imports to the kingdom so much fear and danger that his
    personal return was most required and necessary.

KENT Who hath he left behind him general?   5

GENTLEMAN The Marshal of France, Monsieur La Far.

KENT Did your letters pierce the queen to any demonstration of grief?

GENTLEMAN Ay, sir. She took them, read them in my presence,
    And now and then an ample tear trilled down
    Her delicate cheek. It seemed she was a queen   10
    Over her passion, who most rebel-like
    Sought to be king o'er her.

KENT   O, then it moved her?

GENTLEMAN Not to a rage. Patience and sorrow strove
    Who should express her goodliest. You have seen
    Sunshine and rain at once; her smiles and tears   15
    Were like a better way; those happy smilets
    That played on her ripe lip seemed not to know
    What guests were in her eyes; which parted thence
    As pearls from diamonds dropped. In brief,
    Sorrow would be a rarity most beloved   20
    If all could so become it.

---

1 no] Q; the Q2 *1 reason?] Q2; reason. Q *5 him general?] *Theobald;* him, General. Q; him, Generall? Q2 *8 Ay, sir] *Johnson;* I, sir *Theobald;* I say Q 10–12 Her ... o'er her] *Pope's lineation; lines divided* ... passion, / Who Q *13 strove] *Pope;* streme Q *15 Sunshine] Sun-shine Q2; Sun shine Q *17 seemed] *Pope;* seeme Q *18 eyes;] eyes, Q2; eyes Q *19 dropped.] dropt; Q2; dropt Q

---

0 SD GENTLEMAN Apparently the same Gentleman that Kent spoke to in 3.1. See 3.1.0 SD n.

1 gone back Steevens (cited by Furness) aptly explains why, in view of his different ending, Shakespeare decided to return the king to France rather than have him present at the battle, as in *King Leir*. Eliminating references to his arrival in the first place obviates the need to send him back later.

3 imports carries with it, involves as a consequence (Onions).

6 The ... La Far Pope emended Q 'Mar-shall' to 'Mareschal', making the word trisyllabic so that the line scanned as blank verse. Steevens, who spelled the name 'le Fer', thought Shakespeare had an impoverished French nomenclature, because the Marshal bears the same name as the common soldier, 'M. Fer', who was *'fer'd, ferreted,* and *ferk'd'* by Pistol in *H5* 4.4.26–31.

7 your letters Compare 3.1.10–20.

9 trilled trickled. Compare Cotgrave, '*Transcouler,* To glide, slide ... trill, or trickle' (Wright, cited by Furness).

11 who The pronoun personifies 'passion'.

13 rage violent outburst of grief (Kittredge).

13 strove See collation: *o/e, u/m* misreading.

15 Sunshine ... tears Proverbial (Tilley L92a). Compare *R2* 3.2.9–10 and Sidney's *Arcadia,* Bk III, ch. 5: 'Her tears came dropping down like rain in sunshine' (Steevens, cited by Furness).

16 a better way i.e. of expressing conflicting attitudes. For various interpretations and emendations, compare Furness: Duthie, pp. 408–9; Hunter.

16 smilets little smiles.

18 which i.e. the 'guests' (= tears).

19 As ... dropped Shakespeare often refers to tears as pearls, as in *Lucrece,* 1213 ('And wip'd the brinish pearl from her bright eyes'; compare *ibid.,* 1548–53) and *TGV* 3.1.226 ('A sea of melting pearl, which some call tears'); eyes as 'diamonds' is a rarer image (compare *Wiv.* 3.3.55). The elegant simile is appropriate to a courtier (Kittredge).

20 rarity something excellent, precious; compare Sonnet 60.11.

21 If ... it i.e. if everyone could make it so attractive.

KENT   Made she no verbal question?

GENTLEMAN   Faith, once or twice she heaved the name of father
               Pantingly forth, as if it pressed her heart;
               Cried 'Sisters, sisters! Shame of ladies! Sisters!   25
               Kent! Father! Sisters! What, i'th'storm? i'th'night?
               Let pity not be believed!' There she shook
               The holy water from her heavenly eyes,
               And clamour moistened. Then away she started
               To deal with grief alone.

KENT   It is the stars,   30
               The stars above us, govern our conditions,
               Else one self mate and make could not beget
               Such different issues. You spoke not with her since?

GENTLEMAN   No.

KENT   Was this before the king returned?

GENTLEMAN   No, since.   35

KENT   Well, sir, the poor distressèd Lear's i'th'town,
               Who sometime in his better tune remembers
               What we are come about and by no means
               Will yield to see his daughter.

GENTLEMAN   Why, good sir?

KENT   A sovereign shame so elbows him: his own unkindness   40
               That stripped her from his benediction, turned her
               To foreign casualties, gave her dear rights
               To his dog-hearted daughters – these things sting

---

*27 pity ... believed] pitie ... beleeft Q; pitty ... beleeu'd Q2; pity ne'er believe it *Pope;* piety not be believed *Oxford*   *29 moistened] *Capell;* moystened her Q; mastered *Oxford (conj. Stone)*   *30–1 It ... conditions] *Theobald's lineation; one line* Q   *38–9 What ... daughter] *Pope's lineation; one line* (daughter *turned under*) Q   *43–5 To ... Cordelia] *Johnson's lineation; lines divided ... mind, / So* Q

22 Made ... question Did she not say anything?
22 question speech.
23 Faith In faith.
27 Let ... believed Either (1) let (it for) pity not be believed (Harbage), or (2) let pity not be believed (to exist) (Steevens, cited by Furness). See collation. The accidental indentation of the line in Q suggests that a letter has dropped out. Blayney conjectures 'Lest' but recognizes that an inkball could not pull out a long *s* from a long *s*/*t* ligature. Oxford emends 'pity' to 'piety' (*Textual Companion,* p. 521). Perhaps Q 'not beleeft' contains a contraction (= not believe it) and an excrescent 'be' was added in proof (NS: J. D. Wilson).
29 clamour moistened i.e. moistened her outcries with tears ('holy water'), thus silencing them. Compare *2H4* 4.5.138–9: 'my tears, / The moist impediments unto my speech'. Warburton (cited by Furness) proposed hyphenating 'clamour-moistened', putting it in apposition with 'heavenly'. Oxford adopts Stone's conjecture, 'mastered' (= overcame; presumably spelled 'maystered' in copy). Q's 'her' is

metrically superfluous, probably attracted from the line above. (See Duthie, p. 409; Stone, p. 184; *Textual Companion,* p. 521.)
29–30 Then ... alone Compare Gen. 43.30, Joseph's dealing with grief alone (Theobald, cited by Furness).
30–1 It is ... conditions Compare Edmond's opposing view (1.2.104–16).
31 conditions dispositions, characters. Compare *MV* 1.2.129.
32 Else ... and make Otherwise one and the same husband and wife ('make').
37 sometime sometimes.
37 in ... tune i.e. when his wits are together; compare 4.6.16.
40 sovereign all-powerful.
40 elbows him Either (1) jostles, thrusts him back, or (2) stands beside him remindingly; haunts (compare *R3* 1.4.145).
42 foreign casualties accidents, chances abroad.
43 dog-hearted pitiless; compare *TGV* 2.3.10–11.

His mind so venomously that burning shame
Detains him from Cordelia.   45
GENTLEMAN   Alack, poor gentleman!
KENT   Of Albany's and Cornwall's powers you heard not?
GENTLEMAN   'Tis so. They are afoot.
KENT   Well, sir, I'll bring you to our master, Lear,
           And leave you to attend him. Some dear cause   50
           Will in concealment wrap me up awhile.
           When I am known aright, you shall not grieve
           Lending me this acquaintance. I pray you, go
           Along with me.

                                                                   Exeunt

---

47 not?] Q2; not. Q   *53–4 Lending . . . me] *Jennens's lineation; one line* Q   *54 SD *Exeunt*] *Pope; Exit* Q

47 powers armies.   **52–3 When . . . acquaintance** Compare
48 afoot on the march.   3.1.23–8.
50 dear cause important business (we are never   **52 aright** rightly, as myself.
told what, but compare 4.6.9–11).

(xxi)   After 4.6.25 Q reads:

CORDELIA   Very well.
DOCTOR   Please you, draw near. – Louder the music there!

(xxii)   After 4.6.32 Q reads:

           To stand against the deep dread-bolted thunder?
           In the most terrible and nimble stroke
           Of quick cross lightning? to watch, poor perdu,
           With this thin helm?

---

1 dread-bolted] *Hyphenated Theobald*   *3 lightning?] *Theobald;* lightning Q*; lightning, Q2   *3 watch,] *Warburton;*
watch Q   *4 helm?] Q2; helm Q

1 deep Either (1) deeply dreaded, or (2) deep-   **3 watch** (1) stand guard, (2) go without sleep.
toned, bass.   **3 perdu** (1) a sentry in an advanced and danger-
1 dread-bolted thunder thunder, armed or   ous position, (2) a castaway, lost one.
equipped ('bolted') with dread, i.e. thunderbolts   **4 thin helm** (1) meagre helmet, (2) scant hair, (3)
conveying dread.   bare head; probably (3).
3 cross zigzag.

(xxiii)   After 4.6.78 ('You see is killed in him') Q reads:

                          and yet it is danger
           To make him even o'er the time he has lost.

1–2 and . . . lost] *Theobald's lineation; as prose* Q

2 even o'er balance up, fill up and smooth over;
i.e. it is dangerous to make him account for what he
has gone through.

(xxiv) After 4.6.82 Q reads:

GENTLEMAN   Holds it true, sir, that the Duke of Cornwall was so slain?
KENT   Most certain, sir.
GENTLEMAN   Who is conductor of his people?
KENT   As 'tis said, the bastard son of Gloucester.
GENTLEMAN   They say Edgar, his banished son, is with the Earl of Kent in   5
   Germany.
KENT   Report is changeable. 'Tis time to look about. The powers of the kingdom
   approach apace.
GENTLEMAN   The arbitrement is like to be bloody. Fare you well, sir.   [*Exit*]
KENT   My point and period will be throughly wrought   10
         Or well or ill as this day's battle's fought.   *Exit*

7–8 Report . . . apace] *As prose, Theobald; two verse lines divided . . . about,* / The Q   *9 SD *Exit*] *After Theobald; not in* Q

1 **Holds it true** Is it confirmed?
7 **Report is changeable** Hence, the Gentleman's
question earlier, 1.
7 **look about** be alert.
9 **arbitrement** decisive action.
10–11 **My point . . . fought** 'The completion of

my lot in life will be worked out, for good or ill,
according as this battle results in victory or defeat'
(Kittredge).
10 **point** object, purpose; compare *Mac.* 3.1.86.
10 **period** full stop, end.
10 **throughly** thoroughly.

(xxv) After 5.1.11 ('To the forfended place') Q reads:

EDMOND   That thought abuses you.
REGAN   I am doubtful that you have been conjunct
            And bosomed with her, as far as we call hers.

2–3 I . . . hers] Q2 *lineation; as prose* Q

1 **abuses** dishonours.
2 **doubtful** suspicious.
2 **conjunct** (1) united, closely joined, (2) con-
spiring (King).

3 **bosomed** (1) close, (2) sexually intimate.
3 **as far . . . hers** i.e. to the fullest extent, all
the way.

(xxvi) After 5.1.14 SD Q reads:

GONERILL   [*Aside*] I had rather lose the battle than that sister
            Should loosen him and me.

1 SD *Aside*] *Theobald; not in* Q   1–2 I . . . me] *Theobald's lineation; as prose* Q; *two lines divided . . .* battell / Then
Q2   *1 lose] *Theobald;* loose Q, Q2

1–2 **lose . . . loosen** Gonerill's word-play
heightens the antithesis.

(xxvii) After 5.1.18 ('Forced to cry out') Q reads:

> Where I could not be honest,
> I never yet was valiant. For this business,
> It touches us as France invades our land,
> Not bolds the king with others whom I fear
> Most just and heavy causes make oppose.   5
> EDMOND   Sir, you speak nobly.

*4 king] King, Q   *4 fear] *Duthie;* feare, Q; fear. *Oxford*

1 be honest be honourable, act with good conscience (Kittredge).
2 For As for.
3 touches concerns, affects.
3 France i.e. the King of France.
4 bolds emboldens, encourages (compare
Abbott 290).
4 with along with.
5 Most ... oppose i.e. very justified and serious

reasons motivate them to fight. Oxford places
a period after 'fear', making this line a separate
sentence and changing the sense to suggest 'just
and heavy causes' on both sides. Muir notes that
'with others whom' occurs also at 5.1.17 and the line
restates the earlier point; he suspects the passage
may be corrupt.
6 nobly Edmond is sarcastic (NS).

(xxviii) After 5.1.23 ('On our proceeding') Q reads:

> EDMOND   I shall attend you presently at your tent.

1 I ... tent Stone, p. 237, suspects the line was
inadvertently dropped from F by a copyist or
compositor.

(xxix) After 5.3.35 ('Or thrive by other means.') Q reads:

> CAPTAIN   I cannot draw a cart nor eat dried oats;
>   If it be man's work, I'll do it.

1 I ... oats i.e. I'm not a horse (or other animal).

(xxx) After 5.3.53 ('hold your session') Q reads:

> At this time
> We sweat and bleed. The friend hath lost his friend,
> And the best quarrels in the heat are cursed

1–4 At ... sharpness] *Theobald's lineation; three lines ending ... *bleed, / ... *quarrels* / ... *sharpnes,* Q   **2** We] Q *corr.,* Q2;
mee Q *uncorr.*

1–6 At ... place Edmond's hypocrisy is patent:
he pretends to safeguard Lear and Cordelia until
they can get a fair trial, but in reality he is stalling to
give the Captain time to fulfil his orders. The lines
motivate Albany's censure of Edmond's presump-
tuousness perhaps better than those retained in F,

which focus rather on Edmond's authority to deal
with the prisoners. (Compare Urkowitz, p. 107;
Stone, p. 238.)
3 quarrels causes.
3 in the heat i.e. of passion engendered by
battle.

By those that feel their sharpness.
The question of Cordelia and her father   5
Requires a fitter place.

4 sharpness] Q *corr.*, Q2; sharpes Q *uncorr.*

4 **sharpness** severity, harshness (Schmidt). See collation. Q corr. may follow copy; but Stone (p. 213), NS, and Greg (*Variants*, p. 179) suspect that the press-corrector thought an *n* was missing and wrongly altered Q uncorr. 'sharpes' (= sharp edges, points; *OED* Sharp *sb*¹2).
        6 **fitter place** i.e. not the battlefield.

(xxxi) After 5.3.195 Q reads:

EDGAR   This would have seemed a period
             To such as love not sorrow; but another
             To amplify too much would make much more
             And top extremity.
             Whilst I was big in clamour, came there in a man   5
             Who, having seen me in my worst estate,
             Shunned my abhorred society. But then, finding
             Who 'twas that so endured, with his strong arms
             He fastened on my neck and bellowed out
             As he'd burst heaven; threw him on my father;   10
             Told the most piteous tale of Lear and him
             That ever ear received; which in recounting
             His grief grew puissant and the strings of life
             Began to crack. Twice then the trumpets sounded,
             And there I left him tranced.   15

ALBANY   But who was this?
EDGAR   Kent, sir, the banished Kent, who in disguise
             Followed his enemy king and did him service
             Improper for a slave.

1–4 This ... extremity] *Theobald's lineation; three lines ending* ... such / ... much, / ... extreamitie Q   *10 him] *Theobald;* me Q   11 Told the most] Q; And told the Q2   *14 crack. Twice] *Theobald;* cracke twice, Q

1 **period** (1) climax, (2) full stop.
    2–4 **another ... extremity** To describe in detail another (tale of sorrow) would add a great deal more (to what I have already told) and exceed the furthest limit (of what is bearable). Compare Furness and *Textual Companion*, p. 526. Edgar, nevertheless, proceeds with Kent's story.
    5 **big** i.e. loud.
    5 **clamour** lamentation; compare xx.29 above.

6 **estate** condition.
    10 **As** As if.
    10 **him** himself.
    13 **puissant** strong, powerful.
    13 **strings of life** i.e. his heartstrings; compare *R3* 4.4.365.
    15 **tranced** in a faint or trance.
    17 **enemy king** Compare 1.1.167–73.
    18 **Improper** Unfitting.

READING LIST

This list includes a selection of books and articles referred to in the Introduction or Commentary along with several additional items that may serve as a guide to those who wish to undertake further study of the play.

Adelman, Janet. *Suffocating Mothers: Fantasies of Maternal Origin in Shakespeare's Plays, Hamlet to The Tempest*, 1992
Berlin, Normand. *The Secret Cause: A Discussion of Tragedy*, 1981
Bevington, David. *Shakespeare*, 2002
Blayney, Peter W. M. *The Texts of 'King Lear' and Their Origins*, 1982
Bloom, Harold. *Shakespeare: The Invention of the Human*, 1998
Booth, Stephen, *'King Lear', 'Macbeth', Indefinition, and Tragedy*, 1983
Bradley, A. C. *Shakespearean Tragedy*, 2nd edn, 1905
Brockbank, Philip. *'Upon Such Sacrifices'*, The British Academy Shakespeare Lecture, 1976
Brown, John Russell. *Shakespeare: The Tragedies*, 2001
Bruce, Susan. *William Shakespeare: 'King Lear'*, 1998
Bullough, Geoffrey. *Narrative and Dramatic Sources of Shakespeare*, Vol. VII, 1973.
Carlisle, Carol Jones. *Shakespeare from the Greenroom*, 1969
Cavell, Stanley. *Must We Mean What We Say?*, 1969
Clare, Janet. *Shakespeare's Stage Traffic: Imitation, Borrowing, and Competition in Renaissance Theatre*, 2014
Clayton, Thomas. 'Old light on the text of *King Lear*', *MP* 78 (1981), 347–67
Cohen, Derek. *Shakespearean Motives*, 1988
Colie, Rosalie L., and F. T. Flahiff (eds.). *Some Facets of 'King Lear': Essays in Prismatic Criticism*, 1974
Colman, E. A. M. *The Dramatic Use of Bawdy in Shakespeare*, 1974
Cox, Brian. *The Lear Diaries*, 1992
Croall, Jonathan. *Performing King Lear: Gielgud to Russell Beale*, 2015
Danby, John F. *Shakespeare's Doctrine of Nature*, 1948, reprinted 1961
Davies, Oliver Ford. *Playing Lear*, 2003
Dobson, Michael (ed.). *Performing Shakespeare's Tragedies Today: The Actor's Perspective*, 2006
Dollimore, Jonathan. *Radical Tragedy: Religion, Ideology and Power in the Drama of Shakespeare and his Contemporaries*, 1984; 2nd edn, 1989
Doran, Madeleine. *Shakespeare's Dramatic Language*, 1976
   The Text of 'King Lear', 1931, reprinted 1967
Elton, William. *'King Lear' and the Gods*, 1966; 2nd edn, 1988
Foakes, R. A. *Hamlet versus Lear: Cultural Politics and Shakespeare's Art*, 1993

Fortin, René. 'Hermeneutical circularity and Christian interpretations of *King Lear*', in *Gaining upon Certainty: Selected Criticism*, 1995, pp. 125–38

Fraser, Russell A. *Shakespeare's Poetics in Relation to 'King Lear'*, 1962

Garber, Marjorie. *Shakespeare After All*, 2004

Gardner, Helen. *King Lear*, 1967

Greenblatt, Stephen. 'Shakespeare and the Exorcists', in *Shakespearean Negotiations*, 1988
   Will in the World, 2004

Greg, W. W. *The Editorial Problem in Shakespeare*, 1942
   The Shakespeare First Folio: Its Bibliographical and Textual History, 1955
   The Variants in the First Quarto of 'King Lear', 1940

Halio, Jay L. (ed.). *Critical Essays on Shakespeare's 'King Lear'*, 1996

Hamilton, Donna. 'Some romance sources for *King Lear*: Robert of Sicily and Robert the Devil', *SP* 71 (1966), 345–59

Hawkes, Terence. *William Shakespeare: King Lear*, 1995

Heilman, Robert. *This Great Stage: Image and Structure in 'King Lear'*, 1948; reprinted 1963

Hoeniger, F. D. *Medicine and Shakespeare in the English Renaissance*, 1992

Holland, Norman N. *The Shakespearean Imagination*, 1964

Holland, Peter (ed.). *'King Lear' and its Afterlife*, *S.Sur.* 55 (2002)

Honigmann, E. A. J. *Myriad-Minded Shakespeare*, 1989
   'Shakespeare's revised plays: *King Lear* and *Othello*', *The Library*, 6th ser., 4 (1982), 142–73
   The Stability of Shakespeare's Text, 1965

Howard-Hill, Trevor. 'The problem of manuscript copy for Folio *King Lear*', *The Library*, 6th ser., 4 (1982), 1–24

Ioppolo, Grace. *Revising Shakespeare*, 1991

Ioppolo, Grace (ed.). *Shakespeare Performed: Essays in Honor of R. A. Foakes*, 2000

James, D. G. *The Dream of Learning: An Essay on 'The Advancement of Learning', 'Hamlet', and 'King Lear'*, 1951

Jorgensen, Paul A. *Lear's Self-Discovery*, 1967

Kelly, Philippa. *The King and I*, 2011

Kennedy, Dennis. *Looking at Shakespeare: A Visual History of Twentieth-Century Performance*, 1993

King Lear: The Sourcebooks Shakespeare, 2007

Kinney, Arthur F. 'Some conjectures on the composition of *King Lear*', *S.Sur.* 33 (1980), 13–25

Knight, G. Wilson. *The Wheel of Fire*, 4th edn, 1960

Knights, L. C. *Some Shakespearean Themes*, 1960

Kozinstev, Grigori. *'King Lear': The Space of Tragedy*, trans. Mary Mackintosh, 1977

Leggatt, Alexander. *King Lear*, Harvester New Critical Introductions, 1988
   Shakespeare in Performance: 'King Lear', 1991
   'Two Lears: notes for an actor', in Lois Potter and Arthur F. Kinney (eds.), *Shakespeare: Text and Theater: Essays in Honor of Jay L. Halio*, 1999, pp. 310–19

Levenson, Jill. 'What the silence said: still points in *King Lear*', in Clifford Leech and
     J. M. R. Margeson (eds.), *Shakespeare 1971*, 1972, pp. 215–29
Lusardi, James, and June Schlueter. *Reading Shakespeare in Performance: 'King Lear'*,
     1991
Mack, Maynard. *'King Lear' in Our Time*, 1965
Maguire, Laurie E., and Thomas L. Berger (eds.). *Textual Formations and
     Reformations*, 1998
Marcus, Leah. *Puzzling Shakespeare*, 1988
Marowitz, Charles. 'Lear Log', *Tulane Drama Review* 8.2 (Winter, 1963)
McAlindon, T. *Shakespeare's Tragic Cosmos*, 1991
McElroy, Bernard. *Shakespeare's Mature Tragedies*, 1973
McKellen, Ian. 'King Lear', in Julian Curry, *Shakespeare on Stage 2*, 2017
McMullan, Gordon. *Shakespeare and the Idea of Late Writing*: *Authorship in the
     Proximity of Death*, 2007
Meagher, John C. 'Vanity, Lear's feather, and the pathology of editorial annotation',
     in Clifford Leech and J. M. R. Margeson (eds.), *Shakespeare 1971*, 1972, pp.
     244–59
Muir, Kenneth. *'King Lear': A Critical Study*, 1986
Neill, Michael, and David Schalkwyk (eds.). *The Oxford Handbook of Shakespearean
     Tragedy*, 2016
Nevo, Ruth. *Tragic Form in Shakespeare*, 1972
Noble, Richmond. *Shakespeare's Biblical Knowledge*, 1935
Ogden, James, and Arthur H. Scouten (eds.). *'Lear' from Study to Stage*, 1997
Palfrey, Simon. *Poor Tom: Living 'King Lear'*, 2014
Patterson, Annabel. *Shakespeare and the Popular Voice*, 1989
Peat, Derek. '"And that's true too": *King Lear* and the tension of uncertainty', *S.Sur.*
     33 (1980), 43–53
Pennington, Michael. *King Lear in Brooklyn*, 2016
Perrett, Wilfrid. *The King Lear Story from Geoffrey of Monmouth to Shakespeare*,
     Berlin, 1904
Pigott-Smith, Tim. *Do You Know Who I Am? A Memoir*, 2017
Reibetanz, John. *The Lear World*, 1977
Ringler, William A. Jr. 'Shakespeare and his actors: some remarks on *King Lear*', in
     Wendell M. Aycock (ed.), *Shakespeare's Art from a Comparative Perspective*,
     1981, pp. 187–93
Rosenberg, Marvin. *The Masks of King Lear*, 1972; reprinted, 1992
Rothwell, Kenneth S. *A History of Shakespeare on Screen: A Century of Film and
     Television*, 1999
Ryan, Kiernan. '*King Lear*: a retrospect, 1980–2000', *S.Sur.* 55 (2002), 1–11
Ryan, Kiernan (ed.). *King Lear*. New Casebooks, 1992
Salingar, Leo. *Dramatic Form in Shakespeare and the Jacobeans*, 1986
Schafer, Elizabeth. *Ms-Directing Shakespeare: Women Direct Shakespeare*, 1998
Shaheen, Naseeb. *Biblical References in Shakespeare's Tragedies*, 1987
Shapiro, James. *1606: William Shakespeare and the Year of Lear*, 2015

Sher, Antony. *The Year of the Mad King*, 2018

Sillars, Stuart. *Painting Shakespeare: The Artist as Critic, 1720–1820*, 2006

Skura, Meredith. 'What Shakespeare Did with the Queen's Men's *King Leir* and When', *S.Sur.* 36 (2010)

Snyder, Susan. *The Comic Matrix of Shakespeare's Tragedies*, 1979
  Shakespeare: A Wayward Journey, 2000

Speaight, Robert. *Shakespeare on the Stage: An Illustrated History of Shakespearian Performance*, 1973

Spurgeon, Caroline. *Shakespeare's Imagery and What It Tells Us*, 1935

Stampfer, Judah. 'The catharsis of *King Lear*', *S.Sur.* 13 (1960), 1–10

Stockholder, Katherine. 'The multiple genres of *King Lear*: breaking the archetypes', *Bucknell Review* 16 (1968), 40–63

Stone, P. W. K. *The Textual History of 'King Lear'*, 1980

Taylor, Gary 'A new source and an old date for *King Lear*', *RES* 132 (1982), 396–413
  'Revolutions of perspective: *King Lear*', in *Moment by Moment by Shakespeare*, 1985, pp. 162–260
  'The war in *King Lear*', *S.Sur.* 33 (1980), 27–34

Taylor, Gary, and Michael Warren (eds.). *The Division of the Kingdoms: Shakespeare's Two Versions of 'King Lear'*, 1983

Thompson, Ann. *The Critics Debate: King Lear*, 1988

Urkowitz, Stephen. *Shakespeare's Revision of 'King Lear'*, 1980

Van Doren, Mark. *Shakespeare*, 1939

Vickers, Brian. *The One King Lear*, 2016

Warren, Michael. 'Quarto and Folio *King Lear* and the interpretation of Albany and Edgar', in David Bevington and Jay L. Halio (eds.), *Shakespeare: Pattern of Excelling Nature*, 1978, pp. 95–107

Warren, Michael (ed.). *The Complete 'King Lear', 1608–1623*, 1989

Weis, René (ed.). *King Lear: A Parallel Text Edition* (2nd edn), 2010

Wells, Stanley. *Shakespeare: A Life in Drama*, 1995

Wells, Stanley, and Gary Taylor, with John Jowett and William Montgomery. *Shakespeare: A Textual Companion*, 1987

Welsford, Enid. *The Fool: His Social and Literary History*, 1935

Whitaker, Virgil. *The Mirror Up to Nature: The Technique of Shakespeare's Tragedies*, 1965

Wiles, David. *Shakespeare's Clown*, 1987

Wittreich, Joseph. *'Image of that Horror': History, Prophecy, and Apocalypse in 'King Lear'*, 1984

Wood, Michael. *In Search of Shakespeare*, 2003